BEACHAM'S MARKETING REFERENCE

Volume I
Account Executive-Market Segmentation

Edited By
Walton Beacham
Richard T. Hise
Hale N. Tongren

Research Publishing
Beacham Publishing

Ref
HF
5415
.B379
1986

Library of Congress
 Cataloging in Publication Data   v. 1
Beacham, Walton, 1943

Beacham's marketing reference/Washington, D.C.: Research Publishing, 1986
      2 v.; 24 cm.

        Bibliography
        Includes index in v. 2

        Describes marketing terms within context of a business environ-
     ment, providing computer software and databases, and a descriptive bibli-
     ography of additional sources.

        1. Marketing—Handbooks, manuals, etc. 2. Marketing—Termi-
     nology. I. Hise, Richard T., 1937– . II. Tongren, Hale N., 1921–
     III. Title. IV. Title: Marketing reference.

HF5415.B379   1986   658.8   86-20271

Library of Congress Catalog Card Number: 86-20271

        Complete Set   ISBN: 0-933833-03-2
        Volume 1   ISBN: 0-933833-04-0
        Volume 2   ISBN: 0-933833-05-9

                    Printed in the United States of America
                    First Printing, September 1986

PREFACE

The sophisticated marketing techniques of American businesses have gained world respect and attention, but the complex and often technical books written about them have given the impression that only mega corporations are able to apply these techniques to their operations.

Beacham's Marketing Reference takes important marketing concepts, from Artificial Intelligence Marketing to Venture Teams, and explains them within a business environment. Alphabetized A-Z, each entry is formatted for quick access. The subheadings are:

Overview
Examples
Benefits
Implementation
Evaluation
Conclusion
Applications to Small Business
Software/Databases
References/Sources
Related Topics and Terms

Beginning with an overview of the concept, each entry traces case histories of the companies who developed or used the technique, its success, and the benefits. Using Product Elimination, for example, which is an evaluation of the profitability of each product in the line, Hunt Foods reduced its product offerings from 30 to 3, and by doing so doubled its profits. For most businesses, regardless of size or type of product, this same concept should become part of the marketing strategy. An automotive supply house, which might stock 50,000 items, must constantly evaluate its line to determine which items are profitable, which ones must be carried as service items, and which ones can be retired from active inventory.

Beacham's Marketing Reference is designed to help business people determine what concepts are important to their operations, and explains how to implement and evaluate the techniques. There is a special section devoted to particular applications to small businesses, plus a section on software and databases which assist in setting up and running daily operations. Finally, each entry includes a descriptive bibliography of the most important sources for additional reference.

Anyone associated with business will find this an invaluable desk reference. Its purpose is to provide a thorough, straightforward overview of both the theoretical and practical aspects of each concept, so that anyone who deals with marketing terms or techniques—consultants, reporters, third party vendors, advertisers, students, executives, librarians, or salespeople—has a quick reference to the tools which American businesses use to expand and evaluate their markets.

013507

As with all Beacham Publishing reference books, the purpose of this series is to assist the reader in using information. That each entry seems clear and easy to understand is a testament to the contributors' knowledge of their field and their ability to sift through the mass of material on each subject. All of the contributors are professors of marketing and specialists in the topics which they are addressing. Many of them are also established consultants who provide their own consulting services to business. They can be contacted through their university affiliations listed at the end of each article.

This series in marketing will be followed by a parallel series in management concepts. Beacham Publishing is continually interested in how readers use our books, and we welcome suggestions for revising this title or ideas for new ones. Write to: Beacham Publishing, 2113 "S" Street, NW, Washington, DC 20008.

Walton Beacham

CONTRIBUTORS

Erin Anderson
Wharton School of Business/
University of Pennsylvania

Rolph E. Anderson
Drexel University

Danny R. Arnold
Mississippi State University

Jessica M. Bailey
The American University

William R. Bart
Kent State University

Richard F. Beltramini
Arizona State University

Vincent Blasko
Arizona State University

Terence A. Brown
Pennsylvania State University

Alan J. Bush
Texas A&M University

Marjorie J. Caballero
Baylor University

Pravat K. Choudhury
Howard University

Terry Clark
Notre Dame University

Jeffrey S. Conant
Texas A&M University

Robert Lorin Cook
Central Michigan University

Michael F. d'Amico
University of Akron

Duane Davis
University of Central Florida

Jeffrey C. Dilts
University of Akron

William P. Dommermuth
Southern Illinois University

Teresa J. Domzal
George Mason University

Joel R. Evans
Hofstra University

Richard J. Fox
University of Georgia

Warren A. French
University of Georgia

Ralph M. Gaedeke
California State University

William R. George
Villanova University

Peter L. Gillett
University of Central Florida

M. Edward Goretsky
George Mason University

Thomas V. Greer
University of Maryland

Gary Guenther
Texas A&M University

John H. Hallaq
University of Idaho

Richard T. Hise
Texas A&M University

Raymond L. Horton
Lehigh University

Kenneth L. Jensen
Berry College

Eugene M. Johnson
University of Rhode Island

Marvin A. Jolson
University of Maryland

W. Benoy Joseph
Cleveland State University

Stephen K. Keiser
University of Delaware

J. Patrick Kelly
Wayne State University

Renee King
Witchita State University

Robert L. King
The Citadel

Frederic B. Kraft
Wichita State University

H. Richard Kropp
University of Georgia

Mary Ann Lederhaus
University of North Florida

James H. Leigh
Texas A&M University

William C. Lesch
Illinois State University

Greg J. Lessne
University of Rhode Island

Larry S. Lowe
Loyola College

George H. Lucas
Texas A&M University

Steven J. Lysonski
University of Rhode Island

Charles S. Madden
Baylor University

Charles L. Martin
Wichita State University

James Maskulka
Lehigh University

Therese A. Maskulka
Lehigh University

Kevin F. McCrohan
George Mason University

Stephen W. McDaniel
Texas A&M University

Michael A. McGinnis
Shippensburg University

James Utah McNeal
Texas A&M University

Ronald D. Michman
Shippensburg University

Lori H. Mitchell
Kent State University

Michael P. Mokwa
Arizona State University

Fred W. Morgan
Wayne State University

Luiz Moutinho
University of Glasgow

Jan P. Muczyk
Cleveland State University

Donald F. Mulvihill
Kent State University

Susan Logan Nelson
University of North Dakota

Larry R. O'Neal
Stephen F. Austin State University

A. Parasuraman
Texas A&M University

Gordon W. Paul
University of Central Florida

Nancy L. Pishkur
Kent State University

D. Rajaratnam
Texas A&M University

David G. Ratz
Kent State University

Pradeep A. Rau
University of Delaware

James E. Ricks
Southeast Missouri State

Warren Rose
Texas A&M University

Marc Rubin
Loyola College

Michael F. Smith
Temple University

Don R. Snyder
Millsaps College

Jane R. Ziegler Sojka
Wichita State University

Mary Ann Stutts
Southwest Texas State University

Sharon V. Thach
Cleveland State University

Hale N. Tongren
George Mason University

Mark B. Traylor
Cleveland State University

R. Viswanathan
University of Northern Colorado

James B. Wiley
Temple University

Terry C. Wilson
West Virginia University

Ronald L. Zallocco
University of Toledo

William G. Zikmund
Oklahoma State University

CONTENTS BY TOPICS

ACCOUNT EXECUTIVE

Overview

Account executives are the individuals in advertising agencies who are responsible for the planning and preparation of advertising for one or more clients. They are the primary liaison between the advertiser and the agency. The account executive is the advertising agency counterpart of the product manager. Both analyze the environment, develop a strategy and put together a plan.

To be a successful account executive, one must be able to extract the best possible work from a wide variety of people. This includes working with diverse personalities such as the creative director and the director of marketing research in the firm as well as the many different personalities found on the client's staff. Account executives, therefore, must be skilled at balancing the demands of their clients with those of their own agency. This is easier said than done, but yet it is a task that is essential if the client, and agency and account executive are to prosper.

Examples

The client looks to the account executive for advice on marketing and advertising strategies. The creative people in the agency depend on the account executive for product information, market analysis and a timetable. Agency management holds the account executive responsible for account profitability. The account executive must be a capable organizer with a good business mind for facts and must be able to communicate well with agency colleagues such as the writer; the art director and the market researchers; outside suppliers such as research houses, graphic arts and media; and of course the client and its staff. The account executive, therefore, must have an analytical mind and be able to communicate effectively.

Account executives must also be comfortable with change. Accounts change hands with frightening regularity, sometimes for capricious reasons. In a single year, millions of dollars in billings shift from one agency to another. For example, when Lee Iacocca became Chrysler chairman, one of his first decisions was to drop the firm's long-time advertising agency, BBD&O, and give the entire account to Kenyon and Eckhardt. Iacocca had worked with Kenyon and Eckhardt while he was president of Ford, and convinced the agency to give up its Lincoln-Mercury account with Ford in exchange for a five-year no cut Chrysler contract. At the time Chrysler's annual media expenditures were between $120 million and $150 million.

Benefits

Effective account executives can leverage the creative talent of their agencies and extend the useful life of a client's campaign. The account executive is the one individual positioned to participate in budget control, strategic planning and the creative process. It is essential for an account executive to draft an effective plan that will serve as the key dialogue between the client and the agency. Elements of this plan include: explaining to the client why they need the plan, situational analysis, problems and opportunities, positioning statements, objectives, strategies, media, creative budget and scheduling. The objective of this plan is to build confidence in the client and ultimately market growth expressed in sales.

Implementation

What do account executives do? Are they born with these skills or do they learn them? To answer the first question, successful account executives are a product of experience. A planned program of increasingly challenging and diverse assignment is the best approach to developing effective account executives. At the minimum, the account executive should like working with numbers, enjoy creative writing, like to solve problems, work in committees and make decisions, work under deadlines, and, in fact, make better decisions under the pressure of a deadline and, most importantly, enjoy making presentations to clients. These represent the types of activities that make up responsibilities of an account executive.

Most account executives start as trainees in some department within the agency. As they gain experience in various functional areas, such as media buying, copywriting, and research, they typically become an assistant account executive. Once this experience is gained, the individual is prepared to assume the responsibilities of an account executive.

Evaluation

One would think that an increase in sales would automatically signal that the account executive had successfully performed his job. This is not necessarily the case. Since the account executive deals with so many different people, success or failure must be shared. Adding to this dilemma is the knowledge that in the advertising business, everyone thinks he has a great idea. One approach to evaluating account executives would be to have the agency track a variety of measures, such as total billings, profitability, and stability of earnings that the account executive had responsibility over for a period of time.

The key to being a successful account executive is to do more than the job description requires. Merely acting as a conduit for communication between the client and the agency will not suffice. To be successful, an account executive must add value.

The role of the account executive is becoming more important. The addition of more technical specialists on one hand, and the trend towards outsourcing traditional agency functions on the other, requires more than ever the coordinating skills of the account executive. It is also apparent that, as account executives become more involved in the planning aspects of client's campaigns, they have an increasing impact on the long-term direction of these campaigns and the resultant sales figures.

Conclusion

To be a successful account executive one must like people. An even temperament is necessary as well because the account executive deals with all kinds of people. During the course of a single meeting, account executives must be capable of mediating disagreements one moment and encouraging creative insights the next. Overall the account executive must be a team player. Account executives must be willing to compromise some of their own skills for the benefit of the client and the agency. Thus, the better the account executive is at working with others, the better his chances of doing a good job.

Applications to Small Business

Many small businesses could certainly use the services that an account executive provides. Traditionally, most small businesses are undercapitalized and therefore are searching for ways to cut expenses. Unfortunately, the advertising budget is one of the first areas that the small business proprietor seeks to cut. This is a mistake. The marginal savings derived from placing advertisements (i.e., buying time or space at the local rate) almost never equal the benefit of having an account executive and the agency staff of people working on the account.

References/Sources

Aaker, David A. and Myers, John G., *Advertising Management,* 2nd ed. Englewood Cliffs, NJ: Prentice-Hall, 1982, pp. 14-15. Discusses the trend toward "creative boutiques" and the implications for account executives and account management in general.

Bloede, Victor G., *The Full Service Advertising Agency.* New York: American Association of Advertising Agencies, 1983, p. 2. Discusses the potential threat to employees of full-service agencies if creative boutiques, media buying services and house agencies continue to expand.

Gardner, Herbert S., *The Advertising Agency Business.* Chicago: Crain Books, 1976, pp. 121-125. Presents a list of the services an account executive should render to the client.

Harper, P., "Quality People Hold Key to Success," *Advertising Age* (March 18, 1985): 40. Advertising is people-intensive; quality people are the cornerstone of an agency's success.

McGann, Anthony F., "Human Resource Planning in the Advertising Agency," *Journal of Advertising,* Vol. 14, No. 1 and 2 (1985): 3. This two-part editorial cites the essential nature of human resources at the typical advertising agency and ironically the lack of long-range planning to manage this resource in most agencies.

Mondroski, Marcia M., Reid, Leonard N., and Russell, Thomas J., "Agency Creative Decision Making: A Decision System Analysis," in *Current Issues and Research in Advertising,* Ann Arbor, Michigan, 1983, pp. 57-70. This article presents a detailed description of how an advertising agency develops a campaign. A description of the role the account executive plays in this process is also included.

Ogilvy, David, *Ogilvy on Advertising.* New York: Vintage Books, 1985, pp. 32-35. David Ogilvy presents his wisdom and practical advice on how to become a successful account executive.

Zeltner, Herbert, "Client-Agency Conflicts," *Advertising Age* (March 5, 1984): M-64 to M-68. The author presents the results of a study on client-agency conflicts.

Related Topics and Terms
Account Manager, Contact Executive

James M. Maskulka
Department of Marketing
Lehigh University

ADVERTISING

Overview

Advertising is a difficult term to define. One of the better definitions is that advertising is a form of nonpersonal presentation and promotion of goods, services, or ideas by an identified sponsor. The difficulty in defining advertising lies in the overlap between the different types of nonpersonal promotion and the different forms in which each may appear. Advertising can serve purposes other than selling a product and can be implemented through all forms of media. Advertising's main objective is to create a positive attitude for the item being advertised, but sometimes this may not be accomplished due to errors in the design of the ad itself.

Examples

Advertising exists in many forms and can be seen just about anywhere. The most recognizable forms are print and broadcast ads, which can be seen in newspaper and magazines as well as heard on television and radio, billboards and display signs, and point-of-purchase displays. Some other material that is considered to be advertising, yet overlaps with other forms of promotion as well as other areas in the marketing mix, includes the packaging of the product, brochures and booklets, posters and leaflets, packaging inserts, and even the company's symbols and logos. The most familiar examples of advertising are television and radio commercials and newspaper and magazine advertisements. Examples of advertising that are less conspicuous include the material provided with coupons (as well as the information on the coupon), the display of the product in a catalog, the listing of the company in the yellow pages, and the printing of a company's logo or symbol on a t-shirt.

Benefits

It is difficult to generalize the benefits of advertising, since it has many forms and uses, but some qualities can be identified. Since advertising is a highly public mode of communication, it accords some legitimacy to the product being advertised and implies that the message being offered is standardized. Advertising is also very pervasive, since the message can be repeated numerous times, and this repetition allows consumers to compare messages from various competitors. Also, the pervasiveness of an advertising campaign connotes a positive atmosphere about the seller's size, popularity, and success. Advertising also amplifies a company's expressiveness, by using print, sound, and color to dramatize the company and its products. It is an effective way to reach numerous and geographically diverse consumers while being relatively inexpensive for cost per exposure.

Implementation

The purpose of advertising is to be consistent with and complementary to a company's total marketing efforts. The following steps are useful when designing an advertising campaign:

1) Establish the objectives for the ad campaign
2) Identify the product features or consumer motives to be featured in the ads
3) Select an advertising agency to prepare the campaign (or prepare it in-house)
4) Determine the media to be used to deliver the message
5) Determine what, if any, supporting promotional efforts are to be used.

The first step in designing an advertising campaign is to determine its objectives. The objectives of an ad campaign differ from a firm's marketing objectives, which relate to profit, by stressing some or all of the following goals: increased sales or market share; improved consumer awareness of the company, its product(s), or its dealers; and to create a more positive attitude toward the company, its product(s), or its dealers. The second step is identifying what is to be said by the advertisement. This step involves determining how the company hopes to achieve the objectives outlined in step one.

The next steps are those that involve the designing of the campaign. This is done by an in-house advertising group or by an outside advertising agency and involves designing a message that relays the information to be stressed, which has been previously determined in steps one and two. Once the message has been conceived, the media in which it is to be used need to be determined, as well as how much emphasis is to be placed on each medium. Also, any supporting promotional efforts that are to be used must be coordinated to coincide with the timing for the ad campaign.

After the total campaign has been constructed, it is evaluated again to ensure that it will accomplish its purpose. Once this has been determined, the campaign is put into operation. After the campaign is over, it should be evaluated to see if it did achieve its goals.

Evaluation

In order to determine the effectiveness of advertising, goals or criteria should be established prior to the campaign, which will serve as a basis of comparison for the post-campaign study. Additionally, for most ad campaigns, a pre-test needs to be conducted to determine if any corrections are necessary in order to prevent misinterpretation. Some pertinent questions that are of use when trying to evaluate an ad campaign include:

Did the message provide the correct information?
Was the information presented interpreted correctly?
How effective was the media selection?

Were the appropriate target audiences reached?
How were the audience's attitudes and/or awareness affected by the message?
How were sales and/or market share affected?

After the advertising campaign has been evaluated, the company must decide whether to continue, modify it, or end the campaign.

Conclusion

Although advertising is an effective way to promote a product, service, or idea, it is not always done correctly. The possibility exists that the message may be misinterpreted or misleading. It is up to the advertiser to ascertain that what is being said is straightforward and correct. Problems in evaluating advertisements may occur due to overlap with other promotional activities; changes in sales may be due to other influences.

Even though the evaluation of advertising campaigns is difficult, they are still an important part of the promotional mix. Advertisement may be a rather impersonal form of promotion, to which the audience does not feel obligated to pay attention or respond, but it is highly public and persuasive, which tends to reflect positively on a company. Through the use of sound, color, and print, advertising can dramatize a message, but care must be taken that this expressiveness does not dilute or distract from the message.

Applications to Small Business

Advertising is just as important for the small business as it is for the large conglomerate. It is necessary for the small business to advertise in order for consumers to know about it. The most effective methods for advertising are through local newspapers and magazines as well as purchasing space in the yellow pages. In areas that are serviced by cable, some channels offer time for local commercials, which can sometimes be produced rather inexpensively. Advertising over local radio is another possibility for small businesses. Of course, the easiest and most inexpensive forms of advertising for small businesses are point-of-purchase displays and display signs, as well as a company's sign outside the place of business.

Software/Databases

AMI. The New York Times, 229 West 43rd Street, New York, NY 10036. Advertising & Marketing Intelligence abstracts includes 125,000 articles dealing with advertising, marketing and public relations. Covering print, broadcast and newer media, AMI provides data about new products, campaigns, billings, rates, test marketing, and executive changes.

BAR. Broadcast Advertisers Reports, Inc., 500 Fifth Avenue, New York, NY 10036. Broadcast Advertisers Reports monitors radio and television networks and 300 local television stations so that users can see when and where products are advertised. Information provided includes the content of the advertisement, its length and program, as well as estimated expenditures for each sponsor.

References/Sources

Bogart, Leo, "Mass Advertising: The Message, Not The Measure," *Harvard Business Review* (September-October 1975): 107-116. Stresses that it is more important to examine how and why advertising works, than to examine just statistics.

Bogart, Leo, Tolley, B. Stuart, and Orenstein, Frank, "What One Little Ad Can Do," *Journal of Advertising Research* (August, 1970): 3-13. Includes a study that analyzes the success of an advertisement based on sales response and communication response.

Hise, Richard T., Gillett, Peter L., and Ryans, John K., Jr., *Marketing: Concepts, Decisions, Strategies.* Houston: Dame Publications, 1984. Chapter 10 discusses advertising management and develops the process for implementing and evaluating advertising.

Kotler, Philip, *Marketing Management: Analysis, Planning, and Control,* 5th ed. Englewood Cliffs, NJ: Prentice-Hall, 1984. Chapter 19 discusses communication and promotion-mix decisions and includes areas on developing the communication message and criteria for using advertising.

Lavidge, Robert J., and Steiner, Gary A., "A Model for Predictive Measurements of Advertising Effectiveness," *Journal of Marketing* (October 1961): 59-62. One of the earliest discussions of measuring the effectiveness of advertising.

Leckenby, John D., and Plummer, Joseph T., "Advertising Stimulus Measurement and Assessment Research: A Review of Advertising Testing Methods," *Current Issues and Research In Advertising* (1983): 135-165. Discusses the various techniques for measuring the effectiveness of advertising.

Morris, Don, ed., *Advertising Age Yearbook 1984,* Chicago: Crain Books, 1984. Section 3 lists the top advertisers in various categories as well as listings for all major advertising agencies.

Schmalensee, Diane H., "Today's Top Priority Advertising Research Questions," *Journal of Advertising Research* (April-May 1983): 49-60. Discusses important topics that need to be studied in advertising research, as identified by advertisers and agencies.

Shanklin, William L., and Ryans, John K., Jr., *Marketing High Technology.* Lexington, MA: Lexington Books, 1984. Chapter 6 includes a section stressing the important differences between advertising and marketing.

Related Topics and Terms

Advertising Agency, Comparative Advertising, Cooperative Advertising, Corporate Advertising, Image Advertising, Institutional Advertising, Marketing Mix, Media Selection, Nonprofit Advertising, Packaging, Standardized Advertising, Target Market.

Gary Guenther
Department of Marketing
Texas A&M University

ADVERTISING AGENCY

Overview

The "advertising industry" in the United States is comprised of four types of organizations: advertisers (or sponsors), advertising media, advertising agencies, and advertising support services (e.g., research organizations and media sales representatives). Only the first two parties must be involved for advertising activity to be conducted. However, nearly every major national advertiser has elected to delegate much of the advertising function to an independent advertising agency. Nearly 100% of all television network, large-circulation magazine, and coast-to-coast outdoor advertising campaigns are created and placed by ad agencies.

An ad agency is typically thought of as a business organization which is free of control by any advertiser, although "house agencies" by definition are owned by advertisers. Agencies are expected to maintain highly qualified "advertising professionals" who are able and available to transfer their expertise from one account to another. Agencies are expected to have financial capacity adequate to enable them to meet their obligations to the media. Most agency income is derived from payment of commissions by the media. Typically the media will not pay the 15% commission to house agencies. Historically, agencies were not allowed by the media to rebate any part of their commissions to clients, although this is no longer the case.

Examples

Advertising agencies in the United States are an extremely heterogeneous lot. In 1984, 14 U.S. agencies each reported worldwide billings in excess of $1 billion. Sixteen agencies had 2,000 or more employees. Most "giant" agencies are located in major advertising centers, primarily New York, Chicago, Detroit, Los Angeles, Minneapolis, Dallas, Boston, Pittsburgh, Philadelphia, and Cleveland. On the other hand, there are thousands of one- and two-person agencies located in cities and towns across the nation. Many of them, however, appear to be more heavily involved in public relations than in advertising work.

By most measures, America's largest ad agency in 1984 was Young and Rubicam (Y&R). This New York-based giant had estimated gross income of $480 million, based on worldwide billings of $3.2 billion. Y&R's U.S. business is believed to have represented about two-thirds of the agency's billings, and about three-fourths of its gross income. Y&R had more than 8,400 employees worldwide. The agency maintained an impressive roster of accounts including, among many others, American Telephone and Telegraph, Lincoln-Mercury, Jell-O, Thomas' English Muffins, Campbell Soup, the U.S. Postal Service, and the 7-Eleven stores. And like most agencies, Y&R experienced both gains and losses among the accounts it represented. "Gainers" included Advil, Canada Dry No-Cal, Ajax Dishwashing Liquid,

Breyers Ice Cream, NYNEX Business Information System Sales Force, Tupperware Home Parties, Humana's Medfirst Division, and the International Harvester corporate account. Its principal losses were Hallmark Cards and USA Today.

Not all major ad agencies are located in principal advertising centers. For example, Henderson Advertising, the nation's 78th largest agency, is in Greenville, South Carolina. From its unlikely home base, in 1984 the agency reported gross income of $11.3 million on billings of $75.4 million. Henderson's 130 employees served Texize, Carlton's Wolf Beer, Rene Junot French Wine, Fotomat, Hanes Printables Division, and Consolidated Foods, among others. Henderson Advertising was unique among larger agencies in that it reported no account losses.

Benefits

The nearly universal use of ad agencies by larger advertisers and by many smaller ones, and the readiness of the media to pay agencies the customary 15% commission, give testimony to the benefits that both parties find in using the services of agencies. Basically, agencies perform three functions. First, they help clients plan their advertising program. Second, they prepare the ads, thereby translating creative strategy into copy and art. Third, they place advertising in the media that will convey the advertiser's message most effectively and efficiently within budget constraints. Some agencies offer additional services, such as marketing, public relations, and research assistance.

Advertisers use the services of agencies for a variety of reasons. Reliance upon an agency typically provides the client with access to a range and depth of advertising talent that few could afford or adequately utilize independently. Further, it is generally accepted that agency personnel have a unique breadth of experience based upon routine exposure to numerous accounts, and increased objectivity in perspective which derives from not being in the client's organization and on his payroll directly. Finally, in view of the pervasive 15% commission system, many advertisers feel that they must "pay" for the agency's services, whether or not they use them. Under this system some advertisers view agencies' basic services as essentially "free goods."

Most media also seem pleased with the range and quality of "benefits" they receive from agencies. It is argued that the present system eliminates the creative burden which would fall on the media, if professional agencies were not furnishing "finished" copy and art. Similarly, agencies handle scheduling details and mechanical production details (e.g., the production of electrotype), requiring little if any additional production effort by the media. Also, since agencies are financially responsible for their clients' media bills, and since agencies have demonstrated financial capacity to meet their obligations, credit risks of the media are minimized. Finally, the media's sales costs are reduced, since media salespeople call primarily on media buyers in the agencies, rather than on the many clients whom they represent.

Implementation

When selecting an advertising agency the advertiser may approach a single agency which is well known and highly regarded by the prospective client, or he may invite solicitations (or "presentations") by any interested agency or by agencies specifically invited to "bid." Some advertisers invite dozens of agencies, necessarily extending the process of selection.

It has been suggested by Burton and Ryan that the advertiser should be satisfied with prospective agencies' responses to the following questions before final selection is made:

(1) What is the quality of the agency's creative work?
(2) What kind of people, in general, head and staff the agency?
(3) Who are the people who will work on the client's account?
(4) What experience has the agency had with the client's kind of product or service?
(5) How important will the client's account be in the agency's account list?
(6) What is the range of agency services, and how does the agency charge for them?
(7) Is the agency's account list made up of leaders, or also-rans?
(8) Does the agency have case histories that demonstrate its skill?

Other factors, such as the agency's age, size, location, credit standing, reputation, and supplementary services, are also considered. However, executives place great importance on a prospective agency's creative ability, market research competency, and avoidance of competitive conflicts. Product proliferation by major package goods manufacturers has significantly increased the likelihood of competitive conflicts within an agency's account list.

An advertising executive (Salz) has suggested that the advertiser should expect six commitments from its ad agency:

(1) Commitment to the success of the client's business.
(2) Knowledge of the client's business.
(3) Open-mindedness.
(4) Honesty.
(5) Leadership from the agency's account people.
(6) Respect for the client's position as advertiser.

The agency-client relationship is a frequently troubled one, resulting in account turnovers. Salz identifies six elements which support successful collaboration between agency and client:

(1) The collaborators continually focused on their common goal.
(2) Their roles were clearly defined.
(3) They were experts in their own areas, and therefore earned the other collaborator's respect.

(4) They trusted each other.
(5) Client authority lines were relaxed.
(6) The collaborators felt free to contribute in areas other than their own, and accept suggestions from others in their own areas.

Evaluation

The substantial number of account turnovers reported regularly in the advertising trade press provides testimony to the continuing evaluation of agencies being made by client firms, and to the incidence of negative findings in those evaluations. Insight into the nature of advertisers' specific concerns about their agencies is provided by a recent study undertaken jointly by the Association of National Advertisers and the American Association of Advertising Agencies. The following factors are most often cited by advertisers as hindering a productive advertiser-agency relationship:

(1) Too much turnover of personnel within the agency.
(2) Agency's inability to adhere to schedules.
(3) Agency's need for too much lead time.
(4) Insufficient involvement of agency's senior management.
(5) Agency's failure to ask the right questions.
(6) Agency's unwillingness to listen to other points of view.
(7) Agency's failure to show initiative.
(8) Agency's failure to follow established lines of communication.

Highly negative evaluations of agency performance may cause the advertiser to terminate his affiliation with that agency. Among the most frequent causes for advertiser-initiated termination are:

(1) Advertiser is dissatisfied with sales, market share, or other "results."
(2) Advertiser "outgrows" the agency through mergers, acquisitions, or normal growth.
(3) Advertiser becomes involved in international markets, while the agency operates only in the home market.
(4) New product developments and/or mergers put the advertiser into product areas already served by the agency, creating conflict of interest.
(5) Advertiser views the agency's services as too limited.
(6) Advertiser re-organization emphasizes use of a single agency or, conversely, use of multiple agencies.
(7) Another agency becomes known as a "hot" agency based upon a series of dramatic successes.
(8) Misunderstandings about charges made by the agency.
(9) Friendships or, conversely, personality clashes.

Frequently, ad agencies resign existing accounts. Most often this is caused by:

(1) Conflicts of interest which grow out of ad agency mergers and acquisitions.
(2) Conflicts of interest which develop from the client's expansion.
(3) Better prospects with a different client in the same product or service category.

Conclusion

In 1984, the U.S. advertising agency industry attained a worldwide gross income of $7.2 billion, based on billings of $49.4 billion. The industry's level of billings and its use by nearly every major national advertiser attests to ad agencies' established role in American business. Just as agencies differ in size and degree of services offered, so does the nature of agency-client relationships. There is no single "best" type of agency for all advertisers, nor a universally "ideal" form of agency-client relationship. The ad agency business is open to change, as indicated by some of them abandoning or modifying the traditional 15% commission system, expanding into international operations, establishing "giant" agencies in the U.S. through aggressive programs of acquisition and merger, and by selling shares of stock to the public. The vital role of ad agencies in American business is secure, although the nature of agency operations will continue to be in a state of flux.

Applications to Small Business

Smaller firms are even less likely than larger ones to be able to afford, and to efficiently use, the full-time services of highly trained advertising professionals. Further, their more limited advertising budgets require even more attention to the resulting effectiveness and cost efficiency. Unfortunately, executives in small businesses sometimes believe that their accounts are less welcomed, or at least less well served, by ad agencies. To a degree this may be true, since ad agency compensation typically is a function of the level of billings generated by the account. A large account results in higher commissions paid to the agency by the media.

However, many agencies (especially smaller independent agencies and smaller operating subsidiaries of larger agencies) welcome smaller accounts. In other situations, the smaller advertiser may be more welcome by agencies if the relationship is based upon fees, rather than commissions.

Local advertisers, whether large or small, should be aware that purchase of local media time and space are generally not "commissionable." Consequently, local advertisers who use the services of ad agencies will typically be charged fees to offset the income which is not received from commissions from the media.

Software/Databases

AMI. The New York Times, 229 West 43rd Street, New York, NY 10036. Advertising and Marketing Intelligence (AMI) abstracts about 125,000 articles dealing with advertising, marketing and public relations. Containing information about account changes, new products and campaigns, billings, rates, executive changes, market research, and test marketing, AMI is an important source for advertising agencies that want to research past campaigns and keep current with developments in their field.

References/Sources

"A.A.A.A.: Report on Agency Costs and Profits," *B/PAA Communicator* (September/October 1983): 9. Reviews the structure of ad agency expense and profit ratios.

Advertising Age: U.S. Advertising Agency Profiles, published annually by Advertising Age, 740 Rush Street, Chicago, IL 60611. Profiles the nation's ad agencies in terms of billings, gross income, accounts gained and lost during the past year, and agency officers.

Association of National Advertisers, *Agency Compensation.* New York: Association of National Advertisers, 1979. A detailed description of ad agency compensation methods and procedures from the advertiser's perspective.

Association of National Advertisers, *Evaluating Agency Performance.* New York: Association of National Advertisers, 1977. A detailed review of procedures for evaluating ad agency performance, presented from the perspective of the advertiser.

Bonsib, Richard E., "Is an Agency Association for You?" *Advertising Age* (April 25, 1983): M-38. An evaluation of the advertiser's choice regarding whether to employ the services of an ad agency.

Heckerback, Roy A., "You Can—and Should—Audit How Well Your Agency Performs as Your Agent," *Industrial Marketing* (November 1976): 68. Emphasizes the advertiser's need to evaluate the ad agency's performance.

Kanner, Bernice, "Client Audits of Agencies Becoming More Common," *Advertising Age* (December 3, 1979): 10. Illustrates the trend among advertisers in reviewing their agencies' financial records pertaining to their accounts.

Salz, Nancy L., *How to Get the Best Advertising from Your Agency.* Englewood Cliffs, NJ: Prentice-Hall, 1983. A practitioner-oriented book which promotes a stronger collaborative relationship between agency and client.

Selecting an Advertising Agency. New York: Association of National Advertisers, 1977. A guidebook for advertisers who are seeking new ad agency relationships.

Weilbacher, William M., *Auditing Productivity: Advertiser-Agency Relationships Can Be Improved.* New York: Association of National Advertisers, 1981. Presents findings of a study of client and agency evaluations of the advertiser-agency relationship, including evaluations of performance of both self and the other party.

Weilbacher, William M., "The 15% Media Commission Is on the Way Toward Becoming a Relic in Ad Agency Compensation Plans," *Marketing News* (June 10, 1983): 1. Insights into alternative means for compensating ad agencies.

Related Topics and Terms
Account Executive, Advertising.

Robert L. King
Department of Business Administration
The Citadel

ADVERTISING BY PROFESSIONALS

Overview

Historically, professionals such as doctors, lawyers, dentists, architects and accountants did not advertise. These professionals felt that their services were so highly personalized that they could not be compared through a vehicle such as advertising. Furthermore, many professionals considered advertising as unprofessional and contrary to their codes of ethics. These ideals began to change in the 1970s when two lawyers from Phoenix ran a newspaper ad for their newly established law practice. This incidence led to the now famous *Bates vs. State Bar of Arizona* case in which the Supreme Court ruled that bar association codes that prohibit advertising by lawyers are unconstitutional. Shortly after the decision, the Federal Trade Commission ruled that the American Medical Association and the American Dental Association could no longer prohibit their members from advertising their fees and services. Today, it is very common to see newspaper, television and even direct mail ads from lawyers, doctors, dentists and other professional groups.

Examples

While all professional groups utilize advertising in the marketing of their services, it is the legal profession that appears to be the heaviest user of advertising. It is not the individual lawyer, but a new wave of national law firms that are rushing to the advertising bandwagon. In fact, many of these large, progressive law firms view advertising as a routine cost of doing business. Firms such as Hyatt Legal Services, Jacoby and Meyers, and Norton Frickey Associates represent the latest trend in high-volume, low-cost legal services. According to the Television Bureau of Advertising, the first nine months of 1983 showed a 61 percent increase over the previous year in dollars spent by the top 20 legal advertisers on television advertising. Hyatt Legal Services, with 117 offices in 17 states, led all attorneys by spending $2,419,300 on television advertising alone. Additionally, the Television Bureau of Advertising reports a 79 percent increase in ad spending by the top 10 legal firms between 1981 and 1982. Jacoby and Meyers, another large law firm, has developed its own in-house ad agency. This legal group spent $613,000 on television advertising in 1983. As the oversupply of attorneys in today's market continues, it is predicted that more and more attorneys will need to advertise for survival.

Currently, additional professional groups, especially dentists, are turning to advertising. With the latest trend of shopping mall dental centers and dental departments in established retail stores, it has been estimated that more than 15,000 dentists are currently advertising. In fact, the entire medical profession is now

17

realizing that advertising is becoming increasingly important in today's very progressive, marketing-oriented health-care market.

Benefits

Advertising by professionals can result in substantial benefits. While many attorneys are scrambling to stay in business in today's very competitive marketplace, the progressive, marketing-oriented law firms are growing. Hyatt Legal Services now employs about 300 lawyers, ranking it among the nation's 15 largest law firms. At its present rate of growth, Hyatt claims it will soon become the largest law firm in America. Another law firm which experimented with direct mail advertising experienced a twenty-five dollar return in legal fees for every one dollar spent on direct mail advertising.

Other professional groups are also experiencing benefits from their advertising. Comprehensive Care Corporation, a California hospital chain, estimates that 30 percent of its business is due to advertising. Dr. Dennis Brooks advertised his skills as an eye surgeon in several television commercials that were aired in Philadelphia. Dr. Brooks was amazed at the number of new patients the ads brought in during the first month of the campaign. All professional groups are now beginning to realize that new business is possible through advertising.

Advertising by professionals not only helps the professional doing the advertising, but the consumer as well. Professional advertising has yielded such benefits to the marketplace as lowering prices and increasing demand for professional services. During the last several years the prices of legal and dental services have decreased. This is due, in part, to the new marketing-orientation that many professionals are now taking. Additionally, advertising by professionals can benefit consumers by providing them with information they previously did not have.

Implementation

Several factors must be considered before a professional decides to advertise his services. First of all, one should not equate advertising with marketing. It is nearly impossible to have an effective advertisement without paying attention to the other elements of the marketing mix. Without a thorough understanding of who the target audience is, for example, an ad by a professional would probably be misdirected. Knowing an audience is the first step in deciding which media to select and what message to develop.

Another important aspect that the advertising professional must consider is what type of information to include in an advertisement. Two of the most important criteria consumers look for are years of experience and areas of specialization. These selection criteria have particular value in that they can be effectively communicated in both print and broadcast advertisements, and indicate the capability of the professional. Other criteria that were found to be particularly useful in attorney advertising included the personable qualities of the attorney, fees charged for services and the extent the same lawyer could be used for all legal needs. Of this latter group, the personable qualities of the attorney is the most subjective and may be difficult to communicate in a print advertisement. However, communicating a personal quality may be important for a professional in generating repeat business. For example, studies have shown that lawyers are often criticized for not explaining legal matters in words the client can understand. Therefore, professionals should design ads which personally relate to the client. Thus, professionals will do better in their advertising after a careful examination of their target audience and the appeals that best fit that group.

Evaluation

Once a professional advertises, several things can be done to test the effectiveness of the advertisement. A procedure which is practiced by many large advertisers is to pretest the ad before it's put into circulation. This can be accomplished by presenting the ad to several people and asking for their reaction. Another approach is to include the ad with several other ads in an attempt to determine how the ad compares with others of comparable quality. A pretest is an easy, inexpensive way to see if something important has been left out or if there is something that should be taken out.

Another recommended procedure for testing the effectiveness is to conduct a test after the ad has been run in an appropriate media. This can be accomplished by keeping track of one or more important benchmarks, such as the number of new clients, awareness level of the firm, and consumers' image of the firm. If one or more of these important benchmarks increase after the ad has been run, one can argue that the implementation of the advertisement was successful.

Conclusion

Despite the many benefits associated with advertising by professionals, it remains a controversial topic. Some of the issues surrounding this area include:

1. Professionals are still somewhat skeptical of advertising despite the fact that studies show consumers are much more likely to accept professional advertising than are the professionals themselves.
2. Many professionals feel that advertising will lessen their credibility or professionalism.
3. Many professionals feel that advertising is not cost effective.
4. The debate continues concerning whether advertising by professionals provides more information for consumers or whether it creates more confusion.
5. The American Bar Association estimates that about 13 percent of its membership has tried some sort of advertising and nearly 25 percent stated that they would use advertising in the future.

Resistance to advertising by professionals may be due to: 1) professionals' fear that advertising will cheapen their image, and 2) professionals' lack of knowledge concerning the benefits of advertising. With the increasing numbers of professionals entering the marketplace, it is inevitable that a greater portion of them will turn to advertising to survive.

Applications to Small Business

While the majority of advertising by professionals is done by national firms with large advertising budgets, the professional in a small practice should not rule out advertising. Advertising is an excellent way to build awareness of a professional in an area. Unfortunately, independent professionals are often too busy to think about advertising their services. Yet, most professionals who advertise are often amazed at the number of new clients that can be generated with a properly executed advertisement.

References/Sources

"Ads Don't Bite into Dentists' Ethics," *Advertising Age* (May 23, 1983): 88. Reports on the number of dentists rushing to the advertising bandwagon.

"Ads Start to Take Hold in the Professions," *Business Week* (July 24, 1978): 123-124. Presents the trends in advertising by professionals.

Bush, Alan J., and Moncrief, William C., "The Effect of Attorneys' Direct Mail Advertising on Credibility: A Study of Attorneys' and Consumers' Perceptions," *Current Issues and Research in Advertising,* Vol. 1 (1985): 161-173. Presents the results of an advertising experiment involving direct mail ads by attorneys. Attorneys and consumers rated the credibility of several attorney direct mail ads.

Bush, Alan J., and Moncrief, William C., "Enhancing the Credibility of Attorneys' Print Advertising: An Experimental Approach," *Akron Business and Economic Review* (Fall 1985): 55-60. Presents the results of an advertising experiment involving newspaper ads by attorneys. Consumers rated several newspaper ads by a fictitious law firm.

Darden, Donna K., Darden, William R., and Kiser, G.E., "The Marketing of Legal Services," *Journal of Marketing* (Spring 1981): 123-134. Suggests how the distribution of legal services can be enhanced. Additionally, the article profiles users and nonusers of legal services.

Greene, Richard, "Lawyers Versus the Marketplace," *Forbes* (January 16, 1984): 73-77. Presents the latest trends in the legal service marketplace.

Humphreys, Marie Adele, and Kasulis, Jack J., "Attorney Advertising," *Journal of Advertising Research* (December 1981): 31-37. Presents the results of a study where consumers identified what they thought were the selection criteria they used when seeking an attorney.

Kincaid, William M., *Promotion: Products, Services, and Ideas.* Columbus, OH: Charles E. Merrill, 1985. Textbook on promotion with a good definition and overview of advertising by professionals.

Lear, Len, "Eye Doctor Is First to Advertise With TV Spots," *Adweek* (July 20, 1983): 31. Gives an example of how an eye doctor increased the number of new clients through advertising.

Moran, Dennis J., "Moving Out of Infancy," *Advertising Age* (December 24, 1079): S-1. An earlier article highlighting the increasing use of advertising by the professions.

Russell, Anne M., "Courting Lawyers Could Pay Off the Ad Agencies," *Adweek* (March 19, 1984): 34. Emphasizes the size of the legal sector in terms of advertising dollars for ad agencies.

Weinrauch, J. Donald, "The Entrepreneurial Physician: Marketing Challenges and Opportunities," *Journal of Small Business Management* (April 1982): 8-14. Emphasizes the importance of marketing to the doctor in a small practice.

Related Topics and Terms
Advertising, Advertising Agency, Magazines, Newspapers, Promotion Mix.

Alan J. Bush
Department of Marketing
Texas A&M University

ADVERTISING CLAIMS BELIEVABILITY

Overview

To substantiate product performance claims today (and to enhance consumers' perceived believability of these claims), advertisers have begun utilizing research results information more and more frequently (e.g., "four out of five doctors recommend"). However, little information has been available concerning how consumers perceive the believability of such advertisements. Several recent empirical investigations have addressed this topic, and together offer a number of insights to advertisers.

Five characteristics of research which potentially impact advertising believability can be identified from existing relevant research. These include the size of the sample (e.g., "10 experts agreed" vs. "100 experts agreed"), the nature of the sample (e.g., "consumers just like you" vs. "experts in the field"), documentation as to who conducted the research (e.g., "in a recent study conducted by the Consumer Product Safety Commission" vs. the absence of any such documentation), the quantitative versus qualitative nature of the results (e.g., "9 out of 10 prefer" vs. "most prefer"), and the magnitude of the claim difference (e.g., "6 out of 10" vs. "7 out of 10" vs. "8 out of 10" vs. "9 out of 10" vs. "10 out of 10").

Examples

A number of companies have reported research results in their advertisements in an effort to show their products as preferred and hopefully increase sales. Pepsico has alluded to taste test results which show Pepsi as preferred over Coca Cola by soft drink consumers. Doctors have been shown to prefer Bayer Asprin over other competitive pain killers. During a Super Bowl, a live taste test among Miller beer drinkers showed Schlitz to be favored by a majority. Ford's owners, through a survey of new car buyers, have been touted as being more satisfied than the owners of other automobiles.

Benefits

If the trend toward advertisers including research results information in their ads is meant to enhance the believability of product performance claims, it is insufficient that the information be reliable—it must also be believable. That is, advertisers must assess the perceived believability of research results information in advertising to determine if their inclusion represents a positive contribution, or is simply regarded as unbelievable or too good to be true.

Implementation

Implementing research results in advertising necessitates several stages. First, a believability scale is needed to reliably and validly measure the construct of advertising believability. As with most applied measurement situations, this stage involves a pretest and analysis. Once the scale is available, a second stage involves testing the empirical variables for assessment (e.g., magnitude of the claim difference) and levels of each for manipulation (e.g., "6 out of 10" and so forth). Additional pretesting is, therefore, required to refine the variables to be included in the final investigation. Finally, the third stage of this process involves an empirical assessment under representative field conditions, including all the relevant variables.

Evaluation

The results of this series of investigations suggest that consumers perceive research results information based upon smaller samples as significantly more believable than those based upon larger samples. However, it does not seem to matter whether the information is based upon a sample of experts versus a sample of consumers. Similarly, no significant differences in perceived believability were found to derive from information documented as having been conducted by an independent testing agency versus information presented without such documentation.

Consumers were found to perceive advertisements containing qualitatively oriented research results information as significantly more believable than those containing quantitatively oriented results. This finding was consistent when controlling sample size (both across sample sizes and within each sample size were manipulated). Finally, it appears that a threshold effect significantly impacts the magnitude of claim difference, such that perceived believability increases to a point of diminishing returns ("7 out of 10"), after which perceived believability declines.

Conclusion

Basically, these results suggest that consumers are not researchers. They seem to perceive the input of a smaller sample of peers as more believable than that of a larger group of potential strangers. While these results undoubtedly reflect uncertainty over experts' specific qualifications, traditional reliance on information from one's peer group was also evident. This finding was also evident in consumers' perceptions toward independent testing organizations. Finally, it seems consumers attribute more believability to qualitative shorthand (e.g., "most") than to quantitative results, which may be regarded as an overutilized creative technique by advertisers.

Applications to Small Business

These results seem to indicate that advertisers should utilize caution in deciding whether or not to present research results information in their advertising, whether or not the information is in fact reliable. While this caution seems directed primarily at large advertisers with sizable research budgets, the same point can be applied to small advertisrs, who often become so involved in day-to-day operations that they resort to emulating creative techniques of their larger counterparts. It is insufficient to conduct research to substantiate product performance claims, or even to obtain positive results. What is necessary is to pretest advertisements containing such information intended to enhance their believability, and this holds true of large and small advertisers alike.

Software/Databases

Most assessments of advertising believability necessitate situation specific investigations, and little "generic" software is available to facilitate this, short of data analysis packages such as the *Statistical Package for the Social Sciences*. However, the believability scale developed in this on-going stream of research has evidenced reliability across multiple applications and may be utilized.

References/Sources

Beltramini, R.F., "Advertising Perceived Believability Scale," *Proceedings of the Southwestern Marketing Association*, 1982, pp. 1-3.

Beltramini, R.F. and Evans, K.R., "Perceived Believability of Research Results Information in Advertising," *Journal of Advertising*, 14, (1985): 18-24, 31.

Coney, K. and Beltramini, R.F., "Believability of Research Results in Advertising: The 'Too Good to be True' Phenomenon," *Proceedings of the American Marketing Association Winter Educators' Conference*, 1985, pp. 135-139.

Related Topics and Terms

Advertising, Attitudes, Believability, Copy Testing, Information Processing, Measurement, Presentation.

Richard F. Beltramini
Department of Marketing
Arizona State University

APPLIED RESEARCH

Overview

The purpose of applied research is to provide information which will aid an organization's formulation of marketing tactics and strategies. The information which is gathered is typically concerned with gaining an understanding of potential buyers' needs and perceptions. Applied marketing research is capable of answering many important questions, among these are:

How much demand is there for a specific new product concept?
What can be done to make it more attractive to the market?
Who is the best market for a specific product?
What is the consumers' image of the organization?
What is the consumers' image of the competition?
What can be done to improve the image?
What media should be used to reach the market effectively?
How effective is the organization's advertising?
How should products be priced?
What channels of distribution should be used for each product line?

Applied research is intended to have a direct and immediate impact upon major organizational marketing decisions. This distinguishes it from basic research which is conducted without great concern for its immediate relevance to practitioners. The following questions are representative of these posed in basic research:

What is the best way to measure involvement?
How does mood affect buying behavior?
What is the relationship between materialism and consumer satisfaction?

These issues are not as directly relevant to managers as are the issues explored by applied research.

Examples

The Creamy Dough Corporation runs a chain of donut shops throughout the southeastern portion of the United States. Total sales were dropping at a rate of 5% a year. To offset this drop in sales the organization considered introducing bagels as part of their product line. Creamy Dough's marketing director realized that applied research needed to be conducted to provide information that would help the organization decide whether the bagel should be introduced. Information about the extent of the demand for the bagel among present customers was needed.

Creamy Dough management did not have the resources necessary to mount an advertising campaign designed to attract new customers, thus present customers were the focus of the research. An additional goal was to obtain a customer profile of present customers and to identify which customers segments were most likely to purchase bagels. Further goals of the research were: 1) to investigate whether bagels would result in additional sales revenue or would encourage customers to buy bagels instead of donuts (cannibalization), 2) to determine whether the sale of bagels would extend the busy hours of operation beyond the present 6:00 a.m.-9:00 a.m. period, and finally, 3) to decide whether anti-semitic sentiments might adversely affect bagel sales.

After formulating the goals for the research, Creamy Dough's marketing director contacted a number of marketing research consultants for the purpose of soliciting proposals. The accepted proposal involved conducting two focus groups and the administration of a questionnaire to a total sample of 1800 present customers from six stores. The questionnaire was to be completed by customers in the stores and was supervised by representatives of the consulting team.

A focus group involves bringing together approximately 8-12 individuals for the purpose of engaging them in a discussion about a product, service or promotional campaign. In this particular instance the focus group revealed that there was at least a minimal amount of interest in bagels. The focus group also provided the researcher with the opportunity to hear consumers' comments about Creamy Dough and bagels in the consumers' own words. This was particularly helpful in the formulation of the questionnaire.

The research goals and the information from the focus group provided the guidance necessary to write the questionnaire. The information generated as a result of administering the questionnaire proved quite useful. The market segment most interested in purchasing bagels from Creamy Dough were women, twenty-nine and younger with a college education. The survey also revealed that these individuals only comprise about 15% of Creamy Dough's customer base. Those who did plan on purchasing bagels indicated they would purchase them instead of donuts as opposed to purchasing them in addition to donuts. Clearly, this would mean that the sale of bagels would tend to diminish donut revenues. Additionally, it was discovered that most people who were interested in purchasing bagels would do it during Creamy Dough's peak time (6:00 a.m.-9:00 a.m.). Finally, the research revealed that approximately 30% of those surveyed believed that bagels were primarily eaten only by Jewish people.

As a result of these findings Creamy Dough management decided not to introduce the bagel. Fortunately, the company conducted the research before making the $200,000 investment in the plant and equipment necessary for the production of bagels.

Benefits

The basic benefit of all marketing research is to provide management with useful insight into the market place. According to Kotler (pp. 195-196), the following are the ten most commonly conducted types of applied marketing research: determination of market characteristics, measurement of market potentials, market-share analysis, sales analysis, studies of business trends, competitive-product studies, short-range forecasting, new product acceptance and potential, long-range forecasting, and pricing studies. The major benefit of performing research in all of these cases is to provide *unbiased* and *accurate* information. If applied marketing research is not conducted, decisions must be based upon management's assumptions about the market place. These assumptions are likely to be flawed for a number of reasons. They may be based upon outdated, inaccurate, and biased information. For example, the president of the Creamy Dough Company had assumed that the bagel was going to be a very popular product among his present customers. The research was conducted over his objections. If the organization had operated under an "everybody loves bagels" assumption, a significant loss would have been incurred.

Implementation

The procedure that needs to be followed to conduct applied research may vary from one project to another. However, the following steps adapted from Zikmund (p. 39) are sufficiently general to encompass most situations:

1. Defining the research goals.
2. Planning the research design.
3. Planning a sample.
4. Collecting the data.
5. Analyzing the data.
6. Preparing the report and formulating conclusions.

A clear and precise statement of the research goals is absolutely necessary. The goals need to be very explicit. A statement such as, "We need to know whether the product will sell" is clearly inappropriate. The goals are the driving force behind the research. Without a clear statement of goals the project will surely fail to meet expectations.

Once the research goals have been stated, the actual planning of the research design can begin. The first question that needs to be resolved is whether primary or secondary data are necessary. Secondary data are data which already exist because they were collected for some other purpose. The first source of secondary data that should be considered is the company's own records. The advantage of these data is that they can be easily and inexpensively accessed. Other external sources of secondary data include trade associations, government agencies, and syndicated services.

Primary data need to be considered if secondary data are not capable of meeting the needs of the project. The two major types of primary data are qualitative and quantitative. The most common form of qualitative research is the focus group interview. This approach is appropriate when:

1. little is known about consumers' perceptions,
2. direct questioning would be inappropriate, and
3. a large scale quantitative survey is precluded.

Qualitative research is considered exploratory and should not be the sole basis for the formulation of strategy. A unique advantage of qualitative research is that it allows consumers to voice their opinions in their own words without being constrained by a rigid questionnaire. Qualitative research typically employs small non-random samples. As a result qualitative research typically can be conducted more quickly and less expensively than quantitative research.

If specific numerical predictions are necessary, then quantitative research should be conducted. The most common form of quantitative research involves administering a survey to a large random (or quasi-random) sample. Questionnaire development requires a significant amount of skill and experience and should not be done haphazardly. Developing a bad questionnaire is easy; developing a good one is very difficult.

Regardless of the type of research, a sampling plan should be developed. The sample needs to consist of a group of people representative of the individuals one wishes to explore. Designing a sample can be a very complex matter and should be explored more fully by consulting the "Sample" article.

The major means of collecting quantitative data are: personal interviews, telephone interviews, and mail interviews. Cost, timeliness, and the ability to generate meaningful data from the appropriate sample are the criteria which need to be employed when choosing the data-collection method. Telephone interviews are frequently used because they tend to be relatively inexpensive and quick.

The data-analysis approach should be decided upon before the data are collected. This is to insure that the data are collected in a manner compatible with the desired analytic approach. The most common and simple means of data analysis are frequency distributions and cross-tabulations. These two approaches present the data in an easy to understand format. The following is an example of a frequency distribution.

	Strongly Agree	Agree	Disagree	Strongly Disagree
I like bagels	17%	20%	35%	28%

From these data it is clear that the majority of those sampled do not like bagels (63% either disagree or strongly disagree with the statement).

The research report is prepared after the data are analyzed. The following are the major sections of an applied research report:

1. Executive Summary   4. Findings
2. Introduction   5. Limitations
3. Methodology   6. Conclusions and recommendations

Evaluation

Before a research project is embarked upon, the project's benefits need to be compared to the costs that will be incurred. If this evaluation reveals that the costs outweigh the benefits, the project should not be undertaken. This cost-benefit evaluation is sometimes difficult to perform because quantifying the benefit of the research is difficult.

Applied research sponsors need to determine whether the work should be conducted by the organization's staff or by outside consultants. This "make" or "buy" decision should be guided by a number of criteria, most importantly, expertise. If the organization does not have the necessary expertise, the research needs to be conducted by outside suppliers. Even if expertise is present within the organization, the need for the objectivity may require using external consultants. One of the strongest reasons for performing research in-house is confidentiality.

Conclusion

Applied research is designed to aid managers in their decision making. It can be viewed as a systematic means of gathering market-related information. As organizations have become more marketing oriented, the incidence of applied research has risen. Financial institutions and health care institutions have only recently become involved in conducting applied research. As this trend continues, those organizations not conducting research will be at a serious disadvantage.

Applications to Small Business

Traditionally applied research has not been conducted by small businesses. The primary reason for this is probably the relatively high cost of such research. Over time, however, the trend has been for more small businesses to embrace applied research. Universities are the most appropriate source of inexpensive and useful research for small businesses. Experienced business consultants are available through Small Business Development Centers at major universities. Additionally, professors may be willing to implement research for small businesses in the form of class projects. This results in an applied learning experience for students as well as benefits for small businesses.

Software/Databases

SAS and *SPSS* are very powerful software packages available for large mainframe computers and microcomputers. *SAS.* SAS Institute Inc., Cary, NC. *SPSS.* SPSS Inc., Suite 3000, 444 Michigan Avenue, Chicago, IL.

The *Marketing News* periodically lists software packages which are available for microcomputers. *Marketing News,* American Marketing Association, Suite 200, 250 S. Wacker Drive, Chicago, IL.

Many sources of marketing data are available for various types of applied research. Most of the major databases and services are listed in the following two directories:

Bradford's Directory of Marketing Research Agencies and Management Consultants in the United States and the World, P. O. Box 276, Dept. A, Fairfax, VA 22030.

International Directory of Marketing Research Houses and Services, American Marketing Association, New York Chapter, 420 Lexington Avenue, New York, NY 10017.

References/Sources

Alreck, Pamela, and Settle, Robert, *The Survey Research Handbook.* Homewood, IL: Richard D. Irwin, 1985. A very pragmatic guide for conducting survey research. Particularly helpful with questionnaire design.

Bureau of the Census Catalog of Publications. United States Department of Commerce, Bureau of the Census. An index of all census data.

Ferber, Robert, *Handbook of Marketing Research.* New York: McGraw-Hill, 1974. A classic in its field.

Higginbotham, James B., and Cox, Keith K., (eds.), *Focus Group Interviews: A Reader.* Chicago, IL: American Marketing Association, 1979. Contains 24 articles on focus groups. The first article by Wells is particularly helpful.

Kotler, Phillip, *Marketing Management: Analysis Planning and Control,* 5th ed. New York: Prentice-Hall, 1984. Presents an overview of marketing. Chapters 6 and 7 are concerned with applied research.

Tull, Donald S., and Hawkins, Pel I., *Marketing Research: Measurement and Method.* New York: Macmillan Publishing Company, 1984. Presents a very well developed perspective on all aspects of the research process.

Zikmund, William G., *Exploring Marketing Research.* New York: The Dryden Press, 1986. Provides a comprehensive and easy to understand approach to applied research.

Related Topics and Terms

Consumer Behavior, Exploratory Research, Focus Group Interview, Internal Data, Market Potential, Market Segmentation, Marketing Information System, Marketing Research, New Product Development, Personal Interview, Product Design, Questionnaire, Response Rate, Sales Forecast, Sample, Secondary Data, Standard Industrial Classification, Test Market.

Greg J. Lessne
Department of Marketing
University of Rhode Island

ARTIFICIAL INTELLIGENCE IN MARKETING

Overview

Recent technological advances in micro-based computer hardware/software have made efficient and effective applications of artificial intelligence to marketing feasible. Artificial intelligence consists of several fields of research including: expert systems (problem solving), computer aided instruction, natural language translators (converting English into a computer language), sensing (voice, vision, and hearing capabilities in computers), and search techniques (used in game-playing). Each field has been applied to marketing as follows: (1) expert systems—as distribution decision support systems, product design aid, customer service tools (equipment malfunction diagnosis); (2) computer aided instruction—as product attributes in educational software aimed at business and educational markets; (3) natural language translators—used to assess large Management Information System databases, new office equipment product design; (4) sensing—used in robotics, military products, handicap support products; and (5) search techniques—used in sophisticated computer games (product design).

Expert systems, used as decision support tools, offer the greatest short-term potential for improving marketing practice. An expert system is defined as a computer that mimics a human expert; using the methods and information acquired and developed by a human expert to solve problems, make predictions, suggest possible actions and offer advice with a degree of accuracy equal to that of its human counterpart. Expert systems have been applied to the following generic categories of problems: interpretations, predictions, assessments, design, planning, monitoring, debugging, instruction, and control.

Examples

Expert system decision support tools are used by several companies including: Clark Equipment Company, which is testing an expert system that assesses dealer parts inventory managers and provides advice to improve dealer inventory management; Westinghouse Corporation, which is using expert systems to answer routine technical questions from customers regarding products, train new salespersons, and guide customer repairs; Digital Equipment Corporation, which utilizes an expert system to aid computer (product) installations by suggesting the proper set of components to be used that meet customer needs at the lowest cost; Xerox, which is applying an expert system to product design specifically to aid the design of very-large-scale-integrated circuits.

Benefits

Expert systems have several major advantages over the decision support tools currently utilized by marketing managers. First, because the rules are independent of each other, program revision is much easier than step-by-step procedural programming (COBOL, FORTRAN). This means less expensive programming. Second, an expert system is capable of explaining its line of reasoning by displaying the rules used to reach a conclusion. Third, and most important, expert systems use heuristic problem solving techniques (rules of thumb) for solving problems and are applicable to many of the more complex, unstructured marketing decisions that involve behavioral variables. Thus, a major advantage of expert systems is fuzzy thinking (developing a line of reasoning based on *uncertain* or *partial* evidence). These complex marketing decisions which individually and collectively have a major impact on marketing performance and costs include: customer service programs, store and warehouse location, inventory ordering and levels, transportation carrier and advertising media selection, freight rate negotiation, sales force training, product development, and pricing decisions. As an example, benefits that can be expected from expert system application to the distribution area of marketing are: 15-30% inventory cost reduction, 4-15% transport cost reduction, 10-25% product availability improvement, and a 5-15% warehouse productivity increase.

Implementation

The implementation of an effective expert system is performed in several stages with a number of major steps in each stage. The stages include: Problem Identification, System Design, System Development, and Testing/Implementation. The Problem Identification stage contains two steps. First, the problem must be clearly defined. Problems exhibiting the following characteristics have the greatest potential for successful expert system application: well-bounded domain, finite options (6-12 maximum), solvability by symbolic rather than analytic knowledge, solvability by an expert in 20 minutes, large number of managers face the problem frequently or one manager with irreplaceable knowledge faces the problem infrequently, available hard data, measureable cost/benefits, and importance to marketing management. Second, project participants and resources must be identified. The principal participants are usually an expert in the problem area and a knowledge engineer who converts the expert's knowledge into a computer program that mimics the expert's reasoning. In addition, a personal computer is necessary along with either an AI language (LISP, PROLOG) or an AI software development tool (see examples in the Software/Databases section).

During the Design stage, expert system goals are identified and the structure of the knowledge base and decision rules are determined. In addition, decisions regarding the type and method of data input/output are decided. It is important at this stage to consider what the expert system is trying to do so that the design can aid, not hinder, the goal. In addition, when designing the structure of the key concepts and relationships, it is worthwhile to use several expert sources such as outside consultants, textbooks, company history or other managers.

The Development stage consists of prototype and operational system development. Typically several iterations with the expert, knowledge engineer and potential users involved are required. It is important to develop modular input/output interface into the system so that the user can concentrate on one specific part of the problem rather than the whole problem. The internal structure of the program should be modular as well, so that new knowledge can be added on a module by module rather than system-wide basis.

Testing/Implementation involves system validation, field testing by potential users, and introduction. Validation of the expert system is accomplished by using numerous samples of input data to generate expert solutions and then comparing these solutions with those of experts. The expert system should be providing the right answers *and* the right reasons. The field test is conducted to determine how easily the expert system: (1) interacts with users, and (2) fits the resources and user capabilities in the field. Implementation may involve some initial training because experts may incorporate some information to solve a problem that is not familiar to the intended user. Some facility should be available to allow users to update the knowledge base because the types of problems that expert systems attempt to solve are usually dynamic and complex. A major attribute of an expert system is its ability to grow, "learn" and change as new knowledge is discovered.

Evaluation

Once implemented, the marketing expert system should be evaluated using all of the following criteria: quality of decisions and advice, correctness of reasoning, quality of user interaction, system effectiveness, and cost-efficiency. The evaluator must be careful in setting measurement standards, selecting measurement methods, and specifying who will evaluate the marketing expert systems.

Conclusion

Despite the significant performance and cost benefits of applying expert systems to marketing, only a few major firms have developed marketing expert systems. However, the recent technological improvements in micro (personal) computers and software development have opened the floodgates. Over one-hundred expert system software development tools have entered the market in the last few years and many firms are engaged in marketing expert system development with distribution and training applications leading the way.

Applications to Small Business

Although most current marketing expert systems are applied to large scale problems in Fortune 1,000 firms, many future applications will address the operational problems confronting small business managers. Since small businesses cannot routinely afford outside consultants, expert systems will provide a low cost alternative method of marketing decision support. Problem areas with great potential for expert system application include: inventory management; local advertising media and content decisions; sale pricing; store layout, design, and location; and product mix decisions.

Software/Databases

Most current marketing expert systems handle problems that are specific to one firm. Thus, only a few expert systems are generic and available for use across firms. However, numerous expert system development tools (software) are available, including the following:

Knowledge Craft. Carnegie Group, 650 Commerce Ct., Station Square, Pittsburgh, PA 15219.

M.1. Teknowledge, 525 University Ave., Palo Alto, CA 94301.

Artificial Intelligence Corp., 100 Fifth Ave., Waltham, MA 02254.

References/Sources

Allen, Mary K., and Emmelhainz, Margaret A., "Decision Support Systems: An Innovation Aid to Managers," *Journal of Business Logistics,* 5, 2 (1984): 128-142. Discusses expert systems as logistics decision support tools.

Cook, Robert L., Helferich, Omar K., and Schon, Stephen, "Using An AI-Expert System To Assess And Train Logistics Managers: A Parts Inventory Manager Application," Proceedings—16th Annual Transportation and Logistics Educators Conference. Anaheim, CA, Oct. 1986. Generic inventory management expert system.

Feigenbaum, Edward A., and McCorduck, Pamela, *The Fifth Generation.* Reading, MA: Addison-Wesley Publishing, 1983. A description of artificial intelligence and Japan's challenge.

Hayes-Roth, Frederich, Waterman, Donald, and Lenat, Douglas B., *Building Expert Systems.* Reading, MA: Addison-Wesley Publishing, 1983. The first textbook in knowledge engineering.

Helferich, Omar K., "A Viewpoint, Computers that Mimic Human Thought. Artificial Intelligence for Materials and Logistics Management." *Journal of Business Logistics,* 5, 2 (1984): 123-127. AI in distribution.

Michaelsen, Robert, and Michie, Donald, "Expert Systems In Business," *Datamation* (1984). A review of expert systems used in business.

Waterman, Donald A., *A Guide to Expert Systems.* Reading, MA: Addison-Wesley Publishing, 1986. Comprehensive review of expert systems.

Winston, Patrick H., *Artificial Intelligence,* 2nd ed. Reading, MA: Addison-Wesley Publishing, 1984. Overview of Artificial Intelligence.

Related Topics and Terms

Decision Support System, Expert Systems, Marketing Software, Micro-Computers.

Robert Lorin Cook
Department of Marketing
Central Michigan University

ATTITUDE

Overview

An attitude is a learned predisposition, or tendency, to respond to an object or class of objects in a consistently favorable or unfavorable way. Attitudes are oftentimes viewed as a person's positive or negative feelings toward something, such as one's like or dislike for a product or service, a specific brand, a particular attribute, a retail outlet, or a corporation. Such dispositional feelings constitute one of the three components of an attitude—the affective component. A person's beliefs or knowledge regarding the attitude object make up the cognitive component, and his intentions to act or behave constitutes the conative or behavioral intentions component. The rationale for including cognitive, affective and conative dimensions in the definition of an attitude is that what a person believes about an object, how he feels about it, and what is planned in terms of behavior toward it, are closely related to one another. Moreover, each aspect provides unique information about the person's attitude toward the object.

Attitudes serve various functions for an individual, and it is important to be aware of the diverse roles that attitudes perform. Attitudes often serve a utilitarian function by assisting an individual to determine quickly whether some object should be approached or avoided. People are generally drawn to things that bring them pleasure and steer clear of those things they do not like or that represent potential threats. Attitudes also may convey something about a person or what he wishes to portray to others. In this sense, the attitude serves a value-expression function. For example, a person who likes "hot rod" automobiles is most likely to be viewed as masculine, aggressive and a risk-taker. Somewhat comparable to the value-expressive function, the ego-defensive function relates to the fact that people sometimes hold certain attitudes to avoid anxiety-producing threats to their ego. For example, a man may like Marlboro cigarettes because he fears being seen as effeminate. Another function of attitudes is that of organization of knowledge. Attitudes serve as bases through which incoming information can be organized. People tend to add information to memory in relation to the organization they have already developed, and this organization usually revolves around the pros and cons of the object. In summary, people form attitudes about things which have some relevance to them, and such attitudes may serve differing functions in carrying out their daily lives.

Examples

The companies and public agencies that have focused on understanding consumer attitudes often report obtaining useful insights into what consumers believe and feel about the product or service in question.

A study conducted for the Federal Trade Commission determined that even after widespread corrective advertising to dispel erroneous beliefs that Listerine cures colds, many consumers continue to hold this mistaken belief. Through their ongoing market research activities, Procter and Gamble detected a declining trend in sales and market share of Crisco shortening among heavy users in the southeast United States. Additional research into the probable causes for the trend revealed that heavy users of shortening hold very positive attitudes toward Crisco in general and toward its differentiating product attributes; yet, it was also learned that some of these consumers had shifted their purchase behavior to a more price-oriented brand and expressed behavioral intentions to continue to purchase in that manner. The Crisco brand manager decided it would be necessary to convince these price-oriented switchers that they should spend the extra money to buy Crisco. A combined media and sales promotion campaign with Loretta Lynn as the spokesperson was implemented. The brand regained its lost market share and fully recouped the expense for the media/sales promotion blitz.

Benefits

There are numerous benefits which may be derived from assessment of attitudes. In many instances, a focus on consumer attitudes is the only feasible means for projecting likely purchase behavior prior to the implementation of a given change in marketing strategy. For proposed new products, a marketer has no choice but to rely on consumer attitudinal reactions to the product concept for making decisions regarding continuation of the development process.

Additional uses of consumer attitude information may result in such tangible benefits as greater profitability and increased market share, and in such intangible benefits as enhanced consumer satisfaction and improved product positioning. Attitudes are occasionally used as vehicles for longitudinal tracking purposes, which may help identify needed strategy changes and other deserving problem areas. Attitudes also serve an important role in market segmentation (e.g., brand loyal versus non-loyal segments) and may help in distinguishing determinant from non-determinant product attributes. Attitudes toward particular product attributes, when coupled with perceptions (i.e., beliefs) of competing brands, are very helpful to marketers for identifying the relative positioning of each brand on the set of attributes under scrutiny. Such information highlights a brand's strengths and weaknesses in the marketplace and allows for voids and other opportunities to be detected.

Implementation

An effective attempt to explore consumer attitudes requires consideration of a number of related issues. These issues include aspects that pertain to attitude content, context and measurement.

The content-related decisions that must be made are extremely important to the overall usefulness of an emphasis on consumer attitudes. A manager first needs to consider the breadth and depth to which attitudinal information is needed, as well as the attitude object to be the focus of study. These decisions involve asking questions such as:

1. What attitude object should be the focus of study—the firm, the product, the brand, etc?
2. Is there a need to ascertain both specific and general attitudes toward the object? If so, what aspects or attributes of the object should be considered?

Related to these decisions, it is necessary to decide on the particular components of attitudes that should be the foci of investigation—cognitive, affective, and/or conative. In most instances, a manager will benefit from knowledge of (1) affect toward specific product or store attributes, (2) beliefs about the extent to which a brand or store is believed to possess particular attributes, (3) overall affect toward the object in general, and (4) behavioral intentions regarding the object. With respect to this second area, the manager should decide whether the beliefs component should be assessed on a comparative or noncomparative basis. A comparative approach utilizes a particular referent, such as an ideal brand or a competitive brand, whereas a noncomparative approach does not specify a particular point of reference. Use of a comparative approach does not, however, guarantee that consumers will in fact view the comparison in a similar manner.

With respect to the areas of attribute affect, overall affect and behavioral intentions, there is evidence to support the case that responses by an individual may vary across situational contexts, such as a person having a strong positive attitude toward a particular brand for certain consumption settings and a markedly weaker attitude for other settings. A manager should assess whether the attitude object under consideration is subject to situational variability, and, if so, whether there is a likely benefit to examining attitude differences across situational contexts. Substantial benefits are likely to be realized when the marketer is partly in control of the situational context, as when advertising can communicate the differential applicability of the brand or store in particular settings or circumstances.

The context for which attitudes are to be assessed is a second important area of concern in implementation. An *ad hoc* attitude survey is usually used to obtain a general perspective of the sentiment among a consumer population and is not generally conducted to provide definitive answers to particular questions of concern to a manager. Planned or purposeful attitude surveys are conducted to track changes in attitudes over time and/or to determine the impact on attitudes of a change in marketing strategy. Timing is very important for a successful, planned attitude survey. In the case of longitudinal tracking, the surveys should be conducted at regular intervals—for example, on a yearly basis—and under similar conditions. For maximum use, the same individuals should be surveyed and their responses matched over time. Use of a different sample for each time period only allows for aggregate changes to be assessed. For examining the effect of a change in marketing strategy, it is important that the attitude survey be conducted only after a sufficient time has elapsed to allow for the change to have its effect. Although attitudes may change over time, these changes are typically gradual, especially when the attitude is an expression of an individual's values or a buffer for his ego.

The third area which needs to be considered for implementation is that of measurement. The manager first needs to address whether attitudes should be assessed with closed- or open-ended questions. Open-ended questions are appropriate for *ad hoc* attitude surveys, and when the manager would like to obtain qualitative feedback about the attitude object in question. Closed-ended questions are usually necessary for tracking changes in attitudes and when one desires to ensure that responses across individuals can be compared, which may be the case in an *ad hoc* survey as well. Closed-ended questions entail providing all respondents with the same, fixed set of response options from which to choose.

Subsidiary issues surrounding closed-ended questions include: (1) the number of response options supplied to reflect the attitude continuum, (2) the extent to which the categories of response options are labeled, (3) whether or not to provide a "don't know" or "no opinion" response option as an alternative, (4) whether or not to have a neutral position as a response option, and (5) the type of "attitude scaling procedure" to employ. In general, the attitude continuum contains labeled end points and is commonly reflected with either 3, 5, 7 or 11 scale points when a midpoint is given for neutral responses, and 4, 6 or 10 when no midpoint is directly given to encourage the respondent to take a stand, positive or negative. Although inclusion of a "don't know" or "no opinion" response option is advantageous for minimizing any response bias from individuals who really do not have an opinion, it does complicate matters when quantitative analyses are performed.

There are several different attitude scaling procedures which may be used, including (1) the semantic differential scale with bipolar adjectives such as good/bad, (2) the Stapel scale, and (3) the Likert scale. These scaling procedures are typically discussed thoroughly in a marketing research text.

Evaluation

Depending on the purpose for the attitude focus, the criteria for evaluating responses will vary. In general, it is important that the manager formulate decision criteria or standards prior to implementation that can be used for determining whether strategy alterations should be made. Ideally, these criteria will be derived from prior attitude surveys and managerial experience. In the case of longitudinal tracking studies, responses from a previous time period typically form the baseline gauge of change. Irrespective of purpose, it is imperative that planned attitude comparison studies employ common measurement procedures and criteria across product attributes, brands, and/or stores. Use of attitude information for defining market segments and targets requires that such other issues as segment accessibility and substantiality be incorporated into decision criteria.

Conclusion

Attitudes are a fact of life. All too often firms fail to take advantage of such information until irreparable damage has been done and important marketing opportunities missed. Judicious use of attitude information is one of the critical requirements for implementing the marketing concept and achieving desired sales and market share levels. Although attitudes tend to be relatively stable in the short run, they do change over time and situational contexts. As a consequence, it is important to consider the impact on attitudes when contemplating an alteration in strategy and to establish a regular program of attitude assessment.

Applications to Small Business

As with any form of marketing research, many small business owners make the erroneous judgment that an attitude survey is prohibitively costly and requires professional expertise. Any manager who can address the substantive issues given under the implementation heading should be fully able to develop an attitude survey for administering to present and perhaps potential customers. A standard survey instrument could be developed and distributed on an as-needed basis to the desired customer base. The analysis phase need not be highly-quantitative for useful insights to be obtained. For examining the impact of strategy changes, more detailed computer-based analysis would likely be worthwhile. Numerous software data analysis packages are available for use on personal computers and small mainframes.

Software/Databases

SAS (Statistical Analysis System). SAS Institute, Inc., Box 8000, Cary, NC 27511-8000. Comprehensive and well-documented software system. Flexible database management support functions and extensive library of statistical analysis programs.

SPSS and SPSS/PC. SPSS, Inc., Suite 3300, 444 North Michigan Avenue, Chicago, IL 60611. Easy to use data analysis package with a wide assortment of statistical procedures, database management facilities, and graphics capabilities. Documentation available.

References/Sources

Assael, Henry, *Consumer Behavior and Marketing Action.* 2nd ed. Boston: Kent, 1984. Chapter 7 is a non-technical treatment of the foundations of attitude theory and measurement. Chapter 8 concerns deliberate attempts to change attitudes and highlights the difficulties of such an endeavor.

Bem, Daryl J. *Beliefs, Attitudes, and Human Affairs.* Belmont, CA: Brooks/Cole Publishing Company, 1970. Reasonably short and readable book-length treatment of early attitude research in social psychology. Chapters 2, 3, 5 and 6 are particularly useful.

Fennell, Geraldine, "Attitude, Motivation and Marketing or Where Do the Attributes Come From?" in *Attitude Research Enters the 80's.* Richard W. Olshavsky, ed. Chicago: American Marketing Association, 1980, pp. 14-33. Excellent discussion of the various inputs to the formation of attitudes and their relevance to marketing decisions.

Fishbein, Martin, and Icek Ajzen, *Belief, Attitude, Intention and Behavior: An Introduction to Theory and Research.* Reading, MA: Addison-Wesley, 1975. Provides an in-depth treatment of the subject, with a thorough discussion of measurement and theory foundations.

Hawkins, Del I., Roger J. Best, and Kenneth A. Coney, *Consumer Behavior: Implications for Marketing Strategy.* Revised Edition. Plano, TX: Business Publications, 1983. Chapters 2 and 13 are useful guides for the uses of attitudes and relevant concerns.

Kinnear, Thomas C., and James R. Taylor, *Marketing Research: An Applied Approach.* Second Edition. New York: McGraw-Hill, 1983. Chapter 11 is an especially useful review of alternative approaches to the measurement of attitudes and the advantages and disadvantages of each approach. Chapter 10 concerns issues of reliability and validity that are germane to measurement of attitudes.

Kirkman, Walter B. "Attitude Research Enters the Financial World," in *Attitude Research Enters the 80's.* Richard W. Olshavsky, ed. Chicago: American Marketing Association, 1980, pp. 180-184. Exemplary description of potential applications of attitudes to managerial decision making.

Lutz, Richard J. "A Functional Approach to Consumer Attitude Research," in *Advances in Consumer Research,* Vol. 5. Ann Arbor, MI: Association for Consumer Research, 1978, pp. 360-369. Readable overview of the various functions served by attitudes.

McDonald, Susan S. and Alfred E. Goldman, "Strategies of Segmentation Research," in *A Look Back, A Look Ahead.* George B. Hafer, ed. Chicago: American Marketing Association, 1980, pp. 30-42. Useful overview of important issues and procedures for using attitude responses for segmentation purposes.

Miller, Kenneth E. and James L. Ginter, "An Investigation of Situational Variation in Brand Choice Behavior and Attitude," in *Journal of Marketing Research* (February 1979): 111-123. Empirical study demonstrated attitude and behavior differences in brand choice across consumption situations.

Wind, Yoram, "Issues and Advances in Segmentation Research," *Journal of Marketing Research* (August 1978): 317-337. Useful overview of approaches to market segmentation. Of particular use are the sections concerning testing of new product concepts and benefit segmentation.

Wind, Yoram and Tyzoon Tyebjee, "On the Use of Attitude Research in Product Policy," in *Moving Ahead with Attitude Research.* Chicago: American Marketing Association, 1977, pp. 147-156. Very useful and comprehensive examination of the potential roles of attitudes in product development, product modification and product elimination decision making.

Related Topics and Terms

Affect, Applied Research, Behavioral Intentions, Beliefs, Cognition, Conation, Concept Testing, Consumer Behavior, Core Customer, Exploratory Research, Feelings, Idea Screening, Lifestyle, Market Segmentation, Marketing Concept, Marketing Research, Motive, Primary Data, Product Differentiation, Product Positioning, Psychographics, Questionnaire, Self Concept, Store Image, Survey Method, Target Market, Values.

James H. Leigh
Department of Marketing
Texas A&M University

THE ATTITUDE-BEHAVIOR RELATIONSHIP

Overview

> In our work, we have found in every study we have done—and there
> has not been a single exception—that there is a very direct relationship
> between attitudes and usage behavior . . . the more favorable the atti-
> tude, the higher the incidence of usage, the less favorable the attitude,
> the lower the incidence of usage (Achenbaum, 1966, p. 112).

This quotation is based upon extensive research conducted by the Grey Advertising Agency. Its importance is clear: successful products are invariably *associated*
with favorable attitudes. Despite the strong association *at any given time* between
attitudes and product use, the research literature shows a maze of contradictory
findings regarding both the strength of the attitude-behavior relationship and the
direction of causality. Through close examination of the attitude-behavior relationship, however, it is possible to place these contradictory findings into a more
systematic framework.

Examples

It seems quite reasonable to assume that most consumers develop a strong, positive attitude towards one or more specific automobiles before they commit themselves to such a major purchase. Yet, many readers will know someone who
strongly prefers, say, a Japanese car but purchases an American car because "people who work for this firm buy American." As another example, consider a frequently purchased, low cost nondurable such as frozen "gourmet" dinners. Given
the low cost, a reasonable consumer's strategy might be to try the product before
deciding his attitude towards it. Each of these examples is consistent with both the
theoretical and empirical consumer behavior literature.

Benefits

The primary benefits that accrue from a proper understanding of the attitude-
behavior relationship come from a better matching of marketing mix decisions with
the information needs of consumers when making different types of buying decisions.

Implementation

The attitude-behavior relationship is an abstract concept and, thus, there is nothing to implement in the form of a specific program. However, the perspective
provided by the role of attitudes in the consumer decision process gives valuable

insights into how to construct a firm's marketing mix strategy, especially in the area of promotion decisions.

Evaluation

It is possible to identify four basic causal relationships between attitudes and behaviors: (1) no causal relationship exists, (2) attitudes cause behaviors, (3) behaviors cause attitudes, and (4) causation is reciprocal. As Kahle and Berman (1979, p. 315) note, each of these positions has a contemporary advocate. There is also substantial support for each position. The problem is to identity the situations in which each of the four basic relationships is likely to hold.

No Relationship Exists. There are numerous explanations for the failure to find a relationship between attitudes and behaviors. First, attitudes can change over time and any number of events can block the expression of a favorable attitude in behavior. Thus, there may be a weak, or even no, relationship when a lengthy time gap separates the attitude measurement and the occurrence of the behavior.

Second, there is the problem of the level of specificity of attitudes and behaviors. Fishbein and Ajzen (1975, p. 292) identify four specificity dimensions: behavior, target object, situation, and time. For example, a person who has a very positive attitude towards good health does not necessarily buy health foods or exercise regularly. A positive attitude toward good health can be expressed in many other ways: e.g., consuming less animal fat and more fiber. Therefore, marketing questions about health foods, should be framed according to how different individuals express in behavior their attitudes toward good health.

Finally, the behavior may not be under attitudinal control. Social norms, for example, frequently cause people to purchase products or brands they might otherwise not select.

Attitudes Cause Behaviors. Kahle and Berman (1979), using recently developed analytical techniques generally referred to as causal modeling, provide clear evidence that attitudes do cause behavior for the four issues they investigated: Jimmy Carter's presidential candidacy, Gerald Ford's candidacy, drinking, and religion. For most people these are likely to be important, high involvement issues. They also seem to fall into the categories of buying situations known as the "learning hierarchy" (see *Situational Variables*). In such buying situations; e.g., buying a car or a major appliance, attitudes are generally formed prior to purchase and cause buying behavior.

Behaviors Cause Attitudes. In recent years, both theories and empirical data have been developed to suggest that, under certain circumstances, behavior can lead to the formation of attitudes and to attitude change. Cognitive dissonance (see this entry) theory provides a clear illustration of how behaviors can change attitudes. Also, an attitude can be viewed as representing an expected level of satisfaction. Should the actual level of satisfaction be different from the expected level, attitudes may change. In selecting toothpaste, for example, the expectation might be that it will whiten teeth. If it doesn't, the consumer's attitude toward the product will change.

Often, the buyer is forced to make a choice before the information upon which an attitude could be based is available. In a low involvement situation, such as choosing toothpaste, the information that might form an attitude exists in unorganized form because of the lack of importance of the choice. In this case, attitudes are likely to develop directly out of experience with the product.

A particularly interesting example of behavior causing attitudes is known as the foot-in-the-door technique. The basic idea here is that by obtaining compliance with a small request, by getting a foot in the door, it will be easier to obtain compliance with a larger subsequent request. Bem's (1972) self-perception theory explains this prediction in the following way. When the larger request is made, the person will reflect back on his previous behavior. This will provide a basis for forming a positive attitude toward the larger request. Among the possible marketing applications of the foot-in-the-door technique are soliciting charitable donations and increasing response rates in marketing research studies.

Reciprocal Causation. Finally, there is the possibility of a reciprocal relationship between attitudes and behaviors (Kelman 1974; McGuire 1967). This seems especially likely to characterize low involvement and avoidance buying situations (see *Situational Variables*) where behaviors lead to attitudes, which in turn lead to new behaviors.

Magnitude of the Attitude-Behavior Relationship. Many examples can be cited of a failure to find even a modest relationship between attitudes and behavior. Although perhaps less numerous, many examples of moderate to strong attitude-behavior relationships can also be cited. Among the marketing examples of moderate to strong attitude-behavior relationships are the use of private label products (Myers 1967), trading stamps (Udel 1965), and a large number of goods and services (Ryan and Bonfield 1975).

Strong relationships are likely to emerge only when attitudes and behavior are measured at the same level of specificity (Fishbein and Ajzen, 1975; Bagozzi and Burnkrant, 1979). For example, as previously noted, there is no logical reason why a person who values good health will necessarily buy health foods.

A recent study by Day and Deutscher (1982) suggests that the source of an attitude may have important implications for the strength of the attitude-behavior relationship. Although purchasing a major appliance is generally a high involvement decision, Day and Deutscher argue that attitudes toward major appliances are formed mainly though casual, low involvement types of learning. Such attitudes are not likely to be strong or even well-organized and, therefore, are likely to change as the decision-making process proceeds once a need to purchase a specific major appliance is recognized. An important exception to this pattern occurs for manufacturers who follow "a full-line, national brand support advertising strategy" (p. 198). The authors suggest that the stronger attitude-behavior relationship observed for such brands results from direct product experience with other appliances in the manufacturer's line. For example, a consumer who has enjoyed a Kenmore (Sears) refrigerator is likely to replace his old dishwasher with a Kenmore.

As noted above, there are many reasons why a favorable attitude toward an object may not be expressed in behavior. In the case of durable goods, for example, if a person owns a brand with a large number of years left on its life expectancy there is little likelihood of a new purchase occurring, whatever the person's attitudes toward brands currently on the market.

There is also the question of whether the behavior is under attitudinal control. Many behaviors are not. For example, a buyer may have a very strong positive attitude towards Honda automobiles. However, if the buyer's employer imposes major sanctions against employees who drive foreign cars, it is unlikely that this buyer will purchase a Honda. Generally, however, purchasing behavior appears to be largely, although not exclusively, under attitudinal control (Ryan and Bonfield 1975).

Conclusion

Knowledge of the attitude-behavior relationship has a number of implications for implementing successful marketing programs. First, one must determine whether the behavior in question is under attitudinal control. For one or more market segments it may not be. Second, promotional goals are very much affected by the direction of the attitude-behavior relationship. Establishing strong positive attitudes before purchase is generally not a critical promotional goal for low involvement goods because attitudes tend to follow purchase and are based upon direct product experience. For such goods it is generally sufficient if the promotional program establishes enough awareness and interest to induce trial use. In marked contrast, high involvement goods will generally require a strong positive attitude before purchase. In both situations, of course, it is critical that the consumer's product use experience be positive. Third, knowing the direction of causality is critical to the development of appropriate marketing research studies. A finding that potential consumers who have not used the product do not have positive attitudes has a number of different implications depending on the direction of the attitude-behavior relationship.

Applications to Small Business

Knowledge of the attitude-behavior relationship is potentially as useful to small business as to large business. Indeed, a proper appreciation of the attitude-behavior relationship is critical in developing an optimal plan for deploying the small firm's usually limited resources for promotion and marketing research.

References/Sources

In addition to the previously cited references, the reader may find the following references useful for developing a fuller understanding of the relationships between attitudes and behavior.

Dawes, Robyn M., and Smith, Tom L., "Attitude and Opinion Measurement," *Handbook of Social Psychology,* 3rd ed., Vol. 1. New York: Alfred A. Knopf, 1985, Chapter 10. An excellent reference for those interested in measuring attitudes.

Horton, Raymond, L., *Buyer Behavior: A Decision-Making Approach.* Westerville, OH: Charles E. Merrill, 1984. Chapter 8. Provides a comprehensive review of attitude theories. The mediating role of intention in the attitude-behavior relationship is discussed.

Mcguire, William J., "Attitudes and Attitude Change," *Handbook of Social Psychology,* 3rd ed., Vol. 2. New York: Alfred A. Knopf, 1985, Chapter 6. A comprehensive treatment of the topic. Difficult reading, but highly recommended.

Related Topics and Terms
Attitude, Cognitive Dissonance, Consumer Decision Making, Convenience Good, Impulse Good, Multi-attribute Attitude Models, Product Involvement, Shopping Good, Situational Variables, Specialty Good.

Raymond L. Horton
Department of Marketing
Lehigh University

BALANCE OF PAYMENTS

Overview

"A country's balance of payments summarizes international transactions and, at least theoretically, is based on the principle of double-entry accounting—i.e., each transaction is represented by a debit and a credit."

According to the above definition, a balance of payments figure reported by the United States government on a monthly or yearly basis represents a net dollar amount which has either escaped from that country into the hands of foreign governments or their nationals, a situation identified as a deficit, or it will be reported as a surplus in the opposite situation. For instance, during the period of the 1980s, the United States has been experiencing several billions of dollars in deficits, with the figure for 1985 as high as $150 billion. In this sense, balance of payments figures can be looked at as a "zero-sum" game. This means that gains by one country will equal losses of the second country that engaged in trade activities with it.

Examples

The concept has its origins with mercantilism which developed during the sixteenth century. In an attempt to gain military power over its rivals, a state would decree trade to be a privilege that it alone can grant to merchants to engage in. Power and wealth were strengthened through the accumulation of vast amounts of gold and silver. To make this possible, exports were encouraged, and similarly, imports were discouraged, since exports were typically paid in gold or silver. Imports, on the other hand, produce short term unfavorable balance of payments, but with the expectation that future returns from such an investment will reverse the tide.

The situation becomes one of balancing the books of a particular country. In the case of the United States, below is a list of major credit and debit accounts with foreign residents.

Debits: Payments to Foreign Residents
    Imports of merchandise
    Transportation services bought from foreign residents
    Purchases of American residents traveling abroad
    Services provided by foreign-owned capital in American production
    Miscellaneous services bought from foreign residents
    Gifts to foreign residents
Credits: Dollar Receipts from Foreign Residents
    Exports of merchandise
    Transportation services sold to foreign residents
    Purchases of foreign residents traveling in the U.S.

Services provided by American-owned capital in foreign production
Miscellaneous services sold to foreign residents
Gifts received from foreign residents
Investments in the United States by foreign residents
Exports of gold

Until 1971, major strength in the United States balance of payments had been a result of trade surpluses and investment income. On the other hand, weak areas have traditionally been military purchases of goods and services in foreign lands under U.S. defense programs such as U.S. troops in Europe and other parts of the world, transportation, tourism, governmental unilateral transfers, and flow of capital abroad both short and long term. Since 1971 the U.S. merchandise balance of trade has been negative except for a couple of years.

Benefits

A country may be willing to pay a penalty for a strong currency to insure a more competitive atmosphere which will benefit its consumers through lower prices and more diversified product selections. In other instances, countries may have little choice in the matter. During the period of the 1970s most nations began experiencing a balance of trade deficit as a result of skyrocketing oil prices. In 1986 trade in oil accounted for about 15% of the value of international trade. For Brazil, net oil imports make up 40% of that country's total imports, and for Japan about 35%. With the tremendous drop in oil prices in 1986, most of the oil importing countries are likely to improve their balance of trade picture. Until the recent drop in oil prices, a strong dollar also penalized indirectly United States trading partners because oil producing countries demanded payments in United States dollars, thus exerting inflationary pressures on their economies.

Economic theory suggests that when a country like Japan accumulates or experiences a huge positive balance of payments, it should begin to experience inflationary pressure since large amounts of monies begin chasing a limited supply of goods. The prices of these goods rise relative to other countries, thus weakening its export activity with imports from other countries becoming relatively cheaper or more competitive. These international forces cause a market adjustment. However, according to an article in the *Marketing News,* in the last few years the whole system has gotten out of whack and the currency no longer self-adjusts. To provide a degree of appreciation for the impact of a balance of payments surplus, authorities estimate that for every one billion in sales, 30,000 jobs are provided.

Implementation

The Great Depression, economic isolation and trade wars during the depression years were followed by World War II. After the war, nations of the free world created the International Monetary Fund whose aim was to stabilize the international monetary system. The IMF operated under the Bretton Woods agreement which fixed the exchange rate of each country's currency at a par value based on gold and the U.S. dollar. According to J. D. Daniels *et al,* the problem with the system was that rigidity replaced stability. Countries had to hold tremendous amounts of foreign reserve currencies and vast amounts of gold to stabilize their own currencies and were not willing to change the par value of their currency through devaluation or evaluation unless a crisis developed. It was feared that large dollar reserves outside the U.S. might ruin the stability of fixed exchange rates. The U.S. economy was also under severe pressure to correct any disequilibrium in the balance of payments. To control the situation, drastic monetary and fiscal policies had to be implemented. But these in turn led to recessions as well as inflationary pressures. As a result of these difficulties, the member countries decided to go off the gold standard and the fixed exchange rate and adopted a floating exchange rate in which the value of each currency would be determined by the market forces of supply and demand. According to Madura a floating exchange rate should theoretically correct any international trade imbalances by impacting those factors that influence the balance of payments situation. Some of these factors that influence the balance of payments situation are purely economic in nature such as relative inflation rates, relative interest rates, relative income levels, and exchange rates. Other factors may be political and are enforced by the government, such as taxes on imports known as tariffs, or the setting of limits on the amount of a particular product that can be imported, known as the quota. Unfortunately the system that attempts to correct a balance of payments problem is not simple and may persist as in the case of the United States at least as late as 1986.

Evaluation

Until recent years, countries engaging in mercantile trade could accumulate vast supplies of gold and silver, and the amount of taxes a state could collect depended upon the wealth of its citizens. Therefore, policies which promoted prosperity, particularly through the encouragement of exports and discouragement of imports, became mandatory. Through such a policy, the state was attempting what would be known today as a "favorable balance of trade," because this condition meant that such a state had a net claim on foreigners. Coupled with the idea of establishing a favorable balance of trade was the notion that a state ought to establish colonies to increase its wealth. During that period, this became the incentive for countries like Spain and Portugal, followed by England and others, to found colonies rich in raw material resources which could be processed by the mother country and exported to others. These mercantilistic countries maintained as much as possible a monopoly with their rich colonies by exchanging manufactured products for raw materials and draining their colonies of their precious metals and other desirable resources.

Although mercantilism, as a major consideration, has been buried, interest or even concern about a favorable balance of trade is still alive. A favorable balance of trade remains as a long term concern of most nations. In the short run, other considerations may require a greater urgency at the expense of balance of trade.

Conclusion

Balance of payments figure is a net amount which is reported as a surplus if the total value of export activities of a country exceeds the total value of import activities. As recently as 1986 countries like Japan and Germany have been experiencing a surplus. Thus, Germany and Japan are said to be experiencing a favorable balance of payments, a condition which historically has its origins in mercantilism. Although in the long run countries strive for a favorable balance of payments, other considerations in the short run may receive a higher priority such as competition and employment. If market forces are allowed to operate freely, the illness, at least theoretically, is supposed to cure itself. However, non-economic factors may hinder market adjustments to correct this situation.

References/Sources

Adams, J., *The Contemporary International Economy.* New York: St. Martin's Press, 1985, pp. 124-148. Balance of payments conditions of Japan, the European community and the United States are compared and the factors that are straining these economies are described such as government interference, interest rates, and exchange rates. The author also elaborates on the impact of a strong dollar on U.S. trade.

Daniels, J. D., Orgam, E. W., Jr., and Radebaugh, L. H. *International Business: Environments and Operations.* Reading, MA: Addison-Wesley, 1982, pp. 232-250. Mercantilism as a forerunner of concepts of balance of payments is exhaustively treated. In addition, the international marketing system developments are traced from the period of their inception up to the current period.

Madura, J., *International Financial Management.* St. Paul, MN: West Publishing Company, 1986, pp. 22-31. The author describes the various accounts and components of balance of payment and provides statistics demonstrating the balance of payment conditions of various groups of countries. He also explains how the balance of payment condition impacts the international debt situation.

O'Keefe, B., "Shooting Ourselves in the Foot—Our Present Trade Deficit Has a Long History," *Marketing News* (March 28, 1986): 20-21. The author provides a historical view on issues and policies relative to foreign trade since Adam Smith's *Wealth of Nations.* Information is also provided on the influence of exports and imports on employment.

Root, F., *International Trade and Investment.* Cincinnati, OH: South-Western Publishing Co., 1984, pp. 33-50, 474-479, and 505-506. A general review of balance of payment is treated at length. The situation is described in accounting terms and a list of debit and credit accounts is provided. The author also deals with various control mechanisms that attempt to control balance of payments disequilibrium.

Spero, J. E., *The Politics of International Economics Relations*. New York: St. Martin's Press, 1985, pp. 63, 102, 258, and 364. A brief treatment of balance of trade and how it relates to exchange rates is described. The author also provides some details on trade between western and eastern bloc countries.

Swann, D., *The Economics of the Common Market*. London/New York: Penguin Books, 1984, pp. 44-46 and 163-164. This book strictly deals with the balance of payments conditions of members of the European Economic Community.

World Economics Outlook, International Monetary Fund, 1985. This is an annual report of the International Monetary Fund which has a wealth of statistics on the economies of various regions of the world.

Related Topics and Terms
Comparative Advantage, European Economic Community, Exports, Multi-National Corporation, Most Favored Nation, Tariffs.

John H. Hallaq
College of Business and Economics
University of Idaho

BENEFIT SEGMENTATION

Overview

Benefit segmentation is a method of dividing a total market into submarkets (market segments) based on the similarity of product benefits sought in a product by consumers. Instead of segmenting a market by some other variable, for example income, and then determining the needs of consumers in each particular income category, benefit segmentation uses needs as the basis for segmenting the market, then profiles the characteristics of consumers in each group. Coupled with demographic data, this direct approach to segmentation offers many insights into the marketing of a product, such as what features to emphasize in advertising, what media to use in advertising, what products are or are not satisfying certain segments of a market, and what segments might be overlooked by competitors. Benefit segmentation is recognized as one of the most widely used methods of segmenting markets.

Examples

In the automobile rental industry, convenience is a major benefit sought by the business segment of the market. As such, most rental agencies cater to this large segment by locating at airports and featuring quick rental procedures. However, Rent-A-Wreck has built a substantial franchise operation by appealing to customers who seek low cost, dependable transportation when their own cars are for some reason unavailable. Therefore, Rent-A-Wreck franchises are located in smaller towns, often next to car dealerships. The cars they rent are used, not new, and their prices are lower than traditional rental agencies. In effect, they have adjusted their marketing mix to appeal to a benefit segment which is different than the one targeted by most national car rental agencies.

A classical benefit segmentation study uncovered four different benefit segments in the toothpaste market. Included in the four segments was a group that was most concerned with brightness of teeth and another group that desired a toothpaste that was particularly effective in the prevention of tooth decay. After segmenting the market by benefits sought, each segment was profiled in terms of demographic characteristics, lifestyle characteristics, and brands strongly preferred. For example, the segment concerned with prevention of tooth decay, labeled the "worrier segment," was composed of large families. They used a great deal of toothpaste, preferred Crest toothpaste, and tended to be conservative. This profiling provided a great deal of useful information in deciding how to market toothpaste to each of the segments.

Benefits

Most market segmentation approaches are based on the assumption that consumers who are similar in one respect, say income or education, will have similar needs, tastes, and will react the same way to marketing efforts. This is not always the case. A group of people who are similar in age, income, and education may all use a product, but for different reasons. For example, tennis shoes may be bought for comfort, because they are inexpensive, or for the prestige lent by their label. In this and many cases, the true division of a market results not from who the customers are but from what they want.

Benefit segmentation, when properly implemented, does an excellent job of identifying different types of customers and understanding those customers. By illustrating important benefits, it guides new product development by enabling a firm to translate benefits into features, which in turn can be stressed in advertising. The process of benefit segmentation also provides a better view of the total market and competition when segments are linked to competitor's products. In effect, it results in a map of the market and suggests possible strategic moves (which segments are ignored or poorly serviced) and tactical moves (how products should be designed, priced, and promoted).

Implementation

There are a number of tasks necessary to implement benefit segmentation. Through survey or past experience, a variety of benefits sought must be generated. For instance, a survey of shampoo users might show that consumers want a product that adds body to their hair, prevents dandruff, repairs split ends, or conditions the hair.

The next step is to group consumers according to benefits strongly desired. Statistical techniques such as Q-factor analysis, cluster analysis, and multidimensional scaling are used to group individuals. All of these statistical techniques look at the relative importance of benefits and cluster or group respondents accordingly. The important point is that while most consumers want many, if not all, of the benefits possible in a product, they tend to emphasize or more strongly desire some benefits over others. Thus, while everyone may want a car to be stylish and get good gas mileage, one segment will forego appearance for economy, while another will spend more on gas to enjoy the prestige of driving a stylish car.

After segmenting consumers by benefits, each segment can then be profiled to find the predominant characteristics of that segment. For instance, respondents to a survey may be grouped into three benefit segments. From each segment it can then be found that the "taste sensitive" group tends to be 20-25 years old, career oriented, active in their community, and have an average of three years of college. This step may be as simple as averaging the ages of everyone in a segment by hand to get the average, or involve multi-step techniques.

Evaluation

Once a benefit segmentation study has uncovered a number of segments, management must decide which segments it should target (attempt to sell to), and make appropriate marketing mix decisions for each of the segments in which it will compete. As in any type of market segmentation scheme, benefit segments must be accessible, measurable, profitable, and meaningful. A firm must be able to identify who is a member of each benefit segment, the size of that segment, and the competition it will face within that segment. This is necessary to determine the profitability of the segment and the probability of success.

Further, a firm must evaluate its own resources to determine if it is able to compete effectively. A segment may be large and attractive but beyond the organization's financial and production capabilities.

Conclusion

Benefit segmentation is widely used because it is the most marketing oriented and most direct approach to segmenting a market. Segments are not developed but uncovered, and are based on needs, not other variables such as age, income, and education.

Tied into demographic variables, benefit segmentation provides a great deal of information about members of a market segment. Benefit segmentation provides answers to many questions such as:

- What new products should be introduced into the market?
- What changes should be made in present products to better fit the needs of a particular segment?
- What products presently on the market are well suited to a particular segment, and, conversely, what needs are not being met by current product offerings?
- How should advertising be developed to emphasize the needs of a particular market segment?

Applications to Small Business

In many instances, benefit segmentation can be a useful and feasible tool of small business. Many small businesses, especially those that deal directly with consumers, can gather enough information to successfully implement benefit segmentation.

Salespeople are a good source of information. After calling on a given territory for a period of time, they usually know what their customers want. A firm can conduct a study of the market by requiring call reports that specifically state customer characteristics such as size of business, average amount or yearly amount of sales to the customer, industry in which the customer competes, location, purchasing set up, and, of course, what benefits customers feel are most important in purchasing the firm's type of product. Call reports can then be grouped by benefits, and characteristics can be tabulated. While every characteristic in a benefit group will not match, there are usually some predominantly similar ones. Given the benefit segments with profiles, management can then adjust their marketing mix. For instance, a supplier of chemicals may find that there is a group of customers who is concerned with safety. The supplier might then start a direct mail program that includes sending monthly bulletins listing changing regulations passed by OSHA and highlighting the safety features or aspects of one product.

References/Sources

Calantone, Roger J., and Sawyer, Alan G., "The Stability of Benefit Segments," *Journal of Marketing Research* (August 1978): 395-404. Study showing that benefit segments are stable in terms of size. Discusses the attributes of segments which are considered important to marketers.

Haley, Russell I., "Benefit Segmentation: A Decision Oriented Research Tool," *Journal of Marketing* (July 1968): 30-35. Illustrates the possible marketing implications of benefit segmentation through the hypothetical segmentation of the toothpaste market.

Malhotra, Naresh K., "Stochastic Modeling of Consumer Preferences for Health Care Institutions," *Journal of Health Care Marketing* (Fall 1983): 18-26. Application of a statistical technique to uncover the value systems of consumers regarding health care.

Peter, J. Paul, and Donnelly, James H. Jr., *A Preface to Marketing Management*. Plano, TX: Business Publications, 1985. Chapter 5 explains the steps of market segmentation and provides examples of benefit segmentation.

Roberts, Alan A., "Applying the Strategy of Market Segmentation," *Business Horizons* (Fall 1961): 65-72. Explains the concepts of market segmentation and benefit segmentation, providing examples and discussing the managerial implications of segmenting a market.

Smith, Wendell R., "Product Differentiation and Market Segmentation as Alternative Marketing Strategies," *Journal of Marketing* (July 1956): 3-8. Discusses the differences between market segmentation and product differentiation. Indirectly provides a basis for benefit segmentation.

Young, Shirley, Ott, Leland, and Feigin, Barbara, "Some Practical Considerations in Market Segmentation," *Journal of Marketing Research* (August 1978): 405-412. Discusses some problems of market segmentation and possible solutions. Presents market segmentation examples and notes situations when market segmentation may not be useful.

Related Topics and Terms

Concentrated Marketing, Market Segmentation, Product Differentiation, Product Positioning, Psychographics, Target Market, Undifferentiated Marketing.

William Bart
Department of Marketing
Kent State University

BRAND AWARENESS

Overview

The brand is the main link between marketers and consumers. If the consumer doesn't have a particular brand of a product in his memory bank, he is unlikely to buy that brand. Creating brand awareness among consumers, then, is the first major step taken by a mass marketer to obtain sales on a continuing basis through a relationship with consumers. Brand awareness does not guarantee sales but it can be predicted that brand awareness becomes brand acceptance and brand preference when compared with those brands consumers do not know about.

Examples

When marketing researchers ask consumers, "When you think of potato chips, what brand comes to mind?" consumers usually have a ready answer. The same is true if they are asked about candy bars, colas, canned green beans, or hundreds of other mass-marketed products. Consumers have a lot of brands on their minds, in fact, usually more than one brand of a product. That is why the first brand that "comes to mind" is very important to marketers. It is probably more meaningful to consumers than subsequently named brands.

Being aware of a brand does not mean that consumers necessarily like that brand. In fact, it may mean they hate it. Consumer researchers have developed classifications for all possible variations of brand awareness. These classifications are as follows.

1. Brand Repertoire—consists of all brands of all products with which a person is familiar. At a moment in time a person may be aware of five percent of the approximately 30,000 national brands. Whatever the total number, it is called the brand repertoire, and it changes as more new brands are introduced or new products are introduced under existing brands.
2. Awareness Set—consists of all the brands within a product line with which a consumer is familiar. The awareness set suggests that brands are ordered in the mind according to products (although it may be that they are ordered according to store types that handle similar products). This list can be very long in the case of soft drinks; short in the case of bottled water.
3. Evoked Set—consists of those brands a person normally considers when making a purchase of a product. These are favored brands of a product for a particular person and probably do not amount to more than two or three at any given time for a product line.
4. Inept Set—consists of those brands that are rejected from purchase consideration of a product. A consumer is aware of the brands that make up the inept set but knows something negative about them that causes their exclusion from the evoked set.

5. Inert Set—consists of those brands a consumer is unsure whether to consider when purchasing a product. The consumer is aware of these brands of a product but knows so little about them that they are placed in a mental holding pattern while awaiting more information about them. Perhaps they are new.

Benefits

In this world of look-alike products, a firm's brand name is about the only thing a competitor cannot copy. Thus, it is a very distinguishing characteristic of a product, and when placed in the minds of consumers through promotion, it gives a firm higher odds of making a sale. For example, if there are one million potential consumers for five brands of a product, and all of them are known by the consumers, each brand has a 20 percent chance of a sale, or a chance of selling 200,000 products. If one brand is unknown, the other four brands probably have a 25 percent chance of a sale, or 250,000 products. For the firm whose brand happens to be the one not known among consumers, there is very little chance of a sale.

These figures assume favorable attitudes toward the five brands which is not always the case. Some brands are in the inept sets of consumers because they are undesirable to those consumers, and some are in the inert set because consumers aren't sure of them. Brands in the inept set have no chance of a sale without more marketing effort. Only those brands in the evoked set can expect to be purchased. Thus, of the five brands, two may be in the inert set, one in the inept set, and two in the evoked set. If this were true for all one-million consumers, the two brands in the evoked set could expect sales of 500,000 units each. Such attractive sales figures are well worth a company conducting research to discover the brand awareness of its brand, and further, to do those things to get its brand in the evoked set of a large number of consumers.

Implementation

Brand awareness doesn't accidentally happen. It is the result of a long-term, intensive marketing strategy. In fact, if brand awareness did not occur as a result of marketing efforts, the marketing efforts would probably be considered ineffective since few, if any, sales would occur, also. Specifically, a company must have its brand not only familiar to consumers but desirable. That is, its brand must be in consumers' evoked sets. To get it there, a firm can expect its brand to move from unawareness to the inert set in which consumers are aware of it but not sure of it, to the evoked set where each time consumers who purchase that product have considered the firm's brand.

To determine the extent and nature of a brand's awareness, a firm can conduct research among a representative sample of consumers. For a brand of cake mix, for example, brand awareness might be determined with a brief set of questions as the following.

1. Which brands of cake mix might you likely buy when you go shopping the next time? (Measures brands in the evoked set.)
2. Which brands of cake mix do you not prefer and are unlikely to buy when you go shopping next time? (Measures the inept set.)
3. Which brand of cake mix are you unsure about considering when you go shopping next time? (Measures the inert set.)

Since by definition a brand could not be located in but one awareness set per person, the number of mentions represents a measure of brand awareness. For a firm's brand, it may have been mentioned 100 times by 100 respondents, or have a 100 percent awareness rate. More important, however, is the more specific measures of awareness in each brand set, particularly the evoked set. For example's sake, assume that the brand is in the evoked set of 20 percent of those that were aware of it, 60 percent have it in their inert set, and 20 percent place it in their inept set. Now, the company knows where it stands in the mind of consumers, and may then set some goals related to changing the minds of consumers.

This procedure provides, also, some information about this firm's competition. For example, if there were typically three brands in the consumer's evoked set, the other two brands represent the main competition. For more exact information on the competition, marketing research can ask consumers to rank the brands in their evoked set by placing them on a ten-point scale with the most desirable brand receiving a ten. Then the other two brands are given relative positions such as an eight for a closely desirable brand and a five for a less desirable but acceptable brand. By multiplying the various values received for a firm's brand by the number of votes, the firm will know specifically how it stands in competition for the consumer's mind and pocketbook.

With these measures as guides, a firm can establish a marketing program to increase the percent of awareness in the evoked set and decrease the size of the inept and inert sets. The large percent in the inert set represents much profit opportunity since those consumers are simply unsure about the brand and could be converted with more useful information about it. The consumers with the brand in their inept sets will be more difficult to change. They have negative feelings toward the brand, probably due to using it, or to its relatively high price, or perhaps because of the types of people associated with the brand. It is possible to reduce consumer negative feelings toward a brand with a specific marketing program, but unless the percentage is high, it is probably more profitable to focus on converting the consumers who place the brand in their inert set and hope the marketing effort to do this will favorably influence the inept set occurrences, also.

Advertising is the most important marketing tool for moving a brand into an evoked set status, although an entire mix of several marketing elements will ordinarily be used for this purpose. Publicity surely will be used because it is so credible, sales promotion efforts such as coupons usually enhance the effects of advertising, and obtaining better shelf display in the stores will make sure that consumers who see the brand advertised will find it when shopping. Personal selling naturally is important in the case of more expensive items and items sold to industrial consumers, but advertising will still play a decisive role in creating positive brand awareness for these products.

The significance of advertising on brand awareness has been demonstrated in many research findings. For example, there is a high correlation between brands with high awareness and the extent of their advertising. Moreover, when consumers are asked to list all the brands they can, when they are classified by product, the largest classifications usually are those most heavily advertised. Finally, where there are a number of products advertised under one brand, such as Del Monte canned goods and Pillsbury baking goods, brand awareness of these brands is higher than usual.

In moving the brand into an evoked set status, advertising, again, is the critical marketing effort, although actual use by consumers of the product is usually necessary. When children are asked what products they want for Christmas (their evoked sets), the brand names are almost always those the children see advertised on television. When consumers are asked to state their preferences for brands of food goods sold in supermarkets, the brands most preferred (those in the evoked set), usually have the highest advertising budgets.

Evaluation

Most brand name merchandisers understand the concept of brand awareness and attempt to utilize it in their marketing strategies. Most advertising has the objective of planting brand names in the minds of people and keeping them there with repetitious messages. Publicity methods are frequently used to get the brand name before the public. Much of the success of the introduction of the Cabbage Patch dolls in the early 1980s was due to effective publicity efforts such as getting the dolls shown on the Johnny Carson show and in a skit on a Bob Hope Christmas show. Companies are always vying for shelf space and display space in the stores. A brand that is able to get an end-of-the-aisle display in a supermarket is not only sure to increase its sales but increase its awareness as well.

All the advertising and promotion notwithstanding, a bad product cannot be moved to the evoked set status or be maintained there. Bad products may be purchased and used, but once their flaws are discovered, their brands are shifted to the inept set. Even use is not necessary in order to place a brand in the inept set. Perhaps friends talk about the negative features of a product or it is mentioned on a television show. When Tylenol was associated with potential danger through poisoning, it was necessary to reintroduce the product with an additional $100,000,000 in advertising and sales promotion to get it returned to an evoked set status.

Finally, competition is so intense for most product brands, that few brands enjoy an increasing evoked set status. Usually the most a company can hope for is to share the evoked set of a large number of consumers with two or three other brands, and to spend a large amount on advertising to maintain this position. Because such a high promotion expenditure is required, profits are often tenuous.

Conclusion

Consumers rarely buy brands of products that are unfamiliar. Marketers know this and allocate a large number of dollars to advertising and other promotional efforts to make their brands familiar. In fact, major brand marketers tend not to compete on the basis of price but tend to out-advertise each other in order to obtain the best position in the consumer's mind.

There has been a major exception to brand awareness theory and its application that began in the 1970s—generic brands. Generic brands, which in reality are no brands at all, have enjoyed modest success in supermarkets, obtaining up to 10 percent of market share for a few products. The inflation of the 1970s was so intense that many consumers were driven to cut costs wherever possible, and generics was one answer.

Being sold in well known supermarkets gave generics some of the status of a brand. Today, with the decline in inflation, the popularity of generic brands is declining also. Perhaps their limited success and their decline suggests that except in adverse conditions, products must have acceptable brand names to succeed.

Applications to Small Business

All brand owners must depend on their efforts to create brand awareness for their success. In fact, a brand name that does not have awareness has little value and will contribute little if anything to profits.

Creating brand awareness is perhaps more difficult for the small business than the large, but it is even more important because of the competitiveness of major brand marketers. It is often difficult for small businesses to spend a large amount on advertising, particularly television advertising. Small businesses often have to rely on word-of-mouth advertising among consumers in order to create brand awareness. This, of course, is a slower process than standard advertising methods for increasing brand awareness. However, because of its personal nature, it is usually more credible and more effective in spite of its slowness. Small businesses may work to use product sampling to influential consumers as a means to increase the awareness of their brands. Putting free products in the hands of people who can influence the consumer behavior of others is not a major expense; yet, it can be very effective because of the credibility of these influentials that recommend the brands to others.

References/Sources

Abrams, Bill, "Shoppers Are Often Confused By All the Competing Brands," *The Wall Street Journal* (April 22, 1982): 33. Describes the kinds and number of brands available to consumers.

Bogart, Leo, and Lehman, Charles, "What Makes a Brand Name Familiar?" *Journal of Marketing Research,* 10 (February 1973): 17-22. A study showing the kinds of brands that are most familiar to consumers.

Day, George S., and Pratt, Robert W., Jr., "Stability of Appliance Brand Awareness," *Journal of Marketing Research,* 8 (February 1971): 85-89. Demonstrates the change that takes place in brand awareness over time for a product category.

McNeal, J. U., McDaniel, Stephen, and Smart, Denise, "The Brand Repertoire: Its Content and Organization," *1983 AMA Educators Conference.* Chicago: American Marketing Association, 1983, pp. 92-96. Presents a study showing the contents and nature of the brands that are on the minds of consumers.

Murphy, Patrick E. and Laczniak, Gene R., "Generic Supermarket Items: A Product and Consumer Analysis," *Journal of Retailing,* 55 (Summer 1979): 3-14. Describes the extent of generic brands among consumer product preferences.

Narayana, Chem L. and Markin, Rom J., "Consumer Behavior and Product Performance: An Alternative Conceptualization," *Journal of Marketing,* 39 (October 1975): 1-6. Provides a good description of consumers' brand awareness sets.

Related Topics and Terms

Brand, Brand Familiarity, Brand Image, Brand Loyalty, Brand Management, Brand Name, Brand Preferences, Brand Sets.

James U. McNeal
Department of Marketing
Texas A&M University

BRAND LOYALTY

Overview

Brand loyalty exists when a consumer deliberately and consistently chooses one product brand more often than competing brands. Almost any consumer may develop brand loyalty after evaluating several alternative choices and determining the most preferred brand based upon both objective and subjective criteria. The reasons for such allegiance may relate directly to the brand's physical characteristics, such as size, weight, color, style, etc., or they may stem from factors such as price, availability, the perceived risk of switching to another brand, the perceived brand image, or some combination.

To a large extent, brand loyalty seems to be brand-specific and consumer-specific in that not all brands enjoy a loyal consumer following and some consumers tend to be more brand loyal prone than others. Nonetheless, it is to the marketer's advantage to cultivate brand loyalty wherever possible.

Examples

The potent impact of brand loyalty was felt in 1985 when the Coca-Cola Company dropped its 99-year-old formula in favor of the "New" Coke. Although many consumers welcomed the change and many were indifferent, a large number of faithful Coke drinkers clearly communicated to Coca-Cola that no substitute would suffice. In effect, brand loyalty was great enough to force Coca-Cola to reintroduce the original brand as "Coca-Cola Classic."

Certain product characteristics seem to be associated with high brand loyalty more so than with lower loyalty brands. Brands that have clearly distinguishable, superior, and salient product attributes seem to have more loyal consumers than competing brands; with other product attributes held constant, the brand with the lower price, higher quality, or better performance will often have the brand loyalty edge.

Other brand loyal product characteristics seem to be less rational. Brands such as Coca-Cola, Ivory soap and Crest toothpaste have loyal consumers largely because these brands were established early in many consumer's lives. To switch brands as an adult would break the nostalgic link with one's past; thus the sentimental value of the brand is maintained through continued loyalty.

Brands that are highly visible and are differentiated largely on an image-basis may also enjoy a following of brand loyal consumers *if* the brand's image is congruent with either the consumer's own self-image or the image the consumer wishes to project. A number of cigarette, alcohol, cosmetic, and clothing brands seem to fall in this category.

Benefits

A strong following of brand loyal customers is *the* single most valuable asset any marketing organization can ever hope to obtain. Consequently, the development and maintenance of such a customer base should be a high-priority objective. The benefits of brand loyalty are numerous. First, a loyal customer base reduces marketing costs. It has been estimated, for example, that it costs approximately six times as much to initially attract a customer as to retain an existing customer. Second, as customers become brand loyal there is a tendency for them to deemphasize the importance of price. And, of course, less price sensitivity translates into higher margins. Third, brand loyal customers play a key role in securing and maintaining distribution to the extent that they demand and expect brand availability from channel members. Last, planning throughout the organization is enhanced in that sales volume among loyal customers is less volatile than among disloyal consumers who tend to be more susceptible to the short-term marketing efforts of competitors.

Implementation

Brand loyalty may be thought of as the "ideal" consequence of a series of steps or stages through which the consumer progresses as he becomes more familiar with the brand. These stages include: (1) initial awareness of the brand, (2) evaluation of the brand's need-satisfying potential, (3) initial trial purchase of the brand, (4) brand satisfaction and confirmation of the brand choice, (5) repeat purchases of the brand, and (6) brand loyalty. Brand loyalty may be cultivated to the extent that marketing efforts positively influence the consumer in each stage, thus allowing for the smooth transition to the next stage.

Differentiating the brand from competitive offerings and frequently communicating brand differences increases awareness and enhances the consumer's evaluation of the brand *if* the differences are meaningful to the consumer. For low-involvement products with few distinguishable attributes between brands, simple maintenance-type advertising to remind the consumer that the advertised brand is "a leading brand" may be the most effective strategy.

Consumer-oriented sales promotions such as cents-off coupons, free samples, and premiums are useful in stimulating trial purchases and encouraging brand switching. The amount of the coupon or other incentive should be great enough to offset the degree of risk the consumer faces in trying an "unproven" brand, but not so great as to eliminate the purchase commitment necessary for the consumer to personally justify the purchase decision at a later date.

The most potent strategy to boost satisfaction with the brand is to ensure that the brand's performance meets consumer expectations and that the consumer receives the benefits touted in pre-purchase communications. Reinforcement messages that remind the consumer of the benefits he received is another possible approach.

Free services or merchandise, quantity discounts, and other customer relationship incentives may be useful in encouraging repeat purchases which help to habitualize the purchase process and may dull the consumer's awareness of competitive offerings. Adequate distribution is critical in encouraging repeat purchases as well, because with many consumers—especially younger ones—store loyalty often supersedes brand loyalty.

Evaluation

It is useful to periodically measure the degree of consumer loyalty toward the brand in order to evaluate the effectiveness of the brand's marketing efforts vis-à-vis those of competing brands. There are over 50 approaches to brand loyalty measurement with an apparent trade-off between validity and ease of administration. Some measures treat brand loyalty as a dichotomous variable (i.e. either a consumer is brand loyal or he is not) while other measures recognize brand loyalty as a continuous variable with several *degrees* of brand loyalty possible. Some so called brand loyalty measures more correctly measure repeat purchase behavior with little attention given to the attitudinal aspects of *genuine* loyalty.

Some of the simpler measurements involve asking consumers which brand they purchase most frequently, whether they would switch brands for an X% price discount, or whether they would purchase another brand or shop elsewhere if their preferred brand were temporarily out of stock.

Analyses of consumer panel diaries often determine brand loyal consumers to be those who purchase one brand disproportionately more than competing brands or those who exhibit a discernible and biased pattern in their sequence of purchases. For example, a consumer might be classified as loyal if 60% of his purchases were for Brand A or if he purchased Brand A three consecutive times during the period.

An attitudinal-based measure of brand loyalty might utilize a loyalty scale with which consumers would be asked to indicate the extent to which they agree or disagree with a series of statements concerning purchase preferences, purchase intentions, importance of price, and the like. Each consumer's brand loyalty score might then be computed by summing the points assigned to the ratings from each statement. For example, five points might be scored if the consumer "strongly agreed" to the statement, "I like Brand X," whereas only one point would be scored if he "strongly disagreed."

Conclusion

Given the numerous and sometimes questionable approaches with which brand loyalty has been measured, it is difficult to draw sweeping conclusions about the concept. Moreover, research suggests that brand loyalty tends to be product-specific and consumer-specific which further limits one's ability to generalize. While some of the product characteristics of brand loyalty were discussed, research that has attempted to identify the characteristics of brand loyal consumers has been less than encouraging. It is clear however that brand loyalty does exist and that successful organizations are those that develop and nurture a brand loyal following of customers.

Applications to Small Business

Relative to the larger manufacturer, the small business manufacturer is often in an advantageous position in that he is likely to be "in touch" with his customers, often has fewer volume constraints, and is often more flexible in his ability to react to changing local market conditions. However, the small manufacturer may also have to cope with higher cost structures and may not be able to ride out prolonged economic downturns and/or competitive threats. Fortunately, these advantages and disadvantages all suggest the appropriateness of a market niching strategy which the small manufacturer may be more effectively able to pursue than his larger counterpart. By serving well-defined niches, of course, the likelihood of high customer satisfaction is enhanced—thereby leading to increased brand loyalty. So, a potent competitive weapon for the small business manufacturer is the development of a substantial brand loyal core of customers within each market niche served.

References/Sources

Carman, James, "Correlates of Brand Loyalty: Some Positive Results," *Journal of Marketing Research* (February 1970): 67-76. Extensive study using panel data examines the relationships between brand loyalty, the shopping process, and individual consumer characteristics. An entropy measure of brand loyalty is also introduced.

Day, George S., "A Two-Dimensional Concept of Brand Loyalty," *Journal of Advertising Research* (September 1969): 29-35. One of the first substantial research projects to explicitly measure attitudinal dimensions of brand loyalty.

Frank, Ronald E., "Is Brand Loyalty a Useful Basis For Marketing Segmentation?" *Journal of Advertising Research* (June 1967): 27-33. Study was unable to find a relationship between brand loyalty and individual consumer characteristics, consumer demand, or consumer sensitivity to promotion.

Guest, Lester, "Brand Loyalty Revisited: A Twenty-Year Report," *Journal of Applied Psychology,* vol. 48, # 2 (1964): 93-97. A follow-up study of prior brand loyalty research. Findings suggest that brand preferences formed early in life often continue into adulthood.

Jacoby, Jacob, "A Model of Multi-Brand Loyalty," *Journal of Advertising Research* (June 1971): 25-31. Theoretical model and exploratory research suggesting that consumers may be loyal to more than one brand.

Jacoby, Jacob and Chestnut, Robert W., *Brand Loyalty Measurement and Man-*

agement. New York: John Wiley, 1978. The most comprehensive review and analysis of brand loyalty research available. This book evaluates prior research, formulates a theoretical model of brand loyalty, and offers some practical guidance for the marketer interested in cultivating brand loyalty. An extensive bibliography is also included.

Kiesler, Charles A., *The Psychology of Commitment: Experiments Linking Behavior To Belief.* New York: Academic Press, 1971. Extensive review of experiments in social psychology that provide a rich understanding of commitment—the underlying concept of brand loyalty.

Related Topics and Terms

Brand Commitment, Brand Preference, Commitment, Consumer Loyalty, Involvement, Loyalty, Product Involvement, Purchase Intentions, Purchase Preference, Source Loyalty, Store Loyalty.

Charles L. Martin
Department of Marketing and
Small Business Management
The Wichita State University

BREAKEVEN ANALYSIS

Overview

There are three major components to any business decision. These are the cost component, the revenue component, and the resultant profit component. Breakeven analysis is an analytical tool that enables a decision maker to analyze the relationships among these components.

In breakeven analysis, costs are classified as either fixed or variable. Those costs that generally do not vary with the output are referred to as *FIXED COSTS* (examples of fixed costs are rent, plant, equipment, and any other financial commitments incurred independent of the level of production). Those costs that generally vary proportionately with output are referred to as *VARIABLE COSTS* (examples of variable costs are labor and material, and promotion and selling costs that directly enter into making and marketing the product). Variable costs may be expressed as TOTAL VARIABLE COSTS associated with certain output; it is the *product* of variable cost per unit times the number of units produced).

The revenue component is usually expressed as the product of total number of units sold of the product and the price per unit of the product.

Thus: TOTAL REVENUE – TOTAL COST = PROFIT

$$(P \times Q) \quad - (TFC + (UVC \times Q)) = \Pi$$

Where: P   = unit price of the product
Q   = number of units produced and sold
TFC = total fixed costs
UVC = unit variable cost
Π = total profits

Rearranging: Π = $(P \times Q) - TFC - (UVC \times Q)$ . . . .(1)
P   = $Q(P\text{-}UVC) - TFC$ . . . .(2)

At the breakeven point: $\Pi = 0$

Therefore: $$Q = \frac{TFC}{P - UVC}$$ . . . .(3)

Where Q is the number of units of the product that needs to be produced and sold to breakeven.

It is important to note the term (P–UVC) is referred to as the CONTRIBUTION MARGIN (CM) per unit. This is the amount available from the sale of each unit of the product, given the price and the unit variable cost, to cover the fixed costs and generate some profit.

The breakeven point in dollars can be obtained by the following formula:

$$BEP \ \$ = \frac{TFC}{1 - \dfrac{UVC}{P}}$$ . . . .(4)

The term $(1-\dfrac{UVC}{P})$ is referred to as the CONTRIBUTION MARGIN PER-CENTAGE rather than contribution margin per unit.

Graphically, the breakeven point analysis can be expressed as follows:

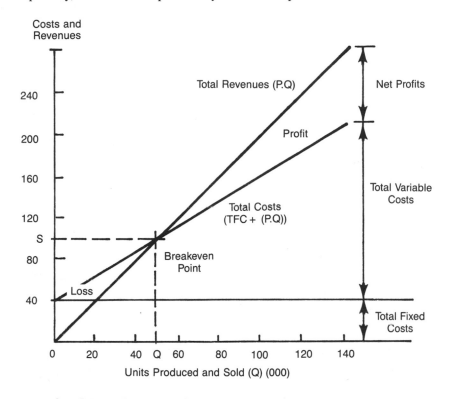

S = Sales at Breakeven; Q = Units at Breakeven

Examples

Ted's Shirt Factory has the following cost structure: rent = $2400.00, equipment costs = $4600.00, labor costs = $10.00 per shirt, and material costs = $2.00 per shirt. The shirts are to be sold at $20.00 each. The breakeven point can be calculated as follows:

$$Q = \frac{TFC}{P - UVC} = \frac{7000}{20 - 12} = 875 \text{ units}$$

$$\$/BEP = \frac{TFC}{1 - \dfrac{UVC}{P}} = \frac{7000}{1 - \dfrac{12}{20}} = \$17,500.00$$

Benefits

Breakeven analysis is one of the most versatile analytical tools available to firms. Besides providing estimates of unit and dollar sales to break even on various investment opportunities, the analysis also enables firms to do the following:

1. Determine levels of sales that must be achieved to attain desired profit goals, given the cost structure.
2. Determine product price levels to attain desired profit goals, given the cost structure.
3. Examine proposed changes in planned expenditures to assess the impacts of these changes in expenditures on the corresponding changes in sales and profit.

Implementation

1. Determine level of sales to achieve stated profit goals.

Since $\Pi = Q(P-UVC)-TFC$ $\dots\dots\dots\dots(2)$

Rearranging $Q(P-UVC) = \Pi + TFC$

Therefore $Q = \dfrac{\Pi + TFC}{P-UVC}$ $\dots\dots\dots\dots(5)$

Where $P-UVC = CM$

To the previous example, add the following: the factory wants to determine the sales level to generate $10,000 in profit.

$$Q = \frac{10,000 + 7,000}{20 - 12} = 2,125 \text{ units}$$

This implies the firm needs to sell 2,125 shirts to attain a profit level of $10,000.

2. Determine Product Price Level

Since $\Pi = (P \times Q) - TFC - (UVC \times Q)$ $\dots\dots\dots\dots(1)$

Rearranging $P \times Q = \Pi + TFC + (UVC \times Q)$

Therefore, $P = \dfrac{\Pi + TFC + (UVC \times Q)}{Q}$ $\dots\dots\dots\dots(5)$

Modify the previous example as follows: the firm's production and sales capacity is 3000 shirts, and the profit desired is $20,000.00.

Therefore, the price to be charged is

$$P = \frac{\$20,000 + \$7,000 + (\$12)\,(3000)}{3000} = \$21.00$$

3. Examine proposed changes in Planned Expenditures.

Since $\qquad \Pi = Q(P-UVC) - TFC \qquad \dots\dots\dots\dots\dots(2)$

Rearranging $\quad Q(P-UVC) = \Pi + TFC \qquad \dots\dots\dots\dots\dots(7)$

This implies that the total contributions from sale of the product is what the business should generate to cover its fixed costs and generate profits. Any expenditure that is to be committed can be looked upon as a form of fixed cost and, therefore, the total contribution generated must exceed the proposed expenditure commitment for the product to be profitable.

Once again, modify the previous example in the following manner: The marketing department of the firm proposes a sales promotional program at a cost of $50,000.00 and this program is expected to increase sales to 2900 shirts at $20.00 per shirt.

Therefore, $\quad 2900(\$20-\$12) = \Pi + (\$50,000)$

Thus $\qquad \Pi = (\$26,800)$

This implies the campaign is not a profitable campaign given the anticipated sales.

Using the same situation, if the firm wanted to know how many shirts need to be sold to obtain a $10,000 profit using the $50,000 sales promotional campaign:

$$Q(\$20-\$12) = \$10,000 + \$50,000$$

Therefore $\quad Q = \dfrac{\$60,000}{8} = 7,500 \text{ units}$

Thus it is evident that the implementation of breakeven analysis involves the manipulation of the basic algorithm established earlier, Total Revenue – Total Costs = Profits.

Evaluation

Breakeven analysis is one of the simplest and most useful tools in management decision making. However, the analysis is not without its limitations. These are:

1. The cost components have to be classified as either fixed or variable, and this may not always be possible or appropriate.
2. The analysis allows for very little fluctuations in costs and therefore, oftentimes is limited to short term analysis.
3. It is an "output" oriented analysis; i.e., fluctuations in costs and revenues are attributed to the output and output alone and the analysis assumes that one is able to sell what one produces, and thus poses no real inventory problems.
4. Adequate adjustments are not built in for environmental changes such as technological changes, economic changes, and the like.
5. The formula assumes a constant price and unit variable cost irrespective of the units involved. In practice, price and unit variable costs may vary according to output.

Conclusion

Despite the limitations, the usefulness of breakeven analysis as a decision making tool is invaluable. The versatility of this tool provides the marketer an avenue of comparison any time two or more desirable alternatives are being evaluated.

The usefulness of breakeven analysis, though the technique is fairly simple, is to:

1. Indicate to a decision maker at what level of sales revenue the business unit will be able to cover its total costs.
2. Determine sales levels that are necessary (given certain prices) to achieve certain profit goals.
3. Determine prices of products, knowing the costs and profit goals.
4. Enable managers to have a quick way to examine any proposed changes in plans and expenditures for increased profits.

Applications to Small Business

The concept of breakeven analysis is also used as "trade-off" analysis in management decision making and "CVP" (cost-volume-profit) analysis in management accounting.

The breakeven analysis is an especially useful tool for small businesses because of its capabilities to analyze many business situations with great ease and simplicity, prior to total business involvement. The analysis can predict with a fair degree of accuracy the profitability of new business ventures, any proposed improvements to the existing business, and the effectiveness of proposed strategic or tactical changes in business operations.

Implementation of breakeven analysis can only increase the decision making capabilities of a small business, thus aiding the achievement of greater performance and profit goals and reducing unnecessary business risks.

Software/Databases

Super Calc, Super Calc-2, Super Calc-3. Cdex Corp. A useful complement to breakeven analysis. Enables the user to make decisions about product pricing, product mix, make vs. buy, and economic order quantity.

References/Sources

Anderson, Roy A., Biederman, Harry A., "Using Cost-Volume-Profit Charts," *Controller's Handbook*. Homewood, IL: Dow Jones/Irwin, pp. 116-141.

Dominiak, Geraldine F., and Louderback III, Joseph G., *Managerial Accounting*, 4th ed. Boston: Kent Publishing, 1985.

Related Topics and Terms

Economic Order Quantity, Elasticity of Demand, Price Strategy, Stock Turnover.

R. Viswanathan
Department of Marketing
University of Northern Colorado

BROKERS

Overview

Brokers, or agents, perform a number of different wholesale functions in distribution channels. They are specialized middlemen, usually independent businesspeople who work on commission, unlike merchant and full-service wholesalers who earn profits by reselling stocks of goods which they own outright. Brokers do not take title to the goods they sell, nor do they usually take possession. Their function is to bring buyers and sellers together to complete a sale. After they do so, they are paid a commission by either the buyer or seller, depending upon which of the two they represent. About 10.4 percent of wholesale sales are made by broker/agents, who make up 9.2 percent of all wholesalers. They sell to wholesalers, distributors, larger retailers, manufacturers, government and some institutions. Others, such as stock and real estate brokers often operate at the retail level, representing individual buyers and sellers. Except for the manufacturer's agents who may have continuing relationships with sellers and customers, most brokers have only a temporary, or one-time-association with either.

There are several types of broker-middlemen:

(1) Manufacturer's Agents carry up to 12 non-competing, similar product lines as self-employed representatives of manufacturers, and operate in exclusive territories. They take commissions as low as 4-6 percent for repeat-sale items but may take as much as 15-20 percent for new items that require harder selling. These brokers sell at prices established by manufacturers and take orders which they forward to manufacturers who ship merchandise and bill customers. See the section on Manufacturer's Agents.

(2) Food Brokers normally handle processed food products and represent several processors in an area. Their function is to get buyers and sellers together, to make sales to chains, larger independent stores and institutional customers. They need to have full information about market conditions, and they may store and deliver goods without taking title to them. Their producer clients specify prices and terms, and the brokers take a 5-7 percent commission on the selling price.

(3) Commission Merchants accumulate goods from local markets and sell them in a central market, sometimes by auction. They are also agent intermediaries but, unlike food brokers, they may have some control over price, and may bid up a selling price or accept any price above a minimum acceptable to their seller-client. They often take possession of goods such as agricultural products, and make them available to buyers for inspection. In addition to these products, they may also accumulate and sell seafood, other commodities and furniture. Commission merchants take about a 5 percent commission.

(4) Selling Agents have a much wider scope of responsibility than do other brokers. They not only sell, but handle all the marketing activities of one or more companies, including advertising, pricing and determining the terms of sale. Instead of limiting these activities to a few items in a producer's line, the selling agent sells the entire output of each firm in a wide geographical area, even in international markets. Commissions vary from about 5 percent in the plywood industry to 20% for silver jewelry. Often, sales agents are used by firms in financial difficulties who are trying to cut costs by eliminating the fixed expenses of marketing departments.

(5) Auction Companies may accumulate goods from a number of individual sources, or from only one, such as a large estate or a business that is being liquidated. They provide a location where buyers may inspect the merchandise, and where buyers and auctioneer (the representative of the seller) may get together and complete sales. The commission varies widely depending upon the type, value and quantity of the merchandise.

(6) Other Brokers, such as real estate and stock brokers, sell unique goods, usually in individual transactions. Real estate commissions are about 5-6 percent of the selling prices, but stock brokers' commissions decline as the transaction value increases.

Examples

Several major manufacturers such as Nabisco and Heinz use food brokers. While Nabisco crackers and cookies are sold in direct channels to insure freshness, Planter's peanuts, margarine and candy are sold by brokers who call on chains and wholesalers. Heinz uses brokers mainly in sparsely populated states where it is not economical to have a separate sales force.

Another example is a sales agent who operated in the food-producing area of northern Illinois where he marketed goods for a number of independent processors. He contacted all frozen-food wholesalers in the state periodically and sent out bulletins on items he thought were good buys. By keeping in close contact with a number of processors, he expanded the range of lines he carried, and was able to offer a wide array of products to his customers. By doing this, he also saved time for customers who would otherwise have to search for suppliers of individual lines. This broker also bought goods in his own name when he came upon a good price that had to be taken up immediately, warehoused the goods and sold them later when prices rose. Here, of course, he was not operating as a broker since he took title to the products.

A commission merchant in Ohio acted as a broker, bringing farmers and bulk buyers together. The broker picked up fresh farm produce from several farmers, transported it to a market in a large city. There, buyers from chain stores, restaurants and smaller groceries inspected the produce, and the commission merchant negotiated the sale.

Benefits

By using brokers, manufacturers and other producers avoid the substantial fixed costs of direct channels, which require a permanent sales force and warehousing facilities. At the same time, producers are able to take advantage of the broker's list of loyal retailers and wholesalers which has been built up over time.

Larger companies find it advantageous to use brokers in selling to wholesalers when some of their lines are not appropriate for their regular channels. Dow Chemical, for example, sells its auto care line through brokers to wholesalers. Because volumes are relatively small compared to Dow's other lines, the company finds it more economical to use brokers than its own salespeople.

Brokers also benefit their customers, since they usually carry lines from several manufacturers. Not only does this permit them to offer a wider variety, but dealing only with one salesperson saves time for the customer.

Implementation

Manufacturers are constantly searching for good, aggressive brokers and agents in order to implement an indirect sales channel. There are several ways in which this can be done:

(1) Contact present and potential customers to get information on how they feel about the integrity and performance of brokers who serve them.
(2) Careful inquiry may reveal which brokers are being used by competitors.
(3) Advertisements in leading industry trade journals should yield brokers who are looking for new lines. A review of their recent sales records will indicate how successful they are.
(4) Trade shows also offer an excellent opportunity to meet brokers and to observe them in action.

Since brokers/agents operate in specific territories, companies must be sure that these territories provide suitable coverage for products being offered. There may be a gap in coverage, or two brokers the company wants to use may overlap in some areas. These are examples of implementation problems that must be resolved before the broker networks are put into effect.

Many companies believe that once brokers have been selected and assigned, they operate independently, and the commission is sufficient incentive for them to sell. But like a regular sales force, brokers need to be contacted periodically and given assistance, such as that provided by missionary support personnel.

Evaluation

Brokers are valuable to manufacturers because they serve their own lists of customers and because their services are comparatively low in cost. But most manufacturers would prefer not to rely on brokers because they are individual businesspeople and have little loyalty to a single supplier. Established wholesalers, on the other hand, usually develop continuing, long-term relationships with producers. They also buy goods in large lots, take title, and pay in 30 days, whereas with brokers, companies must carry their own inventories, ship, bill and collect from individual customers. Thus, manufacturers need to periodically evaluate their distribution systems, the performance of their brokers, and the total costs of using brokers versus wholesalers or their own sales force. These factors should be considered:

(1) Does the broker represent so many manufacturers that any one of them is not effectively represented?
(2) Does the use of brokers, whom the manufacturer does not control, result in loss of needed direct contact with the market?
(3) Do any of these conditions exist in the market? (a) Would it be less economical, overall, to use a different channel? (b) Is there a need to expand or contract the market rapidly? (c) Is the market seasonal, small or scattered? (d) Is the broker's customer list important to the selling firm?

Conclusion

Generally, retailers prefer to deal with a single broker who carries a wide variety of products than with ten manufacturer's salespeople. Producers, however, deal with a broker only when they have no alternative, or when there are substantial savings to be had, because the producer is at the broker's mercy. If the broker finds a better source for the product, a manufacturer could be without a distribution channel overnight. Also, companies lose contact with their market by using this channel, and if the broker demands that prices be reduced, a firm often has no alternative. These problems come about because the broker is more oriented toward customers than suppliers, because suppliers are easier to get. Nevertheless, there are many examples of long-term relationships between manufacturers and brokers, but producers need to carefully review the circumstances surrounding each situation where brokers might be used, rather than making general decisions.

Applications to Small Business

Despite the drawbacks of manufacturer-broker relationships, most small producers would find it difficult to exist without them. Unless these companies have the resources or the need to establish their own sales forces, and unless they have access to regular wholesalers who will carry the products, brokers are the only alternative. They provide sales experience, established customer lists and a fixed, predictable selling cost. By selecting competent brokers through the methods described earlier, manufacturers can get a foothold in the market without incurring heavy initial sales costs. Smaller companies that cannot afford missionary support for brokers can use the less expensive trade shows to get exposure to potential customers at minimum cost, making the selling job easier.

Software/Databases

Since brokers do not usually carry inventory or perform the billing function, any standard software for maintaining lists is suitable. Manufacturers, however, can evaluate broker performance by using the "Stanger Sales Model" which helps to make choices between this channel and direct selling, and "Stanger Rep Evaluator" which evaluates brokers on short and long term order-getting performance. From Wm. M. Stanger, 264 Ashland Rd., Summit, NJ, 07901.

References/Sources

Brobow, E., "Suddenly An Urge to Boost Their Potential," *Sales and Marketing Management* (June 1982), special report. Lists and discusses the three major advantages offered by brokers versus direct sales forces.

Buskirk, Richard H., *Principles of Marketing*, 4th ed. Hinsdale, IL: Dryden Press, 1975, pp. 369-78. A complete discussion of brokers, their advantages and disadvantages and how to locate good ones.

Giges, Nancy, "Grocers' Middlemen Step to the Forefront," *Advertising Age* (Oct. 11, 1982): M19. Discusses the various ways in which large food companies such as Nabisco and Heinz, use food brokers.

Helmers, Henrick O., "Industrial Distribution of Specific Parts: A Case Example," *Marketing in a Changing World*. Chicago: American Marketing Association, 1969, p. 199. Points out the market factors relating to the use of brokers for both producers and customers.

Mintz, Steven, "S&MM Spends a Day in the Field with a Food Broker," *Sales & Marketing Management* (June 1982): special report. A narrative of what brokers do, how they sell and what methods they use.

U. S. Department of Commerce, *Statistical Abstract of the United States*, 105th ed. Washington: US Government Printing Office, 1985, pp. 414, 790. Provides data on the wholesale trade including the part played by brokers.

Related Topics and Terms

Drop Shipper, Manufacturer's Agent, Merchant Wholesaler, Rack Jobber, Selective Distribution, Wholesaling.

Hale N. Tongren
Department of Marketing
George Mason University

BUYING POWER INDEX

Overview

A widely used source of consumer market data is the *Survey of Buying Power* published each July by *Sales and Marketing Management* magazine. The survey reports consumer market data using a variety of information sources. These demographic and socio-economic data are reported for the 316 largest metropolitan areas as well as for states and counties.

The survey provides population by age groups and number of households; total retail sales broken into six major categories; effective buying income (EBI) and a buying power index. The Buying Power Index (BPI) is often used as a measure of relative market potential for frequently purchased consumer products. The Buying Power Index is based upon three factors: the area's share of the nation's disposable personal income, retail sales, and population. The Buying Power Index for a particular area is calculated using the formula:

$$BPI_i = \frac{5I_i + 3R_i + 2P_i}{10}$$

where: I_i = percentage of U.S. disposable personal income in area i

R_i = percentage of U.S. retail sales in area i

P_i = percentage of U.S. population in area i

The Buying Power Index is not appropriate for limited demand, high priced goods. The further a product is removed from being a mass marketed item, the more need there is to make modifications to the index based upon more appropriate measures.

Examples

The basic factors comprising the Buying Power Index provide marketers with an in-depth profile for any metro area, county, city, or state. They allow companies to identify specific markets and focus their marketing efforts on those having the highest potential. The BPI can be used to develop strategies, target specific local markets, design sales territories, set quotas, and evaluate sales performance.

The Schwinn Bicycle Company of Chicago has used the *Survey of Buying Power* and its BPI for over 25 years in setting sales quotas and reviewing sales performance. Schwinn compares a specific market's population with the previous year's sales and computes a "bikes-per-thousand" ratio for the market being investigated. A quota for the market is then developed by multiplying the BPI for that particular market by projected U.S. sales. By comparing the quota with actual sales, Schwinn is able to determine whether its dealers are reaching the prospective market potential. Regional distribution centers adjust their inventories accordingly and the number and location of dealerships is partially based upon the use of the BPI.

The ABC-TV sales department has used the *Survey of Buying Power* for targeting viewer areas where they seek to obtain new advertisers or new local broadcasting affiliates. In preparing presentations to potential affiliates, data and households, population by age group and total population are used to target markets that match the standard ABC-TV demographic profile of the average viewer of their programs. The sales department of ABC-TV has also used this source for projecting five-year profiles of advertising markets used in setting sales quotas or expanding territories.

The *Survey of Buying Power* has been used to identify sales potential on a market-by-market basis for co-op advertising allocations. Allocations are based on objectively projected sales quotas on a market-by-market analysis. In this manner, ad dollars are used to generate projected sales rather than as a payment to dealers or distributors who have already made a commitment to buy.

Benefits

The use of information obtained from the *Survey of Buying Power* has several major benefits to users. The most basic and useful measurement in the *Survey of Buying Power* is the Buying Power Index. This index combines multiple factors into a measurement of a market's ability to buy expressed as a percentage of the U.S./ Canadian potential. As a single market measure, the level of accuracy has been documented. As a ready source of marketing data, the *Survey of Buying Power's* information has proved both relevant and reliable.

Implementation

The *Survey of Buying Power* has been utilized as a desktop reference for state, metro and country statistics since 1929. The method of implementing this information depends upon the marketing decision to be made. The BPI can be used as reported, or a customized index can be developed, depending upon its application.

A frequent use of the BPI is in estimating market potentials. For instance, a home delivery pizza operator interested in starting a regional system of franchised stores used the BPI to assess market potential. Each store was to have exclusive territorial rights and it was estimated that the total regional potential would reach $50 million annually. Franchises would then be sold in any town where the store might have sales of more than $350,000 a year. He would advertise in *Pizza Today* and the regional edition of the *Wall Street Journal* to attract potential franchisers. Upon examination of the applicant's business credentials, it was necessary to determine if the area had enough buying potential to justify a franchise.

An application from Athens, Georgia, indicated that market as having a Buying Power Index of .518. Since the total national potential is $50 million, this amounts to a potential of $259,000 (equals $50,000,000 x .00518) in Athens, Georgia. Since a successful store sells over $350,000 annually, the franchiser leaned toward not awarding the franchise. However, it was necessary to adjust the market for additional factors such as competition in the market, local market uniqueness, such as the presence of a heavy concentration of college students and seasonal conditions.

The Buying Power Index is calculated using the area's percent of U. S. income, percent of U. S. retail sales and percent of U. S. population. For instance, the Buying Power Index for Orlando, Florida, might be calculated as follows:

Percent of U.S. Income	$0.356 \times 5 = 1.780$
Percent of U.S. Retail Sales	$0.431 \times 3 = 1.293$
Percent of U.S. Population	$0.322 \times 2 = \underline{0.644}$
	$3.717 \div 10 = .372$ BPI

Thus, an area with only 0.322 percent of the U.S. population has 0.372 percent of the national sales potential because of higher average retail sales and income. This is evidence that the metro area is attracting patrons from surrounding counties. The BPI expresses sales potential in relative rather than absolute terms. However, specific estimates can be obtained by multiplying the BPI times national sales figures. For example, if national sales of a brand of under-counter can openers is projected at 1.5 million units, the BPI would indicate sales to the Orlando metropolitan area to be 5,580 units (1,500,000 x .00372 = 5,580).

The variables and weights used in the Index reflect the potential for frequently purchased, popularly priced consumer products. Because the index is not appropriate for limited, high-priced goods, some firms select their own variables and weights and create indexes which are felt to more accurately measure the potential for their products.

The first step in calculating a custom BPI is to isolate the population and/or household factors that apply to the targeted audience. For instance, if the product is an under-counter automatic coffee maker, an area's total household count rather than a specific age group is more important. The next step would be to select the income group most appropriate for the product. If it were a premium-priced product only those households with incomes of $50,000 and over might be used. The third step would be to select the retail outlet or store group category that is appropriate for distribution, such as general merchandise stores. Once these factors have been selected, the process is as follows to establish the BPI for a premium-priced home entertainment center.

Step 1: For each area to be indexed, use factors associated with premium-priced centers such as

$$\frac{\text{Area's Households}}{\text{Total U.S. Households}} = \text{X\%}$$

$$\frac{\text{Market Households with Income over \$50,000}}{\text{U.S. Households with Income over \$50,000}} = Y\%$$

$$\frac{\text{Markets General Merchandise Sales}}{\text{U.S. General Merchandise Sales}} = Z\%$$

Step 2: Determine the importance of each factor and assign a weight

Factor 1 (demographic) = 60%
Factor 2 (economic) = 20%
Factor 3 (distribution) = 20%

Step 3: BPI = (.6 x X%) + (.2 x Y%) + (.2 x Z%)

The same approach would be used for each area targeted. The figure arrived at would be a relative indicator allowing a comparison of the buying power of the specific area with the total.

The standard or customized BPI can find use in sales planning, marketing applications and advertising. Firms often select their own variables and weights and create indexes which are a more accurate measure for their particular products than the standard BPI available from the *Survey of Buying Power.*

Evaluation

When using the BPI to measure market potential, it is necessary to first clearly define the market to be investigated and understand the buying behavior of the market. This is necessary because the *Survey of Buying Power's* BPI is based upon frequently purchased, popularly priced consumer products. It is not appropriate for limited demand, high-priced goods; and it is not particularly useful in estimating potential in industrial markets. However, for a readily available multi-factor index, it may be most useful for a wide variety of marketing decisions.

In addition, the *Survey of Buying Power* provides relevant and reliable statistics that are frequently used by marketers. However, it should be remembered that these are limited to metro areas. For certain companies and products, major metropolitan areas may not be the most important targets. As population shifts away from urban centers, rural areas may become more attractive as potential markets.

A number of alternatives to traditional metro/county measures have been developed for specialized markets. Arbitron's Areas of Dominant Influence (ADIs) or the Audit Bureau of Circulations newspaper markets have emerged as more useful alternatives for individual industries. In 1973, *Sales and Marketing Management* created its *Survey of Buying Power—Part II* to provide information with similar geographical bases. In addition to data on ADIs and newspaper markets, five-year projections for all metros and metro counties are provided. Rankings of individual merchandise line sales for seven major categories are included in Part II. Marketers needing more specialized information in terms of media markets have found this a valuable information source.

Conclusion

The *Survey of Buying Power* provides marketers with a convenient single source of relevant demographic, economic and distribution information. This information has been found to be most useful for a wide variety of sales and marketing applications. The buying power index developed from the *Survey of Buying Power* provides marketers with a useful general purpose multi-factor index. Users need to recognize the buying circumstances applying to their product and make the necessary adjustments.

Applications to Small Business

The Survey of Buying Power (Part I and Part II) provides an information base that can be used in several ways by small businesses. Statistics on merchandise sales such as apparel, groceries, appliances, health and beauty aids show a product market share and provide the small business marketer with a more accurate way to estimate potential sales of particular product lines by metro markets than is possible with other methods. This can result in improved planning as well as better targeted strategies for these smaller businesses.

In addition to existing metro population and economic and distribution information, five-year projections provide small business organizations with the ability to identify those markets having high growth or little or no growth. This has been found useful for sales force allocation, retail location and media spending. The *Survey of Buying Power* can provide the basis for allocation of advertising dollars among local markets. Information on population, BPI and retail sales for newspaper markets can be used for improving cost and coverage of media expenditures. By analyzing the strength of a newspaper market's retail sales for a given store category, small businesses have found it useful to gauge the effectiveness of newspaper advertising, direct mail, and coupons prior to committing promotional dollars.

Software/Databases

There are numerous software programs that accommodate the information found in the *Survey of Buying Power*. *Sales and Marketing Management* publishes an annual directory of PC-based sales and marketing applications software. This annual directory provides the vendor title of software package, and specific application as well as the purchase price and computer model or operating system. Three recent software programs that can be used with the Survey of Buying Power data base are:

The Sales Manager. Market Power, 11780 Rough and Ready Road, Rough and Ready, CA 95975. Provides territory, account and sales force management information.

Marketrieve. International Digital Systems, 699 East Industrial Park Avenue, Manchester, NH 03103. Provides lead tracking, forecasting and market analysis.

Maps III. 25 Associates, 1600 Orrington Street, Evanston, IL 60201. This program aligns sales territories by integrating company data (or secondary source information) with U. S. geography.

The Survey of Buying Power Data Service provides a complete and comprehensive in-depth marketing service that goes beyond the *Survey of Buying Power* in information and detail. This is available in a single volume at the cost of $269.95.

References/Sources

Berman, Barry, and Evans, Joel R., *Retail Management: A Strategic Approach.* New York: Macmillan, 1983, pp. 197-200. Provides an illustration of using the *Survey of Buying Power* for retail site selection.

Lumpkin, James R., and Darden, William R., "Relating Television Preference Viewing to Shopping Orientations, Lifestyles, and Demographics: The Examination of Perceptual and Preference Dimensions of Television Programming," *Journal of Advertising,* 11 (No. 4, 1982): 56-67. Consumers prefer sets of television programs rather than programs of one specific type. These groups vary by lifestyles and demographics but not on shopping orientations. The three demographic descriptors were age, education, and income.

"SBP-II: Pieces of the Marketing Puzzles," *Sales and Marketing Management,* 133 (October 29, 1984): 7-14, 41-174. This provides additional survey of buying power with information breakdowns by metro merchandise sales, five-year metro projections, and media markets.

Survey of Buying Power, Sales and Marketing Management, July 22, 1985. Annual edition that features metro market statistics on population, effective buying income, and retail sales. The July issue is devoted to the *Survey of Buying Power.* If purchased separately, the cost is $65. A yearly subscription to *Sales and Marketing Management* (which includes the annual *Survey of Buying Power*) is $36.

Vaughn, Ronald L., "Demographic Data Banks: A New Management Resource," *Business Horizons* (November-December 1984): 38-42. Much of the information from the Census Bureau in forms that are helpful to marketers is included in the *Survey of Buying Power.* The types of organizations providing data services and the types of services they make available are reviewed.

Weymes, Ed, "A Different Approach to Retail Sales Analysis," *Business Hori-*

zons (March-April 1982): 66-74. The product life cycle concept is applied to an assortment of products in one store. This system monitors the movement of a product through its life cycle in a particular store. The *Survey of Buying Power* could be utilized as an information source for such a proposed matrix.

Zeithaml, Valerie A., "The New Demographics and Market Fragmentation," *Journal of Marketing,* Vol. 49 (Summer 1985): 64-75. Changing demographics will result in fragmentation of traditional mass markets for grocery products and supermarkets. This article focuses on the way that these changing demographics and family roles may affect retailers and manufacturers of grocery products.

Related Topics and Terms
Census of Population, Disposable Personal Income, Effective Buying Income, Household, Market Potential, Merchandise Line Sales, Metropolitan Statistical Area, Retail Trade, Shopping Good, Specialty Good, Standard Industrial Classification (SIC), Standard Metropolitan Statistical Area (SMSA), Trading Area.

Gordon W. Paul and Duane L. Davis
Department of Marketing
University of Central Florida

CABLE TV ADVERTISING

Overview

Advertising on cable television has become an increasingly popular phenomenon over the last several years. From its crude beginnings in the 1940s, cable television has improved to the point where it is currently competing against the traditional networks for advertising dollars. Initially, cable allowed home television reception through a coaxial cable rather than the traditional off-the-air signals. Television dealers were the first to experiment with the concept of coaxial cable in an attempt to sell more television sets. A primary purpose of the early cable systems was to clarify TV signals. The early growth of cable TV can be attributed to the effectiveness of cable in areas that had limited or no television services. In 1950, 70 communities had cable systems, and approximately 14,000 homes were being served. By 1983, A.C. Nielsen Co. reported that nearly 40 percent of all U.S. households were wired for cable television. Others estimate that cable television could reach 60 percent of all U.S. households by 1990. Thus, the tremendous growth in cable television represents enormous opportunities as well as challenges for advertisers in the next several years.

Examples

The growth in the cable television industry is causing many national advertisers to pay increasingly more attention to the cable networks. In fact, major advertisers like Procter and Gamble and General Foods have reduced their ad spending on network TV in favor of cable TV. Cable networks such as CNN (Cable News Network) reported that additions to their growing lists of advertisers include such organizations as Sears, American Express, General Mills, Quaker Oats, and Shell Oil. Additionally, Anheuser-Busch has recently signed a $25 million, five-year contract with ESPN, the Entertainment and Sports Programming Network. Therefore, it appears advertisers are clamoring to take advantage of the growth and impact of cable television.

Not only are these major companies advertising more on cable, but they are investing more money to produce television shows specifically for cable television. For example, major advertisers such as Kraft, Exxon, and Bristol-Myers are experimenting with programming and commercials on the cable networks that will ultimately enhance their corporate image. These companies are creating programs and advertisements that are virtually impossible on network TV. Provocative ideas such as "infomercials"—3 to 10 minute commercial messages—have been run on cable TV. Bristol-Myers and General Foods are experimenting with programming that is created and sponsored entirely by them. Such options as these would be prohibitively expensive on network television.

Benefits

Cable television offers its advertisers several important benefits. Perhaps the most important benefit that initially lured many advertisers to cable television was the low cost associated with cable programming. Many national advertisers have been pleased with the relatively low cost of producing material for cable. For example, estimates of $3,000 to $15,000 for a half-hour of client-supported programming have been given for cable television. These costs are substantially less than those on network television. Another related advantage of cable television is that advertisers can usually select a better programming environment for their ads on cable than on network television. For example, advertisers of health-care products may choose to advertise their products on the Lifetime (Health) Network. Advertisers of sporting goods and childrens' products may find the environment for advertising their products much more effective on such cable networks as ESPN (Sports Programming) and the Disney Channel.

Perhaps the greatest advantage cable television offers to its advertisers is its ability to pinpoint an audience. Since its inception, cable television has been positioned as a form of media that can offer advertisers relatively inexpensive rates and selective target audiences. If an advertiser utilizes the broadcast or traditional networks, it will cost a lot of money and chances are the ads will be reaching more people than they need to. The benefit of cable is that it is "narrowcast." That is, advertisers can target an audience and avoid throwing money away on people who don't care and don't listen. In fact, networks such as CNN promotes that they can offer advertisers this "narrowcasting" by providing them with an upscale audience.

Several studies have corroborated the fact that audiences viewing cable television are different from those audiences who do not subscribe to cable. A recent study indicated that a typical cable subscriber would have a higher incidence of: 1) a three-to-four person household, 2) the lady of the house in the 35-54 age group, 3) white collar occupations, 4) households with teenagers present, and 5) whites more than blacks. Others have concluded that subscribers of cable television tended to have a greater interest in electronic devices, had higher incomes, a younger median age, more owned their own home, and had a larger household size. Therefore, it appears that cable television can offer advertisers several unique benefits.

Implementation

Several important aspects must be considered before placing an advertisement on cable television. First, the nature of the individual cable network and their audience composition must be considered. There has been much controversy surrounding the issue of whether or not advertisers are really benefiting from the uniqueness of the cable environment. That is, advertising mass marketed products on selective cable networks like Lifetime or ESPN may be defeating the purpose of cable television advertising. Advertisers must first match their products to their target audience before seeking out the appropriate cable network that reaches that audience. Otherwise, the relatively low cost of cable advertising can be wasted.

A thorough understanding of the various cable networks alternatives is imperative before the implementation of an advertisement on cable TV. For example, research has shown that several of the first cable networks (WTBS, WGN, CNN, etc.) may in fact appeal to more "broadcast" audiences than some of the newer cable networks. Superstations such as WTBS and WGN may offer the advertiser of mass marketed products an excellent advertising vehicle at a low cost. However, the more recent additions to the cable arena like Lifetime, the Nashville Network, the Disney Channel, and MTV offer the advertiser very unique, yet selective audiences. These are very important considerations for an advertiser contemplating the use of cable television.

Evaluation

In only a few years, cable television has gained respect as a viable advertising vehicle among many major companies. This is particularly evident by the vast amount of advertising dollars that are being shifted to cable from the traditional broadcast networks. However, there are still some who have doubts when it comes to using cable television for advertising. These doubts include:

1) Because of the growing number of cable channels, cable audiences will continue to be significantly smaller than those of the broadcast networks.
2) Coverage of markets can be very spotty or fragmented.
3) Too many cable services and channels can cause consumer confusion.

In evaluating cable television as an advertising vehicle, the majority of individuals involved with advertising believe the benefits outweigh the problems. Advertisers are still, and will always be interested in a younger, better-educated, target audience that's available to them on the cable networks. In fact, many experts are predicting the recent movement in the U.S. away from the mass market to the more splintered consumer groups will continue. This important trend strengthens the attractiveness of cable TV advertising in the future.

Conclusion

Despite the many advantages of advertising on cable, there are those who are still skeptical of its value as an advertising vehicle. Some of the trends, benefits, and criticism of cable television are as follows:

1. Approximately 40 percent of all U.S. households are currently wired for cable. By 1990, that number is expected to increase to 60 percent of all households.
2. Many large, national advertisers were quick to utilize cable networks for their advertising.

3. People in cable households are significantly different than people who do not have cable in their households. Most importantly, cable viewers earn more money, are younger, and better educated than individuals in non-cable households.
4. Cable audiences tend to be significantly smaller than those of network television audiences.
5. A great deal of fragmentation, and therefore confusion, exists in today's marketplace concerning cable networks.
6. Cable television offers advertisers "narrowcasting"—i.e., selective target audiences.

The controversy surrounding the cable industry is likely to continue, but so will the number of advertisers rushing to place ads on the cable networks.

Applications to Small Business

While the majority of advertising on cable has been by national advertisers, small businesses should not rule out advertising on this unique medium. Local ads by small businesses are currently being run on several of the cable networks. The same benefits (i.e., lower cost and selective audiences) the national advertisers receive from cable TV can also be realized by the small business. The major difference the small or local business will experience is the even smaller audience that the local cable ad will generate versus the national cable ad. However, if a small business wants to reach a very selective or narrowcast audience, and wants to use TV, cable television is the medium to use.

References/Sources

Barban, Arnold M., and Krugman, Dean M., "Cable Television and Advertising: An Assessment," *Journal of Advertising* (1978): 4-8. Presents the historical development of cable television and assesses its impact for future advertisers.

Bush, Alan J., and Leigh, James H., "Advertising on Cable versus Traditional Networks," *Journal of Advertising Research* (April/May 1984): 33-38. This study presents an analysis of advertising on the cable networks and compares it to traditional television advertising.

"Cable Advertising: Growing Blip on Media Radar," *Broadcasting* (February 16, 1981). Reports on the trends and growth of cable advertising.

Garfield, Robert, "Fragmented Cable Can't Attract Ads," *USA Today* (October 21, 1983): 1. Article discusses some of the problems cable TV is having in attracting advertisers.

Gloede, Bill, "National Advertisers Eye Cable: Researchers Ponder Its Audience," *Editor and Publisher* (March 7, 1981): 22. Article discusses some of the earlier problems cable had in attracting advertising dollars.

"Marketing: The New Priority," *Business Week* (November 21, 1983). Article discusses many of the latest trends in the U.S. marketplace which are increasing marketing's role in today's business.

Marx, Nancy E., "Sponsors Start Making Shows to Plug Goods on Cable TV," *Wall Street Journal* (August 25, 1983): 21. Article gives several examples of companies producing their own shows on the cable networks.

Metzger, Gale D., "Cable Television Audiences," *Journal of Advertising Research* (August/September, 1983): 41-47. A study which profiles various characteristics of cable audiences.

Rothe, James T., Harvey, Michael, and Michael, George, "The Impact of Cable Television on Subscriber and Nonsubscriber Behavior," *Journal of Advertising Research* (August/September, 1983): 15-23. A study which compares various behaviors of cable versus non-cable households.

"Why Advertisers are Rushing to Cable TV," *Business Week* (November 2, 1981): 96. Article gives examples of companies using cable TV for advertising and the reasons why cable as an advertising medium is continuing.

Related Topics and Terms
Advertising, Advertising Agency, Direct TV Marketing, Promotion Mix.

Alan J. Bush
Department of Marketing
Texas A&M University

CAPITAL BUDGETING

Overview

Capital budgeting has historically been used by accountants and finance planners to choose alternatives, from an array of tangible assets, which will best satisfy the company's profit objectives. For example, capital budgeting techniques can tell a company's manager which parcels of land to purchase, which types of machines to lease, which types of inventory to stock.

In recent years, there has been increasing support for a theory that capital budgeting techniques are as applicable to a company's marketing operations as they are to the management of their tangible assets. The applicability has surfaced for three main reasons. First, like equipment, machines, inventory, and land, various dimensions of marketing can be considered assets, such as the company's sales force, new products, channels of distribution, advertising, and marketing research. Second, these marketing assets frequently involve expenditures that approach the size of capital expenditures made for tangible assets. For example, a large company will invest millions of dollars to develop and maintain a sales force. Third, marketing dimensions of companies involve time periods exceeding one year. In one study, the effects of advertising expenditures were believed to involve about seven years, those for channels of distribution almost 15 years.

Examples

There are essentially three basic capital budgeting techniques which can be used to evaluate various marketing alternatives.

In the *pay-back* method, a company will determine how long various new product possibilities, for example, will take to recoup their initial investment. Those new products which "pay back" their up-front outlays the quickest are preferred to those which require longer periods of time. Many firms will establish a cut-off figure which serves to eliminate new products whose projected pay-back periods exceed the standard. At one time, for example, Procter and Gamble rejected any potential new product whose expected pay-back period exceeded two years.

The *average rate of return* approach includes the calculation of the average return on the initial investment over the asset's projected life and a comparison of that figure to a company's desired rate of return. If a new product incurred an initial investment of $100,000 and over three years (its projected life) was expected to generate $30,000, $40,000, and $40,000, its average rate of return would be 36.7%:

$$\left(\frac{\overset{\text{Year 1}}{\$30,000}}{\$100,000} + \frac{\overset{\text{Year 2}}{\$40,000}}{\$100,000} + \frac{\overset{\text{Year 3}}{\$40,000}}{\$100,000}\right)3 = (30\% + 40\% + 40\%)/3 = 36.7\%$$

If the desired rate of return is less than 36.7%, this is an attractive new product alternative. Products with the highest rates of return are, of course, the most desirable. In a study of large U.S. corporations, the average rate of return method was preferred by 24% for sales management decisions and by 21% for channels of distribution decisions.

The *present value* capital budgeting approach recognizes the time value of money; that is, when profits are returned to the company from its marketing operations. In order to use this capital budgeting technique, the company decides on a desired rate of return, then divides this rate of return—raised to the power equal to the year involved—into the estimated yearly profits. In order for the marketing asset to be considered attractive, the total of the present values must exceed the value of the original investment. The following example illustrates the above concepts. It assumes that a new product has an initial investment of $100,000, that $40,000 a year in profits is expected to be generated by the product over its useful life of six years, and the company wants a 10% rate of return. The calculations would be as follows:

$$\underset{\text{Year 1}}{\frac{\$40,000}{(1.10)^1}} + \underset{\text{Year 2}}{\frac{\$40,000}{(1.10)^2}} + \underset{\text{Year 3}}{\frac{\$40,000}{(1.10)^3}} + \underset{\text{Year 4}}{\frac{\$40,000}{(1.10)^4}} + \underset{\text{Year 5}}{\frac{\$40,000}{(1.10)^5}} + \underset{\text{Year 6}}{\frac{\$40,000}{(1.10)^6}} =$$

$$\$36,364 + \$33,058 + \$30,053 + \$27,321 + \$24,845 + \$22,586 = \$174,227$$

Since the sum of the present values, $174,227, exceeds the initial investment of $100,000, this project would be desirable.

Many large companies employ the present value technique when making marketing decisions. For example, about 25% of *Fortune 500* companies used the present value approach for the areas of channels of distribution, marketing research, and new product development.

Benefits

Capital budgeting forces companies to apply a rigorous process for making marketing decisions. Another advantage is the profitability orientation explicitly involved with most capital budgeting approaches; firms, thus, are constrained to evaluate their marketing operations on the basis of contribution to their bottom line.

By using capital budgeting in assessing marketing programs, other areas of the firm are more likely to view marketing as contributing assets to the company.

Capital budgeting techniques provide marketing executives with the capability of prioritizing marketing decisions. For example, if companies were using the present value technique to assess new product candidates, the one with the highest ratio of total present value to initial investment would be developed first, the one with the next highest would be developed next, and so on.

Implementation

A major constraint on funding products is the total amount of funds available. This constraint needs to be coupled with the standard of performance the company has established. These concepts can be illustrated by the information below for potential new products:

Product	Investment Cost	Cumulative Investment Costs	Present Value	Profitability Ratio ((4)/2)
A	$100,000	$100,000	$200,000	2.00
B	150,000	250,000	280,000	1.87
C	80,000	330,000	120,000	1.50
D	250,000	580,000	300,000	1.20
E	120,000	700,000	130,000	1.08

If sufficient funds are available, products A-E would all be desirable ventures because their present values exceed their investment costs. Product A is most desirable because it has the highest ratio of present value to investment cost. Suppose that the company has $600,000 to invest in new products. This figure indicates that products A-D should be pursued, but not product E because its investment cost of $120,000 would cause the budget ceiling of $600,000 to be exceeded.

Dealing with risk is a major implementation aspect of capital budgeting. A variety of techniques can be used to handle risk. One approach is to increase the rate of return used in the capital budgeting equations. If this is done in the present value equation, for example, the resultant total present value will be reduced, thereby making it more difficult for the marketing option being considered to have a present value sum in excess of its original investment cost. Another approach to handling risk is to assign probabilities to the estimated profits and then use that lower figure in the capital budgeting calculation. For example, consider the information below:

	Profit	×	Probability	=	Adjusted Profit
Year 1	$500,000	×	0.8	=	$400,000
Year 2	$200,000	×	0.7	=	140,000
Year 3	$300,000	×	0.6	=	180,000
Year 4	$200,000	×	0.8	=	160,000
Total	$1,200,000				$880,000

If the initial cost for the investment is $1,000,000 and a payback period of four years is used, the original investment can be paid back within four years if the unadjusted profit is used, but it can not be paid back by that time if the adjusted profit, which recognizes risk, is used.

Decreasing estimated sales and increasing operating costs are two other ways to account for risk in the capital budgeting process. Both approaches reduce the estimated profit for the investment, thereby making it more difficult for the investment to meet any prescribed performance levels.

Decreasing the useful life of the investment gives the asset fewer years to meet profitability requirements. Increasing the amount of the original investment outlay results in higher profits being required to recoup this original investment figure.

A major implementation problem is that of persuading marketing practitioners not accustomed to applying financial tools to their operations to accept and use capital budgeting. Acceptance and utilization are more likely to occur if marketing executives can be shown how capital budgeting can help them to do a more effective job and that it is not a substitute for their decision-making authority.

Evaluation

When evaluating the effectiveness of capital budgeting techniques for marketing decision-making, 43% of *Fortune 500* companies indicated that they were "very effective." Slightly less than half (46.9%) perceived them as being "somewhat effective" and only 2% believed them to be "ineffective." Eight per cent of these companies stated that they were unable to assess the effectiveness of their capital budgeting applications.

In assessing various aspects of the marketing area's use of capital budgeting methods, three major difficulties were emphasized by these large corporations. About one-third of the firms cited "estimated sales" as the single most important difficulty. "Accounting for the factor of risk" was identified by 27.3% of the companies. Close to one-fifth (19.9%) of the respondents named "getting the techniques accepted and implemented." Other difficulties encountered were estimating operating costs, determining useful life of an investment, determining acceptable rates of return, and estimating original investment outlay.

Conclusion

Capital budgeting techniques can be an important aid to marketing executives' decision-making responsibility but should not be a substitute for these responsibilities. Executives should be aware of the shortcomings inherent in these techniques, and should implement capital budgeting in a manner that leaves room for them to exercise their own intuition and judgment.

Forecasting difficulties—particularly those associated with forecasting sales and operating costs, and hence, profits—appear to be the major stumbling block in using these formulas. Due to this problem, it is advisable for management to employ different estimates for sales and operating costs (which will yield varying profit estimates) when working the capital budgeting formulas. When different estimates are used, management should consider most seriously those marketing alternatives which receive consistently favorable evaluations.

Applications to Small Business

Capital budgeting concepts can assist small businesses in deciding which marketing alternatives to choose. They appear to be particularly relevant for decisions involving marketing research, advertising, sales management, new product development, and channels of distribution.

Sophisticated computer hardware is not a necessary condition for the small business which wants to apply capital budgeting to its marketing operations. Thus, the small business owner or manager should not be frightened by the complexity or cost factors involved. Many capital budgeting problems can be quickly solved with the use of pen and paper. For those calculations which are somewhat more involved—such as those using the present value approach—there are several hand-held electronic calculators costing under $100 which can quickly do the required operations. The Hewlett-Packard 12-C is a good example.

Software/Databases

Capital Budgeting Analysis, Groundstar Software Systems. Provides a schedule of investment alternatives which supports management decision-making responsibilities.

References/Sources

Adler, Lee, "Time Lag in New Product Development," *Journal of Marketing* (January 1966). Develops the notion that new products generally take longer than one year to develop. Uses a study of 42 new products to prove the hypothesis.

Dean, Joel, "Does Advertising Belong in the Capital Budget?" *Journal of Marketing* (October 1966). Asserts that advertising belongs in the firm's capital budget since advertising's effects occur over years' time and advertising outlays are substantial.

Dean, Joel, *Managerial Economics*. Englewood Cliffs, NJ: Prentice-Hall, 1951, pp. 554–555. A strong argument for including advertising, new product development, and channels of distribution in a firm's capital budget.

Hise, Richard T., and Strawser, Robert H., "Applications of Capital Budgeting Techniques to Marketing Operations," *MSU Business Topics* (Summer 1970): 70-75. Discusses a survey of the extent to which 190 *Fortune 500* companies apply capital budgeting techniques to channels of distribution, sales management, advertising, marketing research, and new product development.

Schiff, Michael, "Are You Making These Mistakes in Marketing Profit Analysis?" *Sales Management* (November 21, 1958): 58. Schiff makes a strong case for considering a company's sales force as a long-term asset capable of utilizing capital budgeting techniques.

Twedt, Dik Warren, "What is the 'Return on Investment' in Marketing Research?" *Journal of Marketing* (January 1966): 62. Twedt advocates that marketing research be viewed as a long-term asset.

Related Topics and Terms

Breakeven Analysis, Expected Value, Gross Margin, Present Value, Profitability Analysis, Time Value of Money.

Richard T. Hise
Department of Marketing
Texas A&M University

CAUSE-RELATED MARKETING

Overview

During the 1980s organizations adopted more aggressive strategies in advocacy advertising, corporate advertising and, most recently, cause-related marketing. Advocacy or issue advertising seeks to present the company viewpoint on some important issue, whether long-run or short-run in nature or whether general or specific. Corporate/image advertising, also called public relations advertising, tries to enhance the image of the company in the eyes of consumers or other publics.

Cause-related marketing allows a company to promote its products and/or services while at the same time benefiting nonprofit organizations with cash donations and extensive publicity. Most cause-related marketing takes the form of a company asking the consumer to purchase the company's product/service in return for the company making a donation to a socially worthwhile cause. Cause-related marketing lets corporations benefit from philanthropic investments by combining charitable contributions with innovative marketing techniques.

Examples

The issues that are most popular in advocacy advertising tend to cluster around energy shortages, environmental concerns, and government regulation. An example of advocacy advertising is a campaign by Mobil Oil Company aimed at encouraging public policies that would help the United States avoid dependence on foreign energy sources, such as more incentives for domestic drilling. An example of corporate/image advertising is Phillip 66's campaign showing a medical innovation developed by the company that helps save a little boy's life.

One of the most ambitious cause-related marketing projects was the Statue of Liberty/Ellis Island restoration project. The philanthropic objective of preserving a national monument, coupled with the sale of specific products, generated huge profits and favorable publicity for many corporate sponsors, including five "founding" sponsors: Coca Cola Company, Stroh's Brewery Company, U. S. Tobacco, Kellogg Company, Chrysler Corporation Dealers, and Eastman Kodak Company.

In fall 1984 Stroh's Brewery Company held a five kilometer "Run for Liberty" in 124 cities simultaneously across the country. U. S. Tobacco offered the consumer a $10.95 nylon tote bag for $5.00 and one proof of purchase; the company would donate $2.00 out of every $5.00 to the restoration project. Kellogg Company allowed consumers to send for free, personalized address labels by mailing two Corn Flakes proofs of purchase to Kellogg which donated 50 cents to the Statue of Liberty Foundation; each of the labels featured Miss Liberty's torch and the foundation's registered trademark: "Keep the Torch Lit". Eastman Kodak Company invited consumers to submit photographs of family members, along with a $10.00 fee, that will become part of a permanent electronic album on display terminals at the Statue of Liberty.

Another company that has implemented several cause-related marketing programs is American Express Company. In 1981 American Express began donating a penny to local worthwhile causes for every American Express card transaction, new card application, traveler's check purchase, or tour package purchased. Local causes included the San Jose Symphony, the restoration of San Francisco's cable car system, Fort Lauderdale Symphony, Chicago's Lincoln Park Zoo, the science museum in Des Moines, and the restoration of George Washington's home in Mount Vernon. American Express has also supported the U. S. Olympic teams as well as Olympic teams in Argentina, Mexico, Japan, United Kingdom, Ireland, and Spain with cause-related marketing efforts. In 1983 American Express began its first national campaign using cause-related marketing—raising funds for the Statue of Liberty. The company began its second national campaign in 1985 with a $6 million cause-related project aimed at raising money for local "hometown" projects while stimulating use of its charge card. American Express donated a penny to worthwhile community projects each time an American Express card was used or a traveler's check was purchased; it donated $1 from sales of new American Express cards and travel packages bought through its travel outlets.

A strategy that is increasing in popularity involves coupon redemption. General Foods donated 5 cents to Muscular Dystrophy, up to $1 million, for each coupon redeemed on eighteen of its brands.

Benefits

Cause-related marketing offers the sponsoring company several benefits: (1) national visibility, (2) improved product positioning, and (3) enhanced corporate image. Promotion of Stroh's Brewery's "Run for Liberty" resulted in 150,000 people entering the first race held in 1985 across the country. The race was so successful that a second race was held later in 1985. Because each person was required to pay an entry fee, Stroh's was able to meet its $3 million pledge to the Statue of Liberty Foundation with no cost to the company. Because the promotions for U. S. Tobacco and Kellogg both required "proof of purchase," these companies not only increased their association with the Statue's restoration, but also generated increased sales and trial purchases of their products.

During the 1983 three-month promotion for restoration of the Statue of Liberty, American Express raised approximately $1.5 million for Miss Liberty while generating a 30% increase in charge-card sales and a 15% jump in membership applications. American Express hopes to raise more than $3 million for more than 150 community development programs through its "hometown" project.

Implementation

The key to successful cause-related marketing lies in appealing to the emotions and popular interests of the general public. The two national campaigns selected by American Express appear to be right on target—donations for restoration of the Statue of Liberty and worthwhile "hometown" projects in America.

The two campaigns built on the already excellent image of American Express gave consumers a responsible, even patriotic, reason to use the services of American Express.

For cause-related marketing to be successful it must be planned like any other marketing campaign, complete with objectives and strategies. Advertising and promotion are of key importance in achieving the goals of cause-related marketing, namely national visibility, increased product positioning and enhanced corporate image. The company's publics/customers must be informed as to the relationship between the company, its products/services, and the worthwhile "cause".

In the case of Stroh's Brewery, marketing research revealed that there were 30 million active runners in the country as a result of the fitness boom and they were used to paying an entry fee for a race. One way Stroh's reached this market was to contact a running club in each of the 124 cities. Before the event was held, network TV ads flashed an 800 number for entering the race and point-of-purchase displays in retail outlets publicized the event and featured tear-off registration forms. Ads were also placed in running magazines to reach the more serious runner. For greater publicity during the event, a radio station in each city was solicited to host the race and the call letters of the local station were featured on point-of purchase displays.

Evaluation

An interesting issue concerns how consumers view corporate efforts toward cause-related marketing. Do consumers see the company making an honest effort to promote the cause? Is it viewed as enlightened self-interest? Or is it seen as attempting to exploit the cause to the benefit of the company by cashing in on a noble cause? What types of causes are consumers more inclined to support? And what impact does cause-related marketing have on the propensity of consumers to purchase the company's product or service? A segment on the ABC News Program "20/20" pointed out possible misuse of funds raised by the Statue of Liberty/Ellis Island Foundation. Cable News Network also reported that a corporation, Casual Corner, was wrongfully exploiting these efforts by representing itself as a Foundation member to its customers when in fact it was not. Thus, well-intentioned corporate efforts at cause-related marketing can backfire and bring negative publicity if the public perceives that the company is simply exploiting the cause for selfish benefit.

Conclusion

Corporate contributions all contain some element of enlightened self interest.

Although the result may not be true philanthropy, cause-related marketing will probably continue to be popular. Compared to corporate or image advertising, much cause-related marketing allows a company to tie support of a worthwhile cause to the purchase of the company's products or service. Everyone involved in the process appears to benefit and hopefully the results to the company are increased sales and enhanced company image.

Applications to Small Business

Most of the examples of cause-related marketing discussed so far have been national campaigns. However, small business can also use cause-related marketing for purposes of increased local visibility, increased sales, and enhanced company image. Small companies can support worthwhile local causes such as homes for battered wives/children, restoration of local parks, and sports facilities for teenage youths. The company simply links donation to the cause to purchase of its product/ service, perhaps through the use of coupon redemption.

References/Sources

Bragdon, Frances J., "Cause-Related Marketing: Case Not To Leave Home Without It," *Advertising Age* (March 1985): 42-47, 67. Describes American Express Company's cause-related marketing program as well as steps that a fund raiser might take to help meld business with social responsibility.

Edelson, Alfred H., "Advocacy Advertising," *Advertising Age* (March 30, 1981): 47-48. Critiques several advocacy advertising campaigns including the energy and environmental campaigns of Mobil Oil and Weyerhaeuser Company.

Haugh, Louis J., "Coupons, Charities Team Up," *Advertising Age* (August 31, 1981): 32. Discusses several major companies that are using cents-off coupons to make charitable donations while at the same time requiring consumers to redeem the coupons.

Josephson, Nancy, "American Express Raises Corporate Giving to Marketing Art," *Advertising Age* (January 23, 1984). Discusses the objectives and strategies of American Express Company's program to raise funds for restoration of the Statue of Liberty.

Moran, Brian, "American Express Has Hometown Appeal," *Advertising Age* (September 16, 1985): 88. Discusses the marketing strategy and commercials used by American Express to raise money for local community groups while stimulating use of its charge card.

Rosenfeld, Judith, "Cashing In On A Noble Cause," *Marketing Communications* (April 1985): 19-27. Describes the promotion techniques used by the six (company) Founding Sponsors of the Statue of Liberty-Ellis Island restoration project, as well as other companies which have developed sales promotion programs to sell products and help restore the statue.

Selwitz, Robert, "The Selling of An Image," *Madison Avenue* (February 1985): 61-69. Discusses companies' use of corporate advertising and cause-related marketing to customers, investors, and regulators.

Related Topics and Terms
Advocacy Advertising, Corporate Advertising, Image Advertising, Issue Advertising, Public Relations, Sales Promotion.

Mary Ann Stutts
Department of Management/Marketing
Southwest Texas State University

CENTRAL BUSINESS DISTRICT

Overview

The central business district (CBD) has traditionally been the heart of retail sales in a community. It is the older central shopping district of a city and is synonymous with the term "downtown." The CBD exists in that part of a city that has the greatest concentration of office buildings, and where vehicular and pedestrian traffic are highly concentrated. Even in large cities the core of the CBD usually does not exceed a square mile. Cultural and entertainment facilities surround the CBD. Consumers are drawn from the whole urban area, which includes all ethnic groups and all classes of people.

The CBD generally contains at least one major department store and a wide variety of specialty and convenience retailers, such as drugstores and restaurants. Because the areas are typically older they have often been the first to deteriorate. In addition, America's urban flight to the suburbs had a devastating effect on the CBD. Increasing crime rates and lack of parking space have further added to the decline of this retail location.

Examples

Some communities, however, have rebuilt their downtown areas and managed to bring the people back. One of the best examples of a turnaround of a CBD is Minneapolis, Minnesota. Its Downtown Council has worked hard to strengthen the downtown area to make it more competitive with suburban shopping centers and to stimulate office construction. The Nicollet Mall, the center of the Minneapolis downtown renewal area, received a $38 million investment. The mall is a totally reconstructed twelve-block section, with redesigned streets shared by pedestrians and public transit. Above-ground "skyways" connect buildings for pedestrians. There are benches for relaxing, and shade trees, flowers and fountains add to the atmosphere. Frequent activities, such as orchestra performances and antique car exhibits, create a sense of excitement.

Faneuil Hall in Boston is a different type of successful CBD renovation. When developer James Rouse took over the $6^{1}/_{2}$ acre site, it had been abandoned for almost 10 years. By creatively using landscapes, fountains, banners, courts and graphics Rouse enabled Faneuil Hall to capture a "spirit of festival." Faneuil Hall has combined shopping, eating and watching activities and made them fun. Today, Faneuil Hall attracts around 10 million visitors annually, about as many as Disneyland in California.

Other major CBD renovation projects include Omni Center (Miami), Water Tower Place (Chicago), The Gallery (Philadelphia), City Center Square (St. Louis), The Market at Citicorp Center (New York), and Grand Avenue (Milwaukee). Baltimore, Pittsburgh and Oklahoma City have also redeveloped their downtown areas.

Benefits

The central business district has several strengths and weaknesses. Some of the strengths are excellent product assortment, access to public transportation, variety of store images within one area, variety of prices, location of headquarters, variety of services, and nearness to commercial and social facilities. Some of the weaknesses are inadequate parking, failure to improve old stores, high rents and taxes, discontinuity of certain offerings, traffic and delivery congestion, travel time for those living in the suburbs, high theft rates, and the declining condition of some central cities.

Implementation

It is crucial to have the support of the people—politicians, corporate leaders and entrepreneurs—behind any CBD renovation. A sure sign of success for the revamped CBD is when the city is able to attract out-of-town investment money.

The resurgence of downtown redevelopment has resulted in diverse solutions to shopping center development problems in urban areas. Unlike suburban mall development in the 1950s and 1960s, when one basic plan was easily transported from market to market, successful downtown redevelopment depends on unique approaches to each project.

Evaluation

Although many CBDs have declined, their share of retail sales is still substantial and a number of downtown areas have been growing. Innovations have begun, such as closing off streets to vehicular traffic, modernizing store fronts and equipment, developing strong cooperative merchants' associations, improving transportation, and integrating a commercial and residential environment.

CBDs have increasingly become tourist destinations. New forces are operating in downtown today—vital, live new forces that just weren't around a decade ago. Retailing brings everybody to the city; offices bring a slice of people. But the one place that brings everybody together is the festival marketplace. The most successful festival retail centers are located where both visitors and residents are combined.

Conclusion

During the last three decades, the CBD has diminished relative to the planned shopping center. However, their share of retail sales is still substantial and a number of downtown areas have been growing.

The future hold for the CBD looks positive. Modernization projects will probably continue. Merchant associations will encourage the development of office buildings, restaurants, theaters, hotels, civic centers, etc. in the downtown area.

Not every city will be able to develop a Faneuil Hall, but the central business district (in most cases) is on the upswing.

Applications to Small Business

Small retailers are able to move into the newly renovated CBD and look forward to a brighter future there than in the past. The CBD which has turned itself around allows a small retailer, such as a unique specialty store, the opportunity to become part of a profitable shopping center if its target market matches that of the CBD's.

Software/Databases

Survey of Buying Power. Sales & Marketing Management, 633 Third Avenue, New York, NY 10017. Provides basic data on retail sales, income and population for the United States, states, counties, and cities. Retail sales are presented for various categories, such as food, general merchandise, and automotive. Percentages of households making various income levels are provided, as are per capita and per household income. Total population and population by various age brackets are available. This source is a gold mine of data for the owners, operators and managers of stores located in central business districts. The data can be used to evaluate their retail area's demographic profile against that of other retail trade areas.

References/Sources

Berman, Barry, and Evans, Joel R., *Retail Management: A Strategic Approach*, 2nd ed. New York: Macmillan, 1983, pp. 214-217. Presents an enlightening discussion of the Central Business District.

Faltermayer, Edmund, "How St. Louis Turned Less Into More," *Fortune* (December 23, 1985): 44-58. Provides the reasons for the resurgence of downtown St. Louis and how the city has learned to manage adversity.

Mitchell, Shawn, "Downtown Renewal? Minneapolis Really Did It," *Stores* (September 1974): 10-12. Discusses the successful Turnaround of Minneapolis' CBD.

Mullins, Jesse, "Oklahoma City Retailing," *Stores*, Vol. 65, No. 6 (July 1983): 30-44. Discusses the development of the Metro Concourse, as it connects all the major business centers in the central business district with a network of fully carpeted, air conditioned tunnels.

Peterson, Eric C., "As Suburbs Fill Up, Developers Seeking New Opportunities are Going to Town," *Stores* (November 1984): 64-68. Addresses the rise in number of downtown shopping centers which not only rejuvenate the CBD but also serve as tourist destinations.

Sibley, Paula, "Finding New Opportunities in Urban Areas as Suburban Sites Lag-Back Downtown," *Stores* (May 1984): 58-64. Successful downtown redevelopment depends on unique approaches to each project.

Slom, Stanley H., "Boston's Faneuil Hall: A Rouse-ing Success," *Chain Store Age Executive* (March 1982): 58, 63. Describes Faneuil Hall in Boston, a successful CBD renovation that has captured a "spirit of festival" by creatively using landscaping, fountains, banners, courts and graphics.

Related Topics and Terms
Lifestyle/Psychographics, Metro Statistical Area, Selective Perception, Specialty Store, Store Location, Trading Area.

Therese A. Maskulka
Department of Marketing
Lehigh University

CENTRALIZATION/DECENTRALIZATION
OF INTERNATIONAL OPERATIONS

Overview

A multinational corporation (MNC) is centralized with respect to marketing decisions if these decisions are made in the home country by headquarters personnel, and decentralized if the decisions are made by personnel in the firm's foreign operations. The extent to which a firm is centralized or decentralized will vary among the marketing mix elements, and companies differ greatly in terms of which decisions are centralized and which are decentralized. Some MNCs add a layer of management at the regional level, which can be viewed as being halfway between being centralized and decentralized. In general, budgeting and product policy decisions tend to be the most centralized while advertising decisions are the most decentralized, but recent evidence indicates all marketing decisions are becoming more centralized.

Examples

It is difficult to judge which approach is better as there are many examples of both centralization and decentralization being used successfully by MNCs. N.V. Philips, the Dutch electronics giant, is very decentralized, although its home office does review performance frequently. Dow Chemical is decentralized geographically into six regional units. American Cyanamid, on the other hand, is highly centralized with nearly all marketing decision-making occurring at headquarters. Similarly, Rank Xerox of Great Britain is quite centralized with respect to decision-making.

Some firms try to have a balanced approach. General Electric has centralized product SBUs (Strategic Business Unit), but has also created decentralized geographic SBUs. Goodyear International allows its field offices to develop their own marketing plans under the guidelines of the firm's marketing objectives, but reserves the right to request revisions at any point. Also, final approval authority at each stage of the development of the field offices' marketing strategies rests with the home office.

Benefits

Both centralization and decentralization have their advantages. The former allows for: 1) closer control of international operations 2) greater assurance that company policies are being adhered to, and 3) company objectives' directing the marketing efforts in foreign markets. Also, a centralized structure facilitates the development and implementation of standardized marketing programs.

The greatest benefit of the decentralized approach is its flexibility and responsiveness to local market conditions, especially in international markets which are often quite volatile. The decentralized structure may also be of benefit when the firm is marketing products that are related to the differing cultures and values in foreign markets. In these instances, local personnel are probably best equipped to develop marketing programs that incorporate an understanding of these unique factors.

Implementation

While many decisions can be decentralized, there are some that should always be made at the headquarters level. The home office should set overall objectives and policies for international markets and should retain control over all marketing budgets. Headquarters should also act as the coordinator of all subsidiary marketing programs and should at least provide the impetus and framework for strategic planning for foreign markets.

Beyond these areas management has considerable latitude as to where international marketing decisions are made. The location of decision-making for a given marketing element should not be based solely on the preferences of top management; rather, the choice should be based on an analysis of foreign market conditions and a thorough assessment of the company's resources, capabilities, and foreign marketing structure.

If the centralized approach is chosen, great care must be taken not simply to extend decisions made for the domestic market to foreign operations. Effective two-way communications channels must be opened between headquarters and foreign subsidiaries, and decisions should be made with the needs of the foreign markets in mind. This requires that headquarters personnel solicit input from foreign managers on important decision matters, and that foreign personnel be made to understand fully the nature of and rationale for the decisions that have been made. It must be demonstrated to them that headquarters understands the nature of their market situations and is empathic to their concerns. To build-in some responsiveness to potential changes in local market conditions, headquarters directives should allow some flexibility on the part of local managers, either through formal contingency plans or by giving leeway in the implementation of decisions. For example, a company may specify that prices are to be lowered 10% if a competitor takes a similar action, or it may allow the local manager to alter an advertising appeal to fit local needs.

In the decentralized structure, the headquarters role becomes that of advisor and integrator of various subsidiary plans. With decisions now being made at the local level, it is the home office that should supply input in the form of objectives, ideas, resources, and techniques. The integration and evaluation of foreign marketing plans should become the focus of the headquarters effort. Periodic reviews of subsidiary activities should be conducted and adequate control procedures developed. Foreign-office managers should understand how their operations fit into the overall structure of the corporation and why their objectives are what they are. Control mechanisms should ensure adequate headquarters authority to correct deficiencies, but should not take away too much autonomy from local managers.

Evaluation

Performance relative to objectives is a major criterion for evaluating the effectiveness of international operations in general, but it should not be the only one used to judge the efficacy of using a centralized or decentralized management structure. Objective performance may be quite satisfactory at the current time, but problems with the decision structure that exist now may not impact performance measures until they have become very difficult to correct. Typically, a more subjective evaluation of how "smoothly" international marketing activities are proceeding should be considered.

Some questions the international marketing manager can ask in assessing the adequacy of the decision structure are: How satisfied with decision-making processes and procedures are local marketing managers? Are there many complaints when a directive is sent from headquarters? Do local managers seem to resent headquarters personnel? Are plans being put into effect on schedule? Does headquarters continually affect major revisions on plans submitted by subsidiaries? Do headquarters managers and subsidiary managers often seem not to know what each other are doing? A "yes" to any of these questions may indicate a problem with the decision-making apparatus of the firm.

Conclusion

There are no hard and fast rules regarding when to centralize and when to decentralize. Both approaches have been successfully utilized by many multinational companies. Research results do, however, allow for some generalizations to be made about what is being done in practice.

Most firms tend to centralize strategic decisions and decentralize tactical decisions. Interestingly, the most-centralized decisions, those concerning objectives and budgets, also seem to engender the most conflict between headquarters and subsidiary personnel. In terms of the marketing mix, product and pricing decisions are usually more centralized than are distribution and promotion decisions. Other factors that have been shown to be related to where international marketing decisions are made include the importance of the foreign operation to the firm, the length of time the firm has been involved in foreign markets, the mode—exporting, wholly-owned subsidiaries, etc.—of foreign market participation, the industry the firm is in, and the cultural diversity of foreign markets.

While useful in a comparative sense, these findings should not be taken as prescriptions for success. The best course for any company to follow is the course that a careful analysis of its own unique needs leads it to.

Applications to Small Business

Smaller companies generally use exporting or licensing arrangements as their mode of participation in foreign markets. As a result, they often are only marginally involved in promotion and distribution activities for their products. Greater control over these factors can be had by contractual arrangements requiring certain promotional approaches or distribution channels. This is equivalent to the centralized approach. The decentralized approach in this situation is to fully allow importers or licensees to make these decisions. While the latter will probably be more agreeable to foreign intermediaries, it is conceivable that they could take misguided actions that would be damaging to the firm's reputation. Some control, particularly over promotion, is generally advisable. The objections of intermediaries can be eased by offering allowances or other incentives for compliance with the wishes of the firm.

Product decisions will, in the case of the exporter, always be centralized out of necessity: there is no one in the foreign markets to delegate the decision to. Pricing decisions will likewise be centralized; the relevant price here is the price charged the importer or the fee paid by the licensee. Retail price setting is generally best left to the foreign intermediary, although the originating firm may offer guidance based on its experience.

Some smaller firms set up their own direct exporting capabilities coupled with foreign sales offices. In such instances, promotion and distribution decisions may be delegated to the sales offices based on the same type of analysis that a larger firm would undertake. Local sales offices' input on pricing and product decisions should also be solicited, but these decisions should remain largely centralized. Depending on local market conditions, it may be advisable, however, to allow the local sales manager some flexibility in setting prices.

References/Sources

Aylmer, R. J., "Who Makes Marketing Decisions in the Multinational Firm?" *Journal of Marketing* (October 1970): 25-30. Reports findings of a study indicating centralization related to size and relative importance of international operations.

Brandt, William K., and Julbert, James M., "Headquarters Guidance in Marketing Strategy in the Multinational Subsidiary," *Columbia Journal of World Business* (Winter 1977): 7-14. Details results of in-depth research into headquarters-subsidiary relationships in large multinational corporations.

Clark, Harold F., Jr. "Successful International Marketing Depends on Centralized Leadership," *Industrial Marketing* (March 1975): 54-58. Discusses decision structures necessary for effective international marketing.

Drake, Rodman L., and Caudill, Lee M., "Management of the Large Multinational: Trends and Future Challenges," *Business Horizons* (May/June 1981): 83-

91. Describes decision and control mechanisms in several U.S.—and European—based multinationals.

Hamel, Gary, and Prahald, C.K., "Do You Really Have a Global Strategy?" *Harvard Business Review* (July-August 1985): 139- 148. Discusses role of headquarters in resource allocation and guidance for firms competing on a global basis.

Hulbert, James H., Brandt, William K., and Richers, Raimar, "Marketing Planning in the Multinational Subsidiary: Practices and Problems," *Journal of Marketing* (Summer 1980): 7-16. Presents recommendations for dealing with marketing problems in subsidiary operations.

Keegan, Warren J., "Multinational Marketing: The Headquarters Role," *Columbia Journal of World Business* (January-February 1971): 85-90. Describes a partially-centralized interactive approach to international marketing as an alternative to decentralization.

Peebles, Dean M., Ryans, John K., Jr., and Vernon, Ivan R., "Coordinating International Advertising," *Journal of Marketing* (January 1978): 38-44. Discusses a "programmed management" approach to international advertising that incorporates elements of both centralized and decentralized structures.

Picard, Jacques, "Determinants of Centralization of Marketing Decision-Making in Multinational Corporations," *Marketing in the 80's: Changes and Challenges* (1980 Educator's Conference Proceedings). Chicago: American Marketing Association, 1980, pp. 259-261. Discusses a study of factors that have an effect on the degree of marketing centralization in a sample of U.S.-based multinationals.

Pohlman, Randolph A., Ang, James S., and Ali, Syed I., "Policies of Multinational Firms: A Survey," *Business Horizons* (December 1976): 14-18. Presents results of a study showing that marketing management decisions are generally very decentralized.

Terpstra, Vern, *International Marketing,* 3rd ed. Chicago: The Dryden Press, 1983. Chapter 16 discusses organizing and controlling international marketing operations.

Weichmann, Ulrich, "Integrating Multinational Marketing Activities Abroad," *Columbia Journal of World Business* (Winter 1974): 7-16. Discusses alternative methods for integrating international marketing operations into the firm as a whole. Centralization is one alternative.

Wills, James R., and Ryans, John K., Jr., "An Analysis of Headquarters Involvement in International Advertising," *European Journal of Marketing,* Number 8 (1977): 577-584. Presents study results indicating that objective and budgeting decisions are more centralized than those for creative strategy and media selection in international advertising.

Related Topics and Terms

Control Mechanism, Decision-Making, Exports, International Marketing, Local Autonomy, Focus of Authority, Management Hierarchy, Management Structure, Multinational Corporation, Organizational Hierarchy, Organizational Structure, Regionalization, Regional Organization, Standardized Advertising.

David G. Ratz
Department of Marketing
and Transportation
Kent State University

CHANNEL CONFLICT

Overview

Channel conflict is a state that exists between firms in distribution systems arising from the interdependence of channel members. Sources of conflict are the distribution of profits, allocation of costs, allocation of tasks, and varying objectives for the members. Channel conflict is particularly high in channels where firms are not integrated through ownership or franchise arrangements as there are no administrative or legal mechanisms for the assignment of rewards, costs, and tasks to the firms. Conflict is likely to be maintained at a functional level. In non-integrated channels, conflict may become dysfunctional causing firms to leave the channel or dissipate their energies on conflict reduction rather than the pursuit of collective economic gain. Because conflict causes firms to focus their attention on the channels rather than on competition and on consumers, conflict reduction is beneficial for channel survival, the firms comprising the channel, and for customers of the channel.

Examples

Examples of channels conflict are included from several industries. In the mid-1970s Coca-Cola marketed Mr. Pibb through independent bottlers, a quarter of whom bottled the competing Dr. Pepper. The Coca-Cola channel had high conflict due to competing products. In the early 1980s Levi Strauss expanded its distribution of its five pocket jean through Sears and J.C. Penney which caused conflict with its traditional department store resellers including Macy's. Sears maintains appliance quality through manufacturing specifications for its independent manufacturers. HBO, as a dominant distributor of pay television movies, has dominated pricing for movies. In 1984, IBM increased the distribution of its PCs through the use of value added distributors (VADs) which increased competition for its traditional resellers. Many of the VADs, in turn, redistributed PCs though unauthorized dealers further broadening the PC channels.

Benefits

The benefits of conflict reduction are increased efficiency and productivity and increased financial benefits for the members. By persuasion of dealers bottling Dr. Pepper to substitute Mr. Pibb, Coca-Cola was able to expand Mr. Pibb's market coverage by nearly twenty-five percent. In reducing the conflict with Levi Strauss, the major department stores expanded their product lines and reduced dependence on Levi. By adhering to the production specifications of Sears, manufacturers of appliances obtain substantial orders while Sears maintains appliance quality. To obtain distribution, movie producers must accede to HBO policies while HBO, in turn, provides financing for movie production in order to assure supply. IBM restored the integrity of its PC distribution system by eliminating some forty of its major VADs in 1985.

Implementation

There are two methods of planning for conflict reduction in channels. The first is for the firms to have generally agreed upon goals for the members. Goal integration can reduce the overall level of conflict within the channel. While general statements of channel policy do not exist, most major supplying firms, such as Coors, will have stated channel strategies which enunciate the expectations for distributors of their products.

The second method involves firms at different market levels acting as members of a unified system. These unified channels structures, vertical marketing systems (VMS), have become the dominant channel mode in consumer markets over the last decade. There are two major types of VMS which fall short of ownership integration of the channel.

The first is the administered system. One firm in the channel coordinates successive stages of distribution primarily through the display of size and exercise of power. Proctor & Gamble has been able to structure channel policy for retail sales of its soap products by maintaining a strong "pull" promotional strategy, frequent store visits by salespersons, and provision of substantial promotional assistance to participating retailers. In return it has received favorable shelf space for its products and the ability to expand its product lines within the stores. General Electric, General Foods, Coca-Cola, and Campbell Soup all command cooperation from distributors in return for displays, promotions, margins, and strong consumer advertising.

The second type of VMS is the contractual system. Firms integrate their goals through contracts which specifying actions. Courts become an outside referee for conflicts that arise. There are three general types of contractual VMS: wholesaler sponsored voluntary chains, retailer cooperatives, and franchise organizations.

Achieving conflict reduction generally means subordinating the firm to larger structures and sacrificing independence. The benefits of conflict reduction may be shown by the growth of the VMS and the dominance of the VMS in consumer product channels.

Evaluation

Once a manager has determined that there is conflict, several questions must be addressed. Can the cause of the conflict be removed so that the relationship can be continued? Can the firm replace the supplier/client with little profit impact? Is there a legal solution, as contained in a franchise or sales agreement, to the conflict? Is the conflict sufficiently disruptive such that the channel relationship should be terminated?

Conclusion

Conflict is inevitable in channel relations due to firm interdependence. Conflicting objectives of firms, allocation of tasks, and allocation of profitability will lead to conflict for channel members.

The problem is not one of avoiding channel conflict, but maintaining systems which minimize conflicts and which allow for conflict reduction when conflict arises. One of the major benefits of the VMS is that there are formal mechanisms within the systems for conflict reduction. For firms in non-integrated channels there is high need for communication between firms so that the level of conflict is held at a non-disruptive level.

Applications to Small Business

Alleviation of channel conflict for the small business person allows the managers to focus on client, supplier, and competitive relations rather than on conflict reduction. However, when conflict arises for the small business, there are very limited means available for reduction of that conflict.

A small firm may seek to maintain numerous suppliers of products and customers for a line to minimize dependence on single firms. The losses incurred on additional orders may be less than the costs of conflict reduction. Small supplying firms may seek to maintain multiple small clients and multiple sources of supply for the same purpose. Cost/benefit analysis will show whether this strategy is appropriate.

If conflict arises the small firm may use negotiation with representatives of the other firm to remove the sources of conflict or to temper the level of conflict. A second means available to the small firm is to network with similar firms which maintain a channel relationship with the focal firm and then to negotiate collectively to reduce or eliminate conflict. The final, and draconian, method of reducing conflict is to threaten termination of the channel relationship.

References/Sources

Brown, James R., and Day, Ralph L., "Measures of Manifest Conflict in Distribution Channels," *Journal of Marketing Research* (August 1981): 263-274. This study sought to measure the level of conflict in terms of frequency and intensity between channel members in automotive channels of distribution.

El-Ansary, Adel I., and Stern, Louis, "Power Measurement in the Distribution Channel," *Journal of Marketing Research* (February 1972): 47-52. This was the first attempt to quantify the amount of interdependence among firms in channel relationships. Provides an excellent model for viewing the potential for channel conflict and the use of power as a resolution mechanism.

Eliashberg, Jehoshua, and Michie, Donald A., "Multiple Business Goals Sets as Determinants of Marketing Channel Conflict: An Empirical Study," *Journal of Marketing Research* (February 1984): 75-88. This study suggests that careful channel selection by firms would result in lower conflict. For extant channels, open communication among members is likely to reduce conflict.

Lowe, Larry S., and McCrohan, Kevin F., "Power in the Channel Dyad by Relative Firm Size and Type of Relationship," in *Contemporary Issues in Marketing Channels*. Norman, OK: The University of Oklahoma Press, 1979, pp. 77-85. This article analyzed power in channel dyads, compared power to power use by members in resolving the conflicts, and looked at specific areas in which conflicts arose and power was used.

McCammon, Bert C., Jr., "Perspective for Distribution Programming," in *Vertical Marketing Systems*. Glenview, IL: Scott Foresman, 1970. Develops fully the variety of VMS in the marketplace. Provides data on the growth of the VMS and develops the advantages of the VMS versus conventional channel systems.

Robbins, John E., Morris, L., and Speh, Thomas W., "Retailers' Perceptions of Channel Conflict Issues," *Journal of Retailing* (Winter 1982): 46-47. This study shows that both the contractual VMS and conventional marketing channel structures may be more effective than the corporate chain channel in reducing conflict-related interactions in the channels.

Schul, Patrick L., Little, Taylor E., and Pride, William F., "Channel Climate: Its Impact on Channel Members' Satisfaction," *Journal of Retailing* (Summer 1985): 9-38. Reports on study of channel firm satisfaction and relation to level of firm autonomy and relationship to channel leader.

Schul, Patrick L., Pride, William F., and Little, Taylor E. "The Impact of Channel Leadership Behavior on Intrachannel Conflict," *Journal of Marketing* (Summer 1983): 21-34. Study showed that channel conflict diminished when the franchiser is perceived to lead emphasizing participation, support, and direction in carrying out channel activities.

Zikmund, William and D'Amico, Michael, *Marketing* 2nd ed. New York: John Wiley & Sons, 1986. Chapter 11, pp. 309-344, contains an excellent discussion of sources of channel firm interdependency, possible channel conflicts among firms, and means of reducing channel conflict available to firms.

Related Topics and Terms
Administered Systems, Behavior, Channels, Channels of Distribution, Conflict, Coordination, Distribution, Distribution Institutions, Distribution Management,

Distribution Systems, Interdependency, Leadership, Physical Distribution, Place, Power, Retailing, Structure, Vertical Marketing Systems, Wholesaling

Larry S. Lowe
Department of Marketing
Loyola College in Maryland

CHANNELS OF DISTRIBUTION

Overview

A channel of distribution consists of a system of external sequential linkages of institutions and environments through which a product flows from producer to consumer. A system is conceptualized as two or more units linked together, formally, by flows or activities to achieve particular outcomes. For example, a text book publisher might sell to a book wholesaler, who sells to a college book store chain, who in turn distributes to its individual college stores, who finally put the books in students' hands. This system, or network, depends on many separate departments working together to produce the books, ship and store them, inventory, price and redistribute them, promote them to the faculty, and finally collect money and restock supplies. The most important elements in channels of distribution are the physical product flow, the ownership flow which passes title, the money flow which passes payment, and the communications flow which not only facilitates information between institutions but also promotes the sale of the product to various institutions.

A fundamental premise of a system is that optimum output for the total system is more important than the output of the individual units in the system's network. The value of the systems' concept is that it can be applied at different levels of aggregation and complexity. For example, Clinique cosmetics may have established drug stores as one channel of distribution. Women, who are accustomed to shopping for cosmetics would have no trouble recognizing a new line of cosmetics in that section of the drug store. When Clinique decided to manufacture cosmetics for men, this particular channel of distribution was not flexible enough since men normally shop only for basic toilet items in drug stores. Second, the term external means that the marketing channel and its environments exist outside of the firm. Frito-Lay, for example, includes supermarkets, convenience stores, drug stores, and discount stores among its channels of distribution. These retail institutions are not part of the Frito-Lay organization. This means that many complex aspects of management such as the negotiating functions of buying and selling, and transportation and storage, may be performed by a few or even a great number of firms which are not controlled by Frito-Lay. The management of this type of marketing channel is said to be interorganizational rather than intraorganizational.

Third, the term "linkages" denotes these activities that connect organizational strategies with the external environment and the firms' internal environment. For example, Johnson & Johnson may "link" its band-aid distribution to a product mix that included other minor emergency items.

The fourth aspect of the channel of distribution definition directs itself to product flows from producer to consumer.

Examples

When such brands as Fritos or Doritos are purchased, the consumer does not purchase them directly from the Frito-Lay organization. These brands are typically bought from a supermarket, a convenience store, a drug store, or even in some discount stores who purchase the product in bulk lot, then distribute them within their stores in whatever manner they choose. Once Frito-Lay sells the product, it exercises no further control over the distribution. Different manufacturers have made fundamentally different decisions on channel selection. For example:

- Avon sells through its own sales force directly to individual consumers either in their own homes or where they work.
- Frito-Lay sells direct to such retail organizations as supermarkets and drug-stores.
- Bic pen sells through wholesalers to supermarkets, discount stores, and drug stores.
- Sanyo sells directly to large scale industrial distributors, abandoning the use of small industrial distributors.
- Ford sells automobiles to franchised dealers, who in turn sell to customers.

Benefits

The individual marketing plans of each firm must be combined and coordinated to develop a marketing channel strategy. This strategy consists of the selection of a target market and the blending of the major decision area—product, promotion, place, and price. The responsibility for all or part of each of these decision areas will be assumed by each of the firms participating in the channel system.

An efficient distribution system provides for:

1. A selling program: These activities provide information to the consumer or industrial user through advertising, sales promotion materials such as point-of-purchase displays, and direct selling efforts.
2. A physical distribution program: Products or services must be dispatched from point of origin to a place where they can be purchased.
3. A service program: For such products as office copiers, home computers, and various types of industrial products, post purchase services should be provided.
4. A market information program: Detailed information must be furnished about buyer characteristics and purchaser reactions to prevailing marketing practices.

Implementation

Conventional Channels are any series of firms or individuals who participate in the flow of goods and services from producer to final user or consumer.

An *administered system* permits the most powerful firm to establish policy and to coordinate distribution functions. Integration occurs when channel members cooperate in achieving goals. O.M. Scott, Kraft, and General Electric are examples of companies which control the administered system.

Contractual channel systems are developed when all the terms pertaining to distribution functions, prices, and other factors are specified in writing for each member of the channel system. Ford and McDonalds' are illustrations.

Corporate owned systems are the most direct method to control the channel system. Some manufacturers own their own retail stores or acquire distributors such as Sherwin Williams. Backward integration occurs when retailers such as Sears or Safeway acquire wholesale or manufacturing facilities.

Evaluation

Distribution may be either direct, such as from manufacturer to retailer (e.g. Ford Motor) or indirect, such as manufacturer through various wholesalers or agents (e.g. Frito-Lay) to reach the final user. *The paramount objective is usually to reach the largest number of customers at the lowest possible cost, while exercising control over the channel system.* Resources need to be mobilized and allocated since many manufacturers, such as Toro in lawnmowers, may have as many as 7,500 distributors or Clairol in beauty products as many as 15,000 distributors. Companies must balance cost against control to evaluate their requirements for establishing either direct or indirect distribution programs. These requirements include product characteristics, costs, the degree of desired control and a host of other factors such as technological or social/cultural changes.

A general analysis of direct distribution reveals that high marketing costs are expected but marketers would have a high degree of control over the marketing program. Direct distribution can be accomplished if the marketer has a strong image and good financial resources. Indirect distribution should involve lower marketing costs, less control, reduced channel management responsibilities, and less demands on financial resources.

Conclusion

The primary focus of channels of distribution is to make the product available for consumption. Marketing channels should be considered as relevant competitive systems. The viability of the channel of distribution will depend upon how well and how efficient coordinate efforts work within the network. For example, it is the entire system of Howard Johnsons that competes with Holiday Inns, or the entire system of Campbell's Soup that competes with Lipton Soup. Successful integration of every facet of the channel will determine the company's success.

Channels of distribution should be considered as systems with collective goals and tasks, and functions to be performed. Therefore, characteristics of interorganizational management are present even though authority may range from formal in the case of General Motors and its dealers to informal as in the case of Campbell's soup and its distribution outlets.

Applications to Small Business

Small retail and wholesale organizations should realize that in many instances they are an integral and necessary link in the distribution system. Therefore, small business can expect greater bargaining power in arranging terms with manufacturers. Small retailers may be successful at some degree of channel control through legislation activity. Such activity may focus upon licensing, Sunday closing laws, and price legislation.

Software/Databases

Electronic Yellow Pages: Wholesalers Directory. Market Data Retrieval, 1 Ketchum Place, Westport, CT 06880. Contains the list of all wholesalers listed in the yellow pages of 4,800 U. S. telephone directories. The information provided includes the names and addresses, telephone numbers, county, four-digit SIC code, city population, and type of listing in the yellow pages, such as bold face or display advertisement.

References/Sources

Lewis, Edward H., *Marketing Channels: Structure and Strategy.* New York: McGraw-Hill, 1968. The evaluation of marketing channels is traced from early Anglo-Saxon trade to Colonial retailers and finally to the merchandise-service mix.

McVey, Phillip., "Are Channels of Distribution What the Textbooks Say?" in *Journal of Marketing* (January, 1960): 61-64. The thesis is advanced that business people may have a limited choice of middlemen and that many small firms find channel systems are developed more by accident than by design.

Michman, Ronald D., "Foundations for a Theory of Marketing Channels," *Southern Journal of Business* (now *Journal of Business Research*), (October 1971): 17-26. This work is concerned with the marketing channel as a total system.

Sturdivant, Fred D., and Grandbois, Donald H., "Channel Interaction: An Institutional-Behavioral View," *Quarterly Review of Economics and Business* (Summer 1968): 61-68. This work uses institutional analysis and a behavioral approach as a basis for comprehending marketing channels.

Related Topics and Terms

Channel Conflict, Distribution Channel, Distribution Management, Franchise, Marketing Channel, and Trade Channel.

Ronald D. Michman
Department of Marketing
Shippensburg University

CHURCH MARKETING

Overview

Churches have historically been hesitant to use extensive marketing techniques. There has been some feeling that these types of activities were more "commercial" than "spiritual," thus inappropriate in a church setting. There is, however, a growing trend among churches to apply some of the marketing techniques used successfully by business organizations. When used appropriately, such marketing strategies can be of great benefit to churches.

Examples

Perhaps the most notable examples of church marketing efforts come from large churches such as Robert Schuller's Garden Grove Community Church, Jerry Falwell's Liberty Baptist Church, and Charles Stanley's First Baptist Church of Atlanta. Likewise, many smaller churches are implementing various marketing strategies from formal marketing research studies to television advertising. Although some in the religious press have strongly criticized this pro-marketing trend, the general attitude of those in the religious field appears to be at least a cautious acceptance of marketing techniques. A major reason for this gradual acceptance could be the steady decline in overall church attendance that has occurred in the U.S. over the past thirty years. As churches found themselves essentially competing with one another, the apparent interest in marketing techniques has grown. In fact, the Southern Baptist denomination, the largest Protestant group in the U.S., has recently instituted a seminary curriculum with a specialty in media and promotional activities for the purpose of training individuals to be "Media Ministers" in some of its larger churches.

Benefits

In order to grow, or even survive, churches today must continually enlist new members in the church and encourage their active involvement in church programs. The recent decline in church attendance has made this task even more difficult. As a result, churches today have a great need for understanding more about the people they desire to serve and a great need for communicating with those people. After all, perhaps more than any other institution, the theoretical justification for a church is to meet people's needs. As church leaders apply marketing principles to determine these needs, and inform people about the service the church can provide, society should benefit.

Implementation

In 1985 a nationwide study was conducted of a cross-section of pastors of various churches and members of the general public throughout the U.S. The purpose of the survey was to explore the views of pastors and the general public toward church marketing. Results from the study indicate that the clergy seems to be more open to church marketing efforts than the general public as a whole, and people who attend church regularly view church marketing as favorably as do the clergy. Overall, the following marketing activities were judged by the general public to be *appropriate* for use by churches (in order of perceived appropriateness, with the most appropriate being first): 1) telephoning or mailing information to members, letting them know about current church activities; 2) providing free transportation for those who wish to attend church; 3) having a special church telephone number that provides information about current church activities; 4) sponsoring a religious play/concert/guest speaker and inviting the general public to attend; 5) providing social and service organizations for church members; 6) formally surveying church members for their evaluations of the programs/activities the church is currently offering or should offer; 7) having a temporary sign on the church property, promoting an upcoming church event; 8) sponsoring sports teams; 9) assigning a host family to assist new members in becoming an active part of the church; 10) providing orientation classes for prospective members; 11) advertising the church with a regular listing in the yellow pages; 12) broadcasting church services on television and radio; 13) actively seeking out and welcoming new families to the community and personally inviting them to church; 14) advertising the church in the local newspaper; 15) obtaining names and addresses of visitors to the church; 16) advertising general religious principles (love, honesty, etc.) through various media; 17) officially acknowledging visitors during the church service; 18) sponsoring a brief pre-recorded telephone devotional message (along with a publicized telephone number) for the spiritual benefit of people in the community; 19) having a church staff member whose primary responsibility is outreach to nonmembers of the church; 20) formally surveying the general public about their church-related needs; 21) advertising the church's attributes (fellowship, fun, spiritual satisfaction, etc.) through various media; 22) having a member of the clergy either telephone or personally contact people who visited the church; 23) advertising the church with a block advertisement in the yellow pages; 24) mailing information about the church to the general public; and 25) formally surveying visitors as to their evaluation of their church visit experience.

The general public survey also showed an overall negative opinion of several marketing activities. Beginning with those judged as being *least* appropriate, these are: 1) persuading members of other churches to join that church; 2) informing people about the church by distributing pamphlets, or other material telling about the church, in public places such as malls and street corners; 3) promoting the church with the use of such items as bumper stickers, pens, and book marks; 4) advertising the church on billboards; 5) surveying the general public about their attitudes toward the church; 6) advertising the church's theological beliefs through various media; 7) having a member of the clergy or congregation randomly contact people, either by telephone or personal visit, with an invitation to attend the church; 8) advertising the church on television or radio; 9) having church members telephone or personally contact people who visited the church; and 10) having special programs designed to encourage members to give more money to the church.

Evaluation

There are several problems inherently associated with marketing, and specifically advertising, in any type of nonprofit organization. These include the intangibility of the product being promoted, the nonmonetary price of the product, the lack of frequency of purchase and behavioral reinforcement, the varying levels of consumer involvement, and the need to reach a large but heterogeneous market. Church marketing, in particular, faces some additional limitations: 1) the clergy may lack skills in this area, 2) the clergy and general public may perceive marketing activities as "business gimmicks", and 3) marketing religion may take significant adjustments for it to be successful. Because church marketing efforts are directed toward a market that generally perceives religion as a very personal and even emotional subject, the use of marketing techniques must take into account the strong personal biases the public has about religion and how they are communicated.

Conclusion

Overall, members of the clergy in the U.S. seem to be open to the use of marketing techniques. Although not quite as positive toward marketing activities, the general public as a whole views most church marketing efforts as being appropriate. In general, "personal" communication methods such as personal visits and recognition of visitors are viewed by both the clergy and general public as more appropriate for church use than "nonpersonal" communication methods such as advertising. However the less involved people are in the church, the more they seem to prefer a nonpersonal approach. In other words, the idea of church members or the clergy going around inviting people to church, or providing special attention to visitors at a church is not as appealing to people who do not attend church frequently. As churches take this kind of information into account in planning various church marketing activities, their efforts to take the "good news" to the world can be done much more effectively.

Applications to Small Churches

Like many small businesses, there is a tendency for small churches to look upon many marketing activities as strictly a cost element rather than an investment. Even small churches can plan and implement low budget but very effective techniques designed to identify the needs of its members and prospective members, design programs to meet those needs, and adequately communicate with its audience.

Software/Databases

Religion Index. American Theological Library Association, Chicago, IL. Covering such topics as church history, history of religions, and related areas in the humanities, social sciences, and current events, *Religion Index* provides indexes and abstracts from over 200 journals.

References/Sources

Cooper, Philip D., and McIlwain, George E., "Factors Influencing Marketing's Ability to Assist Non-Profit Organizations," *Proceedings of the Annual Meeting of the Southern Marketing Association* (1980): 314-318. Presents a method for assessing the marketing environment with reference to assisting non-profit marketing efforts.

Culliton, James W., "A Marketing Analysis of Religion," *Business Horizons,* 2, 1 (Spring 1959): 85-92. An early assessment of the possibilities for applying marketing principles to a church setting.

Dunlap, B.J., Gaynor, Patricia, and Roundtree, W. Daniel, "The Viability of Marketing in a Religious Setting: An Empirical Analysis," *Proceedings of the Annual Meeting of the Southern Marketing Association* (1983): 45-48. Points out the slow adoption of marketing techniques by churches and presents the results of a study assessing the clergy's attitudes toward, and their use and knowledge of, marketing.

Engel, James F. and Norton, H. Wilbert, "Effective Evangelism: A Matter of Marketing?" *Christianity Today* (April 15, 1977): 12-15. Presents an assessment of the positive impact marketing techniques can have when applied to a church setting.

Fehren, Father Henry, "The Selling of the Church," *U.S. Catholic,* (December 1980): 39-41. The author presents his views on why churches should not use the same selling techniques as are used by businesses.

Kotler, Philip, *Marketing for Nonprofit Organizations,* Englewood Cliffs, NJ: Prentice-Hall, 1982. A comprehensive text for applying marketing techniques to any type of nonprofit organization. Churches, however, are given little attention in this book.

Krohn, Franklin B., "The Sixty-Minute Commercial: Marketing Salvation," *The Humanist* (November-December 1980): 26-31, 60. Addresses the marketing techniques used by television preachers.

McDaniel, Stephen W., "Church Advertising: Views of the Clergy and General Public," *Journal of Advertising* (1986). Presents an analysis of perceptions regarding the appropriateness of various advertising media and messages for church advertising.

———, "Marketing Communication Techniques in a Church Setting: Views on Appropriateness," *Journal of Professional Services Marketing* (1986). Presents survey results regarding perceptions of nonpersonal and personal communication techniques and marketing research practices used by churches.

Noble, C. Norman, "Advertising Your Church," *Christianity Today* (November 18, 1977): 30-31. Provides recommendations for churches wishing to advertise.

Rothschild, Michael L., "Marketing Communications in Nonbusiness Situations Or Why It's So Hard to Sell Brotherhood Like Soap," *Journal of Marketing,* 43, 2 (Spring 1979): 11-20. An assessment of the differences between public/nonprofit and private marketing environments.

Related Topics and Terms

Nonbusiness Marketing, Nonprofit Marketing, Professional Services Marketing, Services Marketing.

Stephen W. McDaniel
Department of Marketing
Texas A&M University

CLOSE

Overview

The close is a stage in the selling process when a salesperson meets with a prospective buyer for the purpose of selling a product. It is often seen as the key stage in the selling process because it is the decision point at which the salesperson learns if he has successfully persuaded the buyer that his product can satisfy the buyer's needs. The close is preceded in the selling process by activities such as prospecting, prospect qualification, preparation, approach, presentation of benefits, and handling preliminary objections. It is followed by post-sale activities, such as thanking the prospect for the order, asking for referrals, and insuring customer satisfaction.

In a well structured sales presentation, the close will be a natural stage in the sequence of events which does not stand out from the rest. In reality, it is frequently a very difficult stage as salespeople fearing rejection either do not close properly, or fail to attempt to close at all. Keys to successful closing are desire for success, preparation in advance of meeting with the prospect, persistence, confidence in asking for the order, and the ability to wait out a decision by the prospect. A critical point for companies to remember in their training and development programs is that the ability to be good at closing does not come naturally. Rather, it is a skill that can be taught and perfected through practice. It is frequently pointed out that good closers are made, not born.

Examples

Salespeople who are effective at closing may have one or two favorite methods of closing, but they also have mastered a large number of closing methods which they can call upon as the selling situation requires. One key factor in determining success is whether the close fits the situation. If it does, the probability of attaining a sale goes up, but if not, even a tried and true close will often fail.

The number of closing techniques which have been considered in articles and texts on selling is quite vast. Over fifty closing methods have been used and discussed, but most are variations on a central core of five to ten closing techniques. Seven of the mostly widely recognized closes are discussed in this section.

The *alternative choice close* is extremely popular due primarily to its simplicity and ease of presentation. Using this option, the salesperson provides the prospect with a choice between something and something. The salesperson asks if five cases is enough to start the process, or should a full order of ten cases be submitted. Another example is the choice between delivery on Friday or Monday. It is important to note that the choice is between two options that are both satisfactory to the salesperson because they result in a sale. Asking if the prospect would like to buy is asking for a choice between something and nothing. Obviously the latter option is not satisfactory for the salesperson.

The *assumptive close* is also frequently employed successfully by salespeople. In reality it is a close which attempts to make the decision for the prospect. The salesperson simply begins to act as if a sale has been made. The order is phoned in or the merchandise is boxed or wrapped as the prospect watches. If the prospect does not stop the salesperson, it is assumed that there is agreement and the sale has been closed. This closing procedure removes from the prospect the discomfort of communicating a decision. Salespeople should be cautioned that this close should only be attempted after all the major objections to the sale have been handled satisfactorily. Attempting this close too early can result in the prospect feeling pushed and responding negatively.

A close which deals directly with a prospect's reasons for buying is the *summary of benefits close*. This close is very popular because it is based on the salesperson reiterating the key product benefits for the buyer. If the benefit evidence is substantial, the prospect will be moved to make this purchase that will solve his problem. The salesperson should watch the prospect's reactions to the initial statement of benefits during the sales presentation. Only those benefits which the prospect sees as important should be included in the summary of benefits close. Some salespeople prefer to hold back one or two key benefits for this close to give the procedure additional impact.

A closing technique which is similar to summary of benefits, but which includes both the positive and negative aspects of purchasing the product, is the *T-account* or *balance sheet close*. With the balance sheet close, the salesperson asks the prospect to write down all the disadvantages of making the purchase decision on one side of the paper (price, disruption during change over, etc.) and all the advantages in a parallel column (product benefits such as cost savings, greater speed, etc.). If the advantages outweigh the disadvantages, the prospect has clear evidence that a decision to purchase should be made.

One technique which attempts to emphasize the urgency of a decision to buy is the *standing-room-only close*. This close indicates to the prospect that if a decision to buy is not made now, the product may not be available, or would only be available at a higher price, in the future. A customer who cannot seem to make the decision to buy would be told that there are only a very few of the items in stock and they have been moving very fast. A future price increase can also be pointed out. Clearly these changes in future options should be realistic. A salesperson standing in front of a mountain of products could not realistically use the standing-room-only close.

The *continuous yes close* attempts to get the customer responding to a series of questions which are almost certain to be answered affirmatively. The prospect is asked whether saving money is important, whether reducing errors is important, or whether he has a desire to have the best product at a competitive price. The final question in the series is asking for the order. The power of momentum is the basic philosophy behind this close.

Closing on a minor point is another technique. This close reduces the magnitude of the decision the prospect is being asked to make. As opposed to asking if the prospect would like to place an order, the question asks for a decision on color, accessories, or package quantity. Such minor decisions are easier to make and the implications of the answer are the same. If the prospect selects red over blue as a color, without any qualifications, in reality a purchase decision has been made.

Numerous variations exist on these basic themes. The key point in selecting the close that is most appropriate is the situation developing during the sales presentation. There must be a logical fit between the technique and the selling situation.

Benefits

The development of the ability to close sales in the members of a company's sales force is absolutely essential to the survival of a company. Without skillful closing, few customers will be assertive enough to make the purchase decision. Salespeople regularly battle inertia and the fear of change. Skillful use of the closing techniques outlined in the previous section is required if these obstacles to sales are to be overcome.

As a salesperson starts each call, he must have an objective for that contact with the prospect. For many products, that objective will be to close the sale, but in other instances a one call sale may be an unrealistic expectation. Products which are high priced or involve multiple individuals in the decision making process often require several calls to complete a sale. In such instances the salesperson must set a series of objectives for the calls. Before concluding each call the salesperson must close on that objective. If the objective is to get the opportunity to demonstrate the product, this will be the point to close on. Other objectives might be: to conduct cost studies, to make a presentation to the committee, etc. By closing on each of these stages, the salesperson will receive feedback on the progress being made toward a sale. If calls are made without efforts to close, the salesperson may invest a great deal of time and money in an account that is not going to buy the product.

Implementation

For many salespeople the greatest roadblock to the successful implementation of a close is fear. Closing should be a natural part of the process. Both parties know why the salesperson is there, but many salespeople cannot bring themselves to attempt to close. They fear rejection. Rejection is difficult for most people to handle, but it must be realized that it is the product not the salesperson that is being rejected. If no close is attempted, the sale will be lost by default. The worst thing that can happen from the attempt to close is that the sale will not be made. Closing must be seen as a time for feedback. The salesperson can learn that the customer does not understand certain benefits, or has unforeseen needs, or even is ready to make the purchase. The failure to attempt a close is a decision to rule out the possibility of progress and eventual success. These facets of closing must be clearly understood by the successful salesperson.

One of the key issues to be addressed in closing is timing. A close must be attempted when the prospect is in the conviction stage of the buying process, and thus ready to make a decision. This stage can be reached at any point from when the salesperson first contacts the prospect to months or even years later. Closing will usually be appropriate at the end of the presentation, after all preliminary objections have been handled to the prospect's satisfaction. An attempt to close too early will be seen as pushy selling. One way to avoid this problem is to use a trial close. A trial close will produce feedback from the prospect without asking for a buying decision. Asking for overall opinions, future procedures, or an agreement on the value of the product are all examples of trial closes. The response to these questions will either reveal additional objections or provide an indication that the time for a full close is now.

The salesperson may be able to determine the appropriate time to attempt a close without the use of a trial close question. Prospects emit signals that, when carefully monitored and evaluated, can tell the salesperson when to close. These cues may be verbal or nonverbal in nature. Verbal buying signals include detailed questions about the purchase process, or asking others for positive support. Nonverbal signals may be more difficult to read. Relaxation in the prospect's mannerisms, careful examination of the merchandise, and leaning forward are all cues that the person is ready to be closed. Obviously, reaching for a purchase order or a wallet is a clear signal that the prospect is already beginning the close. If these signals are ignored, overselling can occur and the deal may be lost. At some point the prospect will question if the salesperson is truly interested in a sale.

Persistence was listed earlier as a key ingredient to successful closing. This relates to the important issue of how many times should a close be attempted. Many salespeople when confronted with a single no will run for cover. Taking this stance will result in passing up a great many sales which could have been made. A frequently used rule of thumb is that a close should be attempted from three to five times before the salesperson gives up. Each successive close will help to identify the problems that must be dealt with before a sale can be made. Each close will call for a new technique which suits the situation as it develops. If a close brings out an objection which cannot be dealt with, it may be wise for the salesperson to terminate the presentation in a positive light. To continue to ask for an order for a product that does not suit the prospect's needs may create bad feelings about the salesperson and his company. If a salesperson finds this problem happening too frequently, it is an indication that prospecting should be done more carefully.

An understanding of the how to, when, and how often of closing must be communicated to salespeople in the company's training program and developed over time as the sales manager works with the salesperson. The development of effective closing skills must be a top priority for those directing the company's personal selling effort.

Evaluation

A close which is employed by a salesperson will be quickly evaluated by the prospect. The salesperson obviously hopes that evaluation will be positive. At the very least, the feedback should be used to identify what must be done before a sale can be made. The prospect may have become confused during the presentation and confused people usually do not buy. Product pricing may be the problem, which calls for emphasizing product benefits or selling a less expensive model. Irrespective of the close employed, if the prospect is not ready to buy, the salesperson must attempt to use this point to acquire as much feedback as possible about the status of the progress toward a sale.

While the evaluation of the close comes fairly quickly, it can be preceded by what often seems like a long period of silence. By employing a close the salesperson has placed the ball in the prospect's court. The prospect must make some type of decision in response to the close. If the salesperson speaks this removes the pressure from the prospect for a response. The salesperson should wait for the prospect's evaluation, no matter how long it takes. As time progresses the pressure for a decision will mount and this will tend to benefit the salesperson.

Conclusion

Closing is a very important part of a personal selling presentation, but salespeople must not treat it as the only phase in the process. Salespeople who are talented closers are also good at prospecting, preparation, presenting product benefits, and following up after the sale. Good closings are a natural part of the selling process, not a major ceremony. Under ideal circumstances, the prospect will not be able to detect the close from the rest of the presentation.

Companies which utilize personal selling must put forth a substantial effort to develop closing skills in their salespeople. These skills include recognizing buying signals and knowing when to close, having a repetoire of closing techniques that can be confidently employed, and having enough self-confidence to ask for the order as many times as necessary. The salesperson should avoid looking at the process from the perspective of winning or beating the customer at some sort of game. A good sale is one in which everyone wins. The salesperson must believe in his product enough to feel comfortable asking for the prospect's patronage.

Applications to Small Business

Many small businesses fail or succeed based on the ability of the people selling their products to close the sale and get the order. A large firm may have more room for salespeople who are not particularly effective closers. Some larger companies have even gone to a special group of sales closers who come in to sign up the business. Most small companies cannot afford this luxury. Their salespeople must be complete players who can prospect, prepare, present, and close. Smaller companies also do not have the resources to devote to sophisticated training equipment. This clearly places the job of developing a sales force of effective closers with the people performing the sales management functions.

Software/Databases

Astra Sales Analysis System, NEC Information Systems, Inc., 1414 Massachusetts Avenue, Boxborough, MA 01719. The *Astra Sales Analysis System* serves as a marketing strategy tool which assesses the performance of individual salesmen. Sales made by each salesperson are provided on a customer by customer basis, invoice by invoice.

References/Sources

Brennan, Frank, *Personal Selling: A Professional Approach.* Chicago, IL: Science Research Associates, 1983, pp. 209–243. A discussion is provided of the role of closing in the selling process and features of successful closing efforts.

Futrell, Charles M., *Fundamentals of Selling.* Homewood, IL: Richard D. Irwin, 1985, pp. 306–327. An in-depth consideration of the closing stage, including a discussion of closing techniques, is provided in Chapter 10 of this selling text.

Henry, J. Porter, "The Ingredients and Timing of the Perfect Close," *Sales Management* (June 1, 1971): 30–35. Guidelines for successful closing are presented in this article.

Lewis, David V., *Power Negotiating: Tactics and Techniques.* Englewood Cliffs, NJ: Prentice Hall, 1981, pp. 182–195. Chapter 13 of this book looks at the role of closing in the negotiation process.

Manning, G.L., and Reece, B.L., *Selling Today: A Personal Approach.* Dubuque, IA: W.C. Brown Publishers, 1984, pp. 361–384. An in-depth consideration of the psychological aspects of closing techniques is presented in Chapter 16 of this text.

Marks, Ronald B., *Personal Selling: An Interactive Approach.* Boston, MA: Allyn and Bacon, 1985. Chapter 12 provides a detailed discussion of closing techniques and strategies.

Pace, Eric, "He Sells The New Boeings," *The New York Times* (March 29, 1981): F6. In this article a successful Boeing executive discusses the key ingredients of closing large ticket sales.

Pickins, Jim, *The Closers.* Shingle Springs, CA: William and Stephen Publishing, 1980. This entire book is devoted to closing from the seller's and buyer's perspectives. A vast array of closing techniques are discussed in this book.

Radick, Mike, "Training Salespeople to Get Success on Their Side," *Sales and Marketing Management* (August 15, 1983): 63–65. This article discusses key aspects of closing which should be covered in effective sales training programs.

Schoonmaker, A.N., and Lind, Douglas S., "One Custom Made Close Coming Up," *Sales and Marketing Management* (June 13, 1977): 118. Buying signals which point to close timing are the key aspects of this article.

Shapiro, Benson P., and Posner, R.S., "Making the Major Sale," *Harvard Business Review* (March-April 1976): 68–78. All aspects of the selling process for large-ticket items, including closing, are examined in this article.

Templeton, Jane, "The Psychology of the Close," *Sales Management* (June 1, 1971): 11–16. This article differentiates closing from a war in which one person wins and the other loses.

Related Topics and Terms

Buying Signals, Objections, Opening, Personal Selling, Prospecting, Sales Presentation.

George Lucas
Department of Marketing
Texas A&M University

COGNITIVE DISSONANCE

Overview

In the course of collecting information prior to making a purchase, a consumer will confront many conflicting product claims. When a final choice is made, these conflicting claims and beliefs are not immediately forgotten. Cognitive dissonance is a condition that exists when an individual holds two contradictory beliefs or cognitions. It can be a problem for the business from which the individual has purchased the product or it can be an opportunity to cement a firm-customer relationship. The cognitive dissonance effect was described a number of years ago by experimental psychologists and has been used to explain conditions that sometimes lead to customer dissatisfaction. Understanding the effect of cognitive dissonance can provide clues for managers trying to design effective policies for dealing with customer complaints. Additionally, cognitive dissonance theory suggests ways to stimulate positive word-of-mouth advertising for a product by recent purchasers.

Examples

Cognitive dissonance can occur at any time during the purchase process, during the gathering of information concerning alternatives, during the evaluation of alternatives, at the time of choice, or after purchase has been completed. It is a natural and integral part of the pre-choice decision process. Marketing strategies generally focus on the post-purchase dissonance because it is that cognitive state that will most likely affect the next purchase cycle. If a consumer purchases an automobile from a dealer after a rather involved search, post-purchase dissonance may be rather high. If the dealer helps the buyer work out dissonant feelings about the purchase, he is less likely to have costly complaints or to go into the next purchase of a car by the consumer with negative feelings held toward his dealership.

A second fairly common example of cognitive dissonance playing a major role in the buyer/seller interaction process is that which occurs when a buyer is confronted by a salesperson with a product claim that directly conflicts with one of the buyer's previously held beliefs. Understanding the nature of cognitive dissonance may enable the salesperson to maintain credibility with the buyer.

Fairly common buying situations that yield high levels of cognitive dissonance might include the following: A consumer discovers a dead battery and shops at six retail outlets for a new battery and buys the most expensive battery he can find, even though three of the batteries seen were at least as good as the one purchased. A man buys a new suit that fits him well but was not the color he wanted. A family buys a video cassette recorder, understanding that the price reduction they received was because of an impending technological improvement in such systems. A husband and wife spend more money than they had agreed to spend on a new car, when several models were available in their budget range.

Benefits

Despite the fact that cognitive dissonance is usually associated with post-purchase problems, there can be some tangible benefits to the seller of a product when a buyer experiences cognitive dissonance. The major benefit is that while working out one's dissonance, the buyer is usually quite vocal in discussing his purchase. One of the most credible sources of information for a potential buyer of a product is someone who has recently purchased the same product. Thus, the dissonant buyer becomes an initiator of word-of-mouth advertising while trying to rationalize his own mixed feelings. A secondary benefit is that the buyer occasionally buys up to a better unit of a product in an effort to reduce dissonance. A final benefit is that in working through the dissonant state, the buyer frequently gives the salesperson an opportunity to build a stronger personal relationship and trust that will result in the buyer returning during the next purchase cycle.

Implementation

Not recognizing or dealing with cognitive dissonance in the purchase process can create very tangible and costly problems for the marketing management of a firm. Customers who experience cognitive dissonance after a purchase tend to find ways to work out their dissonance. Sometimes that happens very quietly and without incident and results in little or no negative consequence for the firm that sold the product. If, however, there is a minor problem with the item purchased during the time that the customer is still dealing with dissonance, the degree of dissatisfaction can be greatly blown out of proportion. Also, if dissonant feelings persist for any period of time, the customer may carry negative feelings toward the product purchased or the firm from which it was purchased into the beginning of the next product purchase cycle. One way of working out dissonant feelings is to make a mental note that the recently purchased brand will be avoided in the next purchase opportunity. Such a problem may be shared by both the manufacturer of the purchased product and the retail outlet that sold the product. It is, therefore, important to address possible dissonance so that these two problems will not become a reality. Such residual feelings and beliefs can increase over time and become a problem that might remove a brand or a store from the set of evoked choices for the customers.

To gain insight into possible strategies that can be used by businesses to help the customer reduce dissonance, the "natural" strategies that are used by customers to gain their own equilibrium should be examined. Each strategy that is commonly used by customers is a form of rationalization but can in some way be facilitated by providing the buyer with certain types of information or support for a belief. First, buyers can change the cognitive elements that were associated with purchase choice. They can upgrade their evaluation of the product by stressing attributes that may not have been as important in the actual buying process. Also, they can rationalize that they had no real choice but to buy the product they selected.

Second, dissonance can be reduced by denying, distorting, or simply forgetting negative information. Sometimes this is done by attributing low creditability to the source from which they obtained that information. Third, dissonance can be reduced by minimizing the importance of the decision that led to the dissonance. Even though buyers sometimes spend hours making a buying choice, they later dismiss the decision as unimportant or trivial.

Fourth, buyers sometimes reduce dissonance by adding new cognitive elements into the evaluation process. This typically happens after the purchase of a new car when, while reading technical manuals, a buyer will "discover" new reasons for his prior purchase which will later be given as reasons that actually led him to buy. This effect has been documented in research studies.

Marketers can use these natural dissonance-reducing strategies to facilitate the process of dissonance minimization. The major ways that the firm can help the dissonant consumer through this state is by: (1) providing him with positive information about the choice he made and reassure him that he made a good choice, (2) providing him with comparative information about his brand and competing brands that supports the choice he made, (3) providing him with information that shows that many other people have made the same purchase choice that he has made, (4) providing him with positive information or opinions of others that may be about attributes that were not a part of his initial evaluation process.

Evaluation

In 1967 Robert J. Holloway identified several factors that tend to contribute to high or low cognitive dissonance in a purchase situation. Dissonance tends to be high when (1) all purchase alternatives seem to be attractive, (2) the product or service selected for purchase has some negative factors, (3) the number of purchase alternatives is large, (4) the alternative choices are very similar, (5) the purchase must have very specific attributes, (6) the purchaser is unsure that the selected alternative will be appropriate, (7) the price or other attribute of the purchase is discrepant with previously held purchase norms, (8) the buyer has little or no prior purchase experience with the item being purchased, (9) the purchase is expected to yield a dissonant situation, or (10) the purchase is made without much forethought, although it is a fairly major item. A number of later authors also found that dissonance is more likely to arise when the item being purchased is a highly involving product. Highly involving products tend to be those that are more costly, alter one's lifestyle in a major way or are something in which the purchaser is very interested.

The major factors contributing to a state of cognitive dissonance can be collapsed into cases of logical inconsistency, violation of cultural mores, inconsistency between a belief and a more encompassing belief, and inconsistency with past experiences. Cognitive dissonance is most likely to arise after a purchase, when a large amount of effort has been expended in search, and when the purchaser feels insufficient justification for the decision made. In short, virtually any inconsistency in beliefs that may be encountered during the purchase can create a state of cognitive dissonance.

Conclusion

Regardless of whether the selling firm sees cognitive dissonance as a threat or as an opportunity, the effect is real. The outcome of the problem can be a lost customer or a customer who tirelessly "advertises" the product to other potential buyers. The outcome is largely up to the seller, as to how the customer will be fed positive information after the sale. At the minimum, dissatisfaction will be avoided or minimized. At the maximum, word-of-mouth advertising will be facilitated and a good customer will be made better. This comparison encourages strategies that would provide the buyer with much positive information immediately after the sale.

Applications to Small Business

Because of the close contact with purchasers, small businesses have a unique opportunity to engage in dissonance reduction strategies and, as a result, prevent some of the unfavorable reactions which can occur in dissonance filled customers. Assuring customers that they purchased an excellent product and offering guarantees often head off later dissatisfaction with the purchase. Helpful sales people and responsive management also build confidence in customers and help alleviate dissonance. The concept of a "complaint" department was more to reduce dissonance than to process returned merchandise.

Small business owners are particularly susceptible to the negative aspects of dissonance. Because dissonance is usually a temporary psychological condition arising from insecurity, the correct way to handle it is through a positive, confident response to problems, but often the small business owner who must confront the customer directly rather than through a complaint chain, responds negatively. For this reason, small businesses should establish set procedures for dealing with dissonant customers. The most important lesson to learn is that dissonance can be converted into a positive experience for the customer, which will result in store loyalty and word-of-mouth publicity.

References/Sources

Aronson, E., "The Theory of Cognitive Dissonance: A Current Perspective," *Advances in Experimental Social Psychology IV.* New York: Academic Press, 1969, pp. 1-34. Although not the most recent, this is probably one of the best review articles written. It was done shortly after the bulk of the experimental work in the field of psychology. Most of it deals with generalized decision-making rather than purchase only.

Calder, Bobby J., "Cognitive Consistency and Consumer Behavior," *Perspec-*

tives in Consumer Behavior, 3rd ed. Glenview, IL: Scott, Foresman, 1981, pp. 258-269. This is a good background review of balance theory and related theories that underlie cognitive dissonance theory.

Crosby, Lawrence A. and Taylor, James R., "Psychological Commitment and Its Effects on Post-Decision Evaluation and Preference Stability Among Voters," *Journal of Consumer Research,* 9 (March 1983): 413-430. Although this deals with a voting issue, it presents an empirical treatment of dissonance in light of involvement.

Cummings, William H. and Venkatesan, M., "Cognitive Dissonance and Consumer Behavior: A Review of the Evidence," *Journal of Marketing Research,* 13 (August 1976): 303-308. This is the best review of dissonance in the context of purchase behavior. It focuses on the weaknesses of some of the empirical studies and cautions the reader to look for alternative explanations of post-purchase behavior. This paper puts dissonance in perspective.

Festinger, Leon, *A Theory of Cognitive Dissonance.* Stanford, CA: Stanford University Press, 1957. This is the work that initiated the theory. Chapters 1 and 2 contain the heart of the theory. Most of the rest of the book is devoted to exploratory testing of certain implications of the theory.

Holloway, Robert J., "An Experiment in Consumer Dissonance," *Journal of Marketing,* 31 (January 1967): 39-44. This article is a straight forward test of the predictions of the theory, but with several dissonance reducing factors manipulated: 1) inducement to buy, 2) anticipated dissonance, 3) information, 4) cognitive overlap. This is a good example of the empirical works on this topic.

Kassarjian, H.H., and Cohen, J.B., "Cognitive Dissonance and Consumer Behavior: Reactions to the Surgeon General's Report on Smoking and Health," *California Management Review,* 8 (Fall 1965): 55-64. A classic study that looks at how consumers deal with dissonance producing information. It also demonstrates some of the difficulties encountered in doing dissonance research.

Korgaonkar, Pradeep K. and Moschis, George P., "An Experimental Study of Cognitive Dissonance, Product Involvement, Expectations, Performance and Consumer Judgment of Product Performance," *Journal of Advertising,* 11, (1982): 32-43. This is typical of studies in recent years that relate cognitive dissonance to other factors in the purchase process.

Related Topics and Terms
Attitude, Buyer, Consumer Behavior.

Charles S. Madden
Department of Marketing
Baylor University

COMMON CARRIERS

Overview

Whenever firms ship or receive merchandise, the transportation function comes into play. Both shippers and receivers demand that their shipments move safely, correctly, completely, and conveniently. If shortages, damages, or delays are encountered, prompt claim settlement is expected. The entrusting of goods to another party, a bailment contract, represents a major decision. The firm attempts to obtain a quality transport service at a reasonable price, and any problems should be resolved to the mutual satisfaction of both parties.

A correct transportation selection offers several benefits to shippers and receivers. Incoming goods arriving on schedule mean that production can continue uninterrupted. Merchandise can be offered for sale immediately, pleasing customers. Transportation costs can be reduced. Claim settlements can be reached quickly. Time delays can be minimized. A smooth flow of goods results.

The transport decision is complicated by the fact that there are a wide number of choices. In addition to the modal choice; e.g., rail, motor, air, water, pipeline, or combination, there are legal choices. Shippers or receivers can choose to move the goods themselves, or they can rely on for-hire firms; i.e., companies whose sole business is related to transportation. Within these two categories of private or for-hire, additional options exist.

Common carriers hold themselves out to serve all who apply without undue preference, prejudice, or discrimination. These firms are required to provide adequate facilities and to provide service at reasonable rates. They publish their rates and charges, and they must accept liability for goods tendered to them. They are subject to fairly intensive economic and safety regulations by either federal or state governments. Even though the deregulatory trend has reduced the regulatory impact, common carriers are still subject to more regulation than any other legal form of transport. Common carriers are said to be "affected with the public interest." Translated, the phrase implies that common carriers perform a vital service to the country; there are no close substitutes for the service; often the carriers are in a position to discriminate; and a certificate of convenience and necessity must be obtained in order to conduct operations.

Examples

There are many different legal forms of transportation in addition to common carriers. The total spectrum of these forms appears in Figure 1. In addition, the characteristics of each form are shown in Table 1. Based on this information, the decision maker has a framework for identifying the various legal choices.

Figure 1
Legal Forms of Carriage

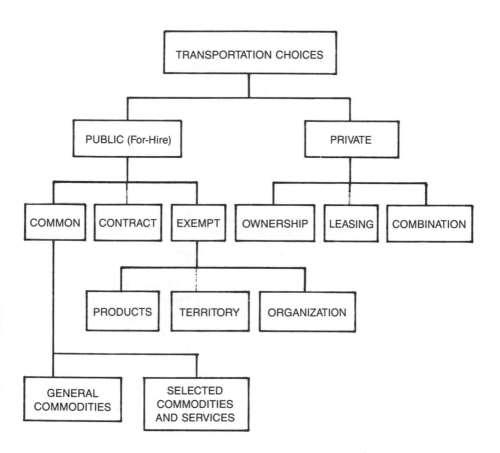

Table 1

CHARACTERISTICS OF THE LEGAL FORMS OF CARRIAGE

Legal Forms of Carriage	Charactertistics
Public (For-Hire)	Agrees to serve all who apply without undue preference, prejudice, or discrimination
Common (All modes of transportation)	Provides adequate facilities and services at reasonable rates
	Delivers goods entrusted to its care with reasonable dispatch
	Publishes rates and charges
	Accepts liability for goods tendered to
	Assumes intensive economic and safety regulations
	Requires a certificate of convenience and necessity from a regulatory body
Contract (Motor, Water and Air Carriers)	Offers a specialized service in terms of equipment and/or products
	Restricts service to a limited number of shippers (1 to 7 persons or firms)
	Receives a permit from a regulatory body in order to operate
	Assumes only modest economic regulation but fairly intensive safety regulation
	Enjoys geographical flexibility and latitude in serving customers
Exempt (Motor and Water Carriers)	Requires no economic regulation
	Open to anyone to enter or exit
	Receives classification because of products carried, territory served, or organization formed
	Negotiates rates—can discriminate
	Assumes no obligations to provide regular service or a quality service level
	Assumes fairly intensive safety regulation
Private	Provides transportation service only for the firm; carrier and owner of goods are identical
(Ownership, Leasing, or Combination-all modes of transport)	Requires no economic regulation
	Assumes intensive safety regulation
	Transporting goods must be incidental to the primary business of the firm
	Enjoys geographical flexibility and latitude in serving customers

Benefits

The choice of common carriage is based primarily on the protection factor. Because of their heavy public service involvement and commitment, common carriers are the most stringently regulated legal form of transport. As a result, shippers and receivers receive maximum protection under the law as well as being supported by the regulatory agencies. The transportation customers also know that the rates they pay are nondiscriminatory; their competitors are also assessed the same charges for comparable service. Common carriers are required to observe scheduled operations as well as providing traffic and equipment interchange with other common carriers.

A fairly high service quality is received from common carriers. Serving the public and specializing in transport operations, common carriers form the backbone of the national transportation system. If protection, dependability, geographical coverage, and service adequacy are required, common carriage is a wise choice.

To this point, common carriage has been related to the various transportation modes. These modes perform primarily line-haul movements from one point to another. There are other common carriers who offer auxiliary services as well. Small packages can best be distributed by the U.S. Postal Service and/or United Parcel Service (UPS). Bus service also can be employed for small shipments over short distances.

Freight forwarders offer another option. These firms provide assembling, consolidating, and distributing services. They act as a carrier in relation to the shipper/receiver, and as a shipper in relation to the common carrier. For international shipments, freight forwarders offer documentation services in order to meet the many requirements of both originating and terminating countries.

Implementation

In resolving a transportation choice problem, the need criterion is most important. Among the broader issues to be decided are the following:

1. What are the inbound and outbound volume requirements?
2. What time-frame requirements exist?
3. What special type of equipment, packaging, or materials are needed?
4. What services other than movement are essential?
5. How much product protection is needed?
6. What degree of dependability and reliability is demanded?

Once these questions have been resolved, the next task is to decide whether to use public or private carriage. Table 2 summarizes the advantages of both types of carriage. Caution must noted regarding private carriage, however. Once the decision to go private has been made, it is extremely difficult to reverse the decision. The investment, the creation of an organizational unit to manage private carriage, and the parts inventory represent major commitments. To discontinue this operation after a short period of time is very costly.

Table 2

ADVANTAGES OF FOR-HIRE AND PRIVATE CARRIAGE

For-Hire or Common Carriage	Private Carriage
Expert, professional service	Improved service through scheduling and delivering
Extensive national and international geographical coverage	Greater control over service and products
Duties and responsibilities are well defined	Flexibility in operations and territory
Shipper protection through economic and safety regulation	Reduced loss and damage claims because goods are not mixed with those of other shippers
Carrier assumption of operating and management problems	Transportation costs can be more economical
Investment is made by the carriers, not the shippers	Specialized equipment and service
Shipper flexibility in using other modes or carriers	Improved customer relations-greater interest in customers by drivers
Transportation charges can be more economical	Use of equipment for advertising-rolling billboards
Extended services through intramodal and intermodal coordination	

Evaluation

Assuming that the firm has made a decision to employ common carriage, periodic evaluation of this service should be made. Both service and cost considerations should be covered in the assessment. The areas of evaluation should include answers to the following questions:

What per cent of all shipments are made on time?

What per cent of all shipments receive customer complaints?

What per cent of all shipments result in claims for shortage, damage, or delay?

How quickly do carriers respond to claims and claim settlements?

How well do carriers respond to special equipment requests?

Can shipments be traced and/or expedited?

What are transportation costs per hundredweight (cwt) or any other measure?

How do these unit costs compare to prior years?

How much are transportation costs as a per cent of the total cost of production or sales?

What additional handling, packaging, or shipping costs are being incurred by using common carriers?

How much are expediting or "hot shot" services?

Conclusion

Common carriers represent the backbone of the nation's transportation system. They supply vital transportation services for both commercial and defense needs. Because of the major role these carriers play, they are "affected with the public interest." Both economic and safety regulations are imposed upon them, thereby providing additional protection to shippers and receivers. Shipments to practically every destination can be performed by common carriers. Although their charges may be somewhat higher than other options, greater protection and prompt claim settlements warrant the higher rates. Because transportation is their primary business, common carriers are movement professionals.

Applications to Small Business

Almost every small business receives or ships goods. These items must arrive promptly, accurately, and damage-free. If goods are damaged, the firm expects quick claims settlement. Efficient transportation facilitates sales, production, inventory control, and profits.

With limited capital, most firms would rather put their funds into their primary business rather than invest in private transportation. To meet their transportation requirements, small business relies extensively on common carriers. In addition to transportation, common carriers also offer advice about packing, documentation, switching services, claim filing, and transport regulations. All of these activities require technical expertise which most small business are not aware of or cannot afford.

Until a firm reaches a size where transportation volume and costs become significant, or when specialized equipment is needed, common carriage represents a sound decision. By entrusting inbound and outbound shipments to professional carriers, management can direct its attention to its primary activities of manufacturing, retailing, or distributing.

Software/Databases

Commercial Trucking Package. The Computer Merchant, Ltd; 571 Main Street, South Weymouth, MA 02190. Provides an accounting and management package for commercial trucking firms, including maintenance, billing, scheduling, and traffic samplers.

References/Sources

Cavinato, Joseph L., *Purchasing and Materials Management*. St. Paul, MN: West Publishing Company, 1984. See Chapter 10 for a discussion about purchasing transportation.

Guandolo, John, *Transportation Law*. Dubuque, IA: William C. Brown Publishing Company, 1965. See Chapter 49 for liability and obligations of common carriers.

Harper, Donald V., *Transportation in America*. Englewood Cliffs, NJ: Prentice-Hall, 1978. Chapter 6 discusses the user choices in a business logistics system.

Rose, Warren, *Logistics Management: Systems and Components*. Dubuque, IA: William C. Brown Publishing Company, 1979. Chapter 3 also relates to transportation decisions as related to common carriers.

Sigmon, Richard R., *Miller's Law of Freight Loss and Damage Claims,* 4th ed. Dubuque, IA: William C. Brown Publishing Company, 1974. A detailed treatment of common carrier liability, loss and damage, and the bill of lading that is presented.

Related Topics and Terms

Carrier Obligations, Claims Procedures, Contract Carriers, Leasing, Legal Liability, Logistics Systems, Private Carriage, Public Carriage, Transportation Choices.

Warren Rose
Department of Marketing
Texas A&M University

COMPARATIVE ADVANTAGE

Overview

Some people in the United States have advocated the idea of self-sufficiency. They question the need for trade with other countries, a situation in which U.S. national security may be weakened since she is forced to rely on others who may be in a position to withdraw essential trade. Even if no risk were involved when trading with others, trading with foreign countries results in a variety of problems and complications. These individuals may argue that the U.S. has most of the resources she needs and has the capability to manufacture products demanded by consumers. Even when resources are scarce, it is possible to substitute products or manufacture synthetic substitutes, so that hypothetically a country like the U.S. could be totally self sufficient. However, in comparing the advantages of substitution to trading, it is usually more cost effective to trade with other countries which have the natural resources. This is the economic "comparative advantage" which is often weighed against the political disadvantages of international trade. The U.S. could, for example, become self sufficient in energy, but to do so would cost a great deal more than trading on the open market and would require social/political judgments, such as reliance on nuclear energy.

Examples

Countries trade because of their need to acquire commodities. Although the United States has a tremendous supply of many natural resources, she still lacks several that are vital to sustain her productive and manufacturing capabilities. For example, the U.S. may not be in a position to manufacture many automobiles, television sets, telephones, and a variety of other goods without certain elements that are needed to accomplish the technological improvements in these products. These need to be imported from those countries that have an abundance of such resources. In other instances, factors such as climate or temperature may make it prohibitive to grow certain crops. Because of an existing absolute advantage or because of some natural endowment, it would seem logical that a country should concentrate on utilizing efficiently its own abundant resources rather than attempting to compete in all commodities.

Benefits

Nations must decide which comparative advantage they will seek or which they will exploit to the fullest extent. The United States, for example, maintains a distinct advantage in computer technology, Britain produces television fare for the U.S. educational television market and France exports fine wines. While these countries have other advantages as well, these goods and services provide foreign exchange that permits acquisition of other goods and services from other countries, as well as providing jobs for its own citizens. Countries able to acquire outputs from other countries that represent their comparative advantages, benefit from higher quality goods, more efficient machinery and technology, and lower prices than domestically-produced goods.

Implementation

The concept of an absolute advantage is very similar to that of an athlete with a natural gift for a particular sport, giving him an edge over most other competitors. On the other hand, just as in sports, even though an individual may not be endowed with a natural talent, such an individual may gain superiority through hard work and training and thus be able to compete against the others. Nations or organizations may be able to accomplish, or acquire such skills that will provide them with an edge over the competition. In the international arena, most acquired advantages are in the area of manufactured goods rather than agricultural goods and natural resources. It is not uncommon, therefore, to see the United States export machinery to Japan and at the same time import machinery from Japan. Each country finds that it is to its advantage to specialize in some goods and import others. Thus, by concentrating effort, efficiency and technological developments in some areas, countries are able to utilize their resources in a manner that provides a competitive advantage.

Evaluation

In his *Wealth of Nations,* Adam Smith stressed the importance of specialization as a source of increased efficiency and output in a world where resources are scarce and human wants, as a result, cannot be completely satisfied. Adam Smith suggested that countries specialize in those goods and services they were good at producing and, in exchange, trade this for products and services that other nations were better at producing. Adam Smith postulated the concept of absolute advantage. Then David Ricardo refined Adam Smith's theory by proposing the principle of comparative advantage. He suggested that a country would have a comparative advantage in the production of goods which it can *relatively* produce more efficiently than other goods. The idea to be stressed is that although a country may have an absolute advantage in the production of two goods, it should concentrate its efforts on the single good in which it has the greatest comparative advantage. A few examples will illustrate this idea. Assume that an individual is the best surgeon in an area. This same individual is also the best cabinet maker in the same location. It makes no sense for this individual to spend part or all of his time hiring his services making cabinets. The same thing can be said about the services of a bookkeeper who is a computer analyst at the same time. A simple numerical example will illustrate the same principle. Regardless of price and other intervening factors, assume that the total productive capacity of England is 50 units of cloth or 10 units of shoes. Similarly, assume that Germany has the capacity to produce 50 units of shoes or 10 units of cloth. It is very easy to see that through specialization, the total output of the two countries will be 100 units, an optimal amount when compared with any other option or combination that each of the two countries may decide to pursue.

The implication so far is that a nation will have all of its factors of production fully employed at all times. This would suggest that the only way in which a nation can increase the production of one good is at the expense of another good. But, if a nation's production factors are not fully employed, a variety of factors play a vital role in enhancing or discouraging these flows despite the dictates of the theory of comparative advantage.

1. *Exchange rates:* The value of the currency of each country can distort the picture. If both currencies were of equal value, the principal of comparative advantage would be operative. As these values fluctuate because of supply and demand market forces, it is conceivable that the trend can be shifted. Although most currencies may not go through dramatic shifts, some do for a variety of reasons such as inflation. Mexico is a case in point. In 1976 the peso was worth 6.9 cents. As a result of several devaluations and depressed economic conditions, the value of this currency in March 1985 was worth 0.45 cents, a very dramatic change. Six months later this dropped to 0.26 cents.

2. *Transportation costs:* Although we may be operating under conditions of free trade, the movement of goods is not free. Not only does one have to consider the actual cost of transportation between two countries, but also the various additional expenses related to shipment of these goods such as packaging and insurance. Furthermore, although such incidents are rare, one can experience a dramatic increase in transportation costs. The closure of the Suez Canal increased the cost of exporting oil from the Middle East. More recently, at the height of airplane highjackings, insurance premiums on these airplanes multiplied.

3. *Per capita income:* It has also been suggested that just because the United States or Japan enjoy a comparative advantage in the production of automobiles, this does not mean that consumers in India will flock to purchase this product even if they desire to possess it. Wants must be backed by purchasing power. When this is not forthcoming, no trade or very little trade will take place.

4. *Tariffs:* Although an assumption has been made that trade will flow freely, in most instances this may be the exception to the rule. No country, no matter how liberal, and that includes the United States, allows free entry of products from other countries. For a variety of reasons, tariffs may be collected on such imports. This has the effect of raising the price of these imports. A point

can be reached where the exporting country enjoying a comparative advantage will have its advantage neutralized as a result of tariffs collected on its exports.

5. *Other factors:* The factors above are the more common ones that can be considered most relevant to the theory of comparative advantages. However, the list has not been exhausted by any means. Other factors can be as oppressive or detrimental. For instance, governmental policies will dictate free flow of trade or lack of it. Today, it is politics and not economic forces that are dictating whether or not products from the United States will flow into Libya. Besides politics, hard currency inventories can dictate whether or not Russia will engage in trade with the United States. Social and psychological factors can also be relevant. In the United States citizens measure their standard of living by the extent of their material possessions. The Faquirs of India may abstain or even denounce material goods to insure their spiritual well-being and purify their souls.

Conclusion

Periodically, throughout modern history, nations seek to ignore or alter the concept of comparative advantage by attempting self-sufficiency or by imposing protective tariffs. Conversely, countries use subsidies to protect domestic industries for which they have no comparative advantages, and to promote markets by selling outputs of these industries at artificially low prices. This technique may be useful in the short term, but often brings about protective tariffs by the customer countries to protect their comparative advantages. Thus, while tariffs and subsidies may be used to protect non-advantage industries, they may induce tariffs by other countries on items for which the producing nation does have a legitimate advantage.

Applications to Small Business

While this discussion has centered mainly upon global concepts, a microcosmic adaptation may be suggested as an operating lesson or guideline for small businesses. In the most recent decade or two, many major companies in the U.S. have attempted to expand their size and scope through diversification. But a number of them found that they were unable to extend the comparative advantage they had obtained for their basic products to entirely different ones, and were eventually forced to divest their incompatibile acquisitions.

Smaller businesses may do well to consider their advantages as well. Restaurants, particularly, find that expansion often causes them to lose their comparative advantage as a small, intimate spot with individually prepared dishes, and they become just another stereotype. So expanding a smaller business that has succeeded because of some specific comparative advantage must be undertaken only if that advantage can be maintained, or if some other attractive advantage can be offered in its place.

References/Sources

Adams, J., *The Contemporary International Economy.* New York: St. Martin's Press, 1985, pp. 17-22. This paper discusses the theory of intraindustry trade, theory of technological competition, and product life cycle theory and how they influence international trade flows.

Anderson, R. E., and Hair, J. F., Jr., *Sales Management: Text with Cases.* New York: Random House, 1983, pp. 553-554. The author describes the U.S. situation today with respect to foreign competition as "an economic Pearl Harbor."

Bhagwati, J. N., ed., *International Trade: Selected Readings.* Cambridge, MA, and London: The MIT Press, 1984, pp. 65-87. Bhagwati discusses comparative advantage as a force behind international trade flows and the factors that weaken those flows are treated using complex mathematical models. This section is recommended for the highly sophisticated, mathematically oriented readers.

Daniels, J. D., Ogram, E. W., Jr., and Radebaugh, L. H., *International Business: Environments and Operations.* Reading, MA: Addison-Wesley, 1982, pp. 24-64. This test traces the development of various theories of international trade and provides statistics on the current level of international trade and compares its nature and magnitude between developed and less developed economics.

Garland, J., and Farmer, R. N., *International Dimensions of Business Policy and Strategy.* Boston: Kent Publishing Co., 1986, pp. 1-15. The authors describe strategic patterns associated with the internationalization of business.

Globerman, S., *Fundamentals of International Business Management.* Englewood Cliffs, NJ: Prentice-Hall, 1986, pp. 29-56. Motivation for going international is described, the various theories of international trade are explained, and an attempt is made to integrate them together.

Leamer, E. E., *Sources of International Comparative Advantage.* Cambridge, MA, and London: The MIT Press, 1984, pp. 45-58. Another mathematical treatment of comparative advantage and international trade for the sophisticated reader. The author formulates various hypotheses to test a number of international trade theories.

Moyer, R., *International Business Issues and Concepts.* New York: John Wiley & Sons, 1984, pp. 1-29 and 81-84. After a discussion of the various international theories, the author suggests the various factors which he thinks led to the demise of the product life cycle theory. In another discussion a case is made for free flow of international trade and against protectionism.

Root, F. R., *International Trade and Investment.* Cincinnati, OH: South-Western Publishing Co., 1984, pp. 209-227. The author discusses inter- and intraindustry forces leading to international trade as a consequence of comparative advantage resulting from dissimilarity of factor endowments of national economies. A number of illustrations through the use of economic curves and graphs are used to demonstrate a nation's benefits from trade.

Spero, J. E., *The Politics of International Economics Relations.* New York: St. Martin's Press, 1985, pp. 99-100. Discusses recent forces of change among developed and less developed nations as a result of some reversals in factor endowments and technology transfer, particularly as a result of a surge in oil prices. This development caused changes in the structure of national economies and comparative advantage.

Related Topics and Terms

Balance of Payments, European Economic Community, Exports, Imports.

John H. Hallag
College of Business and Economics
University of Idaho

COMPARATIVE ADVERTISING

Overview

There are two ways to define comparative advertising. One is "competitive brand advertising that makes an explicit comparison with one or more competing brands." This is the more popular view of comparative advertising with many well-known examples: Bayer and Tylenol, Pepsi and Coke, the Blatz taste tests, and so on.

But what about advertisements such as Avis' admission of being number two, which makes them try harder; or the box of competing laundry detergent with concentric orange circles, partially hidden behind a pile of clothes; or Wendy's question about the beef in competing fast food hamburgers? In these and similar ads, there is no explicit mention of Hertz, Tide, or McDonalds, but the message is intended to be comparative. So a second, more accurate definition of comparative advertising is "advertising in which an explicit brand comparison is *recognized* by the audience."

Based on this second definition, the competing brand need not be actually named—the only requirement is that consumers think the comparison is taking place and that a specific brand is the target of the comparison.

Examples

Most comparative advertisements, especially for consumer services and packaged goods, make superiority claims for the sponsoring brand over the competing brand: Blatz tastes better than Miller, Behold outshines Pledge, and Burger King's flame-broiling beats McDonald's frying.

Other comparative advertising has claimed comparability, such as the Ford LTD's ride with Rolls Royce. In one classic case, the Opel claimed inferiority to the Volkswagen Rabbit—presumably, to build credibility for other claims.

Contrary to popular notion, comparative advertising in the U.S. was never illegal, so long as the claims were truthful. There are examples of comparative ads from colonial days, but the proliferation of comparative ads did not begin until 1972, when the FTC openly encouraged comparative advertising as a means of providing more information to consumers. Before this, advertisers had engaged in the comparisons commonly known as "Brand X" advertising. Rather than making explicit comparisons, the sponsoring brand would be compared to "Brand X," "another leading detergent," the "high-priced spread," etc. This reflected a kind of gentlemen's agreement in the advertising industry not to engage in "name-calling."

Some advertisers felt that the FTC's position would usher in a new era of vicious, destructive advertising. They predicted that consumers would be confused and unable to identify which was the sponsoring brand and which was the target brand, and that advertising would lose whatever credibility it had as claims and counter-claims went back and forth. None of these consequences has come about, and there are still some questions about the effect of comparative advertising.

Benefits

A number of research studies, especially in the mid-1970s, focused on the effectiveness of comparative advertising. In general, the results have been mixed, and almost every study had some methodological shortcoming. What follows is a summary of most of this research, broken down by some commonly used measures of advertising effectiveness:

1. Brand Recall: mixed results, with some studies showing comparative advertising as more effective than noncomparative, and others showing no difference.
2. Content Recall: balance of the evidence is in favor of comparative advertising over noncomparative or Brand X advertising. However, these studies were done when comparative advertising was just gaining popularity, so some of the results may be colored by the newness of the technique to consumers.
3. Liking for the Ads: there is some evidence that consumers like comparative advertisements more than Brand X ads, but not any more than they like noncomparative ads. Again, this could be the effect of the novelty of the technique when the research studies were conducted.
4. Attitude Change: there is little evidence that comparative ads improve consumers' attitudes toward the sponsoring brand, nor that they hurt attitudes toward the target brand. Attitude change, however, is difficult to measure in most advertising research studies, such as the ones reported here, that rely on one or two exposures to the advertisement. Attitude change is often a long term process, requiring repeated exposure to the advertising message.
5. Credibility: the balance of evidence is that comparative ads are less credible than noncomparative ads. In many instances, however, it is not important to have highly credible ads. For some packaged goods, it often matters less that consumers find the ads believable, but that they instill enough curiosity about the brand to get consumers to try it.

Implementation

Despite the lack of evidence showing clearly the effects of comparative advertising, there are some general guidelines about when comparative advertising should and should not be used in a strategic marketing sense.

First, comparative advertising is more useful for firms that are new or that wish to position themselves against well-known—and usually larger—competitors. Comparative advertising is a questionable tactic for firms that dominate their markets. Thus, it may be appropriate for Burger King and Wendy's to compare themselves with McDonald's, but it would probably be a mistake for McDonald's to retaliate with its own comparisons.

Second, there are some brands that, while not dominant in their markets, have certain well known and desirable positions. KitchenAid dishwashers and Mercedes Benz are thought to be top-of-the-line, but are far from major market share brands. While both brands have found themselves the targets of comparative advertising, both should hesitate to respond in kind.

Third, it is more useful if the sponsoring brand has a distinct, enduring advantage over the "target" brand. Datril claimed comparative effectiveness with Tylenol, but said its price was lower. Tylenol responded by cutting prices below Datril in selected markets, and then claimed Datril's ads were untruthful in all instances.

Fourth, there are some markets in which segments of consumers consider comparative advertising to be "bad form." One of these is financial institutions, and another seems to be public utilities (e.g., gas versus electric). There are peculiarities about these markets that make strong comparative advertising inadvisable. In one instance, a group of consumers reacted to a test of a comparative TV ad by saying it looked like an act of desperation by the sponsoring utility company.

Fifth, comparative advertising should probably not be used if claim credibility is of major importance.

Evaluation

A key test, of course, of the effectiveness of comparative advertising is whether comparative advertising has resulted in improved sales of brands. This information is hard to come by, since many advertisers have no way of telling, or are reluctant to release the results. Even if they know, there is often the tendency to color the reports, depending on whether one was an advocate of the campaign or not.

Conclusion

While comparative advertising has not spelled doom for the advertising industry, neither has it been a sure-fire cure for the marketing ills of companies that have used it. Since there are some risks, as well as gains, associated with comparative advertising, companies that are considering it should engage in thorough testing before making major commitments to comparative campaigns.

Applications to Small Business

The disadvantages of comparative advertising listed above apply particularly to small businesses which are attempting to capture a local market. As long as the small business is competing against national giants, consumers will be sympathetic to the "little guy," but when the little guys begin competing against each other with comparative advertising, consumers may perceive it as in bad taste. Healthy competition is a national characteristic which Americans enjoy, but it must always be done fairly, and without belittling the opponent. It is frequently a good idea to give the competition credit for some good feature which does not affect the benefit being offered. For example, a clothing store advertising lower prices might say: "Bob's might offer you a free football calendar, but you'll never pay lower prices on name brand fashions than at Harry's." Another approach to undercut the potential distastefulness of comparative advertising is to include good-natured humor, or unqualified "experts" whose opinions are valued for the wrong reasons. A photo shop, for example, comparing its developing services to a competitor might use a child to exclaim how terrific the prints are, based on the content of the photos (himself or an animal) rather than on the quality of the developing.

While most small businesses do not have large advertising budgets, and when they do advertise they tend to promote a single feature or product in order to capture a target market, there can be select advantages to comparative advertising even for the smallest business. First, is name recognition. Comparative advertising tends to be more memorable. If an unknown company compares itself to an established company, consumers might remember the two together; whereas, they might forget the name of the new company. Second, comparative advertising can generate more business for both companies by increasing product awareness and telling consumers two places they can find an item. Third, the company not involved in comparative advertising can frequently turn a negative to a positive. "You might pay a little more at Bob's, but you'll never have a problem returning the pink tie with alligators your mother-in-law gave you for St. Patrick's Day."

In summary, small businesses considering comparative advertising should know their market well, establish goals for what they hope to achieve by comparing themselves to other companies, and thoroughly test the advertising before going public with it. When producing the ad, the small businessperson should probably rely on an objective ad agency for advice about creating the ad campaign, but he should never relinquish control of the boundaries of acceptability which he believes his audience will accept.

Software/Databases

ADTRACK. Kingman Consulting Group, Inc., St. Paul, MN. Indexes all advertisements of one-quarter page or larger, appearing in 148 major U.S. consumer magazines. Indexing is by product name, company name, and ad content.

References/Sources

Barry, Thomas E., and Tremblay, Roger L., "Comparative Advertising: Perspective and Issues," *Journal of Advertising* 4 (1975): 15-20. A summary of issues raised by advertising practitioners about the effects of comparative advertising on consumers and on the industry in general.

Boddewyn, J.J., and Marton, Katherin, *Comparison Advertising: A Worldwide Study.* New York: Hastings House, 1978. This book discusses comparative advertising in the U.S. and other countries, particularly arguments for and against, as well as regulatory considerations.

Chevins, Anthony C., "A Case for Comparative Advertising," *Journal of Advertising* 4 (1975): 31-36. This article is a history of comparative advertising, with speculations about its effectiveness, and suggestions for its use by advertisers.

Goodwin, Stephen, and Etgar, Michael, "An Experimental Investigation of Comparative Advertising: Impact of Message Appeal, Information Load, and Utility of Product Class," *Journal of Marketing Research* 17 (May 1980): 187-202. This study found little advantage of comparative ads over Brand X or supportive advertising. On only one measure, liking for the ad itself, was the comparative advertisement superior.

Jain, Subash C., and Hackleman, Edwin C., "How Effective is Comparison Advertising for Stimulating Brand Retail?" *Journal of Advertising* 7 (1978): 20-25. Across 12 product categories, brand name recall was higher for the comparative ad than for the noncomparative in an immediate post-test. In a 24-hour delayed post-test, this advantage disappeared, however.

Levine, Phillip, "Commercials that Name Competing Brands," *Journal of Advertising Research* 16 (December 1976): 7-14. An empirical study that showed little support for comparative advertisements in several product categories. The tone of this study was highly argumentative, and the researcher seemed critical of comparative advertising from the outset. The study was sponsored by Ogilvy & Mather which had publicly announced it was opposed to the use of comparative advertising.

Prasad, V. Kanti, "Communications Effectiveness of Comparative Advertising: A Laboratory Analysis," *Journal of Marketing Research* 13 (May 1976): 128-137. Found little difference between a comparative and Brand X advertisement for a fictitious brand of movie camera. The exception was lower credibility for the comparative advertisement among those who preferred the target brand (Kodak).

Shimp, Terence A., and Dyer, David C., "The Effects of Comparative Advertising Mediated by Market Position of the Sponsoring Brand," *Journal of Advertising* 7 (1978): 13-19. This study used a fictitious fast food chain against McDonald's and found copy recall was greater and credibility was lower for the comparative versus a noncomparative ad.

Traylor, Mark B., "Comment on 'An Experimental Investigation of Comparative Advertising: Impact of Message Appeal, Information Load, and Utility of Product Class,' " *Journal of Marketing Research* 18 (May 1981): 254-255. A sharp criticism of the Goodwin and Etgar methodology, with implied criticisms of other empirical studies on comparative advertising.

Ulanoff, Stanley M., "Comparison Advertising: An Historical Perspective," *Marketing Science Working Paper,* February 1975. An interesting history of comparative advertising with many examples.

Wilkie, William L., and Farris, Paul W., "Comparison Advertising: Problems and Potential," *Journal of Marketing* 39 (October 1975): 7-15. A discussion of comparative advertising from the standpoint of regulatory agencies, the media, and advertisers. This article raised a number of research issues that helped launch much of the empirical work on comparative advertising.

Related Topics and Terms

Advertising, Advertising by Professionals, Advertising Claims Believability, Attitude, Brand Awareness, Brand Name, Competitive Edge, Product Positioning.

Mark Traylor
Department of Marketing
Graduate School of Business
Cleveland State University

COMPETITIVE SCANNING

Overview

Competitive scanning involves the systematic, constant surveillance of the activities of a company's competitors. Companies that engage in competitive scanning can benefit in a number of ways. However, benefits are likely to occur only if firms follow the various guidelines which the experts recommend for competitive scanning programs.

Scanning of competitors is a part of any company effort to monitor the environment. In addition to competition, the environment includes technology, legal/political arena, the economy, and societal norms and values. It can be argued that competitive scanning should be the major element in any system to scan the environment. Competitor analysis is viewed by many executives as the starting point for their companies' strategic plans.

Competitive scanning systems have a number of important, basic functions. They can be used for defensive intelligence, passive intelligence and offensive intelligence. Avoiding surprises from competitors is the main objective of the defensive intelligence function. Passive intelligence is designed to obtain benchmark data for objective evaluations of what competitors are doing, whereas offensive intelligence is designed to identify opportunities.

There are a number of important aspects of competitors' activities which may be monitored through competitive scanning. These include competitors' prices, market share, new product plans, strengths and weaknesses, basic goals and objectives, plans or strategies for achieving these goals and objectives, sales data, new markets, profitability data, acquisition plans, and research and development activities.

Examples

A large number of well-known companies have established formal departments to keep tabs on their competitors. Scott Paper designates the responsibility for monitoring competition to the marketing research and research and development departments. Westinghouse Electric allocates responsibility for monitoring competition to its consumer product research department. IBM's commercial analysis department monitors competitors. Citicorp has an executive whose title is Manager of Competitive Intelligence. Sperry Rand uses a staff group to watch competitors; the group reports directly to the president. Borden Chemical's consumer products division devotes a large amount of time to the purchase and evaluation of competitors' products.

Benefits

There is evidence that companies which have competitive scanning programs are more likely to be successful than these without a competitive scanning effort and are less prone to downturns. These results occur because these companies are able to alter their competitive strategies when appropriate. Some examples include:

1. Changing pricing strategy
2. Redesigning products
3. Reevaluating advertising or promotional campaigns
4. Modifying product packages
5. Adjusting trade discounts
6. Changing sales force tactics and strategies
7. Avoiding legal entanglements
8. Changing distribution patterns

A recent study of the competitive scanning practices of 92 high-growth companies revealed that the most frequent strategic adjustments occurred in pricing, costs, acquisitions, and new product development. For example, one company said that its competitive scanning operations enabled it to find out that Kodak was developing a disc camera and film and that they were able to display their own disc camera and film next to Kodak's on the day the new products were introduced.

Implementation

Two major sources of information can be used to gather data about competitors: published sources and field data. Published (or secondary) sources have the advantage of low cost, but lack timeliness, depth, and have a low level of aggregation. Field data essentially involve interviews with people in the industry or observers of the industry. Field data are timely and address significant issues more directly.

Companies have traditionally shown some strong preferences in regard to specific techniques used to acquire information concerning competitors. These include:

1. Feedback from sales personnel
2. Examination of competitors' advertisements
3. Examination of competitors' products
4. Reading competitors' manuals, catalogs and other literature
5. Talking to competitors' customers
6. Scrutinizing trade association publications
7. Reading business magazines and newspapers
8. Attending professional and technical meetings
9. Studying competitors' annual reports
10. Using directories containing information about competitors
11. Subscribing to government publications
12. Talking to competitors' suppliers
13. Studying competitors' 10-K reports

Evaluation

An effective competitive scanning program will involve a number of dimensions. Specific organizational responsibility for the scanning effort must be assigned. The office in charge should not be located in any particular functional area, and the competitive scanning officer should report to the company's chief executive officer. If companies make major decisions at the headquarters level, a centralized competitive scanning effort is recommended because personnel can fit various pieces of information together for a composite idea of competitors' current endeavors and future plans. On the other hand, if the firm makes decisions at divisional or strategic business unit (SBU) levels, a decentralized competitive scanning program is more appropriate.

At least one analyst and an assistant or secretary are probably required for medium- or large-scale companies and these individuals' sole responsibility should be competitive scanning.

If companies use outside firms to keep tabs on competitors, they can count on paying about $3,000 yearly for information about one competitor. Salaries and expenses for an internally operated competitive scanning program involving the number of personnel indicated above will probably run $50,000 to $60,000 a year.

In order to incorporate an effective competitive scanning program, companies need to assess the quality of the information obtained about competitors and determine which type of data is the most helpful. Information acquired must be used to alter tactics and strategies.

Companies need to ensure that their competitors are not deliberately misleading them to cause them to pursue wrong courses of action. For example, false information has caused companies to direct their products to inappropriate market segments, institute different production capabilities for product materials which were not needed, and develop a new product that was not needed by the market.

Conclusion

Despite the many significant benefits accrued by companies which engage in competitive scanning, evidence exists that many companies are not keeping tabs on their competitors or not doing so very effectively.

Approximately two-fifths of companies contacted about their competitive scanning efforts did not have such a program in operation. Those with competitive scanning efforts tended to locate them in a functional area, usually marketing, rather than give them separate organizational status. There was a reluctance to assign the competitive scanning department sufficient numbers of people or to provide them with a sufficient budget. Companies tended to emphasize data collection methods which were able to easily and quickly collect data about competitors and were inexpensive, but did not provide very meaningful information. A great deal of emphasis was placed on obtaining information about competitors' marketing operations, but little emphasis was placed on acquiring data about other functional areas or top managements.

Applications to Small Business

Small businesses need to keep tabs on their competitors. Because their competitors are usually geographically close to them, small businesses can use a variety of direct methods for determining what their competitors are doing.

The owner of a grocery store, for example, can "visit" competitors' stores and check on their prices, merchandise mixes, displays, and so on. A restaurant owner can have friends sample competitors' food and beverages and report back. A manufacturer can purchase a competitor's product and take it apart in order to discover materials used, quality of workmanship, and how it operates.

Less direct methods for assessing competitors are also available to the owner or manager of a small business. Articles in local newspapers, speakers at business luncheons, and yellow-page listings can be very helpful in providing information about competitors.

Since a small business may frequently consist of the owner or manager and only a few other employees, there is a tendency to direct all efforts toward the company's day to day operations and problems while ignoring opportunities for competitive scanning. This is unfortunate because small businesses, especially those in their early years, are quite vulnerable to tactics and strategies of their competitors. Thus, in order to protect themselves, they must allocate some of their time to finding out what the competition is doing.

Software/Databases

PTS F&S Indexes. Predicasts, 200 University Circle Research Center, 11001 Cedar Avenue, Cleveland, OH. An excellent source to begin collecting information about competitors. Over 6,000 business, trade, government, and corporate publications are indexed and articles on specific companies and industries are abstracted.

D&B Million Dollar Directory. Dun's Marketing Service, Parsippany, NJ. Provides basic information on 115,000 United States companies that have a net worth of $500,000 or more. Both public and private corporations are included. Data available are company name, address, SIC codes, annual sales, number of employees, and officers.

References/Sources

Cleland, David I., and King, William R., "Competitive Business Intelligence Systems," *Business Horizons* (December 1975): 19-28. Provides a plan for collecting, evaluating and disseminating information about competitors.

Cleland, David I., and King, William R., "Information for More Effective Strategic Planning," *Long Range Planning* (Fall 1977): 59-64. Discusses the types of information required for competitive scanning programs.

Hershey, Robert, "Competitive Intelligence for the Smaller Company," *Management Review* (January 1977): 18-22. Presents inexpensive ways that small companies can obtain data about competitors.

Jagetia, Lal C., "Developing an End-Use Intelligence System," *Industrial Marketing Management* 10: 101-107. Provides recommendations as to how industrial manufacturers can collect data about competitors.

Montgomery, David B., and Weinberg, Charles B., "Toward Strategic Intelligence Systems," *Journal of Marketing* (Fall 1979): 41-52. Discusses how to collect information about a company's environment, including its competitors.

Porter, Michael E., *Competitive Strategy*. New York: The Free Press. Discusses the information required for competitive scanning systems and the means available to collect this information.

Schendel, D.E., Patten, G.R., and Riggs, J., "Corporate Turnaround Strategies: A Study of Profit, Decline, and Recovery," *Journal of General Management* (Spring 1976): 3-9. Demonstrates the importance of competitive scanning.

Wall, Jerry L., "What the Competition is Doing: You Need to Know," *Harvard Business Review* (November/December 1974): 162-166. Provides the results of an extensive survey of companies' competitive scanning programs.

Related Topics and Terms
Business Intelligence Systems, Competitive Intelligence, Competitive Strategy, Intelligence Systems, Strategic Intelligence Systems, Strategic Planning.

Richard T. Hise
Department of Marketing
Texas A&M University

CONCENTRATED MARKETING

Overview

Concentrated marketing is a market coverage strategy in which the firm chooses to focus its marketing effort on one market segment or a few submarkets. Rather than cultivating the total market or most of its segments, as is the case with undifferentiated and differentiated marketing, concentrated marketing is designed to satisfy a smaller market target.

Concentrated marketing, or targeting one segment within the total market, is a suitable option for firms with limited resources. The strategy is especially appealing to new, small firms that lack the working capital and marketing expertise of their competitors. A single market segment coverage strategy is also a popular option for firms with highly specialized capabilities that meet the needs of a single segment of end-users in the market.

Examples

Several examples of concentrated marketing illustrate how a firm can achieve a strong market position in the segment it serves. Volkswagon has concentrated on the small car market for years. The Beetle became known as a car specifically designed and aimed at buyers wanting economy and sound performance in their transportation. Saab concentrates on the luxury/sport segment with its 900s and 900 Turbo models. Rolls-Royce, on the other hand, has a world-wide reputation as selling the ultimate expensive, luxury automobile.

Playschool concentrates its marketing of toys for preschoolers; Hewlet-Packard concentrates on the high-price calculator market segment; and retailers located along Rodeo Drive (Hollywood, California) cater to the most luxurious promenade in a community whose primary industry is pampered indulgence.

Astute retailers catering to teenagers recognize the importance of concentrated marketing. To attract high school students, for example, retailers might concentrate on "Greaseballs" (submarket including farmers and wrestlers), "Rah-Rahs" (submarket consisting of popular conformists with few intellectual or political interests), "New Wavers" (submarket that is fashion-conscious in an attention-getting way), "Apes" (submarket consisting of the smart students who are known to outsiders as "encyclopedias"), "Zobos" (submarket consisting mostly of female students distinguished by their high political consciousness and bag-lady fashion look), or on "Resistors" (submarket that defies fashion trends as evidenced by their uniform of T-shirts, sweatshirts, and chinos).

Benefits

Through concentrated marketing a firm can achieve a strong position in its chosen market segment. Concentrating on a single segment allows a firm to know thoroughly and understand its market. As a result, it can meet and respond to the specialized needs of the segment in a way that would not be possible with an undifferentiated marketing approach. In the process, the firm can acquire a unique reputation as is evidenced by the examples cited previously. In short, the firm can achieve competitive advantage by dedicating itself to one segment exclusively.

Concentrating on a segment of the total market may result in various operating economies because of specialization in production and marketing. If the firm can thus achieve cost advantages vis a vis competitors, the firm will be an above-average performer in the industry. As a result, concentrated marketing allows a firm to maintain profitable operations.

Implementation

Several factors need to be considered in employing concentrated marketing as a market coverage strategy. The factors are: company resources, product homogeneity, product age, market homogeneity, and competition.

Firms with limited working capital and marketing expertise may have little choice but to select a single market target. Limitations in financing, personnel, and promotion budgets favor a focus on only one segment in a market.

Products which are perceived to be homogeneous by consumers call for either undifferentiated or differentiated marketing, rather than concentrated marketing. Products perceived to be heterogeneous, on the other hand, are candidates for concentrated marketing, notably during the early stages of the product's life cycle.

When consumer needs or wants are diverse, concentrated or differentiated marketing is appropriate. The firm needs to ascertain what needs or wants are not fully satisfied by competitors and then develop a marketing mix designed to more fully satisfy them.

When competitors practice undifferentiated or differentiated marketing, opportunities may exist for a firm to exploit a smaller segment of the market. To do so profitably, the segment has to be identifiable, accessible, and of sufficient size and purchasing power to warrant a concentrated strategy. If such a segment has growth potential and is of little interest to competitors, it would be especially suitable for concentrated marketing.

Evaluation

Concentrated marketing involves a relatively high risk. For one thing, if demand or customer buying patterns suddenly shift, a firm may find that it has nothing to fall back on. Moreover, if new competitors with more resources appeal to the same segment, sales may decline substantially, resulting in severe cash flow problems and possible bankruptcy.

By focusing on a single segment, a firm might become so pre-occupied with its current customer base that it neglects to spot and respond to opportunities elsewhere in the market. Or, having acquired a special reputation, a firm might find it extremely difficult to re-position itself in light of changing market conditions.

Conclusion

Concentrated marketing is a market coverage strategy designed to appeal to a smaller market target than is the case with undifferentiated or differentiated marketing. By focusing on a single segment, firms are in a position to more fully satisfy the needs or wants of the particular segment. As a result, firms acquire a reputation of being a specialist.

The major risk of concentrated marketing is that the segment is vulnerable when market conditions change. The segment may be attacked by competitors and/or adversely impacted be de-regulation, technology, economic conditions, or cultural/ social changes.

Applications to Small Business

Small firms typically lack the financial resources of entrenched competitors. Consequently, a strategy of concentrated marketing is particularly appealing to such firms. Small businesses have numerous opportunities to offer a specialized product or product line targeted for a narrow segment of submarket. Market segments requiring special customer services are also common targets for small firms. At the retail level, examples of concentrated marketing employed by small businesses include restaurants, beauty salons, apparel stores, gift stores, food stores, and sporting goods outlets.

Software/Databases

Wonderwoman. CACI, Inc., 1815 N. Fort Myer Dr., Arlington, VA 22209. A current database of demographic and buying power facts and forecasts. Manipulates income and sales potential data for markets of any size or shape. Include counties, states, etc.

References/Sources

Biggadike, Ralph, *Entering New Markets: Strategies and Performance.* Cambridge, MA: Marketing Science Institute, 1977, pp. 12-20. Examines the strategies of forty firms that entered a market occupied by incumbant firms.

Cook, James, "Where's The Niche?" *Forbes* (September 24, 1984): 54.

Presents a critical look at the danger of designing too many options into U.S. automobiles.

Kotler, Philip, *Marketing Management*. Englewood Cliffs, NJ: Prentice-Hall, 1984, pp. 267-71 and 410-413. Discusses the terms "undifferentiated," "differentiated," and "concentrated" marketing. These terms were originally suggested by the author.

Resnik, Alan J., and Mason, Barry, "Marketers Turn to Counter Segmentation," *Harvard Business Review* (September-October, 1979): pp. 100-106. Discusses how marketers can analyze the profitability of a strategy of offering simpler products with lower price tags.

Smith, Wendell R., "Product Differentiation and Market Segmentation As Alternative Marketing Strategies," *Journal of Marketing* (July 1956): 3-8. A classic article discussing the alternative marketing approaches.

Steinberg, Bruce, "The Mass Market Is Splitting Apart," *Fortune* (November 28, 1983): 76-82. Demonstrates that the simplicity of undifferentiated or mass marketing has vanished.

Townsend, Bickley, "Psychographic Glitter and Gold," *American Demographics* (November 1985): 77-82. Shows why it is important to continually monitor the marketplace over time and across product categories because values and lifestyles are constantly changing. Has important implications for concentrated and differentiated marketing.

Whalen, Bernie, "Tiny Saab Drives Up Profits With Market-Niche Strategy, Repositioning," *Marketing News* (March 16, 1984): 14-15. Discusses Saab's concentrated marketing strategy.

Wind, Yoram, "Issues and Advances in Segmentation Research," *Journal of Marketing Research* (August 1978): 317-337. Reviews the status and advances in segmentation research.

Related Topics and Terms
Benefit Segmentation, Differentiated Marketing, Market Penetration, Market Segmentation, Product Differentiation, Product Positioning, Reposition Strategy, Target Market, Undifferentiated Marketing.

Ralph M. Gaedeke
Department of Management
School of Business and Public Administration
California State University, Sacramento

CONCEPT TESTING

Overview

New product failures are a major concern of marketing organizations. Much literature has been directed at understanding the causes of new product failure and better ways to predict product success. Concept testing is one method to estimate consumer reactions to a new product or service before the product is fully developed. This saves the time and cost of development while allowing the marketer some insights into whether or not it is financially advisable to create and market the product.

Concept testing is a form of exploratory research, and was developed to reduce product failure, increase the return on funds invested in designing and marketing new products, and to predict better and understand consumer responses to new products and concepts. One goal of exploratory research, and accordingly concept testing, is to learn more about a given marketing situation before a major commitment is made by the organization. Specifically, concept testing allows for concept evaluation, target market identification, and product position placement. It also provides the company an opportunity to make improvements on the product concept while still in the product design stage. In essence, it is an early screening mechanism to help anticipate how consumers will respond to the final product when (and if) it is presented in the market place.

Examples

There are many different ways to use concept testing. Service organizations may benefit from concept testing to see how well a new or additional service will be accepted by the current customer base. For example, a hospital was considering a new form of billing to expedite the payment process. Before initiating the service, they held two focus groups, each with twelve previous users of the facility, to test the idea of the new billing procedure. After exposing the group members to the concept statement, they proceeded to evaluate how well it was understood, how believable were the benefits of the procedure, the potential advantages and disadvantages of such a billing procedure, and their overall propensity to be attracted to such a system.

Such discussions can turn into an iterative approach to evaluating and refining the overall concept. As comments are made, the concept can be adjusted (improved), given input from the group. The new improved concept can then be tested and further refined. The number of iterations is dependent upon the complexity of the concept design and the willingness of the manager to keep testing the new concept.

If the concept is well defined, concept testing can also be performed using non-personal interviewing techniques. A well-known hair care facility in Toledo, Ohio was considering expanding to a new location with a new concept in hair care. To test how acceptable the product would be to the surrounding customer base, a telephone interview was conducted in which the following brief concept statement was read: "A new contemporary hair cutting and styling service is considering opening a store in the Uptown Shopping Center. This new salon would offer hair cuts for about $7.00 and styles for $12.00, and would not require any appointments. You could simply walk in when you wanted a hair cut or styling."

The respondent was then asked, "Do you think that you would use such a facility if it were available in the Uptown Shopping Center?" The answer choices read were 1) definitely would use, 2) probably would use, 3) probably would not use, and 4) definitely would not use. Several other questions were also asked in an effort to better understand exactly what type of hair care center was most appealing to the respondent.

By testing the concept before committing to the project, the hair care facility was able to estimate usage and customer reaction. Note that this type of non-personal data collection technique is best suited when the concept and potential customer base are well defined.

Benefits

The benefits of concept testing are numerous. In addition to the advantages listed earlier, such as understanding customer reactions, defining the target market, and product position placement, concept testing also provides an objective appraisal of the concept by outside judges.

Oftentimes, pressures cause managers to hastily approve a product before testing. If concept testing were an accepted and expected practice, managers would not be willing to accept the responsibility of product introduction independent of some formal testing. Secondly, product managers are often given specific goals to meet in a given time period. Therefore, product introductions are pushed through in order to meet the given objectives. The results of concept testing could be used to slow down the pressure to have a new product reach some arbitrary deadline. Finally, there is often pressure to introduce a product that has strong backing from influential members of the corporation. By a mandatory testing procedure, the introduction decision becomes more objective than subjective.

Implementation

Concept testing and advertising copy testing are often difficult to distinguish and separate from each other. Copy testing is designed to learn about the readers' reaction to the copy or advertising message. Concept testing is performed to evaluate the reaction to or acceptance of the actual product concept. Therefore, when the concept statement is designed it merely describes the product; it does not attempt to "sell" the product or describe the product in terms of benefits. Positioned between a copy statement and a concept statement is an embellished concept statement that includes some "sell." Specifically, this is a concept statement that has some promotional words included.

Before implementing a concept test, four questions must be answered. First, what will the concept statement be? As mentioned above, the statement may take on one of two forms. It may be a straight concept statement or it may include some "sell." To decide which statement design is best, an analysis of the product is helpful. If the product is very new and has few or no competitors, a bland or straight concept statement is best. The purpose of the test is to learn about the appeal of the new product. However, if the product is entering a well defined competitive product class it is more realistic to use a concept statement that has been embellished. This is needed since the product must be positioned against the competitors. If the statement includes a strong product position clause, the test may be referred to as a concept position test. In this case, not only the concept is being tested but also the position and the "sell" phrases.

Another consideration when writing the concept statement is the number of concepts or concept statements being tested. If there are many statements to be read, it is best to use more bland or straightforward concept statements without any sell. If a position test is desired, the number of statements should be limited.

It is important to note that recent literature has supported that there is a great deal of interaction between the reaction to the concept and the reaction to the words used to describe the statement. Specifically, the same concept idea described by different copy writers received statistically different scores. This indicates that it is not the concept in isolation being tested, but it is the concept in conjunction with the copy or word choice that is being tested. Because of this interaction, it is suggested that the less "sell" in a concept statement, the better or more pure the concept test will be.

The second issue is the design of the test itself. There are two distinct methods of concept testing. The first type is to test the concept monadically, which means to test the concept without explicit comparison to its actual or potential competitors. This type of test is best when the competition is hard to define or there is not a detailed search process involved in buying this product. Two comments have been made about this testing procedure. First, researchers say comparison is inherent and that it does not have to be explicitly introduced into the testing procedure. Secondly, it has been shown that this testing procedure has been a good predictor of actual product acceptance.

The alternative method of testing is called competitive environment testing. This type of testing implicitly introduces the respondents to the competition in addition to the concept being tested. It is said to be a more realistic type of testing since actual print ads for the concepts are prepared and actual competitors' ads are used. This method is best when there is a considerable amount of search involved in the purchase process and the general level of knowledge about the alternative competitors is relatively low.

The third consideration when designing the concept test is to develop the questioning series. There is a considerable amount of discussion regarding whether or not the price should be included in the concept statement or left as a variable to be discussed in the interview. If the product is entering an established product class and the prices are in a fairly tight range, price is probably not a significant variable. However, if the product is a new offering and the price will have an impact on the acceptance, price could be an important issue. If this is the case, there are two available options. Various price levels could be used in the concept statements. Using the example above, the concept would be read stating that hair cuts would be $7.00; the next statement would read that hair cuts would be $9.00, and so forth. The change in the acceptance level would be attributed to the price changes. Alternatively, the concept statement could be read without mentioning any prices and the respondents asked what price they would expect such a service would cost and/or how much they would be willing to pay for such a service.

The second concern with respect to the questioning series is the volume of usage projected for the consumer in a given time period. Specifically, if the objective of the concept test is to estimate acceptance and expected usage, it is necessary to 1) project how much of the product would be used in a given time period, and 2) estimate repeat purchase behavior (assuming the product was found to be acceptable after the first use). Such information is possible to obtain through objective questions; however, the data is tentative at best since the respondents have not actually used the product.

The ability of the concept test to predict the long term success of the new product introduction is the last issue mentioned. The tester must define the actual goal of the concept test with respect to what measures will be used to define a "success."

The decisions in the four areas listed above are not mutually exclusive. Overall, the decisions will be influenced by the objective of the test, the time and money that the organization is willing to invest, the number of concepts to be tested, and the type of product or service being tested.

Evaluation

The ability of concept testing to accurately predict consumer acceptance has been questioned for several reasons. First, it is often the case that the concept tested and the product offered on the market are not identical. Secondly, the product may match the concept but may be positioned differently in the market. In both cases, the test is not an accurate assessment of the market's reaction since the product is not being marketed in the same fashion that was presented in the test. Third, the time lapse between the completion of the test and the offering of the product may have afforded a change in the marketing environment. Specifically, competitors' reactions or economic changes may impact the consumers differently now than they did during the testing period. This situation also interferes with how well the test will predict the actual acceptance levels.

Alternatively, there is no information available on how many potentially good products did not pass the concept test because of a poorly written concept statement or an inappropriate questioning series.

Finally, there is also some interest regarding how well the concept test can predict repeat purchase behavior since the product has not actually been used. Repeat purchase is also strongly dependent on the counter moves of the competition. Buyer behavior is a key element in the long-term success of the product so consequently it is a concern to management.

Generally, concept tests are a fairly good source of information if the concept tested is identical to the product offered and possible changes in the marketing environment are monitored and taken into consideration.

Conclusion

Concept testing has proven beneficial in forewarning management as to how the consumer will react to new products. However, it does not predict adoption rates or the potential frequency of purchase. This suggests that the benefits of concept testing are limited to providing information about the immediate reaction or the first trial potentials of the product. Considering the vast number of product failures and the associated expense of a product failure, a well executed concept test definitely has a place in the product development stages of marketing.

Applications to Small Business

Concept testing can be used by large and small firms alike. The actual implementation of the testing procedure is the same; however, since the distribution area of the smaller firm may be somewhat limited, smaller firms may rely more on qualitative research from focus groups and other personal interviews than on collecting mass quantities of quantitative data.

References/Sources

Haley, Russell I., and Gatty, Ronald, "The Trouble with Concept Testing," *Journal of Marketing Research*, (May 1971): 230-232. The results of a study which shows the interaction between the concept and execution of the test are shown. The authors suggest that concept testing is in reality copy testing.

Moore, William L., "Concept Testing," *Journal of Business Research*, Vol. 10, No. 3 (1982): 279-293. This article gives a complete treatment of concept testing.

Tauber, Edward M., "Why Concept and Product Tests Fail to Predict New Product Results," *Journal of Marketing* (October 1975): 69-71. This article discusses the limited predictive capabilities of concept testing.

Tull, Donald S., and Hawkins, Del I., *Marketing Research Measurement and Method,* 3rd ed. New York: MacMillan, 1984. Chapter seventeen discusses the statistical methods used in concept testing data analysis.

Zikmund, William G., *Exploring Marketing Research,* 2nd ed. New York: CBS College Publishing, 1986. A brief introduction to concept testing is included in chapter four.

Related Topics and Terms

Applied Research, Commercialization, Idea Generation, Idea Screening, Product Design

Lori Mitchell
Department of Marketing
Kent State University

CONSIGNMENT SALE

Overview

A consignment sale is a unique agreement, usually between a wholesaler and a retailer, whereby the retailer agrees to take possession and a reasonable degree of responsibility for merchandise offered to sale. The seller, however, retains title to the goods as well as control of the channel of distribution. More specifically, the retailer provides floor or shelf space where goods may be displayed, maintains the goods in an orderly way, assures normal security and collects money for each sale. The wholesaler provides the merchandise, sets prices, marks them on items and takes back any unsold goods. He may or may not stock the shelves or arrange displays. In effect, the wholesaler consigns stock, but does not sell or transfer it to the retailer unit after a final sale is made. At that time, the retailer pays for merchandise sold and deducts a commission from the selling price.

Examples

There are several different methods of consignment selling. Consignment is the normal means of supplying such products as salted snacks, bakery goods and other items where freshness must be assured. Salespeople who work for the manufacturer routinely re-stock shelves or racks, replacing merchandise that has been sold and removing past-dated items. The store manager pays for the goods sold at the time they are replaced.

Another example of consignment selling is illustrated by a supplier who consigns merchandise such as cosmetics or housewares to supermarkets or specialty items such as sunglasses to service stations. The suppliers re-stock the merchandise and collect from retailers as described earlier. The Hanes Corporation uses this method to distribute L'Eggs hosiery products. A single display rack of the egg-shaped panty hose packages generates well over $1500 a year in profit.

Craftsmen or small-product entrepreneurs who develop unique products will often consign prototypes to gift or other specialty stores to determine if there is a market, and what prices should be charged. In these cases, the seller must offer exceptionally high margins to retailers, at least until the products begin to sell well, because the untried goods take up valuable selling space that could be used to display items with proven sales records.

Individuals also bring used clothing or other items to so-called Consignment Stores where they are displayed for sale to the public. The seller retains title to the merchandise and may reclaim it at any time, but sometimes a handling fee must be paid. The seller is paid only after a sale is completed. But the store takes a commission, often 50 percent or more, from the sales price.

Benefits

Consignment selling can help a seller break into an important market or to get a new individual account. In one case, a salesperson for a shirt manufacturer offered a retailer 120 extra days to pay for merchandise if he would carry the shirt line in his new store. But a competitor's salesperson made an even better offer. The full line of this brand would be put into the store on consignment, and the shirts would be paid for as they were sold. To make the deal even more attractive, the salesperson would maintain the inventory and stock the shelves. The second salesperson made this offer because the retailer had indicated he was pressed for cash during the expansion.

Retailers will also accept new merchandise on consignment when demand is unknown. The first order for a product may be handled this way, but sellers should agree to the arrangement only if they are anxious to have the product displayed. At the same time, the retailer benefits because the new items can be carried on a trial basis at no cost or risk. Consignment is also useful to retailers when they have exhausted their open-to-buy account, since it provides additional merchandise that could not be had otherwise.

Some sellers are anxious to sell on consignment because it permits them to control resale prices. This control can assure them a higher than normal return because, with the retailers' lower margin, the seller has extra protection with the controlled higher selling price.

Implementation

Although retailers assume no apparent risk in making consignment sales, they must recognize that sellers may be offering inferior goods on consignment because the goods cannot be sold through normal channels. To guard against this possibility, retailers should carefully inspect all consignment merchandise before it is placed in stock. If it is inferior, the image or reputation of the store may be damaged.

Retailers should also examine the consignment option carefully and satisfy themselves as to why a supplier is willing to accept this type of sales arrangement, and even push for it. In addition to assuring that the merchandise is of acceptable quality, retailers should determine if the vendors will really accept merchandise previously delivered on consignment if it does not sell or becomes shopworn. Some sellers claim that items were damaged or were not properly displayed, and demand payment for them. These and other points of potential disagreement should be negotiated in detail with the vendor at the outset, because the consignment method requires close cooperation between both parties. When implementing any type of consignment sale, retailers should also set a definite trial period, and specify in advance what will constitute a successful test.

Evaluation

Retailers need to maintain close control over the profitability of consigned goods because their margin is often lower for such goods than for other merchandise. This method should be considered only as a temporary arrangement. Larger chains may use consignment selling consistently for goods that are different from those normally carried because it may be too costly for chain warehouses to distribute comparatively low-volume lines, but smaller retailers sacrifice profits by accepting lower consignment margins over the long run. In evaluating the success and profitability of consignment selling, the following points should be considered:

1. Has the merchandise's trial period been long enough to determine whether or not it should be carried on a permanent basis? If the trial period has been completed, the consignment arrangement should be terminated. If the trial is successful, the goods should be purchased through normal channels in the future.
2. Could the floor or shelf space be used to better advantage than for the consigned merchandise?
3. Is the consignment vendor offering a reasonable profit margin? If the normal retail margin is 40%, consignment margins should be from 26 to 30%.
4. Has the vendor set a reasonable retail price for the merchandise?
5. Is the incentive to sell consignment merchandise the same as it is to sell goods the retailer owns?

Conclusion

Consignment selling is the only reliable method and channel that can be used for short shelf-life convenience goods, where the seller must consistently assure that stock is fresh and that outdated items are removed. It may also be used when retailers want to offer lines that are not carried by their normal wholesalers. Yet, many retailers are reluctant to use this method of selling. They realize its advantages, but know consignment is not the most advantageous way for vendors to sell, so they fear the merchandise may be poor quality or overpriced. Nevertheless, if retailers use proper safeguards when implementing consignment selling, it can be a useful method for carrying new lines of merchandise, fads or seasonal items at little risk. For the long run, however, straight purchase is the better method if a potential for future sales becomes apparent.

Applications to Small Business

Some smaller businesses depend on consigned goods to a major extent, sometimes for as much as 50 per cent of their inventory. Smaller distributors and retailers of expensive appliances, industrial or farm machinery and other high-cost, slow-moving items find it financially difficult to maintain inventories, so they make special consignment-type arrangements with manufacturers. In these, producers furnish display models for dealers and the dealers periodically place orders to cover anticipated sales with regional manufacturers' sales offices. The merchandise is shipped to a local public warehouse where it is held in the dealer's name, although title does not pass. When the retailer makes a sale, the goods are delivered directly from the warehouse to the customer, and the dealer is billed for the cost of the goods, storage fees and delivery. Nevertheless, the extra costs for the dealer are normally less than those incurred by carrying inventory.

Software/Databases

Since the basis of consignment selling relieves retailers of detailed record keeping, and involves them only to the extent of providing space and making the sale, they need no special software. For vendors, any micro database package for processing marketing information should suffice for keeping records on consigned inventory. One such package is *Prospector.* Concord Management Systems, Box 31108, Raleigh, NC, 27622.

References/Sources

Dalrymple, Douglas J., and Parsons, Leonard J., *Marketing Management,* 3rd ed. New York: Wiley, 1983, pp. 476-478. Provides examples of how consignment selling may be used for high-cost equipment and machinery, and how physical possession and ownership may be separated.

Duncan, Delbert J., and Hollander, Stanley C., *Modern Retailing Management,* 9th. ed. Homewood, IL: Irwin, 1977, pp. 344-345. Examines consignment selling from the standpoint of retailers and how they should deal with suppliers.

Redinbaugh, Larry D., *Retailing Management,* New York: McGraw-Hill, 1976, pp. 233-234. Discusses the advantages and disadvantages of consignment selling for both retailers and vendors.

Related Topics and Terms

Channel of Distribution, Convenience Good, Discount Store, Display, Impulse Good, Inventory Control, Open-To-Buy, Physical Distribution, Trial.

Hale N. Tongren
Department of Marketing
George Mason University

CONSUMER BEHAVIOR

Overview

Consumer behavior is the study of consumers and the decision-making processes, external factors, and individual characteristics that they use in making purchase decisions. The decision process under high-involvement conditions has been modeled by various researchers including Bettman, Howard and Sheth, and Engel and his colleagues with the early models being later expanded to include low-involvement decisions as well. In addition to the decision-making process, a variety of external and internal variables can affect the consumer's ultimate purchase decision. Among the external factors that can be influential in the purchasing decision process are socio-economic factors, family and reference group influences and cultural and subcultural variables. Internalized psychological variables such as motivation, attention, personality, attitudes, and learning are also considered to play a significant role in the understanding of consumer behavior.

Examples

Obviously the study of consumer behavior primarily involves how consumers make the decision to buy a particular product. In addition, however, the consumer behavior discipline is interested in a variety of other behaviors both prior to the actual purchase and after the purchase has been made. The search process, the consumption process and, in some cases such as in the purchase of a house, the disposal process, are all instrumental to the ultimate purchase decision.

As a result of studying the psychological processes consumers use in making a purchase decision, several decision-making models have been suggested.

A simplified model of a high-involvement consumer behavior decision which might be used to purchase a house or a car, for example, involves five main stages: problem recognition, information search, evaluation of alternatives, purchases, and postpurchase evaluation. In the problem recognition state, the buyer becomes aware of a discrepancy between an ideal state versus an actual state. There are several situations which may lead to problem recognition. For example, the consumer's stock of goods may be depleted, thus necessitating a purchase decision. In addition, motive arousal such as a basic drive (i.e., being hungry), autistic thinking (i.e., thinking about food), or an environmental stimulation (i.e., the smell of food) can create problem recognition.

The second stage of the decision process, the information search, involves both an internal memory search as well as an external search for information. A number of factors will help determine the extent of the internal memory search. First of all, the quantity and quality of existing information as well as the consumer's ability to recall that information will affect the amount of information currently accessible to the consumer. Secondly, the perceived level of risk—in terms of financial risk, social risk, and commitment—tends to motivate external search. Finally, the consumer's lack of confidence in his decision-making skills also tends to minimize internal search in favor of external searching.

Once the internal memory search has provided all of the information available, an external search is undertaken if still more information is required. The external search involves gathering pertinent information about the product from a variety of external sources such as reference groups, opinion leaders, family members, sales clerks, point of purchase displays, and product packages. Although the information itself may not cost any dollars, the search process is far from free. Among the costs that may be associated with the external search for information are: time costs, cost of gasoline and parking, psychological frustration, and time spent away from leisure activities.

The next step, evaluation of alternatives, involves a comparison of products considered to be viable alternatives. Using a heuristic, or rule of thumb, the consumer decides upon the salient attributes for the product and then evaluates each brand accordingly. Once an acceptable product has been selected, the buyer is ready to move on to the purchase stage of the process.

During the purchase stage, the consumer physically purchases the product. Depending upon the particular product, issues such as price, delivery, service, and warranty may be negotiated between buyer and seller during this stage of the decision process. The brand selected in the "alternatives" stage of the decision process is not necessarily the brand that is purchased; product availability, particularly in the case of stock outs, may influence the consumer's ultimate purchase regardless of the original brand selected.

Finally, after purchasing and using the product, the consumer will evaluate it during the post-purchase evaluation stage and determine whether or not the product lives up to expectation levels. The eventual outcome of this stage, satisfaction or dissatisfaction, feeds back into the initial stages of the purchase process to influence repeat purchases.

The decision process for low-involvement products, such as basic grocery items, is a simplified variation of the high-involvement model. The initial stage, problem recognition, is the same for both models. In the low-involvement version, however, the purchase may be made prior to the evaluation of alternatives. Since there is little risk involved with a low-involvement decision, it is beneficial to forego the costly search and evaluation steps of the process until after the purchase has been made. Therefore, it is not until the third and final stage of the decision process, the alternative evaluation stage, that an actual comparison of products occurs.

Benefits

The benefits of understanding consumer behavior are numerous. First and foremost, in order to fully utilize the marketing concept, it is essential that the marketer know his customer. Not only does the study of consumer behavior help him identify his customer, but it also gives him insight into the decision process as well as the external variables and psychological constructs that influence the purchase decision. By understanding these variables, the marketer can hopefully influence the purchase process.

In addition, the study of consumer behavior is helpful to consumers themselves by providing governmental agencies with information necessary to institute and regulate public policies such as package labeling. By helping consumers improve their buying skills, the study of consumer behavior opens their eyes to marketer influencing (i.e., manipulation) attempts.

Implementation

In addition to examining the decision process, the study of consumer behavior also involves examining both the external variables present in the environment and the psychological constructs unique to each individual which influence the product purchase.

Reference groups, or the groups of people with whom an individual associates, are important to the decision process since individuals take on many of the same qualities of the group to which they belong. In addition, groups have the power to influence their member's behavior. By using reward or coercive power, a group either rewards or punishes an individual for his behavior. Legitimate power is used by evoking the individual's internalized values such as his patriotic duty. Expert and referent power are frequently used in advertising messages. Expert power results from an individual's expertise in the group whereas referent power results from a feeling of identification an individual has with the group.

A consumer's socioeconomic status also plays an important role in the purchase process. Socioeconomic status is largely determined by an individual's source of income, occupation, housing, and education. Warner's Index of Status Characteristics ranks individuals on the basis of certain objective criteria such as house type, or occupation.

Cultures and subcultures are particularly significant when studying consumers in the United States due to the diverse population. Culture includes intangible concepts as well as values and acceptable behavior patterns. Subculture consists of the values and behaviors unique to certain races, ethnic groups or other human characteristics. Hence, cultural and subcultural differences may dictate considerably different preferences and buying patterns for various consumers.

In addition to external factors, a number of psychological constructs unique to each individual are also pertinent to the understanding of consumer behavior. Motives, or those internal energizing forces that orient a person's activities toward a goal, can be combined to form either: (1) motive linking, which occurs when various levels of generality are used; (2) motive bundling, when two or more motives are combined; and (3) motive conflict, where major motives conflict in the marketplace. For example, a person may be motivated to visit a dentist out of fear for future dental problems without preventive maintenance as well as a desire to have white teeth. Hence motives can be both negative and positive, and an individual can act on more than one motive at a time.

Learning and memory can also affect consumer behavior. Very simply, learning can be defined as a relatively permanent change in behavior or cognitions which results from experience. Both psychological theories of classical conditioning and operant conditioning are used in marketers' analysis of consumer learning.

Memory, or the ability to recall information stored in the brain, is particularly crucial to the search stage of the decision process. Whereas short-term memory can be thought of as the workspace for information processing, long-term memory is a relatively permanent storehouse for information. The amount of information an individual is able to process, as well as how that information is processed, are highly individual traits.

Attitude, another significant construct in understanding consumer behavior, is considered to be a learned predisposition to respond in a consistently favorable or unfavorable manner towards an object, idea or individual. Attitudes, in general, remain relatively stable throughout an individual's lifetime.

Finally, personality is another psychological construct which can be influential in the purchase process. Although there are as many definitions of personality as there are researchers who attempt to define it, they all seem to agree that personality tends to be consistent throughout an individual's lifetime. Although marketers have tried to match particular products with personality types, such as risk takers versus risk avoiders, the results have been inconclusive.

Evaluation

Consumer behavior can be researched and evaluated using several different research methodologies depending upon what aspect of consumer behavior is being examined.

To understand the decision process, protocol analysis, information integration or informational monitoring research approaches are frequently used. Methods such as word-association tests, projective tests, or depth interviews are used as cognitive measures. In addition, a variety of observational techniques, both unobtrusive and obtrusive, such as eye movement analysis, are used to investigate consumer behavior. Finally, surveys in all forms—telephone surveys, mail surveys, and personal interviews—are used in descriptive research as well as in experimentation.

Conclusion

Although a relatively recent discipline, the study of consumer behavior has progressively enriched the understanding of why people buy and how the decision to buy is made. Many areas within the discipline, however, are particularly ripe for further research. While the study of how an individual makes a decision is difficult enough to understand, the problem is further complicated when the decision involves a group of people; hence, family decision-making offers new challenges to the consumer behavior researcher. Attitude theory, well advanced by Fishbein and his multiattribute model, still leaves questions unanswered despite the modifications made in the extended model. While personality research has been studied by psychologists for a significant amount of time, its relation to the field of marketing needs additional investigation. Finally, related topics such as the adoption and diffusion of new products as well as the role of opinion leaders can be extremely helpful in furthering understanding of consumer behavior.

Applications to Small Business

The application of consumer behavior research to small business is similar to applications used by larger businesses. Probably the most recent use of consumer behavior in a nontraditional setting is investigating how consumers use, purchase, and evaluate services. Since the service industry provides an intangible product, understanding the purchase process is similar yet unique from the typical product purchase decision. In addition, the study of consumer behavior in relation to nonprofit donations provides a relatively new application of the discipline which could be instrumental in helping charitable organizations understand, and ultimately, solicit their constituents.

References/Sources

Bettman, James R., *An Information Processing Theory of Consumer Choice.* New York: Wiley & Sons, 1969, Chapters 1-3 summarize information processing and provide an outline of his decision model.

Coleman, Richard P. and Rainwater, Lee, *Social Standing in America: New Dimensions of Class.* New York: Basic Books, 1978. Discusses variables included in determining social class.

Davis, Harry L., "Decision Making Within The Household," *Journal of Consumer Research* (March 1976): 241-260. Recaps research on family decision-making and discusses problems associated with past research methods.

Engel, James and Blackwell, Roger, *Consumer Behavior.* Chicago: The Dryden Press, 1982. Appendix compares three decision process models; the Howard-Sheth model, the Howard model and the Engel Blackwell model.

Fishbein, Martin and Ajzen, Icek, *Belief, Attitude, Intention and Behavior: An Introduction to Theory and Research.* Reading, MA: Addison-Wesley, 1975. Chapters 1 and 2 review theories of attitude and highlight proposed theory.

Howard, John and Sheth, Jagdish, *The Theory of Buyer Behavior.* New York: Wiley and Sons, 1969. Chapter 2 summarizes a theory of buyer behavior with four sets of constructs: input variables, output variables, hypothetical constructs, and exogenous variables.

Kassarjian, Harold H., "Personality and Consumer Behavior: A Review," *Journal of Marketing Research* (November 1971): 409-418. Review of research on the personality variable and its relation to marketing.

Kotler, Phillip, *Marketing for Non-Profit Organizations.* Englewood Cliffs, NJ: Prentice-Hall, 1975. An application of marketing and consumer behavior research to non-profit organizations.

Loudon, David L., and Della Bitta, Albert, *Consumer Behavior.* New York: McGraw-Hill, 1984. An overview of consumer behavior research and applications.

Morrison, Bruce John, and Dainoff, Marvin J., "Advertisement Complexity and Looking Time," *Journal of Marketing Research* (November 1972): 396-400. Provides an example of eye movement analysis to evaluate advertisements.

Rogers, Everett M., "New Product Adoption and Diffusion," *Journal of Consumer Research* (March 1976): 290-301. Summary and discussion of adoption and diffusion literature.

Related Topics and Terms

Adoption Process, Attitude, Consumer Heuristics, Diffusion Process, Information Processing, Motive, Multiattribute Model, Opinion Leader, Protocol Analysis, Questionnaire.

Jane R. Ziegler Sojka
Department of Marketing and
Small Business Management
The Wichita State University

CONSUMER HEURISTICS

Overview

Heuristics, or rules of thumb, are routinely used by consumers when evaluating a number of product alternatives prior to purchase. By using one or any combination of the various heuristics, the consumer is able to systematically screen and evaluate the products available for purchase; thus saving time and energy. While some rules may be as simple as "buy American," or "always buy the least expensive," the actual process that a consumer uses to apply these rules may, in fact, be quite complicated.

Examples

Although researchers are not certain exactly how many heuristics consumers use, ten basic categories are generally accepted. Which precise rule or rules are used by the consumer is contingent upon the task, the particular situation, and the individual.

The majority of heuristic rules can be broadly classified as either compensatory or noncompensatory. In compensatory heuristics, a negative product attribute such as a high price or poor quality may be offset by a positive ranking on another product characteristic such as a free installation or a strong warranty. That is, brand strengths may compensate for product weaknesses. Using the *linear compensatory* heuristic, for example, product alternatives are described through multiple attributes and then these scores are either added or averaged. Since each product is evaluated by the sum total of its attributes, information processing occurs by brand comparison.

A noncompensatory rule, on the other hand, automatically eliminates any brand in which one attribute is considered unacceptable by the level of standards set by the consumer. Hence, noncompensatory heuristics are frequently used in conjunction with other decision rules as a method to winnow the choice set to a more manageable number before evaluating the remaining products in greater detail. Using the *conjunctive* heuristic, just one example of a noncompensatory rule, minimum acceptable standards are specified for each product dimension. If a brand does not meet the minimum cut-off point, it is automatically eliminated regardless of how well it might rate on other attributes.

Another example of a noncompensatory heuristic is the *lexicographic* rule in which attributes are sequentially ordered in terms of importance to the consumer. Product choices are evaluated on the basis of the most important attribute. If two or more products are evaluated similarly, the consumer then compares them on the basis of the next most significant attribute until the tie is broken and one brand is preferred. Note that, unlike a compensatory decision rule, a high value on one attribute can not compensate for a weakness on another product dimension.

In addition to the *linear compensatory, conjunctive* and *lexicographic* heuristics, consumers also use other heuristics, including affect referral, general information, disjunctive, sequential elimination, elimination by aspects, lexicographic semi-order, and additive difference. These heuristics vary in information required and processing difficulty.

Benefits

Heuristics provide the time and value conscious consumer with a road map for decision-making—a mechanism for the efficient search and evaluation of competing product alternatives.

Without the guiding influence of heuristics to streamline the choice process, one of two clearly unacceptable behaviors would dominate: (1) consumers would suffer from frustration and information overload caused by the incomprehensible task of synthesizing all available product information, or (2) the choice process would be reduced to one of mere random selection in which no information is processed and no brand preferences are developed.

Thus, by mediating these two extremes, heuristics enable the consumer to: (1) save valuable time and energy, (2) circumvent frustration and information overload, and (3) choose an alternative based upon salient and relevant criteria.

An understanding of consumer heuristics also benefits the marketer. By suggesting which heuristic the consumer "should" use, and by controlling the order and amount of product information, for example, the marketer can influence the choice process.

Implementation

In the study of heuristics, it is important to see how a consumer would apply a particular heuristic to make a purchase decision. As an example, suppose a consumer used a conjunctive rule to determine which calculator to purchase. After collecting information on three different brands of calculators available, he then determines the minimum acceptable cut-off points for the attributes he considers significant in a calculator. Suppose Brand A carries a 90 day warranty. By the standards set by the consumer, a one year warranty is considered the absolute minimum acceptable; hence Brand A would be eliminated as a potential purchase. Suppose Brand B, on the other hand, carries a one year warranty, but was judged by the consumer to be rated as only fair in terms of functions. Since the consumer determined a good rating on functions was the minimum acceptable standard, Brand B would also be removed from the potential purchase set. Finally, an evaluation of Brand C reveals that it carries a one year warranty as well as being rated excellent by the consumer in terms of calculator functions and is judged to be above the minimum standards set for the remaining attributes. Hence, Brand C would be purchased in this example.

The lexicographic rule extends the disjunctive rule so that additional evaluative criteria can be incorporated, if necessary, to make a decision. Thus, if a choice can not be made by using the most important criterion, additional criteria can be considered based on their importance to the consumer. Using this decision rule, all brands would be evaluated on the basis of the most important criterion. Take for example, another hypothetical consumer desiring to purchase a calculator. Based on his budget, he has determined that price is the most important criterion for his choice of calculators. Suppose Brand A sells for $9.00, Brand B sells for $9.00 and Brand C sells for $12.00, and the individual has set $10.00 as the maximum amount he is willing to pay. Hence, Brand C would be eliminated as a viable alternative. However, to decide between Brands A and B, the consumer would have to consider the second most important attribute. Suppose ease of use was considered to be the next most important attribute and that Brand A was evaluated to be very easy to use while Brand B was considered to be somewhat difficult to use. As a result, the consumer would choose to purchase Brand A.

It is important to note that the evaluation of product attributes is purely subjective. Hence, consumers using the same heuristic rules, and evaluating the exact same set of brands could conceivably choose different products depending on how each evaluates the different Brands' attributes. In addition, the hierarchy of attributes, which also affects the ultimate choice tends to vary from consumer to consumer. Thus it becomes obvious that individual characteristics play an important role in determining the final outcome of the decision.

Evaluation

It is not always clear which heuristic a consumer may have employed in a given situation, because the measurement of heuristics—like most other psychological processes—is a difficult task. Bettman (1979), however, outlines six methods researchers use to study consumer heuristics.

1. *Correlational methods,* such as brand belief surveys, first ask respondents (i.e., consumers) to evaluate the attributes for a set of known brands. Next, respondents rate their overall preference for each brand. The researcher then *estimates* a separate brand evaluation score for each heuristic which he correlates with the consumer's *actual* brand preference rating. It is then inferred that the heuristic with the highest correlation is the one actually employed.

2. *Information integration approaches* do not require respondents to reveal their own beliefs; rather respondents are asked to match specific belief levels with specific evaluation levels. Special analysis of statistical variance techniques is then used to determine the predominant heuristic.

3. *Protocol methods* require the respondent to think out loud as he shops. Comments are recorded and later analyzed to determine which heuristic was used.

4. *Information monitoring approaches* typically involve asking respondents to

select pieces of brand attribute information from a display board arranged in a matrix fashion with each row representing a different brand, for example, and each column representing a different attribute. Respondents select pieces of information represented by the matrix cell values until they are able to make a choice among the brands. By analyzing the sequence of information selected by each respondent, the researcher is able to classify respondents according to the heuristic used.

5. *Eye movement analysis* involves the use of a sensing apparatus that tracks the consumer's sequence of eye movements as he examines a number of product alternatives. The sequence of movements is then analyzed to determine which heuristic was employed.

6. *Response time analysis* may be applied by measuring the elapsed time required for a consumer to select a product from a group containing several choices. The longer the elapsed time, supposedly, the greater the information processing effort required. Thus, some insights are gained as to the heuristic employed or the number of attributes evaluated.

Conclusion

Not only can heuristics help consumers simplify the decision process, but they can also be helpful to marketers who can influence the purchase decision by suggesting which heuristics and which attributes the consumer "should" use. In studying heuristics, however, it is important to recognize when consumers are most likely to use them. Many of the same factors that come into play when determining the amount of search activity to be undertaken also affect the use of heuristics. The more urgent the need, the more likely a simplistic heuristic such as "buy American" will be used. In contrast, the more significant the product or the more complex the alternatives, the more likely complex heuristics will be used.

In addition, consumers do not always use the same decision rule; consumers will tend to apply different rules under different circumstances. Also, the use of two rules to make one decision is not uncommon; protocol analysis studies have found that consumers may use a noncompensatory heuristic to initially screen alternatives followed by a compensatory rule to evaluate the remaining alternatives.

Finally, it is important to remember that heuristic research is still in its infancy. Additional research is necessary to fully understand the heuristic concept, how it is applied to consumer purchases, and how marketers may best benefit from an understanding of the topic.

Applications to Small Business

Small businesses—especially manufacturers and retailers—are currently in an advantageous position to successfully apply heuristic theory. Capitalizing upon consumer heuristics must begin with the recognition of three key points. First of all, the consumer's choice of a particular brand often depends upon which heuristic is employed and/or upon which product attributes the consumer considers relevant when implementing the heuristic. Secondly, an individual consumer may, over time, utilize several different heuristics and several different attributes. Finally, the selection of specific heuristics and attributes depends upon several task, situation, and individual factors. By manipulating the marketing mix, the small business marketer can influence some of these factors—and thereby influence the choice of heuristics and attributes, as well as the purchase decision itself.

Of course, many task, situation, and individual factors are beyond the influence of marketing action, but some are not. For example, the marketer may be able to manipulate the amount of pertinent information processed by the consumer, and the order by which it is processed. To illustrate, if a small business manufacturer believes his brand to be the overall superior brand, he might advertise and promote the importance of *several* "equally critical" attributes, thus prompting the consumer to select one of the compensatory heuristics and weigh brands according to the touted attributes. Conversely, a competitor whose brand was clearly superior on only one or two attributes might ignore or downplay the other attributes in hopes that the consumer would apply the lexicographic heuristic.

A second factor the marketer might influence is the ease of obtaining product information. Sometimes the consumer will discount, temporarily bypass, or totally disregard otherwise key attributes if the information about those attributes is difficult to obtain. The breakfast cereal shopper may disregard the price-per-ounce attribute, for example, if competing brands are packaged in several different sizes making extensive calculations necessary to determine the lowest price-per-ounce choice.

Finally, knowledgeable consumers with limited past experience in specific product categories are more likely to rely on the heuristics and attributes suggested by marketers. As consumers gain knowledge and experience with the product category there is tendency to utilize the affect referral heuristic and thus evaluate brands in a wholistic fashion: an overall positive, negative, or indifferent evaluation of each brand—regardless of specific attribute evaluations. Consequently, the small business marketer should ensure that the consumer enjoys a positive first experience with the brand followed by the implementation of a brand-name recognition strategy.

References/Sources

Assael, Henry, *Consumer Behavior and Marketing Action*. Boston: Kent Publishing Co., 1984. Decision making strategies discussed in chapters 2 & 20.

Bettman, James R., *An Information Processing Theory of Consumer Choice*. Reading MA: Addision-Wesley, 1979. Chapter 7 presents a thorough and rigorous overview of heuristics, their implementation and factors that influence their usage by consumers.

Duncan, Calvin P., and Olshavsky, Richard W., "External Search: The Role of Consumer Beliefs," *Journal of Marketing Research* (February 1982): 32-43. Study establishes that the heuristic-type beliefs consumers have about the marketplace and their own capabilities influence the extent to which they externally search for information.

Engel, James F., and Blackwell, Roger D., *Consumer Behavior.* Chicago: Dryden Press, 1982. Chapter 17 discusses the choice process and the effects of its outcome.

Grether, David, and Wilde, Louis, "An Analysis of Conjunctive Choice: Theory and Experiments," *Journal of Consumer Research* (March 1984): 373-384. Uses the conjunctive choice rule as a formulated constrained optimization problem.

Olshavsky, Richard, and Acito, Franklin, "An Information Processing Probe into Conjoint Analysis," *Decision Sciences,* 11 (1980): 451-470. Used protocol analysis to identify actual choice rule used by respondents.

Svenson, Ola, "Process Descriptions of Decision Making," *Organizational Behavior and Human Performance,* 23 (1979): 86-112. Good overview of heuristic research and specific decision rules.

Related Topics and Terms
Beliefs, Choice Heuristics, Choice Models, Choice Strategies, Compensatory Decision Rules, Conjunctive, Consumer Behavior, Consumer Decision Rules, Consumer Information Processing, Decision Rule, Disjunctive, Evaluative Criteria, Information Processing Strategies, Lexicographic, Non-compensatory Decision Rules, Rules of Thumb.

Jane R. Ziegler Sojka
Charles L. Martin
Renee King
Department of Marketing
and Small Business Management
The Wichita State University

CONSUMER PANEL

Overview

A consumer panel refers to a group of consumers who agree to provide information about themselves over time. Many companies rely on consumer panels for information about how consumers buy both new and established products. In addition, consumer panels may be used to track consumer reaction to changes in marketing strategy including pricing, distribution, and promotion. Consumer panels may be preferred to one-shot surveys of consumers because panel information permits tracking of the changes in the behavior of individuals over time. In addition, it is often possible to obtain more information from panel members who are questioned on several different occasions. Panel information may be more accurate than one-shot surveys because panel studies receive higher rates of response. Panel members can be trained to minimize reporting and recall errors. Consumer panels are not without their problems, however, as they are costly to establish and maintain. Considerable effort is necessary to ensure that the panel is representative of the firm's customers.

Examples

There are two major types of consumers panels: continuous and interval. The same information is gathered on a repetitive basis from members of continuous panels. For example, two commercial research firms, MRCA (Market Research Corporation of American), and NPD (National Purchase Diary, Inc.) operate continuous panels containing over ten thousand households. Members of these households record in purchase diaries such information as brand name, store name, and purchase price for both packaged goods, such as cereal, and soft goods, such as clothing, that they purchase. Panel members mail their diaries to the commercial firms weekly or monthly, depending on the frequency of purchase of the items in the diaries. These commercial firms provide information about the relative market shares of competitive products, as well as other information about the purchase behavior of panel members, to client companies on a fee basis. Yearly subscription costs to a continuous panel may range between $50,000 to $150,000 depending on the type and amount of information needed by the company.

Other methods, such as pantry audits, daily telephone interviews, or observation of behavior with mechanical devices may also be used to gather information about members of continuous panels. A. C. Nielsen uses audimeters which are attached to panel members' television sets to monitor television viewing habits of member households. The results, called Nielsen Ratings, can be made available to advertisers and networks within 24 hours after shows have been aired. Nielsen supplements the ratings with the results from viewing diaries which identify the age and sex of viewers watching the televised shows.

BehaviorScan, a system developed by Information Resources, Inc., uses checkout scanners installed in supermarkets and drug stores to track the buying habits of more than 35,000 households across 14 U. S. geographic areas. Itemized information about each purchase made by panel members is stored on a computer file. It is not necessary for panel members to record their purchases in diaries; they simply present a plastic card for identification purposes during checkout.

Members of interval panels, also called mail, omnibus, and standby panels, are contacted only when information is needed. Generally, different information is collected from these panel members each time they are contacted. For example, they may be asked about their buying habits and attitudes toward microwave cooking on one occasion and their car purchase behavior on another survey. Thus, the same behavior is not tracked for a selected group of individuals over time.

NFO (National Family Opinion, Inc.) and CMP (Consumer Mail Panels Division of Market Facts, Inc.) are two commercial operators of interval panels. Both firms have thousands of names of households who have agreed to answer mail questionnaires. They can select samples of households from their pools which are demographically balanced to match the characteristics of the U. S. population. In addition, these firms can provide a sample of cooperative respondents with specific characteristics such as certain ages, income groups, or residents of selected geographic areas.

The cost of obtaining information from interval panels is dependent on the specific needs of the client firm. Firms may be able to obtain information at a cost of less than $5 per completed interview if they are able to use the multi-client studies provided by NFO and CMP. These studies involve monthly mailings of several short questionnaires to a balanced sample of households. These questionnaires are designed to fit the needs of the clients who contract for the study. Generally, 70% or more of the panel members who receive these multiple questionnaires complete and return them. Each client firm receives the results from their individual questionnaire.

Benefits

Information available from consumer panels can help firms make better marketing decisions. Continuous consumer panels help firms monitor shifts over time in the purchasing patterns of both their customers and the buyers of competitive products. Stouffer Foods used the results of consumer panels to help shape its successful line of frozen diet entrees, Lean Cuisine. In the case of Fruit Float, one of the hottest new products of 1973, NPD panel data helped the manufacturer recognize a potential problem. Although the product appeared to be an apparent success, with more than 10% share of the $110 million packaged pudding/whipped dessert market 5 months after introduction, an examination of purchases of panel members disclosed that the product had a very low rate of repeat purchase. Most of the sales consisted of first time triers; market share for the product fell below 5%

by the end of the product's first year.

Continuous panel information can be used to gauge the effectiveness of promotional programs. The United Dairy Industry Association used household purchase data from an MRCA panel to measure the response of consumers to promotional deals for dairy products. They found that promotional deals result in substantial increases in the level of purchase of dairy products.

Panel data can help firms develop a better understanding of certain market segments. A study of the eating habits of members of the NPD panel disclosed some surprising facts, including that people classified as naturalists eat french toast with syrup in addition to "natural foods." In another study using MRCA data, apparel shoppers were found to buy their apparel from different types of stores. Certain apparel shoppers, for example, split their patronage between department and specialty stores.

Purchase information gathered from continuous consumer panels is generally more accurate than information collected with a one-shot survey. Consumers are more likely to misreport their purchase behavior if they are asked to recall purchases made in the past. They may forget some purchases and incorrectly report the details such as price or brand for other purchases. Panel members are asked to record their purchases in their diaries on a daily basis. Mechanical methods such as checkout scanners can produce even more accurate records of consumer purchases.

Panel data can also be more reliable because relatively few panel members fail to cooperate in providing requested information. In general, 70% or more of a sample of panel members return their completed diaries or other types of questionnaires to panel operators on time. Mail surveys of nonpanel members frequently experience response rates of less than 25%.

Another advantage of consumer panels is that it is possible to gather more information from panel members than with a one-shot survey. Demographic, attitudinal and product ownership items can be gathered from each panel member in a separate interview. Consequently, other surveys of panel members can be devoted exclusively to the areas of primary interest to the firm which conducts or sponsors the study.

Panel data can also be relatively less costly than other methods of gathering the same data. One reason is that the cost of selecting and recruiting a sample of participants can be spread across the numerous sets of data collected from panel members. It is not necessary to incur these sampling costs each time a study is conducted.

Implementation

Consumer panels should be used if management is convinced that the benefits from their use exceed the cost of acquiring the information from these panels. Assuming there is a need for consumer panel information, the next step is to decide how to gather that information. It may be more economical to gather the needed information through a one-time survey than a continuous study of the behavior of a panel of consumers. One-time surveys can be relatively efficient methods of providing profiles of the characteristics of both present and potential customers.

The actual establishment of continuous consumer panels requires considerable time and effort. Panel members have to be recruited; only about 10% of the people contacted agree to participate in panels. It is especially difficult to recruit the very rich, the very poor, blacks and other minorities. New panel members need to be recruited continuously to replace panel members who drop out of the panel. Panel dropout rates of 10 to 20% per year are common. In addition, it is generally necessary to add new members to the panel as the original members age to ensure that the panel is representative of a dynamic population.

Panel members need to be trained how to record their purchase behavior. It is also necessary to continue to monitor the reporting behavior of long time panel members to ensure that they are providing complete and accurate information.

Considerable effort is required to code, edit and analyze panel information. For example, NPD has to process the diaries returned by its 13,000 member households every month. These diaries contain more than 20 items of information for each brand or product purchased by the household during the month.

Panel operations are generally too costly for firms to establish and maintain themselves. It can cost $100 or more per household to recruit and train panel members. Annual operating costs can also exceed $100 per household. Businesses who need panel information may find it more economical to use commercial panel firms. Although MRCA established the first commercial panel in 1941, the number of commercial panels has expanded rapidly with approximately 100 national panels available today. It is necessary to evaluate these panels carefully prior to selecting one as a supplier of panel information.

Evaluation

Management needs to determine which commercial panel operations provide the needed information with the desired degree of accuracy. Cost of the panel information also must be evaluated as part of the decision involved in selecting a commercial supplier of panel data. An evaluation of the types of information available from commercial panel operators would include determination of whether the firm's products and markets were covered by the panel.

The characteristics of panel members need to be examined to determine if there are sufficient numbers of panel members who are customers of the firm. National continuous panels are generally constituted to provide adequate market coverage for firms who market products purchased by the majority of the U. S. population. Their coverage may be inadequate for firms who market either in limited regions of the U. S. or sell products such as home sewing machines which appeal to a small portion of the population. If the market coverage offered by available continuous panels is inadequate, firms should consider using a sample of the members of an interval panel such as NFO or CMP. These panel operators are able to select a sample with specific characteristics from their pool of consumers who have agreed to answer mail questionnaires.

Timing of availability of panel information should also be considered when selecting commercial consumer panel services. In the case of some marketing decisions, such as those involving new products or new promotional campaigns, it may be critical to have access to information about consumer behavior immediately following the actual purchase or viewing of commercials. Speed of response of panel operators may be much less critical for established products or other types of decisions.

Issues concerning the accuracy of available panel data include sampling, questioning, and analysis procedures. Firms should examine the samples used by panel operators to ensure that the characteristics of panel members are similar to those of the population of interest to the firms. Panels may not be representative because many consumers refuse to be members of panels and many who do join drop out in the first year of membership. Responses of panel members may be influenced by the questions they are asked. Reputable panel operators institute numerous procedures, including considerable training and careful study of the impact of question wording on responses, to ensure data accuracy. Established analysis procedures are also a necessity to ensure that panel results are consistently edited, accurately coded, and analyzed to provide needed information. Standardized reports provided by commercial firms may not fit the needs of firms. Most commercial suppliers are willing to either develop specialized reports or to provide computer tapes of the raw data for firms who request them.

The cost of purchasing information from commercial firms is generally significantly less than if a firm decides to establish and maintain its own panel. However, the cost of purchased panel data varies with each commercial firm and the types of reports needed by the firm. Generally, the cost increases as the requests of a firm become more specialized. Special data analyses and data tapes are added costs because the commercial firm cannot spread the cost of this service among all its clients who subscribe to the more general services. Companies who purchase data tapes from commercial panel operations need to assess both the time and effort needed to develop the computer systems and the support personnel necessary to generate specialized reports from these data tapes.

Conclusion

Most firms have used consumer panels for information about the purchase and media behavior of consumers of their products and services. A study of 59 companies revealed that 63% currently use consumer panels; usage is highest among manufacturers of consumer goods and advertising agencies and lowest among industrial companies and the financial services. Those firms which do not use consumer panels may either not feel a need for panel information or there may not be any commercial firms who provide panels which cover desired markets or products. The cost of establishing and operating a panel is generally prohibitive for a single firm. It is generally more economical to purchase panel data from a commercial firm which spreads the costs of its panel operation among many client firms.

Firms which are considering use of panels need to realize differences among panels. Some provide continuous reports from panel members while interval panels provide a sample of consumers who have agreed to respond to mail questionnaires. Information may be gathered from panel members through surveys and observation.

Applications to Small Business

Consumer panels can be an important source of marketing information for small businesses, particularly manufacturers, wholesalers, and retailers. Information from continuous panels can help them track behavior of their consumers over time. In addition, interval panels can be valuable because they can help small businesses find samples of customers for their specific product or localized market without the expense of screening all members of the population. Of course, the small business manager needs to carefully examine the information offered by any commercial research firm to ensure it meets the needs of his company.

Software/Databases

PC/NEWPROD. New Product Planning Model, Applied Decision Systems, 33 Hayden Ave., Lexington, MA 02173. Can be used in conjunction with consumer panels to project five-year sales volume and profit contributions for new products based on estimates of trial, repeat purchase and units bought per purchase.

References/Sources

Carman, James M., "Consumer Panels," *Handbook of Marketing Research.* New York: McGraw-Hill, 1974, pp. 2-200—2-216. Discusses techniques used to analyze panel data.

Cotton, B. C. and Babb, Emerson M., "Consumer Response to Promotional Deals," *Journal of Marketing* (July 1978): 109-113. Provides an example of the use of panel data to measure the impact of different promotional strategies on product sales.

Elrod, Terry, and Winer, Russell S., "An Empirical Evaluation of Aggregation Approaches for Developing Market Segments," *Journal of Marketing* (Fall 1982): 65-74. Uses data from purchase records of consumer panel to test criteria for aggregating customers into market segments. Consumer response proved a superior segmentation variable.

Hisrich, Robert D., "Response Quality of Consumer Mail Panels: An Exploratory Investigation," *Akron Business and Economic Review* (Fall 1983): 20-24. Results of a study of members of a consumer mail panel suggest that quality of response depends on degree of interest of panel members in completing questionnaires.

Markus, Gregory B., *Analyzing Panel Data.* Beverly Hills: Sage, 1979. Demonstrates the use of different models including Markov, Wiggins, Coleman, and loglinear models to analyze panel data.

Parfitt, John, "Panel Research," *Consumer Market Research Handbook.* London: McGraw-Hill, 1972, pp. 143-177. Discusses use of panel services available in Great Britain. Techniques for forecasting sales using panel data are presented.

Poston, Carol, "Dear Diary Panel . . . Electronics is Changing the Monitoring of Consumer Behavior," *Advertising Age* (February 9, 1981): s-12,13. Highlights the impact of use of computer technology in consumer panel operations.

Sudman, Seymour, and Ferber, Robert, *Consumer Panels.* Chicago: American Marketing Association, 1979. Presents an excellent primer of the issues involved in operating and using consumer panels. A detailed reference of consumer panel information is provided.

Wind, Yoram, and Lerner, David, "On the Measurement of Purchase Data: Surveys Versus Purchase Diaries," *Journal of Marketing Research* (February 1979): 39-47. Discusses a study which links individual consumers' survey responses to their panel diary recordings. Results cast considerable doubt on the accuracy of survey data in measuring individual respondent brand purchase behavior.

Related Topics and Terms
Continuous Panel, Diary Panel, Interval Panel, Mail Panel, Marketing Research, Omnibus Panel, Standby Panel, Tracking Studies.

Stephen K. Keiser
Department of Business Administration
University of Delaware

CONSUMERISM

Overview

Consumerism is a concept that became popular in the mid-1960s as consumers became increasingly dissatisfied with product performance and safety, misleading and deceptive business practices, and inadequate handling of complaints to redress these problems. It refers to the efforts of individual consumers, organizations, government agencies, and professional associations to protect people from practices of both business and government that infringe upon their rights as consumers. President John F. Kennedy first enumerated these rights in a special "consumer interest" message to the 87th Congress in 1962, as follows:

1. *The right to safety*—to be protected against the marketing of goods which are hazardous to health or life.
2. *The right to be informed*—to be protected against fraudulent, deceitful, or grossly misleading information, advertising, labeling, or other practices, and to be given the facts needed to make an informed choice.
3. *The right to choose*—to be assured, wherever possible, access to a variety of products and services at competitive prices and, in those industries in which competition is not workable and Government regulation is substituted, assurance of satisfactory quality and service at fair prices.
4. *The right to be heard*—to be assured that consumer interests will receive full and sympathetic consideration in the formulation of Government policy, and fair and expeditious treatment in its administrative tribunals.

Consumerism is not a recent phenomenon in the marketplace, but a long-run movement that periodically has a resurgence in response to economic, social, technological, political-legal, and ethical changes in the business environment. Each period of consumer unrest has been stirred by some catalyst—declining real income, higher prices, or publicity given some product tragedy, safety or health hazard, or misrepresentation. But, the root problem in all cases seems to be a credibility gap, i.e., people's lost confidence in the ability or willingness of business self-policing and existing government regulations to protect them.

Examples

Consumer rights has been an increasingly important issue since the nineteenth century when the Industrial Revolution ended the close relationship between production and consumption. The current wave of consumerism which began in the 1960s has been described as kaleidoscopic in nature because its scope has continuously changed and shifted. Beyond the issues of product performance, product safety, product information, the handling of complaints, and deceptive business practices, the consumer movement began to include a spectrum of new concerns about the quality of the physical environment—(air, water, and noise pollution), discrimination (race, sex, age), and societal injustice, and such disparate issues as automobile safety, truth in packaging and lending, meat inspection, high food prices, gas pipeline safety, tire performance, cigarette advertising, "empty calories" of breakfast cereals, hospital care, low-income housing, coal mine safety, radiation control, public utility rates, effectiveness of drugs, dangers of insecticides, toy safety, and misleading television advertising (especially aimed at children).

Widespread publicity given to societal problems made consumers more aware of weaknesses in existing laws and their enforcement. General dissatisfaction with the impersonalization of the marketplace further stimulated the consumer movement. Widespread use of computers tended to frustrate consumers in trying to resolve complaints or correct a billing error. Mass marketing and new technology, while improving living standards, increased physical and psychological distance between sellers and buyers.

Businesses and governments still have much work ahead of them in responding to consumerism. According to a recent nationwide sample of 2,500 households by the U.S. Office of Consumer Affairs (OCA), 70 percent of consumer complaints about unsatisfactory products and services are never remedied. OCA researchers concluded that most private industries and government agencies are inept in handling consumer complaints and do an inadequate job of informing the public how to file and follow through on their complaints.

Benefits

The consumer movement has brought about many benefits over the years that have helped all Americans enjoy a higher standard of living and a better quality of life. A significant distinction of recent consumer movements from those of the 1900s and 1930s is the development of means to translate dissatisfaction into effective pressure on government. More than four times as much consumer protection legislation has been enacted in the past three decades than in all the previous years of the twentieth century together. This outpouring of protective legislation was spurred by numerous consumer spokesmen who were not only able to identify and publicize problems, but also able to follow up with workable programs for federal legislative action.

Great changes have been made in the previously slow response of business and government to consumerism. A number of firms have developed formal programs and made real commitments to resolve consumer issues. Many manufacturers have devised specific programs to help consumers to get their complaints resolved. Maytag introduced Red Carpet Service in 1961 to improve its appliance repair service. In 1967, Whirlpool created its Cool-Line which provides a 24-hour, national, toll-free, 7-days per week telephone service to answer customer problems. In addition, Whirlpool set up over 1,200 nationwide franchised repair and service outlets for its products. Frigidaire makes an Award of Merit to dealers and service units that meet rigid service standards. Zenith established a customer relations department in 1968; Motorola created an Office of Consumer Affairs in 1970; and RCA implemented a consumer affairs office at the corporate level in 1972. Procter & Gamble provides toll-free complaint numbers on its consumer packaged products. Some companies have long-standing, outstanding records of consumers orientation. For example, J.C. Penney adopted its "the customer is always right" consumer philosophy in 1913; Macy's established a Bureau of Standards to test merchandise in 1927; and Giant Food developed its own consumer bill of rights in 1974 which added "the right to redress and right to service" to Kennedy's original four rights.

Most individual companies join trade associations to represent their views as a group, and many of these trade associations have responded to consumerism by coordinating and distributing research findings, developing consumer and company education programs, establishing product standards, and handling complaints. The Major Appliance Consumer Action Panel (MACAP) is an effective educational and complaint-resolution program sponsored by the Association of Home Appliance Manufacturers, the Gas Appliance Manufacturers Association, and the American Retail Federation. The Bank Marketing Association stresses a Financial Advertising Code of Ethics (FACE) for member firms; the Direct Mail/Marketing Institute sets industry guidelines and operates a consumer action line; and the National Retail Merchants Association has a Consumer Affairs Committee and provides information to the public. The Better Business Bureau (BBB) is the largest and broadest business-operated trade association involved with consumer issues. It emphasizes self-regulation as an alternative to government legislation. The BBB publishes educational pamphlets and books, investigates complaints, supervises arbitration panels, conducts consumer affairs audits, provides ethical behavior guidelines, holds symposia, publicizes unsatisfactory practices and identifies the firms involved, and has local offices throughout he country.

Consumers are constantly pushing standards higher, demanding more candor and broader recognition of social responsibilities from business and government. Although Americans have achieved enormous benefits from the consumer movement, business and government still have much to do before reaching that elusive goal of all successful organizations—providing customer satisfaction.

Implementation

Following his declaration of the rights of consumers in 1962, President Kennedy created a Consumer Advisory Council to represent consumers. Then two years later, President Johnson appointed Esther Peterson as his Special Assistant for Consumer Affairs and established the President's Committee on Consumer Interests. Soon, a torrent of bills were introduced at all levels of government as many politicians saw consumer legislation as an "inexpensive" way to build an impressive domestic legislative record and placate irate consumers in an inflationary period. Some of the laws enacted were: 1965 Fair Packaging and Labeling Act; 1966 National Traffic and Motor Vehicle Safety Act; 1966 Child Safety Act; 1966 Cigarette Labeling Act; 1968 Consumer Credit Protection Act; 1968 Child Protection and Toy Safety Act; 1970 Fair Credit Reporting Act; 1972 Consumer Product Safety Act; 1974 Equal Credit Opportunity Act; 1975 Truth-in-Leasing Act; 1975 Consumer Product Warranties Act; 1975 Fair Trade Laws; 1977 Debt Collection Act.

President Nixon established a new Consumer Protection Division in the Department of Justice to defend the public from several specific unfair and deceptive practices, such as "bait and switch" advertising, selling used goods as new, and misrepresenting price reductions. The Consumer Product Safety Commission (CPSC), established in 1972, is the federal agency with the major responsibility for product safety. During the period from 1975 to 1982, one third of all 1976 to 1980 model U.S. cars were recalled by the CPSC, including 45 percent of 1980 models. The CPSC has issued product recalls for many millions of items, besides automobiles. It has also banned products such as flammable contact adhesives, easily overturned refuse bins, certain asbestos-treated products, and Tris (a flame retardant used in children's clothing that was linked to cancer).

Although many older Americans were taught from childhood that "you can't buck the system or fight city hall," public crusaders like Ralph Nader have demonstrated to others what one determined individual can do even against the giants of industry.

Evaluation

Early business reaction to consumerism might fairly be described as largely critical and defensive. At first, many businesspeople seemed to share the attitudes that (1) consumerism destroys public confidence in the free enterprise system, (2) the market is self-regulating, and (3) government legislation tends to deprive consumers of freedom of choice. Some businessmen even tried to dismiss consumerism as merely a fad that would soon pass. But foresighted business leaders saw consumerism not as a threat but an opportunity to get a jump on competition by being among the first to respond positively to consumer desires in the marketplace.

Most successful and respected leaders of business and government organizations recognize that no one can predict consumer expectations for they are infinitely elastic—bounded only by individual imagination. But, any perceived gap between these continually rising expectations and product or service performance will likely lead to consumer dissatisfaction and a demand for legislation. The U.S. Chamber of Commerce states that an organization can operate at any one of four basic attitude levels: (1) obeying the law, (2) meeting the recognized public demands, (3) anticipating new social initiatives, or (4) leading the way. It is largely up to top management in business and government to initiate positive on-going programs to keep up with consumer needs and ensure the success of their organizations.

Conclusion

Instead of posing a threat to free enterprise, consumerism can offer an opportunity to progressive businesspeople to gain a competitive advantage. Anticipation of passage of new consumer legislation—then being the first to provide this extra customer protection—can measurably enhance the company's offerings in the marketplace. Too often, the businessperson is likely to see only the good aspects of his own product and react defensively to any criticism of it. He tends to assume that if the attackers knew as much about his product as he does, they would think as he does. Such an attitude is understandable, but it is also dangerous to business health because consumerism is a strong force and business policies must be designed to deal responsively with consumer issues; the government will implement laws protecting consumer rights that businesses refuse to product. Consumerism should be viewed as an opportunity—not a threat. Businessmen who respond positively to this long-run force will gain a significant advantage over those who ignore or attempt to deny the basic "rights of consumers."

Applications to Small Business

Consumerism has and will continue to affect all businesses, whether large or small. Although big business may have the finances to conduct highly publicized programs in response to consumerism, such as setting up toll-free "hot lines" for consumer inquiries or complaints, small business owners can do similar things in a smaller way. For example, the small business owners can make sure that all store personnel are trained to treat customers with courtesy, to listen to their concerns, to be as helpful as possible, and to ensure that all complaints are handled promptly and fairly to retain the goodwill and patronage of customers. Paraphrasing Tom Peters, co-author of the best-selling book, *In Search of Excellence:* "If you treat customers with simple courtesy, you'll be virtually alone because few other businesses do it." Today's customer seldom ever hears a "thank you" from store clerks when paying for a purchase.

Small businesses are generally much more in touch with their customers and thus more likely to know what consumer concerns are before large businesses do. By responding quickly and sensitively to consumer needs, wants, and complaints in the marketplace, small businesses can secure profitable competitive niches for themselves.

Software/Databases

Various consumer databases and some software programs have been generated by such government agencies and consumer organizations as the U.S. Office of Consumer Affairs (OCA), American Council on Consumer Interests, Common Cause, Consumer Federation of America, Consumers' Research, Consumers Union, Environmental Defense Fund, Federation of Homemakers, National Resources Defense, Nader Organizations, National Consumers' League, National Home Economics Association, Public Interest Research Group, and the Sierra Club. Moreover, many commercial research organizations periodically conduct research on various research issues that are oftentimes reported or summarized in newspapers and magazines.

References/Sources

Anderson, Rolph E., "Consumer Dissatisfaction: The Effect of Disconfirmed Expectancy on Perceived Product Performance," *Journal of Marketing Research* (February 1973): 38-44. Discusses the relationships between consumer expectations and product performance.

Dameron, Kenneth, "The Consumer Movement," *Harvard Business Review* 17 (Spring 1939). Provides the background on the depression that spurred an increase in consumer activism.

Marketing News (February 22, 1980): 8. An interesting study of consumers' attitudes toward various consumer-related problems.

Related Topics and Terms

Attitudes, Cognitive Dissonance, Environment, Ethics, Expected Value, Federal Trade Commission, Marketing Concept, Selective Perception, Social Responsibility.

Rolph E. Anderson
Department of Marketing
Drexel University

CONTAINERIZATION

Overview

Containerization refers to the use of a fairly large shipping container for the movement and storage of goods between and among different transportation modes. The container may be a box, bin, cage, or highway trailer, with or without wheels. Almost any type of cargo can be containerized.

The objective of containerization is to enable the shipper to be assured of the prompt and undamaged arrival of the total shipment. Door-to-door service is obtained, and the only time the container is opened is for customs inspection. In addition to door-to-door service, containers also are used for port-to-port movements as well as for door-to-port/port-to-door shipments. Dry cargo shipments are the most common use of containers, but shipments for such cargo as refrigerated goods, liquid bulk materials, livestock, automobiles, and lumber and mill products frequently employ some form of container.

The dimensions and capacities of intermodal containers vary. A typical container carries between 22,000 and 50,000 pounds. It measures eight feet by eight feet in width and height, while the length varies between 10 and 40 feet. Barge containers can carry from 750,000 to over 900,000 pounds, while aircraft containers house shipments which weigh between 10,000 and 15,000 pounds.

Examples

Sears Roebuck had been making shipments from Chicago to Denver by rail to reduce transportation costs. It discovered that costs of unloading the rail shipments and transferring them to motor carriers amounted to over 80 cents per 100 pounds. By using piggyback service, highway trailers on rail flat cars, the firm claimed annual savings of over $100,000. By using containers for overseas shipments, the American Rice Company was able to minimize damage claims by an estimated $80,000 a year. Intermodal container shipments were utilized by the Phillips Petroleum Company to effect a reduction in service time from the Gulf Coast to the Middle Atlantic states by three days.

Benefits

The use of containers offers several benefits, including:

1. Protection from handling, shock, temperature, dirt, moisture, and contaminants;
2. Prevention or minimization of theft and pilferage;
3. Elimination of extra handling;
4. Completion of door-to-door service to customer;

5. Reduction in transportation charges;
6. Extension of container reuse; and
7. Facilitation of intermodal service, thereby obtaining the benefits of more than one transport mode.

Implementation

To employ containerization, shippers should be aware of the various options available to them. These choices are as follows:

1. Interchangeable container—the most common method which is adaptable to flatbed trucks, rail cars, barges, and oceangoing vessels.
2. Trailer-on-flatcar (TOFC)—highway trailers placed on rail flatcars.
3. Container-on-flatcar (COFC)—intermodal containers detached from the highway trailer chassis and placed on rail flatcars.
4. Roll-on-roll-off (Ro-Ro)—highway trailers and rail cars are driven directly on and off specially-adapted ships.
5. Barge-on-Board (Lash/Seabee)—cargo is loaded on barges, which in turn are loaded on an oceangoing vessel. At destination, the barges are removed from the ship and towed to final destination.
6. Container-on-Airplane (birdyback)—aircraft containers called "igloos" are placed on highway trailers.

Having identified the various containerization choices, shippers must determine what their intermodal needs are. To help in this determination, such factors as packaging materials, containers, volume levels, weight, dimensions, and product characteristics are considered. In addition, the factors of customer requirements, the use of more than one transport mode, materials handling equipment, and storage facilities impact on a containerization decision must be taken into account. From a cost perspective, container costs must be measured against the previous costs of transportation plus handling costs, losses from pilferage or damage, and extra packaging costs.

The implementation of a containerization program also demands standardization to the greatest extent possible. For example, if a firm plans to use both motor and rail service on an intermodal basis, the designated carriers will advise which container size is best accommodated in their respective systems. The lack of agreement over standardization continues to plague the transportation industry. Therefore, it is incumbent upon the shipper to learn which sizes are best handled by the carriers expected to handle the firm's business. Questions of reusability and return of empty containers also should be resolved prior to making a containerization investment.

Evaluation

Once the decision to containerize has been made, shippers should evaluate the system periodically in order to determine its effectiveness and efficiency. To assist in the process, the following questions must be answered:

Are customer reactions favorable?

Are they receiving improved transport service in terms of delivery time and condition of goods?

What is the amount of claims being filed and awarded?

How does this amount compare to pre-containerization?

How do transportation and handling costs compare to similar costs before containerizing?

What are the transportation and handling costs per hundredweight or other measure?

What is the degree of container utilization in terms of days?

What are the container investment costs in terms of hundredweight or other measure?

Are the benefits of intermodal shipments being realized to the extent that the inherent advantages of each mode are maximized?

What system exists for the return of empty containers and what are the additional costs?

Are packing costs increased or decreased as a result of employing containerization?

What additional materials handling costs are being incurred, and what is the degree of utilization of this equipment?

What are total logistics costs and how do they compare to pre-containerization costs?

Conclusion

There are several basic conclusions to be drawn about containerization. First, it facilitates the movement of goods to customers and to the firm, benefiting from the use of more than one mode of transport. Second, containerization increases the probability of goods arriving in a safe and good condition, thereby minimizing loss, damage, and delay claims. Third, total logistics costs should be reduced, primarily because of the lower handling costs. Fourth, technology is dynamic in this area, suggesting that containerization advancements should be reviewed annually.

There are also precautions to be observed. A high degree of utilization must be obtained to justify the container investment. Because of the lack of standardization agreements, compatibility with the carriers' systems is required. The operating issues of returnable and reusable containers must be resolved prior to purchase. Finally, it should be understood that while transportation and handling costs will be lowered, container costs and materials handling equipment costs will be increased.

Applications to Small Business

Any small business which ships or receives goods in carload or truckload quantities is a likely candidate for containerization. In addition, a firm which engages in importing and/or exporting activities generally will participate in some form of containerized shipments. The advantages of assuring the prompt and safe delivery of goods as well as the minimizing of handling costs are obtainable. Facilitating the documentation process and reducing legal liability between carriers represent additional benefits of containerization.

The impact on small business is extensive. Increased customer satisfaction is obtained, thus providing a sales stimulant. Logistics costs should be greatly reduced, particularly transportation, packaging, and handling costs. By increasing sales and reducing costs, profit should rise. Inventory control also will be enhanced because of improved delivery times and a reduction in damaged goods. By using containerization, the firm also strengthens its competitive position.

Before embarking on a containerization program, however, the small business firm should consult the various transportation carriers that are likely to move the goods. The lack of container standardization, differences in transportation charges, and the technology change rate all have a great impact on containerization. Consultation also is urged because of the need for additional materials handling equipment to accommodate containerization. Storage facilities also may have to be redesigned to handle containerized freight.

In summary, the small business firm that can utilize containerization should do so. Containerization is the most practical way to transport goods intermodally, and the benefits greatly outweigh the costs.

References/Sources

Exporters' Encyclopedia. New York, NY: Dun & N. Bradstreet, 1983. This book contains information about import regulations and procedures required for shipping to every country in the world, with special sections on packing and containerizing.

Farris, Martin T., "T.O.F.C.: A Coordinated Transportation Service," *Modern Transportation: Selected Readings.* New York, NY: Houghton Mifflin, 1967. Excellent discussion on rail and truck transportation.

An Introduction to Materials Handling. Pittsburgh, PA: Materials Handling Institute, 1966. Basic information about equipment, procedures, and technology relating to materials handling, including containerization.

Ports of the World, 19th ed. Philadelphia, PA: Insurance Company of North America, 1985. Information is presented about the various port facilities throughout the world as well as helpful assistance on the use of containerization.

U.S. Department of Commerce, *A Basic Guide to Exporting.* Washington, D.C.: Government Printing Office, 1983. Mechanics and guidelines for exporting, including a discussion on transportation and containerization.

————, *Ocean Freight Rate Guidelines.* Washington, D.C.: Government Printing Office, 1982. Factors to be considered in shipping goods by ocean vessels are assessed.

Related Topics and Terms
C.O.F.C., Containers, Igloos, Intermodal Distribution, Intermodal Variations, Materials Handling, Multimodal Movements, Piggyback, T.O.F.C.

Warren Rose
Department of Business
Analysis & Research
Texas A&M University

CONTROL

Overview

Planning, implementation and control are the three major elements of basic management. Control refers to the systematic examination and appraisal of operations to ensure decisions that are consistent with a firm's strategic objectives and business thrust. Measurements are an inherent part of control, and are used to track stated objectives. There are four categories of controls in marketing: 1. Sales/Customer, 2. Performance, 3. Profit/Cost, and 4. Strategic.

Examples

Included in the first category, Sales/Customer, are detailed breakdowns such as geography, product type/size/grade/color/brand, discounts, credit terms, order size, commission, customer size, and sales method; e.g., telemarketing or direct. Many firms also use ratios such as sales force to sales, advertising to sales, sales promotion to sales, marketing research to sales, and sales administration to sales. Which analysis is used depends on the information that is available, and what is most logical for a particular circumstance. Controls are customary within an industry. For example, market share, the percent of total product sales for one firm, is customarily used to compare competitors within the consumer packaged goods industry. Market share is not used as extensively for industrial goods because accurate data is not often available. Most companies perform some type of analysis with respect to sales or customers, but often these measurements could use substantial improvement.

The second category, Performance, also contains a variety of measures that are meant to be indications of efficiency. Some common measurements that are used include number of sales calls per day, cost per sales call, entertainment per sales call, advertising cost per 1000 buyers, number of inquiries, % of sales on deals, inquiries per demonstration, economic order quantity, inventory, and transportation costs.

The third category, Profit/Cost, involves financial analyses directed toward marketing areas. The basis for this analysis is the P&L statement, and includes items such as billings, bookings, margins, and expenses. Segmental analysis allows measurement of the financial impact within a market segment, thereby providing a reliable basis for decisions such as product addition, modification, or elimination.

The fourth category, Strategic, is intended to assess the overall marketing strategy of the firm. One common method of evaluation is to ask employees how well the firm is doing in marketing, and compare the results from year to year. A second method is a marketing audit, which is a comprehensive, systematic examination of a firm's marketing. Items examined include environment, strategy, organization, systems, productivity and functions. It is preferable for an audit to be performed by an independent entity rather than internally for the same reason that firms use outside accounting auditors. An audit is costly and generally advisable only every three to five years.

Benefits

The four categories of control explained above provide a firm with data which will assist in making product and marketing decisions. With a consistent control system in place, companies can judge their growth patterns relative to their goals, to their past performance, and to their fiscal capabilities. Too frequently companies use "intuitive" control systems, and while those might suffice to make short run decisions, long term planning should be based on performance patterns, and the relationship of patterns in one segment of company operations to the others.

Implementation

Information constraints may make it initially difficult to track results for each objective that a firm sets. Even within a firm, measurements can differ from division to division due to differences in information availability. Standardized measures are not as important as usable and obtainable measures that track the efficiency and progress of a particular objective. Accounting data is a good starting point, but accounting systems were not designed to address marketing problems and are seldom focused enough to be of use to a marketer. For example, a firm might be making a profit overall, but the profit is coming from only 20% of the customers while the remaining 80% are actually diluting profits.

It is advisable not to overdo implementation of a control system. Managers can easily find themselves inundated by paper and data, but information necessary to make effective decisions is missing or hidden in the quagmire of paper. The key is to plan a control system, and allow evolution of that system as the manager and the firm change.

Evaluation

The end result of managerial control is to make decisions about addition, elimination, or modification of activities. It is not a simple or inexpensive decision to add a product to the line, to eliminate a product that has considerable sunk costs, or to modify a product that has historically been successful. Consider Coca Cola and their long history of only one product with the name Coke. Additions, eliminations, and modifications of their cola line alone make national news, and the decisions to change are not simple ones.

An important aspect of control evaluation is the feedback loop. A common mistake companies make is to collect and analyze information, externally from customers or internally from the sales force, and provide little or no feedback to the decision makers and managers that could use the information to make better decisions. With respect to sales information, for example, weekly monitoring, monthly reviews with responsible persons, quarterly reviews with top management and related functions, and annual reassessment of markets and structures provide the necessary feedback loop. Simply adding marketing aspects to the quarterly financial review forces attention to the marketing issues.

Conclusion

The need for control is reflected in the filtering of new product ideas:

Initial Ideas	58
Ideas that pass the Initial Screen	12
Ideas that pass Concept Development	3
Ideas that pass Market Testing	2
Ideas that become Commercial Successes	1

Without control mechanisms the firm would be investing in 57 ideas that would ultimately be unsuccessful in the marketplace, an obvious waste of time, money, and effort. Other areas of marketing have similar results with control measures; consequently, control is an area that could use substantial improvement in most companies.

Applications to Small Business

Most small business control systems are limited to accounting analysis. One study indicated that the smaller the business the poorer the controls in terms of setting objectives and measuring progress toward those objectives; nearly half of the companies surveyed had no marketing controls, and more than half did not know profitability of individual product lines.

Software/Databases

Marksman Market Analysis. Control Data Business Information Services, 500 W Putnam Ave., Greenwich, CT 06830. Gives access and *control* over voluminous internal and external sales data. For use by marketing executives.

Promoter. Management Decision Systems, Inc., 200 Fifth Ave., Waltham, MA 02254. Decision-support system for marketing managers, helps evaluate and improve effectiveness and profitability of consumer goods promotions.

References/Sources

Booz, Allen, Hamilton, *The Management of New Products,* 1968. A consulting firm survey and report detailing success rates of new products.

Kotler, Philip, *Marketing Management,* 5th ed. Englewood Cliffs, NJ: Prentice-Hall, 1984, chapter 24. This is an excellent overall text, and the chapter on control is the most specific available.

Mossman, Frank H., Crissy, W.J.E., and Fischer, Paul M., *Financial Dimensions of Marketing Management.* New York: John Wiley, 1978. Chapter 2 provides a thorough discussion of segmental analysis.

Related Topics and Terms

Critical Path Method, Idea Screening, Management by Objectives, Market Share, Marketing Audit, Marketing Information System, Marketing Plan, Profit and Loss Statement, Profitability Analysis, Sales Quota, Segmental Analysis.

Terry C. Wilson
Department of Marketing
West Virginia University

COOPERATIVE ADVERTISING

Overview

Cooperative advertising is any advertising for which the cost is shared by two or more businesses, each of which should benefit from the advertising. The most common form of cooperative advertising is *vertical cooperative advertising,* which involves the retailer and the retailer's suppliers (usually manufacturers, but sometimes wholesalers). It is "advertising mutually sponsored by a manufacturer and retailer that is placed locally by the retailer and sells a branded product to local consumers." For advertising the manufacturer's product according to the manufacturer's program specifications, the retailer is reimbursed at a specified rate. Although rates vary widely, a somewhat standard reimbursement procedure is that the retailer and the manufacturer each pay half the cost.

Retailers also sometimes receive a variation of vertical cooperative advertising—*promotional advertising allowances.* These allowances are offered periodically by manufacturers to support specific promotional programs or drives. The allowance is usually based on a percentage of the invoice value of the promotional merchandise offered by the manufacturer to the retailer, such as 5 percent off-invoice.

Another cooperative advertising form becoming increasingly common is *horizontal cooperative advertising,* or joint advertising. Many variations are possible; all the independent jewelers, pharmacies, realtors, or insurance agents, for example, may join in sponsoring advertising campaigns to professionalize their public image. Shopping centers or downtown shopping area associations often advertise for the benefit of all members. On a national scale, manufacturers of complementary goods such as outboard motors and boat hulls may jointly advertise. The following discussion, however, focuses on vertical cooperative advertising.

Examples

Most retailers who carry products (rather than service retailers) use some form of cooperative advertising. The use varies by trade lines among manufacturers and by type and size of stores among merchants. Recent estimates show that the following percentages of ad budgets are co-op: discount stores, 20%; jewelers and furniture and household goods stores, 30%; clothing merchants, 35%; shoe stores and department and specialty stores, 50%; food stores, 75%; and television, radio, and appliance dealers, 80%.

Although no one has precise figures on how much co-op advertising is used, industry leaders and observers indicate the total made available to retailers may be as much as $10 billion per year. In addition, it is estimated that over $1 billion of this total *is not used by retailers.* Although television and radio broadcasters are making inroads, about 75% of co-op ad dollars are used for local newspaper ads. Co-op funds represent roughly one-fourth of all retail advertising media dollars.

Benefits

Proper utilization of cooperative advertising can lower costs or increase advertising volume, result in more professional-looking ads, and tie in with the prestige of a manufacturer's national advertising campaign.

Implementation

The first major problem faced by retailers interested in cooperative advertising involves finding the co-op deal opportunities. Although the Federal Trade Commission's (FTC) *Guide 8* insists that it is the "seller's duty to inform" every competing dealer about the availability of co-op plans, the seller is free to choose the means of notification. Consequently, all retailers are not necessarily notified about all co-op deals available for the products they carry. Approaches and sources of co-op information include: (1) send a form letter that asks for co-op funds to each of the store's sources of merchandise, (2) check with appropriate trade associations, (3) check with local media and related organizations, (4) check various directories of co-op advertising sources, and (5) watch other stores' ad for indications of previously unknown opportunities.

After the appropriate co-op opportunities are chosen, the retailer must sign a contract with the vendor. Although there is no standard form, most contracts contain three basic parts. First, *allowances* must provide for proportionally equal payments to all stores as required by the FTC. The allowance may be (1) a fixed dollar amount, such as $1000 for each major Christmas promotion; (2) a fixed percentage advertising cost, such as 50 percent of the cost of any and all advertising the merchant uses for the product involved; (3) a fixed percentage (i.e., 5%) of retailer's dollar purchases from the vendor; or (4) a specified dollar amount (i.e., $3) per unit for each unit purchased from the vendor. The allowance can be raised during the year to stimulate local advertising that coincides with top sales opportunities and the manufacturer's heaviest national advertising.

Second, *performance requirements* are normally clearly stated in co-op contracts. Common performance requirements include restrictions on media (i.e., prohibiting weekly newspapers), specific time periods in which the advertising can appear, and limitations specifying how much the retailer can change the sponsor's preapproved advertisement.

Third, *billing for reimbursement* can be rather complex. Although the procedures vary, most allow the retailer a specific time period such as 30 or 60 days to bill the manufacturer. Each bill or claim must include supporting evidence such as a newspaper tearsheet or affidavit of broadcast plus a notarized copy of the actual script. An invoice must also be included that shows total cost, the retailer's share, and the balance due from the manufacturer.

Evaluation

Improperly used or overused, cooperative advertising can do harm to the local merchant. The following points should be kept in mind.

First, co-op ads should be used only when they truly fit in with the store's overall advertising and marketing plans. Indiscriminant use of cooperative advertising opportunities will result in poor performance. Too much can be spent and it can be spent on advertising the wrong merchandise.

Second, overusing cooperative advertising can decrease, rather than increase, a store's total profit in at least two common situations. One occurs when virtually all of a store's ad budget is spent on co-op programs—little or no money is left for image-building institutional ads that set the store apart from competitors. The second situation occurs when a store thrives primarily because of traffic generated by fast-moving staple times with a low unit price. Since little or no co-op funds are typically provided for these goods, overusing co-op funds means that the advertising budget is being spent for bigger ticket items that are normally sold as a result of the high traffic generated by the lower price items.

Third, if the advertising budget is used solely to match co-op offers, the retailer may miss opportunities to exploit seasonal buying trends peculiar to the local market or neglect profitable or traffic-building departments or lines.

Fourth, the administrative duties associated with co-op contracts can be confusing or neglected. This can result in time-consuming correspondence, late payments, or even eventual non-payment of the vendor's share.

Conclusion

Used properly, cooperative advertising should serve as a bridge linking the planned, long term, promotion plan of a manufacturer with the overall marketing and advertising plans of the retailers. If a manufacturer's plans, however, are not compatible with the retailer's, the retailer should not use co-op advertising. Essentially, co-op advertising is appropriate when the retailer would have spent the same dollars on the same merchandise regardless of the co-op rebate.

Applications to Small Business

Cooperative advertising is especially beneficial to small retailers. In addition to stretching the advertising budget, other benefits include: (1) possible lower per-unit ad rates from media for doing a larger total volume of advertising, (2) the use of the manufacturer's professionally done art and copy, (3) allows tie-in with total national marketing programs that often include special displays and other sales-stimulating literature and devices, (4) increased traffic, (5) sometimes manufacturers pay 100% of cost of color, and (6) identification with national brands.

References/Sources

Arnold, Danny R., Capella, Louis M., and Smith, Garry D., *Strategic Retail Management*. Boston: Addison Wesley, 1983, p. 486. Discusses vertical cooperative advertising, promotional advertising allowances, and horizontal cooperative advertising.

Crimmins, Ed, "A Co-op Myth: It Is a Tragedy That Stores Don't Spend All Their Accruals," *Sales and Marketing Management* (February 7, 1983): 72-74. Discusses why stores and the media find it acceptable to not use all the cooperative advertising funds available.

Golden, Lawrence G. and Zimmerman, Donald A., *Effective Retailing*, 2nd ed. Boston: Houghton Mifflin, 1986, pp. 299-301. Discusses distinction between horizontal cooperative promotion and vertical cooperative promotion.

Haight, William, *Retail Advertising*. Morristown, NJ: General Learning Press, 1976, pp. 195-211. Presents a broad and extensive discussion of cooperative advertising, primarily from the retailer's perspective. Topics include common types, scale, growth, reasons, limitations, problems, budgeting, and contracts.

Sales and Marketing Management (May 16, 1983): 65-94. This is a special section on cooperative advertising containing many examples, tips, and guidelines.

The Buyer's Manual, Merchandising Division of the National Retail Merchants Association, 1965, pp. 94-99, 107-108. Discusses how cooperative advertising works, including its advantages, problems, costs, and tips on how to use it.

Related Topics and Terms

Advertising, Media Selection, Newspapers, Promotional Allowances, Promotion Mix, Push Strategy, Sales Promotion

Danny R. Arnold
Department of Marketing
Mississippi State University

DECLINE STAGE

Overview

The decline stage of the product life cycle is, in most renderings of the product life cycle (PLC), the fourth stage. It also is the final stage of that cycle, the stage in which the PLC curve moves downward until, at last, no sales at all are being made. Some authors use the term "obsolescence stage" rather than "decline stage," and others depict it as the penultimate rather than the ultimate stage of the cycle with "product death" being the last stage. Further, some render the product life cycle in five or even three stages, rather than the more widely used four-stage formulation of introduction, growth, maturity, and decline.

While decline of a given product's sales may frequently be traced to innovations from competing industries which make the product obsolete and cause market decline, various factors may play a role. Fashion is one such factor, as is new product development within an industry. Other shifts in the environment of marketing can also lead to a product's decline and "death." Buyers' concerns about health, the environment, rising costs, and alternative uses of funds are just a few of these.

The decline stage of the PLC has many characteristics but among the most easily noted are these. First, there is an absolute drop in industry sales which may be gradual or abrupt depending on the speed with which the new or alternative product is passing through the earlier stages of its own life cycle. In either case, the drop in sales signals the end of the maturity stage of the PLC. Second, marketing efforts are likely to be diminished overall, but also are likely to become more selective as organizations attempt to hold on to remaining core market buyers. Third, price is commonly seen to decline as sellers try to hold customers or buy time until more lasting solutions to the problems of decline can be found. Prices are then frequently observed to stabilize, then actually *rise*, reflecting the inelastic demand of the remaining core buyers. Fourth, as total industry sales fall the number of competing firms dwindles. It is common that a few remaining firms, facing a diminished but inelastic demand, reap considerable profit.

Examples

The product life cycle concept was originally intended to reflect industry sales. That is, the PLC is a depiction of unit sales for, say, automobiles *in toto* rather than for particular brands or models of cars. It is common, however, to use the PLC as a way of thinking about the rise and fall of particular types of cars such as the Willys or Edsel. This discussion focuses primarily on a product class rather than on particular brands.

Many products have declined from once high sales but remain on the market today. Their sales have diminished to a small fraction of what they once were, but they have escaped "death." Among these are gas lights, coal stokers for home furnaces, horse-drawn carriages, wind-up record players, and a host of musical instruments such as the sackbut and viola da gamba. Selecting the most familiar of these, the gas light, one can easily trace its decline.

During the 1800s the gas light was the most widely used means of indoor and outdoor lighting. Gas had largely replaced the earlier sources of light, candles and oil lamps, and was a major improvement over these. Gas lights could burn indefinitely without the need to constantly replenish the fuel. Gas lights were safer than "old fashioned" sources of light. They also cast a steadier glow than the flickering candle or oil lamp. But a major competitor, Edison's incandescent lamp, quickly drove the gas light into the decline stage of its product life cycle. The electric light, an innovation and a new competitor, made the gas light obsolete as consumers quickly accepted a product that represented an improvement over gas light just as the gas light had once been an improvement over previous lighting means.

There occurred a clear, unmistakable drop in gas light industry sales. Style changes and other "improvements" offered by makers of gas light fixtures could do nothing to stem the trend. Though some consumers stuck with gas lighting longer than did others, downward adjustments in price and promoting the benefits of gas lights did little to forestall the inevitable near-disappearance of gas lights. Within a decade of the introduction of Edison's light the gas fixture was becoming an oddity. Street lights, which had of course also been gas fueled, were converted to electricity and the old lamplighter who strolled the streets at dusk existed exclusively as the subject of nostalgic songs.

There are, however, still gas lamps today, though they are almost never used for indoor home lighting. They are used as camping lights and as decorative post lights outside homes. Few firms manufacture these products, and while the product selection offered by manufacturers is adequate for market needs it is far less than the selection of lights offered when gas lighting was the norm. The surviving firms that make gas lights address profitable marketing opportunities since their customers (campers and well-to-do home owners) want gas lights and can obtain them from only a few suppliers. Demand is thus relatively inelastic.

Much the same pattern is true of other obsolete products mentioned. Makers of horse-drawn carriages were once found in every hamlet. Now their number is small, but their product is in demand by people who strongly desire, for whatever reason, to drive about in horse-drawn vehicles. Blacksmiths, too, once faced many competitors. Now they have almost none, and the few remaining smiths are well-paid by the comparatively few remaining horse owners.

Though it is something of an abuse of the original product life cycle concept, the pattern of decline noted here can also be seen in the obsolescence and "death" of individual brands of products. For example, the automobile is very much in demand but the Willys, Kaiser, Edsel, Crosley, and many others are long gone from the new car market. Yet, their decline and "death" notwithstanding, there remains a trade in these cars among collectors of unusual autos. Further, there is healthy business in supplying parts for cars like these. These parts are often rebuilt scrap pieces, but are also made-to-order, small quantity items. The nation needs very few suppliers of parts for Kaiser automobiles, but the few that remain do very well financially because of the existence of inelastic demand and small numbers of competitors.

The above examples were chosen because their histories are essentially complete, but there are more modern stories of decline. Eight-track audio tapes have been in decline since the advent of the cassette. Cassettes themselves will soon decline as compact discs gain popularity. Forty-five r.p.m. records are in their decline stage. Slide rules have declined and "died" as have several artificial sweeteners in the face of competition from aspertame. Coffin sales have declined as cremation has become more commonplace.

Can a product ever reverse a pattern of decline or even "come back from the dead?" Numerous example of this phenomenon can be found. Nostalgia accounts for many of these, as does fashion. Candles are obsolete as major sources of light but many are sold to those people who appreciate their warm glow on special occasions. Ipana brand toothpaste was off the market for years until a small company bought the rights to the name and returned it to buyers who were old enough to remember the once-number one toothpaste brand.

This suggests one final point. A product whose life cycle appears to have peaked, then entered its decline phase, may in fact be entering a period of "false decline." That is, the "decline" may simply be a temporary downturn. A sales drop in the decline stage of the PLC is *permanent*. In the early 1960s, for example, the PLC of television sets took a noticeable dive, but the introduction of "perfected" color television soon afterwards buoyed the market again. Obviously, television was not in its decline stage after all. Like all marketing management tools, the PLC is only a guide or framework for thought. The PLC curve cannot replace judgment, and should not be used as an absolute guide to strategy formulation.

Benefits

As has been shown, a product entering its decline stage can benefit some organizations. Obviously, the firm whose new products are forcing out the old ones benefits, as do the sellers of obsolete products who remain to cater to a small residual market characterized by inelastic demand. The last blacksmiths and carriage makers exemplify this group. Yet other firms can benefit from the decline stage of a product life cycle, albeit in a "lefthanded" way. Some firms whose products have reached the decline stage of the PLC seek new products on which to build even greater successes. Some are able to improve their products to slow the continuous market decline. But it is also true that many organizations are unable to cope and are forced out of business.

The decline stage of the PLC is, in a way, the base on which the entire product life cycle concept is built. After all, why should a manager attempt to use the PLC at all if not to avoid decline and, if this is impossible, to prepare to market other offerings when current products do slip into decline? In a sense, it is the decline stage that "focuses the manager's mind" on the need for planning. It should be noted that several books have been written suggesting strategies appropriate to the stages of the PLC. These strategies are also addressed briefly in virtually every general marketing text. These dwell largely on "milking" potentially profitable sales to core market members. This is a reasonable course of action if the manager is certain that the product is truly in decline. To follow this course blindly, however, is to make the PLC's intimation of "product death" a self-fulfilling prophesy.

Implementation

In general, marketing managers do not seek to implement or bring about the decline of their products' life cycles. However, wise managers do prepare to make the best of the decline situation once it actually occurs. Several courses of action are available to managers.

Marketing managers may seek to cater to a residual core market if that market has the economic wherewithal and has demonstrated a relatively inelastic demand for the product. This combination of characteristics has kept many products on the market for decades after their general popularity has waned. Patent medicines, such as Father John's or Lydia Pinkham's, remained available for many years even though most people believed the companies making them were long out of business. The manufacturers, however, kept the products on the drug store shelf, at a premium price, and did no advertising or product improvement at all. In other words, these companies "milked" the products, selling them, with virtually no effort, to aging buyers who would pay almost any reasonable price for these old stand-by products. When the market finally got too small to justify any marketing effort at all the products were finally allowed to "die."

Another possibility is to divest, to sell off the declining product while it can still attract buyers. Often the sale is made to a smaller company that can maintain itself on the diminished sales of an elderly product. Thus, when a large, well-known firm rids itself of one or more products, it often can sell the name to a small, virtually unknown company that can justify maintaining a product no longer attractive to larger organizations.

A third possibility, of course, is to simply withdraw from the marketplace and sell off any assets associated with the manufacture and marketing of the good. Certain products are truly "dead and gone" and no organization would care to attempt to maintain them on the market. Such products as ink eradicator, slide rules, 78 r.p.m. records, and non-electronic calculators are examples.

One other possibility exists. That is to attempt to breathe new life into a dying product. Black and white TV has survived a long "decline." Most black and white TV's are either sold as second or third sets to families who have one or two color sets, or have been downsized for portability like the Sony Watchman. Of course such efforts could possibly lead to a rise in sales of black and white TV's, suggesting that the decline of this product was in fact a "false decline."

Evaluation

The decline stage of the PLC is signaled by a drop in sales volume. Further, if the sales drop is permanent the decline is not "false." Oddly enough, many managers are not aware of their products' approach to and entry into the decline stage of the PLC. While some industries may be characterized by companies that keep sales figures secret, total unit sales for most products can be charted using government or other secondary data. In other words, it is usually not difficult to actually draw a "real world" PLC since the life cycle is really nothing more than a chart reflecting unit sales. It is therefore possible to develop and utilize a genuine product life cycle and to plot brand or corporate sales figures against it.

If a marketing manager takes the time to chart a product life cycle he can evaluate the degree of product decline, the permanance of such a decline, and the apparent effects of attempts which have been made to slow, halt, or even reverse it.

Conclusion

The decline stage of the product life cycle is, in a sense, the foundation upon which the entire PLC concept is built. It is the inevitability of the decline most products face which justifies all the marketing efforts aimed at avoiding the final stage of the PLC. Further, once the decline stage is encountered the marketing manager must make the important decision of "when to get out of the market." Made too soon this decision can cost the manager lost sales. Made too late it can leave the manager holding assets that are no longer sellable.

Applications To Small Business

One reason why the approach of the decline stage of the product life cycle often goes unnoticed by marketing managers is the tendency for those managers to spend so much of their time "putting out fires." Emergencies seem always to develop in marketing's dynamic environment. It is often the case that the operator of a small business has as many fires to put out as do the managers of larger organizations while also having fewer resources at his disposal. These circumstances may result in the small business operator having far less time than is necessary to devote to medium and long range planning. Preparing for the decline of a product is likely, therefore, to be a matter left undone by the small business manager even though the decline of one or more products might easily devastate a smaller operation.

The small business manager, then, must face a familiar problem. The decline stage of the product life cycle is an important fact of life that must be addressed even though the manager has less time and fewer resources than those piloting larger organizations. Many texts have been written which deal with the planning process in the small business context. These may be helpful in coming to grips with the need to plan for the decline stage of the product life cycle even when time and resources are limited.

Software/Databases

Because the product life cycle is essentially a unit sales chart, any number of packages may be used to analyze sales data and to develop charts. Among the many packages capable of such work are SPSS-X, SAS, and GPSS. SPSS-X and SAS are familiar to most users of computers and are available in PC adaptations. The following software may also be helpful in putting the PLC concept to work.

Arthur D. Little/Online. Arthur D. Little, 25 Acorn Park, Cambridge, MA 02140. Provides coverage of forecasts and reports and is up-dated monthly.

Find/SVP Reports and Studies Index. Information Clearing House, 500 Fifth Avenue, New York, NY 10036. Describes industry and market research reports available nationally and internationally. It is up-dated quarterly.

References/Sources

Barksdale, Hiram and Harris, Clyde, "Portfolio Analysis and the Product Life Cycle," *Long Range Planning* (December 1984): 74–83. Relates the product portfolio and the product life cycle, identifying two kinds of decline products, the "war horse" which can carry on into the future and "the dodo" which should be dropped from the portfolio.

Bennet, Roger C. and Cooper, Robert, "The Product Life Cycle Trap," *Business Horizons* (September-October 1984): 7–16. Argues that companies with declining products are established companies which have lost the ability to innovate, and offers some solutions to this dilemma.

Fierman, Joyce, "How to Make Money in Mature Markets," *Fortune* (November 25, 1985): 47–53. Describes techniques used by firms whose markets are in decline or late maturity stages of the product life cycle.

Harrigan, Kathryn Rudie, "Managing Declining Business," *The Journal of Business Strategy* (Winter 1984): 74–78. Discusses proper administrative posture for decline including managing a product in its decline stage and knowing when to exit a market.

————, "Strategic Planning for Endgame," *Long Range Planning* (December 1982): 45–48. Describes strategies for firms facing seemingly irreversible declining demand.

————, *Strategies for Declining Businesses.* Lexington, MA: D.C. Heath, 1980. A book-length treatment of declining businesses and the strategic options they have.

Harrigan, Kathryn Rudie and Porter, Michael, "End-Game Strategies for Declining Industries," *Harvard Business Review* (July-August 1983): 111–120. Discusses declining markets, barriers which prevent exiting from these markets, competitive conditions, and choosing a strategy for decline.

Kaufman, Allan M., "Pulling the Plug on the Brand Life Cycle Theory," *Madison Avenue* (May 1983): 60–63. Argues that life cycle theories have caused the untimely deaths of products which could have remained successful competitors.

Kerr, Jeffrey, "Assigning Managers on the Basis of the Life Cycle," *The Journal of Business Strategy* (Spring 1982): 58–65. Discusses management styles, performance and rewards at all stages of the product life cycle.

Luck, David J., *Product Policy and Strategy.* Englewood Cliffs, NJ: Prentice-Hall, 1972. Discusses product strategies throughout the life cycle including what the author calls "product senility."

Magnani, Lou, "Born Again," *Madison Avenue* (June 1984): 8, 12–15. Argues that it is easier and cheaper to resurrect old products than to introduce new ones and offers a number of appropriate marketing strategies.

Sheth, Jagdish N., *Winning Back Your Market*. New York: John Wiley & Sons, 1985. Book-length treatment of steps taken by firms that faced declining market situations.

Thietart, R. A., and Vivas, R., "An Empirical Investigation of Success Strategies for Businesses Along the Product Life Cycle," *Management Science* (December 1984): 1405–1423. A study of 1100 businesses to determine the influence of strategic actions on market share and cash flow. Includes an excellent reference list.

Wasson, Chester R., *Dynamic Competitive Strategy and Product Life Cycles.* Austin, TX: Austin Press—Lone Star Publications, 1978. Book-length treatment of product life cycles and competitive marketing strategies.

Wernerfelt, Birger, "The Dynamics of Prices and Market Shares Over the Product Life Cycle," *Management Science* (August 1985): 928–939. A mathematical treatment of the Boston Consulting Group hypothesis that growth of market share should be maximized early in the product life cycle, never late when "harvesting" should occur.

Related Topics and Terms
Environment, Growth Stage, Introduction Stage, Laggard, Late Majority, Product Life Cycle, Product Revitalization.

Michael F. d'Amico
Department of Marketing
University of Akron

DEMARKETING

Overview

Demarketing is the systematic attempt through marketing to reduce or limit demand for consumption of a specific product or service on a temporary or permanent basis. Such attempts are a consequence of excessive demand or unwanted demand which may have a bearing on an organization's long-term objectives, or a society's concern for the well-being of its citizens. Hence demarketing can be applied to private or public sector goals. The conventional practice of marketing generally deals with the problem of increasing or stimulating demand in conditions of over-supply. This traditional notion views marketing as a way of identifying customers for existing products or developing new products for unmet preferences. The use of the marketing mix (i.e., price, product, place and promotion) by practitioners becomes central to this goal.

As some experts point out, the bulk of marketing literature emphasizes: defining the firm's objectives, knowing the relevant market, and satisfying consumer desires. Such a framework is useful if the firm wishes to sell more. But consider a changed situation when undersupply, shortage or harmful consumption is apparent. Then, the traditional marketing activity of building demand is no longer appropriate; the conventional approach becomes superfluous in the face of excessive demand. A firm in such a situation confronts problematic customer-mix and marketing-mix decisions. Demarketing can be employed as a mechanism to reduce total demand, or types of demand and uses, for a product to a particular level of supply. Once a firm recognizes that demarketing is necessary, all the major marketing tools can be applied. As marketing scholars suggest, the marketing mentality is as relevant to the problem of reducing demand as it is to the problem of increasing demand.

Examples

Demarketing activities predominately fall into two categories: 1) general demarketing which deals with lessening total demand and 2) selective demarketing which deals with discouraging demand in specific customer segments. In the case of general demarketing, a firm tries to discourage customers from purchasing their product or service. Often temporary shortages result from excess demand as was the case with Kodak's Instamatic Camera and the Wilkinson Sword new stainless steel razor blade in the early 1960s, Coors Beer in the 1970s, and Honda Cars in the early 1980s. Each of these cases was corrected once supply was satisfied through plant expansion, allocation or increased competition.

Selective demarketing is useful when an organization wants to reduce the demand from selected market segments. Such segments may be undesirable because they are less profitable or have a detrimental impact on the demand of other profitable segments. Some examples would be a restaurant that wishes to dissuade poorly dressed or ill-mannered customers; fashion designers who want to make their fashions popular only with the affluent; or the country club that seeks only members of high-ranking professional status. Some marketing experts cite that Gresham's law might operate when the "cheaper" segments drive out the "dearer" segments from the firm's clientele.

Benefits

Demarketing efforts can result in substantial benefits or long run success for the firm or organization. The use of demarketing by Parker Brothers to recall its hazardous Riviton toy in the 1970s did not injure the goodwill of the firm and lessened the likelihood of legal liability. Demarketing activities by public agencies decreased apathy toward seat belt use. Another successful well known application was the demarketing of infant formula in Third World nations by Nestle Corporation and others. Their demarketing efforts brought an end to the boycott of their products instigated by alarmed consumers.

Implementation

An effective demarketing campaign first begins with a decision regarding a general or selective approach. In general demarketing, a firm must deter demand or allocate their products to certain dealers and customers. Some ways of lessening demand are reducing advertising, sales promotion, or salespeople's efforts; altering ad messages; increasing purchase costs either through price or the time needed to buy the product; reducing product quality and limiting distribution. Product allocation is another method to demarket a product. Kotler and Levy (1971) outline four solutions to allocation: 1) first-come, first-serve basis; 2) proportional demand basis where a customer is given a proportion of available supply; 3) favored customer basis where valuable customers are given preference; and 4) highest bid basis where those who will pay more receive the goods.

Choosing which segments to demarket and the specific means to do so is problematic. Marketing theorists recommend a host of methods to accomplish this goal such as discouraging a customer's hope for product availability; providing inferior service to unwanted segments to indicate their business is not wanted; instructing salespeople to give less attention to members of these segments; and limiting access to information or sources of these products to chosen segments. A firm practicing selective demarketing must be mindful of the ethical problems raised when it discriminates against some customers, sometimes leaving a customer without any option for purchasing a product elsewhere.

Evaluation

Once a demarketing campaign is implemented, a firm should operate with an understanding of demand elasticities and cross elasticities. Care must be taken not to injure demand for the future when greater supplies become available. If allocation is used, discretion is needed so as not to disappoint customers to the degree that they discontinue their business altogether and choose another supplier or alternative. A firm must confront the following questions when engaging in demarketing activities:

1. When does a situation warrant specific demarketing activities? Do some situations require different demarketing activities?
2. What techniques and methods should the firm use to lessen total and selective demand? Does the firm have the skills to demarket thoughtfully and skillfully?
3. How should the firm allocate its products to different segments?
4. How can these less important segments be identified and then approached?
5. What are the different demand elasticities and cross elasticities of various segments?
6. Should senior management play a role in selecting demarketing activities?
7. Do the demarketing activities have ethical concerns such as discrimination?

Conclusion

Demarketing should not be regarded as merely marketing in reverse where the product, price, place and promotion decisions are used to lessen demand. Arranging the optimal marketing mix is problematic. Firms must be careful not to reduce short-term demand so drastically that surpluses develop in the long run. Furthermore, extreme care must be exercised not to alienate current and future customers to the degree that long run demand is injured. When demarketing is successfully executed, the firm can enjoy a viable future and a more stable, predictable short run.

Applications to Small Business

In the early stages of developing a business or during periods of great demand for its products, a firm may have to methodically limit its supply to some customers and discourage others. In such circumstances, a small firm can successfully use demarketing activities to manage this problem. Unfortunately, some small businesses will offend some clients and lose their business forever. A firm must be circumspect to determine if it wishes to limit general or selective demand. Usually some customers are less valuable than others.

Implementing a sound demarketing campaign begins with altering elements of the marketing mix. Once the key elements are changed, the firm should monitor frequently the efficacy of the demarketing. Extreme care must be taken not to discriminate against some clients; otherwise serious loss of goodwill or legal suits may prevail.

Software/Databases

Some companies have established on-going procedures to monitor demand for their products according to market segments. These same companies also use forecasting methods to assure that future demand will be attuned to product availability. Available commercial software allows firms to keep a history of demand by segments and a forecast of demand by these segments. If demarketing is necessary, the database can help in carefully selecting segments.

Sales History (S/H). MCBA, Z441 Honolulu Ave., Montrose, CA, 91020. Provides period-to-date and year-to-date sales figures for products and compares them to similar periods in previous years.

References/Sources

Bates, D.L., and Dillard, John E., "Social-Demarketing—General Management's Policy Guide in a Supply Based Recession," *Journal of General Management* (Spring 1976): 81-88. Presents ideas on the effective use of demarketing as a policy by senior management.

Clement, Douglas, "Nestle's Latest Killing in the Bottle Baby Market," *Business and Society Review* (Spring 1978): 60-64. Identifies the issues confronting Nestle before it demarketed infant formula.

Cullwick, David, "Positioning Demarketing Strategy," *Journal of Marketing* (April 1975): 51-57. Outlines the approaches that can be taken to use demarketing as a successful marketing strategy.

Frisbie, Gil A., "Demarketing Energy: Does Psychographic Research Hold the Answer?" *Journal of the Academy of Marketing Science,* 8, 3 (1980): 196-211. Discusses the results of a psychographic study to examine consumer purchasing patterns in short supply areas. Provides strategy implications for demarketing.

Jacobs, Bruce A., "Ross Labs Finds the Formula," *Industry Week* (December 8, 1980): 71-72, 74. Presents the approach used by Abbott Labs to demarket infant formula.

Kinnear, Thomas C., and Frey, Cynthia J., "Demarketing of Potentially Hazardous Products: General Framework and Case Studies," *Journal of Contemporary Business,* 7, 4 (1979): 57-68. Reports the success of demarketing seatbelts and cigarettes and gives theoretical insight on consumer behavior.

Kotler, Philip, "The Major Tasks of Marketing Management," *Journal of Marketing* (October 1973): 42-49. Lists and discusses uses of marketing other than demand building.

Kotler, Philip, and Levy, Sidney, "Broadening the Marketing Concept," *Journal of Marketing,* 33 (January 1969): 10-15. Stresses that marketing can be used for purposes other than selling products.

Kotler, Philip, and Levy, Sidney, "Demarketing, Yes, Demarketing," *Harvard Business Review* (November-December 1971): 14-30. Develops an excellent review of demarketing as a policy and how to implement it.

Papadopoulos, Nicolas G., "Shortage Marketing: A Comprehensive Framework," *Journal of the Academy of Marketing Science* (Winter/Spring 1983): 40-60. Describes the issues a firm should consider when using demarketing to manage shortages.

Post, James E., and Baer, Edward, "Demarketing Infant Formula: Consumer Products in the Developing World," *Journal of Contemporary Business,* 7, 4 (1979): 45-50. Presents the need for demarketing of infant formula.

Teel, Sandra J., Teel, Jesse E., and Bearden, William O., "Lessons Learned From the Broadcast Cigarette Advertising Ban," *Journal of Marketing* (January 1979): 45-50. Gives a summary of the effectiveness of demarketing cigarettes.

Uhring, Nancy E., "Demarketing Health Care: Responding to the Needs of Market Segments," *Akron Business and Economic Review* (Winter 1979): 21-25. Discusses demarketing of health care for specific market segments.

Related Topics and Terms
Broadening the Concept of Marketing, Recession Marketing, Shortage Marketing.

Steven J. Lysonski
Department of Marketing
University of Rhode Island

DEMOGRAPHIC FACTOR

Overview

Demographic factors, such as age, sex, family size, income, expenditures, occupation, marital status, education, family life cycle, religion, race, nationality, and social class, are statistics that are used to describe the size, composition, and distribution of the population. These factors can be readily identified, obtained, measured, and analyzed. The size, distribution and nature of the population in any geographic market are major influences on marketing.

In the United States, there are now more one-person households than ever before; the oldest baby boomers are now approaching 40 and the youngest just leaving college; nearly 70% of women from 25 to 39 years old now work—double the rate of 25 years ago; fertility is at near record low levels; the elderly market continues to grow at a remarkable rate; the agricultural population continues to shrink; and discretionary income is rising. These are but a few examples of descriptive demographics. In response to such changes in the environment, marketers have to develop appropriate marketing strategies to reach changing demographic target markets.

Examples

To appeal to changing demographic markets, Stouffer Foods developed products such as Lean Cuisine, a unique line of frozen prepared food that offers quality, taste, and variety at economical prices. Stouffer's one- and two-serving packages are designed for today's smaller families and the increasing number of women working outside the home. In response to declining birth rates, Gerber Products Company branched out into life insurance, day-care centers, nursery furniture, infant and children's apparel, and children's car seats and play pens. In response to the aging of the baby-boomers, Levi Strauss added Levis for Men "with a skosh more room" for mature men. The company also added fuller jeans for women, youthwear for children aged 2 to 14, infantwear, and a line of maternity clothes, pants, and denim jumpers.

Safeway supermarkets, which used to appeal to the traditional family of four, with 85 percent of shopping done by women on Saturday mornings, now appeals to smaller families, teenagers, and working women. Safeway changed its approach to attract "the jogging generation"; i.e. two-income families with the adults aged 25 to 44. Stores remain open longer and many nonfood departments have been added. The growth of the elderly has led Elizabeth Arden to add the Millennium cosmetic line for the mature woman, magazine publishers have introduced new magazines such as "50 Plus" and "Prime Time," and some hotels give room discounts of 50 percent and restaurant discounts of 25 percent to older guests.

228

Benefits

Significant growth opportunities can be realized by targeting the new demographic markets. Because the United States is going through an era of notable demographic change in many areas, an awareness of demographic statistics can help marketing managers plan strategies for adapting to the transition from mass markets to demographic-specific market segments. For example, the shift to an older population, notably those aged 65 and over, provides growth opportunities for medical care, travel, entertainment and restaurants. The mobility of the U.S. population, such as the shift to West South Central and Mountain regions, provides growth opportunities for regional brands. The increasing number of affluent consumers represent lucrative markets for IRAs, luxury autos, vacation homes, leisure-oriented activities, restaurants, and other goods and services. The increase of women in the labor force offers new growth opportunities for automobiles, clothing, restaurants, time-saving appliances, prepared foods, prewrapped goods and personal services such as day care centers, nail care, and home care services, aimed at the working women.

Implementation

Implementing strategies that are consistent with the changing demographic profile of the U.S. market requires the development of a consumer demographic profile based on the most current statistics available. A market-product grid is then developed for a particular demographic market segment and an estimate of the market size made. If the market segment is judged to be viable, an appropriate marketing program can be developed and implemented. Implementation strategies require an awareness and understanding of population statistics and trends as well as the impact thereof on the consumer purchase process. It requires knowing where to obtain relevant demographic statistics (see Reference/Sources).

Evaluation

When using demographic factors it should be noted that the statistics may be dated and thus lead to misleading interpretations as to their significance and impact on the firm. Furthermore, summary data may be too broad and not reveal the opportunities (and risks) in local markets or for specialized product and service categories. In addition, it should be pointed out that the batting average on longer-term demographic predictions may be just short of being dismal. For instance, demographers have consistently underestimated the surge of women in the labor force and the early retirement of older men. Demographers' failure to give early enough warning of the exploding numbers of very old people exacerbated the financial troubles of Social Security and Medicare. Failure to anticipate the movement to the South and Southwest left a number of northern metropolitan areas with excess power and water capacity.

It is also essential to recognize that demographic factors alone do not indicate why and how consumers make purchase decisions and what the appropriate marketing strategy might be for any particular demographically identified target market. For example, how should a firm approach the rapidly increasing Hispanic market? Should Hispanics be treated as a monolithic, homogeneous group or segmented according to country or region of origin? Do Hispanics, for example, differ in their product and/or brand preference based on their ancestral roots? Given this nation's rapidly rising Hispanic population (a demographic description), few firms will be able to ignore this potentially lucrative opportunity in the years ahead. To sell successfully to this market, however, firms must understand more than simply demographic factors, such as consumer decision-making practices, and motivation.

Conclusion

An understanding of demographic factors; i.e., the size, composition, and distribution of a population, is necessary to determine growth opportunities marketers have, as well as the limits of options available. Marketing's environment changes constantly. Demographic factors are one of the most important forces in the environment to which marketers have to respond. The appropriate marketing response requires keeping track of the changes in demographic factors. Appropriate marketing programs can then be planned and implemented based on the demographic (and behavioral) profile of the customer.

Applications to Small Business

Demographic factors are of relevance to all firms regardless of size. Small businesses, however, may be in a better position to respond more quickly to demographic changes, provided such changes can be spotted or forecast on a timely basis.

Local manufacturers, wholesalers, and retailers should keep track of the changing demographic factors in their respective markets. One way to help accomplish this is to be aware of the newspapers, trade journals, and magazines that publish annual market profiles for their city of metropolitan trading area. A few newspapers publish surveys of product/brand preferences and buying habits on a wide range of consumer products and services, along with demographic data for the respective geographic area.

Software/Databases

A number of companies provide commercial software designed specifically to retrieve demographic data. Three of them are:

Supersite. C.A.C.I. Inc., 1815 N. Fort Myer Dr., Arlington, VA 22209. Provides on-line retrieval of demographic data (census and updates) for any area.

Max. National Planning Data Corp., P.O. Box 610, Ithaca, NY 14850. Provides on-line demographic data-retrieval systems.

Bankmarket. Innovative Systems Inc., 341 Fourth Ave., Pittsburgh, PA 15222. Provides marketing database and household census data.

References/Sources

American Demographics. This is a monthly magazine providing an excellent guide to demographics in America. Of particular value are articles which sharpen ones understanding and use of demographic data. Feature articles focus on various topics, such as, "How To Read A Demographic Report," "Going For Brand Loyalty," "Three Stages Of Health," "Computer Mapping," and "Rating The Test Markets." Another feature entitled "Business Reports" shows how companies use demographics in developing or marketing a new product, in siting a store, in planning for corporate growth, or in creating an advertising campaign.

United States Government Statistics. The largest single publisher of detailed demographic statistical data is the Bureau of the Census. Much of the data is arranged by state, county, standard metropolitan statistical areas, or city, and some of it also by census tract, block, congressional district, standard industrial classification industry, and so forth. The Economic Censuses in particular (retail, wholesale, service industries, agriculture, construction, manufacturers, mineral industries, and transportation) are a major source of essential facts that can be used by market researchers for such purposes as determining market potential, forecasting economic conditions, forecasting sales, analyzing sales performance, determining sales territories, allocating funds for advertising, and selecting sites for new stores or plants. The censuses comprising the Economic Censuses include: "1982 Census of Agriculture," "1982 Census of Construction Industries," "1982 Census of Manufactures," "1982 Census of Mineral Industries," "1982 Census of Retail Trade," "1982 Census of Service Industries," "1982 Census of Transportation," "1982 Census of Wholesale Trade," "1982 Enterprise Statistics," and "1982 Census of Population." The Bureau of the Census also publishes several series for current population statistics, including: "Population Characteristics," "Population Estimates and Projections," and "Consumer Income."

Nongovernmental Statistical Reports. A number of commercial firms or associations provide statistical services. Some of these are: "Commodity Year Book," Jersey City, NJ: Commodity Research Bureau; "Dun's Census of American Business," Parsippany, NJ: Dun's Marketing Services; "National Economic Projections Series," and "Regional Projections Series," Washington, DC: National Planning Association; "Predicts Basebook," Cleveland: Predicasts, Inc.; "Predicast Forecasts," Cleveland: Predicasts, Inc.; "Standard & Poor's Statistical Service," New York: Standard & Poor.

Many trade journals publish annual statistical, outlook or survey issues that are potentially of value in collecting up-to-date statistics focusing on the industry which the journal covers. Among the better known professional and trade magazines are:

Advertising: "Advertising Age," "Adweek," "Journal of Advertising Research," "Marketing and Media Decisions"

Marketing: "American Demographics" (see discussion above) "Marketing News," "Business Marketing," "Industrial Marketing Management," "Journal of Consumer Marketing," "Journal of Marketing"

Marketing Research: "Journal of Marketing Research"

Purchasing and Physical Distribution: "Chilton's Distribution," "Modern Materials Handling," "Packaging," "Purchasing," "Traffic Management"

Retailing: "Chain Store Age Executive," "Chain Store Age," "Direct Marketing," "Discount Merchandising," "Discount Store News," "Drug Store News," "Journal of Retailing," "Merchandising," "Progressive Grover," "Shopping Center World," "Supermarket News"

Sales Management: "Marketing Times," "Sales & Marketing Management"

Wholesaling: "Industrial Distribution."

Related Topics and Terms
Disposable Personal Income, Environment, Market Potential, Nielson Reports, Sales Forecast, Secondary Data, Standard Industrial Classification.

Ralph M. Gaedeke
Department of Management
School of Business & Public Administration
California State University, Sacramento

DEPARTMENT STORE

Overview

Today's popular department store is an outgrowth of the old-fashioned general store that can still be found in small rural communities. A department store is a large retailing business unit that handles an extensive variety (width and depth) of products and is organized into separate departments for purposes of buying, promotion, service, and control. Pricing is usually competitive, while product quality ranges from average to very good. Service varies, depending on the department store's target market.

The Bureau of the Census defines a department store on the basis of three characteristics. First, at least twenty-five people are employed. Second, the merchandise assortment must include some items in each of these lines: dry goods and household items, family wearing apparel and furniture, home furnishings, appliances, and radios and TV sets. Third, if sales are less than $10 million per year, no more than 80 percent of the sales can come from any one of the lines. If sales are greater than $10 million, there is no limitation on the percentage of sales for any line, as long as the combined sales of the smallest two lines are at least $1 million.

Examples

Many department stores are part of large diversified chains, such as Mercantile, Batus, Dayton-Hudson, May, Carter Hawley Hale, R.H. Macy, Allied Stores, Associated Dry Goods and Federated. Some of these giants own everything from off-price stores to specialty stores. However, among the department store companies, the most successful continue to be R.H. Macy and Mercantile, both remaining devoted to the department store concept.

Some department stores, such as Hudson's or Macy's, sell furniture and appliances as well as dry goods and family wearing apparel. Other department stores, such as Saks Fifth Avenue, do not carry home appliances and concentrate solely on apparel. Many department stores, like Neiman Marcus, have substantial mail order sales.

Leased departments exist in many department stores. Companies will pay the department store rent to occupy their space and sell their merchandise or services. Department stores benefit from leased departments because they increase the variety of merchandise sold and they do not have to incur the time and expense of training specialized salespeople. The lessee obtains the heavy traffic usually generated in the department store.

Department stores usually dominate the shopping center in which they are located. These "anchor tenants" account for large percentages of shopping centers' total space and sales and generally claim credit for attracting shoppers to the shopping center. In a large regional or super regional shopping center, three or four department stores may be found. Because of their dominant position in malls, department stores frequently are able to extract favorable leasing terms and other concessions from developers—much to the consternation of the non-department store tenants.

Benefits

From a retailing perspective, a department store has the greatest assortment of any retailer, provides a variety of customer services, dominates the stores around it, is frequently a fashion leader, and has strong credit card penetration. Department stores have been very innovative over the years; for example, the first type of retailer to advertise prices was a department store. The department store was the first retailer to develop a one-price policy. Most recently, department stores have adopted automated checkout facilities.

From the customer's viewpoint, department stores allow them to do the majority of their shopping (in some cases even their food shopping) under one roof. Most often, the department store enjoys a good reputation by offering a liberal exchange policy, money back guarantees, full refunds, etc. Often a customer will patronize a store he can trust even if department store prices may be significantly higher than some of their discount competitors.

Implementation

Many medium-sized and large department stores use organizational structures that are a modification of the Mazur plan, first presented in 1927. The Mazur plan divides all retail activities into four functional areas: 1) *merchandising*—buying, selling, stock planning and control, and planning promotional events, 2) *publicity*—window and interior display, advertising, planning and executing promotional events (in cooperation with the merchandising department), advertising research, and public relations, 3) *store management*— merchandise care, customer services, purchasing store supplies and equipment, store maintenance, operating activities, store and merchandise protection, personnel, and workroom operations, and 4) *accounting and control*—credit and collection, expense budgeting and control, inventory planning and control, and record keeping.

These four areas are organized with the use of line (direct authority and responsibility) and staff (advisory or support) components. For example, the controller and the publicity manager provide staff services to the merchandising divisions, but within these staff areas personnel are organized on a line basis. The buyer, under the Mazur plan, has complete responsibility for controlling expenses and reaching profit goals within his department.

The growth of branch stores has caused three alternative forms of the original Mazur plan to emerge: 1) the parent organization operates the branch (known as mother hen with branch store chickens), 2) each branch is treated as a separate store with its own buying responsibilities (known as a separate store), and 3) selling responsibilities are separate from buying responsibilities. Buying is centralized, and branches become sales units with equal organizational status (known as equal store).

Evaluation

Department stores are now facing strong competition on various fronts for a number of reasons. First, the geographic expansion of some aggressive department store chains is placing these outlets into direct competition with existing stores, illustrated by Bloomingdale's moving into the Dallas and Miami areas. Second, J.C. Penney and Sears have embarked on significant store renovation programs and are increasing their fashion emphasis to attract more upscale consumers. Third, off-price chains have been taking customers away from department stores by featuring branded merchandise at low prices. Fourth, specialty stores are competing on the basis of distinctive product lines, strong store image, a better selection, and an attractive atmosphere.

What are department stores doing to protect their position in the market? They are developing more private-label merchandise, refusing to deal with suppliers that sell to discounters, opening their own off-price chains, showing a greater interest in fashion leadership, running sales more frequently, and moving toward a boutique (store-within-a-store) orientation. However, these strategies are not foolproof. For example, by running sales more frequently, customers who may have paid full price for an item now will wait since he knows he can "get it on sale by waiting a few weeks."

Conclusion

In many department store organizations, the emphasis has traditionally been on effective merchandising and opening new stores rather than on managing the ongoing business effectively. However, the combined effects of the 1981 recession, rapid store expansion, and entry of new retail concepts into the marketplace, are posing managerial dilemmas today for many department store organizations.

Dayton-Hudson, Macy's, and Federated Department Stores are recognizing the parallels between their own experiences and those of their nonretail counterparts, they are beginning to build general management skills among their senior executives and to reorient their organizations toward strategic thinking about the questions: "What business are we in? Who is our target market? How can we distinguish ourselves from our competitors in the mind of our target customer?"

There are those who believe a shakeout is near in the department store industry. When this will occur and what will be the result is difficult to determine. However, those department stores which are developing a strategic viewpoint will be better prepared for the future.

Applications to Small Business

Traditionally, small business observed and often copied the large department store. Today, however, the small retailer is being more innovative and is presenting a greater threat to the retail giants, especially if they have accurately determined their target market. Many small retailers have been so successful with specialized product lines that department stores have been forced to drop these items, such as sporting goods.

Software/Databases

PTS F&S Indexes. Predicasts, Inc., 200 University Circle Research Center, 11001 Cedar Avenue, Cleveland, OH 44106. Over 6,000 business, trade, government, and corporate publications are indexed. Access by company name and industry is provided. This source is a good place to start when desiring information on the department store industry and specific companies.

References/Sources

Berman, Barry, and Evans, Joel R., *Retail Management: A Strategic Approach*, 2nd ed. New York: Macmillan, 1983, pp. 96-98 and 250-255. Presents a detailed discussion of the department store concept.

Cornwall, Deborah, J., "Say Goodbye to the Merchant Mystique," *Business Horizons*, 27 (5), (September-October 1984): 78-82. Strongly suggests the managerial perspective of retailers must shift from that of running a store to running a business.

Crask, Melvin R. and Reynolds, Fred A., "An Indepth Profile of the Department Store Shopper," *Journal of Retailing*, Vol. 54, No. 2 (Summer 1978): 23-32. Based on two nationwide surveys, this study provides a detailed portrait of the frequent department store shopper.

Gable, Myron, Gillespie, Karen R., and Topol, Martin, "The Current Status of Women in Department Store Retailing: An Update," *Journal of Retailing*, Vol. 60, No. 2 (Summer 1984): 86-104. This study replicates the work of Gillespie (1977-1978) that examined women's status in the managerial ranks of department store retailing. A comparison was made of the composition (male versus female) of the boards of directors of the nation's 25 largest publicly owned department store firms with that of its 25 largest industrial firms.

Ingene, Charles A., and Lusch, Robert F., "Market Selection Decisions for Department Stores," *Journal of Retailing*, Vol. 56, No. 3 (Fall 1980): 21-40. A model is developed which incorporates the effects of managerial actions and environmental demand variables as predictors of retail demand.

Mazur, Paul M., *Principles of Organization Applied to Modern Retailing.* New Brothers, 1927. A pioneering work; developed the organizational structure for department stores which is still being utilized today.

McQuade, Walter, "Making a Drama Out of Shopping," *Fortune* (March 24, 1980): 105-107. Burdine's (a division of Federated Department Stores) is highlighted with their imaginative approach to merchandising.

Rich, Stuart U., and Portis, Bernard D., "The Images of Department Stores," *Journal of Marketing*, Vol. 28 (April 1964): 10-15. Reports the results of a study of 4500 women shoppers. Discusses the different types of appeals in department stores, the different customer characteristics, differences in shopping behavior, and differences between the imagery of suburban branch department stores and their "parent" stores in the city.

Related Topics and Terms
Chain Store, Large Retailer, Mass Merchandiser, Retail Giant.

Therese A. Maskulka
Department of Marketing
Lehigh University

DERIVED DEMAND

Overview

Derived demand refers to the fact that the need for industrial goods is generated indirectly from the demand for the consumer goods or services they are used to make or provide. This implies that small changes in demand for consumer goods will cause large changes in demand for the factors of production of those consumer goods. The demand for all industrial products can be traced to and is derived from consumption at the end-user or household level, although that demand may be very remote from the industrial product. Industrial customers do not purchase goods and services because of their own personal needs or desires but rather to produce other goods or services for their customers. The industrial customer's demand is derived from the demand for their products by their customers. As a result of derived demand, industrial marketers often find it difficult to predict demand for their products. This concept may be the single most important point that must be understood by industrial marketers, and it is the major difference between consumer and industrial marketing. Since the demand for all industrial products can be traced to the final consumer, changes in consumer spending patterns may have major repercussions for the entire economy, and, therefore, even industrial marketers must monitor changes in final consumers. Even more importantly, relatively small fluctuations in final consumer demand may result in much larger fluctuations in the demand for capital goods used to produce the products sold in the consumer market.

Examples

A simple example helps to illustrate the far reaching effects of the concept of derived demand. When final consumers began to conserve electricity in response to high energy prices, the demand for electricity decreased. This resulted in a decrease in the demand for new generating equipment by the utilities, which resulted in the manufacturers of the generating equipment reducing their purchases of component parts and subassemblies for that equipment. When the sales of component parts for the generating equipment fell, the manufacturers of the component parts, in turn, reduced their orders for steel and specialty metals from raw material extractors. Even further, the decrease in the demand for extracted materials lowered the need for heavy mining machinery, causing the extractors to reduce their purchases of that machinery. Thus, the producers of heavy mining machinery can trace the demand for their product back all the way to the final consumers' demand for electricity. Changes in population or social patterns, such as later marriages, fewer children, or increased leisure time, also, can have major effects on the demand for industrial products.

Benefits

When end-user demand for a consumer product increases, the resulting changes in demand for the industrial goods used to make that product may increase by an even greater amount. In this case, the industrial marketer is faced with greater potential for sales increases. These increased sales may frequently occur without the beneficiary having to incur additional expenditures for demand-increasing efforts, such as advertising. Thus, derived demand increases' higher sales may be accompanied by increased profits as well.

Implementation

Industrial marketers must consider the effects of derived demand in their efforts to forecast demand for their products. They must look not only to their own customers when forecasting demand, but also to their customers' customers, and so on, down to the demand at the end-user level.

Since these demand increases are frequently not the result of the industrial marketer's efforts, there is a tendency for them to not be prepared when sales increases in other industries ripple back to them. By knowing what effects increases in demand in other industries will have on their own demand, industrial marketers can be adjusting work force size, raw materials, production schedules, and inventory levels.

Similarly, on the down side, industrial companies need to be able to predict the effects that demand contraction in other industries will have on their own demand levels. They are then in a position to adjust work force size, raw materials, production schedules, and inventory levels.

Evaluation

Due to the volatility of derived demand, the effects of a small fluctuation in ultimate consumer demand may result in large fluctuations in the demand for some industrial goods or services. The classic example of this volatility of derived demand took place during the depression years between 1929 and 1932. During these years, a 20-point drop in the physical production of consumer goods, based on an index of 100 points, resulted in a 65 point decrease in capital spending for equipment; when sales of consumer goods fell, the need for new equipment used to produce those consumer goods fell to a much greater degree.

More recently, decreases in consumer demand for oil and gas during 1974-1975 and 1980-1981 resulted from OPEC price increases. This drop in consumer demand caused a dramatic decrease in the demand for equipment used to produce the fuels. Demand, of course, may shift in the opposite direction as well, in which case increases in consumer demand, although signaling increased opportunity for the industrial marketer, may also result in sharper increases in the demand for factors of production, leading to shortages of materials, production capacity, and labor.

Some industrial marketers have attempted to soften the effects of derived demand by trying to influence end-user demand for their industrial products. Although NutraSweet is an industrial product sold to food manufacturers, the artificial sweetening ingredient has been promoted to final consumers in an attempt by the manufacturer to gain greater control of demand. For many years, aluminum producers have urged final consumers to use aluminum cans and containers because, although the consumer never comes in direct contact with the aluminum producer, the ultimate consumer has a major influence on the demand for this industrial product.

Conclusion

The possible effects of derived demand are widely accepted, and industrial marketers must work within this framework which affects all areas of marketing decision making in one way or another. Although the subject has not received a great deal of attention in the marketing literature, its importance cannot be overstated. The industrial marketer may, however, be able to limit the injurious effects of derived demand in several ways. First, increased market research may be used to forecast consumer demand in related consumer markets as well as in the industrial market, leading to more accurate estimates of demand. Second, diversification of product lines, markets and operations may decrease the impact of the volatility of derived demand on an organization. Thus, although end-user demand may adversely affect one product or market, other products or markets which are not affected by the shift in consumer demand would lessen the overall impact on the organization. As mentioned previously, promotion may be adjusted, and, finally, flexible pricing policies which allow firms to reap larger profits during "boom" periods to make up for the decreases in profits during "busts" may also be employed to limit the effects of changes in end-user demand on the individual organization.

Applications to Small Business

The concept of derived demand and its effects are applicable to small industrial businesses as well as large. However, small businesses may find that a greater portion of their demand is subjected to the fluctuations of derived demand. Thus, like their larger counterparts, they need to be able to predict increases and contractions in derived demand.

Due to limited budgets, however, small firms generally do not have the resources to conduct extensive primary studies of demand modifications in other industries and develop sophisticated forecasting models based on those data. But they can use published sources to obtain these estimates. Because their environment is more local, small businesses can keep tabs on businesses in their area that provide them with sales and adjust their demand figures accordingly. For example, a small paper manufacturer may study carefully the circulation figures and projections for the local newspaper, if the paper is one of the manufacturer's largest customers.

Software/Databases

PTS U. S. Forecast, Predicasts, Inc., Cleveland, OH. Provides abstracts of short term and long term forecasts for the United States. Forecasts include the general economy, all industries, specific products, and end-users. Sources include trade journals, business and financial publications, major newspapers, government reports, and special studies.

References/Sources

Ames, B. Charles, and Hlavacek, James D., *Managerial Marketing for Industrial Firms.* New York: Random House, 1984. Discusses the implications of derived demand and the effect shifts in population or social patterns may have on the industrial firm.

Berndt, E.R., and Wood, D.O., "Technology, Prices and the Derived Demand for Energy," *The Review of Economics and Statistics* (August 1975): 259-268. Looks at the derived demand concept using the demand for energy as an illustration.

Bishop, William S., Graham, John L., and Jones, Michael H., "Volatility of Derived Demand in Industrial Markets and Its Management Implications," *Journal of Marketing* (Fall 1984): 95-103. Presents examples of the effects of derived demand for several products, and marketing strategies to lessen the volatile effects of that demand.

Clark, J.M., "Business Acceleration and the Law of Demand: A Technical Factor in Economic Cycles," *Journal of Political Economy* (March 1971): 217-235. Seminal presentation on the subject of derived demand.

Douglas, Edna, *Economics of Marketing.* New York: Harper, 1975. Discusses the concept of derived demand with basic economic explanations.

Haas, Robert W., *Industrial Marketing Management.* Boston, MA: Kent Publishing, 1982. Basic industrial marketing text which contains a good presentation of the concept of derived demand and presents an example of the complex relationship between demand for consumer products and demand for the associated factors of production.

Hill, Richard M., Alexander, Ralph S., and Cross, James S., *Industrial Marketing.* Homewood, IL: Richard D. Irwin, 1975. Contains a discussion on the meaning and consequences of derived demand, with several examples.

Hutt, Michael D., and Speh, Thomas W., *Industrial Marketing Management.*

Chicago, IL: Dryden Press, 1981. Discusses the concept of derived demand, including examples.

Industrial Marketing Committee Review Board, "Fundamental Differences Between Industrial and Consumer Marketing," *Journal of Marketing* (October 1954): 152-158. Lists derived demand as a fundamental difference between industrial and consumer marketing.

Kotler, Philip, *Principles of Marketing.* Englewood Cliffs, NJ: Prentice-Hall, 1983. Contains a brief introductory discussion of derived demand with respect to industrial marketing.

Robinson, Patrick J., Faris, Charles W., and Wind, Yoram, *Industrial Buying and Creative Marketing.* Boston, MA: Allyn & Bacon, 1967. Discusses some of the effects of derived demand and the related decisions faced by businesses.

Smith, William L., *Macroeconomics.* Homewood, IL: Richard D. Irwin, 1970. Presents a general discussion on the topic of derived demand.

Vaile, Roland S., Grether, E.T., and Cox, Reavis, *Marketing in the American Economy.* New York: Ronald Press, 1952. Contains the classic example of the volatility of derived demand, the changes in production during the Depression.

Webster, Frederick E., Jr., *Industrial Marketing Strategy.* New York: Wiley, 1979. Contains a discussion of derived demand and stresses the need to analyze all levels of demand rather than demand at the industrial level only.

Related Topics and Terms
Demand, Industrial Demand, Industrial Good, Industrial Market, Industrial Marketing.

Nancy Pishkur
Department of Marketing
Kent State University

DIFFERENTIATED MARKETING

Overview

Differentiated marketing is a market coverage strategy in which the firm decides to operate in several segments of the market and designs separate offers to each. In contrast to undifferentiated marketing, differentiated marketing tailors its offerings to several different segments. Each segment of the market consists of groups of customers with different, or heterogeneous, needs. Consequently, each segment requires a distinct marketing mix.

Differentiated marketing is widely practiced by firms in both the consumer and industrial markets. By offering a marketing mix designed to serve the specific needs of each market segment, firms hope to generate a greater number of total sales in each segment and more product loyalty in each of these submarkets. Additionally, firms hope to strengthen the consumers' overall perception of the company with the product or service category. When a firm chooses differentiated marketing as its market coverage strategy, it is practicing multiple market segmentation. Using differentiated marketing exploits the differences between market segments by tailoring a unique marketing mix for each segment, rather than inducing each of the segments to purchase one product with a single marketing program designed for everyone.

Examples

Differentiated marketing is a market coverage strategy employed by most automobile manufacturers today. Ford Motor Company, for example, offers product versions for the general purpose market segment via small-sized cars, such as Escort and Lynx, medium-sized cars, Tempo, Taurus, and Topaz, and large-sized cars, LTD, Crown Victoria, and Sable. The company offers different versions for the sports car market segment via the medium-priced Capri, and Mustang, and the high-priced Cougar and Thunderbird. Ford Motor Company offers different entries for the luxury market segment, the medium-priced Lincoln and high-priced Continental.

To meet Japanese competition, Ford Motor Company is taking a more personalized approach toward Californians. On certain models, such as Thunderbird, Ford offers Californians special options such as improved paint finishes and sporty wheels. Advertising is different too. Commercials aired in California show Fords at state landmarks such as Yosemite National Park. This strategy has been very effective. Thunderbird became the No. 1-selling domestic car in California in 1984 and 1985.

Coca-Cola abandoned undifferentiated marketing as a market coverage strategy years ago. Today's consumers are offered a wide choice of products to meet the needs of distinct segments of the total soft drink market. The company has expanded beyond its traditional one product nondiet cola drink by introducing "New Coke." It has expanded into the diet cola market by offering Tab, Fresca, and sugar-free Sprite. To appeal to the nondiet, noncola drinkers, it offers Sprite, Fanta, and Mello Yellow. To appeal to the segment desiring natural ingredients, it offers soft drinks with fruit juice. In addition, Coca-Cola offers many of its entries in different sizes and types of containers.

The grocery division of Beatrice markets a kosher Wesson vegetable oil to the Jewish population in the Northeast, and Mexican cuisine to Latinos in the Southwest. Cigarette companies are appealing to smokers with entries targeted to meet specific taste preferences, tar and nicotine preferences, and price preferences. Furthermore, such entries are differentiated based on demographics such as age and sex. For smokers wanting a designer cigarette, J.J. Reynolds Tobacco Co. introduced Ritz cigarettes, a female-skewed brand billed as the nation's first designer cigarette.

Although farm products such as fresh fruits and vegetables are, by and large, offered to consumers via undifferentiated marketing, a number of firms are using differentiated marketing to appeal to particular segments, rather than the mass market. Castle & Cook is selling both pineapples and tomatoes under the Dole brand. Campbell Soup recently began selling avocados under its label and mushrooms under its Campbell's Farm Fresh label. The company is also testing spinach, lettuce, cucumbers, and tomatoes under the Pepperidge Farm name. The rationale underlying these differentiated marketing approaches is to address the needs of a market segment which desires consistent, good quality produce that tastes freshly picked all year round.

From these examples it becomes evident that an undifferentiated marketing approach is no longer adequate in today's fragmented markets. With increased domestic and foreign competition, firms are taking advantage of greater industrial flexibility and supplementing their principal lines with products and marketing programs aimed at specific kinds of buyers.

Benefits

Differentiated marketing typically results in higher total sales than undifferentiated marketing. Given alternative choices, customers may continue to buy or buy more than is the case when only one product entry and marketing mix is available. Using differentiated marketing allows the firm to exploit the differences between market segments by tailoring a specific marketing mix to each group of customers. Customers are usually better served because products offered are specifically designed to meet the needs of specific segments.

A policy of differentiated marketing also allows a firm to withdraw from a segment of the market that proves unprofitable or where there has been a change in needs or wants. A firm can thus direct its efforts toward other market segments. Given the dynamic nature of the environment in which firms operate, new market segments continually evolve, thereby providing sales opportunities to those who spot and respond to changes in the marketplace.

Implementation

In choosing a differentiated marketing approach, firms need to consider the following factors: company resources, product homogeneity, product life cycle, market homogeneity, and competitors' strategies. Although there are no formulas to indicate for every case the nature of each of these factors that would call for differentiated marketing, a number of broad guidelines can be used to determine when differentiated marketing is most appropriate.

If a firm has a considerable amount of working capital and marketing expertise, differentiated marketing is appropriate. Products which are not perceived by consumers as being homogeneous are especially suited to differentiation, as with the examples cited previously. Products which are in the late growth stage of the life cycle or which are in the maturity phase of the life cycle are suited for differentiated marketing. Competitive pressures during these stages of the product's life cycle typically result in modified marketing mixes aimed at smaller segments of the total market. If the needs of consumers are different in a given market; e.g., car market, soft drink market, cigarette market, etc., differentiated marketing is in order. When competitors practice differentiated marketing, undifferentiated marketing would be a mistake.

Differentiated marketing can be based on the product itself, the distribution system by which it is sold, the pricing strategy employed, or the promotion mix used. The specific means for differentiation are peculiar to each industry. The rationale underlying differentiated marketing requires that a firm choose attributes that are different from those of competitors.

To implement differentiated marketing as a market coverage strategy, firms need to practice market segmentation effectively. Essentially, a firm needs to identify market segments, ascertain whether the segment is accessible, and determine whether the segment is large enough to be profitable.

Evaluation

Differentiated marketing typically results in higher total sales than undifferentiated marketing, but it also results in higher production and marketing costs. The production and marketing requirements of servicing many different segments increase the costs of doing business. Production costs may be higher due to smaller sales volume realized for each product version. Product modification costs may be significant due to increased engineering and tooling costs. Inventory costs are generally higher when inventories of several differentiated products have to be kept compared to the inventory costs of keeping only one product. Other marketing costs, notably promotion expenditures, rise when different market segments need to be reached with different promotional tools or advertising campaigns.

To practice differentiated marketing, it is necessary to weigh the risk of differentiation against the cost of differentiation. Several questions need to be addressed, such as: What is the financial status of the firm? What marketing expertise is available? What are competitors doing? How is the market evolving? Unless questions such as these are answered, a firm may find it has oversegmented its market, resulting in too many marketing mixes. An additional risk associated with differentiated marketing is that differentiation may not be sustained because competitors tend to imitate a successful differentiation strategy. Furthermore, bases for differentiation tend to become less important to customers as the competition increases.

Conclusion

Differentiated marketing is a market coverage strategy whereby a firm decides to operate in several segments of the market. For each segment, a unique marketing mix is required to satisfy groups of customers with different, or heterogeneous needs. Given the demise of the mass market, a differentiated marketing approach is followed by a growing number of firms today.

The major benefit of differentiated marketing is that it usually results in more sales than undifferentiated or mass marketing. On the other hand, increased production and marketing costs result when a firm serves several different market segments. The costs of differentiated marketing need to be recognized and weighed against the risks of undifferentiated and concentrated marketing.

Applications to Small Business

Small business firms enjoy several advantages vis-à-vis large firms. The willingness and ability to offer personalized customer service, familiarity with customers and local markets, close ties to the community, and overall management flexibility are advantages to be exploited through differentiated marketing.

Consumer market segments being served by a product requiring a high proportion of services are excellent targets for small firms. When segments of the market seek heterogeneous technical or personal services, differentiated marketing may not be cost-effective for large firms, whereas small firms serving local markets are often in a position to profitably differentiate their marketing mix for two or more segments. To be sure, small firms generally lack the resources to employ an undifferentiated marketing approach, whereas differentiated or concentrated marketing are viable market coverage strategies.

Software/Databases

Atlas AMP 2. Strategic Locations Planning, Suite 123, 4030 Moorpark Ave., San Jose, CA 95117. Target marketing studies and advertising analysis.

PC-MDS. Scott M. Smith, Department of Marketing, Brigham Young University, Provo, UT 84602. Statistical applications for marketing research, psychological applications such as lifestyle for differentiated marketing segments, strategic planning in marketing and brand management.

References/Sources

Bartos, Rena, "Over 49: The Invisible Market," *Harvard Business Review* (January-February, 1980): 140-49. Discusses the market of consumers past 49 years of age that must be segmented to understand the opportunities for expanded sales.

"Bringing Up Baby: A New Kind of Marketing Boom," *Business Week* (April 22, 1985): 58-59, 62, 65. Discusses how the changing consumer demographics are having a substantial impact on marketing approaches.

"Coffee Companies Pitch To A More Discerning Drinker," *Business Week* (May 28, 1984): 72-73. Shows why major coffee manufacturers are changing from an undifferentiated marketing approach to a differentiated marketing approach.

Cook, James, "Where's The Niche?" *Forbes* (September 24, 1984): 54. Presents a critical look at the danger of designing too many options into U.S. automobiles.

Hall, Trish, "Brand-Name Produce Hits Stores—But Will It Really Taste Better?" *Wall Street Journal* (September 23, 1985): 33. Discusses the rationale underlying differentiated marketing approaches pursued by companies in the produce business.

Kotler, Philip, *Marketing Management.* Englewood Cliffs, NJ: Prentice-Hall, 1984, pp. 267-271. Discusses the terms "undifferentiated," "differentiated," and "concentrated marketing." The terms were originally suggested by the author.

Moran, Brian and Horton, Cleveland, "John Scully: Marketing Methods Bring Apple Back," *Advertising Age* (December 31, 1984): 1, 22, 23. Presents Scully's strategy of developing various Apple computers targeted to specific segments such as schools and small businesses.

Resnik, Alan J., and Mason, Barry, "Marketers Turn to 'Counter Segmentation,' " *Harvard Business Review* (September-October 1979): 100-106. Discusses how marketers can analyze the profitability of a strategy of offering simpler products with lower price tags.

Shiver, Jube, "Firms Get Personal In Sales Quest," *Los Angeles Times* (February 27, 1986): 1. Shows why a differentiated marketing approach is called for in selling various products, including automobiles, grocery items, computers, and magazines.

Smith, Wendell R., "Product Differentiation And Market Segmentation As Alternative Marketing Strategies," *Journal of Marketing* (July 1956): 3-8. A classic article discussing the alternative marketing approaches.

Steinberg, Bruce, "The Mass Market Is Splitting Apart," *Fortune* (November 28, 1983). Demonstrates that the simplicity of undifferentiated or mass marketing has vanished.

Wind, Yoram, "Issues And Advances In Segmentation Research," *Journal of Marketing Research* (August 1978): 317-337. Reviews the status and advances in segmentation research.

Related Topics and Terms

Benefit Segmentation, Concentrated Marketing, Marketing Penetration, Market Segmentation, Product Differentiation, Product Positioning, Repositioning Strategy, Target Market, Undifferentiated Marketing.

Ralph M. Gaedeke
Department of Management
California State University, Sacramento

DIRECT MAIL

Overview

Direct mail is a mass medium that delivers an advertising message directly to individual prospects through the U. S. Postal Service or through private services. In 1984, direct mail accounted for $13.8 billion of the more than $88 billion spent on advertising media—15.7 percent of total media dollars. These figures have been rising steadily over the past several years and are expected to continue to rise. Direct mail as an advertising medium has the advantages of selectivity, intensive coverage, flexibility, personalization, uniform production quality, fewer immediate distractions, and response measurement.

Examples

Many different kinds of businesses use some form of direct mail marketing: retailers advertise special sales and distribute catalogs; financial institutions announce new services; insurance companies sell their policies; industrial firms pre-sell clients before their salespeople call; and various manufacturers sell directly to the consumer, bypassing the middle man.

For example, the Neiman-Marcus Christmas catalog is the epitome of Texas class. It is big, expensive, colorful, and innovative. In 1983 more than 1.5 million books were mailed to past customers and potential customers. As expected, this catalog was well received, and within 45 days following distribution of the catalog, more than 60 units of a novel product offering, a Chinese Shar-pei dog, had been sold at a price tag of $2,000 apiece.

When sales of one of its staple products, Pro Banthine, a peptic ulcer medication, began to decline, Searle Laboratories chose direct mail to attack the problem. Anamorphic art, distorted images which can be seen in proper perspective with a special mirror called an anamorphoscope, were placed on the covers of Searle brochures. The mailings created involvement as the mirrors had to be assembled in order to view the art in proper perspective. The mailings were headlined "Providing a Proper Perspective" as Searle wanted its target market, the physician, to view Pro Banthine in a new way. As a result of Searle's direct mail campaign, decline of prescribing stopped and, in fact, the campaign generated an 18.3% prescribing increase.

Benefits

Although the cost per person reached is higher for direct mail than for most other advertising media, direct mail does offer some distinctive advantages. First, the audience can be carefully selected to avoid wasted coverage. It is possible to limit contact only to those who qualify as real prospects. Since a mailing list is used, each piece can be personalized with the name and address of the recipient and even with other bits of information such as birth date. Multiple mailings enable the advertiser to achieve high frequency with direct mail. Further, serial mailings can be employed to maintain a high level of interest as the advertiser reveals the message through a series of attention-getting mailings.

Direct mail commands the immediate attention of the recipient and is less likely to be diluted by environmental distractions than are other media. Direct mail lends itself well to response measurement, unlike many other advertising media. Sales volume, number of orders, average order size, repeat orders, returned inquiry cards, new memberships, and information requests are only a few of the ways in which direct mail effectiveness can be assessed.

Finally, direct mail marketing can be used to expand a firm's reach to additional target markets, to supplement other media advertising, and to distribute samples or coupons to prospective buyers. An association was able to achieve a membership level of 110,000 by using direct mail programs. A retail jewelry chain estimates an average sales ticket of more than $70 for mailings to their house file of buyers.

Implementation

As with any advertising endeavor, the critical first step is to determine the objectives of the direct mail effort. All decisions as to which mailing list to use, how to design the mailing package, what the offer should be, and how much should be spent depend on what the advertiser intends to accomplish. Once the advertiser establishes the objectives, several stages are involved in implementing a direct mail campaign.

First, the key to an effective direct mail campaign is to select the right target audience for the mailing. This is done by the use of various mailing lists, and each type has its own particular strengths and weaknesses. The *house list,* a company's list of its customers, is potentially the very best kind of list to use. It has the advantage of pinpointing individuals who have already bought from the advertiser and who, consequently, are likely to buy again. *Mail response lists* are "rented," often through list brokers, or from other companies and are composed of someone else's customers. Response lists may be virtually as good as house lists if they are kept up-to-date ("cleaned" regularly) and if the kinds of products sold are similar to those sold by the advertiser. *Compiled lists* are generated from other lists—for example, the yellow pages. However, since 22 percent of the nation's population relocates to a new address each year, these lists quickly become obsolete. It has been estimated that the average mailing list changes more than 28 percent a year.

The next step is to design the mailing package. The advertiser must decide whether to retain development of the package or to use an advertising agency or free-lance designer and writer. But regardless of who designs the campaign, the procedure is basically the same. A typical mailer includes a sales letter, a brochure, and a response device. Decisions must be made concerning size and shape of the mailing pieces, the texture and the color of the paper used, whether there will be any special production requirements, how to word the offer, and how much to spend.

Production itself will usually be done by a local lettershop, although some large advertisers have internal facilities to handle large jobs. These activities involve not only the printing itself but also stuffing, sealing, affixing labels, sorting and coding, calculating postage, and delivery to the post office.

Evaluation

Evaluation of the direct mail mail campaign is more easily accomplished than with many other types of campaigns since a direct response is usually solicited. It then becomes a routine matter to count the number of response cards, the new members, the items sold, or the coupons redeemed as a result of the mailing.

There are numerous guidelines for designing an effective direct mail advertising package. As in all other media, the positioning is critical as a product can be different things to different people depending on how it is presented and the make-up of the audience. Even the offers themselves can be positioned. An advertiser will likely get different responses to a "Four for $1.00" appeal versus a "Buy three for $1.00 and get one FREE!" approach.

The letter is the backbone of any direct marketing campaign. Long letters (8-12 pages) have been known to achieve a high response rate. Advertisers should be ruthless in cutting out nonessentials, passive verbs, and redundancies but careful to tell the whole story. The first sentence of the letter acts as a headline and should be so designed. Type size should ideally be 10-11 point at least, and the right margin should never be justified.

The P.S. is important because it virtually functions as a subheadline. That is, the P.S. is the second item the recipient looks at after the first sentence. Copywriters should construct the P.S. as a teaser line to induce the recipient to read the entire letter or as a summary that restates the essence of the offer.

The body of the letter should be comprised of short paragraphs—a maximum of six sentences—with a lot of white space between sentences and between paragraphs. Sentences should be short and easy to read, and the vocabulary should be highly understandable.

Response devices should always be a part of the mailing since they increase response rates tremendously. They should be noticeable and easy to use. Such features as prepaid postage, pre-addressed labels, and even a pencil included in the mailing have been found to increase response rates.

Finally, a general rule-of-thumb is to use a number ten envelope. Self-mailers never outpull the number ten, nor do any of the other envelope sizes.

Conclusion

Direct mail marketing as an advertising medium and as a marketing tool has grown dramatically for several reasons. The ever-increasing numbers of women in the work force strongly indicate that they have less and less time to shop. Consequently, buying through the mail is a real time-saver as it eliminates the hassle of driving across town, negotiating the parking lot, and waiting in line to check out. At home, consumers can shop at their leisure, choosing just those items that meet their individual needs.

Direct mail can be personalized by addressing the recipient by name. It can be coupled with specialty advertising or premiums to enhance involvement with the message, and direct mail provides the advertiser with concrete feedback on how well the advertising effort is working.

As a medium for business-to-business advertising, direct mail has some special advantages. In industrial advertising, the market is often relatively small, so each potential customer can be individually targeted. Direct mail can be used to pre-sell a customer or introduce a product before the salesperson makes a call. Since sales calls cost a company an average of more than $200 each, direct mail can be extremely cost effective if it helps reduce the selling time of an average call.

Applications to Small Business

Direct mail offers the small advertiser essentially the same benefits that it offers the large advertiser. The difference lies predominantly in the size of the advertising budget. Small businesses generally have a somewhat limited and reasonably identifiable clientele. For this reason, a targeted medium like direct mail can often achieve specific objectives that no other medium can match. Additionally, direct mail allows the small advertiser the option of selectively targeting those customers that have been historically the most profitable. Such a strategy greatly enhances the efficiency of each media dollar spent.

Direct mail can be implemented by a small advertiser who is operating with a relatively small budget and yet can be extremely effective in reaching realistic advertising goals. Further, the small advertiser can tailor a mailing package to reflect local customer needs as well as local competitive market conditions. Finally, direct mail provides the small advertiser with an opportunity to measure advertising effectiveness in terms of sales, new customers, product trials, or information requests.

Software/Databases

Alvin B. Zeller Mailing Lists, Alvin B. Zeller, Inc., 475 Park Avenue South, New York, NY 10016. Provides a large number of mailing lists for the direct mail marketer, including lists for businesses, executives, doctors, dentists, attorneys, accountants, engineers, teachers, churches, schools, organizations, students, farmers, and all residents of the U. S. Names are available by states, counties, cities, metro areas, and zip codes.

References/Sources

Bauer, Carol H. *The Law and Direct Marketing*. Publications Division of DMMA (Direct Mail/Marketing Association, Inc.), 1980. Provides concise summaries of pertinent legislation including list use, mail and phone solicitation, delayed delivery, and guarantees.

Bivins, Jacquelyn, "The Sale Is In the Mail," in *Chain Store Age Executive* (March 1984): 44-54. Identifies trends in catalog sales by retailers.

Direct Mail Advertising & Selling for Retailers, National Retail Merchants Association, 1978. A compilation of 28 professional ideas on how to use the various facets of direct mail marketing to maximize profit.

Direct Mail in Focus, Direct Mail/Marketing Association, 1979. A summary of 1978-79 focus group opinion research studies conducted by Goldring & Company to define the broad outlines of consumer characteristics and habits related to direct mail.

Gillet, Peter L. "In Home Shoppers—An Overview," in *Journal of Marketing* (October 1976): 81-88. Reviews findings on in-home shoppers and points out further research needs.

Hansen, Robert A. *National Survey of Consumer's Attitudes Toward Direct Mail Advertising*. MASA International, 1979. Two-volume national survey of consumer attitudes toward direct mail advertising—covers attitude, readership, and action or usage for every direct mail category.

Higgins, Kevin T. "Boom Time for Cataloging Is Quieting Down," in *Marketing News* (August 2, 1985): 11-13. Points out reasons for the trend of companies being more selective in catalog mailouts, focus on upper-income consumers.

Hodgson, Richard S. *Direct Mail and Mail Order Handbook,* Dartnell Corp., 1980. The "Bible" of direct mail; filled with information from "how-to" tidbits to major marketing principles.

_____, *How To Work With Mailing List,* Direct Mail/Marketing Association, 1976. A presentation of the essentials to good list management—starting a mailing list, evaluating results, list sources, and working with brokers.

Horchow, Roger, *Elephants In Your Mailbox*. New York: Truman Talley Books, 1980. Confessions of "The Catalogue King" supply secrets of success and big mistakes in mail order activities.

Klein, Bernard, *Directory of Mailing List Houses*. B. Klein Publications, 1977.

Lists approximately 2,000 listhouses, brokers, compilers, list managers, and list owners who rent their lists (with notation of specializations).

Lewis, Herschell Gordon, *Mail Order Advertising.* Englewood Cliffs, NJ: Prentice-Hall, 1983. Offers rules for creative mail order writing and guidelines for setting up direct response advertising.

Mayer, Edward N. Jr. and Roy G. Ljungren, eds. *The Handbook of Industrial Direct Mail Advertising,* 1972. Handbook designed especially for industrial advertisers with instructions on how to integrate direct mail into the marketing and advertising mix, what lists to use, etc.

McQuade, Walter, "There's a Lot of Satisfaction (Guaranteed) in Direct Marketing," in *Fortune* (April 21, 1980): 110-124. Study on the growth and penetration of direct mail through an increasing array of product lines and technological advances in the field.

Ross, Maxwell, C. *How To Write Successful Direct Mail Letter Copy.* Direct Marketing/Mail Association, 1976. Includes a 20-point checklist to help write better copy.

Simon, Julian L. *How To Start and Operate A Mail-Order Business.* New York: McGraw-Hill, 1976. Discover the least expensive and most effective ways to promote a selected product—define its market, create ad and mail-order copy.

Related Topics and Terms
    Account Executive, Advertising, Advertising Agency, Catalog Merchandising, Catalog Selling, Copywriting, Direct Marketing, Direct Response, Inquiries, Letter Shop, List Broker, Mailing Lists, Mail Order House, Media Selection, Offer, Promotion Mix, Response Device, Response Rate.

Marjorie J. Caballero
Department of Marketing
Baylor University

DIRECT SELLING

Overview
Direct Selling is a form of product distribution that involves direct-to-consumer marketing through personal presentation and demonstration of goods and services, primarily in homes. In 1983, direct selling represented a contribution of $8.5 billion to the U. S. economy and provided employment for 4.9 million independent direct sales people across the country.

Examples
In 1983 Mary Kay Cosmetics, whose products are sold by some 200,000 independent beauty consultants world-wide, recorded $323.8 million in sales. Net income was $36.7 million. These products are sold by independent sales consultants through a modified party plan system in which the cosmetics are demonstrated and used by all attendees. The emphasis is on in-home teaching rather than selling.

While Cameo Coutures, Inc., producers of lingerie and loungewear, is considered a party-plan company, over 25% of sales are made on a one-to-one basis. The retail price range on Cameo lingerie varies from $17.00 to $134.00, and an average Cameo show grosses $175. At a 25% commission, a couturier (sales representative) would earn $43.75, while a strong regional manager can make from $36,000 to $50,000 per year.

Avon is one the most well-known direct selling companies with annual sales of nearly $3 billion. Avon's selling strategy emphasizes the one-on-one, door-to-door approach using approximately 1.3 million independent sales representatives and operating in more than thirty countries.

However, not only are clothing and cosmetics sold directly, but also such products as books, home decorating items, home cleaning products and appliances, cookware, cutlery, and insurance.

Benefits
Personal service is one benefit offered by direct selling that is often lacking in traditional retail service. Customers like to feel that they are being given individualized attention; they also appreciate a relaxed atmosphere in which to ask questions and learn more about the product. Direct selling offers customers the convenience of shopping at home without the annoyance of traffic, crowded parking, lack of sales assistance, and waiting in check-out lines.

From the seller's perspective, the opportunity is available to fully explain product features. Obligation is another advantage of direct selling from the seller's perspective. Many prospects buy on the basis of friendship.

Implementation

The first step in implementing a direct selling program is to determine whether the product or product line lends itself to being sold directly.

Ideally, the product should exhibit some form of exclusivity to set it apart from comparable product lines. Exclusive features may be price, design, packaging, or additional features and benefits. It helps if the product requires a demonstration, particularly if the customer can be directly involved. Many successful products are oriented to home and family, such as cookware and home furnishings. Finally the product should have repeat and/or multiple sales appeal. Cosmetics, food supplements, and apparel must be replaced; food containers, toys, and jewelry offer a variety of "versions" so that multiple-item purchases occur.

If the product lends itself to direct selling, an effective distribution plan must then be developed. The party plan is one of the most widely used approaches in direct selling. "Party plan" is the term applied to group selling, of which there are several variations. In most cases, the product is not only displayed, but also demonstrated in use, often with party guests participating. At a "tasting party," guests sample food products; at a home decorating party, guests observe various configurations and applications of decorating items; at an apparel party, guests model clothing.

One-on-one selling, which includes door-to-door, is employed when a sales representative calls on the prospect at home. This approach is used by Avon, Stanley, the Southwestern Company, Electrolux, and many others.

An underlying principle in a direct selling approach is that salespeople earn a commission on what they sell. Very few direct selling companies try to apply any type of salary approach at the sales representative level. In fact, most salespeople are recruited as independent contractors and work on a part-time basis, thus eliminating much of the overhead costs associated with more traditional sales forces.

However, most direct selling companies implement a promotion and rewards system based on performance. Those who have moved up the organizational ladder are often responsible for recruitment and training of new sales representatives.

The multilevel approach is the fastest-growing area of direct selling. Under this type of plan, sales representatives earn graduated commissions based on increased personal sales and/or sales of those they have sponsored into the organization. This system can become extremely profitable for someone who is willing to invest extra time and effort. As the group of those sponsored either directly or indirectly by an individual continues to grow, sales commissions, bonuses, overrides, and discounts increase. As a result, direct selling has produced many wealthy and successful business people.

Evaluation

Party plans can be used successfully for selling lower-priced products. Although individual sales are lower, the lesser commission is offset by multiple sales and greater volume generated by group selling and additional bookings. The party atmosphere is conducive to consumer purchasing behavior and also to recruiting others into the program. Parties produce a high degree of customer interest and involvement as guests have the opportunity to experience the product directly. Successful party plans provide representatives with increasing incentives and goals as they progress to managerial and executive levels within the organization.

The company that chooses a one-on-one plan for product distribution often is selling a high-ticket item. Some examples of these are vacuum cleaners, encyclopedias, cutlery, and home security systems. While sales of such items yield substantial commissions, the products also require considerable selling time and effort. Thus, the reward for this type of salesperson is more likely to be individual rather than group achievement, and the reward system should be designed to reflect this orientation.

Sales meetings, training sessions, and recruitment are often conducted through branch offices. Under this distribution plan, new leads are generated through referrals as well as cold canvassing. Even more than those under the party plan, sales managers who operate under one-on-one selling must be experienced in recruiting, training, and motivating the sales force as well as experienced in prospecting for customers and making good sales presentations.

The one-on-one method usually takes longer to show substantial market penetration (12 to 18 months) than does the party plan. However, neither approach can be evaluated accurately until a trial period of approximately two years has been completed.

The multilevel structure of distribution and compensation has often been confused with the illegal and unethical pyramid schemes of a few years ago. However, pyramids differ from multilevel marketing in the following key respects:

1. They emphasize recruitment—that is, the selling of distributorships—rather than the selling of products.
2. Pyramid schemes required prospects to invest very large nonrefundable sums of capital, usually in the form of purchasing nonreturnable inventory.

In contrast, multilevel marketing builds on a solid economic base. Distributorships must be earned by selling the product and thereby producing specified levels of sales volume. Thus, rewards are closely linked to performance, and ambitious people have essentially equal opportunities to progress upwards in the organization.

Conclusion

During the past 20 years, direct selling has been one of the fastest-growing areas of marketing. Customers appreciate the convenience, the personalized service, and the unique, high-quality products offered by many direct sellers. Customers give high marks to direct selling compared to retail selling with respect to: 1) helpful-

Media Decisions (March 1985): 98-99. Cites reasons for traditional consumer package goods marketers' move toward the use of direct marketing in trying to build their businesses.

Shook, Robert L. *Ten Greatest Salespersons*. New York: Harper & Row, 1978. A text containing interviews with today's ten top salespeople on how they explain their success.

Skolnik, Rayna, "Shaklee Shares the Good Life," *Sales & Marketing Management* (October 9, 1978): 33-36. An overview of the activities leading to the continuing success of Shaklee, manufacturer and distributor of nutritional supplements, cosmetics, and household items.

Stem, Edward, *The Direct Marketing Market Place*. Hillary Publishers, 1980. Directory of major direct marketing companies, suppliers, prominent individuals, agencies, consultants, media buyers—with names, addresses, phone numbers, products, services, chief executives, sales and advertising volume, etc.

"There's No Place Like Home," *Sales & Marketing Management* (June 18, 1979): 85-86. Research article which uses graphs to depict the results of using the two different types of direct-selling methods.

Related Topics and Terms

Buyer, Canned Presentation, Close, Demonstration, Direct Distribution, Door-to-Door Selling, Dyadic Interaction, Marketing Plan, Multilevel Marketing, Party Plan, Personal Selling, Planned Presentation, Promotion Mix, Prospecting, Sales Branch, Samples, Telephone Selling.

Marjorie J. Caballero
Department of Marketing
Baylor University

DISTRIBUTION INTENSITY

Overview

Companies can choose from one of three possible distribution intensity alternatives—intensive distribution, selective distribution, or exclusive distribution—which denote three degrees of market exposure. Intensive distribution, as the name suggests, is the strategy of attempting to gain access to as many resellers or to establish as many of the company's own units as possible within the region. Selective distribution is the policy of screening resellers and picking only a few to carry the product or establishing just a few company units in the region. Exclusive distribution is the selection of one reseller or establishing one company unit in the region to carry the product.

Examples

Intensive Distribution

Manufacturers of convenience goods and standardized industrial goods generally try to place their product with as many outlets as possible. For example, a company like Bristol-Myers desires widespread distribution for their product Bufferin, since the buying habits of consumers are predicated on convenience of purchase. The dominant factor in marketing of convenience goods is place utility. Since brand insistence is relatively weak, maximum exposure is essential. Although intensive distribution is required, it is unlikely that the manufacturer will be able to depend upon the retailer for much promotional assistance. The manufacturer will probably assume most of the responsibility and cost of advertising and point-of-purchase materials. In the case of marketing Bufferin, the retailers are drug stores and supermarkets that carry numerous other competing products and other product lines. In this situation, the product is one of several thousand sold by the retailer so that strategic shelf placement and other merchandising aids cannot necessarily be expected by the manufacturer.

Selective Distribution Policy

Between the policies of intensive and exclusive distribution is selective distribution or the policy of selling to a limited number of resellers in a particular market. This type of arrangement affords the manufacturer more coverage than exclusive selling but does not overextend its resources as the case might be with intensive distribution. Established and new companies use this policy profitably since distributors and dealers can be gained by offering them selective distribution. Generally, a better than average selling effort is expected, and adequate market coverage is realized with more control and reduced costs than with intensive distribution. Such firms as Cluett Peabody and Company, manufacturer of Arrow shirts; the Simmons Company, manufacturer of Beautyrest mattresses; Jantzen, manufacturer of sportswear; and Jonathan Logan, manufacturer of ladies-ready-to-wear clothes, follow a selective selling policy.

Exclusive Distribution

Some manufacturers hope to attain more selling support and to be able to exercise more control over the selling outlets' policies on pricing, promotion, credit, and other functions by deliberately limiting the number of intermediaries handling their products in particular geographic areas. An agreement is entered into between manufacturer and distributor or dealer. Usually the manufacturer agrees to permit the distributor to be the exclusive seller in a given territory. The distributor agrees to aggressively sell the manufacturers' product. Examples of companies marketing their products using this method are Hickey Freeman with men's clothing and C.F. Hathaway Company with men's shirts.

Benefits

Intensive Distribution

(1) Wide coverage of distribution outlets; (2) extensive brand recognition; and (3) high brand turnover.

Selective Distribution

(1) Distributors and retail dealers will give preferential treatment to the brand because of relatively limited competition; (2) the retail dealer, from a status standpoint, may find it advantageous in the local community; and (3) the retail dealer will likely join in cooperative advertising campaigns reducing costs to the manufacturer and at the same time enlarging the promotional effort.

Exclusive Distribution

The main reasons for granting exclusive distribution agreements are the following: (1) to obtain market access if dealers believe that protection against intrabrand competition is needed and they would decline to handle the product without such a stipulation; (2) as a motivational means to increase the distributors' sales efforts; (3) to control the character and uniformity of the resellers' operations; (4) strong sales forecasting capability; and (5) a high degree of dealer loyalty and cooperation.

Implementation

Intensive Distribution

A decision to use as many resellers of a particular type as possible to distribute the product is usually based on a combination of factors. Generally, distribution saturation is attempted if the product price is relatively low and if buyers frequently purchase the product but are willing to accept a substitute product. Companies marketing such products as cigarettes, soft drinks, and inexpensive glass and dinnerware frequently use an intensive distribution policy. Furthermore, these companies often use multiple channels, especially differentiated by type of retailer, to saturate the market with the product.

Selective Distribution

The more selective the distribution pattern, the greater is the expected selling effort from the dealers. Also, the more intensive the distribution, the less selling effort is anticipated on the part of any one reseller. A good rule of thumb is that the more expensive the product, the lower the stock turn is, or the more important the repair service, the more of a tendency there is for the policy of highly selective distribution to be chosen.

Exclusive Distribution

The buyer may welcome such an arrangement since a continued source of supply is assured. This can be especially important in periods of shortages. Prompt delivery when re-orders are placed is usually another advantage of exclusive distribution. If the manufacturer promotes the product effectively, the profit potential of the product may well justify the concentration of selling efforts on the part of distributors and retail dealers. This distribution policy is usually more effective in medium and small-size cities. Manufacturers may use a selective distribution policy in cities with more than one million people and an exclusive policy for cities and towns with less population.

Evaluation

A critical factor in strategically positioning a firm in the competitive marketplace is the selection of the correct distribution intensity. Distribution intensity decisions and channel management are vital for the operation of the distribution system. The choice of strategy and the adjustment of strategy are essential management concerns. A pivotal role of distribution intensity decisions and channel management was indicated as Zenith, in the television market, moved away from exclusive to selective to intensive distribution. In contrast, Ethan Allen moved away from intensive distribution towards more selective distribution policies which were supported by various services and assistance from the manufacturer. The degree of market coverage and channel support is an essential factor in servicing customer needs and achieving channel objectives.

Conclusion

Strategic Outcomes: Exclusive distribution: (1) high degree of channel control; (2) strong sales forecasting capability; (3) high degree of dealer loyalty and cooperation. *Selective distribution:* (1) maintenance of channel standards; (2) moderate degree of channel control; (3) subject to price competition and dealer desires to reduce number of competitive outlets. *Intensive distribution:* (1) low degree of channel control; (2) wide coverage; (3) wide customer recognition; (4) high brand turnover; (5) fierce price competition.

Applications to Small Business

Both middlemen and retailers should weigh the cost of intensive, selective, and exclusive distribution, while manufacturers should consider problems of fulfillment, advertising, and returns before selecting the distribution method. Drug stores, for example, must balance the cost of shelf space, stocking, inventory control, and storage when deciding whether to carry two or ten brands of shampoo. Manufacturers must decide if distributing shampoo to every drug store, or only to selected drug stores of a certain size or location, is more cost effective. Intensive distribution often requires expensive advertising or deep dealer discounts.

Retailers can be greatly assisted by local market surveys and buying patterns. Market segmentation and tastes greatly effect the type of distribution required, as does the emotional appeal of a product. If, for example, certain television programs are especially popular in a town, then it may be necessary for a retailer to carry only the advertised items rather than a complete line of similar products.

Unit costs and product uniqueness will also greatly affect the method of distribution. Buyers of televisions seldom demand a particular brand as long as the same features are available in a competitive model. Small businesses are in an excellent position to ask for manufacturer support and discounts if they understand their market and the manufacturer's competition.

Software/Databases

Market Potential. Donnelley Marketing Information Service, 1351 Washington Boulevard, Stamford, CT 06902. Using primarily the 1980 *Census of Retail Trade,* Market Potential provides consumer expenditures for over 20 types of retail outlets, such as department stores, grocery, drug, furniture, and variety. These data are available for a number of areas, including states, counties, tracts, CMSAs, PMSAs, MSAs, SMSAs, SAMIs, and Zip Codes.

References/Sources

Bucklin, Louis P. "Retail Strategy and the Classification of Consumer Goods," in *Journal of Marketing* (January 1963): 50-55. One of the early studies showing the relationship between the types of consumer goods and distribution policies.

Jain, Subbash C., *Marketing Planning and Strategy.* Cincinnati, OH: South-Western Publishing, 1985. Chapter 15 develops a framework for strategic implementation.

Michman, Ronald D. and Stanley D. Sibley, *Marketing Channels and Strategies.* 2nd ed. Columbus, OH: Grid Publishing Company, 1980. Chapter 10 develops a channel program for these distribution policies.

Rosenbloom, Bert, *Marketing Channels: A Management View.* 2nd ed. New York: The Dryden Press, 1983. Chapter 5 presents a graphic illustration of distribution intensity levels.

Stern, Louis W. and Adell L. El-Ansary, *Marketing Channels.* 2nd ed. Prentice-Hall, Englewood Cliffs, NJ: 1982. Chapter 5 demonstrates the pitfalls of intensive, selective, and exclusive distribution policies.

Related Topics and Terms
Distribution Intensity Decisions, Distribution Policies, and Distribution Programs.

Ronald D. Michman
Department of Marketing
Shippensburg University

DROP SHIPPER

Overview

Wholesalers, that is intermediaries who buy and sell merchandise and thus take title to the goods they handle, are often categorized into two major groups. The first of these consists of "full-function" or "full-service" wholesalers, those that provide a full array of services to their clients. The second group includes the "limited-function" wholesalers, those who offer a reduced number of services eliminating, for example, delivery or the granting of credit. Drop shippers are limited-function wholesalers who avoid the delivery function by arranging for the shipment of goods directly from a manufacturer to a retailer, industrial user, or other buyer. Almost every sort of wholesaler occasionally resorts to this practice, but only wholesalers who perform the bulk of their business in that manner are properly called drop shippers. Several thousand establishments of this sort operate in the U.S. and account for billions of dollars in sales. Drop shippers are known by many other names. Among them are "desk jobber" and "direct mill shipper." The term can also be used as a verb as in "drop ship the merchandise to customer X."

Drop shippers usually operate from spartan offices and perform few services other than the selling function. Since they do not handle the goods they sell they have no warehouses but *do* take risks that attend ownership, and must collect from customers and/or extend credit at their own risk. In short, even though the drop shipper never takes possession of the merchandise sold, he owns the goods and is responsible for financing, risk-taking, and other functions except delivery. Delivery is handled by the producer who, of course, ships directly to the retailer, industrial user, or other buyer.

Examples

Because the drop shipper's method of operation permits elimination of warehousing and "double handling" as the merchandise makes its way from producer to buyer, this type of intermediary operates most successfully in situations where goods are bulky and relatively inexpensive in comparison to their bulk. It is also helpful if buyers typically purchase those goods in large lots. Therefore, such products as lumber, coal, building blocks and bricks, metals, and petroleum are among the goods most likely to be drop shipped. The drop shipper's cost of doing business in these lines is typically far below that of other types of wholesalers. In the lumber trade, for example, it is traditional that drop shippers have a cost of doing business half that of "regular" wholesalers who maintain lumber yards and inventories.

Many drop shippers are "one man operations" operated by individuals with experience in the industries they serve. They are often salespeople formerly employed by manufacturers who see an opportunity to "pirate" old customers from

266

their former employers by offering those customers reduced prices. Other drop shippers are semi-retired people who can use their experience and contacts to make a reasonable number of sales with a minimum amount of effort and virtually no investment in assets. In Fairfield, Connecticut, one former lumber yard owner is a drop shipper for nails which he ships directly to construction sites. His "investment" in his business is his experience, two telephones, and rented space in the loft of the lumber yard he formerly owned.

The activities of drop shippers often inspire "regular" wholesalers to operate their own drop shipment business in an attempt to gain the sales that otherwise go to drop shippers. Such action is not without risks, however. Customers given a low price on drop shipped goods may expect the same low price on ordinary purchases. Too, drop shipment sales may cannibalize "regular" sales, sales that produce a far higher margin. Furthermore, manufacturers may resent the fact that the performance of limited functions by drop shippers can mean that the manufacturers themselves must perform some of the functions the drop shipper has avoided.

Benefits

Benefits of the drop shipper's mode of operation accrue to both the drop shipper and to customers purchasing goods via a drop shipper. Drop shippers may begin business with a minimum investment in offices and equipment. In general, it is their expertise and experience in a field of activity that they offer. Manufacturers may provide drop shippers with a small supply of sample merchandise and expect the drop shippers to develop customers for it. In other words, drop shippers are supposed to know who wants to buy in quantities suited to the drop shipping approach to doing business. Like brokers, then, they bring buyers and sellers together. Unlike brokers, however, they take title to the goods they sell. This is a benefit to the supplier who avoids the task of extension of credit to buyers and the resulting risks.

The drop shipper's way of operating brings obvious benefits to the customers employing this means of purchase. Customers expect and get substantial savings over the "regular" prices charged by intermediaries who stock and handle goods. Too, they can deal with a local businessperson rather than a distant manufacturer. In some cases, manufacturers may not want to deal with retailers or industrial users except where a drop shipper is involved. This is because the drop shipper, who may be known to the manufacturer, assumes the risks of collection from the customer, a person who may not be known to the manufacturer. Lastly, the buyer using a drop shipper can have carload or other sizable quantities of goods delivered where needed, such as to a construction site, avoiding the task of assembling a suitable quantity of goods from "regular" wholesalers.

This last point suggests a limitation inherent in the drop shipper's way of conducting trade. That is, buyers must be able to purchase in large quantities or, at the least, in quantities in which the manufacturer normally packs and ships products.

Many buyers cannot use such large quantities of goods, or may only be able to buy in such quantities once in a while, such as at the beginning of a selling season.

Implementation

It is not difficult for an individual with a certain familiarity with a given industry to become a drop shipper. The investment is small and the greatest risk is the chance that purchasers will fail to pay their bills. Some drop shippers reduce this risk by demanding that buyers pay for merchandise at the time it is ordered. In such a case the drop shipper is no longer performing the credit function and will likely have to reduce prices to reflect that fact.

These conditions are also true of wholesalers who do take possession of merchandise in the normal course of their operations. These intermediaries may chose to drop ship merchandise on occasion and can do so with relative ease. In some states a commercial license may be required or other regulations met. These are, in virtually every case, *pro forma* requirements which are easily fulfilled.

Business people seeking to implement a drop shipping operation may find that it is necessary to advertise or otherwise promote this service. But because these intermediaries are usually familiar with the relatively narrow fields in which they operate; e.g., the building supplies field, appropriate advertising media directed at specific target market groups are usually not difficult to identify. In most cases, assistance in developing promotions will be available from the media, such as the publishers of directories or trade publications. Drop shippers may also employ personal selling techniques, calling on specific customers to inform them of available services.

Evaluation

The performance of a drop shipping operation may be difficult to gauge for several reasons. In the case of the "pure" drop shipper, the intermediary who does not deal in any other than drop shipped goods, standard evaluative tools are applicable. Profit and loss statements, sales data and trends, and other figures can be used to determine whether or not the drop shipping operation is profitable enough to satisfy the owners. Because the owners are likely to be former manufacturers' sales representatives, or employees of wholesalers or retailers of the goods they are now drop shipping, some of their "payback" comes to them in the form of satisfaction or a feeling of independence in operating their own (typically small) businesses. Thus the operation of the firm often involves achieving personal as well as financial goals.

Since most wholesalers who normally take possession of their merchandise also do some drop shipping, evaluation of their drop shipping performance is complex. This is because the intermediary *might* have sold the very same merchandise through normal, higher margined means, but drop shipped it instead. As was noted earlier, it is not difficult for a wholesaler to cannibalize "normal" sales in favor of sales that employ drop shipping. Further, since most "regular" wholesalers engage in drop shipping from time to time it is difficult to find data that describe drop shipping operations specifically. Trade magazines dealing with specific industries may be of some help, as might the Small Business Administration. Texts dealing with wholesaling typically cover drop shipping operations in one or two pages (out of 700 or more). The *Statistical Abstract of the United States* makes no mention at all of drop shippers, nor does the U.S. Department of Commerce publication *Current Business Report*. Even the U.S. *Census of Wholesale Trade* does not treat drop shippers specifically, lumping them in with other types of merchant wholesalers.

No entry for "drop shipper" appears in either the *American Statistics Index*, the *Encyclopedia of Associations* or the *National Trade and Professional Associations of the United States*. Business people seeking guidance through published sources must, for the most part, check specific industry or product categories.

Conclusion

Despite the paucity of information available, drop shipping is an important activity, especially where bulky, relatively low cost materials are involved. Cement blocks, nails, and lumber are often drop shipped to building sites where they are needed. Further, since a drop shipper's major asset is likely to be a knowledge of the industry served, this type of business provides an opportunity for experienced individuals to begin their own businesses with relatively little upfront investment.

Applications To Small Business

The concept of drop shipping, wholesaling products for which one holds title but does not take possession, can be utilized in almost any line of trade! Some very large wholesalers drop ship merchandise from time to time, as might some small wholesale operations. The "pure" drop shipper is likely to be a small business, however. Little investment is needed to begin operations. It is not unusual to find a drop shipper who has been in business for years operating a one-person office containing modest equipment and located in an unimpressive building or neighborhood. The drop shipper's major asset is a knowledge of the industry served. For this reason the drop shipper is typically a former sales representative dealing in the products handled or former owner or employee of some other type of business related to the industry served.

Despite the attractiveness that undertaking a drop shipping operation might hold to an individual who, willingly or not, finds himself anxious to begin an independent business, there is always a risk of failure. Fortunately, drop shippers can minimize monetary risk because their operations are essentially "invisible" to their suppliers and customers. Drop shippers process orders by mail or telephone and can work out of their homes or other limited facilities. No warehouses need be built, no materials handling equipment purchased, no stock is maintained.

Of course, any business characterized by ease of entry is likely to be competitive. Consequently, drop shippers tend to be localized operations. They most commonly start out small and stay small. However, the chance for a person with experience in a given line of goods to operate an independent business continues to prove attractive.

Software/Databases

Considerable amounts of spreadsheet software with applicability to drop shipping operations are available. *Lotus 1-2-3*, for example, may be used to analyze a number of marketing problems. Since the drop shipper's operation is based in good measure on effective order processing the applicability of computers is obvious.

Less readily available are data directly pertaining to drop shipping operations. Drop shipping is often only one part of the operations of "regular" wholesalers, and is likely to get "mixed in" with figures describing wholesaling operations in general.

Lotus 1-2-3 for Marketing and Sales by Michael Laric and Ronald Stiff, Prentice-Hall Inc., Englewood Cliffs, NJ 07632. Offers an overview of how *Lotus 1-2-3* may be used to assist in analysis of marketing related considerations such as pricing, demand, and costs.

Electronic Yellow Pages-Wholesalers Directory. Market Data Retrieval, Inc., Westport, CT 06880. Lists all types of wholesalers throughout the U.S. and is updated quarterly.

References/Sources

Beckman, Theodore N., Engle, Nathanael H., and Buzzell, Robert D., *Wholesaling*. New York: Ronald Press, 1959, pp. 169–171. Offers a textbook-length treatment of wholesaling operations, providing a typically brief discussion of drop shippers. Despite the age of this text, it is still in wide circulation, reflecting the lack of attention given this field in recent decades.

Burns, Lawrence, Hall, Randolph, Blumenfeld, Dennis, and Daganzo, Carlos, "Distribution Strategies that Minimize Transportation and Inventory Costs," *Operations Research* (May-June 1985): 469–490. Explores methods for minimizing distribution costs contrasting direct shipping with delivery to more than one customer and shows direct shipping to best fit economic order quantity models rather than the shipping need of the supplier.

Zikmund, William and d'Amico, Michael, *Marketing*. New York: John Wiley and Sons, 1986, pp. 367–369. Contrasts full-service and limited-service wholesalers, and discusses drop shippers and their operations. A chart showing the flow of paperwork, fees, and merchandise is included.

Related Topics and Terms
Broker, Channel of Distribution, Commodities, Industrial Market, Manufacturers' Agent, Physical Distribution, Wholesaler.

Michael F. d'Amico
Department of Marketing
University of Akron

EARLY ADOPTERS AND EARLY MAJORITY

Overview

If the frequency of adoption of a new product is plotted against time, the result is a bell-shaped curve. This curve can be conveniently divided into 5 sections, corresponding to the five classifications of adopters: innovators, early adopters, early majority, late majority, and laggards. The early majority is the third group of consumers to adopt a product after the innovators. They constitute approximately 34% of all of those who will ever adopt the product. The early majority is influenced in their buying behavior by the early adopters while they, in turn, exert considerable influence over the late majority and laggard adopter categories. The early majority tends to accept a new product just before the "average" adopter. He is socially active, but seldom a leader, and he likes to deliberate for some time before making a decision. While this group is willing to take some risks in trying new things, it prefers risks to be tempered by the experiences of the early adopters.

The early majority provide the link between the more adventurous innovators and early adopters, and the more cautious late majority and laggards because they hold an important place in the new product introduction strategy. Because of the sheer size of the group (34% of all those who will adopt the product) they, along with the late majority (also 34%) are the ultimate target of new product strategies. The early adopter category with only 13.5% of the total is really only a stepping stone to these greener pastures.

Examples

Rita is in the early majority when it comes to cosmetics. She has a wide circle of friends, and is generally liked, but she is definitely not the trend setter for her circle. With regard to her make-up, she is trendy, but not a trend setter. As a matter of fact, she gets most of her ideas in how to get "dolled-up" from Alice, an early adopter. Rita admires Alice's pluck, but she had to sit back and think things through very seriously before she followed Alice's example and dyed her hair green. The local Young-face cosmetics rep decided that she could make more in commissions if she could get people like Rita to come to her presentations. However, when she found that Rita was somewhat reluctant to show up, the Young-face rep decided to develop a strategy to bring her in. Her plan was threefold: first of all, she was going to encourage a number of early adopters, like Alice to come to her presentations, by offering a much more contemporary line of products. Secondly, she was going to offer gifts to the early adopters for every five women they brought with them. Finally, when she got the women into the presentation, she was going to tone the great-grand style preferred by many of the early adopters down

272

somewhat, so as to appeal more to the cautious risk takers like Rita. Her plan took a little longer to work than she expected; however, she did eventually break into the early majority market in her area.

Revlo, the manufacturer of a new industrial ink, decided to target the early majority segment of its ink purchasers in order to gain a stronger foothold in the market. Their plan was threefold. First of all, they secured lengthy testimonials from some of the most respected opinion leaders among the ink purchasers. Secondly, they sent out these testimonials along with a generous set of free samples to those they had identified as possible early majority. Finally, they followed this up a month later by sending their sales force for personal contact and to give demonstrations to their target prospects. As a result, Revlo's inks had captured 20% of the market by the end of the year.

Benefits

Being able to identify the pertinent group of early majority can give a company a substantial edge in developing its new market and products. While the key to entering a market is the early adopter, the key to gaining market share begins with the early majority.

The early majority is an important group of adopters for three reasons: first of all, they are a large group, comprising 34% of all those who will ever adopt the product. Secondly, they provide the essential link between the risk-taking early adopters, and the risk-averse later adopters. Finally, the early majority is important because it represents the beginning of the more stable part of the market. The early adopters and innovators may be flashy, but they tend to be fickle. The early and late majorities and the laggards provide a stable core for future planning.

Implementation

Putting together a program which target markets the early majority in a particular market is not an easy matter. Effective programs require a number of steps. The first step is to identify exactly who the early majority are. It is important to be able to specify in concrete terms what the group is. This description may take on a number of forms: geographical, race, religion, income, age and occupation. Getting the information to develop such a description is also difficult, but it can be achieved in two different ways: either by conducting extensive analytical surveys of the market, or by using pre-existing mailing lists. Regardless of the method used, perfection is not possible. Rather, what most often emerges is a reasonably close approximation of the early majority group.

The second step is to identify the early adopter group in the market being considered. This can also be achieved by either an analytical survey, or by using pre-existing mailing lists. The early adopter is perhaps a little easier to identify because of the more distinct characteristics of the group.

The third step is to identify the nature of the relationship between the early majority and early adopter categories in the market under consideration. Understanding this relationship is important because early adopters have a strong influence on the adoption patterns of the early majority. In particular, three characteristics of the relationship should be investigated: the nature of the social system, the nature of the communication process within the social system, and the expected rate of adoption. First of all, the social system constituting the market should be identified and described. This system may take on the characteristics of individuals, informal groups, organizations, or governmental units. The question to ask is, what are the fundamental units of the market under consideration, and how do they relate to each other? Second, the nature of the communication process within the social system/market should be evaluated. The fundamental phenomenon to investigate is how the units of the social system communicate with and influence one another. This communication and influence process can take the form of face-to-face, telephone, group meetings, trade publication, print, radio and visual mass media. Finally, the rate at which new ideas, or new products are adopted in the social group/market should be carefully evaluated. When the time of individuals adopting a new product is plotted cumulatively over time, the result is an S-shaped curve. While most new products have this S-shaped curve, there is some variation in the slope of the "S". The slope of this cumulative adoption curve will have implications for the timing and implementations of the marketing strategy.

The fourth step is to develop a marketing plan which exploits the relationships between the early adopter and the early majority. It must be remembered that interest in early adopters comes from their influence over the early majority; the focus of strategic planning is on the early majority. An effective marketing strategy would thus be two-pronged. The first prong would be to direct marketing efforts towards the early adopters, so that the early majority can eventually be affected through them. Thus, communications channels appropriate for targeting the early adopter must be identified. The second prong of the marketing strategy would be to facilitate adoption of the product by the early majority *directly*. Here appropriate channels of communications must also be identified. The tone of the messages should be in keeping with the cautious risk taking behavior of the group. Furthermore, because of the tendency of the early majority to deliberate before adopting new products and ideas, advertising communications should provide information suited to serious deliberation. Moreover, the use of stereotypical early adopters in the advertising communications may also facilitate product adoption.

All market planning should be prefaced with, and influenced by, the results of the analysis suggested above in step three.

Evaluation

The whole point of target marketing the early majority is that they are the key to market share. Furthermore, they are essential to reaching the other 50% of the market who will adopt the product at a later date. As a result of this, a two stage evaluation process is appropriate. The first stage requires that the process of adoption of the new product by the early majority be monitored. This can be determined by a careful analysis of sales trends, as well as by in-store interviews.

The second stage of the evaluation process requires that the adoption of the product by the rest of the social group, but particularly the late majority, be monitored also. This stage of the evaluation can also be achieved using sales analysis in store interviews, as well as geographic and demographic analysis of the market.

Conclusion

While there is a great intuitive appeal in analyzing and target marketing the early majority, few firms actually seem to be using it as an approach to the introduction of new products. The main reason for this is the great difficulty of actually identifying the early majority, in an operational way. Furthermore, the *actual* diffusion process of a new product within a given population is not nearly so clean as theory would suggest. Nevertheless, the concept of identifying the early majority does provide marketing strategies with an orienting framework for planning purposes.

Applications to Small Business

The value of the early majority to the small business is that it provides a framework within which to develop marketing strategies. Even though the concept often proves difficult to implement, it can provide insights into such questions as: What markets can be approached after an initial acceptance of the product by the early adopter? How can that market be increased? What messages are appropriate for that market?

The insight provided by the concept is all the more valuable to the small business because it can be dealt with in a semi-intuitive way, with perhaps only a modest outlay of capital.

References/Sources

Engel, James F., Kegerreis, Robert J., Blackwell, Roger D., "Word of Mouth Communication by the Innovator," *Journal of Marketing* (July 1969). Deals with the extent to which innovators communicate information about new products to potential purchasers.

Hise, Richard T., "New Product Acceptance Overlap: A Measure of General Innovativeness," *Akron Business and Economic Review* (Summer 1971). Reports a study about the extent consumers are innovators of multiple products.

Ostlund, Lyman E., "Identifying Early Buyers," *Journal of Advertising Re-*

search (April 1972). Describes the characteristics of innovators of new products.

Robertson, Thomas S., "The Process of Innovation Diffusion and Innovation," *Journal of Marketing* (January 1967). Discusses the general process through which innovations are diffused throughout a social system.

Robertson, Thomas S., and Meyers, James H., "Personality Correlates of Opinion Leadership and Innovative Buying Behavior," *Journal of Marketing Research* (May 1967). This study examines personality by factors which are associated with innovativeness.

Rogers, Everett M., *Diffusion of Innovations*. New York: The Free Press, 1962. This is the classic work on the topic of diffusion of innovations. Chapters 6 and 7 discuss adopters of innovations.

Related Topics and Terms
Adoption Process, Diffusion Process, Innovator, Laggard, Late Majority, Target Market.

Terry Clark
Department of Marketing
University of Notre Dame

ECONOMIC ORDER QUANTITY

Overview

An important function in marketing is the management of inventory. One of the best known and most basic decision models for inventory control is the Economic Order Quantity. A widespread fallacy among some business managers involves the attempt to "maximize sales while minimizing inventory levels." The problem with these objectives is, of course, that maximizing sales is difficult when merchandise is not available on the shelf. Rather, the objective should be to carry just enough inventory to meet demand, but not so much that excess costs are incurred. This is the purpose of the EOQ model, and careful use of it can result in a higher proportion of customer orders filled, fewer back-orders, fewer customers lost to competition and a substantial reduction in inventory costs. The model is designed to answer these questions for business managers: (1) When should an item be reordered? and (2) What quantity should be ordered?

Examples

Most firms that carry inventory find as few as 10% of the items stocked by a firm account for as much as 90% of the sales. While it is vital to assure that a high proportion of the 10% is in stock at all times, it is also important that a minimum, yet adequate, level is maintained for the remaining 90%. Both are necessary in order to keep inventory carrying costs down.

One firm's policy was to set high and low limits on all items based on average sales and re-order lead time. For one of its items, annual sales were 24 units and the unit cost was $127. Since it took two months from the time an order was placed until it was delivered, the firm set a low limit of 4 and ordered 20 when it was reached. Using EOQ, the reorder quantity was calculated to be 6, indicating it was more economical for the firm to order a small quantity more often. Overall, the firm was able to reduce its inventory carrying costs by one-third by applying the model, and to decrease the number of stock-outs at the same time.

Supermarkets and other large stores are now able to keep perpetual inventory records by using electronic checkout devices. This system also made it possible to apply the EOQ model to every item in inventory, and to streamline inventory control.

Benefits

In addition to the basic benefit of determining the most economical quantity to reorder, the model forces managers to examine the details of their holding and ordering costs. In the process of gathering these data preparatory to using EOQ, firms found that many warehouse costs, such as receiving, initial storing and inventory record entries for receipts were classified as holding costs. This procedure tended to reduce ordering costs, making it appear that frequent reordering was the most efficient way to control inventory levels. By proper re-allocation of costs, the number of re-orders was reduced substantially, for many items.

Implementation

Firms using the EOQ model as part of an overall inventory control program, are able to exert close control over individual items, and to respond quickly to changes in costs or demand. The model compares the costs of carrying inventory to the costs of processing re-orders. In other words, it compromises between (a) holding small amounts of inventory and re-ordering often and (b) holding larger inventories and reordering less frequently. The following chart illustrates the basic idea of the model.

ECONOMIC ORDER QUANTITY

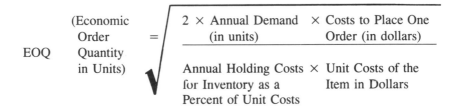

EOQ $=$ (Economic Order Quantity in Units) $= \sqrt{\dfrac{2 \times \text{Annual Demand (in units)} \times \text{Costs to Place One Order (in dollars)}}{\text{Annual Holding Costs for Inventory as a Percent of Unit Costs} \times \text{Unit Costs of the Item in Dollars}}}$

There are three basic steps which managers must follow in order to use the model:

(1) Calculate a re-order point for each inventory item as follows:

First: Determine how many days it takes, on the average, from the time an order is placed until merchandise is received.

Second: Multiply the result by the average daily sales of the item.

Third: Add to the result the number of extra units which, in the manager's opinion, are needed to cover unanticipated demands, delivery delays, etc.

When the inventory reaches the point just calculated, additional quantities should be ordered.

(2) Next, the costs to hold inventory should be calculated, usually as a percentage of the total inventory value. These "holding costs" include rent or mortgage payments, the cost of capital invested in inventory, materials handling equipment, warehouse and clerical personnel, insurance, and taxes and utilities.

(3) Then, determine the costs of reordering, including paperwork expenses, filling out forms, obtaining quotes, letters, phone calls, invoices, bills of lading, payment of bills, as well as handling and storing costs for incoming material.

In the following sample calculation, an Auto Supply firm maintains an average inventory of all items totaling $150,000. Its carrying cost for this inventory is $22,500, or 15%. Processing one re-order costs the firm $5.00.

It wants to calculate the EOQ for a carburetor air filter, with annual sales of 1,500 units and a unit cost of $4.00:

$$\text{EOQ} = \sqrt{\frac{2 \times \text{Average Annual Sales} \times \text{Cost to place 1 reorder}}{\text{Annual Holding Cost (\%)} \times \text{Unit cost of item}}}$$

$$= \sqrt{\frac{2 \times 1500 \times \$5}{.15 \times \$4.}} = \sqrt{\frac{15,000}{.60}} = \sqrt{9000} = \underline{95}$$

Thus, it is most economical for the firm to order 95 when the limit is reached.

Evaluation

Companies considering using the EOQ model can compare inventory investments by using past records to simulate what investments would have been by applying EOQ whenever low limits were reached, and what they actually were. It is also possible to simulate what levels of customer service would have been attained, but the process for this evaluation would be more complex than a straight dollar comparison.

As with many quantitative techniques and models, however, any evaluation of the effectiveness of the final reorder quantity determined by the EOQ model must involve the judgment of inventory managers. The manager should be aware, for example, that the model assumes a constant demand rate, based on an average calculation. But seasonal items, for example, will need higher rates in the model during the high season and lower ones for other periods.

One factor the model does not consider is the level of customer service desired by a firm. Thus, management must evaluate results to balance the minimum total inventory cost with the customer service level necessary to maximize profits. Since increased carrying costs are associated with fewer stock-outs, the reorder quantity may often be somewhat higher than the optimal point from the model.

Conclusion

The Economic Order Quantity model is one approach that managers can use either by itself, or as a step in the development of low cost operating policies for inventory control. All the information needed for the model is normally available in business or other organizations that carry inventory in quantities large enough to warrant use of a control system.

A useful feature of the model is its determination of a basic optimal reorder quantity that managers may adjust according to their personal knowledge of seasonal trends, erratic demand, delivery delays and other variables.

Applications to Small Business

Smaller retail, wholesale, manufacturing and service businesses can use the EOQ model to advantage. It may be used with equal ease in both computer and manual inventory control systems. In the latter, many firms apply it only to the small proportion of items that account for the largest proportion of sales, since the greatest cost benefit will be realized from that group.

Using adaptations of the EOQ model, small businesses that hold inventories with high unit value can control backorders, using the Planned Shortages model. Companies may also calculate economic order quantities when suppliers offer quantity discounts, using another model adaptation.

Software/Databases

There are a number of inventory control software packages that include EOQ and EOQ-extended models. Some of these are:

(1) IBM—*Production Information and Control System* GE-20-0280-2.

(2) Detroit's Best Dist., Inc., 6900 Wagner St., Detroit, MI, 48210. *Cash Register and Inventory Maintenance Program.* Tracks sales and inventories, for use by retailers.

(3) 4-6-5- World, 224 Anacapa St., Santa Barbara, CA, 93121. *Inventory Control Autoplate.* Tracks, controls, counts and manages inventories for small to medium-sized companies.

References/Sources

Adkins, Alvin C., "EOQ in the Real World," *Production and Inventory Management* (4th Qtr. 1984): 50-54. Illustrates how variations in carrying costs can change inventory levels and reorder frequency.

Anderson, D. R., Sweeney, D. J., and Williams, T. A., *Management Science,* 2nd ed. St. Paul: West Publishing Co., 1979, pp. 497-521. A step-by-step descriptions of the EOQ model and an example of how it operates in an industrial situation.

Edwards, J. D., and Roemmich, R. A., 1975, "Scientific Inventory Management," *MSU Business Topics,* 23, 5 (1979): 41-45. Discusses the use of scientific and quantitative methods in inventory systems.

Homsany, Michael P., "Lot Size Rules: Act II," *Production and Inventory Management* (1st qtr., 1983): 17-26. Examines the lot-size theory and provides examples as to how it should be used and interpreted.

McLaughlin, Frank, and Dickhardt, R., *Quantitative Technology for Management Decisions.* Boston: Houghton Mifflin, 1978, pp. 104-119. Discusses Economic Order Quantity and other quantitative methods for inventory management.

Render, Barry, and Stair, Ralph, Jr., *Quantitative Analysis for Management.* Newton, MA: Allyn and Bacon, 1982, pp. 195-213. Discusses the EOQ model and variations thereto such as planned shortages, setting low limits and demand rates.

Related Topics and Terms

Control, Demand, Internal Data, Inventory Control, Forecasting, Physical Distribution, Reorder Point, Safety Stock, Stock Turnover, Wholesaler.

Hale N. Tongren
Department of Marketing
George Mason University

ELASTICITY OF DEMAND

Overview

Elasticity of demand (or price elasticity of demand) is the measure of sensitivity of quantity demanded of a product to a price change of the product. Elasticity of demand is expressed as the ratio of the percentage change in the quantity demanded of a product to the percentage change in the price of that product.

$$\text{Elasticity of demand} = E = \frac{\text{Percentage change in quantity demanded}}{\text{Percentage change in price}}$$

If the percentage change in quantity demanded is greater than the percentage change in price ($E > 1$), the demand is said to be elastic. If the percentage change in quantity demanded is less than the percentage change in price ($E < 1$), the demand is said to be inelastic. If the percentage change in quantity demanded is equal to the percentage change in price ($E = 1$), the demand is said to be unitarily elastic.

The elasticity of demand for a product depends upon the following factors:

1. Whether there are close substitutes available for the product in the market place. The more close substitutes available, the more elastic the demand.
2. The portion of consumer's income being spent on the product. The greater the portion of income spent on the product, the more elastic the demand schedule.
3. Whether the product is a luxury item or a necessity. Luxury items tend to have a more elastic demand schedule than necessary items.
4. The number of product uses. The greater the number of product uses, the more elastic the demand schedule tends to be.
5. The time frame within which the evaluation takes place. In the short run, most demand schedules tend to be inelastic.

Examples

Products which have a number of close substitutes, products which require a larger monetary outlay, products that are perceived as luxury items, products that have many uses, all tend to have elastic demand schedules. Conversely, products which have no close substitutes, products that require a smaller monetary outlay, products that are necessary, and products that have fewer uses all tend to have inelastic demand schedules.

The demand schedule for gasoline would tend to be inelastic because of the lack of close substitutes available (there are many brands of gas but no substitute for it). The housing market will fluctuate drastically to changes in interest rates (price of loans) because of larger monetary outlays on the consumers' parts to acquire the houses. The demand schedule for medicinal products (necessities for people who are sick) will tend to exhibit inelastic tendencies when compared with demand schedules for diamonds and jewelry (luxury items) which will tend to be elastic.

Benefits

Understanding the nature of elasticity of demand for a particular product or service will enable the management to make sound pricing decisions. The increases and decreases in total revenues due to price changes can be anticipated, explained, and controlled if managers can determine the elasticity of demand for their products or services. Total revenues and consequently, the resultant profits could be adversely affected if the wrong price changes are implemented.

Implementation

In effectively implementing the elasticity concept, one must establish the relationship between price changes of products and the corresponding changes in the total revenues generated. Total revenue is calculated by multiplying the number of units sold of a product and the unit price of that product.

Once data has been collected regarding the price changes of the product and the revenue streams associated with these price changes, the ensuing analysis will enable the decision maker to determine the elasticity of demand for the product.

If the price and total revenue move in the same direction, then the demand schedule is inelastic. That is, as price is increased, total revenue generated also increases and as the price is decreased, the total revenue generated also decreases.

If the price and total revenue move in the opposite direction, then the demand schedule is elastic. That is, as the price is increased, the total revenue generated decreases, and as the price is decreased, the total revenue generated increases.

Evaluation

Once the elasticity of demand has been determined for the product, management must determine the strategies and tactics necessary for product performance improvement. These include:

1. the evaluation of the nature of the close substitutes available in the market for the product,
2. the reevaluation of product pricing strategy based on the demand elasticity of the product,
3. repositioning the product if necessary in the market, based on the new pricing strategy.

Conclusion

In spite of the fact that elasticity of demand provides management with the ability to better price and market their products, it often the measurement of elasticity of demand that may present a problem. Elasticity measures a product's sensitivity to price changes in the past and, therefore, its usefulness for predictive purposes may be limited. The usefulness of elasticity of demand for decision making should be approached with caution.

Elasticity of demand does not reflect the qualitative aspects of the product. Therefore, all around effective marketing decision-making may be hampered. Elasticity of demand may not be used to extrapolate into the future because of its dynamic nature. And finally, it is a statistic that reflects consumers' behavior patterns of the past and therefore does not lend itself to predicting consumer behavior patterns for the future.

Applications to Small Business

A number of small businesses, manufacturers and retailers alike, handle products that are very sensitive to the market forces of supply and demand. The elasticity of demand is a function of a number of product characteristics such as: substitutability, product uses, and the type of product (convenience or luxury item). Therefore, in investigating the elasticity of demand for a product, management will have to evaluate in depth the competitive forces in the market and the target market the particular product is aimed at. This evaluation will enable management to determine the most effective marketing strategies for the product and thus result in improved product performance in sales and profits.

The data for determining elasticity of demand should be most readily available from the company's existing sales and performance records. By analyzing these records, management can identify products that can generate increased revenues and with proper cost controls the overall profit picture of the firm should be improved.

Software/Databases

Making Key Business Decisions with the VisiCalc, VisiCalc Advanced Version and VisiCalc IV Programs. Cdex Corp. Allows the user to make decisions about product pricing, product mix, make vs buy, and economic order quantity which will improve the return on sales.

References/Sources

Bach, George Leland, *Economics,* 9th ed. Englewood Cliffs, NJ: Prentice-Hall, 1977, pp. 664-665. Provides a concise explanation using differential calculus.

Dolan, Edwin G., *Basic Economics*. Chicago: The Dryden Press, 1977, pp. 292-298. Discusses the concept of elasticity and the measurement problems well.

Leftwich, Richard H., *The Price System And Resource Allocation,* 4th ed. Chicago: The Dryden Press, 1970, pp. 38-48. Provides a brief analysis of elasticity of demand using simple mathematics.

Maxwell David W., *Price Theory And Applications in Business Administration.* Beverly Hills, CA: Goodyear Publishing Co., 1970, pp. 48-58. Provides an excellent mathematical analysis and interpretation of the elasticity of demand concept and its usefulness.

Related Topics and Terms
Demand, Demand Schedule, Price Elasticity.

R. Viswanathan
Department of Marketing
University of Northern Colorado

THE ELDERLY MARKET

Overview

Older American consumers and the market segment they comprise has been studied extensively since the mid-1950s when it became increasingly apparent that this group would grow rapidly in absolute numbers, affluence and influence in the marketplace. Today, the emphasis is less on the sizable and profitable market that exists, but more on its potential as the baby boom hump in the population moves relentlessly through time toward middle and old age.

In 1985, there were over 17 million elderly between the ages of 65 and 74. The 75 to 85, or "aged" group has about 8.5 million while the "very old", over 85, total only about 2.7 million. In the next ten years, the "elderly" will grow to 19 million, the "aged" to 11 million and the "very old" will increase 50 percent, to 4 million. The entire group, now about 11.6 percent of the population, will soar to 16 percent when the peak of baby-boomers reach the age of 60 to 65. Clearly, this market will demand even more attention from marketers in the future than it has in the past.

Examples

Size, itself, does not necessarily constitute a market, but the older population is becoming an increasingly affluent group. For households headed by persons 60 to 64, per capita discretionary income was $3700 in 1980. But for those 65 and older, it was the highest of any age group, or $4100, which is more than double the $2000 amount for persons in the 30-39 group. And discretionary income continues to increase for older consumers.

By 1995, more than 37 percent of married households over 65 will have incomes of $20,000 and more, up from only 28 percent in 1980. While this may not seem to be affluence, it has been estimated that the spending power of older households is over 30 percent greater than their cash income. This is due mainly to the "imputed" income many of them receive from mortgage-free home ownership (no monthly payments), tax benefits on Social Security income and large personal exemptions (lower taxes), no children left at home (lower expenses), and the numerous special discounts on goods and services they receive.

Not only is the older segment more affluent than ever before, but they are healthy and active in the market as well. Less than 10 percent live with their children, and about 5 percent are in institutions. But those two groups are mainly "very old," and a large proportion of the "elderly" and "aged" are still living in individual households.

Benefits

With about 27 percent of the U.S. national budget devoted to programs for, and direct payments to, the older population, and the political pressure the elderly exert to maintain or increase these benefits, the market appears to be assured for some time to come. Added to these are private pension payments, investment income and, in the future, IRAs. The group's annual purchasing power is estimated to be between $60 and $200 billion. These data strongly suggest substantial potential benefits for marketers who pursue this segment.

Implementation

Those who enter the older market segment in the future will be markedly different than those in the past or even those in it today. Increasingly, businesses will encounter older people in the marketplace who appear, act and buy in a manner that resembles much younger consumers. Fewer of them will have experienced the Great Depression which instilled a fear of debt and emphasis on saving. Today's elderly consumer is more likely to have a credit card than is the population as a whole.

Older consumers today are not particularly cost conscious, and while many are ardent shoppers, they do not always go shopping to make purchases. They are more likely to shop in department or specialty stores than are younger consumers who favor discount stores. This characteristic may change as "new" elderly enter the segment. Both males and females often "shop" as a recreational, exercise or entertainment activity. Retailers, particularly, need to recognize this tendency, and avoid hard-sell tactics on older "lookers" who may decide to return and buy later, if they are treated courteously.

While many younger consumers use in-store information such as unit pricing, open code dating and nutritional labeling, older buyers generally do not. For example, about 90 percent of the total population said they used unit pricing, while only 60 percent of the elderly did, but not nearly as often. Older shoppers consider having a place to rest while shopping, more help in locating products, package carryout, and courteous treatment more important than product data.

Producers and retailers must approach this market cautiously. In the past, products that were promoted exclusively for the elderly, such as special foods and clothing, failed because the elderly do not like to be reminded they are old. They consciously avoid advertising themes that are directed specifically toward them and their recall for such messages is substantially lower than it is for general audience themes.

Evaluation

Retailers, particularly, have a range of choices when deciding if the older market is worth pursuing. Primarily, the question will be whether or not the market is large enough to warrant special promotions or inducements. If it is, then what types of approaches are likely to attract these consumers without alienating them or present customers? If the market is not large enough today, is it likely to grow in the near future?

If a firm does decide to actively cultivate the older market, the following specifics might be considered:

Will the present type of products attract the market, or must others be added?

Is there sufficient depth in the lines to satisfy needs of this market, or must the depth be expanded?

Will special discounts be offered to older customers? How can the discounts be offered without offending these customers?

If discounts are offered overtly through store signs or advertising, will they be considered discriminatory by other customers?

If a store actively pursues this market, will it get an "old folks" image, and lose its younger customers?

What advertising and promotion media are available to reach this market? Should older models be used in the advertising?

Conclusion

While marketers are generally aware of the older market segment, they have been reluctant to take aggressive action for a number of reasons. The youth syndrome, inherent in today's culture, rejects the aging process by avoiding references to it. Thus, many products and services may not be suitable for older consumers today. Yet the increasing youthfulness and activity of these consumers, together with their unique experience base compared to earlier elderly groups, should blur the actual and perceived differences between younger and older buyers.

This does not mean that older consumers will eventually respond to the same or similar approaches as do younger ones. Styles designed for other age groups may not be becoming to the elderly, or may be difficult to take on and off. And as the number and active age of this segment increases—many are highly mobile in their eighties—retailers must provide minimal comfort and assistance.

Applications to Small Business

The potential to capitalize on the older market is more likely to be available to smaller than to larger businesses. The elderly tend to be personalized shoppers. Although they visit the larger malls frequently, to shop in major department stores, they do a substantial amount of shopping close to home. They like to be recognized in stores and depend more on assistance from salespeople than do younger shoppers, particularly for apparel and other specialty purchases.

Smaller stores are more capable of advertising by word-of-mouth and promoting their products or services through neighborhood Seniors' organizations than are larger ones. Fashion shows, demonstrations of new kitchen appliances, travel slide shows and similar promotions not only inform consumers about business offerings, but they also provide a direct communication channel for special discounts and inducements. These methods are much less expensive than direct advertising, and they prevent any change in store image perception on the part of present customers.

Software/Databases

Client and Prospect Profiler. Marketing Institute International Corp., Suite 108, 600 W. Service Rd., Box 17130, Dulles Int'l Airport, Washington, DC 20041. Helps professional service and business organizations apply strategic data to marketing plans. Helps firms focus on those organizations offering the most sales potential; and helps identify key networks and market segments (elderly) to concentrate on.

References/Sources

Bartos, Rena, "Over-49, The Invisible Consumer Market," in *Harvard Business Review* (Jan/Feb 1980): 140-148. Describes the increasing affluence of older consumers and their buying habits.

Bearden, William O. and J. Barry Mason, "Elderly Use of In-Store Information Sources and Dimensions of Product Satisfaction/Dissatisfaction," in *Journal of Retailing* (Spring, 1979): 79-91. Reports the extent to which elderly know about, and use information available in stores and how satisfied or dissatisfied they are with products and services.

French, W. A. and M. Crask, "The Credibility of Media Advertising for the Elderly," in *AMA Educator's Conference Proceedings.* B. Greenberg and D. Bellinger, eds. Chicago: American Marketing Assn., 1977, pp. 74-77. Discusses the types of media and extent they are used by older consumers, the believability of messages from these media, and the effects they have.

Lazer, William, "Inside the Mature Market," in *American Demographics,* (March 1985): 23-25+. Presents a profile of demographic and growth data for the older market.

Lumpkin, James R. and B. A. Greenberg, "Apparel Shopping Patterns of the Elderly Consumer," in *Journal of Retailing,* (Winter 1982): 68-89. Determined that the elderly were likely to be less cost conscious for many types of products than were younger consumers.

Mason, J. Barry and W. D. Bearden, "Profiling the Shopping Behavior of Elderly Consumers," in *The Gerontologist,* 18 (1978): 454-461. Discusses how the shopping habits of younger and older consumers differ.

Riggs, Carol R. "Reaching the 50+ Market," in *Dun and Bradstreet Reports,* (March/April 1985): 28-32. Presents a profile of the elderly and their likes and dislikes in the marketplace.

Tongren, Hale N. "Imputed Income Expands the Consumer Credit Market," in *Journal of Consumer Credit Management,* (Winter 1978): 82-87. Illustrates how various benefits for the elderly enhance the purchasing power of lower incomes.

_____, "Retailing to Older Consumers," in *Progress in Marketing Theory and Practice,* Southern Marketing Assn., (1981): 93-96. Reports that older consumers are more likely to buy apparel items and less likely to purchase hard goods than are younger ones.

Related Topics and Terms
Consumerism, Family Life Cycle, Gerontology, Market Potential, Marketing Mix, Marketing Plan, Retail Strategy, Sampling, Target Market

Hale N. Tongren
Department of Marketing
George Mason University

ELDERLY MARKET SEGMENTATION

Overview

Whether a firm is offering a good or a service, the product can be either mass-marketed (sold to everyone), or channeled to only one or a segment of the market (one, or several groups of consumers who are particularly interested in the product). The older market, depending on how it is defined, is one example of a segment. It consists of that portion of the entire population over a certain age: 50, 60, or 65. Another group of the population segmented by age might be consumers from 20 to 34. In this age group, all members are consumers, and the amount and assortment of purchases they make might be expected to increase as age increases. In the older segment, however, the amount purchased is likely to decrease and the assortment will change significantly as age increases. For this market, the question becomes: are there sub-segments that have specific marketing requirements and how are these sub-segments defined?

Examples

Many firms, alert to the increasing influence and affluence of the older population, have expanded product and service lines adapted to its several age or lifestyle segments. This has been done effectively without alienating other segments the firms serve. In a direct mail promotion, a travel agency provided a pamphlet on the elderhostel programs, mentioning only that the agency hoped the information would be useful, and briefly explaining the services offered by travel agencies. The response was a flood of inquiries from older consumers who were not aware that agencies charged no fee for their reservation services.

An appliance service firm in a metropolitan area gave demonstrations to Senior Citizen's clubs on how to trouble-shoot and repair home appliances. They had hoped to increase sales of repair parts to what they saw as a market that could not afford service calls. While their parts business failed to improve, their service call business increased over 10 percent, mostly from newly retired older consumers who were impressed by the firm's perceived honest effort to help them save money.

Benefits

Initial approaches to the individual segments of the older market can bring secondary beneficial effects through word-of-mouth advertising. A restaurant that served a younger clientele found that it was nearly empty from its 5 PM opening until about 7:30 PM, and considered opening later until it tried offering an early-bird discount on all meals from 5 to 7 PM. At first, only a few older customers came in, but after two weeks, word about the unadvertised discount had spread and the restaurant was half filled with seniors, mostly in their 60s and 70s. Similarly, a drug store in an older suburb added a line of rental wheel chairs, and other physical comfort devices for the very old. Not only did this line add substantially to profits, but the prescription business nearly doubled at the same time.

Implementation

Implementing a program designed to attract older consumers requires a basic understanding of the types of segmentation that may be used. Generally, though, the market cannot be segmented on the basis of amounts spent expressed as percentages of income. Except for medical and utility costs, age itself has little influence on expenditures, and when health and income permit them to do so, older consumers largely duplicate the expenditure patterns of younger ones.

There are, however, possible segments that can be isolated and approached. In one study where elderly consumers evaluated their own buying styles, the largest group (34.6%) said they were Conspicuous Consumers who were more stubborn, dominating and egotistical than their peers, and that they bought certain brands to impress their friends. The next largest group (25.4%) said they were more candid and confident, but tended to buy unknown brands. The remaining 40% consisted of four small groups, the largest of which was 11% of the total.

The elderly can also be segmented in terms of how they feel about themselves, and the lifestyles they lead. These "active old" are a segment that will continue to buy goods over a wide age span while the "inactive" and "infirm" segments will buy more personal and medical services.

Most differences among groups of older consumers, however, have been observed in the retired vs. employed categories, but there are also differences between these for the 55 to 65 and the 65+ age groups. While today's older, employed consumers generally follow the buying practices of the population as a whole, retired males, in particular, become much more involved in all phases of the buying process. But females who work in the home are affected very little when the male retires, since their routine activities stay about the same. This relationship is likely to change, however, in the future, when both household members must adjust to retirement at the same time.

Evaluation

Whether the market for any one firm should be segmented by age, by lifestyle or by employed retired will depend on the products or services offered, the age-mix of the market or other factors such as the amount of retirement income and shopping habits. In the process of determining the most applicable method of segmentation, the following points should be considered:

Is there a large proportion of the market population in or nearing the age of 50? Approaching 60? Over 70?

Are there a number of active, flourishing Senior Citizens' groups in the market area?

Do these groups tend to engage in social or political activity?

Are there newsletters, newspaper columns or other print media that reach older consumers?

Are there local television programs or radio station formats that deliver an older audience? What ages are involved?

What is the median income of the older population? Does it vary as age increases? How much variation is there?

What proportion of older households own and still use automobiles?

Conclusion

More recently, marketers have defined the older market threshold at the age of 50 rather than at 60 or 65. They have also recognized that sub-segmentation is needed to describe more precisely the products and services required by each of these narrow groups. Unlike other market age segments which encompass about fifteen years, the older segment covers thirty or forty years, and market behavior may be expected to vary widely within this span. Thus, the over-50 group may not be treated as a homogenous market.

Another important characteristic of the older market that will have a significant effect in the next twenty to thirty years is the entry of younger-old, in their fifties, who have lived in an era of widespread social change and economic prosperity with emphasis upon youthfulness and health. These recent entries are likely to behave quite differently in the market than today's elderly and to remain actively in it for longer periods. These factors suggest that lifestyle rather than chronological age may be a useful sub-segment for the future.

The employed retired categories should also be considered in combination with lifestyle, since there is evidence of marked changes in buying procedures following retirement. Consumers have more time to comparison shop in different stores and for different products or services. Moreover, their needs and desires also change and retirees will be looking for new stores and shopping areas to fill these new demands.

Applications to Small Business

Although larger retail firms and producers have begun to provide a widening range of goods and services to older buyers, there is probably a greater potential for small businesses to sub-segment this market since they are more accessible to it. Retailers, especially, should be aware that retired consumers can shop during slack periods and would be likely to do so if properly motivated. Hobby stores and home improvement supply stores can schedule do-it-yourself classes for the newly retired segment. Travel agencies can work with Senior Citizens' organizations to sponsor tours designed for older sub-segments who no longer want to plan trips themselves. Sports and recreational equipment businesses can appeal to the lifestyle segment that tries to stay young by sponsoring appropriate activities and demonstrating equipment at Senior Citizens' organizations. Similarly, health food outlets can provide lectures on proper nutrition. Because many older consumers are difficult to influence by advertising, these approaches to specific groups should take its place. For upper-age segments, total care homes, medical appliances, personal comfort items, medical products that aid sleep or digestion and short vacation tours should be offered.

Software/Databases

ON SITE. Urban Decision Systems, Inc., 2032 Armcast Ave., Box 25953, Los Angeles, CA 90025. On-line demographic retrieval and analysis. Also COLOR-SITE demographic and user data grid for identification and analysis of markets (elderly demographics).

Sammamish Data Systems, Inc., 1413 77th Ave NE., Bellevue, WA 98008. *Market Statistics Basic Demographics and Marketing Data Bases* is the latest economic and demographic data by county to aid in identifying elderly markets.

References/Sources

Barak, B., and L. Schiffman, "Cognitive Age: a Non-Chronological Variable" in *Advances in Consumer Research,* Vol. 8, Ann Arbor, MI: Assn. for Consumer Research, 1980, pp. 602-606. Determined that women from age 60 upward were more likely not to believe they felt or looked their age than were women from 50 to 59.

Bartos, Rena, "Over 49: The Invisible Consumer Market" in *Harvard Business Review* (Jan/Feb 1980): 140-148. Proposed six sub-groups in the over-50 segment, of which 3 had market impact.

French, W. A. and Richard Fox, "Segmenting the Senior Citizen Market," in *Journal of Consumer Marketing* (Winter, 1985): 61-74. Sub-segmented older consumers into 3 groups based on the levels of adjustment to advancing age, and discussed how these levels influenced market activity.

Lederhaus, M., F. DeZoort, and P. Phillips, "An Analysis of Singular and Multidimensional Measures to Profile Older Adults: Macro Implications for the Marketer," in *Proceedings, Southern Marketing Association* (1983): 168-171. Found that there was no difference in terms of expenditures for purchase behavior among three over-60 age groups.

Meadow, H. Lee, S. Cosmas, and A. Plotkin, "The Elderly Consumer: Past,

Present and Future," in *Advances in Consumer Research,* Vol. 8, Ann Arbor, MI: Assn. for Consumer Research, 1981, pp. 742-747. Examines the use of chronological age as a factor in sub-segmentation and suggests other bases for it.

Reinecke, John A. "The Older Market: Fact or Fiction," in *Journal of Marketing* (January 1964): 60-64: Reported that the over-65 market segment was a homogenous one and that there was no basis for sub-segmentation on expenditures as a percentage of income.

Sherman, E. and L. Schiffman, "Applying Age-Gender Theory from Social Gerontology to Understand the Consumer Well-Being of the Elderly," in *Advances in Consumer Research,* Vol. 11, Provo, UT: Assn. for Consumer Research, pp. 548-552. Suggested that 55+ consumers be sub-segmented into 3 age groups, and each of these into gender, for a total of 6 groups.

Tongren, Hale N. "Measuring Brand Centrality for Younger and Older Consumers," in *Marketing: Theories and Concepts in an Era of Change,* Southern Marketing Assn. 1983, pp. 72-75. Reported that 65+ consumers were more likely than those aged 50-59 to accept brands of convenience staples other than their regular brand.

Towle, J. G. and C. Martin, Jr. "The Elderly Consumer: One Segment or Many," in *Advances in Consumer Research, Vol. 9* (1976): 463-468. Identified 6 lifestyle sub-segments within the older market of which two were the largest and most market-influential.

Related Topics and Terms
Consumer Behavior, Convenience Good, Demographic Factor, Differentiated Marketing, Economics of Age, Family Life Cycle, Lifestyle, Psychographics, Self-Concept, Senior Citizen Discounts.

Hale N. Tongren
Department of Marketing
George Mason University

ENVIRONMENT

Overview

The marketing environment of a company is all areas outside the marketing department over which it has little or no control and which affect its ability to relate to its customers. This is a major area that must be constantly monitored in order to keep up with new opportunities or obstacles which may occur from changes in the environment. Many forces affect the environment, and the successful marketer needs to keep informed about all of them. Monitoring the environment is costly in terms of time and money, but the advantages obtained easily outweigh these costs. Significant benefits from monitoring the environment include being informed about recent technological advances, new government legislation affecting businesses, changes in socioeconomic/demographic trends, factors affecting suppliers or customers, and any changes within the company. While monitoring the environment may be difficult to achieve, it must be done in order for the company to remain competitive.

Examples

The marketing environment can be separated into two main areas: the microenvironment and macroenvironment. The microenvironment consists of the people or organizations who are closely connected with the company and are in its immediate environment. The macroenvironment consists of those areas which are not as closely connected to the company; they are forces which affect the microenvironment.

The most important microenvironmental forces includes the company's suppliers, as well as its dealers and distributors, and also the ultimate consumer. Other factors include the competition, the community in which the organization operates, and factors within the organization, such as the company's employees and its stockholders. Examples of companies who effectively monitor the microenvironment include Scott Paper Company, who designates this responsibility to the marketing-research and research-and-development departments. Several companies also monitor their competitors. Examples of these include Texas Instruments, Inc., Sperry Rand Corp., and Westinghouse Electric, which delegate this responsibility to the consumer-product research department.

The macroenvironment is broader in scope and includes less distinct areas. These areas include economic and technological forces. Political and legal aspects are also a part, in addition to demographic and socio/cultural forces. A final area of concern that cannot be discounted is foreign countries. Examples of macroenvironmental forces that have affected companies are the ban on hexachlorophene in 1972 by the Food and Drug Administration, the increase in mobile home sales due to the decline in the ability of families to purchase conventional homes, an increase in vitamin sales, trends toward buying natural foods, and awareness of nutrition.

The classifications under the macro- and microenvironment are not clear-cut. The forces under these main areas are determined by the particular industry (or industries) in which the company operates, in addition to the location of the particular company.

Benefits

At a very basic level, monitoring the marketing environment is preventative in nature. That is, it prevents the company from remaining uninformed about recent trends and developments. As the monitoring becomes more involved, the information can be used to react to changes, and perhaps even predict future variations. The benefits of reacting to changes in the environment are even more numerous, ranging from just keeping up with the competition to being the first to react to new developments and leading the way in new technologies or markets. Monitoring and reacting to the environment can help prevent a company's stagnation and eventual loss of competitiveness.

Implementation

Monitoring of the marketing environment can be done in several different ways. One way is to utilize market research studies which focus on demographic and socio/cultural forces, as well as attitudes and preferences of consumers. They can also be used to stay in tune with the attitudes and needs of suppliers, dealers, and distributors. The environment within the firm can also be studied to determine corporate attitudes and opinions, as well as employee satisfaction. Measurements of market share, market potential, and a company's sales growth (or decline) can be obtained using marketing research techniques.

A second way to monitor the environment is through public relations. Although public relations is predominantly used as a promotional tool, it can be used to monitor such environmental forces as media coverage of competitors, as well as the individual firm, and also the attitudes of the media towards the company.

Marketing intelligence is yet another way of monitoring a company's environment. This method not only monitors the activities of competitors, but also technological innovations and breakthroughs. This can be done in-house, as with Citicorp's Manager of Competitive Intelligence. Lobbyists, another specialized intelligence group, keep the company informed about the political and legal environment.

Several ways also exist for a company to influence its environment. As mentioned earlier, public relations is one method to influence a company's external environment. This is but one part of the firm's promotional mix, which is used to inform the public about the organization, and the products or services it has to offer. Internally, the company can influence its employees through company newsletters, fringe benefits, and "extracurricular" activities, such as company picnics and athletic leagues.

Reacting to environmental information and predicting what will happen is referred to as strategic planning. This is especially important for high technology firms because of the volatility of their environment.

Evaluation

Just because a company monitors the environment does not mean it will survive. In order to remain competitive, a company must be able to react to the information obtained from monitoring. In many instances, the environment may present obstacles and constraints that must be overcome in order for the company to perform effectively. Another problem is determining what areas of the environment to monitor. For major conglomerates, as well as for many other companies, it is often difficult to determine who their actual competitors are. Yet another problem is determining what technological advances are of importance. A company benefits from monitoring the environment only if it can evaluate the information obtained, to determine how much of it is useful.

Conclusion

One means for highly competitive companies to stay ahead is to monitor and react to their environment. The major questions to be considered are:

—What areas should be monitored?
—How valuable is the information obtained?
—How much should be spent on monitoring?

Several ways can be used to monitor the environment, as well as to influence it. The successful marketer will utilize as many of these methods as possible in order to adequately keep track of environmental fluctuations and help the organization to remain competitive. The most important lesson to be learned is that as much information should be obtained as possible and should be studied and acted upon.

Applications to Small Business

The environment affects small businesses just as much as it does large conglomerates. The only difference is in the degree of involvement in the environment and the magnitude of the information to be obtained. Small, local businesses are more affected by local and regional variances than are multinational corporations, and are especially susceptible to community influences. They have to be just as aware of their small, local environment as larger firms are of their larger environments, sometimes even more so, since minor environmental deviations will have a greater effect on a small business with less of an ability to withstand these deviations.

Software/Databases

Federal Register Abstracts. Capital Services International, Washington, DC. Provides comprehensive coverage of federal regulatory agency actions as published in the *Federal Reporter,* including regulations, proposed rules and legal notices issued by federal agencies, laws, presidental proclamations, and executive orders.

References/Sources

Churchill, Gilbert A., Jr., *Marketing Research: Methodological Foundations,* 3rd ed. Chicago: The Dryden Press, 1979. Chapter 1 briefly covers how marketing research can be used, and provides examples of information that can be obtained.

Hise, Richard T., Gillett, Peter L., and Ryans, John K., Jr., *Marketing Concepts, Decisions, Strategies.* Houston, TX: Dame Publications, 1984. Chapter 4 provides a brief overview of the marketing environment and its impact in certain areas.

Kotler, Philip, *Marketing Management: Analysis, Planning and Control,* 5th ed. Englewood Cliffs, NJ: Prentice Hall, 1984. Chapter 3 discusses marketing environment in detail.

Shanklin, William L., and Ryans, John K., Jr., *Marketing High Technology.* Lexington, MA: Lexington Books, 1984. Chapter 8 deals with strategic planning and what a company needs to do to implement a strategic marketing plan.

Related Topics and Terms

Industrial Spying, Lobbying, Marketing Information System, Market Research

Gary Guenther
Department of Marketing
Texas A&M University

EUROPEAN ECONOMIC COMMUNITY

Overview

The European Economic Community, a result of the 1957 Treaty of Rome, is an effort to create a regional economic group. such entities are frequently called trade blocs. It is in reality somewhere between a customs union and a common market, despite the popular term "common market" that writers, consumers, and even some E.E.C. officials often use.

Trade blocs consist of the following types in order of sophistication and complexity: regional cooperation groups; free trade associations; customs unions; and common markets. A regional cooperation group is a limited, specialized arrangement in which two or more nations cooperate on a small number of economic factors. Typically these are quite specialized and often related to each other, such as navigation, flood control, irrigation, water purity, and hydro-electricity. A free trade association permits free movement of products among its member nations. An example is the European Free Trade Association, in which several non-E.E.C. countries hold membership. A customs union adds to the free trade association concept the standardization of tariffs against all non-member countries. A common market is by definition an entity which permits the free flow of all goods, services, labor, and capital. The E.E.C. still does not have free trade in a few types of goods and has made only modest progress on the free flow of capital.

The General Agreement on Tariffs and Trade, a 1947 treaty which the United States and other non-communist nations have signed, prohibits discrimination in the restrictions which a signatory nation might have against imports. However, this treaty contains a provision permitting regional groups of countries to seek economic benefits by forming trade blocs. In doing so, such countries can discriminate in favor of each other and against the remainder of the world's signatories of that treaty. In order for it not to be a violation of the treaty, there must be a formal organization with clearly spelled out purposes and objectives. The E.E.C. is such an organization.

The E.E.C. was envisioned by its founders as simultaneously a practical way to stimulate further economic development, encourage private and public technological research, provide an opportunity for business firms to grow and prosper, allow consumers access to a wider range and assortment of goods and services, enable consumers to benefit from the increased number of competitors, allow capital markets to function efficiently, and make job mobility more feasible. Moreover, meaningful economies of scale could be realized in some lines of industry in some individual small countries of Europe only if there were an entity like the E.E.C.

The original E.E.C. members were France, West Germany, the Netherlands, Belgium, Luxembourge, and Italy. Britain, which had rejected membership at the formation of the organization, joined in 1973 along with Ireland and Denmark. Norway planned to join at that time, but the electorate of that country voted it down in a referendum. Greece joined in 1982 and Spain and Portugal in 1986. The lower level of economic development in these last three caused delay in membership and a transition period for taking on all obligations of membership.

The E.E.C. is by far the most advanced of all trading blocs in the world. Others include the Latin American Integration Association, Central American Common Market, Andean Pact, Caribbean Common Market, Association of Southeast Asian Nations, and Economic Community of West Africa.

Examples

Business organizations which were already in place in western Europe before the creation of the E.E.C. have had the greatest opportunity to make use of its potential. For example, a large Italian automobile company still centralizes its facilities in Italy but can distribute its automobiles throughout the E.E.C. nations. It gains economies of scale in production. Without this treaty organization this company probably would have had to build a branch plant in each country in which it was interested, or reduce its costs to the point at which its cost advantage could offset the import tariffs. Regardless of cost relationships, quotas on imports would have been an interference without the existence of the E.E.C.

Several American firms of certified public accountants and several American marketing research agencies are all able to provide services to clients in several adjoining countries from one office. Support services and equipment can be used more effectively and inexpensively in this manner. Esoteric professional specialists can be used efficiently, thus justifying their costs to have on the staff. In a similar way an American insurance company is able to coordinate personal selling and claims service for several adjoining countries from one office. Several American, French, British, Dutch, and West German advertising agencies provide services in each of several countries that are culture-specific but back them up with centralized planning, research, and support services.

A large American camera and electronics maker uses one centralized facility in Enschede, the Netherlands for all of its physical distribution of finished goods from its two European manufacturing plants and imported parts and finished goods from the United States.

On the other hand, a large manufacturer of electronics and home appliances has used the E.E.C. by having a network of interlocking plants and assembly points plus carefully selected unaffiliated manufacturing suppliers under contract for certain components and parts. One of the world's largest manufacturers of margarine, toiletries, detergents, soaps, and cleaning supplies found foreign trade extremely difficult before the E.E.C. was set up. Because of historical and cultural reasons, this organization found it necessary to maintain headquarters in both the Netherlands and Britain. After Britain joined the E.E.C. this company was able to make planning, production scheduling, channels of distribution, logistics, inventory control, and promotion more rational and economical.

Several retail chains of specialty shops, particularly in apparel and shoes, have become trans-European. However, most large department stores have hung back, presumably because of their high visibility, local leadership roles, and a tradition of conservatism. Nevertheless, both a Dutch and a British department store company have several branches in nearby countries now and are monitoring progress and further opportunities. Three American department store companies have entered the E.E.C., but all three have been disappointed at the difficulty of using fairly standardized merchandising operations in several places simultaneously. They have also found it difficult to predict demand on hundreds of categories of goods, some of which are related to the specific cultures involved.

Benefits

There are many practical benefits for business organizations. The key factor is that barriers to trade in finished goods, parts, components, supplies, and the capital goods from which the consumer goods are made are drastically reduced. Specifically, tariffs on manufactured products among nine nations were eliminated over a period of year. In the three nations that joined recently, Greece, Spain, and Portugal, tariffs will be phased out over a period of years. One must note that there has been relatively little liberalization of trade in agricultural goods in the E.E.C. This situation is explained in part by the great political involvement of the member governments in farming questions, the complex set of subsidies to agriculture that has evolved through time, the overcapacity in many types of agricultural products, and the number of marginal farms and farmers.

A major area of benefit is the movement of labor. Of great significance is the ability of people to move in search of more economic opportunity, or of workers to be transferred by their employers with a minimum of government paperwork and delay. Previously such relocation was almost impossible unless one went through lengthy formal procedures. It is not practicable for a company to move large numbers of unskilled or semi-skilled workers, but it is quite feasible to transfer skilled workers, professional staff, and managers. Independent service professionals, such as medical doctors, dentists, consulting engineers, architects, and computer specialists can move if they satisfy the minimum educational and training preparation specified by E.E.C. agreements. Moreover, non-professional licensed persons, such as barbers, hairdressers, and master plumbers, can now relocate so as to serve themselves and the public where they are most needed.

Implementation

European manufacturers are taking steps to become transnational in order to reap the advantages of the E.E.C., and more alert, aggressive non-European manufacturers are doing the same. Professional service organizations see major opportunities Any interested firm must plan for entry, and a good starting point is to contact the E.E.C. headquarters in Brussels or its delegation in Washington, D.C. In the meanwhile within the E.E.C. the regulation of marketing and trade is being made more similar from country to country. Regulation of advertising content and media is being harmonized among the members. Some economies of scale in both the creation of the advertisements and the media time and space are becoming feasible. Various other types of consumer protection are in preparation, such as warranties and uniform product liability.

Evaluation

Without question the E.E.C. has accomplished a great deal in a short time. Nevertheless, the E.E.C. reached virtually an impasse in the 1982-1984 period because of fundamental disagreement on budgets and how they were to be prepared and spent. The traditional requirement of unanimity for decisions has been a major stumbling block. A tentative understanding has been reached that hereafter policy questions will be divided into two levels of importance, those so significant that unanimity is highly desirable and those of lesser significance where a solid major-ity will be sufficient for a decision. Whether this will work is very much in doubt.

There was no agreement among the E.E.C.'s founders on the appropriate level of political integration. Whether there will be integration of monetary systems and taxation systems and related matters is hotly disputed. There is a European Parlia-ment, at first indirectly but now directly elected, but it has little real power. The formation of a United States of Europe is the objective of many people. It appears that Britain is less supportive of political integration than the other members. Although not consistent, France appears to be the most supportive of political integration. On the other hand, France has often discouraged and/or delayed pro-gress on business cooperation and economic change.

Conclusion

Despite the great number of significant benefits to individual companies and the general public, many companies, both in and outside the E.E.C., have taken no advantage of the opportunities. This fact may be explained by several factors, among them the following: lack of awareness; awareness but lack of practical un-derstanding of the nature of the E.E.C.; lack of a sincere desire to grow; and a corporate culture that resists change. In particular, U.S. organizations, except for the very large, have traditionally been less aggressive about foreign markets than their counterparts in other developed nations.

Applications to Small Business

Countless small businesses of most types can make use of the E.E.C. In particu-lar, it is feasible for small manufacturers from outside the E.E.C. to find additional markets for their products there. Because there is now a market approaching continental proportions, small foreign manufacturers without their own overseas marketing staff can use one export house in their own country or one import house in an E.E.C. country and gain distribution throughout the 12 countries. Various export-import houses offer varying bundles of marketing services to small companies.

References/Sources

Dornbusch, Rudiger, *Macroeconomic Prospects and Policies for the European Community.* Brussels: Centre for European Policy Studies, 1983. Compares the advantages of further integration to the economic dislocations and political risks. Considers difficulties of establishing uniform policies.

Fishwick, Frank, *Multinational Companies and Economic Concentration in Europe.* Brookfield, VT: Gower Publishing, 1982. Considers the threat to survival of small and medium-sized European companies and the potential new competitive mix in Europe.

Foxall, Gordon, "Cooperative Marketing in European Agriculture: Organizational Structures and Market Performance," *International Marketing Review* (Spring-Summer 1984): 42-57. Critically examines the role and efficiency of agricultural marketing co-ops in Europe.

Greer, Thomas V., and Thompson, Paul R., "Development of Standardized and Harmonized Advertising Regulation in the European Economic Community," *Journal of Advertising* (Summer 1985): 23-33. Analyzes the history of regulation of advertising and the trend away from setting regulatory policy at the national level. Contrasts the drives for consumer protection and efficient operation of the multinational EEC market.

Hu, Yao-su, *Europe Under Stress: Convergence and Divergence in the European Community.* Boston: Butterworths, 1981. Examines the fundamental economic, political, and cultural conflicts and the likelihood of future cooperation.

Hutchinson; J. M., "International Marketing Techniques for Engineers," *International Marketing Review* (Autumn-Winter 1984): 51-59. Orients the engineering profession to international marketing opportunities. Compares to domestic marketing experiences.

Kerr, Anthony J. C., *The Common Market and How It Works.* New York: Pergamon Press, 1983. Examines the organization structure, lines of authority, the internal bureaucracy, and the efficiency of work performance. Political realities are considered.

Markin, Robert, and Williams, Karen, *Competitive Law: Antitrust Policy in the United Kingdom and the E.E.C.* London: Sweet and Maxwell, 1984. Analyzes evolution and present status of anti-trust policy at the national and EEC levels. Considers likelihood of future uniformity.

McGovern, Edmond, *International Trade Regulation: GATT, the U.S., and the European Community.* Globefield, Exeter, U.K.: Globefield Press, 1982. Examines the economic and political assumptions and biases of the three entities. Considers prospects for compromise and effects on Third World.

Seers, Dudley, and Ostrom, Kjell, *The Crises of the European Regions.* New York: St. Martin's Press, 1983. Analyzes relative economic health of the competing regions of Europe and the political/historical rivalries and current roles.

Stucki, Hans-Ulrich, and Altenburger, Peter R., *Product Liability: A Manual of Practice in Selected Nations.* Dobbs Ferry, NY: Oceana Publications, 1980. Provides technical and legal information and guidance on liability. Gives comparisons and contrasts.

Tracy, Michael, *Agriculture in Western Europe—Challenge and Response 1880-1980,* 2nd ed. Brookfield, VT: Renouf U.S.A., 1982. Documents evolution of agriculture and national and international policies toward agriculture. Analyzes basic inconsistencies and irrationalities in the industry and its regulation.

Walters, Peter G. P., "Export Information Sources: A Study of Usage and Utility," *International Marketing Review* (Winter 1983): 34-43. Reports survey evidence on what sources of information are utilized and their relative value to the users. Separates data by size of exporter.

Related Topics and Terms

Common Market, Consumerism, Customs Union, Economic Integration, Expatriate Personnel, Exports, Free Trade Association, Imports, International Business, International Marketing, International Trade, Multinational Corporation, Regionalism, Trade Blocs, Trade Balance.

Thomas V. Greer
Department of Marketing
University of Maryland

EXPATRIATE PERSONNEL

Overview

For organizations engaged in international business, expatriate personnel are those employees who are not citizens of the country in which they are working. Expatriate personnel are generally home-country nationals (citizens of the country in which the organization is headquartered), but the term also applies to third-country nationals (citizens of neither the country where they are working nor of the headquarter country of the firm). The difficult dilemma of deciding between hiring local nationals or expatriate personnel is faced by all types of organizations. Although the emphasis is generally on the negatives associated with the use of expatriate personnel—such as the high costs incurred by the organization, time consuming preparations for expatriate assignments, unhappy expatriates and their families, and the problems of repatriation—in instances where home or third-country nationals have qualities or expertise not available in the local labor force, expatriate personnel may play a critical role to the organization's success.

Examples

Large and small organizations alike have employed expatriate personnel with varying degrees of success. A U.S. engineering company encountered insurmountable problems with its expatriate personnel in Italy, and traced the cause of many of their problems to an unhappy American executive's wife who was able to arouse unhappiness in other spouses. The spouses' unhappiness resulted in poor morale among the expatriates, which in turn resulted in missed deadlines and other problems. Other organizations, such as the Peace Corps, rely heavily on expatriate personnel and have developed successful programs to minimize problems. Because expatriate personnel are likely to cost an organization significantly more than foreign nationals, the company must be sure that the expatriate's effectiveness is worth the added expense.

Benefits

Although many American organizations attempt to hire local nationals when possible, the important role of the expatriate cannot be overlooked. Historically chosen for top-management and middle-management positions, expatriates generally bring a level of technical knowledge, background, or experience which may not be available locally, especially in less developed countries. Expatriates are also chosen over local nationals because they are typically familiar with the organization and its policies, products or services and, especially when beginning operations in a foreign country, the expatriate's knowledge of the organization may be necessary for the subsidiary's success. Expatriates may also be called upon to infuse new methods, developed at home, into a foreign subsidiary. In addition, an expatriate may lend a level of prestige to the organization in some countries. Generally, an expatriate will be used if the organization believes that a home-country or third-country national will in some way be more effective in the position than a local national.

Implementation

The focus of much of the literature on the subject of expatriate personnel has been on the problems encountered by expatriates and their organizations; a high failure rate, estimated to be at least 30%, high costs to the company, and loss of career opportunities, to name a few. However, proper selection, training, and a properly implemented program for expatriate personnel can significantly reduce the problems encountered by expatriates and their families.

Selection of an expatriate employee is critical. Not only must the potential expatriate be technically capable of the foreign assignment, he must also be mentally capable of handling the move. The potential expatriate must have a favorable outlook on an international assignment, and many companies are now evaluating the outlook of the employee's family, as well, since unsuccessful family adjustment is the most important reason for expatriate dissatisfaction. In addition, potential expatriates should be able and willing to accept and work within the framework of the local customs and practices of the country, and have the flexibility to adapt to the local environment. Between 15% and 20% of expatriate turnover is due to the inability of the expatriate or the expatriate's family to adapt to the foreign environment. Individual organizations may have additional requirements for expatriate personnel, depending upon the job and organizational policies. These may include certain technical skills, interpersonal skills or qualifications, knowledge of a foreign language, and the ability to work and make decisions independently, far removed from home office influence. Organizations must also consider local prejudices in choosing expatriate personnel, which may render certain candidates ineffective in a particular area, such as a very young manager in Japan. Many organizations go through a lengthy selection process in order to avoid problems later.

Once a candidate has been selected, an extensive orientation program is often necessary to prepare the expatriate and his family for the international assignment. Information should be presented to the expatriate and the expatriate's family which will help them gain an understanding of the cultural, political, and economic environment of the assigned country, as well as information regarding compensation, allowances, transportation, housing, taxes, and provisions for readjustment to the corporate structure upon return. Language training may be made available, and, if possible, the orientation program should include an opportunity for the family to visit the country before the actual move is made. Upon arrival in their new country of assignment, the expatriate and family should be given a period of two to four weeks to get settled and further oriented to the country.

Involvement with expatriate personnel does not end when the expatriate is placed, but rather must continue while the expatriate is abroad and upon repartriation to the home country. A major problem is keeping the expatriate in the foreign assignment for the duration of the assignment. The attrition rate may be very high, as experienced by a construction contractor who started out in Saudi Arabia with 155 American expatriates and within two months was left with only 65 of those employees.

A common complaint of expatriate personnel is that they are forgotten by their employers, and often return to find they have been passed over for promotions or there is no longer a viable position for them in the organization. Thus, companies must closely monitor employees while they are abroad, keeping them in mind with respect to opportunities within the organization. In addition, a re-orientation and de-briefing program is often necessary when expatriates return to their home country, especially when the assignment has been a lengthy one. The repatriation process is critical because the employee often makes the decision to exit the organization at this stage.

Evaluation

The decision of whether to send an expatriate or hire a local national depends upon many factors, including the preferences of the organization, the assignment in question, and the location of the assignment. The requirements of the expatriate and the length of stay also differ among organizations and types of assignments.

Typically, if the position can adequately be filled by a local national, the company will do so. If for some reason, however, an expatriate employee will be more effective in the position, and if the use of expatriate personnel is acceptable to the government of the country, an expatriate may be advisable. Although assignment durations differ, it is generally thought that it is best to agree to a specific assignment duration at the onset of the assignment, although some expatriates are permanent, either taking one assignment or moving from one expatriate position to another.

Conclusion

In the past, many organizations have haphazardly attacked the problems of expatriate staffing, resulting in multitudes of examples of poor performance and failure. The future, however, looks brighter. As more organizations adopt an international outlook and integrate careful selection, orientation, and repartriation programs into all levels of the organization, the successful use of expatriate personnel is sure to increase. Rather than assume expatriates are always the answer, businesses today are more likely to make each staffing decision individually and choose expatriates when they are likely to be more effective than a local national in an assignment.

Applications to Small Business

Expatriate personnel may be utilized by organizations of any size which are actively involved in doing business in other countries. The use of expatriate personnel by small businesses may vary from a lone expatriate salesperson who serves as the only link between a small business and its foreign market to a small subsidiary in a foreign country which is staffed entirely with expatriate personnel.

References/Sources

Acuff, Frank L., "Awareness Levels of Employees Considering Overseas Relocation," *Personnel Journal* (November 1974): 809-812. Emphasizes the importance of providing potential expatriates with full information about all the factors involved in working abroad, especially assuring the employee that his or her safety, security, and social needs will be met.

Conway, Michael A., "Reducing Expatriate Failure Rates," *Personnel Administrator* (July 1984): 31-38. Suggests a systematic approach to overseas staffing which unifies the aims and functions of the three processes of selection, orientation, and repatriation.

Daniels, John D., Ogram, Ernest W., and Radebaugh, Lee H., *International Business: Environments and Operations*. Reading, MA: Addison-Wesley, 1979. Chapter 23 examines the major alternatives for recruitment, selection, training and compensation of international managers.

Dwyer, Gilbert E., "Which Candidates are Most Likely to Succeed in Overseas Assignments?" *Management Review* (July 1982). Suggests employee characteristics to aid in the selection process for expatriate personnel.

Green, Walter E., and Walls, Gard D., "Human Resources: Hiring Internationally," *Personnel Administrator* (July 1984): 61-66. Presents a discussion of three "pure" ways to obtain personnel for foreign operations and also looks at compensation of expatriates.

Harris, Phillip P., and Harris, Dorothy L., "Training for Cultural Understanding," *Training and Development Journal* (May 1982). Considers the importance of the cultural dimension to expatriate personnel. Expatriates must be able to accept cultural differences and understand the culture of their assigned country.

Heenan, David A., "The Corporate Expatriate: Assignment to Ambiguity," *Columbia Journal of World Business* (May-June 1970): 49-54. Considers the special problems of the expatriate businessperson in dealing with the multinational employer, the country of assignment, and the expatriate's own personality.

Howard, Cecil G., "The Expatriate Manager and the Role of the MNC," *Personnel Journal* (October 1980): 838-844. Presents results of a survey of 81 expatriate managers and their families in which they discussed problems encountered in their assignments and subsequent repatriation. Also includes recommendations to avoid many of these problems.

Illman, Paul E., *Developing Overseas Managers—And Managers Overseas.* New York: AMACOM, 1980. An account of international personnel considerations covering topics which are critical to the success of an American organization that operates internationally.

Noer, David M., "Integrating Foreign Service Employees to Home Organizations: The Godfather Approach," *Personnel Journal* (January 1974): 45-52. Discusses the problem of repatriation and presents a system for alleviating some of those problems.

Rahim, Afzalur, "A Model for Developing Key Expatriate Executives," *Personnel Journal* (April 1983): 312-317. Looks at several problems experienced by expatriate executives and presents a model for the development of multinational management.

Roberts, John C., "Section 401 (k) and the Expatriate Employee," *Personnel Administrator* (July 1984): 18-21. Presents some of the compensation problems associated with expatriate personnel and the alternatives available to them.

Shahzad, Nadeem, "The American Expatriate Manager: Present and Future Roles," *Personnel Administrator* (July 1984): 23-28. Considers the importance of expatriate personnel problems experienced by the expatriates and the organization, and discusses prospects for expatriates in the future.

Sieveking, Nicholas, Anchor, Kenneth, and Marston, Ronald C., "Selecting and Preparing Expatriate Employees," *Personnel Journal* (March 1981): 197-202. Discusses using an orientation program as a method for selecting expatriate employees, orientation programs themselves, and following up expatriate employees.

Tung, Rosalie L., "Selection and Training of Personnel for Overseas Assignments," *Columbia Journal of World Business* (Spring 1981): 76-88. Presents an argument for a contingency approach to the selection and training of personnel for overseas assignments, supported with the results of an empirical study on the selection and training procedures used by a sample of 80 U.S. based international organizations.

Related Topics and Terms
Expatriate Executives/Managers, Home-Country Nationals, International Marketing, International Personnel, Repatriation, Third-Country Nationals.

Nancy Pishkur
Department of Marketing
Kent State University

EXPECTED VALUE

Overview

The term "expected value" has its roots in probability and statistics. The general meaning of expected value is not the literal translation; i.e., the likely or anticipated value in a probabilistic situation. Rather, the expected value is a weighted average of values associated with possible outcomes which occur according to respective probabilities. Thus, the expected value is ordinarily not even one of the possible values. The expected value is the long-run average value that would prevail over many identical repetitions of a probabilistic process. This is a special case of the general fact that the long-run average value over a sequence of probabilistic situations, not necessarily identical in structure, is the average of the expected values associated with the individual situations.

The concept of expected value plays a key role in decision analysis. Uncertainty is reflected by the probabilities attached to the alternative "states of nature." These states could be potential outcomes of a random process or could be alternative potential scenarios. In any event, one of these states is realized, and the payoff to the decision-maker is determined by the state and specific action taken. One often uses the decision criterion to choose the action having the highest expected value or payoff. The rationale is that this strategy is optimal in the long-run because the long-run average payoff is the average of the individual expected payoffs as mentioned earlier.

Examples

Consider the simple experiment of tossing a fair die. Six outcomes, corresponding to the six faces of the die, are possible. Let the value associated with each outcome be the number of dots that appear on the shown face. Hence, the possible values are 1, 2, 3, 4, 5 and 6. Under the assumption that the die is fair, the respective probabilities are all one-sixth. The expected value is 3.5. The interpretation is that over many independent tosses of this fair die, the average number obtained in the long run will be 3.5.

Most introductory texts in probability and statistics initiate the reader to the concept of expected value in the context of gambling. The expected value is referred to as the product of the amount the player can win and the probability that the player will indeed win. A "fair price" to play such a game is the expected value because paying this price for each play results in the long-run average gain/loss of zero. Many examples, involving roulette wheels, card games, and so forth, are used to drive home the meaning of expected value.

Benefits

The concept of expected value provides a valuable framework for analyzing alternative actions. Even though the probabilities associated with the potential outcomes often must be subjective rather than empirical in nature, the structure is still quite useful. The process of developing a matrix of payoffs for each combination of possible state and action is often very valuable in itself. This exercise helps to define the problem, and problem definition is many times the most difficult task in developing a solution.

Implementation

The key to applying the concept of expected value to decision problems is the fact that it represents the long-run average. The laws of probability dictate that over a large number of separate probabilistic situations, the average payoff will be close to the average of the expected values associated with the individual situations. Hence, by pricing individual policies so that the expected value to the insurer is positive, insurance companies are basically guaranteed of a positive cash flow by the laws of probability. That is, across many individuals, each representing a probabilistic situation for the period of insurance, the average payoff to the insurer is guaranteed to be quite close to the average of the individual expected values. Because each expected value is positive, the insurance company is basically guaranteed of having a positive cash flow.

The same logic applies to decision making in a marketing setting. If one approaches each decision by analyzing the expected value associated with each alternative, and chooses that alternative with the highest expected value, the decision maker is in a sense acting optimally. Again, the laws of probability suggest that over many such decision-making scenarios, the average value or payoff associated with the decisions will be "close to optimal".

Consider a simple example of this approach to decision-making. Suppose a firm is faced with deciding the level of inventory of a product to cover a prescribed period of time. For simplicity, suppose demand for this period of time can be 0, 1, 2, 3, 4, 5 or 6 units. Hence, the possible actions are to begin the period with 0, 1, 2, 3, 4, 5 or 6 units. The probabilities associated with the various demand levels are shown in the table below. The table below also shows the hypothetical value or payoff to the firm associated with each possible combination of demand and inventory. These payoffs of course are based on the profit margin for the items, cost of the items, salvage value, and so forth.

PROFIT TABLE

Probability	Demand	Inventory						
		0	1	2	3	4	5	6
.05	0	0	-2	-4	-6	-8	-10	-12
.10	1	0	1	-1	-3	-5	-7	-9
.25	2	0	1	2	0	-2	-4	-6
.30	3	0	1	2	3	1	-1	-3
.20	4	0	1	2	3	4	2	0
.05	5	0	1	2	3	4	5	3
.05	6	0	1	2	3	4	5	6
EXPECTED PROFIT		0	.85	1.40	1.20	.10	-1.60	-3.45

Shown in the marginal row at the bottom of the above table are the expected values associated with the possible actions. For example, the expected profit associated with an inventory of one unit is found as follows: $(-2)(.05) + (1)(.1) + (1)(.25) + (1)(.3) + (1)(.2) + (1)(.05) + (1)(.05) = .85$. On the basis of the probabilities assigned to the possible market situations, the optimal decision is to stock two units. This action has the highest expected value.

Analogously, the expected value of demand is 2.85 units, which clearly demonstrates the fact that the expected value is not the anticipated or most likely value. The most likely value is called the mode—3 units in this example. Also, the fact that the expected value is not necessarily one of the outcome values is again demonstrated.

It is important to point out that once the decision is made the outcome will be one of the listed possible outcomes. Hence, the firm may indeed suffer a loss by stocking two units, as would be the case if the demand was 0 or 1. The only consolation is that over many similar decisions all approached in the same manner, the average payoff to the firm should approach the average expected value associated with those decisions, i.e., the average maximum expected value. Thus, the average payoff across a long sequence of identical problems, all having this structure, would be close to $1.40.

Occasionally, it is better to look at payoffs in terms of their utilities as opposed to monetary values. In other words, the value of money is factored into the overall evaluation of the decision alternatives. As a simple example, consider a person waiting for a bus with only 75¢ while the required bus fare is $1.00. The value to this person of the additional 25¢ is far more than face value. That is, the person might well be willing to gamble the 75¢ he does have against 25¢, even though the chances of winning and losing are equal. This individual has a tremendous utility for gaining an additional 25¢ or more, and basically very little concern over losing the 75¢ currently owned. Analogously, a firm facing a business decision might have a tremendous negative utility for a large monetary loss, and not an equal positive utility for an equal monetary gain. The decision analysis should reflect these feelings or opinions regarding the value of money. Hence, utilities are often substituted for monetary values to account for this phenomenon.

The concept of expected value is very important to the process of setting quality control standards. For example, suppose that the weight or volume of actual product placed into a container during the packing operation is probabilistic in nature. That is, the actual amount inserted into the package by the filling process is not exactly the same from package to package but rather can be several or many values with varying probabilities. One objective might be to control the process so that the expected value of product packed into a single unit is equal to some criterion value. Hence, one would be guaranteed that over a large manufacturing run of product, the average product volume or weight would be very close to the quality target.

A specific area of statistics where the term expected value assumes its literal meaning; i.e., an anticipated or likely value, is the analysis of contingency tables. The most simplistic use of market research data is the construction of cross-tabulations in which a random sample of survey respondents is cross-classified according to two factors. The resulting table is called a contingency table. For example, a random sample of 1000 female heads-of-households could be cross-classified according to their favorite brand of cake mix and the household's annual income. Having constructed such a table, the researcher seeks to determine whether preference for cake mix is independent of household income; i.e., cake mix preference is consistent across income groups. To test this hypothesis, the researcher calculates the expected value or expected frequency for each cell of the table. If cake mix preference and household income are independent, the expected value for each cell of the table is the product of the percent of the sample who prefer the brand in question and the percent of the sample falling into the particular household income category and the size of the sample. Hence, the expected number of people in the lowest income bracket preferring Duncan Hines cake mix is the number of respondents in the sample times the percent of the sample preferring Duncan Hines times the percent of the sample in the lowest income bracket.

The table would be analyzed by comparing the expected value for each cell with the observed value for each cell, using what is called the Chi-square test for independence. The test statistic simply sums across the cells of the table the squared deviations of observed from expected values divided by the respective expected values. The resulting test statistic is compared to the Chi-square table to determine whether the results are statistically significant. "Abnormally" large values of the test statistic indicate statistical significance, and the hypothesis that cake mix preference and household income are independent would then be rejected in favor of the alternative that preference for cake mix does vary with income bracket.

The table below shows a hypothetical cross-tabulation for the example discussed above.

INCOME BRACKET

		Low	Medium	High	
CAKE	Duncan Hines	150	140	110	400
MIX	Betty Crocker	100	90	10	200
PREFERENCE	Pillsbury	110	120	70	300
	Other	40	50	10	100
		400	400	200	1000

The expected value for the cell corresponding to high income and preference for Duncan Hines would be: $(1000)(.40)(.20) = 80$. The contribution to the overall Chi-square statistics for this cell would be: $(110-80)^2/80 = 11.25$.

Evaluation

The first steps in applying the expected value logic to a decision problem are to analyze the situation and develop the structure. The alternative states, their corresponding probabilities, and possible actions must be identified. Also, a system for determining value of payoff for each combination of state and action must be developed. Then, the expected value of each action can be determined. The sensitivity of the choice of action to the probabilities can be analyzed. Because the probabilities are often subjective rather than empirical, the impact of adjusting these values on the choice of action should be analyzed.

It is often possible to revise initial probabilities by collecting data which provides information regarding the actual situation. The initial probabilities, called "prior probabilities," are updated, based on the collected data, to "posterior probabilities." The expected values are recalculated based on the revised probabilities, and the appropriate action is taken. Further, one can compound a decision problem by including an option to collect information, typically imperfect, and taking the action indicated by the information. In order to evaluate this option, the expected value of the additional information must be calculated and compared to its cost. The marketing research literature contains discussions pertaining to the calculation of the expected value of additional information.

Conclusion

Expected value has many business applications ranging from deciding whether to introduce a new product to establishing quality control procedures for day-to-day operation of a manufacturing plant. In a general decision-making context, expected value provides a simple vehicle for evaluating alternative possible actions under uncertainty. It also provides a means for identifying a long-run optimal strategy.

Applications to Small Business

The decision-making structure suggested by using the optimal expected value or payoff decision criterion has value to small businesses as well as large businesses. In fact, in many cases the problem structure may be far less complex for small businesses than in the case of large businesses. Further, the emergence of micro-computers and associated software facilitate using sophisticated decision models at the small business level. The inventory-demand model displayed in the example would certainly appear to be applicable to small retail businesses.

Software/Databases

Spread-sheet software such as VisiCalc or Lotus 1-2-3 can be used with a personal computer to analyze decision problems. The payoff table could be constructed, and the calculation of the expected values associated with the actions could be programmed. This would facilitate evaluating the sensitivity of the solution to the assigned probabilities and the assumptions involved in calculating the payoffs.

Most statistical software packages; e.g., SAS or SPSSX, contain programs or subroutines for performing the analysis of cross-tabulations.

References/Sources

Feller W., *An Introduction to Probability Theory and Its Applications*. New York: John Wiley & Sons, 1957. Section 1 and 2 of Chapter IX are devoted to random variables and expectation; sections 3 and 4 of Chapter X contain a discussion of "fair" games.

Ferber, R. ed., *Handbook of Marketing Research*. New York: McGraw-Hill, 1974. Chapter 3 of Part A contains a discussion of expected value, payoffs, states of nature, subjective probabilities, and the value of additional information.

Freund, J. E., *Statistics A First Course*. Englewood Cliffs, NJ: Prentice-Hall, 1970, pp. 78-81. Defines expected value and its use in a decision-making context.

Hodges, J. L. and Lehmann, E. L., *Basic Concepts of Probability and Statistics*. San Francisco, Holden-Day, 1964. Sections 5.3 and 5.4 are devoted to the calculation of expectation, and contain several examples.

Kohler, H., *Statistics for Business and Economics*. Glenview, IL: Scott, Foresman, 1985. Chapter 10, pp. 409-420, contains a discussion of the analysis of contingency tables.

Schlaifer, R., *Probability and Statistics for Business Decisions*. New York: McGraw-Hill, 1959. The book is devoted to the use of expected value as a decision-making tool, and the revising of prior probabilities based on sample information.

Tull, D. S. and Hawkins, D. I., *Marketing Research Measurement and Method.* New York: Macmillan, 1984. Chapter 3 is devoted to the value of additional information in a marketing research decision-making context.

Related Topics and Terms

Expectation, Decision Theory, Expected Utility, Mathematical Expectation, Mean, Posterior Probabilities, Prior Probabilities.

Richard J. Fox
Marketing Department
University of Georgia

EXPLORATORY RESEARCH

Overview

Marketing research is typically subdivided into three types—exploratory, conclusive and performance-monitoring. Conclusive research entails an extensive and usually expensive investigation to help a manager evaluate alternative courses of action and determine which one to take, and performance-monitoring research is just as the name implies—research aimed at assessing the performance results of the course of action followed. In contrast, exploratory research is used as input for the early stages of a manager's decision-making process. It represents a preliminary investigation of a decision-making situation with a minimal expenditure of time and money, compared to the other two types. It is characterized by flexibility and an orientation toward discovery.

Exploratory research is appropriate when searching for potential problems and opportunities, when seeking new insights or hypotheses regarding the decision situation being confronted, when seeking a more precise formulation of the decision problem and identification of the relevant variables in the decision situation, and when identifying alternative courses of action. Exploratory research usually serves as a precursor to conclusive research.

Examples

Prior to the introduction of the Susan B. Anthony dollar coin, a series of focus group interviews were conducted with representatives from retailing organizations, since retail clerks would be the primary collectors and dispensers of the coin. They could also relate their own feelings as consumers. Significant problems with the coin were identified in these sessions. These problems included its similarity to the quarter, its bulkiness compared to the dollar bill, and the lack of an unused compartment in cash registers for storage. The coins were, however, introduced to the market as planned; interest waned after the novelty effect wore off, and the coins now assume a large portion of the government's stockpile of existing coinage.

A metropolitan public library commissioned a conclusive study of its user population for the ostensible purpose of identifying which one of several alternative sources of action would be most favorably received. Contrary to expectations, focus group interviews with library users revealed that the survey questionnaire for the conclusive study would need to be modified to reflect the distinctive jargon used to describe library facilities and the widespread nontraditional uses for the library (e.g., shelter, social interaction). Moreover, the courses under consideration were found to be in need of substantive modification.

A multi-phase exploratory research study was conducted by a trade association whose membership had a vested interest in the mechanics of the mandatory beverage-container deposit and redemption law passed by Michigan voters. The study commenced six months before the law went into effect and entailed: (1) a comprehensive examination of Oregon's experiences with its "Bottle-bill" (i.e., a case history study using library sources), (2) completion of depth interviews with market intermediaries and with industry and packaging experts, (3) acquisition of product movement data from a syndicated data source, and (4) retrieval of industry performance statistics compiled by the trade group (i.e., internal secondary data search). These data inputs were used to formulate alternative decision scenarios and the courses of action that the industry as a whole might take to accommodate changes imposed by the legislation.

Benefits

Benefits of exploratory research include enhanced utilization of conclusive research, improved managerial decision making, better understanding of the marketplace, and elimination of unwarranted expenditures for unnecessary conclusive research.

Implementation

Secondary data and literature are developed for some purpose other than the decision task at hand (as opposed to primary data specifically collected for the decision) and should always be consulted prior to investing in primary data collection. Secondary data are relatively inexpensive and easily accessed (many are available in local libraries and company files).

Internal secondary data include accounting and production data and past marketing research reports. External secondary data sources are subdivided into those in the public and private domains. In the public domain, there are many community and university libraries across the United States that have extensive holdings of business-related materials, such as corporate annual reports, general business publications (e.g., trade association and industry periodicals, newspapers, handbooks), academic publications and government documents. The *Statistical Abstract of the United States* is a summary volume of the myriad of data regularly collected by government agencies and should be consulted first when government documents are investigated. The *Business Periodicals Index* is an excellent reference resource for locating data and articles on particular topics.

Apart from sources available in the public domain, syndicated data sources regularly collect market data that may be acquired for a fee. The familiar Nielsen television program ratings, the SAMI wholesale movement of goods reports, Dun & Bradstreet's Market Identifiers, and Starch *Readership Reports* are but a few of the large-scale syndicated data sources available. In addition, there are many small market research suppliers that collect and sell syndicated data that pertain to a specific industry or locale. M/PF Research, Inc. serves the Dallas/Fort Worth housing industry with regular reports on the real estate market in the area. Preston

Publishing Company provides similar services for oil and gas drillers. Trade associations are a particularly useful way to locate syndicated sources, and many of them also supply such data to their members which may be acquired by nonmembers for a fee.

Case histories and experience are intensive investigations of analogous or related situations to those being confronted; they may provide a useful means of identifying important considerations and possible courses of action. Such information may be obtained from secondary data sources, through observation of the related situation, and/or through surveying individuals involved. For example, a sales manager confronted with a change from a straight commission compensation plan to a salary-plus-commission plan would likely benefit from consultation with managers who have experienced similar changes in corporate policy.

Somewhat like experience surveys, a depth interview is a one-on-one probe of a particular topic with someone knowledgeable of the subject matter. The aim is to get beneath the surface of a person's typical response and explore his underlying motives, needs and values. It is appropriate when: (1) the subject matter is highly confidential, emotionally-charged or embarrassing, (2) strong social views exist and conforming tendencies would be likely in a focus-group setting (see below), (3) the behavior or decision-making patterns are complicated or superficial responses will likely be given, and (4) the respondent is a professional or the topic concerns his job.

Often used synonymously with the term, "exploratory research," the focus group interview is a widely-applied technique to explore virtually any topic in depth. It is characterized by a small group of individuals (usually 8-12 in number) conversing about a topic under the direction and leadership of a moderator, who is usually a trained industrial psychologist. The atmosphere of the group setting is designed to be informal and free-flowing in the hope of providing stimulation of group interaction and the possibility of something unexpected and useful surfacing. Typically, participants are recruited in such a way that friends, spouses and "repeaters" are excluded from participation in order to minimize the possibility of undermining group interaction.

Another type of exploratory research is used to identify any problems with a survey questionnaire or its administration prior to implementing the study on a larger scale. Typically a survey will be pretested on a small sample of the representative population. Data generated from this pretest are used to determine if there are any modifications to the basic procedure and survey instrument which need to be made. Although pretesting may help identify glaring problems, testing on a small scale may be insufficient for all problems to surface.

Evaluation

Secondary data are usually not exactly what the researcher needs. However, it is frequently possible to develop satisfactory estimates using several different sources by making judicious assumptions and performing simple numerical transformations. For example, estimates of demand for industrial lubricants could be obtained by using county or state industry employment data in conjunction with data or lubricant use per employee. When only rough estimates are needed, such data manipulations can be very useful.

Case histories and experience surveys offer the advantage of the inferences being drawn from an entire and real situation which may provide more accurate data than would otherwise be available. However, there is a large element of subjectivity inherent in this approach and a tendency to overgeneralize.

The primary advantages of the depth interview approach are the depth and richness of the responses that may result. Drawbacks include: 1) the need for highly trained, skilled and paid interviewers, 2) subjective responses which make content analysis difficult, and 3) the length of the interview (i.e., over one hour) makes participation burdensome for the respondent.

Advantages of the focus group interview that are often cited include: it offers the potential for providing hypotheses worthy of testing in a conclusive study, it assists in questionnaire construction and fieldwork design of a conclusive study, the findings can be readily understood by clients, and it helps bridge the gap between marketing managers and their customers. On the other hand, disadvantages include the possibility of an ineffective moderator (which can bias group results and cause costly mistakes if it misdirects subsequent research efforts), the microscope-magnification effect (i.e., by focusing on a particular topic, it assumes a greater importance than exists in everyday life), and data can be interpreted as one desires (which is biasing in its own right). Each of these disadvantages can generally be minimized through the use of a respected research supplier that regularly conducts focus groups.

Conclusion

Exploratory research serves useful purposes in eliminating some of the uncertainty surrounding a manager's decision making and offers the potential for enhanced efficiency and effectiveness in the use of expensive conclusive research procedures. Although not intended for providing definitive answers that will enable a manager to select "the" appropriate course of action, exploratory research procedures can help clarify the decision problem, identify possible courses of action, and provide important inputs to conclusive research that may be able to supply the needed answers. All firms, large and small alike, can and do benefit from use of the relatively inexpensive and fast exploratory research alternatives available.

Applications to Small Business

Small businesses, like large operations, need information upon which to base their decisions and like their larger counterparts, small businesses can benefit from engaging in exploratory research. However, unlike large businesses, the owners and operators of smaller companies can frequently use exploratory research to get tentative answers to research questions, thereby avoiding the need to conduct further research and incurring the time and cost involved.

This benefit of exploratory research for small businesses can occur for several reasons. First, small businesses will usually be serving a relatively small geographic area. Second, they will have fewer customers. Third, they will need to use fewer suppliers. Fourth, they are competing with a handful of companies.

References/Sources

Andreason, Alan R., "Cost-conscious Marketing Research," *Harvard Business Review* (July-August 1983): 74, 75, 78, 79. Dispels prevailing false beliefs about marketing research and demonstrates how exploratory research methods can be easily and cheaply implemented in small business contexts.

Bellenger, Danny N., Bernhardt, Kenneth L., and Goldstucker, Jac L., *Qualitative Research in Marketing,* Monograph Series #3. Chicago: American Marketing Association, 1976. In-depth discussion of various exploratory research techniques—focus group interviews, depth interviews and projective techniques.

Bonoma, Thomas V., "Case Research in Marketing: Opportunities, Problems, and a Process," *Journal of Marketing Research,* 22 (May 1985): 199-208. Explores the case history approach as a research method. Provides a four-stage model of the research process.

Boyd, Harper W., Westfall, Ralph, and Stasch, Stanley F., *Marketing Research: Text and Cases,* 6th ed. Homewood, IL: Irwin, 1985. Chapter 3 provides a detailed discussion of the case history approach to exploratory research, and a good overview of other approaches as well.

Buncher, Martin M., "Focus Groups Seem Easy to Do and Use but They're Easier to Misuse and Abuse," *Marketing News* (September 17, 1982, Sec. 2): 14-15. Discusses improper use of focus groups as a conclusive research tool and offers guidelines for effective use as an exploratory research tool. Variants on the traditional focus-group procedure are given.

Calder, Bobby J., "Focus Groups and the Nature of Qualitative Marketing Research," *Journal of Marketing Research,* 14 (August 1977): 353-364. Reports on various uses of focus groups and evaluates them in relation to philosophy of science considerations and relevance to subsequent conclusive (quantitative) research.

Comer, James M. and Chakrabarti, Alok K., "The Information Industry for the Industrial Marketer," *Industrial Marketing Management,* 7 (1978): 65-70. Provides an overview of the mechanics of the provision and use of secondary data sources for the industrial marketer. Offers guidance for usage by large and small firms with differing usage rates.

Cox, Keith K., Higginbotham, James B., and Burton, John, "Applications of Focus Group Interviews in Marketing," *Journal of Marketing,* 40 (January 1976): 77-80. Provides three examples of the effective use of focus group interviews to assist in developing and implementing conclusive research. Strengths and weaknesses of the approach are considered.

Dupont, Thomas D., "Exploratory Group Interview in Consumer Research: A Case Example," *Advances in Consumer Research,* Vol. 3. B.B. Anderson, ed. Atlanta: Association for Consumer Research, 1976, pp. 431-433. Good example of how focus group interviews serve the important function to guide the design and conduct of a large-scale quantitative (conclusive) survey.

Goeldner, C.R. and Dirks, Laura M., "Business Facts: Where to Find Them," *MSU Business Topics* (Summer 1976): 23-36. Provides a detailed annotated bibliography of secondary data sources available in government and business reference libraries.

Johnson, H. Webster, Faria, Anthony J., and Maier, Ernest L., *How to Use the Business Library,* 5th ed. Cincinnati: South-Western Publishing Co., 1984. Excellent "how-to" guide on locating secondary information sources. Step-by-step instructions given. Detailed compendium of available sources, organized by content area.

Katz, Arthur S., "Inexpensive Research: Analyze Sales Data Hidden in Your Files," *Marketing News* (September 17, 1982, Sec. 1): 6. Provides several examples of uses of internal secondary data.

Kinnear, Thomas C., and Taylor, James R., *Marketing Research: An Applied Approach,* 2nd ed. New York: McGraw-Hill, 1983. Chapter 4 provides a discussion of how and when exploratory research may be of assistance to decision making and subsequent conclusive research. Chapters 5 and 6 are useful for identifying alternative data sources for exploratory research. Focus group interviews are discussed in Chapter 13 (pp. 374-379). The appendices of Chapters 5 and 6 contain valuable annotated listings of available syndicated and library secondary data sources, respectively.

Kudla, Ronald J., Krampert, William A., and Sader, Harold M., "Follow These Guidelines to Get The Most Out of One-On-One Interviews," *Marketing News* (September 17, 1982, Section 1): 3, 18. Identifies important considerations in conducting depth interviews with managers.

Lautman, Martin R., "Focus Groups: Theory and Method," *Advances in Consumer Research,* Vol. 9. A.A. Mitchell, ed. Ann Arbor: Association for Consumer Research, 1982, pp. 52-56. Critical analysis of practical issues in the use of focus groups in marketing research contexts. Provides useful description of types of information sought from focus group participants.

Percy, Larry, "Using Qualitative Focus Groups in Generating Hypotheses for Subsequent Quantitative Validation and Strategy Development," *Advances in Consumer Research,* Vol. 9. A.A. Mitchell, ed. Ann Arbor: Association for Consumer Research, 1982, pp. 57-61. Useful companion to article by Calder cited above. Provides several solid examples of the utility of focus group research for developing hypotheses to be tested in a conclusive manner.

Robey, Bryant, "10 'Shortcuts' to Evaluating Demographic Statistics: Think About What Lies Behind the Numbers," *Marketing News* (September 17, 1982, Sec. 1): 9-10. The editor of *American Demographics* identifies a number of ways to evaluate 1980 census data for accuracy.

Seymour, Daniel T., "3-stage Focus Groups Used to Develop New Bank Product: Explanation, Team Task, and Group Discussion Phases," *Marketing News* (September 17, 1982, Sec. 2): 11. Provides example of use of focus group interviews for product concept testing.

Wasson, Chester, R., "Use and Appraisal of Existing Information," *Handbook of Marketing Research.* R. Ferber, ed. New York: McGraw-Hill, 1974, pp. 2-11 through 2-25. Detailed analysis of sources and uses of external secondary data.

Wells, William D., "Group Interviewing," *Handbook of Marketing Research.* R. Ferber, ed. New York: McGraw-Hill, 1974, pp. 2-133 through 2-146. Analyzes the strengths and weaknesses of focus group interviews and offers guidance for the preparation and conduct of such interviews.

Wish, John, Slade, Rod, and Emerson, Susan, "Marketing Literature: How to Find it with a Computer," *Journal of Marketing,* 42 (April 1978): 12, 13, 135. Provide data that reveal large differences in on-line, computer-assisted literature search services.

Related Topics and Terms
   Case History, Depth Interview, Focus Group Interview, Pretest, Qualitative Research, Secondary Data.

James H. Leigh
Department of Marketing
Texas A&M University

FAMILY DECISION MAKING

Overview

Family decision making is the process through which a family or other group of affiliated people goes in arriving at a choice. In the market place, the process might also be called family buying behavior. No single person in a family group makes a buying decision without being influenced in some way by other members of that same family unit. While most of the consumer research that has been done has been based on individual buying behavior, a substantial part of larger or more expensive purchases arise out of a joint purchase decision made by more than one buyer. Many firms have based their marketing strategies on the assumption that family buying behavior is really the result of a group of individual decision processes. Research in this area suggests that family buying behavior is different and far more complex than individual buying behavior. This difference and complexity yields a very dissimilar set of marketing strategies that will affect every element of the marketing mix.

Examples

Typical attributes of buying decision situations that tend to be made by families are (1) relatively large dollar purchases (2) complex purchases, requiring a variety of expertise and evaluative skills, and (3) non-routine and highly involving purchases. Several types of family decision making behavior can be identified. All involve multiple parties, but may be dominated by one party. Husband dominant, wife dominant, syncratic (joint), and autonomic (husband or wife seemingly making the decision alone but in a way that would be acceptable to their spouse). It has been suggested that the dominance or degree of cooperation can change across the stages of the decision making process; i.e., what may start as a wife dominant process may later end up syncratic (joint) at the time of purchase.

The selection and purchase of a house has been shown to be a syncratic (joint) buying process for families. The purchase of an automobile tends to be slightly husband dominant with some role specialization concerning colors and interiors generally assumed by the wife. Most research suggests that insurance is usually purchased autonomically by husbands with some confirmation by the wife in the later stages of purchase. Thus, there is no single pattern that forms that best example of a family buying decision. Despite the irregularity of this process, many firms still use such research about family buying to plan marketing strategies.

Benefits

Using and understanding the process of family buying can be very helpful to the marketing strategies of a firm. A home builder in the Southwest found that by

325

training their salespeople to understand the interspousal decision process they were able to greatly improve the number of closed sales. A major automobile dealership has redesigned its way of selling to couples by having a second salesperson work with wives who wish to understand all of the interior options in selecting a new car. In most purchase processes involving both spouses, there is a real danger of either forcing one spouse into a higher level of involvement than he or she wants, or that of ignoring a spouse. Either can be deadly to a sale without the salesperson ever knowing what caused the missed sale. Most firms that recognize the differences among the various types of family decision processes enjoy a major competitive advantage.

Implementation

To effectively use strategies that recognize the family decision making process, firms must first understand how families view their products or services. For example, if a firm is in the travel business it is important to understand that families tend to see the purchase of a vacation package as a joint decision with one spouse (hard to predict which one) starting the search process, but with no final decision made until both spouses concur. Agents for such a firm would have to understand that part of the enjoyment of the vacation arises from selecting the destination and that both parties have role specializations. Simply being aware of that process with its many variations can keep a travel agent working constructively with a couple rather than working against the natural flow of their decision process.

A major problem exists in many family buying situations when the process involves the presence of conflict between the spouses in making a choice. If a salesperson is not aware of the need to help manage conflict in the buying process, the sale may be lost and the couple may associate their frustration with the firm and the salesperson.

Firms selling life insurance must understand that, in most cases, the policy is sold to the male, with only certain key aspects of the service which interest the wife. Exceptions are plentiful, but by understanding the possible structures of dominance, autonomy, and syncracy, the marketer can quickly adjust to the role sharing and role specialization that is present in a couple's relationship.

Evaluation

In order for management to determine whether their products or services must be viewed from the standpoint of the family buying process, there are a number of questions that must be asked:

1. Are couples both involved in the buying situation?
2. Is each spouse asking questions about different aspects of the product or service?
3. From start to finish, does the typical couple take a long time to arrive at a choice?

4. Regardless of who starts the buying process, do both spouses get involved before a purchase is made?
5. Do couples frequently differ in what they want in buying the product?

If most of those questions could be answered "yes" from a firm's experience in selling, then family decision strategies should become part of the marketing approach. In terms of evaluating how well salespeople handle family purchasing, the following questions yield insight into the effectiveness of their strategies:

1. Are salespeople being trained to deal specifically with couples?
2. Has the firm's marketing research taken into account the need to study the roles of both spouses independently as well as their interactive relationship in buying?
3. If research is being done using the couple as the unit of analysis, are the findings then being translated into strategies for product design, advertising, and personal selling?

If the answers to any of these questions are negative, the firm needs to reexamine the way it is handling family buying.

Conclusion

Most firms in the U.S. have never effectively dealt with the family buying process for their products or services. There are several reasons for this shortcoming:

1. The family buying process is very complex and despite a significant amount of research in the area, there is still no well accepted model of how the process works.
2. The rapid development of numerous, competing models of individual consumer behavior has encouraged firms to ignore the greater complexity of family buying behavior.
3. Even when the research has been done by firms to understand family buying of their products, it has been difficult to articulate those findings into actionable strategies.
4. Even when strategies have been developed as a result of family buying patterns, it has been difficult to overcome the biases of sales training that typically assume that the selling process is aimed at a single buyer.
5. In nearly forty years of academic research concerning family buying, the total body of accumulated knowledge is still quite incomplete.

Most firms that wish to respond to this extremely important area must still rely on product-specific research findings. Even with all of these drawbacks, the advantages of researching and thinking about product strategies from a family buying process perspective are very encouraging.

Applications to Small Business

Many products that are manufactured or retailed by smaller businesses are sold to families that buy using interspousal decision making. At first look it may not appear that smaller firms would have the resources to identify key aspects of the family decision process concerning their products or services. It must be recognized, however, that what a smaller firm lacks in resources is frequently made up for by being closer to the customer. A series of informal observations about how couples buy the firm's products can, over time, accumulate to a very effective body of actionable knowledge. A beginning place for incorporating the awareness of family decision making is to look at the firm's strategies relative to the needs of family units.

A second approach is to talk with couples after they have purchased the firm's products (or not!). While the smaller firm usually cannot justify a formal, complex research study of family buying behavior concerning its products or services, it can undertake a careful process of observation and informal experimentation to determine what strategies facilitate the family buying unit.

References/Sources

Davis, H.L., "Decision Making Within the Household," *Journal of Consumer Research* 2 (February 1976): 241-260. This is probably the best single review of the major findings of the literature in an organized and readable manner.

Davis, H.L. and Rigaux, B.P., "Perception of Marital Roles in Decision Processes," *Journal of Consumer Research* (June 1974): 51-62. Although this article is over ten years old, it remains as a very insightful and useful view of husband and wife interaction and role specialization in the buying process.

Kelly, R.F., and Egan, M.B., "Husband and Wife Interaction in a Consumer Decision Process," *Proceedings of the 1969 Fall Conference.* American Marketing Association, 250-258. This is still a classic in the family decision literature and provides strategic insights for product planning or promotion. It may be a bit more difficult to find than the other articles, but is useful.

Sheth, J.N., "A Theory of Family Buying Decisions," *Models of Buying Behavior: Conceptual, Quantitative, and Empirical.* New York: Harper and Row, 1974, 17-33. The value of this piece is in its explanation of the major differences and similarities between individual buying behavior and family buying behavior. Sheth based the proposed model on the major constructs of the Howard and Sheth buying behavior model. This can be helpful in understanding of the basic issues.

Related Topics and Terms

Buyer, Consumer Behavior, Family Life Cycle, Group Decision Making, Personal Selling, Role Conflict.

Charles S. Madden
Department of Marketing
Baylor University

FAMILY LIFE CYCLE

Overview

One of the personal factors of the individual which influences his consumer purchases is the stage of the family life cycle. Nine stages of the family life cycle have been identified, all of which are useful in understanding the forces which shape consumption in adult consumers. These forces include age, marital status, the presence or absence of children in the home and the ages of the children. It is widely believed that buying is best understood as a correlate of the stage of one's family development rather than as a response to any one demographic variable. The family life cycle concept is concerned with how consumption behavior changes over time as a result of attitude development, role changes, and the effects of maturity, experience, and aging.

Examples

Many research studies have identified relationships between the stages of the family life cycle and buying differences among adults.

Bachelor Stage. Persons at this stage are single but not living at home with their parents. Having few financial burdens and being fashion and recreation conscious, they live in their own apartments; purchase cars, vacations, basic furniture and kitchen equipment; and acquire the necessities for the mating game. Members of this group represent attractive opportunities to marketers of apartments, vacations, furniture, music, and restaurants. The U.S. automobile industry has targeted several of its sportier models to members of this group.

New Married Stage. These couples are generally still young but have no children; consequently, they are financially better off than they will be in the near future. Since their emphasis is on marriage and the establishment of the home, this group has been documented as having the highest purchase rate and highest average purchase of durable items. Members in this stage are attractive prospects for the sale of such items as houses, refrigerators, stoves, sensible and durable furniture, and vacations. Kroehler Manufacturing Co. found, through marketing research, that interest in furniture buying is greatest among this group.

Full Nest I. These young adults have their youngest child under age 6. Seeking more living space, they are at the peak of their home purchases and the nadir of their financial security. Such products as the following are attractive to them: washers, dryers, all baby-related products, televisions, vitamins, chest rubs and cough medicines. Baby food producers, like Gerber and Beechnut, have successfully targeted members of this stage.

Full Nest II. Couples at this stage have children, the youngest of which is 6 or over. While their financial position is improved, these couples to tend buy in quantity. They are attractive markets for such products as bicycles, music lessons, cleaning materials, and many foods. Schwinn bicycles were, traditionally, targeted toward members of this stage. Likewise, until recently, families at this stage were McDonald's primary target.

Full Nest III. These couples are older yet they still have dependent children. Their financial positions are improved since many wives of this segment work, as well as some of the children. Members of this stage are frequent purchasers of tasteful furniture, non-necessary appliances, dental services, magazines, boats, and auto travel.

Empty Nest I. Members of this stage are still in the work force, but no longer have children living at home. Since home ownership is at its peak among such couples, home improvements are among their frequent purchases. These couples are also interested in travel, recreation, and self-improvement, so they invest in vacations, luxury goods, making contributions, and giving gifts. Many travel agencies have successful marketed vacation packages to these individuals.

Empty Nest II. These older couples, likewise have no children living at home, but the heads of the households are retired from the workforce. In keeping with the subsequent reduction in income, these individuals tend to keep their homes. They purchase medical appliances and aids which assist with sleep, digestion, and general health.

Solitary Survivor I. This individual, having lost his/her spouse is still a member of the labor force. There is a tendency among members of this group to sell their homes and seek smaller living quarters. They are attractive targets for the sales of such items as condominiums, apartments, and those related to health care.

Solitary Survivor II. This individual is without spouse and is no longer a member of the workforce. This consumer has many of the same medical needs as the aforementioned aging group and is an attractive target for the sale of pharmaceuticals, dentures, health foods, nursing homes, transportation, entertainment, books, televisions, and various forms of mild recreation. Also, members of this group seek attention and security.

Benefits

The family life cycle concept is a convenient means by which the marketer can segment the vast array of consumer buyers. Based on trends in earning power, needs, and motives, the sea of adult consumers can be classified into groups related to product preferences and differences in purchases. Also, the family life cycle concept is an intuitively appealing means of understanding the total behavior of the consumer which is influenced by a combination of major factors: cultural, social, psychological, as well as personal.

Studies have found relationships between the stages of the family life cycle and buying differences of white goods, bicycles, pianos, furniture, and different types of energy. These findings can be useful in devising promotional messages which effectively communicate with the target market and in developing new products which meet each group's unique needs.

Implementation

The family life cycle is only one of many variables which describe buyers and relate to purchasing differences. As with lifestyle, personality, geographic location, demographic characteristics, and benefits sought, just to name a few, the family life cycle can be an integral part of setting the parameters for the market segmentation process.

First, the marketer must decide what kinds of market segments he desires, such as those which distinguish purchasers from non-purchasers or those which differentiate heavy users from light users. Once the type of segments desired is clearly defined, the marketer must ask if stage of the family life cycle relates in any way to those segment differences. Does membership in the Bachelor stage, for example, serve as an indication of a tendency to purchase a product? Or a tendency to be a heavy user of a product? If a link is found between the family life cycle and the desired market segments, the stages of the cycle can serve as the means of the dividing the market and the basis for establishing different marketing appeals.

Once membership in a stage of the family life cycle and the determined segment attributes have been measured, the relationship between the two is determined via such procedures as cross-tabulation, correlation analysis, factor analysis, cluster analysis, automatic interaction detection (AID) analysis, discriminant analysis, multidimensional scaling, and canonical analysis. The marketer is then able to determine if membership in a stage of the family life cycle is an indicator of differential purchase behavior.

Evaluation

The usefulness of this concept is limited to how well the stages of the life cycle describe the progression of the average U.S. household over time. It is by this criteria that belief in and use of the concept has weakened in recent decades. Changing U.S. demographics indicate that Americans of the 1980s are marrying later in life; that they are electing to have fewer, if any, children; that about 50% of all marriages end in divorce; that more than half of all wives work outside of the home; that many households are made up of single adults or adults who are not married to each other; and that many children are raised by only one parent who may or may not have ever been married. Today, it is estimated that only one-sixth of all U.S. families can be described as "typical;" i.e., husband, wife, and two children. Consequently, it is sensible for a marketer to question the validity of the concept in relationship to his product. There are many instances in which the family life cycle concept has shown no significant relationship to purchases or product preferences.

Recently, additional life cycle stages have been identified which relate to psychological passages or transformations in adults. Though these stages have not been documented as being predictive of purchase behavior, it is reasonable to think that they may have an influence on consumption patterns and should, therefore, be considered in the marketing process.

The marketer seeking to use the family life cycle concept as a tool for market segmentation or strategy development should ask the following:

- Do the family stages of consumers being targeted generally conform to the stages of the family life cycle concept?
- Is purchase or use of the product being offered known to be related to the stages of the concept?

Conclusion

There are many companies which rely on the family life cycle concept as a means of segmenting the market and as the basis for specifying the marketing strategy. It has proven to be a successful tool for housing developers, marketers of durable appliances, and sellers of all baby-related products. Some skepticism has been raised in recent years concerning the concept's validity and applicability in light of changing U.S. demographics, and attempts have been made to modernize or re-structure the family life cycle stages to reflect those concerns. The number of stages has even been expanded to include the childhood and teen years.

Applications to Small Business

Many small businesses achieve success by pursuing market niche strategies which allow them to specialize and achieve profitability with their low market shares. The family life cycle is a useful means of identifying attractive market niches. The small business owner is well equipped to provide high levels of service and specialized customer attention which would be valued by those at the Solitary Survivor stage, like free home delivery and easy payment terms. In addition, the small business can offer features in products and services which would appeal to those at the New Married Stage, like romantic vacation packages and smaller capacity home appliances. The possibilities are endless since many of the niches associated with the stages of the family life cycle are of negligible interest to market leaders.

References/Sources

Bailey, Jessica, "Small Business and the Elderly," *1985-SBIDA Conference Proceedings: The Challenge of Small Business Management Assistance Unification,* Small Business Institute Directors' Association, 1985, pp. 325-329. This article highlights the reasons why small businesses should target consumers in the latter stages of the family life cycle.

Gould, Roger, *Transformations.* New York: Simon & Shuster, 1978. Details a theory of life-cycle transformations in adulthood.

Haas, Robert W., and Wotruba, Thomas R., *Marketing Management: Concepts, Practice and Cases.* Plano, TX: Business Publications, 1983. Chapter 4 explains how the family life cycle concept can be useful in the market segmentation process.

Kotler, Philip, *Marketing Management: Analysis, Planning, and Control,* 5th ed. Englewood Cliffs, NJ: Prentice-Hall, 1984, pp. 131-132. Details the family life cycle concept as a personal factor influencing consumer behavior.

Lansing, John B., and Morgan, James N., "Consumer Finances over the Life Cycle," *Consumer Behavior.* Lincoln H. Clark, ed., Vol. 2. New York: New York University Press, 1955. Relates the stages of the family life cycle to income, expenditures, assets, debts, and feelings of financial security.

Lazer, William, and Culley, James D., *Marketing Management: Foundations and Practices.* Boston: Houghton Mifflin, 1983, pp. 391-394. Offers an expanded family life cycle which includes childhood and teen years.

Markin, Rom J., Jr., *Consumer Behavior: A Cognitive Orientation.* New York: MacMillan, 1974, pp. 447-453. Discusses the family life cycle concept as a key component in understanding the influence of the family on purchase behavior.

Murphy, Patrick E., and Staples, William A., "A Modernized Family Life Cycle," *Journal of Consumer Research* (June 1979): 12-22. This study attempts to adapt the traditional life cycle concept to the new family structures found in America.

Myers, James H., and Alpert, Mark I., "Determinant Buying Attitudes: Meaning and Measurement," *Journal of Marketing* (October 1968): 13-20. This article discusses measuring item attributes and interpreting results when doing segmentation research.

Sheehy, Gail, *Passages: Predictable Crises in Adult Life.* New York: E.P. Dutton, 1974. Outlines a theory of the psychological life-cycle stages of adulthood.

Social Research, Inc., "Furniture Buying and Life Stages," *Understanding Consumer Behavior,* Martin M. Grossack, ed. Boston: The Christopher Publishing House, 1964. Relates changing patterns in furniture purchases to changes in life cycle stages.

Wells, William D., and Gubar, George, "Life Cycle Concept in Marketing Research," *Journal of Marketing Research* (November 1966): 355-363. Details the characteristics and purchases of the stages of the family life cycle.

Wind, Yoram, "Issues and Advances in Segmentation Research," *Journal of Marketing Research* (August 1977): 323-332. This is a good discussion of methodology issues which arise when doing segmentation studies.

Related Topics and Terms

AID Analysis, Canonical Analysis, Cluster Analysis, Correlation Analysis, Cross-tabulation, Demographics, Discriminant Analysis, Elderly Market, Factor Analysis, Multidimensional Scaling, Segmentation, Target Market.

Jessica M. Bailey
Department of Marketing
The American University

FOCUS GROUP INTERVIEWS

Overview

The focus group interview brings together a small number of individuals in a group format for an open, in-depth discussion focused on some research topic of interest to the client. In contrast to the structured individual interview in which the information flow is unidirectional, between the interviewer and respondent, the group setting encourages the ideas and opinions of each individual to be considered and discussed by the group. A skilled moderator guides discussion in a nondirective manner to encourage group interaction, overcome individual inhibitions, and to probe topics in some depth. Focus group interviewing is categorized as qualitative research, because data are not numeric, but are the result of the moderator's subjective interpretation of the meaning of the verbal and non-verbal content of group discussion.

Focus group interviews in marketing research appeared about thirty years ago as a successor to clinical depth interviews for the extensive probing of consumers. Today, focus group interviews are one of the most frequently used techniques in marketing research. A 1977 survey of U.S. companies found that nearly half had used focus groups. Over 80 percent of consumer goods firms had used them. Focus groups are undoubtedly more widely used today.

Examples

The focus group interview is generally considered as a quick, relatively inexpensive, and flexible method for identifying consumers' perceptions, attitudes, desires, and behaviors toward a topic area. As such, focus group interviews are often used in the initial stages of a research project as an exploratory research method to help generate hypotheses and to identify and pretest questionnaire items. Focus group interviewing serves many marketing decision needs, from generating new product ideas, to assessing consumer opinions on new product concepts, brand comparisons, packaging, and advertising copy. Heaviest usage is among consumer packaged-goods companies. The variety of research uses is suggested by several examples of focus group research.

An electric utility company initially used focus groups to examine consumer opinions of and resistance to proposed utility rate increases, for use in its rate negotiations and to generate advertising campaign ideas. The hypotheses developed from focus groups were then quantitatively measured in a follow-up telephone survey of a large, random sample of consumers in the company's trading area. Owens-Corning conducted a series of fifteen focus group interviews with automotive tire dealers to learn what key benefits and merchandising aids would best help dealers sell fiberglass radial tires. Observing dealer groups revealed that dealers talked extensively about their fears that earlier problems with bias-belted fiberglass

335

tires would recur with the fiberglass radial tires. As a result, Owens-Corning marketers reworked sales themes and promotional copy for the fiberglass tires.

Focus group research is spreading widely beyond industrial and consumer goods companies. Newspapers are using them as a guide in planning new features and graphics. Lawyers are using them to pre-test trial arguments. Universities have reported success in using them to tailor in their recruiting and fund-raising efforts, and public-service organizations find them helpful in determining how to allocate funds.

Benefits

Focus groups are especially useful in exploratory stages of research. Compared with structured interviews, focus groups are easier to set up, less expensive, and generate results more quickly. Persuading subjects to join a focus group is usually easy. A videotaped session typically runs from one and a half to two hours in length, and costs under $2,000. Evaluation and reporting of results can follow within several days.

The interview length and lack of tight structure allow the moderator considerable flexibility to take advantage of unexpected responses and probe areas previously thought unimportant. The small-group environment typically consists of 8 to 12 persons not personally acquainted but sharing common backgrounds. The group encourages participation, offers emotional support and a sense of group rapport that allows the moderator to explore sensitive topic areas more effectively than in individual interviews.

Implementation

Focus groups can be used for a variety of purposes:

1. To provide background information for research personnel and their clients. Observing and directly experiencing focus group customers' reactions to their products can be valuable to executives having little in common with their customers, and in new or rapidly-changing markets where their experience is limited.
2. To generate hypotheses about the way consumers think or behave. The purpose here is exploring research to help define problems which can be analyzed and confirmed through further quantitative research.
3. To structure survey questionnaires by uncovering relevant questions and response categories.
4. To test and evaluate new product concepts. This popular use of focus groups explores how potential consumers perceive a new product concept and evaluate its abilities to meet their needs.
5. To generate new product ideas or stimulate new ideas about existing products.

6. To find explanations for results of other quantitative studies.

Focus group sessions are organized in different ways depending upon the research purpose. A common approach in new product development research is to move the focus group through three stages. First, group members discuss products they use for a particular need or situation, with little moderator intervention. Next, the moderator guides members to discuss among themselves how they rate alternative products. Finally, the moderator probes their feelings about why they favor some products over others.

Most experts report that ideal focus group size is from eight to twelve people per session. Socially and intellectually homogeneous groups are most productive. One advertising agency almost never puts married, full-time housewives with children at home in the same group as unmarried, working women, believing their lifestyles and needs are completely different. While there is disagreement as to the importance of good recruiting, most researchers agree that individuals should have some experience with the product category being studied, and persons with previous focus group experience should not participate.

The physical environment is important. The atmosphere should be relaxed to encourage discussion. Client observation of sessions is valuable. Observation through a one-way mirror allows unobtrusive note-taking and monitoring of nonverbal communications within the group. Videotaping allows further observation by the client and moderator before drawing conclusions.

The moderator's role is of prime importance. Moderators must establish group rapport and guide the discussion through relevant topics, encouraging individual spontaneity and group interaction. The moderator also analyzes and interprets the data from the session. Thus, moderators should possess considerable verbal ability, interviewing skills, and insights into group behavior, as well as knowledge of the subject at hand.

Evaluation

The increasing popularity of the focus group method reflects its use as an exploratory research tool to uncover marketing problems and opportunities and to guide follow-up research. Focus groups are especially well-suited for new product concept and prototype testing, studying advertising and packaging changes, and advertising copy formulations.

Despite its use in marketing research since the 1950s, there are no set guidelines for interviewing, no formulas, and no strategems commonly prescribed by its users. Researchers disagree about when focus group interviews are appropriate and how research should be done. Perhaps the most serious problem that has intensified with higher costs of quantitative research is the use of focus groups as the sole source of information in planning and decision-making. While the technique can provide considerable data at modest cost, the results are based on small, non-random samples that cannot be projected to the entire market. Focus group interviews are easy to set up but can be difficult to moderate and interpret; hence, easily misused. Researchers may be misled by the seeming simplicity of the method. For example, in the problem analysis task of new-product research, respondents may not be able to perceive what problems they have with product use, or may be unable or unwilling to verbalize them.

Other limitations have been noted by various sources:

1. Research findings are suggestive only; the investigation does not follow scientific methods.
2. The method risks client misinterpretations of singular comments.
3. Focus groups require trained moderators to generate useful data and to minimize biases in its observation and interpretation. Highly-skilled moderators are scarce.

Conclusion

The focus group interview is one of a number of effective qualitative research techniques that can be profitably employed to help marketing managers make better decisions. Its growing popularity reflects its adaptability to such decision areas as new product development, advertising campaigns, and evaluation of existing marketing strategies. Organizations find that quick focus group interviews can provide insights that help bridge the gap between marketing management at the manufacturing level and the product end user. Focus groups can generate hypotheses in the preliminary stages of research, and help guide questionnaire construction, lessening the risk of addressing the wrong problem in the wrong manner.

Focus groups have a number of limitations. Poorly trained moderators can bias group results, or fail to uncover relevant information, a costly error if it misdirects later research. Many users caution against generalizing from focus group results to the entire market. There are considerable differences of opinion about the appropriateness of focus group research in meeting different decision needs, on the need for respondent homogeneity, the skill requirements of moderators, and rules for determining the number of focus groups needed.

Applications to Small Business

Focus group interviews represent a practical research tool for a variety of smaller organizations. The new business establishing a consumer database may find focus group interviews helpful in gaining familiarity with its customers. Nonprofit organizations in the service sector, such as community hospitals and public libraries, have successfully used focus groups of their patrons to elicit ideas and evaluate different aspects of their marketing programs.

The small business with little market research experience which faces tight funding should be aware that numerous organizations of all sizes now provide focus group research capabilities, often including complete physical facilities for conducting interviews. Single focus group sessions may be produced for $1,500 to $2,000, including incentive payments to recruit participants. Some smaller organizations have used focus groups as an inexpensive alternative to more expensive consumer surveys. These organizations should caution against relying on focus groups as conclusive data that reliably represent behavior of its market segments. As focus groups are not scientific, controlled research, validity of findings must always be questioned.

Software/Databases

Focus group interviewing involves qualitative research and thus does not lend itself to computerized data collection and analysis. There is commercial software designed to develop and maintain consumer panels for selecting individuals for focus groups. Two of them are:

"GEMS'™ Group Experience Management System." Sophisticated Data Research, Inc., Atlanta, GA. Provides consumer panel management for selecting, recruiting, and managing an updated file of candidates for focus groups.

Looking Glass. Sigma Research Company, Fort Lee, NJ. Provides a computer program for focus group panel maintenance for IBM PC's and similar machines.

References/Sources

Bellenger, Danny N., Bernhardt, Kenneth L., and Goldstucker, Jac L., *Qualitative Methods in Marketing.* Chicago: American Marketing Association, 1976. Chapter 2, "Focus Group Interviews," is a useful, readable discussion of focus group research.

Calder, Bobby J., "Focus Groups and the Nature of Qualitative Marketing Research," *Journal of Marketing Research* (August 1977): 353–364. A thoughtful analysis of the focus group technique from a philosophy of science perspective. Argues that commercial researchers confuse three distinct approaches to focus groups, and underestimate the complex nature of qualitative research. Develops implications for using focus groups.

Cox, Keith K., Higgenbotham, James B., and Burton, John, "Applications of Focus Group Interviews in Marketing," *Journal of Marketing* (January 1976): 77–80. Briefly discusses focus group interviews and three examples of practical applications.

Fern, Edward F., "The Use of Focus Groups for Idea Generation: The Effects of Group Size, Acquaintanceship, and Moderator on Response Quantity and Quality,"

Journal of Marketing Research (February 1982): 1–13. Fern questions the value of the moderator in focus groups in the idea generation task.

Goldman, A.E., "The Group Depth Interview," *Journal of Marketing* (July 1962): 61–68. Author views the group-depth interview as a clinical approach.

Hess, John M., "Group Interviewing," in R.L. King, ed., *New Science of Planning*. Chicago: American Marketing Association, 1968, pp. 193–196. An early accounting of focus groups in marketing research, comparing advantages of group versus individual depth interviewing.

Higgenbotham, James B., *Focus Group Interviewing: A Reader*. Chicago: American Marketing Association, 1979. A compilation of some of the best articles on the subject.

Journal of Data Collection (Fall 1985). Chicago: Marketing Research Association. An applied marketing research journal. This issue contains several articles on focus groups.

Lange, Judith, "When Using Qualitative Research To Generate New Product Ideas, Ask These Five Questions," *Marketing News* (May 14, 1982): 15. Offers practical suggestions for using focus groups. *Marketing News*, a bimonthly publication of the American Marketing Association, also has occasional articles on focus groups oriented toward practitioners in their Special Marketing Research issues.

Related Topics and Terms
Depth Interviews, Focus Groups, Focused Groups, Group-Depth Interviews, Group Interviewing, Motivation Research, Nonsurvey Research, Qualitative Marketing Research.

Peter L. Gillett
Department of Marketing
University of Central Florida

FRANCHISE

Overview

Franchising is a method of marketing and distributing a product and/or service. Traditionally, the term "franchise" has been associated with the right to distribute another's product in a given trade area. This form of "product" franchising differs from the newer, more complex "business format" concept, which has received greater attention in recent years. "Business format" franchising involves the development and licensing of an entire operation—marketing of a unique, patterned way of doing business. Central to any franchise arrangement is a contractual relationship, which specifies the rights and obligations of the franchisor (the company offering the franchise) and the franchisee (the independent party that will own the business). In return for a consideration, a select number of independent parties are offered the opportunity to engage in a business and/or sell a product or service developed by the franchisor, using the latter's trade name and expertise.

Examples

Although fast-food operations typically come to mind, examples of franchising may be found in many areas of our economy. Franchising has been employed in the marketing and distribution of automotive products (Goodyear Tire Centers), business services (H & R Block), general merchandise (Coast to Coast Stores), health services (Diet Centers), home electronics (Curtis Mathes), furnishings (Pier 1 Imports), motels (Holiday Inn), printing (Kwik-Kopy), real estate (Century 21), recreation (Putt-Putt Golf Courses), rentals (A to Z Rental Centers), specialty foods (Hickory Farms), specialty clothing (Athlete's Foot), tools (Mac Tools), and other product-service categories.

Of the differing types of franchise systems, "product" franchising dominates the field in terms of sales. Auto dealerships and gasoline service stations typify this form. However, the "business format" concept has been responsible for much of the growth in franchising during the past twenty years. This form of franchise involves a total business concept, in which everything from store motif to merchandising is coordinated so as to achieve a given image that will appeal to a particular market segment. In establishing such an arrangement, franchisees are often required to make a capital investment and to pay an initial franchise fee and/or continuing royalty or service fees. In return, they are granted the right to operate a franchise in a prescribed manner in a given trade area for a specified period of time. As part of the franchise package, they may receive various assistances, including: financing or help in securing a loan, site location services, initial and on-going training, standardized operating manuals, record-keeping services, centralized purchasing, and advertising and promotional support.

National Video provides an example of the nature and growth of the "business format." The following profile was obtained from various sources, including several franchise directories, such as Bond's *Source Book of Franchise Opportunities* and the Department of Commerce's *Franchise Opportunities Handbook*. The operation consists of a network of retail stores that rent and sell video recorders and related software. Within a period of three years, the franchise grew from zero to over 560 stores nationwide. Presently, they have over 950 stores in all 50 states and Canada, with licenses in a number of foreign countries.

National Video franchisees are required to make an initial cash investment of $10,000—$20,000 when the outlet is opened and a total financial commitment of $60,000—$160,000, depending on the location, level of inventory, and nature of store design. A non-recurring payment of $16,000 is requested up-front to cover the franchisor's cost of locating, qualifying, and training the franchisee. A continuing royalty fee of approximately 4% of gross sales and an advertising fee of 2% is required. In return, the franchisees are granted the privilege to operate in a specified manner in an exclusive territory for an initial contract period of 5 years, with renewal periods of 5 years. Although direct financing is not provided, assistance in securing a loan is. A package of benefits, including a national identity, group purchasing, promotional support, and tested operational procedures are provided.

Benefits

A franchise system provides mutual benefits by combining the capital and entrepreneurial spirit of the franchisees with the strength of an established, more experienced franchise operation. This pooling of resources and coordination of activities among the parties enables a greater market impact and operational economies than those which may be achieved alone.

Franchisors are able to penetrate the market more quickly while conserving their limited capital, by establishing a distribution system that builds on the investment made by the franchisees. Performance in the local market, and thus revenue (e.g., royalty fees) is likely to be enhanced by a more highly motivated businessperson, who has a vested interest in the outcome. While franchisees manage the day-to-day operations of their businesses in a prescribed manner, the franchisor may be free to focus greater attention on planning efforts that are designed to improve the franchise program. As the operation grows, greater economies in purchasing, promotion, and other areas may occur.

The franchisees benefit from the experience that a franchisor has gained from opening and operating similar outlets. They have access to a well-coordinated source of goods and services, in which initial and on-going training and assistances are provided. The standardized program facilitates operational economies in the form of group purchasing and cooperative advertising and enables the franchisee to compete in the local market with an established market identity. With a more marketable business package and the backing of a reputable franchisor, local financing may be more readily available on more favorable terms.

Implementation

The development and implementation of a franchise program involves considerable market planning, a substantial financial commitment, and the use of outside professional help in the areas of law, finance, and marketing. A franchisor may require a period of several years to develop, test, and market a "business format" concept, before the initial franchise operation is opened. Outside professional services, costing a minimum of several hundred thousand dollars, are necessary in the preparation of the legal documentation, operations manual, training system, and franchise sales program.

Initially, a prototype operation may be established and tested. It is then revised and standardized so as to provide a model for future outlets. This serves to completely specify the nature of the operation, including: the operational procedures, assistances, and controls that will be employed; the expected costs, profit margins, and fee schedules involved; and the nature of the organizational support system required. The operating manuals, training program, and contractual agreement are then developed based on this formulation. Of critical importance is the contractual agreement, since it sets the environment for the future business relationship. Before a contract may be executed, the Federal Trade Commission requires that a potential franchisee be provided with a full disclosure regarding the franchise offer and a substantiation of any claims made. Various states may require further documentation.

Next, a sales program is developed to attract potential investors. Inquiries may be generated by various methods, including the placement of ads in key financial, trade, or local publications. The *Wall Street Journal* is a commonly used advertising medium. Selection of qualified franchisees is critical to the organization's overall success. Although the criteria employed varies, the candidate's financial background, related business experience, and personality (e.g., willingness to accept some risks and work with the supporting organization) are commonly mentioned areas of concern.

Evaluation

The success of a franchisor in penetrating and serving a market with a well-coordinated, competitive offering is highly dependent upon the effective performance of its franchisees. Consequently, franchisors are interested in the economic performance, control, and adaptability of these operations. Sales and operational performance may be monitored routinely to determine a unit's compliance with established standards. Occasionally, a more comprehensive evaluation may be employed. This may involve such questions as: Is the franchisee willing to make the necessary effort to maximize revenue? Is the local merchandise assortment consistent with the desired market image? Are franchisees willing to modify their operations to capitalize on change in the environment?

Franchisees may be more concerned with personal achievement, operational freedom, and a satisfactory level of return. Although contractually dependent upon a franchisor, many franchisees tend to view themselves as independent businesspersons, and may evaluate the franchise relationship in that context. In attempting to satisfy local market demand, they may desire the freedom to offer products other than the standardized line required. Continuing assistance programs, for which they pay a fee, may not be considered as adequate or appropriate. For example, a national advertising program may not be consistent with local conditions or available in all markets. Store management assistances may be valued less as a franchisee gains operational experience. A franchisor's request to maximize sales, in the hopes of increasing their own revenue (e.g., royalty fees calculated as a percentage of sales), may be viewed as inconsistent with the achievement of a satisfactory return and a desire to maintain some degree of operational freedom.

Given the enduring nature of the franchise relationship and the difficulty of changing it without penalty, a thorough evaluation of the initial franchise decision should be conducted. All too often, many individuals have approached this decision without adequately considering the merits of the situation or employing the use of professional help in that review process. Prior to entering into any business agreement, aspiring franchisees should consider the potential profitability of the relationship, the nature of the initial and continuing support provided, the extent of contractual restrictions on their operational freedom, as well as a thorough self-evaluation of their own qualifications to engage in such a business.

An evaluation might begin with the use of a franchise directory, such as the previously mentioned *Franchise Opportunities Handbook*. This will provide information by which to compare alternative franchises within a given industry. The Better Business Bureau and the International Franchise Association (a trade association of franchise companies) are possible sources. Existing franchisees might also be contacted. If the franchise is privately-held, the investigative services of Dun and Bradstreet or other fact-finding organizations might be employed to obtain or confirm information regarding the franchisor. Information regarding a particular type of business may be generated by various data sources, including Ganly's *Small Business Sourcebook*. The above evaluative process might be structured by employing a series of questions suggested by the Small Business Administration's publication, *Franchise Index/Profile*. During this review process, the services of an experienced lawyer and accountant are critical to a determination of the suitability of the proposed business relationship.

Conclusion

Franchising is an increasingly important force in our economy. It continues to offer individuals, who might not otherwise have the opportunity, the chance to open their own business. It also enables undercapitalized business firms to expand more rapidly in the marketplace. According to the Department of Commerce, retailing dominates the franchising field, accounting for almost ninety percent of all franchise sales. Franchising has been employed by over 1,800 companies in approximately forty different industries, involving a total of more than 481,000 outlets. Presently, these franchise systems account for one-third of the total retail sales in the United States.

Applications to Small Business

Most individuals who start a small business for the first time are inexperienced. They may not know best where to locate the business, what merchandise to carry, where to buy it, how to market it, and so on. According to the Small Business Administration, many of these firms will fail within the first five years of operation. Although they may be hard working individuals, their inexperience in planning and management may condemn their operations to an early failure. The International Franchise Association has argued that franchising may allow these individuals to realize their entrepreneurial objectives, yet minimize the risks attendant to starting and running a business. Although debate continues as to the relative level of risk involved, several independent studies have indicated that many franchisees would not be self-employed without the existence of franchising.

Despite its apparent attractiveness, potential investors should approach franchising cautiously. Initial expectations may differ from the actual experience. Past surveys have indicated some concerns among franchised dealers regarding the adequacy of the franchisor's product line, their continuing support, and the fairness of the contractual agreement. A lack of an initial understanding of the contractual requirements may have contributed to this. Many franchisees enter the relationship without employing the professional services of an experienced attorney. Furthermore, they may not have fully realized the extent to which their operational freedom would be limited. For example, a franchisor may tightly control the type of merchandise offered locally and the manner in which it is sold, so as to maintain the distinctiveness and uniformity of the franchise program. Furthermore, there have been cases of outright abuse and fraud. Consequently, attention must be given to a thorough investigation of the franchise company, as well as to a self-evaluation of one's own aspirations and business goals.

Software/Databases

Personal computers and spreadsheet software, such as Lotus 1-2-3, may be used to analyze a number of marketing-related problems of interest to both service and product retailers. Sources of the software and examples of how it may be applied are indicated below.

LOTUS 1-2-3. Lotus Development Corporation, 55 Cambridge Parkway, Cambridge, MA 02142. A computer spreadsheet program.

Michael F. Laric and Ronald Stiff, *LOTUS 1-2-3 For Marketing and Sales.*

Prentice-Hall, Inc., Englewood Cliffs, NJ 07632, 1984. Presents an overview of the Lotus 1-2-3 spreadsheet program and how it may be applied to various marketing-related problems, including demand analysis, cost analysis, pricing, and retail analysis.

References/Sources

Bond, Robert E., *The Source Book of Franchise Opportunities*. Homewood, IL: Dow Jones-Irwin, 1985. Provides data on 1,400 domestic and Canadian franchise operations, with observations on how to interpret and use the information.

Bruno, R. Richard, "Franchising: Business Review," *Journal of Consumer Marketing* (Fall 1984): 47-56. Discusses the nature of franchising, its advantages and disadvantages, the legal requirements and procedures (using a flow-chart format) that a franchisor needs to consider in establishing a franchise.

Bruno, R. Richard, "Capital Reserves and Expertise Are Mandatory before Taking Plunge into Business Franchising," *Marketing News* (February 17, 1984): 3. Cautions potential franchisors as to the nature of the commitment required in developing and implementing a successful franchise program.

Directory of Franchising Opportunities. Babylon, NY: Pilot Books, 1985. Includes information on approximately 700 franchise operations.

"Franchising: Opening the Doors to Expansion," *Retail Week* (February 1, 1981): 28-31. Provides an overview of franchising, with a focus on "business format" franchises and the growth potential in non-food retailing.

Ganly, John, Sciattara, Diane, and Pedolsky, Andrea, eds., *Small Business Sourcebook*. Detroit, MI: Gale Research Company, 1983. A guide to information services and sources for 100 types of small businesses.

Goodman, Jacob, "Franchisor—Franchisee Relation Requires Delicate Balance," *Marketing News* (February 17, 1984): 4. Discusses the nature of the business relationship and the need to balance the interests of both the franchisor and franchisee.

Hackett, Donald W., *Franchising: The State of the Art*. Monograph Series no. 9. Chicago: American Marketing Association, 1977. Provides an overview of franchising, with a discussion of franchisor management strategy and major trends.

Hunt, Shelby D., "The Socioeconomic Consequences of the Franchise System of Distribution," *Journal of Marketing* (July, 1972): 32-38. A discussion of the functional and dysfunctional consequences of franchising.

Norback, Peter G., and Norback, Craig T., *The Dow Jones—Irwin Guide to Franchises*. revised edition. Dow Jones—Irwin, Homewood, IL, 1982. Provides information on over 500 franchising companies, and includes a discussion on how to evaluate the franchise offer.

Pagan, Jr., Rafael D., "Franchising is Nightmare for Some Investors," *Marketing News* (February 17, 1984): 7. Discusses the nature and importance of evaluating a franchise offer.

Small Business Administration, *Franchise Index/Profile*. Washington, DC: U.S. Government Printing Office, 1973. Provides a structured evaluation process, consisting of a series of questions that a potential franchisee should consider.

Smart, Albert, *The How To's of Retail Franchising*. New York: Chain Store Publishing Corp., 1982. Provides an overview and discussion of the trends, the nature of the franchise agreement, and the financing and regulatory aspects of franchising.

Stern, Louis W., and El-Ansary, Adel I., *Marketing Channels*. 2nd ed. Englewood Cliffs, NJ: Prentice-Hall, Inc., 1982. Chapter seven provides a description and comparative evaluation of the franchise system and alternative methods of organizing the channel of distribution.

U.S. Department of Commerce, Industry and Trade Administration, *Franchise Opportunities Handbook*. Washington, DC: U.S. Government Printing Office, 1985. Provides information on over 2,000 franchising operations and sources of assistances offered by federal agencies and business counseling services; includes an annotated bibliography and a checklist for evaluating franchises.

U.S. Department of Commerce, Industry and Trade Administration, *Franchising in the Economy 1983-1985*. Washington, DC: U.S. Government Printing Office, 1985. Survey results of 1,877 franchisers, classified by type of business, describing the number, average sales and investment requirements, and renewal/termination data regarding franchise operations.

Vaughn, Charles L., *Franchising: Its Nature, Scope, Advantages and Development*, rev. ed. Lexington, MA: Lexington Books, 1979. A comprehensive discussion of the nature, scope, and history of franchising, its advantages, as well as practical information of interest to potential franchisors and franchisees.

Related Topics and Terms

Administered System, Channel Conflict, Channel Coordination, Channel of Distribution, Channel Management, Channel Performance, Channel Power, Channel Structure, Contractual Marketing System, Conventional Marketing Channel, Corporate Marketing System, Dealership, Exclusive Distribution, Federal Trade Commission (FTC), Interorganizational Relations, Programmed Distribution System, Retailing, Selective Distribution, Small Business Administration, Specialty Store.

Jeffrey C. Dilts
Department of Marketing
University of Akron

GENERIC BRAND

Overview

A generic brand is a distributor's brand that does not have a traditional brand name on its label. Distinctive colors, designs, or other brand marks may be used but generic products are distinguished by the absence of a traditional brand name. A generic brand is a plainly packaged, less expensive version of a product such as paper towels, canned fruit, potato chips and coffee filters. Generics are often priced as low as 30% to 40% below national brands and 20% lower than store brands. The lower price is possible due to lower-cost packaging and labeling, minimal advertising and promotion costs, and lower-quality ingredients. Generic brands began appearing in 1977 in U.S. supermarkets and drugstores, and captured sales from national and store brands. Generics seemed to have reached a peak in their market share in 1982. Since then, their market share has dropped to about 9%. Generic purchasers tend to be from middle or higher incomes, from larger households, and an average age bracket of 35 to 45. These consumers of generics are found to be less brand loyal and more store loyal than purchasers of native brands and retailer brands.

Examples

Generic brand products are found in over 300 product categories. They range in diverse products such as motor oil, tennis shoes, health and beauty aids, vitamins, drugs, underwear, cigarettes, and beer.

Generic brands initially appeared in Jewel stores in Chicago and have spread to over 80% of all supermarkets in the U.S. They have captured over 10% of sales volume in categories such as canned foods, paper/plastic/aluminum foil products, and baking ingredients/condiments. In 1984, in the granulated sugar category, generic brands obtained a 44% share of dollar sales. Generic brands with shares of over 10% dollar sales are found in canned foods such as apricots, oranges, sausages, spinach, mushrooms, pears, pineapple, carrots, beans, potatoes, peaches, tomatoes and chili. In the paper/plastic/aluminum foil products' category, generic brands have high shares among products such as coffee filters, paper and plastic plates, aluminum foil, paper napkins, paper towels, garbage bags and facial tissue. In the baking ingredients/condiments category, generics have high shares in products such as granulated sugar, baking soda and powder, powdered milk, evaporated and condensed milk, frosting mix, honey, coffee creamers, tomato paste, pepper, solid shortening, tomato-sauce, salt, vinegar and cooking wines, jellies and preserves. Other product categories where generics have over 10% of dollar sales are potato chips, lemon and lime juice, apple juice, soft drinks, cat litter and deodorant, grape juice, iced tea mix, semimoist dog food, breakfast drink mixes, and chlorine bleach.

Benefits

Retailers have offered generic brands at prices 30% to 50% lower than nationally-advertised brands and 10% to 15% lower than retailer private label items. These savings have had a strong appeal to consumers who have been affected by inflation, unemployment and other economic ills. The buyers of generics tend to be concentrated in middle income, large households that are price conscious and predisposed to the selection of lower priced alternatives. These consumers possess a relatively low level of brand loyalty and tend to be store loyal. They see generic brands as offering good value.

Retailers who add generic items broaden their customer base and this allows them to generate the high volumes needed to be profitable. Retailers who do not carry generics run the risk of consumers perceiving them as having higher prices than their competitors who offer generic brands, and this can hurt retailers' sales. Although generic brand consumers rarely go from store to store shopping for the lowest price on individual items, they will change their store loyalty if they perceive that a store is not making an effort to keep prices down. Generic brands can serve as an important, highly visible means of generating that confidence in customers.

A second, though lesser, benefit is being able to use less visible shelf space. If a customer knows that a store carries generics, they are willing to look for generic brands on lower shelves or less frequently used parts of the store.

Profit margins on some generic items are the same as national brands. If consumers feel that they can buy more of an item because the price is cheaper, then the seller's profits will increase proportionally.

Finally, larger retailers can occasionally produce their own generic brands using local resources. When this is possible, profits can be significantly increased.

Implementation

Generic brands have made their greatest impact in the commodity-type categories. They have achieved highest sales volume among canned goods, condiments and baking products, and paper/plastic/aluminum products. These categories are comprised of non-food items or foodstuffs that are ingredients or supplements to a meal. These products are purchased by consumers when quality is of lesser importance than price. Marketers of generics should maintain the present price differential offered by generic brands. If generic brands are not offered at lower prices, customers will probably stop purchasing them, since generic brand purchasers possess a low level of brand loyalty.

Generic brand purchasers tend to be store loyal and they concentrate their shopping in only a few stores. Therefore, adding generic brands may not result in attracting new customers away from stores which already stock generics. Discount stores which already attract bargain shoppers might induce buyers to purchase generic brands there rather than at their local supermarket, thereby increasing sales.

Promotion at the point of purchase is crucial. A common approach is to place generic products in a conspicuous location such as a center aisle or an aisle near the entrance to the store. This strategy maximizes the impact on customers who are looking for the generic items. The disadvantage of this strategy is that it does not facilitate direct price comparisons. To facilitate price comparisons, generic brands should be placed on shelves adjacent to their most directly competitive private label and national brands. Another approach is to have a separate generic section to show consumers that the retailer offers generics. Placing high turnover generics in this section would provide promotion of other generic offerings to customers.

To reduce the quality gap between national brands and generics, the consumer can be educated to accept and benefit from the quality level of generic brands in certain usages, for example, the use of generic canned tomatoes as an acceptable alternative in preparing a casserole. The objective here is to appeal to the price conscious consumer while at the same time recognizing the lower quality level of generic brands. This lowering of expectations can reduce the risks of customer dissatisfaction.

Evaluation

The critical requirement for success is to have a clearly defined marketing strategy for generic brands. This strategy should include a clear positioning of the products, realistic pricing, and a systematic review procedure for evaluating the performance of the product and for removal of weaker performers. Criteria for evaluating the sales and profit contributions of generics as well as absolute minimum acceptable performance standards should be defined. Some of the key factors affecting the sales, profitability, inventory, and space performance of generic brands are production costs, product-development costs, cost of materials used, packaging costs, warehousing costs of raw materials and finished products, advertising, quality control, administrative costs, return on investment, impact on store traffic, market-share, competitive position, and investment requirements.

Questions that may be asked are: Is the price acceptable? Will greater expenditures for in-store promotions improve sales or profits? Will a change in retail outlets improve sales? Will a change in retailer discounts help? Should the product be located elsewhere in the store?

Conclusion

Generic brands have made a significant impact in the market place and have demonstrated their long-term viability. Retailers and manufacturers need to respond with long-term strategies and avoid short-term tactical moves that can jeopardize products as well as retail outlets. In order to attract consumers, generics must be positioned as alternatives that offer value and consistent quality. Buyers of generics tend to be from middle-income, large households that are price conscious. The price differential offered by generics is crucial to meet the needs of the generic brand purchaser. Generic brands have been introduced in diverse product categories. They have also been introduced in categories such as beer and cigarettes where extensive advertising has been a traditional practice. The successful entry of generics into competitive brand markets indicates the importance of generic brands for meeting the needs of segments of the market place.

Applications to Small Business

For small businesses, generic brands offer the potential for making profits by entry into the lower price segment of the market where there is no brand loyalty. Advertising and promotion costs for generic products are substantially lower and this is advantageous to small businesses which have limited capital. Packaging and labeling costs are also lower when compared to branded products. These savings in costs reduce the costs of production and marketing and thus reduce the capital required to be in business.

Strategic long-term decisions about the kind of generic products to manufacture and market, product quality, pricing, retail outlets and location of products in stores need to be carefully made. Profit and sales objectives should be carefully defined. Generic brands have fared well among commodity-type product categories and entry into these categories may be profitable.

Software/Databases

Business Accounting Control System—Point of Sales System. American Business Systems, Inc., 3 Littleton Road, Westford, MA 01866. This inventory control system provides continuing indications of inventory levels for retailer's merchandise. This capability can be used to identify slow-moving items and those which are close to being out-of-stock.

References/Sources

Cunningham, Isabella C. M., Andrew P. Hardy, and Giovanna Imperia, "Generic versus National Brands and Store Brands," in *Journal of Advertising Research* (October/November 1982): 25-32. Examines the characteristics of consumers who prefer national, store, generic brands, and those with no brand preference.

Harris, Brian F. and Roger A. Strang, "Marketing Strategies in the Age of Generics," in *Journal of Marketing* (Fall 1985): 70-81. Reviews past manufacturer and retailer strategies with generic products and makes recommendations for future strategies.

Hawes, Jon M. *Retailing Strategies for Generic Brand Grocery Products.* Ann

Arbor, MI: UMI Research Press, 1982. Documents over 400 articles that discuss the marketing of generic brand grocery products.

Hawes, Jon M. and William F. Crittenden, "A Taxonomy of Competitive Retailing Strategies," in *Strategic Management Journal* (No. 3, 1984). Surveys U.S. supermarket chain store organizations to determine the relative success of different retail strategies.

Kono, Ken and Michael D. Bernacchi, "Are Generic Products a Fad or a Long-lasting Marketing Phenomenon? The Future of Generic Products," in *Marketing In the 80's: Changes and Challenges*. Chicago: American Marketing Association, 1980, pp. 191-194. Analyzes sales patterns and repurchase rates for generics.

McEnally, Martha R. and Jon M. Hawes, "The Market for Generic Brand Grocery Products: A Review and Extension," in *Journal of Marketing* (Winter 1984): 75-83. Reviews and synthesizes the demographic and psychographic characteristics of consumers of generic brand grocery products.

Murphy, Patrick E. and Gene R. Laczniak, "Generic Supermarket Items: A Product and Consumer Analysis," in *Journal of Retailing* (Summer 1979): 3-14. Examines buyers and nonbuyers of generics and their characteristics.

Schutte, Thomas F. "The Semantics of Branding," in *Journal of Marketing* (April 1969): 5-11. Analyzes the semantics of branding and proposes a set of brand terms and definitions.

Wilkes, Robert E. and Valencia Humberto, "A Note on Generic Purchaser Generalizations and Subcultural Variations," in *Journal of Marketing* (Summer 1985): 114-120. Reports the findings of a survey of generics purchasers and their perceptions, and examines ethnic effects on generics purchasing.

Zbytniewski, Jo-Ann and Walter H. Heller, "Rich Shopper, Poor Shopper— They're All Trying Generics," in *Progressive Grocer* (March 1979): 92-106. Examines buyers and nonbuyers of generics and their characteristics.

Related Topics and Terms
Generic Brand Grocery Products, Generic Grocery Products, Generics, National Brand, No-frills Products, No-name Products, Plain Labels.

D. Rajaratnam
Department of Marketing
Texas A&M University

GOVERNMENT MARKET

Overview

Government markets include city, state, and federal procurement authorities. Large by any dimension, they represent great marketing opportunities and problems for firms. Federal procurement alone represents the world's largest volume for any customer group. Military and civilian installations purchase goods and services ranging from complex space vehicles to paper clips and from janitorial services to technical studies on subjects such as genetics and geriatrics. Governmental authorities buy food products, medicines, machinery, equipment, ships, airplanes, paper, ink, furniture and clothing. They also contract for construction projects including housing, offices, warehouses, bridges and dams. In short, the government market buys just about every category of commodities and services available. While many business firms are involved in city, state, and federal activities, thousands of contracts worth billions of dollars each year bypass firms who do not know of or understand Government buying needs.

Examples

There is more consistency in the organizational structure, operating procedures, and purchasing practices of the agencies at the federal level than at the state level. The marketing firm that desires to sell products to the federal government must understand how the agencies are organized, whether procurement is centralized or decentralized, and what types of products and services are used by each. The federal agencies involved in purchasing fall into the areas of defense or non-defense. Purchasing in the defense arena is accomplished by (1) centralized procurement done by each military service for the various operations under its control; (2) procurement from a consolidated military supply agency; (3) procurement from a non-defense supply agency; and (4) local procurement for base operations from local sources of supply.

Centralized procurement is accomplished by each military service. Procurement operations for the Army are for the most part the responsibility of the U.S. Army Materiel Command. The Navy Materiel Command has the responsibility of procuring and managing the logistic system for the Navy. Requirements of the U.S. Marine Corps are merged with the Navy requests. The Department of the Air Force is organized such that procurement is handled by three principal programs: (1) Systems Procurement, (2) Support Procurement, and (3) Base Procurement.

The Defense Supply Agency is directly responsible to the Secretary of Defense for providing supplies and services used in common by the military services. The General Services Administration was established primarily to service the non-defense sector but it is also responsible for the acquisition of strategic and critical materials. For base operations, the military services have established many regional and branch procurement offices.

One of the major dissimilarities between state and federal buying is the organizational proximity of the chief purchasing official to the chief executive in each state government.

In some states, the purchasing official reports directly to the Governor and in other states is separated by one organizational position. State and local spending is usually in the hands of separate groups responsible for education, highways, public welfare, hospitals, health, police protection, fire protection, sewerage, sanitation, parks and recreation, natural resources, housing and urban development, airports, water transport and terminals, parking facilities, correction, libraries, and public buildings.

Benefits

Opportunities are available to sell to all levels of government, and it has recently been reported that defense contractors made more than twice as much profit on federal government work as on commercial business, when their gains are measured against what they had invested in plants and other assets. Profits on sales, as distinguished from those on assets, were also higher, averaging 9.2 percent in 1984 compared with 8 percent profit on commercial business for these same contractors.

Implementation

Once a determination has been made to enter the government marketplace (federal, state, or local), much early marketing efforts are required; e.g., knowing the intended customer, potential competitors, and the supplier's own capabilities and interests. For each opportunity, identify specifics of the requirement. If the supplier has not made a similar item before, it is important to know the item before it is bid. Next, the supplier must examine the effect of the contract on their operations. Project this effect over the life of the contract. Review the procurement request in detail and discuss the request with government personnel as allowable. Identify specification details to assure that the supplier has the interest and capability to respond. Make the bid decision. To do this, establish whether the requirement is real; i.e., whether government funds are available, and whether a firm decision has been made by the government to proceed. Compare total sales and estimated profits with alternative opportunities. Also analyze competitive activities and likelihood of award. For a positive bid decision, prepare a proposal and/or a price estimate. Check them completely. Forward the proposal/bid on time. Prepare for possible negotiations and carefully review contracts before signing.

Evaluation

Active participation in government markets does not assure success. Preparing bids and proposals takes time and corporate resources and thus contractors should bid only to win. A study by a major government contractor showed the following statistics for one year's proposal activities. Of 866 Requests for Proposals (RFPs) received, they turned down 575. It looks like a large portion, but the figure was not large enough. Of the 291 proposals made, 114 RFPs were anticipated; i.e., their progress was tracked for as long as 2 to 3 years. Of the 114 anticipated proposals, they won 70, or 61 percent. The other 177 proposals of the 291 made were for RFPs with no advance notice. They won 56 of these, for a win rate of 32 percent, or half the win rate of the "hot" RFPs. Even worse, they submitted, 136 unsolicited proposals, and won 36 of them, for a win percentage of 26 percent, i.e., losing three out of four.

Based on the experiences of bidders who have suffered losses or defaults while performing Government contracts, the following warning signs have been identified: failure to read with meticulous care the solicitation, its attachments, and specifications; excessive optimism in assessing the task, the risk, and in-house capabilities; bidding on unreliable drawings, purchase descriptions, and specifications; bidding based on guess estimating, instead of cost estimating based on factual data; bidding under too much pressure of time; a new contractor performing on a previously established-source contract; accepting an impossible time frame; accepting tasks beyond the state-of-the-art; and buying production quantities of components before the design has been tested and accepted.

Conclusion

The opportunities and advantages to doing business with government agencies have been proven many times over. One would think that just about every firm would be fighting to get its share, yet this isn't so. One year the General Services Administration identified $73 million worth of contracts, each worth $50,000 or more, for which there had been fewer than four bidders. A recent report by the Comptroller General of the United States identified that federal procurement reform aimed at increasing the use of competition still needs support.

Much can be learned about government procurements and the perhaps surprising fact is that the government, federal, state, and local, will help. Every agency with procurement responsibilities holds seminars, prints "how-to" brochures, and/or announces procurement intentions.

Applications to Small Business

The U.S. Small Business Administration (SBA) works closely with the principal purchasing agencies of the Federal Government in developing policies and procedures that will lead to increased contract awards to small business concerns. At the same time SBA provides a wide range of services to individual small businesses to help them obtain and carry out Government contracts.

These are some of the important ways in which the agency assists small business concerns:

SBA Procurement Center Representatives are stationed at major buying centers of the Federal Government to assist small firms with contracting problems and to advise them on how to do business with the Government. They also assure that appropriate procurements are set-aside for small business, provide additional opportunities for small firms to participate in unrestricted procurements, request changes in specifications that are too restrictive, initiate "breakouts" on sole source purchases and review and evaluate the overall small business programs of purchasing centers. SBA Representatives carry out the same type of program at smaller buying installations on a liaison basis.

Through its Certificate of Competency program, SBA provides an appeal procedure for the small business that faces loss of a Government contract award because the purchasing office does not believe it is sufficiently capable to meet contract requirements so as to assure satisfactory performance.

The SBA provides small business owners with information on Government buying methods, products and services bought and agencies that buy them, necessary steps in getting on bidders lists, and related matters.

SBA field offices help bring together Government prime contractors in need of subcontractors and small businesses that have the required facilities.

SBA's regional offices maintain inventories or listings of the productive facilities of small business concerns in their areas, and refer prime contract and subcontract opportunities to listed concerns that furnish needed product or services.

Software/Databases

The U.S. Small Business Administration has established a computer-based program to improve potential Government contract and subcontract opportunities for interested small businesses which are organized for profit and independently owned and operated. The Procurement Automated Source System or PASS is designed to be responsive to the requests of Government Agencies and major corporations for profiles of potential bidders.

PASS uses the latest technology in computers, remote video display terminals, and data retrieval techniques. It will permit small firms registered with PASS to have their capabilities available if requests are made by Federal procuring offices or purchasing agents of prime contractors. The matching will be accomplished by the comparison of keywords which the small business has used to describe its capabilities on the PASS data form. Registration is free and entirely voluntary.

References/Sources

Cohen, William A., *How to Sell to the Government*. New York: John Wiley & Sons, 1981. This book describes the various activities that must be mastered to succeed in marketing to the government—how to make presentations, where to look for requirements, how to write proposals, and how to negotiate effectively.

Cummins, J. Michael, "Incentive Contracting for National Defense: A problem of optimal risk sharing," *The Bell Journal of Economics* (Spring 1977): 168-185. Analyzes risk sharing in defense contracting within an insurance framework with moral hazard present. The model specifies conditions under which risk sharing between the firm and the government can be expected to occur, and identifies the important exogenous characteristics of the firm that determine the equilibrium set of contract terms.

Entrikin, Richard L. and Peterson, John K., "Competition in Government and Industry Procurement Contracting", *Industrial Marketing Management,* 10 (1981): 273-276. Explores government and industry procurement officials' perception of inhibiting factor importance to competition in Federal contracting.

Hynes, Cecil N. and Zabriskie, Noel, *Marketing to Government.* Columbus, OH: Grid, Inc., 1974. A paperback book detailing the federal and state buying procedures and how best to market your goods and services.

Schill, Ronald L., "Buying Process in the U.S. Department of Defense", *Industrial Marketing Management,* 9 (1980): 291-298. The article (1) compares the key differences between the buying behavior of the defense organization with commercial buying behavior, (2) addresses key policy and strategy concerns of the Department of Defense within the 1980s, (3) addresses areas of proposed and completed policy changes, and (4) briefly identifies significant research efforts and opportunities for marketing practitioners.

U.S. Department of Commerce, *Commerce Business Daily.* Government Printing Office, Washington D.C. Every weekday this service brings hundreds of new business proposals for products and services wanted or offered by the U.S. Government. The contents address unclassified requests for bids and proposals, procurements reserved for small business, prime contracts awarded, federal contractors seeking subcontract assistance, and upcoming sales of Government property. Also included are Government research, development leads and information on current foreign government procurement offers in the United States.

U.S. Small Business Administration, *U.S. Government Purchasing and Sales Directory.* Washington, D.C., 1977. The small businessman will find in the Directory an alphabetical listing of the products and services bought by the military departments, and a separate listing for the civilian agencies. Both sections are keyed to the purchasing offices that buy such products and services. Additionally, the Directory includes an explanation of the ways in which the Small Business Administration can help a business obtain Government prime contracts and subcontracts.

Wilson, George C., "Arms Work Found Highly Profitable", *Washington Post* (November 28, 1985). Reports on a study conducted for the U.S. Navy which conflicts with an earlier report by the Defense Department claiming that the defense industry received on "equitable return for its involvement in defense business".

Related Topics and Terms

Acquisition, Bidding Strategy, Contract Pricing, Contracts, Industrial Market, Negotiation, Procurement, Proposal Writings, Purchasing, Subcontracting.

M. Edward Goretsky
Department of Marketing
George Mason University

GROWTH STAGE

Overview

A product, after initial commercialization, usually goes through an S-shaped sales pattern over time before it reaches a point of wide acceptance in the market-place. The lower tail of this curve corresponds to a period of slow growth in sales, and is called the Introduction Stage. Immediately following the introduction stage is a period of rapid growth, commonly referred to as the growth stage of the product life cycle. This stage is, in turn, followed by a tapering off of the rate of sales growth, represented by the top tail of the S-curve, and this leads into the maturity stage. The curve is shown below:

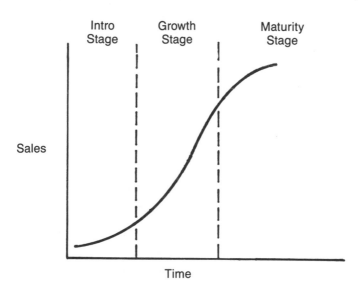

The growth stage is marked by a number of features beyond simply a rapid growth in sales, and these features have many implications for marketing strategy decisions.

Examples

A number of generalizations may be made about the growth stage of the life cycle. It is characterized by a broadening of the target market beyond the narrow group of early-adopters who purchased the product during the introduction stage. This market expansion brings an increase in the size of the overall market and accompanying profits, which may attract new competitors. Some recent examples of the growth stage will help explain these features. The compact car segment of the US automobile market grew slowly through the 1960s and early 1970s until skyrocketing oil prices in the late 1970s brought rapid growth. Volkswagen was a leader in this market, but as the market expanded, other manufacturers brought out competitive small cars.

Another example is found in the video games market. In its early stage, the market offered only a limited number of arcade games. But these whetted the interest of consumers and, with improved technology, the market grew rapidly in both the arcade and home segments. This growth attracted a number of toy manufacturers such as Mattel and Coleco, as well as electronics producers such as Texas Instruments. The proliferation of products and heavy price competition caused several companies to leave the market in the early 1980s. This pattern is similar for most types of products in the growth stage and has important lessons for the marketing decision-maker.

Benefits

Marketing managers should be alert to the signs that accompany the movement of a product from the introduction to the growth stage. An understanding of these signs would also include knowledge of the appropriate decisions that should be made in each of the following areas:

Target Market: During the growth stage, the product gradually finds acceptance in wider segments of the population. These segments are considerably less innovative and risk-prone than the market that purchased the product in the introduction stage. In the growth stage the market has some knowledge of the product since it is no longer entirely new.

Product: The product itself undergoes some changes during the growth stage. Modifications that enhance it and clearly differentiate it from competitive products greatly increase its acceptance by the new target market. Such modifications may include minor changes in the physical product as well as new sizes, colors and packaging.

Promotion: During the growth stage, the promotional support for the product must be increased substantially. This entails more widespread advertising in different media designed to reach the new segments. The informational content of the advertising may be greater, depending upon the "newness" of the product.

Distribution: As in the case of promotion, the growth stage requires wide distribution through new types of outlets. Designer clothing, for example, moved during the growth stage from exclusive department and specialty stores to mass merchandise and discount outlets.

Price: As both the size of the market and competition increase in the growth stage, prices gradually become lower. Demand changes from inelastic in the introduction stage to somewhat elastic in the late growth stage.

Implementation

For the marketing decision-maker to employ the best marketing mix during the growth stage, it is first necessary to develop a definite measure to determine when the growth stage of a product actually begins. Such a measure should also take into account the distinction between the growth stage of the product category as a whole and the growth stage for the firm's individual brand or model. This distinction is important because both the product category and individual brands will have life cycles similar in shape, but will not correspond to each other on a one-to-one basis. For example, fruit-flavored drinks such as Slice may be in the growth stage, although the soft drink market as a whole is in the maturity stage.

The marketing decision-maker should begin by developing a measure of the overall potential for the product category. This task requires a considerable degree of experience and judgment. If a new diet soft drink is contemplated, estimates of the potential per capita consumption must be made for all soft drinks. Thereafter, estimates of the share that diet drinks can attain will also have to be determined. Once these data are available, a measure of the current saturation of the market, i.e., a ratio of the size of the market at present to its overall potential, can be worked out. The growth stage would then be at the intermediate level of saturation, and the marketing manager can use sales data to monitor this factor on an ongoing basis.

Other factors indicative of a growth stage, such as rapid increases both in the sales rate growth and in the number of competitors entering the field, may be assessed to aid in decision making for products in this stage. When the decision-maker observes these factors operating in concert, it will be clear that the first phase of the growth stage has begun. This phase continues as long as the rate of sales increases. When growth slows, the second phase begins. Prices begin to be under considerable pressure, and there is a shakeout in the market with smaller, marginal producers dropping out. This two-phase distinction is important because a decline in profits may indicate that phase two is about to begin, and only the shrewd marketer can steer his product through this hazardous phase and into maturity, by employing proper strategies.

Evaluation

Thus far, many of the features of the growth stage have been identified, and a number of questions have been suggested that decision-makers should address during this stage. Specifically, some of these are:

1. What is the market potential for the product category, and what share of this potential can a specific brand expect to attain?
2. Has there been a recent increase in the rate of sales growth for the product?
3. What is the competitive situation? Are new competitors entering the market?

Once the decision-maker has determined that the product is clearly in the growth stage, various other questions can help determine appropriate marketing decisions:

1. What information about this product should be included in the promotional program so as to increase its acceptance to new market segments?
2. What media will best reach the wider market?
3. Are wider distribution channels needed to reach this market?
4. When will prices begin to feel competitive pressure?
5. What economies of scale in the production and marketing of this product are possible, in order to assure survival in the second phase of the growth stage?

Conclusion

The growth stage of a product's life cycle has many unique features which require close attention of marketing managers. It is the most profitable of all the life-cycle stages, yet it is also the most hazardous and requires close attention, not only to recognize when it begins but to choose proper strategy throughout its phases.

Applications to Small Business

Small businesses would be well advised to consider carefully the appropriate marketing decisions in the growth stage. This is because it comes soon after a period of slow growth and heavy cash outflow during the introduction stage. Without proper resource planning smaller firms may not be able to exploit the opportunities of the growth stage for sheer lack of resources. Some of the frequent problems include a lack of manpower and inventory when sales start to grow rapidly. An accompanying shortage of space, plant and equipment is also likely.

It is inherently more difficult for small businesses to determine market saturation points because these firms are faced with narrow, vaguely defined markets. Also, after a period of low sales growth, the business may be attitudinally unprepared for the explosive increases that characterize the growth stage. For these reasons, smaller firms must develop the judgment necessary to read market signs of the growth stage. Failure due to inadequate planning in a market with growth opportunities is more difficult to face than failure in a declining market.

Software/Databases

As in the case of other stages in the product life cycle, most companies can track the relationship between sales and overall market potential as a function of time, if they have maintained a proper sales database. Commercial software that may assist in this process is +*Forecast* from Computer Software Consultants, Inc., 180 State St., Binghampton, NY, 13901. Generates short term forecasts for economic variables such as sales demand.

References/Sources

Balachandran, V., and Jain, S., "A Predictive Model for Monitoring PLC," *Relevance in Marketing/Marketing in Motion,* Chicago: American Marketing Association, 1972, pp. 543-546. Illustrates a quantitative approach to monitoring the product life cycle.

Catry, Bernard, and Chevalier, Michel, "Market Share Strategy and the Product Life Cycle," *Journal of Marketing* (October 1974): 29-34. Explains the relationship between the stage in the life cycle and a product's market strategy.

Clifford, Donald K., Jr., "Leverage in the Product Life Cycle," *Dun's Review* (May 1965): 62-70. Identifies critical management decisions in each of the stages of the life cycle.

Davidson, W. R., Bates, A. D., and Bass, S. J., "Retail Life Cycle," *Harvard Business Review* (November-December 1976): 89-96. Applies the product life cycle to the retail situation in which many small businesses may find themselves.

Day, George S., "Diagnosing the Product Portfolio," *Journal of Marketing* (April 1977): 29-38. Discusses some of the pitfalls of misreading the growth stage.

Hise, Richard T., *Product/Service Strategy.* New York: Petrocelli Charter, 1977. Chapter 8 discusses each stage of the life cycle.

Levitt, T., "Exploit the Product Life Cycle," *Harvard Business Review* (November-December 1965): 81-94. Explains how firms may make optimal decisions at each stage in the life cycle.

Smallwood, John, "The Product Life Cycle: A Key to Strategic Market Planning," *MSU Business Topics* (Winter 1973): 29-35. Discusses the strategic marketing implications of the product life cycle.

Wind, Y., *Product Policy: Concepts, Methods and Strategy,* Reading, MA: Addison-Wesley, 1982. Chapter 3 discusses each stage of the life cycle.

Related Topics and Terms
Advertising, Competitive Edge, Decline Stage, Early Adopter, Introduction Stage, Maturity Stage, Product Life Cycle, Sales Forecast, Saturation.

Pradeep A. Rau
Department of Business Administration
College of Business & Economics
University of Delaware

HEALTH CARE MARKETING

Overview

Health care marketing is an integrated management process which includes the analysis, planning, implementation, and control of programs that promote mutually satisfactory relationships between an institution and its key publics. These publics may include patients and their families, health care professionals, employers, third party payers, government agencies, social service agencies, donors, volunteers, and the general public, among others. Major elements of the marketing process include market opportunity analysis, strategic market planning, market segmentation, target market selection, marketing mix decisions (product, price, promotion, and distribution), and management control (evaluation and monitoring) of marketing programs. Effective marketing strategies are those that maximize "customer" satisfaction among the institution's key publics without compromising the institution's mission and long term goals. As competition in health care becomes more "generic," with new types of health care providers (e.g., for-profit hospital chains, freestanding emergency care centers) competing against traditional providers (e.g., community hospitals), marketing becomes a necessary ingredient for survival and long term success. There is growing evidence that marketing is being integrated into the management strategies of health care organizations.

Examples

A large 772-bed nonprofit hospital in a southern Ohio city found that a newer suburban hospital was causing it to lose business. The suburban hospital had built a small suburban medical complex to better serve a growing population in the city's southern suburbs. The city hospital hired a new administrator who instituted an aggressive public relations program to promote the hospital's many strengths. This program resulted in much national publicity for the hospital, which contributed to increased referrals from physicians. The hospital also marketed to suburban physicians by offering special inducements (e.g., cheap office space). The improved relations with physicians helped the hospital to stem its eroding market share.

Market surveys conducted by the same community hospital uncovered opportunities for serving new market segments. One service which was developed as a result of the market survey—an inpatient alcoholism treatment program—has reportedly filled 27 beds about 90 percent of the time.

When Albert Einstein Medical Center in Philadelphia introduced a campaign, dubbed "HOSPITAL-ity," to motivate hospital staff members, from doctors to orderlies, to be more courteous to patients (e.g., "make eye contact;" "introduce yourself;" "explain what you're doing"), patient ratings of the staff's "interest in patient as a person" increased from 43 percent in 1982 to 85 percent in 1985.

A Detroit radiologist was in danger of going bankrupt because he was not getting enough referrals from other physicians. Advice from a marketing consultant led him to market his services directly to the public. He now operates two walk-in centers where a woman can go without a referral and get a complete breast examination for less than $200. He also developed a program of informational advertising to educate women about breast examinations.

Benefits

Marketing, when properly implemented, can help a health care institution to lower its breakeven point (e.g., by deleting unprofitable programs); reduce unit costs (e.g., by building a larger patient base through specialization); reposition its business by introducing new services (e.g., outpatient dialysis, home health care, executive wellness); and strengthen its ties to "key influentials" in the marketplace (e.g., physicians, patients, philanthropic organizations, etc.).

Segmentation strategies can help the organization to customize its services to the needs of key groups of customers. Special services (e.g., sports medicine) can be highly profitable if the target markets for such services have been clearly identified and their size, buying power, and motives well defined. Segmentation strategies, based on systematic market research, can contribute to the development of responsive marketing programs. For example, the Cleveland Clinic offers maximum security, luxury suites for dignitaries and celebrities.

A computerized marketing information system can provide administrators with timely information on the productivity of various business units, the institution's effectiveness in serving various market segments, changes in the internal and external environment of the organization, and the impact of various marketing programs that are being implemented. The MIS can also help the organization to develop forecasts and strategic planning models.

Implementation

Effective marketing begins at the top. No marketing program can succeed unless there is a clear understanding of what modern marketing is, and the changes in resources allocation, organizational structure, and corporate behavior that a marketing orientation entails. No hospital, nursing home, group practice, or HMO can succeed unless there is a philosophical commitment to the "marketing concept" from the highest levels of the institution (top administrators; board of trustees) all the way down the organization chart to the lowest levels where primary care is provided to patients by the institution's staff, where switchboard operators and receptionists greet callers, where business office cashiers and credit managers deal with patients' families, and where parking attendants and cafeteria busboys interact with patients, staff members, and the general public. This type of organization-wide commitment is essential to the success of a health care institution's total marketing effort. Neglect of this area can undermine even the most expensively

mounted promotion and publicity effort. Inservice marketing workshops and training sessions for staff members, combined with a judicious use of incentives to
reinforce such a customer orientation, are mechanisms that can help to implement
marketing changes in an organization.

Implementing marketing in a health care organization requires attention to many
details: market analysis; marketing research; strategic market planning; program
development, modification, and elimination; new program launching; pricing of
services; accessibility to and physical delivery of services; planning promotions;
coordinating fund development; and monitoring and evaluation of marketing programs.

Attention to these and other related details is the responsibility of the marketing
director, who should report to the executive director of the organization. The lines
of communication, authority, and responsibility for this position can be problematic, especially in organizations where marketing is a relatively recent formal activity. However, active support from top management can help to overcome the initial
resistance that department/program heads and others may have toward the marketing director's new role in the organization. In a mature marketing organization, the
top marketing executive will have either line authority over department/program
heads—which is not far-fetched if the chief of programs is well trained in marketing
and has a marketing staff reporting to him—or will serve in a staff capacity as the
head of marketing services for the organization. In a small health care institution,
the marketing director may have to wear several hats; in larger institutions, the
marketing staff may consist of specialists in research and data analysis, forecasting,
public relations, fund development, and other areas.

If the institution is not ready to hire a marketing director, a commitment to
marketing can still be made by acting on one of the following options: invite
marketing experts in the community to sit on the board of trustees or serve on an
advisory panel; form a marketing executive committee, consisting of key staff
members, trustees, and marketing experts from the local business community; hire
a marketing intern from a local university's graduate program in business or public
administration; retain a paid or volunteer consultant to assist in marketing planning
and to coordinate marketing programs with local advertising agencies and the media; or hire an outside consultant experienced in health care marketing.

The primary marketing tasks that a health care organization must perform are no
different from those which are performed by other organizations, both in the profit
and the not-for-profit sectors. These tasks include: market and competitive analysis, target market selection, positioning decisions, marketing mix programming,
patient satisfaction surveys, and other measures of monitoring program effectiveness. But the success of marketing programs in any organization is predicated upon
the support that the marketing staff will receive from the rest of the organization.
This support will not come automatically. But good communication between marketing and other departments, utilizing clear and persuasive explanations of how a
department will be affected by specific marketing programs and why such pro-

grams are needed, can help to win support. Whereas the support of board members and top administrators is essential in developing a marketing commitment, the cooperation and willing support of middle managers (e.g., program heads, nursing supervisors, department heads) can be critical to the success of day-to-day marketing decisions.

Evaluation

Marketing programs can be evaluated in several ways. Common measures include:

- sales volume—e.g., occupancy rates by department; number of admissions; revenues generated by program; grants and donations procured; utilization rate for specific therapies.
- customer and market factors—e.g., market share changes; penetration into new markets; changes in case mix; new referrals obtained; repeat patronage.
- customer satisfaction and feedback—e.g., patients' ratings of satisfaction with hospital stay; unsolicited responses; employee morale; physician satisfaction; customer attitudes and perceptions of services obtained.
- public image and perception of institution relative to competitors.
- financial and productivity measures—e.g., profitability of specific programs; cost analysis; productivity of marketing programs; tracking of costs, revenues, and profits over time.

Conclusion

The structural changes taking place in the U.S. health care industry threaten the survival of many traditional institutions. New programs, new competitors, and new institutional forms have emerged: market-specialized health maintenance organization; preferred provider organizations; for-profit hospitals; outpatient surgery centers; executive wellness programs; employee assistance programs; independent physician, dentist, and nursing group practices; hospices, nursing homes and intermediate care facilities; and home health care programs. An industry-wide shakeout is predicted, where institutions with tenuous market positions or those lacking a distinctive competitive advantage may be forced to liquidate, merge with other institutions, trim services, or enter into joint or cooperative ventures with other neighboring institutions.

Strategic market planning, with bold, innovative marketing programs, will be needed to survive this shakeout and ensure long term success.

Applications to Small Organizations

Small organizations, such as dental practices, neighborhood clinics or mental health centers, intermediate care facilities for the handicapped, and small hospitals, may appear to be handicapped by their size because small operating budgets may leave little flexibility to hire a marketing director, let alone a marketing staff. But smallness can be a competitive advantage (greater flexibility, lower break-even points, more responsive management). Furthermore, marketing effectiveness is dependent, not on titles or the presence of a specialized staff with marketing diplomas, but on the ability of key administrators to assume responsibility for the performance of key marketing tasks or to delegate them to others within or outside the organization.

Small nonprofit organizations can use volunteer expertise from local colleges and universities. As an alternative, they might consider hiring a part-time or full-time marketing/fund development director. The salary for this position could be funded, at least initially, from a foundation grant. Small, for-profit health service organizations and group practices should invest in professional advice from a marketing consultant who specializes in the marketing and management of health care services. Small organizations can also benefit by retaining the services of a reputable local or regional marketing/public relations/advertising services agency which can relieve the health care organization of many routine marketing operations (e.g., preparation of sales brochures, conducting patient surveys, developing advertising campaigns, preparing press releases for the media, etc.).

In sum, the decision that health care administrations in institutions, both large and small, must make is not "should we market?" but "how well should we market ourselves?" Finding the right answers to the second question can spell the difference between survival and extinction.

Software/Databases

Case Mix Manager. Ernst & Whinney, Cleveland, OH 44115. Available for micro or main frame. Integrates clinical, revenue, and costing data by patient; identifies product line trends; assesses product profitability. Other packages for health care operations and marketing management include *The Budget Manager, Case Mix Forecaster,* and *Clinical Review System.*

Expert Choice. Decision Support Software, Inc., 1300 Vincent Pl., McLean, VA 22101. Accommodates quantitative data and subjective judgments for decision analysis ranging from strategic planning to product selection. For IBM PC/XT or compatible.

Macro Track. Black River Software, 118 N. Marshall, Suite 150, Winston-Salem, NC 27101. Generates automatic forecasts for key sectors of the economy (eg., GNP, inflation, retail sales, interest rates, etc.). Designed to help managers plan sales and pricing, set credit policy, decide on financial outlooks, etc. Available for Apple II series or for IBM PC/XT compatibles.

MEDLINE. U.S. National Library of Medicine, Bethesda, MD. Indexes articles from over 3,000 international journals published in the United States and 70 countries. Medline shows its citations from three printed indexes: *Index Medicus, Index to Dental Literature* and *International Nursing Index.*

SPSS (Statistical Package for the Social Sciences). SPSS Inc., Suite 3300,444 N. Michigan Avenue, Chicago, IL 60611. Popular statistical package to perform analysis of market research data, from simple cross tabulations to sophisticated multivariate analysis. Now also available in a microcomputer version called SPSS/PC.

State Profiles. Woods & Poole Economics, Inc., 1974 Columbia Road, NW, Washington, DC 20009. Provides economic and demographic data for each state's counties, MSAs, CMSAs and TV-ADIs. Available in hard copy, magnetic tape, and floppy disk.

Statgraphics. STSC Inc., Rockville, MD 20850. An integrated, interactive system with more than 300 functions for data analysis, data management, and statistical analysis. Offers powerful graphics capabilities. Designed for IBM-compatible microcomputers.

References/Sources

An Annotated and Extended Bibliography of Health Care Marketing. Chicago: American Marketing Association, 1984. Contains a comprehensive listing of recent books and articles on health care marketing.

Berkowitz, Eric N. and Flexner, W.A. "The Marketing Audit: A Tool for Health Service Organizations," in *Health Care Marketing—Issues and Trends.* Germantown, MD: Aspen Systems, 1980, pp. 245-253. Shows how a marketing audit can be conducted and the benefits of conducting an audit.

Building Marketing Effectiveness in Health Care. D. Terry Paul, ed. Proceedings from the Academy for Health Services Marketing's Fifth Annual Symposium on Health Services Marketing, American Marketing Association, Chicago, 1985. Papers cover marketing within the organization, implementing marketing advancements, creative health care promotion, marketing research, marketing alternative health care services, etc.

Froebe, D. et al., "Variables Influencing the Consumer's Choice of Nursing Homes," *Journal of Health Care Marketing* (Spring 1982): 25-33. Describes four most important factors which consumers used to select a nursing home.

Healthcare Market Research: Reports, Studies, and Surveys 1985. New York: FIND/SVP, 1985. Describes more than 700 commercially available market research reports related to the health care industry, equipment, supplies, companies, etc. Reports are listed by topic and each gives a succinct description of the scope, date, price, and publisher.

Hisrich, R.D., and Peters, M. "Focus Groups: An Innovative Marketing Research Technique," *Hospital and Health Services Administration* (July-August,

1982): 8-21. Describes how focus groups can be conducted and discusses the uses of this technique in the health care setting.

Joseph, W. Benoy, Zallocco, Ronald, and Markovic, Paul, "Strategic Market Planning in Hospitals: Results of a Nationwide Survey," *Developments in Marketing Science,* Vol. 8 (1985): 346-350. Reports survey findings on strategic market planning practices of U.S. hospitals.

Korneluk, Greg, N., "Launching a Successful Satellite Clinic: A Marketing Approach," *Medical Group Management* (September-October 1981): 56-58. Discusses a systematic marketing approach for developing marketing strategy, based on a study of the market environment, site selection, pricing, target markets, and consumer needs.

Kotler, Philip, "Strategies for Introducing Marketing into Nonprofit Organizations," *Journal of Marketing* (January 1979): 37-44. Presents a general, but highly readable, discussion of why marketing is important for nonprofit organizations and how marketing techniques and concepts can be implemented in a typical nonprofit.

MacStravic, Robin, *Marketing Health Care.* Germantown, MD: Aspen Systems Corp., 1977. A general marketing textbook for health care institutions.

MacStravic, Robin, "The Demise of an HMO: A Marketing Perspective," *Journal of Health Care Marketing,* Vol. 2 (1982): 9-16. Analyzes failure of a Tacoma HMO and explains planning steps necessary for successful establishment of an HMO.

Whittington, F. Brown, Jr., and Dillon, Ray, "Marketing by Hospitals: Myths and Realities," *Health Care Management Review* (Winter 1979): 33-37. Explores five myths of marketing by hospitals and reports survey findings about the perceptions of hospital administrators concerning the appropriateness of various marketing techniques.

Zallocco, Ronald, Joseph, W.B., and Doremus, H., "Strategic Market Planning for Hospitals," *Journal of Health Care Marketing,* Vol. 4 (1984): 19-28. The application of strategic market planning models to hospitals is discussed with an example of the G.E. business screen model applied to a large urban teaching hospital's product portfolio.

Related Topics and Terms
Competitive Strategy, Consumer Decision Making, Hospital Marketing, Marketing of Nonprofit Organizations, Professional Services Marketing, Services Marketing.

W. Benoy Joseph
Department of Marketing
Cleveland State University

IDEA GENERATION/SCREENING

Overview

Idea generation applies mostly to the development of new products or services, but can be used to identify alternative solutions to many types of problems. In the area of development, a company seeks to instill creativity into the management process, and into the people who manage the process. Creativity is the ability to see things in a new way and from that insight generate something new. It is the ability to make a connection between two very dissimilar ideas through sensitivity to ordinarily inane objects, events or facts. Idea screening follows the generation process, and is a sorting process to filter the more productive ideas and guide resources that must be allocated in the technical development phases. Screening is meant to insure that resource allocation is consistent with the business mission and strategy.

Examples

There are two sources of new ideas for a firm, internal and external. Within the company, ideas can be found in any of the functional areas through employee suggestions, but the most common are marketing, research and development (R&D), and production. Product managers, sales personnel, applications engineers, installers, service workers, and warranty claims are the most common areas within marketing. Product designers, materials engineers, and process engineers are the areas within R&D. Industrial engineers, quality control and packaging are areas within production that are fertile grounds for new ideas. External to the firm, customers, distributors, dealers, and consultants often perceive solutions that are creative because they are not involved with the daily routines within the company that often stifle creativity. New technical solutions to problems can be found in patent attorney's files, from licensors, independent investors, competitors, materials suppliers, research labs, universities, and technical consultants. One firm that actively seeks new ideas is Hallmark cards of Kansas City. They sponsor movies and cartoons on company time, and pay the way for employees to visit art galleries, watch plays, and window shop; all in a search for creative new ideas.

Benefits

There is ample evidence suggesting that the innovator, the first one to market with an idea, is the one that reaps the most awards. By being first to market an innovation, other companies must play catch up. It is possible to gain the largest market share, get the best ROI, and carve a sustainable competitive advantage in the marketplace.

While many ideas are the result of the purposeful development, others come spontaneously. An employee of the 3M company, reported the *Wall Street Journal,* thought of note paper that could be stuck in books, to telephones, etc. using a small strip of adhesive on the back that would hold, yet peeled off easily. These notes, now called "Post-It" reap about $40 million in sales.

Implementation

Several methods of generating new ideas are common. First is "brainstorming," which is simply getting a group of people to focus on a problem and generate solutions to that problem. Brainstorming sessions should be freewheeling, non-critical, and primarily interested in the quantity of ideas rather than the quality. Second is focus groups, which take 8 to 12 users or potential users of a product and ask them about potential solutions. The idea is that users are often the best equipped to provide solutions that are outside the culture constraints of the producer company, and listening to users is the core of the marketing concept. Third is synectics, which takes a group of people with widely varied backgrounds and asks them to generate ideas. By utilizing different backgrounds, the transfer of ideas from one area to another often produces unique solutions. Fourth is word association, which asks potential users what they associate with words that commonly describe a product or service. This method is commonly used with consumer products to name products and test potential advertisements. Fifth is attribute listing, which takes attributes of a current product and puts them together in various combinations to arrive at new solutions. Ways to modify each attribute, and then combinations of attributes, can lead to improvements in a product or service. Sixth is forced relationships, which ask potential users to determine bundles of attributes or groups of products to invent new products that combine the most important attributes and form a unique solution. For example, an office equipment manufacturer might use all the objects commonly found in an office environment and consider combinations of those objects to invent new concepts. Seventh is morphological analysis, which singles out the most important dimensions of a problem, and then examines all the relationships among those dimensions. Dimensions are usually defined by asking end-users which attributes are most important to them. And finally are analogies, taking similar circumstances and extrapolating the reasoning to form solutions to a particular problem. As is usually true with analogies, the lesson is seldom obvious until the situation is abstracted.

Evaluation

Evaluation of new product ideas should be done with an idea screening process. Initially no idea should be rejected because it appears implausible. There may be considerable opportunity behind an obviously absurd solution. It should be part of the idea screening process to determine the feasibility and risk associated with each new idea. Production and marketing that are convergent with current methods present the least risk, while divergence in production and marketing presents a greater risk because the company knows less about new products and markets than the products and markets in which they are already involved. A typical example is an industrial products company that envisions an opportunity with consumer products. The two areas generally require very different expertise, and companies often find themselves woefully lacking in knowledge and success in the area that is traditionally divergent to their company. Screening should insure a proactive position in a changing environment, a sustainable competitive advantage, a match between capabilities of the firm and its resources, assumptions which are explicit, and a sufficient focus on market needs.

Conclusion

Innovations resulting from ideas must be subjected to a rigorous screen as the ideas progress from early development to eventual market introduction. Generating ideas is the lifeblood of the firm because it leads to innovation and growth. Screening ideas insures a market focus and success in introducing new products and services. Idea screening is more qualitative than quantitative, and should not be an inhibiting factor in the idea generation process. Idea generation and screening are part of the overall new product development control process.

Applications to Small Business

Several areas are worth considering for the small business. First, businesses should allow sufficient time to define a problem or opportunity, rather than say "Let's get on with it." A little more time can avoid treating a symptom as a problem, and facilitate understanding the assumptions that are being made. Second is to promote the talent of thinking by setting objectives, defining problems explicitly, and devising alternative solutions. Third is to enhance evaluative thinking ability, and broaden perspective. Short courses, seminars, workshops, and travel are common methods for obtaining new ideas and perspectives. Fourth is to watch for unanticipated solutions and ideas. These usually become apparent after talking with employees and colleagues, and are often a function of being aware of subtle changes in the environment in which the business operates. Fifth is the use of constructive criticism. Such criticism might produce controversy, but at the same time increase morale and productivity. Sixth is a people orientation that reduces inhibitions and enhances confidence. The rule is to guide rather than tell. The seventh and final method is to be involved with monitor groups. These are usually found in trade associations or similar industry organizations. Involvement with such groups enhances the ability to envision new solutions and methods.

Software/Databases

Query. Management Science Associates, Inc., 5100 Centre Ave., Pittsburgh, PA 15232. Used to search and subset a database to find new brands and market opportunities; *Market Impact* is an interactive system for concept evaluation and new product forecasting, planning and control.

References/Sources

Bonasso, Sam, "Can We Be More Creative?" *Civil Engineering* (January 1983). A brief discussion of applying creative ideas.

Crawford, C. Merle, *New Products Management.* Homewood, IL: Irwin, 1983. An excellent text that has a substantive section on idea generation.

Drucker, Peter F., *Innovation and Entrepreneurship.* New York: Harper & Row, 1985. A book of practice and principles containing many examples.

Poze, Tony, "Analogical Connections—The Essence of Creativity," *Journal of Creative Behavior,* Vol 17, 4, 1983. An article discussing analogies in the creative process.

Rose, L.H. and Lin, H., "A Meta-Analysis of Long Term Creative Programs," *Journal of Creative Behavior,* Vol 18, 1, 1984. A discussion of learning creative postures through training programs.

Tyler, Leona E., *Thinking Creatively.* San Francisco: Josey Bass, 1983. A readable book that has ideas on expanding awareness.

Young, Arthur, *Innovation: The Agenda for American Business, 1985.* A consulting firm study of innovation management practices in 400 U.S. companies.

Related Topics and Terms

Competitive Edge, Concept Testing, Control, Focus Group Interview, Innovator, Marketing Concept, New Product Development, PIMS, Preliminary Investigation, Product Design, Roll Out, Test Market.

Terry C. Wilson
Department of Marketing
West Virginia University

IMPULSE GOOD

Overview

An impulse good is essentially what its name implies, a good purchased on impulse or whim, and without any prior thought or planning. Usually, impulse goods are considered to be a sub-segment of convenience goods since they would fit into that classification if they were bought to satisfy ongoing needs, rather than immediate desire. Generally, impulse goods have been described as goods that are mass marketed, mass advertised, not necessities, small sized, quickly consumed, low priced and easy to store. But recent trends suggest that impulse items no longer need to possess those characteristics although they continue to be primarily convenience goods. It is also possible that specialty or shopping goods could be bought on impulse, given a consumer's supply of money, and a conducive set of circumstances. A wealthy shopper may see a display of $200 cameras and buy one on whim. Another shopper looking for a $50 dress may see an attractive one at $300, and buy it on impulse. In the development of marketing strategy, however, these are exceptions rather than the rule, and do not fall into the impulse goods category.

Examples

There are numerous items and products that are routinely purchased on impulse in certain situations. Candy mints at the cashier's counter in restaurants, drug stores and similar establishments are one example. Another is the array of candy, gum, magazines, lurid tabloids and other items, often 100 or more, that face consumers in supermarket checkout lines. Most of these items are stocked elsewhere in the store, so if they are bought at the checkout location, the purchase is a pure impulse one.

Other types of "temptation" products that are normally purchased as convenience goods are placed in heavily traveled aisles in a store in order to provide maximum consumer exposure. The candy counter in many department stores is near an entrance in the main aisle so consumers will pass it both entering and leaving.

Also, a consumer may buy a Coca-Cola from a vending machine on impulse, but if the same buyer were to pick up a six-pack of Coke during a regular shopping trip, it would be a convenience item.

Benefits

The concept of impulse goods has been used by retailers for many years to increase sales of lower-priced items, coercing consumers to spend the small change they have just received from other purchases. But the day when most consumers buy grocery items from a list and ignore other displayed items may be fast disappearing. More recently, changing lifestyles have brought about a substantial increase in impulse buying, mainly among busy singles and two-income families.

There are four types of impulse purchases:

    (a) Pure Impulse: A purchase with no real basis or benefit except to satisfy a momentary whim. Candy, popcorn or a soft drink are pure impulse examples.

    (b) Reminder Impulse: A display reminds a consumer to buy a product. A shopper has not thought about aspirin until he sees a display, which reminds him the supply at home is low. He buys some.

    (c) Suggestion Impulse: A display suggests a use for a new item. A shopper sees a display for a new type of milk that can be stored without refrigeration. He thinks it will be just the thing to take on camping trips.

    (d) Planned Impulse: A special in-store incentive to buy. A shopper sees a 50-cents-off special on a brand of detergent he does not usually buy. He needs detergent, and buys several boxes at that price.

These are examples of how knowledge of selling and buying techniques for impulse items benefits both retailers and consumers. By recognizing them, and providing different displays and incentives for each type, sales should be stimulated.

Implementation

Retailers need to understand the basic concepts of the impulse buying process, particularly in today's marketing environment. Instead of a few items at the cash register, the entire stock of a supermarket, and many items in other stores, may be considered to be impulse goods. Thus, they should be arranged and displayed so that consumers have maximum exposure to as many items as possible as they move through the store. Location is extremely important. If a shopper wants a bottle of anchovie-stuffed olives, he will seek them out even if they are stocked in a dark corner. But if they are displayed prominently, many shoppers will take a jar, just to try them. But if the buyer does not see them at the right time, the sale may be lost forever.

Supermarkets must have straight aisles for carts to pass easily, so they depend upon end-aisle displays and "special" signs. But many department stores have moved toward the boutique concept where aisles are zig-zagged around displays and sales areas, increasing consumer exposure and impulse purchasing. Here, the consumer needs to see a product and buy it immediately. If not, the temporarily perceived need will probably disappear. In a supermarket, however, if a shopper needs something for dessert, one impulse item or another will be bought eventually.

Evaluation

The types of items that sell well as impulse goods vary according to the type of store and the economic area in which it is located. In affluent areas, displays of gourmet foods or imported sweaters foster heavy impulse buying. In other localities, special prices, one-cent sales and coupons stimulate planned impulse purchasing. In evaluating the operation of impulse-oriented strategy, questions such as these should be asked:

(1) Are promotional programs aimed at getting consumers into the stores? e.g., special incentives, loss leaders.
(2) Are special offers or reduced prices highlighted with displays or signs to attract attention?
(3) Are displays for new items prominently placed and their attributes made clear, to attract suggestion impulse buyers?
(4) Are packages designed to catch the shopper's eye, and self-sell the product?
(5) Are impulse items selected so they are likely to appeal to the specific target market served?

Conclusion

Impulse shopping today involves a much wider variety of goods than it has in the past. Lifestyles of many consumers mitigate against orderly and planned convenience good shopping. Instead, consumers rely more and more on in-store cues. Rather than shopping specifically for a pot roast, potatoes and green beans, a consumer enters a store looking for "something for dinner" and cruises the aisles until an attractive product triggers an impulse buy. Thus, impulse goods can include most convenience goods when they are bought to satisfy a strong current need. Intensive distribution is a must, and manufacturers need to assure their displays are well-placed so as to catch the consumer's eye.

Applications to Small Business

Smaller retailers should use the same techniques as larger ones: displays, price incentives and promotion to bring shoppers into the store. Fast moving items should be located so that consumers must pass displays of impulse-type items in order to get to them. Smaller manufacturers should concentrate more on packaging and on personal selling direct to retailers. Heavy consumer advertising may not be necessary unless there are several competitive products in the same channels, because consumers are likely to depend upon in-store cues and make impulse purchases.

Software/Databases

Retailers can track sales of impulse items in aisle displays or shelf-marked price specials, using a number of inventory control software packages, or other packages integrated with scanner checkout.

Sales Planner. Mastersoft, Inc., 4628 N. 17th St., Phoenix, AZ, 85016. Produces all elements of a sales plan, including staffing, quotas, revenue and unit sales. Also, *Sales Productivity and Reporting* monitors performance against sales plans produced by *Sales Planner.*

References/Sources

D'Antoni, Joseph S., Jr., and Shenson, Howard L., "Impulse Buying Revisited: A Behavioral Typology," *Journal of Retailing* (Spring 1973): 65. Describes results of study that determined the characteristics of impulse goods.

Bellinger, Danny N., Robertson, Dan H., and Hirschman, Elizabeth, "Impulse Buying Varies by Product," *Journal of Advertising Research* (December 1978): 15-18. Suggests that some products are more susceptible to impulse buying than others.

Evans, Joel R., and Berman, Barry, *Marketing.* New York: Macmillan, 1982, pp. 135, 216 and 493. Presents various definitions and applications for impulse goods.

McCarthy, E. Jerome, *Basic Marketing,* 6th ed., Homewood, IL: Richard D. Irwin, 1978, pp. 283, 553. Provides descriptions of impulse goods, how they are bought and how retailers and producers should handle them.

Nisbett, Richard E., and Kanouse, David E., "Obesity, Hunger and Supermarket Shopping Behavior," in *Perspectives in Consumer Behavior,* H. Kassarjian and T. S. Robertson, eds., Glenview, IL: Scott Foresman, 1973. Describes a method of measurement of unplanned, or impulse, buying.

Stern, Hawkins, "The Significance of Impulse Buying Today," *Journal of Marketing* (April 1962): 59-62. Discusses the four types of impulse goods and how they relate to consumer in-store behavior.

Related Topics and Terms

Automatic Vending, Convenience Goods, Display, Inventory Control, Rack Jobber, Self-Service, Staples, Unplanned Purchases.

Hale N. Tongren
Department of Marketing
George Mason University

INCENTIVES FOR SALESPERSONS

Overview

A company should attempt to motivate its salespeople through a group of set incentives that will encourage them to strive for the best possible results in quality and quantity of sales. This type of motivation involves replacing individual goals with group objectives. Individual needs can be satisfied by the set incentives which the company presents in turn for positive results in selling the company's products.

Incentives can be categorized into two dimensions: monetary and nonmonetary. Monetary incentives include commission, sales incentives or bonuses, and stock options. They also include rewards such as fringe benefits, and facilitators such as company cars and expense accounts. Nonmonetary rewards include recognition, trips, prizes, increased responsibilities, larger territory, larger offices and new titles, better working conditions, office help, information, and congenial coworkers.

Examples

Monetary incentives and rewards are expected by salespeople. The four basic methods of compensating salespeople are: (1) straight salary, (2) straight commission, (3) bonus, and (4) combination plans.

Straight salary: Under this method, a salesperson is paid a fixed amount of money for work during a specific time. This method has the advantages assuring the salesperson of a steady income and developing a sense of loyalty toward the customer. It also gives the company more control over the salesperson. Since the salesperson's income is not based directly on results, the company can ask the salesperson to undertake activities that are in the best interest of the company even though they may not lead to immediate sales.

Commission: The commission plan includes a base and a rate. The base is typically unit sales, dollar sales, or gross margin. The rate is expressed as a percentage of the base, such as 10 percent of sales or 8 percent of gross margin.

Bonus: Under bonus plans, salespeople are paid a lump sum of money for outstanding performance. Bonuses may be awarded monthly, quarterly, or annually. They are always used in conjunction with salary and/or commissions, and thus are part of combination plans.

Combination plans: Frequently, two or three of the basic methods are used to create a combination plan. Combination plans offer the greatest flexibility for motivating and controlling the activities of salespeople. They can incorporate the advantages and avoid the disadvantages of salary, commission, and bonus plans. The principle disadvantage of combination plans is their complexity. Since the plans combine several elements they can be misunderstood by salespeople and misused by sales management.

Nonmonetary compensations also motivate salespeople. Recognition in various forms is growing as a primary sales incentive tool. There are basically two approaches. First, the salesperson can be given increasing responsibilities, perhaps in terms of a larger territory, additional product lines, more customers, or more prestigious accounts. The salesperson's responsibilities can also be extended in a managerial direction. He might, for example, be asked to train new salespeople or to prepare a special analysis of competition in his territory. A second type of nonmonetary compensation is the prerequisite, familiarly called a "perk." These include new titles (perhaps sales engineer or account representative), larger offices or personal parking slots.

Benefits

Specifically, a good incentive plan should accomplish the following objectives:

1. Motivate salespeople to perform at their best level by providing an incentive with sufficient clarity so that it will encourage selling and related job responsibilities and reward outstanding performance.
2. Provide an equitable relationship between the work being done and the level of compensation. It is important that this relationship be perceived as equitable by the sales force.
3. Attract and retain desirable salespeople, and provide sufficient stability to allow adequate support and economic security.
4. Provide a means whereby management has the flexibility to maintain an optimum balance between costs and sales.
5. Be clear, easy to understand, and relatively easy to administer in order to minimize the costs of implementation and administration.

Implementation

Monetary compensations alone are not sufficient motivators. Their absence, however, might result in dissatisfaction. Certainly, the most important example here is an adequate base salary. In almost all types of selling, the salesperson is guaranteed some minimal level of income. Even in sales jobs compensated solely on commission, salespeople are permitted to draw against future revenues, up to a certain amount each month.

The presence of any of these monetary factors does not completely motivate most salespeople. Their absence, however, causes dissatisfaction, and therefore, has a negative effect upon salesperson motivation. The manager who desires to positively motivate his salespeople will turn to monetary factors that more directly relate to sales performance. They will also turn to one of the various forms of recognition as a reward. Prizes and plaques awarded publicly among peers can be a major augmentation to compensation programs.

Motivated employees must have (1) some recognition, (2) some degree of security, and (3) some pressure to perform at the optimum level.

Evaluation

A periodic review of incentive programs is necessary. It is a rare compensation plan that continues to satisfy both the individual salesperson and organization. Thus, sales manager and salesperson should recognize that the compensation package should be subject to continuous review, with adjustments as necessary. Many authorities suggest that any new compensation formula first be "tested" against the historical performance of a representative group of salespeople. By calculating compensation using the new formula on past performance, it is possible for the sales manager to determine what the effect of the compensation package would be. If the package does not produce "reasonable" results, it obviously should not be instituted.

Conclusion

Incentives have both monetary and nonmonetary components. The components of the compensation package for each individual salesperson should be determined on a systematic basis. The procedure should include matching the organizational and salesperson's individual objectives, operationalizing this match as a compensation formula and periodically reviewing that formula to be sure that it accurately reflects current conditions.

Applications to Small Business

Although sales incentives are vital in assuring the successful operation of sales forces in large firms, these incentives are even more important in smaller companies because below average performance on the part of a single salesperson may cause a break between success and failure. But incentives may be more difficult for small firms to offer because margins may be lower. Thus, nonmonetary incentives such as titles, office space, and personal recognition by the company's executive may be coupled with smaller monetary incentives. Also, some base compensation, however small, could replace the straight commission plans normally offered by smaller businesses.

Software/Databases

The G.I.S. program by Management Planning Systems, Inc., 8282 S. Memorial Dr., Tulsa, OK 74133.

market, without consideration of the industrial market, would be shortsighted for many businesses. The industrial market, and thus, industrial products, represent unlimited potential for many organizations. Producing and selling industrial goods rather than consumer products may offer businesses other advantages as well. The buying decisions for industrial products are generally assumed to be more rational than those for consumer products. An international market often exists for industrial goods, and, although the customer base for industrial goods is much narrower than the base for consumer goods, the price and resulting profit per product is typically higher for industrial products.

Implementation/Evaluation

Due to the extreme diversity of industrial products, and the differences in the demand for those products, a closer look at the classification system is necessary.

Products categorized as heavy or major equipment are basically capital goods which, due to their high unit purchase price, are usually charged to a capital account rather than treated as a current expense. Because of the high cost of major equipment, companies selling this type of industrial good may have to offer loans, arrange financing, or offer lease agreements to their customers. Heavy equipment is of two general types: multi-purpose equipment, also known as standard equipment, and single-purpose or specialized equipment. The demand for heavy equipment, especially specialized heavy equipment, is often confined to one industry. Unlike some other industrial products, purchasers of heavy equipment normally use the equipment rather than integrate it into their final product.

Light equipment, also called minor or accessory equipment, is generally characterized by its significantly lower price tag than heavy equipment, its standardized nature, and its more routine purchase by businesses. Often used in an auxiliary capacity, accessory equipment is not permanently affixed to the buyer's physical plant, and, like a small tractor, for example, may be used in many different departments or in many different industries. Minor equipment is often sold through many more outlets and with less negotiation than heavy equipment.

Component parts include all products that are purchased for the purpose of inclusion into the final product of the industrial organization. Component parts may or may not be modified by the industrial purchaser, and some components, such as tires on automobiles, for instance, may even retain their identity in the finished product. Component parts are usually marketed as OEM (Original Equipment Manufacturers) products, but, in cases where the identity of the product is retained, a replacement market for repair or service facilities and other outlets may also exist. Component parts are often purchased on the basis of the purchaser's specifications for a specific contract period, and buying decisions are often based on uniformity, reliability, quality and delivery.

A fourth type of industrial good is process materials, which includes all types of processed materials not considered component parts. Most process materials, unlike component parts, cannot be identified so that they can be recognized in the finished good. Since process materials tend to be purchased on specifications developed by the trade, government or buyer, as with chemicals and pharmaceuticals, individual purchase decisions are often negotiated and based on price and service. Few process materials have a replacement market.

Raw materials include all products generated by the extractive industries which are then sold with little or no modification. They are generally purchased in large quantities and bought or sold on the basis of recognized standards. Raw materials are most often marketed by various kinds of agents, especially brokers.

The class of industrial goods which includes standardized products that are used up or worn out by the purchaser in the operation of its business is referred to as operating supplies. Operating supplies are often bought in small quantities or purchased on a routine basis.

Conclusion

Although industrial products are diverse in nature, all industrial goods can be measured based upon the value and satisfaction a customer derives, both personally and organizationally, from the industrial marketer and his or her products. Just as in marketing consumer goods, the industrial customer buys more than the physical product; he buys reliability, risk reduction, friendship, efficiency, or status. Thus the industrial marketer must look beyond the physical product in developing a marketing strategy.

The industrial product classification will determine, to a great extent, the types of marketing efforts which are necessary. Although other classification systems exist, ranging from three classes to at least ten classes of industrial goods, all are based on the same areas as the classification system presented here, and are merely more or less detailed.

Applications to Small Business

Small businesses may be engaged in either selling industrial goods or selling to industrial good manufacturers. Many small businesses supply component parts or process materials to industrial manufacturers, who, in some cases, act only as an assembler of the components rather than an actual manufacturer.

References/Sources

Corey, E. Raymond, *Industrial Marketing*. Englewood Cliffs, NJ: Prentice-Hall, 1983. Contains cases which provide insight into the differences among the six classes of industrial goods.

Haas, Robert W., *Industrial Marketing Management*. Boston: Kent Publishing

Co., 1982. Reviews the six categories of industrial products, providing examples of each.

Hill, Richard M., Alexander, Ralph S., and Cross, James S., *Industrial Marketing,* Homewood, IL: Richard D. Irwin, 1975. Presents a discussion of the general classification system used for industrial products and examples of each category.

Industrial Marketing Committee Review Board, "Fundamental Differences Between Industrial and Consumer Marketing," *Journal of Marketing* (October 1954): 152-158. Explains the major differences between industrial and consumer goods.

Jackson, Donald W. Jr., Keith, Janet E., and Burdich, Richard K., "Purchasing Agents' Perceptions of Industrial Buying Center Influence: A Situational Approach," *Journal of Marketing* (Fall 1984): 75-83. Discusses five of the classes of industrial goods and their definitions.

Nystrom, Paul H., ed., *Marketing Handbook.* New York: Ronald Press, 1948. Considers ten classes of industrial goods, further refining the classification system presented but very similar in content.

Robinson, Patrick J., Faris, Charles W., and Wind, Yoram, *Industrial Buying and Creative Marketing.* Boston: Allyn & Bacon, 1967. Considers various bases for classifying industrial goods.

Vaile, Roland S., Grether, E. T., and Cox, Reavis, *Marketing in the American Economy.* New York: Ronald Press, 1952. Contains an early reference to the classification of industrial manufactured goods (thus omitting raw materials) into three broad classes: equipment (heavy and light), fabricated materials and parts (component parts and process materials) and supplies. They note that the three classes they provide may be further refined.

Vinson, Donald E., and Sciglimpaglia, Donald, *The Environment of Industrial Marketing.* Columbus, OH: Grid, Inc., 1975. A collection of readings in industrial marketing.

Webster, Frederick E., Jr., *Industrial Marketing Strategy.* New York: John Wiley & Sons, 1979. Discusses categories of industrial goods with explanations.

Webster, Frederick E., Jr., and Wind, Yoram, *Organizational Buying Behavior.* Englewood Cliffs, NJ: Prentice-Hall, 1972. Explains differences between consumer and industrial marketing and differences in the way consumer and industrial products are bought and sold.

Related Topics and Terms
Component Part, Heavy (Major) Equipment, Industrial Product, Light (Acces-

sory) Equipment, Manufactured Good, Operating Supplies, Process Materials, Raw Materials.

Nancy Pishkur
Department of Marketing
Kent State University

INDUSTRIAL MARKET

Overview

In the narrow sense of the term, the industrial market consists of approximately twenty per cent of the business establishments in the United States. These are the ones in the U.S. Bureau of the Census categories of agriculture, forestry, and fisheries; contract construction; manufacturing; mining; and transportation and other public utilities. This definition does not include retailing, wholesaling, finance, insurance, and real estate, services, or government as these are usually treated as separate entities.

The industrial market is concerned with the buying and selling of raw materials; machinery, both heavy and accessory; semi-finished goods; parts and subassemblies; and supplies. All of these goods either enter into a finished consumer good or aid in its production. Besides buying and selling, which entails seeking sources of supply and finding buyers, industrial distributors perform the other marketing functions: assembly and dispersal through storing and transportation; financing and risk-bearing through pricing, credit, and leasing; market research and information; and marketing management. Although there are independent middlemen within the various industrial segments, the marketing functions often are performed by divisions within manufacturing or distribution companies.

This market is characterized as one in which the units are concentrated geographically. It is made up of fewer and larger buyers than in other markets, with professional or rational purchasers. There has been an increase in leasing of machinery which decreases the level of capital expenditure. Demand for all types of industrial goods is derived from the demand for the finished consumer product. Most purchases are made directly from the producers and there may be some reciprocity between buyers and suppliers.

Examples

The large processors of basic materials, such as U.S. Steel, are at one end of the industrial continuum and the producers of a small component part, such as Cleveland Mold Company that, by cohesion, makes a self-lubricating gear for Ford Motor Company, is at the other.

Small companies, such as the "wildcatters" in the oil industry, are present in the industrial market, representing around thirty per cent of the oil field supply transactions. The supplier, the oil field industrial distributor, a merchant wholesaler, often leases drilling rigs, pipe, and rock bits, becoming, in reality, a partner in the exploration.

Owners of patents covering items necessary to manufacture certain products may not wish to be involved in marketing their unique products, so they will sell to distributors in the proper segment of the industrial market.

Benefits

The industrial market provides a means whereby manufacturers and processors may obtain the materials needed to produce their end products which may be used either by other manufacturers or by ultimate consumers. To ensure continuing availability for production, long term contracts that specify delivery times are often established. Very few fabricators start with ores, timber, or chemicals but rely on the controllers of basic raw materials to turn them into sheet steel, sized lumber, or solvents.

The rights to use machinery are controlled by the owners of patents covering the devices. Heavy machinery, often referred to as capital, is purchased infrequently and either paid or written off through long time periods.

Like materials, semi-finished goods, parts, and subassemblies are bought from those who control their processing, again often through patents. Again, long-term contracts are entered into to ensure inventory in terms of production schedules.

Supplies, those items necessary to allow physical production to run smoothly, such as lubricating oils, do not become a part of the finished product. Such items are used by many diverse industries. In some industries, such as oil well development, the rock bit used to drill the hole for the casing is considered a supply.

Because of the specialization by manufacturers, as indicated above, the producer of consumer end items (i.e., an electric toaster) may obtain all materials needed for the production process without having to incur the capital costs required to make each of the various industrial goods himself.

Evaluation

The organization of the industrial market in terms of specialized production of goods makes it possible for many other industrial and consumer goods to be made. Such specialization probably makes for a higher degree of efficiency and cuts down on the capital needed by those producing consumer end products. These should make for lower costs and, hence, lower prices for the end product.

On the other hand, specialized machinery or critical parts controlled by a monopolist or by patents may lead to excessive prices or limitation of inventory that will cut down on end items or competition. Either situation may cause prices that will limit effective demand for the end product.

It is probable that, in general, the industrial market is such that more items at lower prices are produced than would be if each manufacturer had to provide all the activities necessary to make the particular products desired.

Such a market situation leads to a question of whether or not a manufacturer or processor will make or buy industrial goods. Another alternative is to attempt integration, either forward, led by the controller of natural resources (i.e., iron ore), or backward by the manufacturer of a consumer end product (i.e., a maker of mining machinery who buys a company making conveyor belts).

A constant problem is to keep up, or ahead of, other firms in terms of new industrial goods that may make the existing product better because of new materials, parts, or machinery. This leads, in some companies, to the establishment of research and development groups, contracting for such work by outside agencies, or pooling resources with similar firms to establish an industry resource.

Conclusion

The industrial market contains twenty per cent of the business establishments in the United States. Its number of transactions far exceeds those of the other market segments.

Although dependent upon derived demand for its products, the industrial market is relatively stable through time. This is true particularly for supplies, common parts and subassemblies, materials, and accessory equipment.

Heavy machinery may have a less stable market except for those that perform operations common to many processes, such as a multipurpose lathe, needed by most manufacturers. Machinery used in a single industry, such as a paper-making, may have volatile demand. Some other principles are:

- –The geographic concentration of professional buyers with rational buying motives allows suppliers to concentrate their selling efforts.
- –The attempt to control sources of supply caused by the need for assured inventories for continued planned production leads to vertical integration in many industries.
- –The industrial distributor often provides the smaller manufacturer with financial aid and management advice.

Applications to Small Business

The industrial market has within it many small business concerns, which often effect suppliers of unique goods controlled by patents or producers of highly specialized consumer products. Small businesses are often encouraged by industrial distributors through credit terms, management advice, and leasing of machinery. In many cases, the distributor actually becomes a joint entrepreneur with the original business. If the innovator controls a needed unique good or process, aid from the industrial manufacturer will often be furnished relative to market information and possible competition.

Although roughly seventy per cent of industrial sales in the U.S. are directly from the manufacturer, industrial distributors and merchant wholesalers, who account for the remaining thirty per cent, also find it desirable to aid the small business concern who can provide a steady market. Since all operators must be rational, professional buyers or sellers, the risks attendant upon innovation or simple market entry will be recognized, evaluated, and encouraged.

Software/Databases

BLS Producer Price Index. Bureau of Labor Statistics, U.S. Department of Labor, Washington, DC. Contains the producer price indexes as calculated by the U.S. Bureau of Labor Statistics. Prices are provided for over 2,800 commodities.

References/Sources

Barr, Joel J., "SIC: A Basic Tool for the Marketer," *Industrial Marketing* (August 1969): 52. How to use the S.I.C. data as aids in making decisions in the industrial market.

Corey, E. Raymond, *Industrial Marketing: Cases and Concepts,* 2nd ed. Englewood Cliffs, NJ: Prentice-Hall, 1976. One of the few textbooks in the field, especially good on the characteristics of the industrial market, the types of goods and services, and the product evaluation process.

Cox, William E., Jr., *Industrial Marketing Research.* New York: John Wiley and Sons, 1979. Methods for the measurement of industrial markets; includes many bibliographic references and a model demand schedule for cranes in the United States.

Enis, Ben, *Marketing Principles,* 3rd ed. Santa Monica, CA: Goodyear Publishing Company, 1960, p. 284. Discusses the three industrial buying situations: the straight rebuy, modified rebuy, and new task.

Fern, Edward F., and Brown, James R., "The Industrial/Consumer Marketing Dichotomy: A Case of Insufficient Justification", *Journal of Marketing* (Spring 1984): 68-77. Indicates that differences between the two markets may not be causally related to practice or theory, have not been tested empirically, nor justified logically.

Finney, F. Robert, "Reciprocity: Gone but Not Forgotten," *Journal of Marketing* (January 1978): 54-58. A brief history of reciprocity, its decline, and future prospects.

Haas, Robert W., *Industrial Marketing Management,* 2nd ed. Boston: Kent Publishing Company, 1982, pp. 6-24. Definitions of market customers, systems, and goods.

Harding, Murray, "Who Really Makes the Purchasing Decision?" *Industrial Marketing* (September 1966): 77. A map of the decision-making for purchasing a test stand for auto engines.

Hill, Richard, Alexander, Ralph, and Cross, James, *Industrial Marketing,* 4th ed. Homewood, IL: Richard D. Irwin, 1975, pp. 101-104. Explanation of vendor analysis.

Hutt, Michael D., and Speh, Thomas W., "The Marketing Strategy Center: Diagnosing the Industrial Marketer's Interdisciplinary Role," *Journal of Marketing* (Fall 1984): 53-59. Discusses the need for marketing interfaces with manufacturing, physical distribution, and technical services; has copious bibliography.

Kotler, Philip, *Principles of Marketing,* 2nd ed. Englewood Cliffs, NJ: Prentice-Hall, 1983, pp. 166-180. A detailed discussion of the industrial market, its characteristics, and its buying operations.

McCarthy, E. Jerome, and Perrault, William D., Jr., *Basic Marketing,* 6th ed. Homewood, IL: Richard D. Irwin, 1984, pp. 226-243. Characteristics of the industrial market and discussion of the Standard Industrial Classification.

Robinson, Patrick J., Faris, Charles W., and Wind, Yoram, *Industrial Buying and Creative Marketing.* Boston: Allyn and Bacon, 1967, p. 14. Presents a buy grid framework for determining the effect of buying phases on the three classes of buying.

Webster, Frederick E., Jr., and Wind, Yoram, *Organizational Buying Behavior.* Englewood Cliffs, NJ: Prentice-Hall, 1972, p. 32. Explanation of industrial buying behavior.

Related Topics and Terms

Derived Demand, Economic Order Quantity (EOQ), Elasticity of Demand, Industrial Good, Merchant Wholesaler, Physical Distribution, Purchasing Agent, Safety Stock, Standard Industrial Classification.

Donald F. Mulvihill
Department of Marketing
Kent State University

INELASTIC DEMAND

Overview

Demand for most products tends to increase as price is lowered and to decrease as price is raised. This general pattern is the basis of the standard downward sloping demand curve portrayed in economic texts. There are two underlying reasons for this pattern, sometimes termed "the law of downward sloping demand." The first is that as price increases the potential buyer is "poorer" than before the price increased. Secondly, as price increases the buyer is likely to seek to substitute other goods for the one whose price is rising. Thus tea or hot chocolate may be substituted for coffee. There are many exceptions to this general rule. Luxury or status items are the most obvious. It might be, for example, that as the price of a high-status brand of automobile falls, fewer of the cars are demanded because the auto has lost some of its luster as a status symbol.

Economists and business people know that as prices vary demand may change. To the degree that demand changes it is said to be elastic. To the degree it remains the same it is said to be inelastic. It should be noted that demand may be more inelastic at certain prices than at others. Thus consumers might continue to purchase steak as the price of steak increases until it reaches some no-longer-acceptable level. At this price, demand for steak may not keep pace as prices rise. For this reason, economists often speak of "arc" elasticity or inelasticity, noting that to get a view of inelasticity or elasticity of demand for a product it is necessary to specify the *portion* of the total demand curve under discussion.

Examples

The degree to which a product fulfills a basic human need is often an index of its inelasticity of demand. A classic example is the demand for insulin. If a diabetic person requires one dose of insulin per day to remain alive that person will seek one treatment per day regardless of the price. If the price were to increase slightly, or double, triple, or go up ten-fold, the patient still would demand just one treatment per day. Notice, too, that if price should fall the patient would still want just one treatment daily. Within reasonable bounds it is safe to say that no price is too high to dissuade purchasers and no price so low as to induce additional product use.

Notice that price inelasticity of demand "cuts both ways." Neither higher prices nor lower prices much affect demand. In the case of insulin and other medicines price affects demand not at all until the price gets so high as to put the product out of the buyer's economic reach. Even if this should occur the buyer would be likely to beg or steal to have the product he needs. This is a case of "perfect" inelasticity of demand.

Although the case of insulin is a bit extreme, many products face demand situations that are quite insensitive to price. Household electricity is one example. The typical householder uses the electricity he feels is necessary for a comfortable life. Toast is made and laundry washed with little real thought given to the "few cents" worth of electricity these tasks consume. If the price of electricity rises a bit, as it does from time to time, does the householder cut back on the use of electricity? How often does he decide not to toast the morning English muffin, eating it untoasted to reduce the monthly electric bill? Some care might be given to turning off the lights when a room is unoccupied, but few buyers of electricity will not make toast, not watch television, and not wash their laundry because the price of power rose. Conversely, should the price of electricity fall somewhat, would the householder eat more toasted muffins, wash more laundry, or watch more television because electricity is now a "better buy?" Probably not. Thus the demand for household electricity is, in general, price inelastic.

A similar phenomenon is noticeable when industrial goods are analyzed. Demand for industrial or organizational goods is generally found to be price inelastic. This is because of several factors found in the industrial buyer's purchase situation. First, the industrial buyer is generally a "rational buyer" who has calculated carefully what he needs to purchase. If such a buyer has analyzed the organization's needs and found that *two* new boilers are necessary to properly run the business, the buyer is unlikely to be impressed with a salesperson's offer of "buy four, get the fifth one free." Secondly, the industrial buyer will purchase nothing at all unless he believes that the product will be sold. When Jeeps are selling well the Jeep manufacturer will pay a higher price for the required number of tires, steering wheels and transmissions because the demand for the final Jeep product is strong. These increased costs can simply be passed along to Jeep buyers. The third factor contributing to the price inelasticity of industrial goods is that most industrial goods constitute a comparatively small part of the final product sold. In the case of a new Jeep, each fender, steering wheel, and even each transmission is but a small percentage of the total selling price of the new Jeep. Therefore, the industrial buyer (Jeep/AMC) is very unlikely to refuse to buy these parts if suppliers raise their prices.

It is obvious that many products will be demanded, if other conditions are right, at almost any price until some upper limit of price is reached. Yet these products do differ in the *degree* to which they are inelastic. Our householder might eat untoasted English muffins and wash clothes by hand if the monthly electric bill jumped from $100 to $500 or $1,000. The insulin user who will *die* without his quotidian dose is even less likely to change purchase habits than the householder is to hang a clothes line and eschew using the electric dryer.

Economists use a simple formula to measure elasticity of demand (E). E is expressed as a ratio, the percent that quantity demanded (Q) has risen or fallen divided by the percent that price (P) was raised or lowered. Several presentations of this formula exist and can be found in any economics text, but the problem remains the same: how much change in demand resulted from the change in price?

The formula yields a numeric "answer" which can be used to compare the inelasticity of demand among several products, or during different periods of time, or under different economic conditions. If the price of product A were cut by 20 percent and quantity demanded were observed to increase by 10 percent the formula $E = \%$ change in $Q/\%$ change in P would be shown as $E = 10/20$. That is, the change in price was greater than the observed change in demand. $E = 10/20 = .5$. If the price of product B were reduced by 50 percent and demand were seen to rise by 10 percent the formula would show $E = 10/50 = .2$. Note that the 20 percent price cut for product A produced a demand increase of 10 percent while a 50 percent price cut for product B yielded the same demand increase of 10 percent. Demand for product B is more inelastic, or less elastic, than is demand for product A. For product A, $E = .5$; for product B, $E = .2$. Thus, the smaller the figure yielded by the formula the more inelastic the demand.

It will be noted that the value of E is less than 1 because the change in quantity demanded is less than the change in the price. This is the very meaning of inelastic demand. For comparison's sake, suppose that a change in price led to exactly the same proportional change in quantity demanded; e.g., $E = 50/50 = 1$. This shows that demand is neither elastic nor inelastic and is usually termed "unity." But if the change in demand is greater than the change in price, if it shows great sensitivity or response to price, elasticity will be greater than 1. For example, price is cut by 10 percent and quantity rises by 50 percent or $E = 50/10 = 5$. When the change in price is *less* than the observed change in quantity demanded, E must always be greater than 1.

This discussion has dwelt on *price* in elasticity of demand, by far the most familiar form of the concept. Others exist, however. One is income inelasticity, which can be exemplified by the fact that as income rises comparatively few additional purchases of potatoes, salt and plain white bread are likely to result.

Mathematical formulas illustrating income inelasticities and other inelasticities are common in economics and business books. Readers will note, however, that they are all modifications of the concept shown above as $E = \%$ change in $Q/\%$ change in P.

Benefits

The concept of inelasticity of demand is of great importance in business though the number of people who actually sit down and attempt to calculate the inelasticity or elasticity of the demand for their own products or those they buy may be limited. Yet, most business people use the concept intuitively. The price of oil and gasoline rose and fell during the 1970s and 1980s. The price quadrupled in the 1970s, fluctuated a bit, then dropped precipitously in the mid-1980s. Yet most Americans continued to own and operate cars, take vacations, and heat their homes. They altered their behaviors somewhat of course, but in general showed their willingness to "pay the price" and their unwillingness to change their lifestyles greatly. O.P.E.C. and U.S. oil companies successfully gauged the price inelasticity of demand and for years made record profits. They thus benefitted from a situation of elastic demand.

A similar situation developed in 1986 when, in the U.S., interest rates fell to levels prevalent ten years earlier, rates that were unthinkable in the early 1980s. Yet, rates charged by VISA and MasterCard remained high, ten percent or more above bank loan rates. Credit card lenders cited many reasons for this phenomenon, and underwent some scrutiny from government agencies. But it seems clear that these lenders calculated, with good accuracy, that Americans would pay a high price for the convenience of credit buying and "instant loans." The lenders estimated the inelasticity of demand for their product and benefitted thereby.

Industrial marketers often benefit from the realization that demand for their products is generally price inelastic. They know that many of their customers are in a position to pass price increases on to their own customers. They may be in the enviable position of being a sole supplier of a product, or the only nearby supplier, or the only supplier who can guarantee quick delivery, or the supplier with the finest reputation. In cases like these the supplier faces a relatively inelastic demand curve and can set prices accordingly though, of course, legal, ethical, and competitive considerations must be met.

Lest it appear that all the benefits of inelastic demand accrue to the seller it should be noted that certain consumers also benefit from the phenomenon. Take, for example, the diabetic who must have that one dose of insulin per day to live. Given that the alternative is death, the drug companies keep the price for insulin quite low. Partly, this is because they wish to charge an "ethical" price, so as to be seen as helping, not gouging, the people who must have their product. Some people might suggest that competition is what keeps the price of insulin low, or that the producers hope to avoid government price controls. But the fact remains that inelastic demand does not always mean high prices to the buyer.

Implementation

Making use of the concept of inelastic demand in a business situation can range from the intuitive application of the concept to exerting a concerted effort to use data, formulas, and other means to develop an assumed demand curve and concommitant coefficient of elasticity. Since inelasticity of demand is demonstrated in the assumed demand curve, some methods of estimating that schedule should be mentioned. Among the tools used for this purpose are: survey of executive opinion, survey of customers, survey of sales force, trend analysis, and analysis of substitutes.

The survey methods (of executives, customers, and sales force) each bring with them attendant risks and benefits. If the organization's executives are seasoned veterans of the marketplace wars, it simply makes good sense to get their opinions on the nature of the demand the firm faces. They may know, for example, that customers are sensitive to price changes or, conversely, that customers seem to purchase what they need almost without regard to price. The survey of executives may be formal or informal but, either way, it makes sense not to pass over this potentially rich mine of information.

The survey of customers is appropriate to certain situations, especially the sale of industrial products. This is so because organizational buyers are usually better able than consumers to judge their buying intentions and are believed to be more "rational" in their approaches to purchasing. Surveying sales force members can be defended on the grounds that these individuals are closest to their customers and should be able to make reasonable estimates of customer reactions to price changes. The risks are that, for their own reasons, salespeople are often tempted to underestimate their future sales totals.

Trend analysis also makes good sense if the organization has sufficient data available to plot sales totals and these have been affected by price changes. The problem, of course, is that basing the future on the past is always risky since conditions might have changed greatly.

Analysis of substitutes is a technique whereby price inelasticity of demand is judged in terms of other options open to the buyer. Suppose the seller is able to determine that a buyer, suddenly deprived of the seller's product, would have to purchase another product at twice what the seller now charges. This suggests that the seller could raise the price currently charged without much fear of losing the customer since the customer's alternative is to pay another supplier twice the current price. Of course, the cost in goodwill lost and the risk of driving the customer to seek additional sources of supply must be considered as well.

The U.S. government, and other researchers, have attempted to develop coefficients of elasticity/inelasticity for several products. However, most work has been done with classes of products rather than specific brands of products. It is known, for example, that as income rises a given percentage of each new dollar is spent on air travel rather than bus travel. These general facts are of some use to firms in the air and bus travel industries and to suppliers of those companies, but provide only a starting point for the development of company-specific estimates of elasticity/inelasticity of demand.

Evaluation

There are several tools available that business people may use to determine the demand schedules they confront and the degree of price inelasticity shown by those schedules. Unfortunately, competitor firms may also employ those same tools and adjust their marketing strategies to fit market conditions and competitive actions. Price inelasticity suggests that prices may be raised with little resultant loss of sales, but the prices of one firm cannot be raised if competing firms are then able to call attention to their own lower prices. In short, it is one thing to discover that demand for a particular good or other product appears to be relatively price inelastic and quite another to determine how to put the information to use.

Identification of situations of price elasticity is one step in a long and complicated managerial process, a process that relies on cogent judgment far more than it
does on formulas or other tools. Like so many other marketing management tools,
the concept of inelastic demand is a *starting point*, not an end in itself. Knowing
that demand appears to be inelastic is just a beginning. What to *do* about this
condition is the real marketing challenge.

Conclusion

The concept of inelastic demand is important to individual organizations and to
the economy as a whole. Many companies face inelastic demand situations in the
marketing of some or all of their products, as earlier examples have shown. Too,
the macroeconomy embraces numerous situations where demand is surprisingly
insensitive to price. Among these is the demand for medical services. Except for
the impoverished, when faced with a medical emergency most U.S. and Canadian
citizens want nothing but "the best" for themselves and their families. News stories demonstrate this daily by reporting the willingness of some individuals to go
anywhere and try anything to overcome their particular infirmities.

Mathematical formulas and graphic depictions of demand schedules can be used
to discover and analyze instances of inelastic demand. Yet it would appear that even
if these are not employed specifically, managers of organizations intuitively use the
concept in their decision making.

Applications To Small Business

Many managers of small businesses are drawn to their fields of endeavor by what
they perceive to be an inelastic demand for that particular good or service. That is,
they feel that their product will always be needed, virtually without regard to price,
because it is so basic. Local roofing company owners, operators of small grocery
stores, and other entrepreneurs are frequently heard to remark "If the roof leaks
you have to fix it" or "People always need food." Unfortunately, it is this kind of
thinking that attracts other entrepreneurs to the same businesses, increasing the
level of competition and driving prices and profits down. What may have been a
case of inelastic demand for a product type thus becomes a widely varying demand
for the product of a single firm. Small business operators, and others for that
matter, should avoid being unduly influenced by the "inelasticity fallacy."

Business operators should attempt to analyze the demand situation they face. It
has been pointed out by many experts that whether or not a manager tries to draw
or calculate a demand schedule that demand schedule still exists. Thus attention to
determining its true nature with as much accuracy as possible is a recommended
course of action for both small and larger businesses. It is entirely possible that the
small business manager may find that demand for his product is in fact price
inelastic. Such inelasticity may be seasonal as it is for the costume rental shop two

days before Halloween or the tuxedo rental shop during the Spring months. Demand may be inelastic for certain products, but not others. The retailer may note that people dicker over the price of necklaces but not over the price of diamond engagement rings.

In short, consideration of instances of inelastic demand and its ramifications can yield considerable payoff to the small business. Thinking beyond intuitive reaction to the phenomena is strongly endorsed by small business consultants.

Software/Databases

Databases dealing specifically with "real world" price elasticity and inelasticity of demand are not widely available. This is because much data is proprietary and because market dynamics diminish the usefulness of historical data.

Business researchers advise that current information is best gathered via monitoring of the business press. This task can be facilitated by the use of the following sources:

Database of Databases. M.E. Williams, Inc. and the University of Illinois-Urbana, Urbana, IL 61801. Provides detailed information on publicly available databases and is updated quarterly.

McGraw-Hill Business Backgrounder. McGraw-Hill Co, 1221 Avenue of Americas, New York 10020. Reviews all McGraw-Hill business publications.

PTS Prompt. Predicasts, 11001 Cedar Avenue, Cleveland, OH 44106. Summarizes information from thousands of publications.

PTS U.S. Forecasts. Predicasts, 11001 Cedar Avenue, Cleveland, OH 44106. Offers historical data, as well as forecasts, for many industries.

References/Sources

Bennett, Sidney, and Wilkinson, J.B., "Pricing Quality Relationships and Price Elasticity Under In-Store Experimentation," *Journal of Business Research* (January 1974): 27–38. Describes results of systematic raising and lowering of prices for the purpose of determining sales response at various prices and the effect of these price changes on the sales.

Guiltinan, Joseph P., and Paul, Gordon W., *Marketing Management*. New York: McGraw-Hill, 1982. Chapter 8, "Pricing Programs," provides an excellent overview of price-elasticity of demand, estimating elasticity, and other pricing considerations.

Hughes, G. David, *Demand Analysis for Marketing Decisions*. Homewood, IL: Richard D. Irwin, 1973. Applies theories, models, and measures developed by economics and other disciplines to the analysis of demand, placing inelastic demand in a broad context.

McKenna, Joseph, *The Logic of Price*. Hinsdale, IL: The Dryden Press, 1973. Addresses inelastic demand, supply, consumers, firms, government and resources as these combine to form markets.

Ohshfeldt, Robert and Smith, Barton, "Estimating the Demand for Heterogeneous Goods," *The Review of Economics and Statistics* (February 1985): 165–171. Discusses limitations of demand estimation and practical applications such as price elasticity, noting that models are theoretically attractive but alternative methods more useful.

Related Topics and Terms

Competitive Edge, Economics, Elastic Demand, Industrial Good, Industrial Market, Market Potential, Pricing, Substitutes Analysis, Trend Analysis.

Michael F. d'Amico
Department of Marketing
The University of Akron

INSTITUTIONAL ADVERTISING

Overview

Institutional, or corporate, advertising (the terms are used interchangeably) is advertising whose objective is to make favorably known the organization behind the product or service being marketed and not the product or service itself. Such advertising features information about the organization and its functions, so that people will have more confidence in it and in the products or services the company provides.

Institutional advertising was one of the earliest types of public relations advertising. Used often by the business corporation, its goal is to communicate to the public the activities of the organization that might otherwise go unreported through other media channels. A business firm, for example, may want to let the public know about its extensive research facilities, its hiring practices, or its active role in community affairs. Some have referred to this type of advertising as "image" advertising or even "corporate image" advertising, owing to its use by corporations.

There are three basic types of institutional advertising an organization can use to achieve its objectives: (1) patronage institutional, (2) public relations institutional, and (3) public service institutional. Each of these types has a different general objective.

Patronage institutional advertising gives reasons why the consumer or business user should patronize the corporation other than the product or service sold. It is based on patronage buying motives and promotes the corporation as a good one to buy from because of such factors as excellent research, convenience of location, and reputation.

Public relations institutional advertising tries to develop a friendly attitude toward the company and its management. It is often used to communicate such ideas as the company is a good place to work, a good citizen of the local community, and the like. It may be written for one or more of the company's customer segments or publics.

Public service institutional advertising promotes noncontroversial topics that are in the general interest of the public, such as prevention of forest fires, reducing the risk of heart attack, or stopping air pollution.

Examples

A good example of patronage institutional advertising is that done by Burlington Industries, primarily in magazines, to persuade readers to patronize apparel with their trademark. The main slogan of the ad reads "At Burlington we see fabric not merely for what it is, but for what it can be." The emphasis is on patronizing their fabrics because of their excellent research efforts.

An example of public relations institutional advertising are the ads of South Carolina Electric and Gas Company. These ads explain that their management is economizing and does not profit from increasing utility costs. The advertising explains that only higher fuel costs have forced them to raise rates. Metropolitan Life Insurance Company has used some good examples of public service advertising. Below a picture of a little girl on crutches and leg braces reads this headline, "If you forget to have your children vaccinated, you could be reminded of it the rest of your life." They offer a booklet to the readers on "Immunizations" and further explain that their company is concerned about people's future health and longevity.

Benefits

The ultimate benefit of improved image is to help an organization develop and maintain satisfactory sales and profits. The goal of institutional advertising is to develop and protect not the brand image or the store image but the corporate image. The corporate image can, in one respect, be the most important of the three images developed and positioned by advertising. Products can be replaced by better models with new names and images more easily than the corporation can change its image.

The totality of impressions people have about a company is its corporate image. The corporate image can also be considered to be the personality of the organization as perceived by its various publics. This personality is formed not on the basis of objective evidence but by impressions received and subjective evaluations made by the various corporate publics. Products, packages, trademarks, brand names, the company name, employees, the marketing program, graphics, and other factors combine to make up the corporate personality. "Every company has a corporate identity from the moment it opens its doors—an identity which represents what it has done to convey to the public what it is."

No company can afford to be without a strong corporate image. Some corporations, such as Hershey Foods and Gillette, rely more on their company names than on their brand names. Others, such as International Telephone and Telegraph Corporation use their corporate image and symbol to give an overall image to a vast array of divisions and subsidiaries spread over the world. Consumerism and a growing public demand for product quality and integrity are further reasons for the development of favorable corporate advertising.

Implementation

The first step in implementing an institutional advertising program is research. Studies conducted by individual divisions of the company on behalf of their own products or services may already exist. While these can be helpful, they usually are not adequate alone for corporate purposes. Therefore, a study should be conducted among those publics vital to the entire corporation as well. It probably would include customer groups, community, stockholders, the financial community, channel members, and others.

The second step is to develop the corporation's own corporate mission. The executive responsible for corporate advertising should help corporations develop some internal consensus on what position the corporation ideally desires. The third step is to do positioning analysis with regard to competitors' position. Corporations can be positioned in a similar fashion to products with respect to their individual marketers.

The fourth step is to set executive advertising objectives. As in other advertising campaigns, budget considerations are part of the analysis. The fifth step is to ensure persistence and unity of message.

The carefully chosen positioning strategy can only be achieved with the use of consistent messages over a reasonable length of time. This demands that every message—even product advertising—matches the company's position in its institutional advertising program.

Evaluation

The institutional advertising program is monitored by tracking studies conducted regularly at appropriate intervals. Depending upon the objectives, the time period may be as short as three months or as long as two years. The original research of the corporate image is used as a base or bench mark against which the current image can be compared. It may not be necessary to repeat the entire study, a simplified form may be sufficient. Not only do tracking studies serve as report cards for the entire program, they also are a source of feedback to be folded into the program as it continues.

Conclusion

Institutional, or corporate, advertising is advertising whose objective is to make favorably known the organization behind the product or service, not the product or service itself. In small corporations, institutional advertising may be handled by the advertising department; in large corporations, by the public relations department. The institutional advertising budget is frequently separated from the product advertising budget and is commonly much smaller.

An image may be defined as a mental picture formed by people concerning a product, service, corporation, or retail store. Images exist whether they are planned and promoted by an organization or allowed to develop by the unguided reactions of people to an organization and its products. Images are built up through the years by the quality of the product produced or handled, the services provided, and the organization's reputation, policies, and marketing efforts. Competitors find it much more difficult to imitate images than products.

Applications to Small Business
The difference between store image and corporate image is probably small or nonexistent; therefore, the small businessman must achieve all the same goals as larger institutions. A small firm will need to position its overall image in the local community or regional market or with distributors just as major corporations do. On the local level "corporate image" means company reputation, so that local department stores might reap as much benefit from advertising their return policy or 50th anniversary as they would advertising a product or sale.

Software/Databases
Research regarding attitude surveys can be processed and a database created for use as a benchmark using SPSS or SASS or ICPSR from SPSS Inc., Suite 3300, 444 North Michigan Ave., Chicago, IL 60611.

References/Sources
Dunn, Watson, and Barban, Arnold M., *Advertising,* 6th ed. Chicago: The Dryden Press, 1985. The authors discuss the mission and overview of institutional advertising.

Garbett, Thomas, *Corporate Advertising.* New York: McGraw-Hill, 1981. The book discusses the various forms of advertising and implementation.

Marguiles, Walter, "Custom Control of Corporate Identity," *Business Horizons,* Vol. XIII, No. 1 (February 1970): 31. The articles cover examples of successful use of ads.

Seitel, Fraser, *The Practice of Public Relations,* 2nd ed. Columbus, OH: Charles E. Merrill, 1984. This text covers the positioning of a corporate message.

Stanley, Richard E., *Promotion.* Englewood Cliffs, NJ: Prentice-Hall, This book has key examples of the three areas of institutional advertising.

Related Topics and Terms
Cause-Related Advertising, Corporate Advertising, Corporate Image, Public Relations, Public Service, Store Image.

James Ricks
Department of Marketing
Southeast Missouri State University

INTERNATIONAL MARKETING

Overview

International marketing involves the marketing of goods and services outside an organization's home country. Multinational marketing is a complex form of international marketing that involves an organization engaged in marketing operations in many foreign countries. The comparative approach to the study of international marketing, or comparative marketing, focuses on the similarities and differences existing among the marketing systems of various countries. It seeks to identify, classify, and interpret the similarities and differences among the systems used to anticipate demand and market products. Many large multinational companies are becoming even more geocentric (world oriented).

The geocentric assumption is that there are major differences from country to country and that these differences are important in the formulation of a national marketing plan, but at the same time there are important similarities among markets, and these similarities must be recognized to develop an effective integrated and coordinated international marketing plan that maximizes the profitability of a worldwide marketing effort.

The process of evaluating the uncontrollable elements in the international environment is a crucial step to be undertaken. These factors include (1) political forces, (2) economic forces and socioeconomic conditions, (3) competitive forces, (4) level of technology, (5) structure of distribution, (6) geography, and (7) cultural forces. Marketers must examine each country completely in terms of the proposed products or services and not rely on an often-used axiom that if it sells or is successful in one country, it will surely sell in another. The focus and emphasis of the multinational approach is on adapting to what is unique in each country and culture.

Examples

The business policy of the Japanese is growth-minded. The primary objectives of Japanese companies are set in terms of sales volume rather than short-term profitability. The essence of this strategy is to increase sales volume at least as fast or faster than any of their competitors. A number of routes to "competitive superiority" used by Japanese companies include: (1) a focus on key factors, which are discovered by market analysis and the study of "winning companies" to assess the reasons why they have succeeded; (2) the adoption of aggressive initiatives, which involves questioning the status quo in the marketplace and adopting unconventional stances; (3) the creative seeking of relative advantage over competitors, to develop market share; and (4) the importance of the degrees of strategic freedom available to a company. Japanese firms have been aggressive users of price competition, where it gains volume and achieves market penetration. The Japanese send study

405

teams into the target country to spend several months evaluating the market and figuring out a strategy. The teams search for niches to enter that are not being satisfied by any current offerings. A key characteristic of their entry strategy is to build market share rather than early profits. They rely on product-development strategies and market-development strategies.

The potential for error in international marketing communications is large. For example, a U.S. airline advertised a "rendezvous lounge" as a feature of its jets, but in Portuguese translation for Brazil, "rendezvous" meant a room hired for lovemaking. Pepsi Cola's international slogan "Come Alive With Pepsi" was translated into German as "rise from the grave."

Colgate-Palmolive launched Cue toothpaste internationally, only to find that in French-speaking countries Cue is a pornographic word. Advertising for Listerine mouthwash showed an intimate boy and girl relationship, with the couple advising each other to use the product to avoid bad breath. In the Far East, such a public portrayal of a boy/girl relationship was objectionable, and the theme had to be changed to two girls.

A manufacturer of water recreation products exported to Malasya, used a prominent green logo on the products. In Malasya green is a symbol of the jungle, danger and disease. Some guidelines for advertising in China include: avoid a glamour appeal in favor of strong price-performance emphasis; tables and charts speak louder than blonde beauties; a serious tone, low key and straightforward, is most effective for industrial advertising in the People's Republic. In China, the most popular color is red; it indicates happiness. Black with gold lettering also elicits a positive response, because it denotes age and stability. Pepsodent was unsuccessful in Southeast Asia because it promised white teeth to a culture where black or yellow teeth are symbols of prestige.

Some other language blunders in international advertising include: the word "napkin" means "diaper" to the English; in German, "Let Hertz Put You In The Driver's Seat" means "Let Hertz Make You A Chauffeur." Other translations have produced insulting or offensive double meanings in Spanish. Frank Perdue of Perdue Chickens had one of his slogans translated too literally. The slogan in English was, "it takes a tough man to make a tender chicken." The slogan was, unfortunately, understood as "it takes a sexually excited man to make a chick sensual."

Benefits

International marketing efforts can result in substantial benefits. Companies might be pushed into international marketing by a weakening of marketing opportunities at home. GNP growth may slow down; R&D and manufacturing costs might escalate and be recovered only by "going global"; governments might become antibusiness; the tax burden might become too heavy; and the government might push businesses into expanding abroad in order to earn more foreign exchange and reduce the trade deficit. Also, companies might be pulled into foreign trade by growing opportunities for their products in other countries. In many instances, products are in different stages in the life cycle in different countries. International marketing may provide opportunities for prolonging product growth and it may extend the product life cycle. Among American companies deriving more than 60 percent of their revenue from abroad in 1981 are Pan Am (92 percent), Exxon (72 percent), Citicorp (67 percent), Texaco (62 percent), Mobil (60 percent), and Colgate-Palmolive (60 percent). Caterpillar, Coca-Cola, Dow Chemical, Ford, Gillette, Gulf Oil, IBM, ITT, Kodak, Pfizer, and Xerox earn about half of their profits abroad, and their foreign operations are growing faster than their domestic operations.

Implementation

Export marketing is made up of the marketing decisions necessary to direct the flow of goods and communications overseas. Once a company decides to sell to a particular country, it has to determine the best mode of entry. Its choices are exporting, joint venturing, and direct investments abroad. Each succeeding strategy involves more commitment, risk, and possible profits. The simplest way to get involved in a foreign market is through export. Companies may or may not modify its goods for the export market. If all of its goods are produced in the home country, a company can export its product in two ways. It can hire independent international marketing middlemen (indirect export) or handle its own exporting (direct export).

A second broad method of entering a foreign market is to join with foreign nationals to set up production and marketing facilities. Joint venturing differs from exporting in that a partnership is formed that leads to some production facilities abroad, and it differs from direct investment in that an association is formed with someone in that country.

When direct investment is used, the company owns production, marketing, and other facilities in foreign countries without any partners. The firm has all the benefits and risks associated with ownership. There are savings in labor, and marketing plans are more sensitive to local needs. Profit potential is high, although costs are also high.

Firms that operate in one or more foreign markets must decide how much, if at all, to adapt their marketing mix to local conditions. A standardized marketing mix approach involves the standardization of the product, advertising, distribution channels, and other elements of the marketing mix for all countries served. It promises the lowest costs because no major changes have been introduced. At the other extreme is the idea of a customized marketing mix, where the producer adjusts the marketing-mix elements to each target market, bearing more costs but hoping for a larger market share and return on investment.

With a backward invention product strategy, the firm appeals to developing countries by making products that are less complex than the ones it sells in its domestic market. In forward invention, the company develops new products for its international markets. This plan is more risky and time-consuming and requires higher capital investments than the other strategies. The best product strategy is one which optimizes company profits over the long term, or, it is one which maximizes the present value of cash flows associated with business operations.

A brand policy becomes more important to the multinational firm as competition tightens in the local markets. If the producer is to gain the advantage of promotional efforts, the consumer must be able to identify the product and to separate it from those of competitors. It is critically important for the international company to evaluate proposed new products in terms of their local-international-global potential. Product design, for example, is a key factor in determining success in international marketing, but international laws and regulations have a major impact on product design. A product must be compatible with the environment in which it is used.

International promotion planning must take into account cultural differences such as customs, the meaning of colors and symbols, and the level of literacy. International promotion planning also depends on the overlap of audiences and languages. The use of media requires international adaptation because media availability varies from country to country. Many multinational companies use a standardized advertising theme around the world. In some cases, the copy should be varied, even in a minor way, such as changing the colors to avoid taboos in other countries.

Media habits vary by country. For example, 36 percent of the French population watches less than one hour of television per week. Only 9 percent of the U.S. population watches this little television. French residents subscribe to 2.4 magazines, while U.S. residents subscribe to 3.7. Every international advertiser must decide whether or not to extend, adapt, or invent for each national market appeals, illustrations, and copy.

Regarding price policies, there is the issue of the terms of trade, which determine real selling prices and the division of such costs as insurance, documentation, packaging and freight between the buyer and seller. A further aspect of price terms is the possible mixing of cash payments and goods in barter or in countertrading agreements. These forms of trading may involve straight barter, compensation deals, counterpurchase agreements or buy-back arrangements. This is of particular significance in dealing with areas like eastern Europe, China, and some of the developing countries, which may lack the foreign currency to pay directly for exports. Pricing differentation may be attractive with a strategy of market concentration, but highly uneconomic with market spreading. Price competitiveness starts with list or declared prices, but must also take into account open and hidden or negotiated discounts from the base price, the value of credit or financing arrangements, extra costs to the customer like packaging, insurance and so on, as well as any secondary purchase costs like local delivery charges or premiums imposed by distributors, or the effect of changing relative currency values.

Manufacturers often price their products lower in foreign markets. The manufacturer may set low prices to build market share, or the manufacturer may want to dump goods that have no market at home. When the manufacturer charges less in the foreign market than in the home market, the practice is called dumping. The basic considerations in international price planning are whether prices should be standardized, the level at which prices are set, the currency in which prices are quoted, and terms of sale. When setting a price level, a firm would consider local economic conditions such as per capita GNP. Marketing entry pricing strategies ranging from penetration (low price) to skimming (first price) practices may be employed and the firm's selection of a pricing strategy directly affects the way all the other marketing strategies are utilized.

International distribution planning encompasses the selection of channel members and the physical movement of products. Distribution systems tend to be different in other countries. The international company must take a whole-channel view of the problem of distributing products to the final consumers. Within-country channels of distribution vary considerably from country to country. There are striking differences in the number and types of middlemen, and in the size and character of retail units abroad. Distribution channels in markets around the world are among the most highly differentiated aspects of national marketing systems. Culture exerts an indirect influence on channels of distribution by its direct influence on attitudes concerning pricing, promotion and the like.

A major goal in distribution policy is to gain full market coverage, thus (1) gaining the optimum volume of sales obtainable in each market, (2) searching a reasonable market share, and (3) attaining satisfactory market penetration. The extreme length of channels typically utilized in international distribution makes control of middlemen particularly difficult. Some companies have solved this problem by establishing their own distribution systems; others issue franchises or exclusive distributorships in an effort to maintain control at least through the first stages of the channels. The speed with which a firm has to penetrate each market is a vital consideration when one is choosing channels of distribution.

In personal selling, the most significant decision is the choice between direct selling efforts, federated exporting, local sales offices, or leaving selling to agents and distributors. The company sales force represents one of the major alternate methods of organizing a company for foreign distribution, and, as such, is on the front line of a marketing organization.

The physical distribution of products into international markets often requires special planning. The processing of insurance, government documents, etc. may be time consuming, and transportation modes may be unavailable or inefficient.

Evaluation

International marketing management must determine what can be done to improve marketing performance, effectiveness, and efficiency. Several aspects related to the strategic and tactical planning, organization, and control process, and to the international marketing mix must be examined. Typical questions which management will ask are:

What is the basic market potential for the product in foreign markets? Does the balance of situational factors suggest that market spreading or market concentration is more appropriate to the company's needs? What actions should be taken by the company? What product factors, if any, offer pricing freedom; e.g., product differentiation, substitutability, specialization? What market factors (market share, competition, etc.), buyer factors (consumer habits, buyer loyalty, etc.), and company factors (profits versus volume, skimming versus penetration, etc.) give pricing freedom? Who are the competitors in the market concerned and how successful are they—sales, market shares, key accounts, etc.? What are the major differences in how the firms in the market do business, such as, organization, distribution, advertising and promotion, and strongest market segments? What differences are there in the competing products? What new product developments are expected, and what directions are competitors taking? What differences exist in the type of services offered by competitors? What are the differences in reputation and image between the competing firms? Are there significant differences in sales organizations, distribution policies, delivery time, and reliability and so on?

Conclusion

The expansion of international operations has resulted in changed organizational structures for many businesses. Within this organizational adaptation, some selected organizational prototypes that have been used are the export management company (EMC), built-in export departments, separate export departments, the international division, regional management centers, the international headquarters company, worldwide product structures, worldwide geographic structures, the matrix organization, umbrella companies, and the interglomerate (international conglomerate). The matrix style structure has opened many creative solutions to organizational problems in international marketing.

While market concentration offers the strengths of specialization, market spreading offers a position of greater flexibility, less dependence on particular export or international markets, as well as allowing product rather than market specialization in some instances. Any choice of the desired combination of market and competitive strategy will have to take into account the firm's objectives, its strategic capability, and the market characteristics.

Applications to Small Business

In some cases, small independent companies have found good international marketing opportunities. Few small businesses in different industries recognize how important international marketing efforts can be to achieve goals such as expansion, profitability (ROI), and pay-back period. Government agencies such as the

Small Business Administration and the U.S. Department of Commerce have available many exporting and international trade aid programs and schemes designed to help small business expand their operations into markets abroad.

A small business firm can go international in different ways without having to be engaged only in occasional exporting. The small company can be involved in active exporting by working with independent international marketing middlemen, by using licensing, by setting some simple form of joint venture, or by using some sort of subsidiary agreement. Besides the alternatives of leaving the international marketing operations to agents and distributors, the small firm can also develop direct selling efforts if the market potential is high. A market concentration strategy should be favored and pursued. Recently, there has been some attention given to the advantages of a "low market share strategy." There are case histories of companies which do not have dominant market shares, but which are profitable and growing. A small market share is not necessarily a handicap; it can be a significant advantage that enables a company to compete in ways that are unavailable to its larger rivals. This suggests that a low market share may be profitable for the company engaged in international marketing—because it costs little to achieve it. The implication is that for the smaller firms which may not be able to reach higher levels of volume, taking a low market share in a number of export markets, and minimizing costs as much as possible, may offer more profitable exporting than a policy of export market penetration.

Small firms in the U.S. are now becoming more internationally minded and are in agreement that many marketing opportunities and challenges of the future lie in international marketing.

Software/Databases

BI/DATA FORECASTS. Business International Corporation, New York, NY. Provides market forecasts for 35 countries over four-year time periods. Data include national income, gross domestic product, exports and imports, goods and services, balance of trade, and consumer price index.

BI/DATA TIME SERIES. Business International Corporation, New York, NY. Provides 317 economic indicators in time series form for up to 131 countries. Production and consumption statistics, balance of payments, national accounts, and demographics, and international trade statistics are emphasized.

References/Sources

Abdel-Malek, T. "Export Marketing Orientation in Small Firms," in *American Journal of Small Business*, Vol. 3, No. 1 (1978): 25-34. This article provides some guidelines on export marketing activities for small companies.

Ayal, Igal, "International Product Life Cycle: A Reassessment and Product Policy Implication," in *Journal of Marketing,* No. 4, (Fall 1981): 91-96. The author examines the relationship between the international PLC and product policy decisions.

Ayal, I. and J. Zif, "Market Expansion Strategies in Multinational Marketing," in *Journal of Marketing,* Vol. 43, No. 2, (1979): 84-94. The authors present some market expansion strategies and their implications for multinational marketing operations.

Baker, James C. and John K. Ryans Jr. *Multinational Marketing: Dimensions in Strategy.* Columbus, OH: Grid, 1975. Special attention should be given to Part III—The International Consumer and Developing Marketing Information; Part IV—Product Policy and Pricing; Part V—Marketing Channels and Physical Distribution; and Part VI—Promotion.

Black, George, "Ten Commandments for International Industrial Advertiser," *Industrial Marketing,* (February, 1981): 60. Interesting article focusing on the basic principles to be followed in international industrial advertising.

Cannon, Tom "Managing International and Export Marketing," in *European Journal of Marketing,* Vol. 14, No. 1 (1980): 34-49. This article gives an overview of international and export marketing management tasks.

Cateora, Philip R. *International Marketing.* 5th ed. Homewood, IL: Richard D. Irwin, 1983. This is a classical book in this field. It covers the most relevant areas concerned with international marketing.

Cavusgil, S. Tamer and John R. Nevin. "International Determinants of Export Marketing Behavior: An Empirical Investigation," in *Journal of Marketing Research,* Vol. 28, (February 1981): 114-119. Interesting article devoted to the analysis of the determinants of export marketing behavior within a company and based on empirical research findings.

Colvin, Michael, Roger Heller, and Jim Thorpe. "Developing International Advertising Strategy," in *Journal of Marketing,* Vol. 44, (Fall 1980): 73-79. The article presents some insights on international advertising strategy formulation.

Davidson, William N. and Phillipe Haspeslagh. "Shaping a Global Product Organization," in *Harvard Business Review,* Vol. 60, (July-August 1982): 125-133. This article deals with the design of a global product organizational structure to increase a company's effectiveness and efficiency in international markets.

Green, Robert T. and Arthur W. Allaway, "Identification of Export Opportunities: A Shift-Share Approach," in *Journal of Marketing,* 49, (Winter 1985): 83-88. An interesting article dealing with the screening process of products and markets in an international context.

Hackett, D. W. "Penetrating International Markets: Key Considerations for Smaller Firms," in *Journal of Small Business Management,* Vol. 15, No. 1 (1977): 10-16. Considerations on how to enter international markets for a small company.

Hill, John S. and Richard R. Still. "Adapting Products to LDC Tastes," in *Harvard Business Review,* Vol. 62, (March-April 1984): 92-101. The authors point out strategies for adaptation to less developed countries' particular needs and tastes.

Johansson, Johnny D. and Hans B. Thorelli. "International Product Positioning," in *Journal of International Business Studies,* Vol. 16, No. 3, (Fall 1985): 57-75. Excellent article on international product positioning, perceptual maps, country stereotyping, and differences across countries.

Keegan, Warren J. "Multinational Product Planning: Strategic Alternatives," in *Journal of Marketing* (January 1969): 58-62. Keegan presents his classic approach to multinational product planning—the five broad options in adapting products and marketing communications.

Levitt, Theodore, "The Globalization of Markets," in *Harvard Business Review,* Vol. 61, (May-June 1983): 92-102. Levitt discusses the important concept of globalization in international marketing.

Peebles, Dean M., John K. Ryans, Jr., and Ivan R. Vernon. "Coordinating International Advertising," in *Journal of Marketing* (1978): 28-34. The authors give some ideas on how to coordinate international advertising.

Piercy, Nigel, "Export Strategy: Concentration on Key Markets vs. Market Spreading," in *Journal of International Marketing,* Vol. 1, No. 1 (1981): 56-67. This article examines the advantages and disadvantages of using market concentration or spreading strategies.

————, "Export Marketing Strategy—Can Firms Afford the Key Market Concentration Strategy?" in *The Quarterly Review of Marketing,* (London, UK), Vol. 9, No. 2 (Winter/January 1984): 1-9. Interesting article on key market concentration as an export strategy.

Ricks, David A. "How to Avoid Business Blunders Abroad," in *Business,* 34 (April-June 1984): 3-11. The article contains examples of international marketing blunders and gives guidelines on how to avoid them.

Robinson, Richard D. *International Marketing Management: A Guide to Decision Making.* 2nd ed. New York: Holt, Rinehart and Winston, 1978. Special attention should be given to the different market entry strategies described by the author.

Related Topics and Terms

Comparative Advantage, European Economic Community, Expatriate Personnel, Multinational Corporation, Standardized Advertising, Trade Balance.

Luiz Moutinho
Department of Management Studies
University of Glasgow, Scotland

INTRAORGANIZATIONAL CONFLICT

Overview

Within any organization, whether large or small, there are functions to be performed by top management, marketing personnel, and non-marketing personnel. Top managers establish the firm's line of business, set overall objectives, and instill a corporate culture (the shared values, norms, and practices communicated to an followed by those working for a firm). Marketers select target markets, set marketing objectives, and implement the marketing mix. Non-marketing personnel perform production, finance, accounting, engineering, purchasing, and other functions. Sometimes, these functions are clearly defined and known by all parties; in other instances, they are more ambiguous and unclear to the various parties. Furthermore, in too many instances, there may be overlapping tasks, contradictory goals, poor communication, and an inappropriate corporate culture. As a result, intraorganizational conflict may result. Through proper planning, this conflict can be reduced.

Examples

A number of companies have improved their performance by recognizing the dangers of intraorganizational conflict and taking steps to avoid or overcome it. These firms are successful because their top managements have not been myopic or complacent. They have been willing to try new techniques to stimulate organizational productivity.

These are some leading examples of companies which have been working hard to minimize intraorganizational conflict. When IBM developed its PC, the firm used a venture team for the first time in its history. IBM knew that new-product planning would be too slow, subject to functional or departmental disputes, and too conservative unless a radically different organizational structure was utilized. After the breakup of AT&T, the firm elevated the role of marketing personnel, who had previously been subordinate to production and engineering personnel. AT&T realized that in its highly competitive post-divestiture status marketing personnel had to have greater and clearer input into decisions.

Procter & Gamble had rough sledding during the early 1980s, as competition intensified and it had difficulties penetrating some international markets. As a result, P & G changed its focus to greater emphasis on brand extensions; and in doing so, it limited the number of organizational levels having control over even the most routine decisions; at the same time, it reduced the paper flow required by its famed memo system. After both its Lisa and Macintosh computers failed to live up to expectations, Apple Computer did away with its autonomous Macintosh, Apple II, and Accessory Products divisions and set up a functional organization. This structure facilitates communications, reduces redundancies, and is less costly than the earlier format; it has also enabled Apple to continue to be profitable during a slow period for the personal computer industry.

Because of its declining market share in the small-car market segment, General Motors has been involved with three innovative organizational structures. First, GM reorganized itself into large-car (Buick, Oldsmobile, and Cadillac) and small-car groups (Chevrolet, Pontiac, and GM of Canada). This was done to better coordinate decisions, more quickly respond to market conditions, and more distinctly differentiate car models. Second, GM entered into a joint venture with Toyota to produce a new version of the Chevrolet Nova. Through this venture, GM set up a plant in California, using the Japanese style of management—complete with worker participation in decisions. Third, GM established an entirely autonomous Saturn subsidiary to make subcompacts. The Saturn division is to be virtually free of all existing GM organizational restrictions and biases.

Sometimes, intraorganizational conflict cannot be resolved without very drastic action. Beatrice removed its chief executive officer largely because of a poor organizational climate, which had led to the resignations of a number of valuable employees. The franchisees of Computerland forced the founder of the company to step aside because they were displeased with his management style and the high level of marketing expenditures. Warner Communications had to sell off its Atari division because Warner's senior management was unable to make the transition from electronics toymaker to home computer maker.

Benefits

By minimizing intraorganizational conflict and maximizing cooperation, a firm can achieve a number of benefits. By clearly communicating the organization's line of business, overall objectives, and corporate culture, personnel from different functional areas can better understand their roles and work together better. Costs can be reduced, since functions will not be duplicated. Innovation can be encouraged. Competition for resources will be lessened. The firm's image will be more precise to the target market. Short-run and long-run plans can be more effectively coordinated.

By restructuring itself from 135 strategic business units to 21, Westinghouse has been able to improve communications, facilitate divisional interaction, lower the duplication of tasks, and better focus its efforts. It is also more flexible and responsive to market changes.

Implementation

To minimize intraorganizational conflict, these steps should be undertaken. First, top management must specify the firm's lines(s) of business and outline short-run and long-run goals. These managers must also determine the corporate culture with which they want personnel to conform, with regard to formality of rules, the level of centralization, the level of interdivisional contact, etc. In general the corporate culture may be bureaucratic, with many rules and tight senior management control; entrepreneurial, with few rules and a high degree of divisional autonomy; or collegial, which has some rules and broad senior management guidelines. A progressive senior management team will recognize that the use of corporate culture depends on the firm's interest in innovativeness and a variety of environmental factors. Sometimes, a company would be best served if the corporate culture varies, such as bureaucratic for mature divisions and entrepreneurial for rapidly growing divisions.

Second, it is imperative that top management communicates company goals and corporate culture to every employee in the firm. It is also the responsibility of these managers to fairly allocate resources, encourage interdepartmental cooperation, set up rewards that emphasize such cooperation, and publicly acknowledge the importance of each functional area.

Third, marketing personnel in the firm must recognize their role and the potential for conflicts with others in the company. The role of marketers should be to research the characteristics and needs of consumers; monitor the activities of competitors, the economy, and external forces, and communicate their findings to other functional personnel. Marketers should also be responsible for developing consumer-oriented product concepts, testing these product concepts with channel members and potential consumers, establishing product features and brand names, product positioning, and product life cycle decisions; choosing transportation and warehousing modes, channel member selection, and providing channel member support; selection of promotion media, cooperative promotion, and message content for promotion; and determining demand-oriented price levels, negotiating channel member markups, setting price lines, and compliance with the Robinson-Patman Act. In virtually all of these tasks, marketing personnel should work with their appropriate counterparts in other departments. Usually, marketing decisions have significant impact on other functional areas; and marketers need to understand this.

These are some of the marketing mix-related decisions often or sometimes made by non-marketing personnel: product—production capacity, size of production runs, frequency of design changes, materials used in product, and the feasibility of product variations; distribution—credit rating of channel members, feasibility of national rollouts, use of company-owned facilities, and the use of overseas markets; promotion—size of the promotion budget, emphasis on marketing versus technical features, sales force compensation, and the use of institutional ads; and pricing—cost-based price levels, terms of sales, level of markup, geographic pricing, and the use of special discounts.

Marketing personnel need to be aware of some of the criticisms made of them by other functional personnel. Production: "Marketing has sold products for applications they were not designed to fulfill." Engineering: "Marketers don't need us as often as we're requested; they use us for credibility." Finance: "Design changes are generally very costly and therefore should be kept to a minimum."

Likewise, non-marketing personnel need to be aware that marketers need a certain degree of flexibility, must be adaptive to consumer needs and market conditions, require frequent and detailed reports, and must capitalize on differential advantages that seem costly and inefficient to these personnel. Non-marketing personnel should understand that marketers sometimes feel that "promotion is too technical," "design changes are too seldom," and "more engineering assistance on customer visits" is needed.

Fourth, although conflicts can almost never be totally eliminated, due to vying for resource allocations, different viewpoints regarding proper decisions, and different backgrounds and personalities of the parties involved, these are some specific suggestions for reconciling differences:

1. Openly discuss disagreements and potential disagreements.
2. Encourage interfunctional and interdepartmental contact and regular communication.
3. Hire personnel who have both marketing and technical expertise, as well as a sense of team spirit.
4. Establish interdisciplinary task forces and committees.
5. Set departmental objectives that take into account other units' goals.
6. Offer interfunctional and interdepartmental rewards.

Evaluation

In evaluating a firm with regard to its organizational climate, these questions should be regularly considered:

—Does the firm have a well-defined organizational mission, a long-term commitment to a type of business and a place in the market?

—Is the corporate culture conducive to an open exchange of information?

—If top management uses a centralized decision making process, are divisional executives allowed adequate input? If a decentralized decision making process is used, are departmental decisions consistent with one another and integrated into a companywide strategy?

—Is innovativeness encouraged by providing necessary resources, encouraging (or at least accepting) risk taking, and rewarding performance by employees at all levels and from all functional areas?

—Are long-run as well as short-run goals set and communicated to all units and/or divisions?

—Are strategic business units utilized, whereby divisions or product lines have managers responsible for linking all functions into strategies aimed at specific target markets? Does each SBU have a senior marketing executive in charge, some control over its resources, precise differential advantages, and defined competitors?

—Are marketing objectives consistent with overall company objectives and the criteria used by other functional areas? When differences occur, are attempts made to reconcile them?

—Is the importance of each SBU and functional area recognized by senior management and by divisional and functional managers?

—Are efforts made to hire personnel with complementary backgrounds, rather than emphasizing one educational and career orientation such as engineering?

—Is top management flexible and willing to react to changing environmental factors and the unique attributes of the firm? Are senior managers aware of the actual organizational climate and responsive to the informal personnel structure that exists within the firm?

—Are employees properly motivated and compensated, and are they encouraged to participate in joint projects and committees?

—Do senior executives regularly meet, both formally and informally, with personnel at all levels in the company to communicate their goals and receive important feedback? Are the penalties for continuing conflicts between departments clearly stated? Are top management's expectations in this area known?

—Are changes in company policy, short-run and long-run strategies, etc. communicated to all relevant personnel? Are the roles of personnel with regard to these changes clear?

Conclusion

The ramifications of poor intraorganizational communication and coordination are well illustrated in a timeless marketing cartoon, which shows the different ways a child's swing may be developed—depending on the perspective of the builder. In the cartoon, the marketing department, sales force, engineering department, and production department each conceive of the swing differently; and, none of them come up with the product desired by the customer—an automobile tire suspended from a rope. The crucial moral of this cartoon is that personnel from different functional areas have divergent perspectives, because of their varying educational backgrounds, job experience, priorities, and personalities. In addition, resources are usually limited, not all personnel can be recognized or rewarded for superior performance, and many people like to exert the power inherent in their positions and are unwilling to give it up. Finally, many times, managers are sheltered from diverse viewpoints and they may be unaware of the organizational climate that surrounds them. As a result, there is a natural, almost unavoidable, tendency for intraorganizational conflict unless a firm makes a conscious effort to avoid or minimize it.

As Gustaf Delin noted: "Conflict, confusion, and uncertainty are now the norm; and there are some severe implications for corporations that strive to 'control' these more fluid, 'unplannable' circumstances. Most companies have to develop a new culture. This does not mean that they must abandon the existing values and myths or the traditional heroes of the old culture. Rather, new values, models, and myths must be given priority. Bureaucrat and controller must coexist with, or give way to, designer and entrepreneur."

Regardless of the difficulties in doing so, each type of firm—large and small, nonprofit and profit-oriented, goods and services, domestic and international—must strive to improve intraorganizational cooperation. As Booz, Allen & Hamilton suggests, this will be enable companies to "realize their goals rather than merely to fantasize about them."

Applications to Small Business

Intraorganizational conflict can have devastating effects on a firm regardless of its size. However, some characteristics of small firms may make them particularly prone to such conflict:

1. Decision making may be undertaken by the owner without adequate input from employees.
2. Owner decisions may not be communicated to employees.
3. The firms may rely on intuition and not properly ascertain consumer needs and characteristics.
4. Employees may not be allowed to make decisions if the owner is unavailable to make them.
5. Rules tend to be more informal and, therefore, less consistent than in larger firms.
6. A clear reward structure may not be in place; and employees may believe that the owner shows favoritism.
7. Budgets may be set on an "all-you-can-afford" basis instead of through an objective-and-task method.
8. There may be not be a clearly defined career path through which employees may progress.
9. The roles of each functional area or department may not be known by employees and this may lead to extensive "turf" battles.

On the other hand, in a small firm, there may be less potential conflict if employees are performing multiple tasks, the owner is working alongside his managers, there is a strong sense of collegiality, and the number of personnel is small.

The owner of a small business must work especially hard to establish an appropriate corporate culture, involve personnel in decisions, and encourage teamwork. Rewards for good performance must be provided and known by employees.

Software/Databases

While there are no specific computer software or databases that deal with intraorganizational cooperation and conflict, integrated software packages can be jointly used by different departments to get a better understanding of the operations of their various counterparts. The results generated by the software can lead to a better understanding of departmental strengths and weaknesses. These are a few examples of PC-based integrated software:

Bisybase, International Microcomputer Software Inc., 633 Fifth Avenue, San Rafael, CA 94901.

Marketemplates, Marketplan International, 5237 James Avenue S, Minneapolis, MN 55419.

Base SAS, SAS Institute Inc., Box 8000, SAS Circle, Cary, NC 27511.

Ingot, Schonfeld & Associates Inc., 2550 Crawford Avenue, Evanston, IL 60201.

References/Sources

Bonoma, Thomas V., *The Marketing Edge.* New York: Free Press, 1985. Discusses the relationship between strategy and acts, identifies marketing implementation problems, and examines management mistakes with marketing and marketing effectiveness and efficiency.

Booz, Allen & Hamilton, *New Product Management for the 1980s.* New York, 1982. Describes the results of a study involving 700 U.S. consumer goods and industrial goods firms, with some emphasis on bureaucratic, entrepreneurial, and collegial management styles.

Delin, Gustaf, "Rewiring Corporate Thinking," *Public Relations Journal* (August 1983): 12-13, 15. Explains the premise that some organizational instability must be introduced, created, maintained, and tolerated if a firm is to grow.

Evans, Joel R. and Berman, Barry, *Marketing.* 2nd ed. New York: Macmillan, 1985. Chapters 2, 3, and 24 examine corporate culture, intradepartmental conflict, and integrating marketing plans.

Gardner, Meryl P., "Creating a Corporate Culture for the Eighties," *Business Horizons* (January-February 1985): 59-63. Compares the work force of the 1980s with that of the 1960s, with particular emphasis on the heterogeneity of current personnel.

Laric, Michael V. and Stiff, Ronald, *Lotus 1-2-3 for Marketing and Sales.* Englewood Cliffs, NJ: Spectrum, 1984. An introductory book and computer diskette that show how Lotus can be used in forecasting, cost analysis and pricing, allocating promotional resources, etc.

McDaniel, Stephen, Futrell, Charles M., and Parsuraman, A., "Social Power

Bases of Marketing Executives: The Relationship with Organizational Climate," *Journal of Business Research* (February 1985): 77-85. Reports on a study of 343 marketing executives with regard to reward orientation, personnel policies, MBO orientation, and status orientation.

Peters, Thomas J. and Waterman, Lawrence, Jr., *In Search of Excellence.* New York: Harper & Row, 1982. All-time business best-seller that investigates the corporate culture and intraorganizational climate at many leading U.S. firms.

Selman, James and DiBianca, Vincent F., "Contextual Management: Applying the Art of Dealing Creatively with Change," *Management Review* (September 1983): 13-19. Examines the need for managers to combine abstract and practical thinking.

Shapiro, Benson P., "Can Marketing and Manufacturing Coexist?" *Harvard Business Review* (September-October 1977): 104-114. A classic article that describes some of the basic perceptual differences between marketing and manufacturing personnel.

Tunstall, W. Brooke, "The Breakup of the Bell System: A Case Study in Cultural Transformation," *California Management Review* (Winter 1986): 110-124. An intensive analysis of the post-deregulation organizational climate of AT&T.

Weinrauch, J. Donald and Anderson, Richard, "Conflicts Between Engineering and Marketing Units," *Industrial Marketing Management* (October 1982): 291-301. Studies the different perspectives of engineers and marketers.

Related Topics and Terms
Bureaucratic Management Style, Channel Conflict, Collegial Management Style, Communication, Corporate Culture, Entrepreneurial Management Style, Environment, Feedback, Functional Organization, Management by Objectives (MBO), Marketing Mix, Organizational Mission, Product Manager, Role Conflict, Strategic Business Unit (SBU), Venture Team.

Joel R. Evans
Department of Marketing and International Business
Hofstra University

INTRODUCTION STAGE

Overview

Products pass through different stages as they move from the point at which they are introduced to the point at which they are widely accepted and finally to the point where they are completely eliminated or are replaced by another product. The first stage in this cycle is commonly referred to as the introduction stage and there are some remarkable similarities in the way consumers adopt various products during this stage. These similarities also have several implications for marketing mix decisions that are appropriate for the introduction stage of a product's life cycle.

Examples

A number of recent examples of the introduction stage of the product life cycle can be cited. The compact disk (CD) player was a revolutionary new concept introduced some time ago. The product provides high quality sound reproduction and also uses small disks which make it much more compact and portable than the conventional record player/changer and record albums. The product found its introduction stage marked mainly by purchases from upscale customers who were music enthusiasts and were impressed by the high quality of sound that the CD player could provide. This is characteristic of the introduction stage of a new consumer durable and similar features can be observed in the recent introduction stages of the home computer and cellular mobile car telephone system.

An example of a consumer non-durable that has recently been in the introduction stage is the high quality frozen entree marketed by many food companies. This product is high priced but it also appeals to an upscale consumer, such as the professional single, because it provides greater convenience along with taste and quality approaching that of freshly cooked food.

Benefits

An understanding of the introduction stage of a product's life cycle can provide many benefits to the marketing manager or decision-maker. The examples provided above illustrate a number of features of the introductory stage of a product and these features have implications for each of the marketing strategy decision areas discussed below.

Target Market: The target market in the introduction stage would generally be upscale consumers with higher levels of income and education who are also likely to experiment with new product concepts.

Product: The product itself provides a distinct product plus when compared with others currently in the marketplace though this would not exclude innovative new

but small businesses have a particularly crucial need to understand the marketing implications of the introduction stage. This is because the introduction stage requires a clear definition of the target market, i.e. the early adopters, and appropriate promotional programs directed at that target market. This may entail a considerable financial commitment and the slow growth of sales in this stage can frequently lead to net cash outflows for which the small business has to be prepared. Furthermore, the implications of the negative cash flow for the other operations of the small business have to be considered.

With regard to implementation, the small business, which most probably has its operations confined to a narrow geographical area, needs a sense for the overall potential in the market. It can then develop a measure of saturation against the overall market potential which will help it determine when the introduction stage begins and, more importantly, when it ends. In many respects this is one of the most difficult tasks for the small business because such measures of potential and saturation are much more difficult to determine for a vaguely defined narrow geographical area than for a large manufacturer looking at the overall national market. Yet, these are tasks that the small business has to undertake because at the end of the introduction stage comes a period of rapid growth which the small business needs to plan for, if it does not want to find itself strapped for resources and in a situation where it has to turn away customers and lose sales to its competition.

Software/Databases

Since the introduction stage is mainly defined by the relationship between sales to overall market potential as a function of time, most companies which have automated their sales record keeping system can monitor the performance of their product during the introduction stage without much difficulty. Commercial software that can help in this task is:

SPARCAST. SPAR, 580 White Plains Rd., Tarrytown N.Y. 10591. Forecasts promoted, non-promoted and incremental volumes and profit, using the SPARLINE concept, integrating the promotion effect and other relevant variables.

References/Sources

Balachandran, V. and Jain, S., "A Predictive Model for Monitoring PLC," *Relevance in Marketing/Marketing in Motion,* F. Allvine (ed.) Chicago: American Marketing Association, 1972, pp. 543-546. Illustrates a quantitative approach to predicting the sales of a new product.

Barnett, N.L., "Developing Effective Advertising for New Products," *Journal of Advertising Research* (December 1968): 13-20. Discusses the advertising needs of a product in the introduction stage.

Booz, Allen, and Hamilton, *Management of New Products*. New York, 1968. Provides detailed recommendations for managing the introduction stage for new products.

Catry, Bernard, and Chevalier, Michel, "Market Share Strategy and the Product Life Cycle," *Journal of Marketing* 38 (October 1974): 29-34. Explains the relationship between the stage in the life cycle and a product's market share strategy.

Clifford, Donald K. Jr., "Leverage in the Product Life Cycle," *Dun's Review* (May 1965): 62-70. Identifies critical management decisions in each stage of the life cycle.

Cox, W. Jr., "Product Life Cycles as Market Models," *Journal of Business* (October 1967): 375-384. Provides a rationale for using the product life cycle as a model for marketing decision making.

Davidson, W. R., Bates, A. D., and Bass, S. J., "Retail Life Cycles," *Harvard Business Review* (November-December 1976): 89-96. Applies the product life cycle concept to the retail situation in which many small businesses may find themselves.

Field, George A., "Do Products Really Have Life Cycles?" *California Management Review* (Fall 1972): 92-95. Critically reviews the existence of different stages in the life cycle of products.

Fox, Harold W., "Product Life Cycle—An Aid to Financial Administration," *Financial Executive* (April 1973): 28-34. Discusses the financial decisions involved in each stage of the life cycle.

Hise, Richard T., *Product/Service Strategy*. New York: Petrocelli/Charter, 1977. Chapter 8 discusses the introductory stage in some detail.

Levitt, T., "Exploit the Product Life Cycle," *Harvard Business Review* (November-December 1965): 81-94. Explains how firms may make optimal decisions at each stage in the life cycle.

Polli, R., and Cook, V., "Validity of the Product Life Cycle, " *The Journal of Business* (October 1969): 390. Provides empirical evidence for the existence of product life cycles.

Savich, Richard, and Thompson, Laurence, "Resource Allocation within the Product Life Cycle," *MSU Business Topics* (Autumn 1978): 35-44. Gives resource allocation and budgeting guidelines for the various stages in the life cycle.

Smallwood, John, "Product Life Cycle: A Key to Strategic Market Planning," *MSU Business Topics* (Winter 1973): 29-35. Discusses the strategic market planning implications of the product life cycle.

Twedt, Dik, "How Long Does it Take to Introduce New Products?" *Journal of*

Marketing 29 (1965): 71-72. Explains the need for various capital expenditures in the introduction stage of a new product.

Wind, Y., *Product Policy: Concepts, Methods and Strategy*. Reading, MA: Addison-Wesley, 1982. Chapter 3 discusses each stage of the life cycle in detail.

Related Topics and Terms

Diffusion Process, Early Adopter, Penetration Pricing, Product Management, Sales Forecast, Saturation, Skimming Price.

Pradeep Rau
Department of Marketing
University of Delaware

INVENTORY CONTROL

Overview

Inventory control is the process of managing inventory in order to meet customer demand at the lowest possible cost and with a minimum of investment. Unlike most conditions or factors in business, inventory is controllable by management. The firm decides how much inventory investment to make. It also decides when to reorder and in what quantities. The location, number, and size of the storage facilities also are determined by management.

Inventory control enables management to increase its profits by fulfilling sales and controlling costs. Revenue is increased when the firm has the merchandise available for sale. Lost sales are minimized. Investment and inventory costs are reduced because of inventory management.

Inventory costs are a significant part of the total investment of procuring or producing goods. These costs vary between 25 and 40 per cent of the actual merchandise or production costs. They include such expenses as ordering, carrying, transportation, review, and lost sales. Thus, attempts to control these elements can provide major savings to the firm, particularly when inventories constitute a large part of the total assets of a company.

Because inventories are an essential part of the investment and operations of most firms, inventory management is crucial to success. Without inventory control, companies face sales losses, obsolete and excessive inventory investment, damaged and pilfered merchandise, and reduced profits.

Examples

There are numerous examples of successful inventory management. Southwestern Bell Telephone Company was able to reduce its inventory investment on a certain piece of equipment by $8 million by increasing the review frequency of this item as well as being able to obtain a time reduction in receiving orders from the suppliers. Westinghouse Corporation discovered that its inventory investment was lowered by $12 million because it insisted on a quicker delivery schedule from its vendors. Hi-Lo Auto Parts focused its attention on the most important items in its multi-item inventories in terms of sales and investment, resulting in annual inventory savings of $55 million through closer monitoring and more frequent ordering policies. Improved documentation procedures enabled the Quanex Corporation to reconcile physical and reported inventories, thereby reducing the need for rush orders and minimizing out of stock items.

Benefits

Several benefits are obtainable from an inventory control program. The following areas are illustrative:

1. Both inventory shortages and inventory excesses are minimized.
2. Ordering systems are demand-oriented and can be developed in order to avoid crisis management.
3. Production scheduling can be facilitated by minimizing materials shortages and delayed purchase orders.
4. Determination of proper inventory levels can result in minimum lost sales.
5. Inventory costs can be reduced through improved ordering policies, lead time reductions, increased inventory review periods, and improved documentation relating to reconciling reported and actual inventories.
6. Investment requirements can be lowered.
7. Profit enhancement is increased through additional sales and reduced costs.

Implementation

Many management tools are available to accomplish effective inventory control. Among the more basic and fundamental applications are the following:

Inventory Classification—Multi-item inventories differ in terms of investment, sales, and critical value. A system of classifying inventory items on the basis of these variables readily identifies products which warrant the most attention and review as well as those items which can be managed with only limited analysis and infrequent order patterns. A basic rule of thumb is that 20 per cent of the inventory items accounts for 80 per cent of the sales or investment. These items deserve intensive management scrutiny because inventory reductions mean substantial investment savings.

Inventory Ordering Systems—When and how much to reorder involve both fixed and variable times and amounts. In deciding which system or combination to employ, management considers demand sensitivity, vendor constraints, number of items bought from a single supplier, inventory costs, and lead times. A fixed time and fixed quantity reorder system is employed to meet average demand. To accommodate uncertain and unpredictable demand conditions, either the time or the quantity factor is varied.

Quantity Discounts—Vendors often establish a varying price structure, dependent upon the quantity ordered. Although a lower price is very appealing, the decision must recognize both merchandise and inventory costs, along with the expected demand or usage of the product. Total cost is the final determinant, with the three cost elements consisting of the merchandise costs, the order costs, and the carrying costs.

Ratio Analysis—In order to determine the amount of inventory carried in relation to total investment and sales, ratio analysis is employed. Inventory turnover is obtained by dividing cost of goods sold by average inventory, while inventory as a percentage of sales gives information as to how much inventory is maintained to support a dollar of sales. Comparative analysis then must be made of the industry norm as well as of the firm's previous performance. Resulting figures above or below the industry or firm norm suggest a closer review and subsequent action regarding inventory.

Evaluation

After employing these and other inventory control tools, management should embark upon an action pattern to improve inventory performance in response to demand, investment, and cost. To assist management, answers to the following questions are needed:

Is the present inventory system meeting the demand from customers or from other departments within the firm?

How much inventory investment should the firm carry in relation to its total investment and to sales?

What cost flow problems are created by inventory investments?

How much are annual inventory costs?

Which particular items in inventory are having the most difficulty in terms of stockouts, frequent reordering patterns, and size of investment?

To what extent has inventory been classified in order to determine the relative importance of each item?

Can relatively minor items be purchased in large quantities, covering demand for several years, in order to narrow the reordering problems?

If the demand of usage for a product is relatively stable, can a reorder pattern be developed which calls for a fixed quantity on a fixed reorder time schedule?

Under what conditions should be quantity discount from vendors be accepted?

If inventory turnover occurs at a much faster rate than industry or previous performance, what areas should be examined? Conversely, if a very low inventory turnover exists, what action patterns should be taken?

How much inventory is needed to sustain each dollar of sales?

To what extent can lead time be reduced in order to lower the amount of inventory investment?

Can physical inventories be taken more frequently in order to reconcile them with reported inventories?

How can more accurate inventory reporting be achieved?

Conclusion

There are several basic conclusions. First, inventory control directly impacts profit performance through revenue stimulation and cost reduction. Second, inventory is controllable; management decisions determine the investment level and reordering policies. Third, inventory costs are not only significant, they are subject to change through management actions. Fourth, operating effectiveness is improved by sound inventory management, particularly in the areas of sales, production scheduling, transportation, and purchasing.

Applications to Small Business

Small business manufacturers, retailers, and distributors are all involved in inventory procurement and management. A large share of their investment consists of inventory, and these firms often carry thousands of different items. To succeed in these ventures, inventory management is a must. By not applying inventory control techniques, management faces lost sales and customers, work stoppages and interruptions, overinvestment, obsolete merchandise, and crisis management. Many of their vexing problems stem from improper inventory management. Stated positively, sound inventory management greatly increases profits.

The development of inventory control practices begins with a commitment to inventory management. Establishment of specific inventory control objectives provides a measurement yardstick. Once demand forecasts have been made, inventory levels and procedures can be developed to meet the demand. Understanding the linkages between inventory management and other units of the firm flags the inherent conflicts involved. More importantly, it underscores the need for developing an inventory action pattern because of the pervasiveness of inventory.

Software/Databases

Astra Inventory Control System, NEF Information Systems, Inc., 1414 Massachusetts Avenue, Boxborough, MA 01719. AICS allows users to identify slow moving or obsolete stock and to reduce the time required for a physical inventory.

Inventory Control for Small Business, Computerware, P.O. Box 668, Encinitas, CA 92024. Allows retailers and distributors to store and update cost and quantity information and produce the following reports: general inventory, profit margin, reorder points, and year-to-date monthly sales.

References/Sources

Adam, Everett E., Jr. and Ebert, Ronald J., *Production and Operations Management.* 2nd ed. Englewood Cliffs, NJ: Prentice-Hall, 1982. Chapters 15 and 16 are particularly valuable in presenting conceptual and practical models for inventory management.

American Production and Inventory Control Society. *APICS Bibliography of Articles, Books, Films, and Audio-Cassettes on Production and Inventory Control and Related Subjects.* Washington, DC: APICS, 1973.

Cooke, William P., *Quantitative Methods for Management Decisions.* New York:

McGraw-Hill, 1985. See Chapter 11 for inventory model development and application.

Epstein, Morris, "You Can Make Stockless Purchasing Work!" *Purchasing World* (April 1983): 50. The article emphasizes how to reduce inventories for production planning.

Hoeffler, El, "GM Tries Just-in-Time American Style," *Purchasing* (August 19, 1982): 67. Discusses reducing parts and raw materials inventories.

Lambert, Douglas M., *The Development of an Inventory Costing Methodology: A Study of the Costs Associated with Holding Inventory.* Chicago: National Council of Physical Distribution, 1975. An analysis of the holding costs of inventory and an attempt to determine the holding costs percentage of merchandise costs.

Plossl, George W. and Welch, W. Evert, *The Role of Top Management in the Control of Inventory.* Reston, VA: Reston Publishing, 1976.

Teplitz, Charles J., "Manufacturers Shift the Inventory Carrying Function," *Industrial Marketing Management,* 11 (1982): 225. The articles describe how purchasers are attempting to minimize their inventory holdings by pushing the burden back to their suppliers.

Turban, Efraim and Meredith, Jack R., *Fundamentals of Management Science.* Dallas, TX: Business Publications, Inc., 1977. Chapter 12 is an excellent source for understanding reorder models, economic lot size, quantity discounts, and service levels.

Related Topics and Terms
Base Stock, Customer Service Level, Demand Deviations During Lead Time, Economic Lot Size, Economic Order Quantity, Inventory Review Costs, Just-in-time Inventories, Kanban, Lead Time Variations, Lot Sizing, Materials Management, Materials Requirement Planning, Safety Stock, Storekeeping Units.

Warren Rose
Department of Business
Analysis & Research
Texas A&M University

IN-STORE SIGNING

Overview

The effectiveness of in-store signing is a much-debated topic. While some retail firms are heavy users of in-store signing, others choose to use signing to lesser degrees or not at all.

In-store signing is a form of point-of-purchase advertising. It involves the placement of a small sign, usually mechanically reproduced, next to a product to increase sales of the signed merchandise. The extent to which individual stores use this method of advertising varies greatly. However, as more retailers attempt to cut labor costs, a trend toward self-service operations is developing. Customers are typically left to select their merchandise with little assistance from scarce sales personnel. Packaging on many items has been removed or abbreviated, eliminating descriptions of the products or their functions. This leaves point-of-purchase signing as an important, but often overlooked, method of communicating sales messages to self-service customers.

Examples

In recent years, researchers at Brigham Young University, in cooperation with the Skaggs Institute of Retail Management, have been involved in three separate studies on point-of-purchase in-store signing. Their interest has grown out of the desire to aid retailers in improving sales volume through this medium.

Phase I

The first study conducted by the researchers by BYU was created to measure the effects of in-store signing in twelve different stores. The average daily sales rate of 33 products was monitored with and without signs for a four-week time period. Products were tested in department, drug/discount, home centers and women's specialty stores. A factorial rotated design was used to validate the test results. Results of this study indicated for all stores an average daily sales rate of 3.81 products without a sign and an average of 4.80 products per day with a descriptive sign. After results of the Phase I study were presented at the NRMA meetings in New York, interest developed in determining the difference in the effectiveness of price-only signing compared with signing that explains some of the product features or product benefits.

Phase II

The Phase II study was conducted to measure the effectiveness of no signs, price-only signs, and benefit signs. Three department stores were used with six identical products per store. Similar tight research controls were used and again a rotated sign condition existed which allowed for each product to alternate between all three sign conditions (no sign, price, and benefit) as well as a sale price and a regular price. This allowed for six sign/price conditions. These conditions and the results expressed again in average daily sales are:

Condition	Average Daily Sales	Change
No sign — regular price	7.66 units	---
Price sign — regular price	6.11 units	-20%
Benefits sign — regular price	7.81 units	+2%
No sign — sale price	15.35 units	---
Price-only sign — sale price	19.07 units	+24%
Benefit sign — sale price	22.96 units	+49%

The conclusion drawn from the Phase II study is that benefit signing is more effective than a no-sign or price-only sign for sale priced merchandise. Also, price-only signing should not be used for merchandise at its regular price.

Phase III

The Phase III study added a variable into the test which had been held constant in both Phase I and II. That variable was external advertising. In both previous tests, the products on sale had not been externally advertised. To test the effects of newspaper advertising and various sign conditions, another completely new study was designed.

The Phase III study was conducted in three discount stores. Six identical products were rotated through three signing conditions and two advertising conditions. All of the products were at sale prices. The conditions and the average daily sales rates are:

Condition	Average Daily Sales	Change
Unadvertised — no sign	8.33 units	---
Unadvertised — price only	7.42 units	-11%
Unadvertised — benefit sign	12.17 units	+46%
Advertised — no sign	9.08 units	---
Advertised — price only	10.83 units	+19%
Advertised — benefit sign	13.17 units	+45%

The results of Phase III clearly indicate that the advertising/benefit sign combination is an effective marketing technique.

Benefits

Results of Phase I indicated that signing could be effective in increasing the sales of products. Small printed signs placed next to products do increase sales. Once signing had been proven to be effective, refinements in signing could be tested. Phase II results clearly indicated that at regular price the benefit sign was slightly more effective than no sign condition but at regular price the price-only sign was less effective and actually had a decrease in sales. The consistency of sale priced or advertised with benefit signs items having 49%, 46%, and 45% increases in sales over the no-signed conditions is an obvious indication that benefit signing is a most effective merchandising tool that retailers can use.

Implementation

The creation of benefit statements for in-store signing should be the responsibility of the buyer or product manager. It is important to recognize the difference between features and benefits. The features are the physical specifications of products. For example, 100% cotton is a feature. The benefits of a 100% cotton fabric are that it is cool, comfortable, and easy to care for; in other words, benefits are the positive results provided by the features of a product. The challenge is to identify two or three of the most important benefits to use on the sign. The benefits provided by each feature, rather than features alone, should be listed. For example, the fabric may allow for *dress or sport use,* the size may be the *tapered body,* the collar style may be the *always in style button-down* collar, the type of permanent press may be for *wash, hang and wear care.*

The message placed on the sign should be created by the buyer or merchandiser most closely associated with the product. All signs should be consistent in style and printed with uniform lettering. A style manual, requisition forms and other documents are available from retail sign printing companies.

Evaluation

Retailers often wonder how many items in a store should be signed. The point when sign saturation is achieved has not been determined. A retailer may want to experiment and decide for himself when signing is most effective. It may be that signing can be used most effectively for products associated with consumption holidays such as Mother's Day, Valentine's or other special holidays where gift giving is appropriate. Every retailer can do his own basic test of a signing program to determine its effectiveness by selecting two similar products and displaying one with a benefit sign while the other receives either no sign or a price-only sign.

Conclusion

Signing is an important communication medium with many uses in today's competitive retail environment. Benefit signing is more effective than price-only signing. The elements of signing overload have not been researched, but the decision not to sign at all cannot be justified based upon prior research on in-store signing. It can and should be used by a wide range of retail organizations.

Applications to Small Business

Small retailers can effectively use in-store signing to increase sales levels. Two additional aspects of significance are that the retail owner or manager can develop the appropriate signs himself (there is no need to get outside help) and the cost involved with developing in-store signs is so low that the increased sales per dollar of cost is quite high.

Since the small retailer is frequently close to his customers, he will have a good opportunity to identify those benefits which are important to them and can incorporate these benefits into the in-store signing strategy. In addition, the small retailer will want to seriously consider the use of advertising with the in-store signing strategy.

References/Sources

The following articles discuss various types of in-store signing methods and their results.

"How In-Store Merchandising Can Boost Sales," *Progressive Grocer,* (November 10, 1971): 94-97.

"How to Turn P.O.P. into Sales Dollars," *Progressive Grocer,* 56 (June 16, 1977): 82-84.

"New Era in Point-of-Purchase: How Will Advertisers Benefit?" *Advertising Age* 265 (October 10, 1958): 21-24.

"Point of Purchase Material Raises Off Volume," *Quick Frozen Foods,* 30 (April 1968): 114.

"Point of Sales in Where Payoff Comes," *Advertising Age,* 30 (April 1968): 2-3.

"Research is Now Needed in Point of Signing Field," *Advertising Age,* 32 (October 1961): 69-70.

Russo, J. Edward, "Value of Unit Price Information," *Journal of Marketing Research,* 14 (May 1977): 193-195.

Woodside, Arch G., and Waddle, Gerald, "Sales Effects of Instore Advertising," *Journal of Advertising Research,* 15 (June 1975): 29-33.

Related Topics and Terms

Display, Impulse Good, Merchandising, Point-of-Purchase, Sales Promotion, Self-Service, Stock Turnover, Store Layout.

Patrick Kelly
Department of Marketing
Wayne State University

KEY ACCOUNTS

Overview

Many astute sales managers believe that the futures of their companies may ride with their key accounts. Developing a sound program for dealing with key accounts will result in a number of benefits for both individual sales personnel and their companies.

In identifying key accounts, five basic methods can be used. In the *profitability analysis* approach, a profit and loss statement is proposed for each account. Key accounts might be designated as those on which the supplier obtains a profit, or obtains a certain level of profit or profit margin (profit/sales).

The *gross margin* method involves subtracting the customer's cost of goods sold from the sales volume it provides to arrive at a gross margin figure. The gross margin is the dollars available for an account to cover the expenses involved with selling and servicing the account. A key account might be a customer which generates a certain level of gross margin or achieves a certain gross margin percentage (gross margin/sales).

The *sales volume* approach involves designating those customers which achieve a certain level of sales volume as key accounts. The figure established is believed to be large enough to cover the costs associated with producing and marketing the products purchased by customers.

The *20/80 analysis* method assumes that a small percentage of customers provide a company with a large percentage of its total sales volume. For example, one manufacturing company estimated that 10% of its customers provided it with 70% of its sales volume. The small nucleus of accounts which give a supplier a disproportionately large percentage of its sales volume are usually considered to be key accounts.

While a customer's present sales volume or profit may not meet minimal standards, its prospects for the future may justify it being regarded as a key account. In the *future potential* method, this decision will be made because of expected future growth, such as that accruing from the development of a new product or landing a large government contract.

Examples

There have been numerous companies which have identified key accounts and developed a program for servicing and retaining them. Some of these key account efforts include:

1. Sales managers for Ducommun Metals and Supply Company of Los Angeles calculate the profit generated by each account and use this figure as the basis for its key account strategy. The Chemicals and Plastics Group of Union Carbide follows the same approach.

438

2. Johnson & Johnson developed a key account program based on its finding that five per cent of its food store customers accounted for 48% of its total sales.
3. Sweda International, a manufacturer of electronic point-of-sale equipment for retailers, has instituted a key account effort stressing top-level participation and vigorous after-the-sale servicing of customers.
4. Pillsbury's key account program stresses close contact with top management of its top chain store grocery customers. Sony's key account program emphasizes calling on the central buying offices of its top retailers.

Benefits

Key accounts are important because they are the customers that account for most of a company's sales and profits. Losing several key accounts, therefore, can have disastrous effects on a company's bottom line. Key accounts also contribute heavily to the salesperson's income, especially if he is paid on a commission basis. The process of identifying key accounts points out not only those that are most valuable to a company and its sales force, but also those that are marginal accounts and not as important. If they know who the key and marginal customers are, management can decide which customers should receive the bulk of the sales force's time and effort and which should receive only minimal time and effort. A system for concentrating salespeople's calls on key accounts can be developed, and a plan for reducing (or even eliminating) calls on marginal accounts can be put into effect.

Another reason key accounts are important is that they are often leaders in their industries and thus may provide valuable feedback about market conditions, new products, and so on. Carolina Steel, for example, has 20 service center salesmen, each with 150 customers. The company considers feedback from customers to be extremely critical.

Implementation

When putting together a key account program there are a number of considerations which company executives need to observe.

After a company's key accounts have been identified, someone should be put in charge of them. The responsibilities of this person are (1) to develop strategies for selling key accounts, (2) to obtain top-level participation with key accounts, and (3) to follow up on the key account program. Since key accounts can make or break a firm, it is only logical that someone be assigned the full responsibility of handling key accounts. This person should have clout. For example, the senior vice president for customer relations at Union Carbide's Chemicals and Plastics Group is in charge of major accounts for seven operating departments with hundreds of industrial products. At Sweda International, the person in charge of key accounts carries the title of Vice President, Major Account Sales.

A comprehensive program must be developed for selling to key accounts. Key accounts are too important to a company to not be approached in a systematic fashion. The consumer sales division of Sony (television and other home entertainment products) "has a national accounts program directed mainly at buying offices of department store chains and home electronics dealers. Coupled with that is methodical follow-up by key account salesmen in the field." At Pillsbury, account managers for grocery products call on buying executives of grocery chains at the regional and headquarters levels.

One of the most important aspects of developing strategies for selling to key accounts is to determine whether the key accounts are receiving enough calls by the company's sales personnel. Companies that do some analysis of their customers will probably find that their key accounts are not receiving sufficient coverage.

As a first step in deciding whether key accounts are receiving enough calls, the company needs to determine what percentage of its total sales volume is represented by key accounts. Then it should see if the key accounts are receiving a similar percentage of the company's total sales calls.

Because key accounts are so important to a company's success, there is often a need for top-level management to become involved with them. Firms that purchase thousands, perhaps millions, of dollars' worth of products per year from a company often expect that company's top executives to spend some time with them. At Sweda International, it is not uncommon for the president to call on key accounts and close the sale. In addition, Sweda's regional sales executives find that they spend about 75% of their time on key accounts. Sony has a national accounts manager who calls on the central buying offices of retailers of its products. Each year, Pillsbury brings top management personnel of its grocery chain customers, such as Jewel Tea and Kroger, to its headquarters in Minneapolis to meet with its top executives. Pillsbury's chairman often is called upon to demonstrate how Pillsbury can meet the needs of these large food chains.

Evaluation

A company's key account program should be evaluated in terms of the objectives specified by the firm's executives for the program. Specific standards of performance should accompany these objectives and the results of the firm's key account efforts should be compared to the expected standards. Below are some critical questions to ask in evaluating companies' key account programs:

1. Was a greater sales volume obtained from key accounts?
2. Was the net profit from key accounts increased?
3. Was the gross margin from key accounts increased?
4. Has a greater percentage of key accounts been retained?
5. Has the average order size of key accounts increased?
6. What percentage of emergency shipments to key accounts arrived on time?
7. Was the order cycle length for key accounts reduced?

8. Was the reliability of shipments to key accounts increased?
9. Was the number of key account complaints reduced?
10. Did sales personnel make their assigned number of calls on key accounts?

Conclusion

Because of the crucial significance of key accounts to a company's bottom line, their business cannot be taken for granted. Therefore, it is recommended that companies develop a structured, formal program to deal with key customers. The program should consist of five major elements. First, key accounts need to be identified. Second, someone in the firm needs to be given the overall responsibility for key accounts. Third, strategies for selling to key accounts should be developed. Fourth, top-level participation in calling on key accounts needs to be obtained. Fifth, the key accounts program needs to be periodically monitored in order to assess the extent to which it is achieving its objectives.

Applications to Small Business

Small companies tend to have fewer accounts than do larger companies. Yet, like their bigger counterparts, their customers are very likely to represent a pronounced 20/80 situation; that is, a handful of customers accounting for a large percentage of the small business' total percentage of sales. For a small operation to lose several large customers would be disastrous; indeed, such a development would seriously damage the firm's profitability and may, in fact, jeopardize its continued existence. Thus, small companies need to have in place a well-designed, key account program.

Because of the limited amount of personnel available in many small businesses, the key account effort will probably need to be headed up by the company's owner, general manager, or chief executive officer. Much of this person's responsibility should include making the actual sales calls on key accounts as well as maintaining subsequent contact with them through service and other follow-up calls.

Small businesses are not as likely to have marketing information systems as larger operations. In general, the costs involved may be prohibitive. However, it is necessary that some type of system be available that will allow executives or owners of small companies to identify key accounts so that a program can be effected to return their business.

Software/Databases

Flexware Sales Analysis Systems, Microfirm Corporation, 1504 East Valley, Industry, CA 91746. The Flexware Sales Analysis System is a good source to use to start developing a key account program because it provides the user with sales analysis by specific customers.

References/Sources

Everett, Martin, "Why the Future of Your Company May Ride With Its Key Accounts," *Sales Management* (May 19, 1975). Discusses the significance of key accounts and presents excellent recommendations for developing a key account program.

"Getting (and Using) Good Feedback from Salesmen," *Industry Week* (January 19, 1976). Stresses the role that key accounts can play in providing feedback about developments in their industry.

"Phone Rings True as Answer to Covering Small Accounts," *Industrial Distribution* (February 1972). Recommends that telephone marketing be used as the answer to efficiently handling small accounts.

Wolfe, Harry Dean, and Albaum, Gerald, "Inequality in Products, Orders, Customers, Salesmen, and Sales Territories," *Journal of Business* (July 1962). An excellent study which shows the existence of key accounts through the use of 20/80 analysis.

Related Topics and Terms

Gross Margin, Marginal Accounts, Marketing Audit, Marketing Information Systems, Profit and Loss Statement, Profitability Analysis, Twenty/Eighty Analysis.

Richard T. Hise
Department of Marketing
Texas A&M University

KEY BUYING INFLUENCE

Overview

Key Buying Influence (KBI) denotes those persons in a household or organization exerting the most influence on product purchases. Identification of the Key Buying Influence, important to product designers, engineers, advertising and sales personnel, is often difficult. Household buying influence is partly idiosyncratic and partly a result of social roles; therefore, the dominant pattern depends on the particular good and the situation. Organizational patterns depend on the product, the effect of the purchase, the structure of the buying firm, and informal power relationships within the buying organization. Nevertheless, identification of, and subsequent marketing efforts directed at the Key Buying Influence(s), are essential to sales success.

Examples

Households. Generally people choose the products which are solely for personal use, even though other members of the household may actually pay for them in the store. Such items include shampoo, cereal, and shaving gear. Other household purchases affect other people and the importance of one of these other family members is often overlooked. For example, a man may be the major consumer of beer, but the woman may be the actual buyer. The actual beer drinker may like 3 brands so the purchaser may determine which brand is really chosen, motivated by the point-of-purchase display, the salesperson, the comparative prices, and her own awareness of different brands. It is in the interest of the beer companies, then, to direct some portion of their promotional efforts at the purchaser as well as the true consumer in order to generate sales. Point-of-purchase materials need to attract the attention of the Key Buying Influence, who in this case, is not the obvious person. More costly or important items—cars, appliances, financial planning—are quite often joint household decisions, although some household members may specialize in information seeking and others as the final deciders. In new car purchases, some research shows that wives tend to do preliminary shopping and make decisions on style and color, while husbands tend to make brand and price decisions.

Organizations. Organizations, like households, may vary greatly in how decisions are actually made. A large capital goods investment may require information and decisions from many levels in the firm. A corporate aircraft order for a major airline may begin with engineers and pilots representing both firms meeting to discuss plane design. If the discussions are satisfactory, then the representatives of the buying firm become key influences affecting the planning and operations managers who are also key decision makers for this purchase by this company. A small airline, on the other hand, simply may choose from existing plane designs and fewer people may be involved.

The purchase of copier paper presents a very different set of actions and circumstances. In a large organization with a central purchasing office, the purchasing agent is the Key Buying Influence. The major decision is the selection of the vendor as there is usually brand switching. With a decentralized purchasing function, the situation is similar to the one of the small firm. Then, users may be the Key Buying Influence for both the brand and the vendor. Smaller quantities and less standardized buying schedules are likely to pertain.

Benefits

Selling requires persuasion of the Key Buying Influence. However, research shows that sales personnel often misidentify who that is. One survey of more than 4,000 executives in a wide variety of industries showed that 61% had seen *no* salespeople in the previous quarter even though they were Key Buying Influence for 1 to 99 different products bought by their firms. Understanding the behavior of firms in an industry and knowing typical decision processes is a necessity for improved sales. Access to Key Buying Influence doesn't guarantee sales, but lack of access certainly minimizes sales.

Clarifying social roles in households means that common assumptions about decision-making have to be rethought. Indeed, sales may be lost where a household member resents the implication that he is not important in the purchase. In 1955, surveys showed that husbands were dominant in car purchase decisions. A new study in 1983 found this true in only one-third as many households. Children are major brand influences for household purchases of snacks, toothpaste, toys, and restaurants. Thus, a firm needs to adopt its policies and train sales personnel just to gain access and acceptance. Failure to do so has severe consequences. Many observers attribute Colgate's gain in market share to the introduction of a new package (the pump) which appealed to children who are the Key Buying Influence in nearly half of all households for toothpaste.

The other benefit, of course, is greater cost-efficiency for a seller, as resources are allocated where they are most effective. Advertising is directed at those making the decision. Salespeople talk to those most responsible and get leads earlier.

Implementation

The first step in determining the probable Key Buying Influence is to understand the purchase process and to assess those likely to be most dominant at each phase. A second step is to determine the blend of influences as they will affect the final outcome of a purchase.

Household. A household may go through seven stages in a purchase situation. At each stage one or several members may be dominant: need identification, information search, criteria establishment, evaluation, purchase, consumption, and disposal.

These stages apply to all but the most routine, habitual product choices. Need identification is the recognition that a purchase might improve some aspect of household operations. Information searches include seeking facts about both product and vendor. Criteria establishment is when a potential purchaser determines what aspects of product/seller matter most. Evaluation of brands and vendor occurs when the criteria are used. Purchase, consumption, and disposal are self-explanatory; they may occur over extended or short periods of time.

For each new buying situation, previous consumption and disposal experience may enter into the evaluation, as will expected use and disposal. The possible difference between shopper and user, or the necessity for joint use of a purchase, means that the Key Buying Influence may not be apparent at the actual sales transaction. Studies of family decision making have identified four marital arrangements for purchase decisions: husband dominant, wife dominant, syncratic (joint) and autonomic (idiosyncratic). Joint decision-making is more likely when: the purchase is seen as involving high risk, when the purchase is important to the whole family, when there are few time pressures, and in certain demographic groups: younger families, childless households, and middle income families. More families now report joint decisions across a variety of products than were reported thirty and ten years ago: life insurance, automobiles, household products. At the same time, research by *stages* of the purchase decision shows that wives, husbands, and children tend to dominate different phases of the decision: wives tend to have more influence at the need identification and information stages, whereas husbands tend to exert more influence over the purchase choice. Children tend to initiate and influence brand choice for products for which they are the primary consumers. The older the children, the more likely they are to be Key Buying Influences. In joint purchasing decisions, as well as in autonomic buying, husbands and wives tend to focus on different aspects of the product with each placing different priorities on certain attributes.

Organizations. Organizations, by their nature, usually have more structured buying patterns than households. However, the systems are not uniform across products or even in the same firm. Analysis of buying behavior has resulted in two classifications (by type of buying experience and by organizational structure) which enable sellers to generalize about *who* buys.

The three types of buying situations identified are called: the straight rebuy, the modified rebuy, and the new purchase. A straight rebuy is a situation where a firm is reordering the same product in the same circumstances. Supplies are often purchased this way. A modified rebuy occurs when a product is not automatically or regularly purchased. Information on new vendors or brands may be sought out. A new purchase occurs whenever the product is wholly new to the firm or when circumstances have changed significantly from the last time a similar product was bought. As one might expect, the number of influences increases as the purchase becomes less routine. Also, and very important, the more the purchase is viewed as complex and new, the more likely it is that those involved in influencing the purchase are higher in status and power in the organization. The degree to which an organization's purchasing is centralized also affects the number and type of influences.

Corey (1978) found that centralized systems tend to enforce standardization in product requirement, reduce the number of possible suppliers and give purchasing agents more direct authority, thus, in effect, making the members of the purchasing department the Key Buying Influence. Organizations with decentralized systems show greater variation in who makes decisions and exhibit more variation in the standards for vendor and product selection. For example, centralized systems stress price more, while decentralized systems demonstrate more concern with customized products and responsive service.

The impact of the purchase on operations also determines who will be a likely Key Buying Influence. Generally, the more risk, financial or other, the more visible, and the more change in operations a purchase involves, the more likely it is that Key Buying Influences will come from outside a purchasing center. Bonoma (1982) has identified six types of buyers, all of whom can influence the final purchase choice: the initiator of the purchase; the user of what is purchased; the gatekeeper who enhances or restricts information and the evaluation of information; the influencer(s), who may be technical specialists or important figures in the organization; the decider, the one who decides and pushes through a final choice; and the purchaser, the one who processes the purchase. Johnson and Bonoma (1981) surveyed purchase decisions in 62 organizations, finding that typically the six roles were filled by four departments (always including engineering and purchasing), three management levels, and seven individuals when capital goods were purchased.

Evaluation

Results of sales calls and sales should be tagged and tracked to determine the effects of targeting to KBIs. The data system designed to organize information about how decisions are made and who makes them, should be constantly revised. Comparisons should be conducted, not only on a before and after basis, but also by organizational type, product type, size, and salesperson. The compensation structure should reflect quality information as well as sales to encourage the development of the program.

Conclusion

Surveys of influence on buying decisions generally demonstrate that purchasing managers and agents believe real buying influence resides elsewhere in the firm. Observational research indicates that purchasing agents tend to influence the choice of vendor, while other managers influence product choice and criteria for purchase.

Applications to Small Business

Locating and selling to Key Buying Influences is especially important for smaller firms. Unlike large, well-known businesses, they cannot rely on the buyer's awareness of their products and services. They must work harder and smarter—that means increasing KBIs' knowledge and gaining access to them to sell. Lacking the large data and research staff resources of large firms, close attention to typical decision patterns in their industries is crucial to business success.

Implementing a Key Buying Influence directed sales effort may start through training of salespersons in ways of recognizing and determining how organizations/households operate, knowing typical patterns, and recording information on the Key Buying Influence in company records. A second step might be to purchase a database listing Key Buying Influences in a firm by product. This enables salespeople to get around their usual reliance on purchasing departments or chance social acquaintances. Tracking the results of such a program should reveal information helpful to total operations: effect on sales, quality of information about competitors and job satisfaction/improved employee performance.

Software/Databases

D&B Million Dollar Directory. Dun's Marketing Services, Parsippany, New Jersey. Provides information on 115,000 U. S. companies with a net worth of $500,000 or more. Addresses, SIC codes, annual sales, and number of employees available for each firm, as well as the names of individuals holding 25 different executive/managerial positions.

References/Sources

Banville, G.R. and Dornoff, R.J., "Industrial Source Selection Behavior—An Industry Study," *Industrial Marketing Management* 2,3 (June 1973). Lengthy, but useful study of vendor selection within firms.

Bonfield, E.H., "Perception of Marital Roles in Decision Processes: Replication and Extension," *Advances in Consumer Research.* Ann Arbor, MI: Association for Consumer Research, 1978, V: 300-307. Provides data on how decisions are made in households for a wide variety of products.

Bonoma, T.V., Dalton, G., and Johnson, W.J., *Industrial Buying Behavior,* Report No. 77 177. Cambridge, MA: Marketing Science Institute (December 1977). Survey of patterns within firms and industries. Includes a section on buying influence and good bibliography.

Bonoma, T.V., and Shapiro, B., *Segmenting the Industrial Market.* Lexington, MA: Lexington Books, 1983. Contains one chapter specifically on buying behavior and Key Buying Influences.

Cooley, J.R., Jackson, D.W., and Ostrtom, L.R., "Analyzing the Relative Power of Participants in Industrial Buying Decisions," *Contemporary Marketing Thought—1977 Educator's Proceedings.* Chicago: American Marketing Association, 1977, pp. 243-246. A study of how buying influence occurs.

Cunningham, Isabella C.M. and Green, Robert T., "Purchasing Roles in U.S. Family, 1955 and 1973," *Journal of Marketing,* 30 (October 1974): 61-64. Comparative study high-lighting changes in family decision-making over time.

Davis, Harry L., "Decision Making within the Household," *Journal of Consumer Research,* 2 (March, 1976): 241-260. Review article of research on household buying.

Doyle, P., and Hutchinson, P., "Individual Differences in Family Decision Making," *Journal of the Market Research Society* 15 (October 1973): 193-206. Contains suggestions for identifying patterns of decision making and segmentation based on those patterns.

"Finding the Real Buying Influence," *Industrial Distribution* (June 1977): 33-39. Managerial focus which provides good guidelines for locating Key Buying Influences.

Gronhaug, K., "Autonomous vs. Joint Decisions in Organizational Buying," *Industrial Marketing Management* 4 (1975): 265-271. Distinguishes situations where many influences may be important from those where only one or a few influences are important.

Johnson, W.J., and Bonoma, T.V., "Buying Center Structure and Dynamics," *Journal of Marketing* 45 (Summer 1981): 143-156. Looks at the effects of centralized purchasing.

Komarovsky, Mira, "Class Differences in Family Decision-Making on Expenditures," *Household Decision-Making.* New York: New York University Press, 1961, pp. 255-265. Useful in sales training for guidelines in evaluating how families are likely to act.

Luffman, G.A., "Industrial Buyer Behavior: Some Aspects of the Search Process," *European Journal of Marketing* 8,2 (1975): 73-107. Investigates how information affects the level of influence and when that influence is important.

Patchen, M., "The Locus and Basis of Influence on Organizational Decision," *Behavior and Human Performance* (1974): 195-221. Guidelines for determining who may be a Key Buying Influence.

Walsh, C.E., "Reaching Those 'Hidden' Buying Influences," *Industrial Marketing* (October 1961): 164-167. Tips to managers.

Related Topics and Terms
Consumer Behavior, Family Decision Making, Purchasing Agent.

Sharon Thach
Department of Marketing
Cleveland State University

LATE MAJORITY

Overview

If the frequency of adoption of a new product is plotted against time, the result is a bell-shaped curve. The curve can conveniently be divided into 5 sections, corresponding to the five classifications of adopters: innovators, early adopters, early majority, late majority and laggards. The late majority is the fourth group of consumers to adopt a product. They constitute approximately 34% of all of those who will ever adopt the product.

The late majority are influenced in their buying behavior to one extent or another by all of the other adopter categories except the laggards, while in their turn they serve as a major influence on the buying behavior of the laggards.

The late majority are just behind the flow of major trends, fashions and tastes of their social system. They tend to be çautious and skeptical, weighing innovations slowly and carefully before adopting them. Their income and educational level tend to be a little lower than average, while their age is a little higher. Ultimate adoption of a new product, or technical innovation, is often the result of economic necessity and social pressure rather than creativity and curiosity on their part. While the late majority are not nearly so socially isolated as the laggards, they are among the least socially active and visible members of their social system.

Nevertheless, the late majority do constitute just over 1/3 of all of those who will ever adopt a product, and are as a result, of great interest to the marketer. Furthermore, because of their basic conservatism in adoption and consumption, the group represents a very stable market once a product is successfully introduced.

Examples

Bobbie is a 50 year old meat packer. He lives in a well-kept but modest 3-bedroom home. He drives a well-kept 13 year old car (because he can put regular, rather than lead free gasoline in it, and thus save a little money each time he fills up). Bobbie works hard, rarely takes a day off from the factory, and likes to go out bowling with the "boys" every Wednesday and Saturday night. He dream is when he retires, to buy a new "John-boat" and spend his days pursuing his hobby, fishing. Although he can only get away once or twice every other week to do some actual fishing, Bobbie spends most of his evenings thinking about it, reading about it, or else wandering around the sporting goods section of one of the three large discount stores near his home, drooling over "what he *would* get!" One thing that Bobbie does spend money on in his trips to these stores is fishing lures—he spends at least $5-$10 every week on an assortment of lures. However, Bobbie cannot bring himself to spend his hard earned money on one type of lure. Although the financial investment is relatively small, Bobbie just will not buy the newer "gimmicky" lures—he's just not the convinced that they work.

O.J. Walton is the local representative for one of the largest fishing goods manufacturers in the country; he is also an acquaintance of Bobbie's. It has come to O.J.'s attention recently, through a passing conversation with the manager of the sporting goods section of one of the local hardware stores, that Bobbie had never purchased any of the line of so called "Hi-tech" lures carried by O.J.'s company. O.J. and the store manager laughed as they talked about it, but O.J.'s thoughts took a serious turn as he walked out of the store. "Why didn't Bobbie buy any of the lures?" "Bobbie was a seasoned fisherman; did this mean that there was something wrong with them?" After some investigation and a chat with a professor from the business school, O.J. became convinced that the problem lay in the fact that Bobbie belonged to the "late majority" adoption group. Realizing that skepticism, and a high degree of perceived risk on Bobbie's part were his main obstacles, he developed the following plan. He knew many of Bobbie's fishing buddies, and he began to move among them, deliberately ridiculing the fact that Bobbie didn't use any "Hi-tech" or "Modern" type lures. He coined a new nickname for Bobby— "grandpa"—and it wasn't long before everyone picked up on the name. Next, he began stopping by Bobbie's house in the late afternoon before Bobbie arrived home from work, to leave "free samples" of the "Hi-tech" lures with Bobbie's wife. His explanation was always that he wanted to get Bobbie's opinion on them. By the month's end, Bobbie had caved in to the double attack of friendly ridicule and "free gifts." He began investigating and trying the lures on his own initiative. Armed with this success, O.J. approached his company headquarters with a strategy to move the late majority to adopt the "High-tech" lures earlier: a series of advertisements which played on mild, friendly ridicule, buttressed by a program of intensive, free sampling. By year's end, O.J.'s strategy had been such a success, that he was promoted to regional manager.

"Pierre's Kitchen" is a small chain of franchised fast food restaurants in the Southwest. Their format is meant to be 19th century French, and their menu is exclusively Cajun. While Cajun food has been a favorite for years in Louisiana, "Pierre's Kitchen" is the first major attempt to bring it out of that region in a fast food format.

Ed Aikin, the Marketing director for the corporation has been receiving a number of calls and letters from disgruntled franchises. Their complaint has always been the same: while many people have been curious about "Pierre's Kitchen," there seems to be a large section of the population which has no interest, and cannot be enticed even to look inside the restaurant. Ed conducted a major marketing research project in order to investigate the problem. What he found was that a large proportion of the people who would not try "Pierre's Kitchen" were slightly older than the population mean, with lower incomes and educational levels. Furthermore, the study showed that while the major portion of this group was not socially isolated by any means, they were not leaders. They tended to be cautious, skeptical and conscious of the risks associated with trying new things. Ed concluded that the large portion of the group in his study were "late majority." Armed with this information, he began to put together a set of recommendations for a marketing plan to get these people into the restaurants. His plan, on the positive side, involved reducing the perceived risk, answering skepticism, and lowering the financial outlay and, on the negative side, introducing a mildly ridiculing advertising theme directed explicitly to the late majority. In particular, Ed recommended a 50% off couponing program two nights per week, backed by a substantially lower pricing structure for a limited time which undercut other fast food restaurants on a local basis. Furthermore, a series of informational-type hand bills were to be printed which explained exactly what Cajun food was, its history and traditions, as well as some information regarding "Pierre's Kitchen" itself. Finally, he suggested a rather clever series of television advertisements in a "talk-show" format, with close-in, tight face shots. The interviewer, on discovering that the person has not been to Pierre's Kitchen, begins to make light fun of him—the music gets louder and louder as the camera jerks to closer and closer shots, until suddenly, the music stops, the person faces the camera and says "all right, all right, I'll try Pierre's Kitchen!" Ed's strategy was adopted by corporate headquarters, and implemented. A follow-up study the following year indicated success: a large portion of the late majority group were either regular customers, or had at least tried Pierre's Kitchen once.

The identification and targeting of the pertinent group of late majority consumers can give a company a substantial edge over the competition. First of all, while the late majority may lack glamour, it is substantial, and can be a major factor in gaining and holding market share. Secondly, since the late majority are relatively conservative and are reluctant to try new things, once they have been effectively reached, they do constitute a very stable market which is not subject to the winds of style and fashion to quite the same degree as some of the other groups. This is of particular importance when products begin to enter the late maturity and decline stages of the product life cycle.

Benefits

Depending on the type of product, most companies must decide whether they will attempt to attract the 34% late majority. If their product line is comprised of standard consumer items for which there is strong competition, then it is imperative that the company develop a late majority strategy. If, on the other hand, the company produces high fashion or high tech products, then promotional money might be better spent on the early majority until the product has been firmly established in the market place. One of the benefits of considering the late majority is in determining how frequently the company must develop new products in order to capture its goal of market share. Understanding the late majority in relation to particular products can force a number of issues pertaining to product development and advertising.

Implementation

Putting together a marketing program which targets the late majority is no easy matter, and effective programs require a number of steps.

The first step is to identify exactly who the pertinent late majority group is. It is most important to be able to define the group in concrete, relevant terms, otherwise the recommendation of specific actions becomes meaningless. The description of the group can take on a number of forms: age, geographical location, occupation, and income. Obtaining such information is not so easy as it may seem, but it can be achieved using a number of approaches. By conducting extensive surveys of the current customer base, and comparing it with the population at large, it may be possible to identify "holes" in the market served. By using pre-existing marketing lists which seem to coincide to a large degree with the group of interest, or by simply equating the late majority with that group which is slightly older, slightly less well paid, and slightly less well educated than the population at large, identification is possible. While this identification is both necessary and helpful, it is by no means exact.

The second step, once the late majority has been identified, is to pin-point and articulate their specific reservations, risk aversiveness, and fears relating to the product of interest. Skepticism is the key to understanding what makes the late majority late in adopting new products. The late majority is reluctant to adopt a new product because they are doubtful that it will be what it claims. This doubt can take a number of different forms; the job of the marketer is to understand and articulate them.

The third step is to identify the *early adopters* and *early majority groups* in the social system of interest. The late majority tend to be influenced in their adoption behavior by these groups. Identifying the groups makes it possible to develop themes and stereotypical characters for advertisements which will have the greatest potential to move the late majority towards the adoption of the product in question in a shorter time.

The fourth step is to identify effective channels of communication. Unless one is able to communicate the marketing message to the group, efforts will have been in vain. While the late majority are not "main-stream" or "state-of-the-art" in terms of their media preferences, neither are they isolated and singular like the laggards. Media vehicles which have a long established reputation for a solid, middle-of-the-road editorial tone should be evaluated for their possible congruity with the group. Such vehicles might include local newspapers and local T.V. news programs. In the absence of a clear, efficient media vehicle, it may not be out of the question, given the natural size of this target market, to use a mass media approach with the focus of the message remaining on the late majority.

The fifth step is to develop a marketing plan which puts all of the previous steps into a rational, realistic strategy. Because of the characteristics of the group, a "push-pull" approach may prove to be useful. That is to say, the group should be accelerated along their normal adoption process using a coordinated "push-pull" effort. This effort would, on the one hand, entice, or "pull" them along using information, financial inducements and general risk reduction methods, and on the other hand, "push" them with mild, good-natured ridicule from stereotypical characters of the early adopter or early majority adoption groups. The "pulls" should be real, tangible, measurable attempts to reduce and dissolve their skepticism. The "push" should be light-hearted criticism of their "fuddy-duddiness" so as to overcome their natural conservatism.

Evaluation

The late majority is a substantial and lucrative group, with much to offer the thoughtful marketer. Careful planning and implementation can result in handsome rewards. However, the implementation of such marketing strategies necessitates an evaluation process. *First of all,* the marketing decision makers should constantly evaluate the nature and composition of their customer group. This evaluation, as mentioned earlier, will reveal "holes" in the customer group served vis-à-vis the population of the social group as a whole. Once such "holes" have been identified as *late majority*, and when a strategy to reach them has been implemented, they should be monitored for signs that they are coming over to the product, and that the marketing strategy has been successful. Secondly the group should be monitored for signs that their skepticism has been overcome, in order that the financial inducements, risk reduction mechanisms and ridiculing ads can be rolled-back. Once the late majority climb on board, the strategy should change to retaining them.

Conclusion

The late majority may be the most difficult of the adopter categories to identify. While their behavior is distinctive, their appearance and characteristics are not. They are only slightly older, slightly less educated and make slightly less money than the population average. They are not reactionary, but cautious and doubting, and just a little late in getting to the station. Conceptually, the idea of the late majority has great appeal, and has value as an orienting framework for planning purposes.

Applications to Small Business

The value of the late majority concept is not so much that it gives the small business person something he can readily see and measure, as it is that it provides a framework for thinking about certain types of marketing problems. Even though the concept is difficult to operationalize, it can provide insights into such questions as: 1) What groups should be targeted as the product enters the late mature stage of the product life cycle? 2) How can new products be made more appealing to large segments of the market? 3) How can a weak growth stage of a new product be pre-empted with latter adopters?

Software/Databases

PC/NEWPROD. New Product Planning Model, Applied Decision System, 33 Hayden Avenue, Lexington, MA 02173. Allows for five-year projections of sales volume and profit based on marketers' estimates of consumer, retail and wholesale behavior. As many as five repeat user groups with differing characteristics can be defined. Trial, repeat purchase rate and units per purchase are the key input variables required.

References/Sources

Engel, James F., Kegerreis, Robert J., Blackwell, Roger D., "Word of Mouth Communication by the Innovator," *Journal of Marketing* (July 1969). Deals with the extent to which innovators communicate information about new products to potential purchasers.

Hise, Richard T., "New Product Acceptance Overlap: A Measure of General Innovativeness," *Akron Business and Economic Review* (Summer 1971). Reports a study about the extent consumers are innovators of multiple products.

Ostlund, Lyman E., "Identifying Early Buyers," *Journal of Advertising Research* (April 1972). Describes the characteristics of innovators of new products.

Robertson, Thomas S., "The Process of Innovation Diffusion and Innovation," *Journal of Marketing* (January 1967). Discusses the general process through which innovations are diffused throughout a social system.

Robertson, Thomas S., and Meyers, James H., "Personality Correlates of Opinion Leadership and Innovative Buying Behavior," *Journal of Marketing Research* (May 1967). This study examines personality by factors which are associated with innovativeness.

Rogers, Everett M., *Diffusion of Innovations*. New York: The Free Press, 1962. This is the classic work on the topic of diffusion of innovations. Chapters 6 and 7 discuss adopters of innovations.

Related Topics and Terms

Adoption Process, Diffusion Process, Early Adopters, Early Majority, Innovator, Laggard, Late Majority, Nonadopter.

Terry Clark
Department of Marketing
University of Notre Dame

LEASED DEPARTMENT

Overview

Some retailers lease space within their stores to individuals or firms who operate these leased departments independent of their host stores. Because leased departments often must conform to all store policies and practices, retail customers typically are not aware of which departments are leased. Licensed departments, as they are sometimes called, are most commonly found within department, discount and variety stores. Merchandise lines sold through leased departments include, but are not limited to, shoes, fine jewelry, millinery and cameras. Beauty shops, restaurants and watch repair shops are also among those frequently leased out. Leasing of departments within retail stores can provide benefits as well as opportunities for lessor (the retail store), lessee (the leased department operator) and store customers alike.

Examples

With many merchandise lines, leasing is a quite common arrangement. For example, it has been reported that about 65% of all major department stores lease their shoe department(s) to outside parties. Furthermore, leased departments represented from 5 to 8 percent of total retail sales in 1983.

Numerous examples of successful leasing partnerships can be cited. Platt Music of Torrence California leases electronics departments in over 100 department stores including May Company, Diamond's and Marshall Field stores. Adam, Meldrum and Anderson of Buffalo leases various shoe departments to Wohl Company. Intelligent Electronics of Philadelphia leases their Todays Computer departments from Strawbridge and Clothier, Kaufmann's Department stores and others. Evans, Inc., of Chicago operates leased departments in Shillito, Stix, Baer and Fuller, Davison's and Sakowitz department stores, as well as others. In addition, it is the world's largest retail furrier selling through its own Evans' Blum's Vogue in Chicago and Rosendorf-Evans in Washington, D.C.

In an innovative move, Goodyear Tire & Rubber Company, the nation's leading tire manufacturer, has negotiated to lease retail tire and service centers from Gimbels, Broadway Southwest, Emporium Capwell and Weinstock department stores. Oriental rug departments have also been successfully leased. The Mink Company of Philadelphia leases space from John Wanamaker stores, as well as Woodward and Lothrop and Stewart's department stores, to sell orientals, broadlooms and area rugs.

Benefits

There are numerous advantages to leased department arrangements. From the perspective of retail store customers, leased departments enable them to purchase merchandise at their favored stores which might not otherwise be available to them due, perhaps, to its low turnover. Leasing may also allow retail managers to offer better selection and variety to their customers in merchandise lines that typically have rather limited assortments.

For leased department operators, leasing space from established stores allows them to share in the goodwill and customer franchise that has been developed, perhaps, over decades. Their traffic and customer drawing power is also greatly magnified since all store customers potentially view and are exposed to leased department merchandise. Likewise, any store advertising benefits the leased department, whether or not the lessee's merchandise is included in the ads. Finally, leasing enables the lessee to spread his operating and overhead costs (such as lighting and heating) across a number of other store-owned departments.

Leasing offers several important benefits to lessors:

(1) Inventory investment is reduced since the leased departments own their own merchandise.
(2) Assortment and depth are increased above that which might exist if the store itself owned the department.
(3) Highly-trained, expert employees who are often difficult to obtain are available through leased department operators in such specialized merchandise lines as furs, shoes, jewelry, optical, and oriental rugs.
(4) Store traffic and sales volume can be favorably impacted through leasing; leased departments on average contribute about 7% of department store sales and about 11% of specialty store sales.
(5) Shared expenses in advertising, heating and cooling and parking services create economies of scale cost savings for retail stores.

Thus, from the standpoint of all participants, including store customers, leasing offers many benefits in retail store operations.

Implementation

Leasing arrangements vary greatly market by market and between merchandise lines. Typically, however, leased operators pay between 8% and 17% of their sales in fees to stores with which they do business. In shoe department leasing, for example, fees generally run between 13% and 14% of sales. Often, leasing fees are negotiated based on store traffic or volume. The amount of space leased also varies greatly. Platt Music reports leasing space ranging from 2,000 to 15,000 square feet from May Company, Diamond's and Emporium Capwell stores for their electronics departments.

One common feature among leasing arrangements is that of operational consistency with store image and policy. Generally, no signs are used to identify a department as being leased to an outside operator. Leased departments also are required to abide by store policies regarding services offered, (such as credit, delivery, layaway, and refunds), hours of operation and pricing. Advertising must also be compatible with that of the store as a whole, including media employed, frequency and copy. Leased departments, too, often must abide by store tradition with respect to storewide sales, both in terms of frequency of occurrence, and markdown percentages. Lessors, however, hire and train their own personnel, and pay them according to their own scales. Often, wages and salaries among leased department employees are higher than those of other store employees, hence they are kept secret to avoid creating ill-will.

Evaluation

The success of a leased department can in part be measured by its profitability but should not be limited to that narrow a scope. From a profit perspective, the most important consideration is whether the same space within the department store environment could be put to better use, either by the store itself or by leasing to another vendor. A related question is whether the existing leased department would be more profitable if located in a different part of the department store. For traditional merchandise, such as shoes or cameras, many statistics are available to measure the success of those departments. For less "tried and true" merchandise, such as computers, where there is strong competition from specialty stores, the profitability must be measured in conjunction with the overall goals of the department store.

A department store's philosophy about concentrated or target marketing vs. undifferentiated marketing can affect how a leased department is evaluated. Leased departments, which offer a department store an opportunity to be more specialized as to type and quality of merchandise, might contribute more to the store's overall performance than the actual profit which that leased department contributes to the balance sheet. Luxury furs, for example, might return a lower percentage than cameras, but the quality of buyer attracted by a luxury fur department could increase sales in related departments owned by the department store, such as better dresses and evening wear. In other words, a leased department contributes to the marketing mix, and must be evaluated both autonomously and in context of larger goals.

Conclusion

The history of leasing among retailers in the nation is, indeed, a long one. One of the earliest successful partnerships was that between Macy's department store and the Strauss family in 1896, which is widely credited with having rescued Macy's from failure. In that same year, the Emporium and the Golden Rule, both of San Francisco, in a novel arrangement, leased out all of their departments to then-leading merchandisers. The short-lived venture failed in 1897, however.

Later, after World War I, and again after the great depression of the 1930s, leasing made great advancements in the retail industry as a whole, but particularly within shoe departments.

Currently, within select merchandise lines, there is somewhat of a lessee's market, and operators of these departments can be very demanding in their terms. Alternatively, there has been a recent trend whereby many discount stores are re-acquiring former leased departments, as did Woolco beginning in 1980, in order to retain revenues and profits themselves.

Leasing, as a whole, is expected to "continue to play a small but significant part in retailing until the 1990s." Moreover, there are evolving some innovative leasing arrangements, such as that for Goodyear Tire and Rubber Company, in which space is being leased to medical, dental and legal clinics in order to improve store volume and traffic. Thus, leasing continues to be a viable option in many types of retail operations.

The growth of leased departments within retail stores was strongest during the 1960's. At that time over 20% of discount store departments were leased to outside vendors. The use of leased departments since then has been on the decline. Today, for example, less that 10% of store departments are leased out. Despite this general decline, leasing arrangements continue to make sense for many types of retailers under varying circumstances. Sears, for example, presently leases over 200 of their service station operations. Many specialized services and departments, such as restaurants and watch repair shops, continue to be leased and the expectation is that these agreements will remain in effect for the foreseeable future. Given the benefits and advantages of leased departments for many retail stores, it is likely that leasing will remain a part of the retail environment, perhaps indefinitely.

Applications to Small Business

Many retailers own small departmentalized businesses such as department and specialty stores. For them, leasing of departments within their stores can be a particularly attractive option, since specially-trained employees can be hard to come by and merchandise budgets are often very limited. Leasing would allow them access to skilled personnel they might not otherwise be able to attract or afford. It would, of course, also enable them to expand their merchandise offering beyond that of their own resources, thus permitting them to compete more effectively with larger stores. Store traffic and volume would likely increase, and expenses could be reduced through shared-cost means. The obvious impediment to leasing for small retailers is that of attracting interested lessees. Leased department operators often seek out high-traffic stores in order to maximize exposure to their goods and thus sales potential. However, if small retailers can identify one-man leased operators and negotiate favorable terms, such an agreement could be mutually beneficial, particularly when compatible merchandise lines are involved. Hence, small retailers should not feel that the leasing option is available exclusively to their larger competitors. A simple cost-benefit analysis can often provide the necessary insight to determine whether or not leasing can be a profit-enhancing venture for small retailers.

Small businesses should also consider requesting a leased arrangement within a local department store. Often, successful small businesses are in a strong position to offer department stores increased prestige or visibility, while the department store can provide a steady and predictable customer base as well as a high quality location for the small business. A local bakery, for example, which enjoys an outstanding reputation for candies and cakes, might enter into a mutually profitable arrangement with a department store to establish a leased department for birthday cakes near the children's toy section.

Software/Databases

Presently there exists no commercially available software for use in evaluating specifically the viability of leasing new or existing departments within retail stores. However, several packages can assist retailers who are considering such a move or who currently lease space. For example, retail software which tracks sales analysis by department and incorporates profitability and ROI on a department by department basis can be useful in this context. Using these types of software would enable retailers to determine the sales volume and profit dollars generated by leased departments and compare them to (1) other departments within the store (2) similar departments which are owned by the store and (3) (in the case of chains) results achieved by the same leased departments operated by various lessors throughout the chain. Typical of such software is:

SALES AUDIT, SALES ANALYSIS. ARIS Associates, New York. A microcomputer-based software package which tracks sales and various financial data by department.

SMALL CHAIN STORE RETAIL DISTRIBUTION. Diversified Computer Management Corporation, Burlingame, CA. Minicomputer-based comprehensive package which tracks sales and other data by store, salesperson and customer.

MANAGEMENT REPORTS. Gary North and Associates, Costa Mesa, CA. Minicomputerized system that develops reports regarding key financial, inventory and merchandising areas of the company.

DOLLAR SALES. Creative Data Systems, Inc., Cleveland, OH. A minicomputer system which collects reports on dollars sold at the store, department and merchandise class level, as well as providing an audit trail reporting system.

In addition to these, several retail chains have developed customized, proprietary software for use in evaluating the results achieved by their leased department operations and analyzing the viability of adding additional leased departments or expanding existing ones.

References/Sources

Anderson, Paul F., "A Financial Approach to the Leased Department Decision," *Marketing 1979 Educators Conference Proceedings*. Chicago: American Marketing Association, 1979. Examines the leased department decision from a financial, rather than a marketing, perspective. Various means of evaluating leased department operations are included.

"The Arguments for Leasing," *Stores*, (July 1977): Provides pro's and con's of leasing of fur departments within retail stores. An excellent discussion of why stores choose to lease out their fur departments is included.

"At Your Service—Outlook for Leased Departments: Brightest and Best in Service Areas," *Stores*, (December 1977): 44. A summary discussion, including operational figures, of leased departments within department and specialty store retailing.

Davidson, William R., Doody, Alton F. and Lowry, James R., "Leased Departments as a Major Force of the Growth of Discount Store Retailing," *Journal of Marketing*, Vol. 34 (January 1970): 42. An insightful perspective on leased department retailing, discussing benefits and obstacles associated with leased department operations.

Flory, Stephanie, "Platt Music Employs a Fashion Approach to Merchandising Consumer Electronics," *Merchandising* (May 1984): 46. This article reviews in detail how one leased department operator successfully merchandises electronic equipment throughout various department stores throughout the country. Leasing practices are also discussed.

Golden, Lawrence G. and Zimmerman, Donald A., *Effective Retailing*, 2nd ed. Boston: Houghton Mifflin, 1986, The authors discuss concisely the nature of leased department operations and management in U. S. retailing.

"Goodyear Mining New Marketing Lode," *Industry Week*, (November 16, 1981): 111. Describes how Goodyear Tire and Rubber became involved in the leasing of space from Gimbel's Department Stores for their auto tire and service centers. The advantages for Goodyear of such an arrangement are highlighted.

"A Lessee for the Floor Coverings Department?" *Stores*, (June 1983): 16-17. Leasing within the floor coverings lines are thoroughly and insightfully discussed in this trade publication of NRMA.

Lowry, James R., *Retail Management*. Cincinnati: South-Western Publishing Company, 1983, p. 401. Chapter 15 of this text discusses thoroughly several aspects of the retail merchandise buying process. A brief treatment of leased departments is provided.

"Retailing: Discount Stores," *Standard and Poor's Industry Surveys*, (December 11, 1980): R123. Provides, on a continuing basis, a survey of recent developments and measures of performance through various segments of the economy including the retail trade.

Rutigliano, Anthony, "Leased Outlets Nab High-End Sales Through Direct Marketing Efforts," *Merchandising* (October 1983): 45. A trade publication article which discusses the leasing of consumer electronics departments within various department stores. Strategies and operational aspects of leasing are emphasized.

Spalding, Lewis A., "Footwear: To Lease or Own?" *Stores* (July 1979): 16. Provides an interesting discussion of practices in the retail industry regarding leased shoe departments. A brief historical perspective is included.

Zimmerman, Robert M. and Salerno, Robert E., *Directory of Retail Software.* New York: National Retail Merchants Association, 1983. A survey publication of the National Retail Merchants Association (NRMA) describing numerous software applications for use by retailers. Software is grouped according to micro, mini, and mainframe computer applications.

Related Topics and Terms

Concessions, Cooperatives, Franchising, Licensed Department, Merchandise Assortment, Merchandising, Retail Productivity, Retail Store Classification, Retail Strategy.

Don R. Snyder
School of Management
Millsaps College

LIFESTYLE/PSYCHOGRAPHICS

Overview

Consumers and target markets have typically been described and differentiated by demographic characteristics. The notion of lifestyle research, also known as "psychographics," was introduced as long ago as 1959. Since then, lifestyle variables have been used to segment markets for practically every product category.

Lifestyle research is the practical application of the social sciences in business to help understand consumer behavior. Lifestyle analysis is more of a technique than a theory. It is a quantitative research procedure that is used when demographic, socioeconomic or product usage data are insufficient in understanding the preferences of consumers.

Examples

The objective of lifestyle measurement is to identify groups of consumers who are similar in their activities, interests and opinions (AIO). Some typical activities measured include work, hobbies, social events, vacations, entertainment, club membership, shopping and sports. Interests range from family, home, job, fashion, food, media and achievement. Opinion dimensions measure how consumers feel about themselves, social issues, politics, business, education, culture and the future.

One lifestyle technique that is growing in its application is VALS (values and lifestyles), developed by the Stanford Research Institute. The VALS typologies are based on data from 30 attitudinal and demographic questions collected via a mail survey of over 5000 adults. There are four major categories in the VALS typologies with a total of nine characterizations of consumers. The first category is labeled "Need Driven." This category is comprised of 'Survivors' described as old, poor, removed from cultural mainstream; and 'Sustainers' described as angry, resentful, minorities living on the edge of poverty. Outer-Directed is the second category, and represents 66% of the population. 'Belongers,' 'Emulators,' and 'Achievers' comprise this group. 'Belongers' are aging, conventional, content, and patriotic middle Americans; 'Emulators' are young, ambitious, and status conscious; 'Achievers' are middle-aged, prosperous and leaders in business and government. The third category is Inner-Directed. In this group, 'I-am-me,' are very young, impulsive, individualistic and in a transitional state. 'Experientials' are youthful, artistic, and oriented toward inner growth. The 'Socially Conscious' are mission oriented, mature, successful and out to change the world. The last category is labeled 'Integrated.' These consumers are psychologically mature, tolerant, understanding, flexible and self-actualizers.

Yankelovich Monitor interviews respondents in their homes on 50 values questions. Their lifestyle analysis divides people into six categories: Aimless, Moralists, New Conformists, Materialists, Retreaters and Forerunners. Needham-Harper Worldwide advertising agency administers questionnaires to 1200 married adults. Their technique divides men and women into categories such as the Chic Urbanite and the Discontented Man.

Many products are designed, marketed and advertised with the aid of lifestyle analysis. Identifying a new and growing American lifestyle segment such as physical fitness has provided a plethora of products. Nike has added a variety of sports and recreational apparel to its traditional line of running shoes. Caffeine-free sodas, "light" packaged foods with less salt and sugar, and prepared frozen entres such as Lean Cuisine have all been brought to market for those consumer concerned about their health and fitness. Time saving appliances such as microwaves and food processors help meal preparation. Time-shifting products such as VCRs allow consumers to watch programs when they want to, rather then when the network schedules them.

Benefits

Lifestyle attributes can be predictors of product preferences and purchasing patterns. The overall lifestyle pattern of consumers helps marketing managers to decide on how to reach specific segments, either by new product design or different advertising campaigns.

When used with demographic data, lifestyle profiles allow more precise segmentation of consumers because the AIO profiles cover a wide range of a person's life. The lifestyle profiles provide a more detailed picture of consumer characteristics. Lifestyle information is particularly valuable in product planning. Marketing managers have more specific and useful guidelines in developing products and services that appeal to existing and emerging lifestyles. Health clubs, "light" product formulations, more natural foods, diet and caffeine-free beverages were all designed to fill the needs of consumers who believe in fitness and good nutrition as part of their lifestyle.

Implementation

Lifestyle information plays an important role in creating advertising, since AIO measures relate closely to the needs, motives and preferences of consumers. Demographics and lifestyles also guide media selection. For example, weight watchers are younger, single, outdoor types that tend to be adventurous and influential as opinion leaders. Sports, outdoor and fashion related magazines would most likely reach this group. They are more likely to watch news-oriented programming on television.

Lifestyle data can be used either in designing new products or targeting promotion for existing products. Because lifestyle data necessarily categorize people into types, these profiles must be carefully coupled with demographics before a product can be designed or promoted in order to account for regional differences among the same types. One example of successfully evaluating consumer types is Ford Motor's marketing of Thunderbirds in California in which the company was able to differentiate particular lifestyle characteristics and add special features to the car which attracted a specific consumer type.

Evaluation

There is some controversy on the value of lifestyle analysis. Some believe that the items used to assess lifestyles do not provide enough distinction among consumers, and that there is still considerable overlap among the groups of consumers that have been segmented on the basis of lifestyle. Also, because the assessment process requires many questions per respondent, it is a difficult analysis to perform. Conversely, lifestyle analysis can provide insights into the behavior of consumers that cannot be predicted by any other variables. The results provide a powerful tool in new product development and in designing advertising that is relevant to the target consumers.

Conclusion

Lifestyle attributes can be predictors of consumer behavior. More specifically, they can enhance a marketer's knowledge of a target market by understanding how consumers spend their leisure time, their money, and what their interests and opinions are on selected topics. Lifestyle patterns can help a marketer design products and marketing programs to reach divergent lifestyle segments and aid in designing products and services that help consumers achieve their lifestyle goals. Although lifestyle research has been criticized for finding only obvious relationships, it is considered a valuable tool in understanding consumer behavior.

Applications to Small Business

Although the VALS, Yankelovich and similar techniques may be too broad and expensive for smaller manufacturers and retailers, it is possible to determine some lifestyle characteristics for purchasers of specific products or consumers in trading areas. Manufacturers may use samples of consumers who return warranty cards as a list to receive more extensive lifestyle questionnaires, using the AIO technique. The replies should provide some notion of the interests, activities, media used, values, etc. that can assist producers in decisions for advertising copy and content, media to use, and product features. Retailers in local areas may rely initially on zip code demographic data for their customer trading area, and then estimate lifestyles by using secondary data such as radio station and TV listener profiles by area, license plate surveys of patrons of upscale, medium and downscale shopping areas, attendance data from commercial and municipal health and recreational facilities, the number of specialty stores in the area (e.g., gourmet food, hobby, fashion) and many other sources. By keeping abreast of the major lifestyles, retailers can advertise to the most profitable segments, in the best media, tailor advertising to those segments, expand stocks of certain product types or augment the variety offered.

Software/Databases

Ghost data system. Pulse Analysis, Inc. PO Box 116, Ridgewood, N.J., 07450. Generates hypothetical sets of statistically related data for use in model and program testing and evaluation. For market, behavioral, psychological, psychographic and statistical research.

References/Sources

Bernstein, P.W., "Psychographics Is Still an Issue on Madison Avenue," *Fortune* (January 16, 1978): 78-84. Explains the role of lifestyle analysis in some critical decisions on marketing and advertising strategy. Describes various lifestyle characteristics.

Glick, Paul C., and Norton, Arthur J., "New Lifestyles Change Family Statistics," *American Demographics* (May 1980): 20-23. Relates the impact of household demographics on lifestyle.

Gutman, Jonathan, and Mills, Michael K., "Fashion, Life Style, Self Concept, Shopping Orientation and Store Patronage," *Journal of Retailing* (Summer 1982): 64-86. Explains the relationship between lifestyle, self-concept, demographics, shopping orientation, and overall fashion sense as these relate to store patronage and shopping behavior.

Mitchell, Arnold, *The Nine American Lifestyles*. New York: Macmillan, 1983. In-depth analysis and description of lifestyles in America.

Plummer, Joseph T., "The Theory and Uses of Lifestyle Segmentation," *Journal of Marketing*, 38 (January 1971): 33-37. Explains the application of lifestyle research in market segmentation.

Wells, William D., "Psychographics: A Critical Review," *Journal of Marketing Research*, Vol. XII (May 1975): 196-213.

Wells, William D., and Tigert, Douglas J., "Activities, Interests and Opinions," *Journal of Advertising Research*, 11 (August 1971): 27-35.

Ziff, Ruth, "Psychographics for Market Segmentation," *Journal of Advertising Research*, 11 (April 1971): 3-9. Explains how attitudes/needs/values can be used to provide the basis for segmentation for a broad class of products.

Related Topics and Terms

Baby Boomer Segment, Benefit Segmentation, Concentrated Marketing, Consumer Behavior, Experience Curve, Key Buying Influence, Market Segmentation, Psychographics, Reference Group, Selective Perception, Target Market, Testimonials.

Teresa J. Domzal
Department of Marketing
George Mason University

MAGAZINES

Overview

A magazine is a periodical type of print media which is aimed at a particular target audience. It is useful to the promotional areas of marketing, because of this segmentation. The main benefits of using magazines as an outlet for promotional activities are due not only to the demographic selectivity but also to the quality of the magazines and the number of people exposed to the magazine. When choosing magazines in which to advertise, marketers must not only look at the readership but at the costs to reach this readership. When evaluating the success of a magazine campaign, the weaknesses of this form of print media must be considered.

Examples

Of the total amount of money spent on advertising in media, the amount spent for magazine advertising ranks second behind television advertisements. Examples of major advertisers in magazines include Philip Morris, Inc. and R. J. Reynolds Industries, Inc., two manufacturers of tobacco products, who have been the leading advertisers in magazines over the past few years. The three American automobile manufacturers were also in the top twenty-five magazine advertisers, as well as several producers of grocery items and consumer goods, including Procter & Gamble Co., General Foods Corp., Johnson & Johnson, and Bristol-Myers Co. Advertisements are not the only form of promotion used in magazines. Magazines can be used in sales promotion, such as for couponing, or in public relations, such as when a corporate executive is invited to write an editorial comment. These promotional campaigns used in magazines come in various shapes and sizes, ranging from a few lines in the classified section to a multi-page insert, in addition to being in color or black and white.

Benefits

Magazines can be of use to marketers based on their segmentation and their quality. Very few magazines exist in today's society that are aimed for mass audiences. Most are targeted for a specific audience, which is smaller and more controllable. This results in magazines having some degree of demographic selectivity and local market selectivity, as well as being regional in nature, which helps advertisers in reaching their specific target markets. The processes in the manufacturing of the magazine determine several other benefits, due to the quality of the reproductions and the durability of the magazine. Magazines are better than the other print media because they have very good reproduction, especially of color, and the paper on which it is produced lasts longer. The readership of magazines explains several other benefits for using magazines. Not only is the life for an advertisement in a magazine relatively long (one week, one month, etc.) but the initial purchaser may not be the only person exposed to the advertisement: there may be some secondary readership, or pass-along readership.

Implementation

The steps in using the right magazines are basically the same steps in the selection process for media: the nature of the product and promotional appeals, the media habits of the target audience, and the costs involved. The cost to be considered is not the total cost of the magazine advertisement, but the cost of the media in relation to the number of people reached. Once a magazine campaign has been decided upon, the decision of which magazines to use is based on quantitative, qualitative, and judgmental decisions.

The quantitative tests relate to the total audience that can be reached by a single magazine campaign. The circulation aspects include the percentage of subscriptions for the magazine, the current circulation, as well as the expected circulation at the time of the campaign. Audience characteristics include the percentages of primary and secondary audiences and target audience coverage, in addition to total audience efficiency.

The quantitative aspects in the selection of a magazines are based on the target audience. These include the exposure opportunity, which is influenced by the time spent reading a magazine and the portions of the magazine that are read, and the relationship of the editorial outlook of the magazine to the proposed audience for the campaign. Another qualitative test involves the amount of reader action required by the campaign. Does the reader merely absorb the information presented or is more involvement required? Does the reader have to send away for more information about the product, or for the product itself? Does the campaign use recipes or coupons, which must be cut out? A final qualitative test concerns the opinions of the reader. This test involves the importance of the publication to the reader, and his overall rating and the interest and confidence in advertisements in the magazine, relative to other magazines.

The judgmental tests to be used are based on aspects not included in the previous two. These aspects include the degree of advertising clutter and the ad volume for the specific category, the ad layout exposure and position opportunities, the presence of compatible or supportive material, the overall appearance of the magazine, the timing for the magazine (weekly, monthly, etc), past experience with the magazine, and the marketer's own attitudes toward the magazine. The judgmental factors are the last ones to be considered and are used to ensure the correct audience is reached by the campaign and that the campaign is noticed.

Most of the national magazines have developed detailed reader profiles, and for certain products can tell potential advertisers exactly what to expect from their ads.

The New Yorker, for example, knows exactly what segment of its readership drinks scotch whiskey, what brands they prefer, and how often they drink it, while *Playboy* can provide even more extensive data about the buying characteristics of its readership. These statistics, combined with regional data and demographics can be extrapolated to project the probable success of other products and markets.

Evaluation

Once the particular magazines have been decided upon for the promotional campaign, the difficulties with using magazines must be considered. The most important difficulty with magazines is the long ad purchase lead time. Some magazines have a six to nine month lead time between when an advertisement is placed and when it will be included in the magazine. This results in long-term commitments for the marketers, and may result in a lack of urgency for using this media. Another difficulty is the waste circulation involved. Not all of the magazines printed will be distributed. The lack of any guarantee of positioning is another consideration when using magazines. The marketer has no guarantee that his advertisement will be in a highly visible location. Also, unlike television, magazines have a limited demonstration capacity, which tends to limit the information that can be provided in a message.

After the specific magazines have been chosen and the promotional campaign is completed, the effectiveness of the magazine portion of the overall media mix should be evaluated. The evaluations should be similar to those for the other media, with the differences being the magazines themselves. The aspects to be evaluated are:

—Was the correct audience reached by the magazine?
—What was the degree of recognition/awareness for the message? Was it acceptable?
—Were the attitudes formed by the message favorable?
—What was the circulation for the particular issue in which the message appeared?

Evaluating the success of magazine advertising is often the most difficult step, requiring sophisticated sampling. On the most basic level, advertisers can test for such elements as name or image recognition from the ad, but beyond that, especially in the areas of attitude toward the ad or product, testing the results is expensive and often inconclusive. The simplest way of measuring response is by having the consumer clip a coupon, take advantage of some offer or discount, or write the company. For a carefully designed and controlled ad, the number of respondents can be used to judge other effects of the ad. Measuring increases in sales volumes also reflects the effect of advertising in a general way once external factors such as seasonal trends and political events have been taken into account.

Conclusion

Magazines are a very useful component of the media mix, but only if they adequately serve the goals of the promotional campaign. They are better than other media in their segmentation and the quality of the reproduction, as well as their long life. Magazines can reach a more specific audience than the non-profit media, and have a better pass-along readership than most of the other print media. Although magazines have a long ad purchase lead time and no guarantee of position, if the magazines in which the campaign is to be included are chosen correctly, these difficulties will not be much of a problem.

One of the main problems involved in the evaluation of a magazine's effectiveness is the subjectivity in the interpretation of the results. This is a problem with most attitudinal studies, and is dependent on the quality of the questionnaire and the credibility of the researcher. This is important, because the effectiveness of the magazine determines its usefulness in future campaigns.

Applications to Small Business

For small businesses, magazines offer a good outlet for informing specific target audiences. In fact, they are probably more cost effective than many of the other media. Magazines that could be useful include not only those that cater to their specific target segments, but also locally produced magazines, which could be used for institutional advertising to gain name recognition. The same objectives and selection processes used by larger corporations should be used by smaller businesses, but on a smaller scale, with costs becoming a more important factor.

Software/Databases

ADTRACK, Kinman Consulting Group, Inc., St. Paul, MN. ADTRACK indexes by product name, company name, ad characteristics, and content of ads all advertisements of 1/4 page size or larger appearing in 148 major U.S. consumer magazines. The 148 titles account for 98% of advertising revenues in major magazines.

References/Sources

Aaker, David A. and Myers, J.G., *Advertising Management*. Englewood Cliffs, NJ: Prentice-Hall, 1975. Chapter 2 describes the process of advertising planning and decision making.

Fajen, Stephen R., "More For Your Money From the Media," *Harvard Business Review* (September-October 1978): 113-121. Discusses the advantages and disadvantages of the different media.

Hise, Richard T., Gillett, Peter L., and Ryans, John K., Jr., *Marketing: Con-*

cepts, Decisions, Strategies. Houston, TX: Dame Publications, 1984. Chapter 10 includes a discussion on the process of media selection.

Kotler, Philip, *Marketing Management: Analysis, Planning, and Control,* 5th ed. Englewood Cliffs, NJ: Prentice-Hall, 1984. Chapter 20 discusses advertising decisions and includes a section on media decisions.

Morris, Don, *Advertising Age Yearbook 1984.* Chicago: Crain Books, 1984. Section 3 provides a list for the top twenty-five magazine advertisers. Section 4 includes important developments in the magazine industry for the year.

Related Topics and Terms
Account Executive, Advertising, Advertising Agency, Advertising Claim, Attitude, Brand Awareness, Cooperative Advertising, Direct Marketing, Issue Advertising, Lifestyle/Psychographics, Newspapers, Psychographics, Subliminal Advertising, Target Market.

Gary Guenther
Department of Marketing
Texas A&M University

MALL INTERCEPT INTERVIEWING

Overview

Mall intercept interviewing involves questioning shoppers in shopping malls (shopping centers). Interviewers, stationed at mall entrances or locations inside the mall, stop shoppers, qualify them, and either interview them immediately or invite the qualified shoppers into central interviewing facilities that are located at the mall. This method of interviewing, which is second only to telephone interviewing in popularity, is a relatively low cost method of conducting personal interviews. Many businesses use mall intercept interviewing to determine consumer reaction to new products. Mall intercept interviews, however, may not provide accurate information about all consumers because certain types of people may not be interviewed either because they do not shop at malls or they refuse to be interviewed while at malls.

Examples

Mall intercept interviews are usually conducted by marketing research firms such as Market Facts, JRP, or Mid-America Research which have obtained exclusive rights from mall owners to interview shoppers in their malls. These firms may have permanent facilities including kitchens, focus group facilities, interviewing rooms, closed-circuit television monitors and computer-assisted interviewing areas located in their malls. There are over 150 permanent mall interviewing facilities in the United States.

Mall intercept interviewing is experiencing growing popularity with most businesses making use of this technique. It is estimated that about one-fifth of nonmail interviews are conducted in shopping malls. The majority of nonmail interviews are conducted by telephone.

Marine-Midland Bank has used mall intercept interviews to determine which of two advertisements most effectively communicates the distinctive features and benefits of the bank's new in-store banking system. The two advertisements were shown to 400 shoppers in central facilities located in two major New York cities. The results of these interviews helped the bank develop a successful advertising campaign for their new in-store banking system.

The Franklin Mint has used mall intercept interviews to determine consumer preference for two different figurines that were to be marketed through the mail. Subsequently, the relative sales of the two figurines mirrored the relative preferences expressed by the shoppers interviewed in malls.

Benefits

Mall intercept interviewing permits in-person interviews without incurring the expenses connected with sending interviewers to the homes of consumers. Door-to-door interviews can cost four times as much as mall intercept interviews because of interviewer time and costs incurred traveling between houses and finding consumers at home who agree to cooperate with the interviewer. Marine-Midland Bank reports that it took three weeks and cost about $20 per interview for their mall intercept study of the advertisements for the bank's in-store banking system.

Mall intercept interviews allow the researcher to show the respondent large, immobile materials such as a television commercial or new products such as video cassette recorders and videodisc players. These materials can be set-up in central facilities and shown or demonstrated to many shoppers. Kitchen facilities available in many shopping malls are valuable for marketers of prepared foods. Shoppers can be asked to taste and evaluate foods immediately after they have been properly cooked in the kitchens.

The visual contact between shoppers and interviewers permits observation of respondent characteristics which is not possible with telephone interviews. Mall interviewers might use these observations either to select specific types of shoppers for participation in the interview or to determine if the respondents appear to understand the questions.

Implementation

Mall intercept interviewing requires a number of decisions which directly relate to the usefulness of the information. The shopping malls and the locations in or outside those malls where shoppers will be stopped need to be selected. The time of day and day of week for the interviews are also critical decisions when planning mall intercept interviews. The actual interview situation requires careful planning to ensure that neither the interviewer nor the questions lead shoppers to either refuse to participate or to provide incorrect answers.

It is desirable to interview shoppers of more than one shopping mall because of the variations among customers of different malls. Some malls may be patronized predominantly by lower or middle socioeconomic classes while other malls may attract primarily upper-class customers. Frequently, the customers of malls can be determined by examining the characteristics of neighborhoods surrounding these malls. The actual malls chosen to be included in the study will depend both on the type of customer of interest and the malls which permit interviews. Owners/ managers of some malls do not permit any interviewing of their customers at the malls.

If possible, shoppers should be sampled at each entrance of the mall because of variations in customers of the stores located near each entrance. If shoppers are sampled inside the mall instead of when they enter the mall, interviewers should intercept shoppers in several areas of the mall to ensure that the sample adequately reflects the characteristics of shoppers of different stores located in the mall.

Shopper interviews should be conducted at randomly selected times of day and on randomly chosen days of the week. Customer characteristics vary by time of day and day of week. For example, weekday shoppers may be more likely to be unemployed than nighttime and weekend shoppers.

If possible, the number of shoppers sampled at each entrance/location, time and day should be proportional to the traffic at each location and during each time period. For example, if 10% of the shoppers of a mall enter by the North entrance, 10% of the customers who are interviewed should be shoppers who entered at this entrance.

Random selection of shoppers as they pass a specific location at a shopping mall can produce nonrepresentative samples. Shoppers who visit the mall frequently are more likely to be included in the sample than those shoppers who visit less frequently. In the case of customers of one shopping mall, reported frequency of visits ranged from once a month or less for about one-third of the shoppers to 6 or more visits per month for slightly less than one-fourth of the mall's customers. Frequent visitors to shopping malls may be quite different from less frequent visitors. Younger customers and women may visit shopping malls more frequently than older customers and men.

Sex, age, and race quotas may be used when selecting shoppers for mall intercept interviews to help ensure that all shoppers regardless of frequency of mall visits are adequately represented in the sample. Sample quotas based on easily observable characteristics such as sex, may not ensure, however, that the sample is representative.

Generally, it is desirable to include a question about frequency of visits to the mall as part of the interviewing process. The results of this question can be used to adjust study findings to reflect the relative importance of shoppers who visit the mall with different frequencies. The responses of infrequent shoppers are assigned disproportionately more weight than frequent shoppers because infrequent shoppers are less likely to be interviewed than shoppers who visit the mall more often.

It may be necessary to offer shoppers incentives to obtain their consent to participate in mall intercept interviews. Many shoppers are not willing to take the time to complete interviews while they are in a shopping mall. Refusal rates for mall intercept interviews have been reported to exceed 50 percent. Shoppers who refuse to participate in mall intercept interviews may be quite different from those customers who are willing to participate.

Interviewers used for mall intercept interviewing should be selected and trained to ensure that they ask questions properly and conduct any other parts of the interviewing process, including product demonstrations, correctly. Similar to other types of personal interviews, the appearance and behavior of mall interviewers may bias answers provided by respondents. Respondents may misunderstand questions or may try to provide answers they feel would please interviewers. Moreover, respondents may give socially desirable answers in response to personally sensitive questions.

Timing of the interviewing process is also important because most shoppers are in somewhat of a hurry. Mall intercept interviews should not require more than 20-30 minutes.

Evaluation

Results of mall intercept interviews can be a useful aid for marketing decision makers. However, it is necessary to evaluate these results to determine the extent of inaccuracies in these results. Users of the data from shopping mall studies should examine both the method used to select respondents for the study and the circumstances surrounding the interviewing process.

Typical questions to be asked about the selection process include: Was the study conducted in malls that have customers who are representative of target markets? Were the sampled customers randomly selected from different areas of the mall and from different shopping days and times? What proportion of the shoppers who qualified for the study refused to be interviewed? Were quotas or weighting procedures used to ensure that the results are representative as far as shopping frequency of respondents?

Interviewer training and supervision are just two aspects of the interviewing process which need to be considered. The interviewer may not be either asking questions properly or accurately recording the responses. The interviewing process may also result in incorrect responses because either the respondent may be distracted by other members of his shopping party or by his desire to start or resume shopping.

Conclusion

Mall intercept interviewing with consumers shopping at malls or shopping centers is a popular method of conducting personal interviews. Conducting personal interviews in a central location such as a shopping center where consumers are available in large numbers can be much less costly than attempting to interview consumers at their homes. Mall intercept interviews also provide the opportunity to prepare and demonstrate products in central facilities. It is not necessary to incur costly transportation and setup costs for in-home demonstrations. These central mall facilities may include kitchens, focus group facilities, and computer-assisted interviewing equipment.

Other types of interviewing such as telephone and mail may be preferred to mall intercept interviews for several reasons, including the cost and the unavailability of certain types of customers. Mall intercept interviewing may be more costly than telephone and mail. In addition, mall intercept interviewing may be inefficient if a marketer is interested in purchasing agents or some other employee of businesses. Telephone interviews or mail surveys of people who are identified beforehand as the type of business person of interest may be less costly and quicker than using mall intercepts.

Applications to Small Business

Many small retailers and other small businesses market to consumers who could be efficiently interviewed in shopping malls. The market areas of these businesses may coincide with the markets served by regional malls.

Mall intercept interviews could be used by small businesses to develop a better understanding of their customers and their needs. In addition these small businesses, which can ill afford marketplace failures, might consider using mall intercept interviews to determine consumer reaction to changes in marketing programs, including product and price revisions.

Software/Databases

Directory of Shopping Centers in the United States. National Research Bureau, Chicago, IL. Provides information on most shopping centers in the United States. Location, number of stores, name of store, type of store, gross leasable area, vacancy rates and owner or developer are available for neighborhood, community, regional, and super regional shopping centers.

References/Sources

Bush, Alan J. and Hair, Joseph F., Jr., "An Assessment of the Mall Intercept as a Data Collection Method," *Journal of Marketing Research* (May 1985): 158-167. Based on the results of a study, authors conclude that the overall quality of data from mall intercept interviews appears to be equivalent to that of telephone interviewing.

Bush, Alan J. and Parasuraman, A., "Mall Intercept versus Telephone-Interviewing Environment," *Journal of Advertising Research* (April/May 1985): 36-43. A comparison of results of mall intercept and telephone interviews of comparable samples of residents in the primary trading area of a southeastern shopping mall showed that both methods produce similar findings about the characteristics of consumers.

Gage, Theodore J., "Field Research: Alive and Well in the Malls," *Advertising Age* (May 23, 1983): 27-28. Provides description of mall intercept interviewing services of Mid-America Research Company. Mall intercept interviewing is compared to door-to-door interviewing.

Gates, Roger, and Solomon, Paul J., "Research Using the Mall Intercept: State of the Art," *Journal of Advertising Research* (August/September 1982): 43-49. Provides an evaluation of mall intercept interviewing on the basis of research management, validity of data, response rates, and questionnaire design.

Harper, S., "Court Hits Lorillard's Triumph," *Advertising Age* (November 3, 1980): 95. Describes a decision by a federal district judge to enjoin Lorillard from using a comparative advertising campaign for Triumph cigarettes, which was based on mall intercept interviews and preference tests.

Lautman, Martin R., Edwards, Melanie T., and Farrell, Bryan, "Predicting Direct-Mall Response from Mall Intercept Data," *Journal of Advertising Research* (October 1981): 31-34. Suggests that mall intercept interviews can be used to predict relative sales of items marketed through direct mail.

Rougeou, John T., "The New Technology for Market Researchers," *Business* (July-September 1982): 49-50. Describes the use of computer-assisted interviews in shopping malls as a method to quickly provide management with shopper reaction to a new package design.

Sen, Arup K., "Bank Uses Mall-Intercept Interviews to Test Ad Concepts," *Marketing News* (January 1982): 20. Describes how Marine-Midland Bank used mall intercept interviews to determine consumer reaction to alternate advertisements for an in-store banking system.

Sudman, Seymour, "Improving the Quality of Shopping Center Sampling," *Journal of Marketing Research* (November 1980): 423-431. Describes procedures for careful sampling of shopping centers and weighting responses by number of shopping trips.

Related Topics and Terms
Central-Location Interview, Depth Interview, Focus Group Interview, Marketing Research, Personal Interview, Questionnaire, Telephone Interview.

Stephen K. Keiser
Department of Business Administration
University of Delaware

MANAGEMENT BY OBJECTIVES (MBO)

Overview

Management by Objectives (MBO) is a "system of management" or a "management philosophy" developed by practicing managers in such companies as General Motors and General Electric over a quarter of a century ago. The practices now embodied in Management by Objectives have been referred to over the years as Management by Results, Work Planning and Review, Goals and Controls, and Goals Management.

> Management by Objectives is a managerial process whereby organizational purposes are diagnosed and met by joining superiors and subordinates in the pursuit of mutually agreed upon goals and objectives, which are specific, measurable, time bound, and joined to an action plan; progress and goal attainment are measured and monitored in appraisal sessions which center on mutually determined objective standards of performance (M.L. McConkie 1979).

The Management by Objective Process

Phase 1. Organizational goals are derived through the strategic planning process from the organizational mission statement and/or the business plan.

2. Each subordinate and his superior jointly set task goals (derived from the organizational goals) and personal development goals for the subordinate for a predetermined period of time. They agree on the means (performance indicators) by which performance will be measured. The entire understanding is reduced to writing and signed by both parties.

3. The subordinate develops an action plan for each goal.

4. Periodic review sessions are held at least quarterly.

5. A performance appraisal on the basis of degree of goal attainment is provided to the subordinate at the end of the period for which the goals had been set.

6. The process is repeated by setting performance objectives for the next period.

The first person to give MBO widespread exposure was Peter F. Drucker, who in 1954 wrote a successful book entitled "The Practice of Management." Further impetus was provided by Douglas McGregor in a now famous *Harvard Business Review* article entitled "An Uneasy Look at Performance Appraisal," and by George Odiorne's many MBO books.

Examples

Management by Objectives has gained widespread acceptance not only in industrial organizations, but also in medical institutions, school systems, universities, and government agencies; and its popularity is not confined to the United States. Approximately 40% of Fortune's 500 largest industrial firms report using MBO. Among them are General Mills, General Motors, Dupont, General Electric, Honeywell, Ford Motor Company, Parke Davis, and Black & Decker. MBO is part of the planning process, the control process, the performance appraisal process, the management development process, and the motivational subsystem of the organization, and as such has its greatest impact when thoroughly integrated with all processes. Yet, some organizations, such as the Wells Fargo Bank use MBO effectively to achieve a limited objective, such as improving the planning process only. Others use it simply to improve the performance appraisal process for managers. In the marketing area of industrial firms, MBO has chiefly been used in the personal selling area.

Benefits

Properly implemented MBO programs have the potential for improving performance, morale, and career planning by engendering greater commitment to organizational goals, reducing uncertainty about superiors' wants and expectations, enhancing subordinates' development, and encouraging participative management.

Implementation

MBO, above all, is a human process and not an administrative procedure or a reporting system. Therefore, it is necessary to integrate MBO with Organizational Development (OD) methodology. OD presupposes, as first order of business, a data-based analysis of needs in the technical, managerial, and human subsystems, using a wide range of diagnostic methods. Different organizations experience problems that are specific to the circumstances an organization faces, and this is true as well for functional areas such as marketing. Once the major impediments are identified, suitable intervention strategies must be selected and their efficacy measured against the baseline obtained during the needs analysis phase. OD also attempts to establish the values and behaviors necessary to support an MBO intervention, such as high trust, openness, a sense of job ownership, and a perception of low risk.

MBO should be implemented at the top of the organization first, then at the next level, and so forth. Moreover, it is important to involve line management in the implementation phase. If staff departments or consultants are solely responsible for introducing MBO, then the participants may not be motivated to take the program seriously.

Evaluation

As with most organizational interventions, how well MBO works to a large extent is a function of how well it is implemented. MBO, if looked at as a mechanistic formula, appears to be easy to teach, easy to learn, and compatible with common sense. But if it is perceived as a series of ritualistic steps, MBO can cause more harm than good, for it is old wine in new bottles; i.e., scientific management for all levels of the organization without the benefit of a systematic method for setting standards and incentives. In other words, it becomes "speed-up," since few managers will accept last year's goals as next year's objectives.

Organizations interested in implementing MBO should be on the lookout for the following typical problems: 1) excessive paperwork; 2) overemphasis on what can easily be quantified; 3) lack of training, especially with respect to setting measurable objectives and measuring progress toward goal attainment; 4) failure to evaluate the means; 5) permitting subordinates to set easy goals; 6) lack of a strong nexus between goal attainment and merit pay; and 7) teaching superiors how to conduct meaningful periodic reviews.

Conclusion

Clearly, MBO is predicated on a number of sound practical and theoretical constructs, such as: goal setting, participation, feedback, reinforcement, planning, control, and results-oriented performance appraisal. The problem with the MBO formula is that it fails to provide specific processes for attaining its explicit and implicit aims. That is why it is essential to combine MBO with appropriate organizational development techniques which provide the necessary vehicles for achieving MBO's aims. Until a fusion of MBO and OD takes place, the four or five-step MBO formula should be viewed with caution, for assimilated in its pure form it will be a placebo at best and, at worst, will either aggravate or induce serious organizational maladies. MBO, in turn, offers OD the structure and performance orientation which the softer OD approaches lack.

Even when MBO has been properly introduced, it is possible that MBO participants can become careless or even bored with MBO after a while. Therefore, it is advisable to stimulate periodically the employees' involvement in order to prevent the "degeneration" or "drifting" of the MBO process. Several strategies can be employed toward that end. First, MBO review sessions can be conducted when it appears that the MBO participants are losing interest. The review sessions could include films, reading materials, case studies, and discussion of problems associated with practicing MBO, as well as feasible solutions to these problems. Second, organizational development approaches, such as team building, can be employed periodically to get MBO back on stream. Third, managers should be evaluated by their superiors at least annually with regard to how well MBO is working in their units. Fourth, consultants, either internal or external, can be brought in from time-to-time to evaluate the quality of the MBO program and to recommend ways of improving the program in those parts of the organization where it is not working well.

Applications to Small Business

MBO is just as applicable to small organizations as to large ones. Small organizations, however, frequently need the assistance of an external change agent, such as a consultant, in order to implement MBO properly and train the participants.

Software/Databases

MBO can be conveniently integrated with most Human Resource/Personnel software products. Examples are:

1) *Profiles/PC.* COMSHARE, P.O. Box 1588, Ann Arbor, MI 48106.

2) *Human Resources Management Service (HRMS).* Control Data Business Centers, 500 West Putnam Ave., Dept. A675, Greenwich, CT 06830.

3) *Human Resource Information Network.* Executive Telecom System, Inc., College Park North, 9585 Valparaiso Court, Indianapolis, IN 46268.

4) *Human Resources Management.* Open Systems, 6477 City West Parkway, MN 55344.

5) *Harris Personnel Manager.* Harris Data Services, Inc., 11629 W. Dearbourn, Milwaukee, WI 53226.

The above software products offer a broad capability, including complete employee profiles and history, education and training management requirements, payroll interface, counseling on career planning and timing, manpower planning, and salary progression.

References/Sources

Carroll, S. J., and Tosi, H. L., *Management by Objectives: Applications and Research.* New York: Macmillan, 1973. A good primer on MBO, which also provides a good review of MBO research.

Etzel, M. J., and Ivancevich, J. M., "Management by Objectives in Marketing: Philosophy, Process, and Problems," *Journal of Marketing* (October 1974): 47-55. Provides insights into the application of MBO in a marketing context.

Hise, R. T., and Gillett, P. L., "Making MBO Work in the Sales Force," *Atlanta Economic Review* (July-August 1977): 32-37. Provides guidelines for integrating MBO into the management of a sales force.

Kleber, T. P., "Forty Common Goal Setting Errors," *Human Resource Management* (Fall 1972): 10-13. Provides a valuable list of pitfalls to avoid.

Kondrasuk, J. N., "Studies in MBO Effectiveness," *Academy of Management Review* (July 1981): 419-430. Summarizes MBO's effectiveness on the basis of empirical studies.

Levinson, H. "Management by Whose Objectives," *Harvard Business Review* (July 1970): 125-134. Offers a thought provoking critique of MBO philosophy.

Mali, P., *Improving Total Productivity: MBO Strategies for Business, Government, and Not-for-Profit Organizations*. New York: John Wiley & Sons, 1978. An excellent guide to measuring performance, especially outside of production and sales.

McConkey, D. D., "20 Ways to Kill Management by Objectives," *Management Review* (October 1972): 4-13. Highlights common mistakes during MBO implementation.

McConkie, M. L., "A Clarification of the Goal Setting and Appraisal Process in MBO," *Academy of Management Review* (January 1979): 29-40. Provides the reader with a precise operational definition of MBO.

Muczyk, J. P., "A Common Surrogate for OD: Dynamics and Hazards of Management by Objectives Applications," *Approaches to Planned Change, Part 2*. New York: Marcel Decker, 1979, pp. 166-179. Contains a thorough critical evaluation of MBO, and illustrates the dependence of MBO on OD.

Related Topics and Terms

Goals and Controls, Goals Management, Management by Results, Performance Appraisal, Work Planning and Review.

Jan P. Muczyk
Department of Management
Cleveland State University

MANUFACTURERS' AGENT

Overview

Manufacturers' agents, also called manufacturers' representatives or "reps," are independent sales agents who contract with manufacturers ("principals") to sell their product lines. They are *not* employees of the manufacturer. The manufacturers' agent firm (often consisting of several partners or stockholders plus employee salespeople and support personnel) pays for its own transportation, entertainment, promotion, and product training. In addition, the firm may carry considerable overhead; this may include a complete office staff, data processing equipment, salaries and benefits for firm employees. The manufacturer's rep firm is compensated by commission on sales of the manufacturers' product. A rep's accounts are within a specific geographic area. The rep carries the products of several different manufacturers. Most contracts specify that the rep cannot sell competing lines, and as a matter or custom, reps sell only complementary lines, regardless of contract terms.

The alternative to a manufacturers' agent is a direct salesperson. Direct salespeople are employees of the manufacturer. The manufacturer usually pays the salesperson's salary, bonus, expenses and benefits and/or commission and the employer usually trains the salesperson. Direct salespeople sell only their employer's products to their customers.

Examples

Such well-known companies as Borden and National Semiconductor use manufacturers' reps exclusively, even though they can easily afford to go direct. Many firms, such as General Foods, use hybrid systems (reps for some product lines or customer types, direct for others). One survey found 50% of U.S. manufacturers using at least some reps, with the figure approaching 80% in certain industries.

Benefits

Manufacturers' reps are gaining in popularity as rising selling costs make expanding or setting up a company sales force prohibitively expensive. Although comprehensive figures are scarce, the Census Bureau estimates that reps now sell around 10% of output in 15 key U.S. industries (in some lines of business, reps account for more than 40% of dollar volume). From 1972 to 1975, reps' sales grew by over 100%. In comparison, manufacturers' own sales forces grew only 77%, giving reps a growing share of industry business.

The most commonly cited advantage of reps is the "economy of scale" they achieve by pooling the products of several manufacturers. With a broader range of product types and brand names to sell, reps are more likely to recoup the cost of a call than are most direct salespeople. This means they can justify calls that are not worth a company salesperson's time. And by shrewdly combining products, reps can generate synergy among the brands, using one to help sell another.

The keystone of agency selling is that agents are paid only for results achieved. Unlike many all-commission company sales forces, the agency, not the manufacturer, assumes all selling costs (including fixed costs, such as running a sales office, and the usual variable costs of selling, such as entertainment). Such a system offers high rewards to achievers—and quickly puts the others out of business. The Darwinian nature of the system attracts, retains, and motivates excellent salespeople, who operate at variable cost to their manufacturers. Further, representation begins as soon as the agency is signed, not when recruiting and training is finished and contacts have finally been developed. In short, reps offer efficiency, variable cost, and immediate results, a package that appeals to any manufacturer.

Implementation

The major advantage of a direct sales force is control. Manufacturers have no authority when dealing with reps. With a direct sales force, even one paid strictly on commission, the company has the legitimate authority of the employer. But along with its benefits, control exacts a price. Setting up and running a company sales force demands the commitment of overhead and management talent. All too often, firms are disappointed with the results.

Deciding whether to fill a sales district with manufacturers' agents or direct salespeople is a difficult task, as there are many tradeoffs to weigh. It is important to choose well, as it is difficult to change from one system to the other. Recent research suggests that manufacturers' agents, *if carefully selected and properly treated,* give excellent results to their manufacturers in a broad range of circumstance, including many situations where direct salespeople are commonly used.

Evaluation

The manufacturer comtemplating a direct sales force must avoid a common pitfall: underestimating costs (especially overhead and turnover costs) and overestimating the sales results to be expected (particularly in the short term).

The manufacturer contemplating an agent must also avoid a common pitfall: signing up the first interested rep and then simply waiting for sales to be made. To obtain good results from manufacturers' agents, the marketer must carefully screen and select from a number of candidate agencies. Then the marketer must make the effort to communicate with and support its agents. The benefit can be high sales at low cost and with little overhead committed. However, the cost of a quick and careless program can be an unproductive relationship and lost sales opportunities.

Principals can become dissatisfied because they perceive they are not getting their "fair share" of the agent's selling time. The most effective way to gain a larger share of the rep's time is to make it pay for the rep to give time to one product line (rather than to another). This can be done by raising the commission rate. However, a high commission rate is usually a red flag that the product is difficult to sell. In this case a high commission rate will not translate into commission dollars and will not motivate the rep. For many manufacturers, it makes more sense to leave the commission rate as is and help make the product easier to sell through better support, product improvements, and market research.

Conclusion

The manufacturers' agent system is an attractive alternative to the traditional direct sales force. As competition intensifies and the cost of a sales call continues to skyrocket, the usage of manufacturers' agents should rise sharply over the next decade.

Applications to Small Business

The rep's advantage applies to all businesses, but smaller businesses are particularly interested in the variable cost structure that the rep system provides. Further, successful, established manufacturers' agents can attract, motivate, and hold high caliber salespeople. Small businesses can "rent" their sales skills even though the businesses usually could not afford such personnel in a direct sales force.

Software/Databases

Geostar. Geographic Systems, Inc., 204 Andover St., Andover, MA 01810. Performs sales and service territory optimal realignment to reduce travel time, increase sales productivity and balance sales/workload potential. For marketing, sales territory planning and distribution planning.

Know Your Client. Execuware, Inc., 4018 Country Club RD., Winston-Salem NC 27104. Permits user to create and retrieve information on thousands of clients, or vendors. For use by sales personnel, small businesses and sales executives.

Prospect Organizer. Dow-Jones Information Services, Box 300, Princeton, NJ 08540. Helps marketers and sales people track prospects from initial leads through allocation to sales territories. Generates reports.

Stanger Rep Evaluator. Wm. M. Stanger, 244 Ashland Rd., Summit, NJ 07901 Evaluates direct and rep field salespeople and regional managers on short and long term orders performance vs. seasonally adjusted averages and on subjective aspects. Also provides typical set of monthly orders, reports overall and by region.

References/Sources

Anderson, Erin, "The Salesperson as Outside Agent or Employee: A Transaction Cost Analysis," *Marketing Science* (Summer 1985): 234-254. Presents a field study on when manufacturers use reps rather than direct salespeople.

Anderson, Erin and Weitz, Barton A., "A Framework for Analyzing Vertical Integration Issues in Marketing," *Sloan Management Review, 1986.* Presents a step by step method of determining whether a rep or direct sales force is appropriate for a given sales district.

Novick, Harold J., "The Case for 'Reps' vs. Direct Selling: Can Reps Do It Better?," *Industrial Marketing* (March 1982): 92-96. Gives an overview of the rep's advantages vis-a-vis direct salespeople.

The Research Institute of America's 1975 staff report, "When, Where, and How to Use Manufacturers' Representatives." Excellent overview of manufacturers' representatives and how to deal with them.

Taylor, Thayer, "A Raging 'Rep'idemic," *Sales and Marketing Management* (June 8, 1981): 33-35. A summary of the trends toward rep usage by industry.

Related Topics and Terms

Organizational Control, Organizational Structure, Sales Force Compensation, Sales Force Management, Sales Organization, Vertical Integration.

Erin Anderson
Department of Marketing
The Wharton School
The University of Pennsylvania

MARKET CONCEPT

Overview

Through re-evaluation of managerial orientations and actions, business leadership continually strives for improved balance between the firm's market offering and the environment in which it exists. A "new" orientation, popularly called "the marketing concept," emerged during the 1950s. Many adherents viewed the concept as a panacea for corporate ills, while critics called it nothing more than a restatement of historical business truths hardly deserving the attention it was receiving.

A Pillsbury Company marketing executive, Robert Keith, can be given substantial credit for popularization of the marketing concept. He evaluated Pillsbury's business history and discovered three distinct stages of managerial orientation:

(1) A production orientation (1900-1930) during which managerial concern was focused on problems of capacity creation, work methods, and volume production. Generally, problems related to manufacturing assumed greater significance than did those related to identification and development of markets.

(2) A sales management orientation (1930-1950) which placed attention on establishing and maintaining a first-rate sales organization, adequately supported by advertising and market research, which could dispose of the firm's production at a favorable price.

(3) A marketing concept orientation (1950-present) which assigns to marketing the responsibility for planning and executing the sale, from inception of the idea through sale to the consumer. The marketing concept shifted managerial emphasis from production to marketing problems, from the product that could be made to the production that consumers wanted made, and from the company itself to the marketplace.

By 1960, interest in the marketing concept had spread beyond the marketing trade press, into the professional academic literature. At that time a more formal definition of the marketing concept emerged: a managerial philosophy concerned with the mobilization, utilization, and control of total corporate effort for the purpose of helping consumers solve selected problems in ways compatible with planned enhancement of the profit position of the firm. Interest in the market concept as a managerial philosophy has continued through the subsequent years.

Examples

General Electric Company was another pioneer in formally adopting the marketing concept. In the late-1950s, G.E.'s Vice President for Marketing noted that the earlier sales concept concerned itself primarily with volume, while the marketing concept represented a true alliance with the consumer, based upon a course of action of mutual benefit. At that time G.E.'s Director of Marketing Services credited adoption of the marketing concept with subsequent decentralization of product businesses into autonomous operations within the organization. G.E.'s President observed that the concept introduced the marketing manager at the beginning rather than the end of the production cycle, and that it would integrate marketing into each phase of the business.

In the 1980s, Mandell and Rosenberg, contemporary marketing academicians, suggest that the marketing concept is used more by consumer goods companies than by industrial goods companies, and that more larger companies have implemented the concept than small companies. Industries considered to be heaviest adopters of the marketing concept include packaged-goods manufacturers, soft-drink makers, appliance manufacturers, automobile manufacturers, airlines, car rental organizations, and department stores. Industries considered to be lightest adopters of the concept include railroads, meat packers, newspapers, small retailers, universities, hospitals, governmental agencies, and the performing arts.

Benefits

In its broadest sense, the marketing concept means that a firm directs all its efforts at satisfying customers at a profit. When successfully implemented, the concept should significantly enhance the firm's probability of success in identifying and selecting new targets of marketing opportunity, developing and introducing new products and services, designing marketing logistics systems, and in making marketing investment decisions generally. Interestingly, adoption of the concept is consistent with long-run profit enhancement, while consciously redirecting managerial attention from short-run profit-making.

Implementation

Since the marketing concept is essentially a managerial philosophy rather than a sequence of actions or procedures, genuinely interested managers often have found efforts toward implementing the concept frustrating. The concept is elusive beyond certain cosmetic changes that many applied to their corporate organization structure. However, the following guidelines should be of assistance in understanding and implementing the concept, which requires:

(1) Company-wide managerial awareness and appreciation of the consumer's central role in the firm's existence, growth, and stability.
(2) Active company-wide managerial awareness of, and concern with, interdepartmental implications of decisions and actions of individual departments.
(3) Company-wide managerial concern with innovation of products and services designed to solve selected consumer problems.
(4) General managerial concern with the effect of new product and service introductions on the firm's profit position, both present and future, and recogni-

tion of the potential rewards which may accrue from new product planning, including profits and profit stability.

(5) General managerial appreciation of the role of marketing intelligence and other fact-finding and reporting units in translating the general statements above into detailed statements of profitable market potentials, targets, and action.

(6) Company-wide managerial effort, based on participation and interaction of company officers, in establishing understood and acceptable objectives which are consistent with enhancement of the firm's profit position.

(7) Formal short- and long-range planning of corporate goals, strategies, and tactics, resulting in defined and coordinated effort of the firm's functional areas.

(8) Creation, expansion, termination, or restructuring of any corporate function as deemed necessary for mobilizing, utilizing, and controlling total corporate effort toward the solution of selected consumer problems in ways compatible with enhancement of the firm's profit position.

Most companies have not yet arrived at full marketing maturity, although a small number may be identified as practitioners of the marketing concept. They include Procter and Gamble, Kodak, General Foods, General Mills, McDonald's, and Avon. Full implementation of the concept will impact most of the firm's consumer orientation, its organizational structuring, marketing planning, product planning, profit planning and control, and marketing intelligence. The simple creation and staffing of the position of Vice President of Marketing need not suggest corporate acceptance or implementation of the marketing concept. The critical issue is widespread managerial acceptance of the philosophy upon which implementation must be based.

Evaluation

On a general level, it is widely accepted that the marketing concept "works." One observer has noted that the essence of the concept is that if people do not want or need what a firm brings to market, they will not buy it. In a sense the concept represents nothing really new to perceptive managers. Its common-sense logic is clear.

The critical question is whether managers put the concept into practice. While no universal tests of implementation exist, a recent noteworthy example can be cited. Hawes and Varble have examined the degree to which firms within the supermarket industry have accepted the concept and made it operational. Earlier evaluation has typically focused on matters such as whether the firm had a marketing research department, used test marketing prior to product introduction, or included a person experienced in marketing on its board of directors. The evaluation by Hawes and Varble employed a more direct approach.

For purposes of the evaluation they defined the marketing concept in terms of three basic tenants: 1) all business and marketing decisions must be consumer oriented, 2) profit, rather than sales volume, is the standard for evaluating marketing performance, and 3) an integrated marketing effort is required. Six-point, Likert-type statements were developed for each of these tenants, and top executives recorded their responses. The extent to which each firm had adopted the concept was measured by averaging the responses to these statements. Subsequently, three categories of adoption were determined on the basis of the average adoption scores computed. While the procedure is imprecise, it seems the best available in evaluating implementation of the intangible and philosophical marketing concept.

Conclusion

Discussion of the marketing concept is now a standard feature of most textbooks in marketing management and strategic marketing. Its introduction in the first chapters of most of these books reflects acceptance of the concept as a basic orientation for students of marketing. In the trade literature, business practitioners continue to discuss and refine the concept, and to question the degree to which they have been successful in implementing it. In all probability, this elusive concept, which captured the attention and directed the thought of marketing academicians and practitioners over the past thirty years, will remain an important part of marketing knowledge and practice.

Applications to Small Business

The management philosophy inherent in the marketing concept is equally applicable to all firms, large and small. Managers of small businesses should avoid over-reliance on the popular slogan: "large enough to serve you, but small enough to know you." While it may be true that there is substantially more managerial contact with customers in small firms, consumer behavior remains an elusive factor. Similarly, the managers of small firms may share a volume-profit orientation with managers of large firms. In conclusion, implementation of the marketing concept should assist managers in all size firms in bringing efficiency and balance to business operations.

References/Sources

Bennett, Roger C., and Cooper, Robert G., "Beyond the Marketing Concept," *Business Horizons* (June 1978): 76-83. A perspective on changing managerial perspectives in marketing.

Borch, Fred J., *The Marketing Philosophy as a Way of Business Life.* New York: General Electric, 1957. A classic corporate statement concerning the meaning of the marketing concept.

Cravens, David W., *Strategic Marketing.* Homewood, IL: Richard D. Irwin, 1982, pp. 5-10. A restatement of the marketing concept with the Susan B. Anthony dollar and Procter and Gamble cited as illustrations.

Hawes, Jon M., and Varble, Dale L., "The Marketing Concept and Organizational Goals," *Marketing: The Next Decade.* Boca Raton, FL: Southern Marketing Association, 1985, pp. 131-134. A survey concerning implementation of the marketing concept in the supermarket industry.

Hirschman, Elizabeth C., "Aesthetics, Ideologies and the Limits of the Marketing Concept," *Journal of Marketing* (Summer 1983): 45-55. Suggests that the marketing concept is not applicable to two classes of "producers": artists and ideologists.

Keith, Robert J., "An Interpretation of the Marketing Concept," *Advancing Marketing Efficiency.* Chicago: American Marketing Association, 1958. A classic statement concerning the meaning of the marketing concept.

King, Robert L., "The Marketing Concept," *Science in Marketing.* New York: John Wiley and Sons, 1965, pp. 70-97. An early comprehensive statement concerning corporate action and commentary related to the marketing concept.

Mandell, Maurice I., and Rosenberg, Larry J., *Marketing,* 2nd ed. Englewood Cliffs, NJ: Prentice-Hall, 1981, pp. 23-32. A useful distinction between a marketing orientation and other managerial orientations.

Vizza, R. F., Chambers, T. E., and Cook, E. J., *Adoption of the Marketing Concept—Fact or Fiction.* New York: Sales Executive Club, 1967. An early, intensive review of the meaning of the marketing concept and its implications for managerial action.

Related Topics and Terms
  Chief Marketing Executive, Consumerism, Intraorganizational Conflict, Marketing Research, New Product Development.

Robert L. King
Department of Business Administration
The Citadel

MARKET PENETRATION

Overview

Market penetration refers to the extent of sales achieved by a product in a specific market. A formal definition is, the ratio of current users (buyers) to current potential users (buyers) of a product class that is achieved by a specific product. As a strategy for growth, market penetration describes efforts to expand sales and/or market share of current products in current markets. Greater market penetration can be achieved by increasing brand usage or loyalty of existing customers, by attracting competitors' customers, or by convincing nonusers in the targeted market segment to try the product. In the early stages of a product's life, market penetration can be achieved by preemptive techniques such as penetration pricing. In later stages, greater market penetration is usually achieved through intensifying or more effectively utilizing elements of the marketing mix. While market penetration has the advantage of being a relatively low cost/low risk growth strategy, if used inappropriately it can be a costly means of achieving relatively modest gains in the market.

Examples

Examples of effective market penetration abound, and demonstrate the diversity of techniques that can be utilized. Firms like Texas Instruments, Black and Decker, and Briggs and Stratton have achieved extensive market penetration via preemptive pricing—setting initial market entry prices low, in anticipation of future cost decreases, in order to build production experience and economies of scale and discourage competitive activities.

Japanese firms have consistently employed a strategy of building excess capacity at initial product development stages in anticipation of future market size and share gains. American firms, which tend to build capacity for shorter-term markets, later find it difficult and costly to catch up as the market continues to expand.

K-Mart has built a dominant position by finding ways to more effectively serve a specific market segment. Their specialized niche as a leader in the general merchandise discount department store area has been achieved by an intensive expansion program, offering products that appeal to a large base of consumers and also have high turnover rates, constantly adjusting store layout and design to meet changing needs of the consumer, and extensive promotions. They have resisted most temptations to change their merchandising philosophy to appeal to other market segments.

Procter and Gamble has a history of effective market penetration. Brand loyalty has played an important role in this success. Specific techniques used to increase brand loyalty are through product quality, extensive reinforcement-oriented promotion, and constant product reformulation as consumer needs and preferences change. Procter and Gamble has also developed specific programs to maintain

493

market penetration levels in the face of increased generic and private brand offerings, the basics of which are strategies of intensified advertising and continued reinforcement of the P&G quality image.

Benefits

Many of the perceived benefits of extensive market penetration have emerged from the Profit Impact of Marketing Strategy (PIMS) study currently being supervised by the Marketing Science Institute. The PIMS data indicates that increased market share and higher ROI are related, at least among the larger firms that form the database. Other benefits attributed to a dominant market share position include: it acts as a buffer to downturns in the economy, when buyers will shift to the largest most reliable supplier; it portrays a positive image to customers and retailers; and it provides the firm a base of power from which to deal for more favorable policies and treatment from both suppliers and buyers. Finally, when compared to other strategies such as market expansion and product development, market penetration is a relatively low cost/low risk alternative.

Implementation

The emphasis in market penetration is on more effective utilization of marketing tools and techniques. Typically, increased market penetration is achieved by increasing the level or intensity of marketing efforts, improving the utilization of techniques in the marketing mix, or lowering price.

Strategies for achieving market penetration fall into two categories—those designed to increase product usage or loyalty among existing customers, and those designed to attract competitors' customers or nonusers of the product. Increased product usage can be achieved by increasing the frequency of usage, increasing the quantity used, finding new applications for current product users, or some combination of the above. Techniques to support efforts in this direction include constantly modifying the marketing program to meet the changing needs of consumers, developing promotions that reinforce positive levels of awareness and attitudes, offering rapid and reliable delivery, and carrying large inventories.

Attempts to attract competitors' customers generally have a higher level of risk because they likely will encourage retaliation. Shorter-term gains can be achieved via trade promotions, dealer discounts and allowances, and aggressive sales. Longer-term share gains at the expense of competitors will have to be based on something more substantial—a lasting competitive advantage.

An additional penetration strategy is to discourage competitors from entering the market. Techniques used to achieve this include penetration pricing, which is setting a relatively low entry level price. The low price tends to yield lower gross margins, build market share quickly, and give the firm a product cost advantage built on the experience curve. The combination of low margins, an aggressive market leader, and a firm building experience advantage will tend to make the market less attractive to potential entrants. Other preemptive strategies that can build market penetration include offering customers such a high level of service that there is no unique opportunity for competitors to exploit, having a high quality sales force, and utilizing intensive advertising.

During the maturity stage of the product's life cycle, penetration increases are generally achieved by more effective utilization of the elements of the marketing mix. Marketing efforts can either be intensified (increase the level of advertising and promotions, increase the sales force, expand the number of retail outlets) or more effectively utilized (use pricing more systematically to build market share, use target marketing efforts to achieve objectives in specific segments, develop better point-of-purchase strategies, modify products to more closely match consumer needs). In general, market penetration is more difficult to achieve at the maturity stage. Competitors are entrenched and will usually fight to maintain market shares, brand loyalty patterns are established, and the market is not expanding rapidly. While share gains are possible, the efficiency of such achievements must be closely monitored.

Evaluation

The value of market penetration as a strategy rests on the proposition that increased market share is associated with increased profitability. There is much empirical evidence that substantiates this positive relationship between market share and profitability. Many of the studies have utilized the PIMS database. Others, however, have suggested that the relationship between market share and profitability is not that clear—that they are both achieved simultaneously because of a third factor, superior overall management of the firm.

There are a number of situations when market penetration would appear to be a more appropriate strategy than other alternatives. One is when significant experience curve effects exist, which is more likely when there are high levels of value added, continuous process manufacturing, and high capital intensity. The second is when market power, which usually accompanies increased market share, is a significant factor in achieving long-term market success. Third is during early development or growth phases of the market. During this time the market is more volatile and gains in market share require less investment than when the market has matured, sales increases have slowed, and brand loyalty patterns are established. Fourth is when the firm has significant marketing management skills or other unique competitive advantages. Finally, competitors' activities must be considered. It is harder to succeed with market penetration when competitors are going to vigorously defend their market position.

If conditions are appropriate for employing market penetration, the next step is to analyze alternative strategies. Attracting competitors' customers is likely to succeed if a comprehensive marketing program utilizing all elements of the marketing mix is employed and if efforts are targeted to a few segments of the market where the competitors' positions are weakest. Encouraging current customers to buy or use the product more frequently is likely to succeed when customers are infrequent buyers and additional benefits not previously conveyed can be highlighted.

Controls to evaluate a market penetration program need to be established. Any evaluation program needs to consider the effectiveness (net gains) and efficiency (the value of gains versus the cost of achieving those gains) of the program. Specific measures of market penetration are:

- *The percentage increase in sales for a market relative to the percentage increase in market growth*. This measure will determine whether sales increases are coming form an expanding market or from superior performance. It is particularly useful in the early stages of the product life cycle before market shares are solidified.
- *Market Share*. This is a good indicator of the level of market penetration, particularly at the maturity stage when growth has stabilized. It directly measures the impact of a penetration program at the expense of competitors.
- *Brand Loyalty Rates*. This is an indirect measure of market penetration that, if increasing, should lead to share improvements in the long-run.
- *Product Usage Rates*. The frequency and quantity of product usage should be monitored when these objectives are established for the marketing efforts.

Finally, efforts to evaluate market penetration need to examine strategic consequences. Some questions that should be considered are:

- What is the likely reaction of competitors? If competitors are strongly entrenched and/or resource rich, how efficient are penetration efforts likely to be?
- What are the opportunity costs of this strategy? Would the resources utilized be more effectively employed in product or market development?
- What are the risks involved? What will the competitive market position be if the program is unsuccessful?
- Are there any possible anti-trust consequences of increasing market share?

Conclusion

Market penetration is a low risk growth strategy that attempts to make substantive gains with existing products in current markets. It is useful during all phases of the product life cycle, although the most appropriate techniques for achieving penetration will vary with market phases.

There are two primary risks in pursuing market penetration. The first is the opportunity cost of not pursuing market or product expansion, both of which can yield greater returns. The second risk involves possible inefficiencies. Share gain objectives may be achieved, but at a cost that outweighs the benefits accrued. Penetration pricing may discourage competitors and yield higher shares for the firm, but it could also lower overall gross margins, particularly in the short-run. Likewise, increased advertising intensity may yield increased market share that is not economically justified given the added advertising costs.

Applications to Small Business

The perception is that market penetration is a strategy only appropriate for large organizations. This perception is reinforced by the fact that the two primary tools of penetration—penetration pricing and more intensive marketing mix efforts—are generally utilized by large firms.

Smaller firms can also find penetration a useful, and perhaps critical, strategic tool. In both industrial and consumer goods, most smaller firms survive by concentrating—doing a better job of serving a smaller more specialized market than competitors. In a sense they rely on achieving greater penetration in a more narrowly defined market.

The techniques used by smaller firms to achieve penetration are different from those used by larger firms, and include: more customization of products and services, a closer working relationship between the firm and the customer, more direct promotional efforts, concentrating on serving the needs of a few key accounts, and providing a more personalized atmosphere in the relationship between supplier and buyer.

The key to successful market penetration by many small retailers and service organizations is a clearly defined, distinctive business serving a specific market need. Once these dimensions of successful strategy formulation are achieved, it is quite possible for a small firm to gain significant market penetration in its defined market. In fact, the success of the market niche strategy depends upon it.

Software/Databases

A market penetration program requires information on market size, the size of specific market segments, sales by the firm overall and within each segment, and brand purchase and loyalty information. Many companies offer data that can be used as baseline information. Some of them are:

Market Statistics, 633 Third Avenue, New York, New York 10017. Offer a PC program that allows for customized target market data from which companies can measure market potential and compare against sales to calculate penetration rates.

National Family Opinion, 2700 Oregon Road, P.O. Box 315, Toledo, Ohio 42691. Provide data based on a consumer panel. Information is available that can determine brand loyalties, purchase patterns, frequency of purchase, etc.

Rezide, Claritas, 201 N. Union Street, Alexandria, VA 22314. Provides up-to-date data on population, household, income and housing characteristics by zip code for the entire U.S. Useful for establishing market potentials.

References/Sources

Aaker, David A., *Strategic Market Management*. New York: John Wiley and Sons, 1984, pp. 232-236. Provides a good discussion of techniques for achieving market penetration.

Ansoff, H. Igor, "Strategies for Diversification," *Harvard Business Review* (September/October 1957): 113-124. Presents and discusses a framework that conceptually explains alternative strategies for achieving intensive growth. Market penetration is one of the strategies discussed.

Beik, Leland, and Buxby, Stephen L., "Profitability Analysis by Market Segment," *Journal of Marketing* (July 1973): 48-53. Discusses the need for and value of attempting to allocate marketing costs to specific market segments. Has implications for measuring the efficiency of programs to improve market penetration rate.

Buzzell, Robert D., Bradley, T. Gale, and Sultan, Ralph G., "Market Share—A Key to Profitability," *Harvard Business Review* (January/February 1975): 97-106. Uses the PIMS database to find an empirical relationship between market share and ROI. Found that a 10% point difference in market share is associated with a 5% difference in ROI.

Buzzell, Robert D., and Wiersema, Frederick D., "Successful Share Building Strategies," *Harvard Business Review* (January/February 1981): 135-144. Discusses factors leading to success in gaining market share. Utilizes the PIMS database.

Day, George S., "A Strategic Perspective on Product Planning," *Journal of Contemporary Business* (Spring 1975): 1-34. Discusses alternative strategies for growth, including market penetration. Summarizes the advantages and disadvantages of pursuing a strategy of building market share.

Fogg, C. Davis, "Planning Gains in Market Share," *Journal of Marketing* (July 1974): 30-38. Identifies and explains techniques for increasing market share and internal processes to develop and implement strategies for market share gains.

Jacobson, Robert, and Aaker, David, "Is Market Share All That It's Cracked Up To Be?" *Journal of Marketing* (Fall 1985): 11-22. Uses the PIMS database to explore the relationship between market share and ROI. Results bring into question the notion that high levels of market share result in higher ROI. The analysis suggests instead that high market share and high ROI tend to be related because a third factor—good management of the business—tends to create both.

Kotler, Philip, *Marketing Decision Making: A Model Building Approach*. New York: Holt, Rinehart and Winston, 1971. Many of the chapters present models useful in evaluating market penetration programs. Particularly useful chapters are chapter 12 on price decision models, chapter 14 on advertising decision models, chapter 15 on sales models for established products, and chapter 16 on brand share models.

Robinson, William T., and Fornell, Claes, "Sources of Market Pioneer Advantages in Consumer Goods Industries," *Journal of Marketing Research* (August 1985): 305-317. An empirical study which finds a positive relationship between order of market entry and market share.

Weber, John A., "Market Structure Profile Analysis and Strategic Growth Opportunities," *California Management Review* (Fall 1977): 34-46. Presents and discusses methods for analyzing strategies, including the concept of Market Structure Profile Gaps. Many of the Profile Gaps discussed relate to the effectiveness of market penetration efforts.

Related Topics and Terms

Brand Loyalty, Diversification, Growth Strategies, Market Development, Marketing Mix, Market Share, Penetration Pricing, Product Development, Product Life Cycle, Product Usage Frequency, Product Usage Quantity, Product Usage Rate, Profit Impact of Marketing Strategy (PIMS), Relative Market Share.

Ronald L. Zallocco
Department of Marketing
University of Toledo

MARKET POTENTIAL

Overview

Market potential is the maximum possible industry demand for a product/service in a specified market and time period. The product/service "industry" for which market potential is to be calculated should be defined as narrowly as possible, but it should cover all offerings of the firm and its competitors that perform essentially the same function. Alternative definitions are: a) all offerings of the firm and its competitors that provide the customer with essentially the same benefits, or b) all offerings of the firm and its competitors that satisfy essentially the same customer wants. The broader the definition of the product/service industry, however, the more difficult it is to determine which firm and competitor's offerings it covers. An offering of the firm or its competitors may be covered by the definition of more than one industry, since a product/service may perform several functions, provide several benefits, and satisfy several wants.

The market for which market potential is calculated usually refers to a specific geographic region, such as the U.S.A., the firm's trade area, or a sales district. If the time period is the present one, the market potential is referred to as current market potential: if it refers to a future period, it is called future market potential. Since market potential refers to an upper limit, current industry sales are a fraction of current market potential and the sales forecast for a future period will be a fraction of the future market potential for the forecast period. Market potentials should be expressed in units rather than revenues in order to simplify comparison across periods.

The concept of market potential is closely related to the concepts of primary and secondary demand. The gap between current industry potential and industry sales represents the maximum increase in demand that could be achieved by the industry regardless of effort; i.e., the maximum possible increase in primary demand. The size of the gap between industry sales and current potential can be suggestive of market strategies and their consequences. For example, early in the product life cycle the gap is likely to be large and it is possible that a firm can increase its sales by increasing industry sales. Later in the product life cycle, however, the gap may be small (the market is saturated) and little opportunity will exist for the firm's marketing efforts to increase *industry* sales. In this situation, whatever increase in sales occurs in response to the firm's marketing efforts, will come at the expense of competitors' market shares; i.e., by an increase in secondary demand.

Industry market potential represents the sales assumed to occur when four idealized conditions are met:

(a) Every *user* (person, family, firm, or whatever) that might use the product/service does use the product/service,

(b) Every user uses the product/service for all the *usages* to which it might be put,

(c) Every user uses the product/service on every *occasion* that he could use it,

(d) For each usage and occasion, every user uses the product/service to the maximum *extent* possible.

Examples

A company that makes canned soup might make the following assumptions in calculating current market potential using a method called "Chain Ratio": All individuals over the age of two could consume soup and similar products. There are 200 million of these people in the U.S.A. during the current period. There are three usages for the product: a) as a component of breakfast, lunch, or dinner, b) as a snack, and c) as an ingredient (i.e., in a sauce). The maximum number of occasions soup might be consumed during a meal is four (4) times a week. The maximum number of times it might be consumed as a snack is five (5) times a week. The maximum number of times it might be used as an ingredient is two (2) times a week. The maximum amount consumed on each occasion is assumed to be 6 oz., 8 oz., and 3 oz. for meals, snacks, and as an ingredient, respectively. The assumption can be combined to estimate current markct potential as follows:

	Usage			
	Meal	Snack	Ingredient	T
Number 200mm people	200mm	200mm	200mm	600mm people
Occasions (per week)	600mm	1000mm	400mm	2000mm occasions
Amount (oz.)	3600mm oz.	x8 = 8000mm oz.	1200mm	12800mm ounces

Thus, the current market potential for canncd soup is estimated to be 12,800 million ounces per week. The firm could refine this estimate by segmenting the users and developing estimates of market potential for each segment. For example, the firm might segment users by age and develop separate estimates for each age segment which would be combined to yield the aggregate current market potential. Likewise, it is not necessary to assume that all people are potential users for all usages. For example, it might be assumed that the maximum percent of the population that could consume soup for meals, snacks, and as an ingredient are 70%, 50%, and 35%, respectively. The numbers for the respective usages in the above example the would be 140 mm, 100 mm and 70 mm, respectively. The corresponding current market potential is 6,940 million ounces per week.

Benefits

Market potential also plays a key role in developing sales forecasts, especially for new products, the design of sales territories, and the setting of sales quotas for these territories. As general rule, regions should be combined into territories so that the territories have equal potentials. The quotas set for these territories should reflect differences in their respective potentials. Likewise, changes of a territory's quota over time should reflect changes in its current market potential.

The number of retail outlets in a market also should reflect the potential for the market. Too few outlets for the potential of a market can result in lost sales. Too many outlets for the potential of the market can result in low sales per outlet, dissatisfaction, and reduced reseller support.

Finally, market potential estimates play a key role in allocating marketing effort across markets, especially the sales force and advertising efforts. For example, if the total potential for five markets were one million units and one market's potential were 150,000 units, then its relative potential would be 15 percent. The firm therefore would allocate 15 percent of the sales force personnel and 15 percent of its advertising budget to this market. These allocations, of course, could be revised to reflect profitability, competition, and other conditions in the market.

Implementation

Estimates of market potential play a key role in four types of marketing decisions: a) identifying present opportunities and future problems, b) setting sales goals and quotas, c) determining the number of retail outlets, and d) allocating sales force and advertising between markets.

Natural changes in the environment (those beyond the firm's control) can provide the firm with opportunities and present it with problems. Examples include changes in the number of potential users (e.g., stemming from demographic swings or structural changes in an economy), usage occasions (e.g., increased frequency of eating away from the home results in fewer occasions for consuming a product with a meal at home), and amount (e.g., changing life styles have resulted in a reduction of the amount of red meat consumption, as well as a reduction in the number of occasions and users). Clearly, these natural changes represent problems for some producers (producers of red meats and food products prepared and consumed in the home) and opportunities for others (producers of chickens, food products prepared and consumed outside the home, and restaurants). While environmental changes such as these may be beyond the influence of the firm, they may be forecast and the forecasts will play a key role in the firm's strategic (long term) decision making.

Evaluation

Firms that attempt to determine market potential for their products or services must consider a number of factors that will influence their estimates. One of these factors is the potential for the industry, related to that of the individual firm. Will increases in industry demand, itself, carry with it increased demand for the firm, or must the firm rely on its own advertising, promotion and other strategies to realize the full potential of its target area? Other factors that should be considered are:

(a) As market potential is approached, at what point do marketing efforts become inefficient (e.g., when does a dollar spent in marketing effort yield a dollar or less in profit?)

(b) Should all products within a category (e.g., stereo equipment) be considered a single market in terms of potential, or should it be separated into single products such as speakers, amplifiers, and accessories?

(c) Are sufficient secondary data available to yield a reasonably useful estimate of market potential?

Conclusion

Larger companies have measured market potential for their products for many years, using a number of different methods, including surveys by their sales force, market share analysis, chain ratio and market buildup. Only recently, however, have current demographic and other pertinent data been available at the local level, by zip code, making it possible for smaller firms to estimate their own potential for both present and new products or services.

Such estimates are not only useful in making location decisions for new businesses and expansion decisions for established ones, but they provide appropriate support for loan applications and for wholesaler-source credit.

Applications to Small Business

Small businesses, in particular, have had difficulty in estimating market potential for retail goods, services and manufactured products. But the availability of demographic and other appropriate data by zip code, county and other smaller geographical units, and the accompanying acquisition of micro computers by smaller firms, have made these estimates easier to make.

The abbreviated chain-ratio method is probably the most appropriate one for small businesses to use. Together with zip code data, the chain-ratio may be used to: determine market potential by (1) matching demographics for each zip code with the demographics of typical users of the product, then (2) estimating the total market by multiplying the number of potential users (those within the zip code possessing the proper characteristics) by the average product usage in a given period, (3) subtracting the proportion of this market that is estimated to be served by present businesses, and (4) estimating the proportion of the remaining market that would be served by the businesses making the estimate.

While this method is anything but precise, the data to make the estimate can be obtained readily, and it enables a firm to determine whether or not it may be able to operate profitably, not only at the calculated market potential, but at increased and reduced levels as well.

Software/Databases

In practice, the numbers required to develop market potential estimates are estimated from appropriate market research and often can be based on secondary data. National and regional government censuses of populations, manufacturers, wholesalers, and retailers are ready sources for estimating the number of potential users. Industry trade associations often can provide information on the frequency and amount of usage.

"Query." JEB Systems, Inc., 57 Main St., Franconia, NH 03580. Searches and subsets a data base to find new brands, dying brands, market problems/ opportunities, or exceptions to any defined criteria.

References/Sources

Armstrong, J. Scott, Denniston, William B. Jr., and Gordon, Matt M., "The Use of the Decomposition Principle in Making Judgments," *Organizational Behavior and Human Performance,* Vol. 14 (1975): 257-263. Provides the basis for the Chain Ratio Method of estimating Market Potential, suggesting that it may be easier to estimate the potential of individual components of a market than the market as a whole.

Crissy, William J., and Kaplan, Robert M., "Matrix Models for Marketing Planning," *Business Topics* (Summer 1963): 48-66. Presents an analytical approach for determining the market potential of individual segments.

Guiltinan, Joseph P. and Paul, Gordon W., *Marketing Management: Strategies and Programs.* New York: McGraw-Hill, 1985. Excellent coverage of the market potential concept, its measurement, and analysis.

Jain, Subhash, *Market Planning and Strategy,* 2nd ed. Cincinnati, OH: Southwestern Publishing Co., 1985, pp. 207-10. Discusses elements of market potential measurement and summarizes them in an excellent pro-forma chart.

Kotler, Philip, *Marketing Management, Analysis, Planning and Control,* 4th ed. Englewood Cliffs, NJ: Prentice Hall, 1980, pp 221-224. Outlines the procedure for estimating market potential by several methods.

Weber, John, *Growth Opportunity Analysis.* Reston, VA: Reston Publishing Company, 1976. Discusses the calculation of industry market potential and provides strategies for increasing primary and secondary demand.

Related Topics and Terms

Benefit Segmentation, Decline State, Demographic Factor, Elastic Demand, Growth Stage, Inelastic Demand, Market Share

James B. Wiley
Department of Marketing
Temple University

MARKET SEGMENTATION

Overview

Market segmentation is the process of dividing a diverse market into groups of consumers with relatively similar characteristics, wants, needs, buying habits, or reactions to marketing efforts. Consumers are grouped on some variable or variables that are relevant to marketing and reflect true differences within the total market. Common variables on which market segments are based include demographic variables (age, income, occupation), geographic variables (region, city, climate), psychographic variables, benefits sought, and usage rates. The process of market segmentation often results in the uncovering of new opportunities, and a definition of market segments often lends guidance to a firm in developing new products, redesigning present products, developing advertising themes, and reviewing the position of competition in the marketplace.

Examples

A firm may segment a market based on one variable, such as age, or, as is often the case, may combine variables when defining a market segment. In another sense, a market may be defined broadly on one level and then further segmented within general categories.

The market for automobiles, for instance, is often broadly divided into three price categories (high, medium, and low) or by type of car (family, luxury, and sports). Any one of these general segments could be further broken down on one or a number of different variables or dimensions. For example, the market for sports cars could be divided on the basis of price levels, resulting in a relatively high price sports car segment, a medium price sports car segment, and a low price sports car segment.

Revlon has divided the cosmetic market into seven segments based on a combination of age and lifestyle categories. Different products such as Charlie, Moon Drops, and Classic Revlon each appeal to different market segments. Different promotion, pricing, distribution, and product decisions are made for each segment, reflecting its unique characteristics. For example, Revlon's Princess Marcella Borghese line of cosmetics was developed for the older, more conservative woman, concerned with status and prestige. As such, the line is very expensive in relation to Revlon's other products, the distribution is selective, and advertising themes revolve around the exclusiveness of the line. J.C. Penney has segmented its market by lifestyle, and has chosen to serve the fashion conscious, contemporary, and conservative market segments. American Express has carved an enviable position in the credit card market by identifying and catering to the "premium card" segment with its Gold Card, introduced in 1966. In 1984, American Express had 3.3 million Gold Card customers that charged 13 billion dollars, as compared to the

4.1 billion dollars charged on second place Visa's Premium Card. Higher rates are charged for the privilege of using the "premium cards," and holders of them tend to use them more often and charge more than the average card holder. This market segment is composed mainly of professionals who earn more than $40,000 per year. In an effort to better serve its customers, increase profits, and continue the premium card segment, American Express has further segmented this segment by offering the Platinum Card, for a $250.00 annual fee, to those customers who have charged more than $10,000 in one year. As a measure of its emphasis on prestige, the card is granted by invitation only, and includes year end itemized statements as well as other expanded services. By 1985, 60,000 customers had accepted American Express' invitation.

Benefits

Through market segmentation, a firm can find new opportunities or different approaches to competition. Crain Communications Inc., in effect, segmented the market for business publications geographically. When it introduced *Crain's Chicago Business* in 1978, it ranked fourth in total ad pages in the business and financial category of Folio Publishing Corporation's Folio 400. Further, this market segmentation scheme has lead to the introduction of *Crain's Cleveland Business* and *Crain's Illinois Business*. Profits at Wal-Mart stores have increased an average of 37% a year since 1974 due in part to gearing its stores to small towns and a market segment which is sensitive to price.

Implementation

There are a number of steps that must be completed to effectively utilize market segmentation. First, a decision must be made as to whether the total market should be segmented or treated as one group. Mass marketing can often lower production, advertising, and inventory costs, and may be appropriate when a market is small, a product is innovative, a product is sold predominantly to heavy users, or the market is dominated by the firm's product. However, at some point, most firms find that market segmentation is necessary.

Once the decision is made to segment a market, segmentation variables must be chosen. Past experience may serve as a guide in choosing variables on which to segment a market. For example, a furniture manufacturer may be aware of the different buying habits and needs of small, independent furniture stores and large furniture retailers, such as Sears, leading to segmentation by size of business. In other cases, segments are developed only after a great deal of research is done on variables by which consumers may be grouped. In any case, segmentation variables must be relevant to the market or product of interest.

After customers are grouped, based on some variable or variables, the size of each segment must be measured and a profile developed. At this point, it is important to determine the present size of the segment, potential or expected growth, who purchases the product, who uses the product, what product features are important to the segment, how the product is purchased, and where the decision maker looks for information about the product. For instance, a cereal producer will want to know that children are often the consumers of cereal and influence the decision to buy a certain brand while mothers are often concerned with nutrition and actually purchase the product, and also that the number of children in the 7-12 year age group is declining. Each piece of information will affect marketing decisions about the product, such as where to advertise and how or whether to change or discontinue the product.

Finally, after segmenting a market, the firm must decide upon its segmentation strategy. It may focus on only one market segment, taking a concentrated approach, or it may develop a marketing mix for each of two or more segments, taking a differentiated approach. In choosing one of the above approaches, consideration should be given to company resources, the nature of the product life cycle, the state of competition, and the nature of the market. For example, a small company may only be able to practice concentrated marketing because of the cost associated with marketing different products to different segments.

Evaluation

To be effective, a market segment must be measurable, profitable, accessible, and meaningful.

It is necessary, for later decisions, to know the size of the market, possible growth patterns, and characteristics of the market. These data cannot be collected if the market segment cannot be identified and measured. For instance, it would be difficult to measure a segment of those people who consume alcohol only because of job related problems.

If a market segment is too small, too hotly contested by competitors, or requires a great deal of marketing effort, it may not be profitable for many companies. However, it is important to note that a segment which is not profitable today may be profitable in the future, and, thus, market segments should be closely monitored for change. This can be seen by the reduced caffeine, calorie, and sodium products now being offered to the health conscious consumers which were not offered ten years ago.

A market must be accessible in the sense that once it is identified it can be reached and served through marketing efforts. A market segment composed of hermits living in caves may not be feasible because of the difficulty in exposing the segment to promotional and distribution efforts.

Finally, market segments must be meaningful. A segment should reflect divisions of the total market that are relevant to marketing the product. Segmenting a market by height may be meaningful to a clothing manufacturer but not a soft drink maker.

Conclusion

Most firms practice some form of market segmentation. It may be as simple as deciding to sell only in a certain geographic area, or it may be very complex, as is the case with many large consumer product companies which combine many bases to segment a market.

Most importantly, market segmentation enables a firm to match the needs of a consumer with the firm's products. By doing so, not only is the market served more efficiently and effectively, but the firm benefits by satisfying consumers and building customer loyalty as well.

Applications to Small Business

While small businesses may not be as sophisticated in marketing segmentation as large organizations, a small business should think in terms of market segmentation. By not attempting to be everything to everybody, a small firm can create an image and focus on a particular customer. Restaurants can cultivate an image of an inexpensive family restaurant or an exclusive establishment that specializes in seafood. An industrial distributor can appeal to only high volume accounts and set up pricing and inventory services that will help to compete in this market segment.

It is not very difficult for a small firm to segment its market. Information can be gathered by talking to customers, suppliers, and a firm's own salespeople. Many industry trade journals and business publications print the findings of original and secondary research that are useful in segmenting a market. Also, a small firm can observe the practices of competition. Once an organization has an idea of how to segment a market, information regarding the size and nature of the market segments can be gathered locally. Sources for these data include *Thomas' Register,* local and state Chambers of Commerce, census data, and local, state and federal offices. For example, a small firm could decide to segment its market by industry and customer size by following the industry norm, and then use *Thomas' Register,* which is broken down geographically and by Standard Industrial Classification, to determine the size of the market segment. A survey of salespeople could then be used to uncover the particular needs and characteristics of each segment.

Software/Databases

MAX Demographic Data Management and Report Systems, National Planning Data Corporation, P. O. Box 610, Ithaca, NY 14581. MAX provides demographic data and five year projections from the 1980 Census for population, households, income, and age. Updated annually, it is a useful starting point for market segmentation strategies based on demographic factors.

References/Sources

Bass, Frank M., Tigert, Douglas J., and Lonsdale, Ronald T., "Market Segmentation: Group Versus Individual Behavior," *Journal of Marketing Research* (August 1968): 264-270. Argues that, contrary to earlier studies, socioeconomic variables are useful in market segmentation. Usage rates of grocery products are analyzed.

Bell, James E., "Mobiles—A Neglected Market Segment," *Journal of Marketing* (April 1969): 37-44. Considers the feasibility of appeals to a market segment composed of "mobiles."

Kotler, Philip, *Marketing Management: Analysis, Planning and Control.* Englewood Cliffs, NJ: Prentice-Hall, 1984. Chapter 8 provides an overview of market segmentation, targeting a market, and positioning a product.

Michman, Ronald D., "The Double Income Family: A New Market Target," *Business Horizons* (August 1980): 31-37. Discusses the implications to marketing of the two income family, offering a variety of examples.

———, "Changing Patterns in Retailing," *Business Horizons* (October 1979): 33-40. Looks at the social, technological and economic trends that are changing the nature of retailing.

Peter, J. Paul, and Donnelly, James H. Jr., *A Preface to Marketing Management.* Plano, TX: Business Publications, 1985. Chapter 5 explains the steps of market segmentation. Provides many examples of segmentation variables.

Pride, William M. and Ferrell, O.C., *Marketing: Basic Concepts and Decisions,* Boston, MA: Houghton Mifflin, 1985. Chapter 2 explains what markets are and how market segments are developed and evaluated.

Roberts, Alan A., "Applying the Strategy of Market Segmentation," *Business Horizons* (Fall 1961): 65-72. Explains the concept of market segmentation, provides examples, and discusses the management decisions affected by segmenting a market.

Wind, Yoram, "Issues and Advances in Segmentation Research," *Journal of Marketing Research* (August 1978): 313-337. A review of the status of market segmentation, in particular data collection, analysis, and interpretation.

Young, Shirley, Ott, Leland and Feigin, Barbara, "Some Practical Considerations in Market Segmentation," *Journal of Marketing Research* (August 1978): 405-412. Discusses some problems of market segmentation and possible solutions. Presents market segmentation examples and notes situations when market segmentation may not be useful.

Related Topics and Terms

Benefit Segmentation, Concentrated Marketing, Demographic Factor, Family Life Cycle, Product Differentiation, Product Positioning, Psychographics, Target Market.

William Bart
Department of Marketing
Kent State University